GW01046265

ADVANCED TEXTS IN ECO[

General Editors

C. W. J. Granger   G. E. Mizon

TESTING EXOGENEITY

Edited by

Neil R. Ericsson and John S. Irons

OXFORD UNIVERSITY PRESS

OXFORD
UNIVERSITY PRESS

Great Clarendon Street, Oxford OX2 6DP

Oxford University Press is a department of the University of Oxford.
It furthers the University's objective of excellence in research, scholarship,
and education by publishing worldwide in

Oxford New York

Auckland Cape Town Dar es Salaam Hong Kong Karachi Kuala Lumpur
Madrid Melbourne Mexico City Nairobi New Delhi Shanghai Taipei Toronto

With offices in

Argentina Austria Brazil Chile Czech Republic France Greece
Guatemala Hungary Italy Japan South Korea Poland Portugal
Singapore Switzerland Thailand Turkey Ukraine Vietnam

Oxford is a registered trade mark of Oxford University Press
in the UK and in certain other countries

Published in the United States
by Oxford University Press Inc., New York

Editorial organization and new material © Oxford University Press 1994

First published 1994

British Library Cataloguing in Publication Data

Data available

Library of Congress Cataloging in Publication Data

Data available

ISBN 0-19-877404-4 (Pbk.)

5 7 9 10 8 6

Printed in Great Britain
on acid-free paper by
Biddles Ltd., King's Lynn, Norfolk

Contents

Preface   vii

Contributors and Their Current Affiliations   ix

Part I   A Framework for Testing Exogeneity   1

  1. Testing Exogeneity: An Introduction   3
    NEIL R. ERICSSON

  2. Exogeneity   39
    ROBERT F. ENGLE, DAVID F. HENDRY, AND
    JEAN-FRANÇOIS RICHARD

  3. The Encompassing Implications of Feedback versus
    Feedforward Mechanisms in Econometrics   71
    DAVID F. HENDRY

  4. Testing Super Exogeneity and Invariance in Regression Models   93
    ROBERT F. ENGLE AND DAVID F. HENDRY

  5. Testing Weak Exogeneity and the Order of Cointegration in
    U.K. Money Demand Data   121
    SØREN JOHANSEN

  6. Tests of Cointegrating Exogeneity for PPP and Uncovered
    Interest Rate Parity in the United Kingdom   145
    JOHN HUNTER

Part II   Testing Exogeneity in Practice   159

  7. Domestic and Foreign Effects on Prices in an Open Economy:
    The Case of Denmark   161
    KATARINA JUSELIUS

Contents

8. A Dynamic Model of the Demand for Currency:
   Argentina 1977–1988   191
   HILDEGART AHUMADA

9. Dynamic Modeling of the Demand for Narrow Money in
   Norway   219
   GUNNAR BÅRDSEN

10. Finnish Manufacturing Wages 1960–1987: Real-wage
    Flexibility and Hysteresis   251
    RAGNAR NYMOEN

11. An Econometric Analysis of TV Advertising Expenditure in
    the United Kingdom   275
    DAVID F. HENDRY

Part III   Extensions to Testing Procedures   309

12. Parameter Constancy, Mean Square Forecast Errors, and
    Measuring Forecast Performance: An Exposition, Extensions,
    and Illustration   311
    NEIL R. ERICSSON

13. Comments on the Evaluation of Policy Models   341
    CLIVE W. J. GRANGER AND MELINDA DEUTSCH

14. Confidence Intervals for Linear Combinations of Forecasts
    from Dynamic Econometric Models   361
    JULIA CAMPOS

15. Testing for Parameter Instability in Linear Models   389
    BRUCE E. HANSEN

Index   407

Preface

A variable is called exogenous if it can be taken as "given" without losing information for the purpose at hand. Specifically, the exogeneity of a variable depends upon the parameters of interest to the investigator and on the purpose of the model, such as statistical inference, forecasting, or policy analysis. Exogeneity thus plays a key role throughout economic and econometric analysis, both theoretical and applied. In the last fifteen years, exogeneity has undergone important clarifications as a concept; and new, easily implemented tests for exogeneity have been developed. On both accounts, the role of exogeneity tests in evaluating the Lucas critique and the re-interpretation of exogeneity in cointegrated systems have been central. The articles collected in this volume include original sources of the clarifications and tests for exogeneity (Part I), numerous empirical applications (Part II), and refinements and generalizations of the testing procedures (Part III). These studies thus provide both the theoretical underpinnings and an empirical template for other researchers in their applied endeavors. This book should be of value to applied and theoretical econometricians, to graduate students in economics, and in general to economists analyzing time series data. A detailed summary of all the articles appears in the final section of Chapter 1, "Testing Exogeneity: An Introduction".

Many of the articles reprinted in this volume originally appeared in a pair of special issues of the *Journal of Policy Modeling* entitled *Cointegration, Exogeneity, and Policy Analysis*. Preparation of those issues suggested integrating them with other papers on exogeneity, and the current volume resulted. With our focus on *testing* exogeneity, and owing to a lack of space, we have (regrettably) omitted many important papers. For the development of the concept of exogeneity, the reader is referred to John Aldrich's (January 1989, *Oxford Economic Papers*) article "Autonomy" and Mary Morgan and David Hendry's (1994, Cambridge University Press) book *Foundations of Econometric Analysis*.

We are grateful for permission to reprint the papers herein, which originally appeared in *Econometrica* (© The Econometric Society, 1983), the *Journal of Policy Modeling* (© The Society for Policy Modeling, 1992, and courtesy of Elsevier Science Inc.), the *Journal of Econometrics* (© Elsevier Science Publishers B.V., 1993), and *Oxford Economic Papers* (© Oxford University Press, 1988).

We owe many thanks to a number of individuals for their roles in the preparation of this volume. We would like to thank the authors of the articles for agreeing to have their articles reprinted and for their promptness in proofreading them under a tight publishing schedule. Jason Pearce, Andrew Schuller, and Anna Zaranko of Oxford University Press provided helpful guidance throughout the preparation of this volume; and we are grateful to the general editors (Clive Granger and Grayham Mizon) and David Hendry for their encouragement and advice in undertaking this project. We also wish to thank George Tavlas for inviting one of us (NRE) to edit the special issues for the *Journal of Policy Modeling*, and for his support and guidance throughout its preparation. All manuscripts for the special issues were refereed anonymously and subjected to the usual standards of acceptance for the *Journal*. Each referee was provided with the author's data, and this led to substantive, fruitful exchanges on empirical aspects of the articles. Our thanks extend to the referees for their contributions in that process. Margaret Gray provided invaluable proofreading for the special issues. Jurgen Doornik kindly let us use his programs for converting T^3 documents to L^AT_EX and for preparing the index. Finally, and importantly, we are grateful to our colleagues at the Fed for providing a conducive and stimulating working environment.

A few notes on the typesetting of this volume are in order. Camera-ready copy was produced by the editors using Scientific Word and L^AT_EX. We believe that this *modus operandi* provided the most timely, accurate, and visually pleasing reproduction of the articles herein. Most papers already existed in computer-readable form and were converted to L^AT_EX. The few articles that remained were processed with an optical character reader and edited. The approximately ninety graphs of empirical results were reproduced with Jurgen Doornik and David Hendry's PcGive Professional Version 8.0.

As a unified collection, it was desirable to standardize certain features of the articles, including (to the extent possible) punctuation, citations, bibliographies, tables, and figure presentation. Known typographical errors in the original articles have been corrected. Editors' and authors' comments appear where clarification in the original article was thought helpful. References have been updated, while keeping original citations intact so that readers may refer to the initially referenced material, where the original and updated references differ. To facilitate citation, all chapters have marginal notes, in which the original pagination appears in square brackets. The marginal pagination is sequential within a chapter, excepting jumps where the original publication contains entire pages of figures and the figures are placed differently herein.

The views expressed in this book are those of the editors and authors. They should not be interpreted as reflecting those of other persons acknowledged, of the Board of Governors of the Federal Reserve System, or of other supporting organizations and foundations.

Federal Reserve Board   NEIL R. ERICSSON
Washington, D.C.   JOHN S. IRONS
September 1994

Contributors and Their Current Affiliations

HILDEGART AHUMADA, Instituto Di Tella, Buenos Aires, Argentina

GUNNAR BÅRDSEN, Norges Handelshøyskole, Bergen-Sandviken, Norway

JULIA CAMPOS, Departamento de Economía e Historia, Universidad de Salamanca, Salamanca, Spain

MELINDA DEUTSCH, Department of Economics, University of California at San Diego, La Jolla, California, U.S.A.

ROBERT F. ENGLE, Department of Economics, University of California at San Diego, La Jolla, California, U.S.A.

NEIL R. ERICSSON, International Finance Division, Federal Reserve Board, Washington, D.C., U.S.A.

CLIVE W. J. GRANGER, Department of Economics, University of California at San Diego, La Jolla, California, U.S.A.

BRUCE E. HANSEN, Department of Economics, Boston College, Chestnut Hill, Massachusetts, U.S.A.

DAVID F. HENDRY, Nuffield College, Oxford, England

JOHN HUNTER, Department of Economics, Brunel University, Uxbridge, Middlesex, England

SØREN JOHANSEN, Institute of Mathematical Statistics, University of Copenhagen, Copenhagen, Denmark

KATARINA JUSELIUS, Institute of Economics, University of Copenhagen, Copenhagen, Denmark

RAGNAR NYMOEN, Research Department, Bank of Norway, Oslo, Norway

JEAN-FRANÇOIS RICHARD, Department of Economics, University of Pittsburgh, Pittsburgh, Pennsylvania, U.S.A.

Part I

A FRAMEWORK FOR TESTING EXOGENEITY

1

Testing Exogeneity: An Introduction

NEIL R. ERICSSON*

Abstract

This introductory chapter describes the concepts of exogeneity and cointegration, focusing on analytical structure, statistical inference, and implications for policy analysis. Examples help clarify the concepts. The final section of this chapter summarizes the remaining articles in *Testing Exogeneity*.

* The author is a staff economist in the Division of International Finance, Federal Reserve Board. The views expressed in this article are solely the responsibility of the author and should not be interpreted as reflecting those of the Board of Governors of the Federal Reserve System or other members of its staff. Helpful discussions with and comments from Lisa Barrow, Jim Boughton, Julia Campos, Jonathan Eaton, Jon Faust, David Hendry, Søren Johansen, Katarina Juselius, Ed Leamer, Jaime Marquez, Will Melick, George Tavlas, Hong-Anh Tran, and Ken Wallis are gratefully acknowledged. I am indebted to Lisa Barrow for invaluable research assistance.

This article is an amalgam of the papers "Cointegration, Exogeneity, and Policy Analysis: An Overview" and "Cointegration, Exogeneity, and Policy Analysis: A Synopsis" from the *Journal of Policy Modeling* (June 1992), 14, 3, 251–280 and (August 1992), 14, 4, 395–400, which are reprinted with permission of the publishers. The first and last sections have been revised and expanded, so marginal references in brackets to the original pagination are sometimes approximate.

1   Introduction

Testing Exogeneity is a self-contained set of readings that discusses the nature of exogeneity and shows how to test for it through numerous substantive empirical examples. The readings are divided into three parts, which are entitled:

(I)   A Framework for Testing Exogeneity,

(II) Testing Exogeneity in Practice, and

(III) Extensions to Testing Procedures.

This section briefly describes the articles in each part, how they relate to each other, and why we are interested in exogeneity, in particular for its role in cointegrated systems. Section 4 gives more detailed summaries of the articles in the volume.

1.1   An Overview of This Volume

Part I considers what exogeneity is and how it can be tested. The articles in this part provide the conceptual, analytical, and statistical background necessary for implementing and interpreting tests of exogeneity. The current chapter (Chapter 1) describes the concept of exogeneity (Section 2) and its relation to cointegration (Section 3), focusing on analytical structure, statistical inference, and implications for policy analysis. Numerous analytical examples help clarify the concepts and their relationships. Engle, Hendry, and Richard (1983) (Chapter 2) is the central reference on exogeneity as a concept. The authors define and distinguish between weak, strong, and super exogeneity, and show how these concepts differ from (and are more useful than) the "classical" concepts of strict exogeneity and pre-determinedness. Hendry (1988) and Engle and Hendry (1993) (Chapters 3 and 4) propose and implement two tests of super exogeneity, one based on tests of constancy and the other based on tests of invariance. Super exogeneity is the concept relevant for valid conditioning when regimes change and so is of particular interest to economists. Johansen (Chapter 5) and Hunter (Chapter 6) are concerned with the interpretation of exogeneity in cointegrated systems. They describe and illustrate tests of weak exogeneity and cointegrating exogeneity, where the former is a necessary condition for super exogeneity and the latter provides the basis for long-term conditional forecasting in cointegrated systems. While all papers in Part I are primarily theoretical in nature, the latter four include empirical illustrations with U.K. money demand data (Hendry, Engle and Hendry, and Johansen) and U.K. foreign exchange data (Hunter), leading us to the substantive empirical applications in Part II.

Part II applies the various tests of exogeneity in empirical models for both developed and developing countries. The first three articles in Part II test for cointegration and exogeneity in models of prices (Juselius) and money demand (Ahumada for Argentina, Bårdsen for Norway). The remaining two articles model wages (Nymoen) and expenditure (Hendry). The exogeneity status of variables in all five studies is critical for economic analysis, and tests of both weak and super exogeneity are conducted as part of a general research strategy for obtaining a congruent and economically interpretable empirical model. In effect, these studies provide a template for other researchers in their empirical endeavors.

Part III consists of papers by Ericsson, Granger and Deutsch, Campos, and Hansen, which develop and refine various tests of constancy and forecast accuracy. As discussed and implemented in Parts I and II, such tests are central to testing super exogeneity. These four papers also include additional applications to money demand, prices, unemployment, expenditure, and reserves.

Section 4 of the current chapter gives more detailed descriptions of the papers in Parts I–III. To put those papers in perspective, Sections 2 and 3 describe the concepts of exogeneity and cointegration respectively, illustrating both concepts and their relations with numerous examples. The remainder of the current section sets the stage by introducing and motivating the concepts of exogeneity and cointegration.

1.2 Exogeneity and Cointegration

Whether or not a variable is *exogenous* depends upon whether or not that variable can be taken as "given" without losing information for the purpose at hand. Specifically, the exogeneity of a variable depends on the parameters of interest to the investigator and on the purpose of the model, whether for statistical inference, forecasting, or policy (scenario) analysis. These three purposes define three types of exogeneity, which Engle, Hendry, and Richard (1983) [Chapter 2] call weak, strong, and super. Through this categorization, Engle, Hendry, and Richard, in conjunction with Richard (1980) and Florens and Mouchart (1985a, 1985b), have helped clarify and refine the concept of exogeneity, building on Koopmans (1950) and Barndorff-Nielsen (1978). Valid exogeneity assumptions may permit simpler modeling strategies, reduce computational expense, and help isolate invariants of the economic mechanism. Invalid exogeneity assumptions may lead to inefficient or inconsistent inferences and result in misleading forecasts and policy simulations. Exogeneity thus plays a key role throughout economic and econometric analysis, both theoretical and applied.

Two new classes of tests for super exogeneity also have been developed recently, one relying on tests of parameter constancy [Hendry (1988)—Chapter 3] and the other on tests of invariance [Engle and Hendry (1993)—Chapter 4]. As the conjunction of weak exogeneity and invariance, super exogeneity is required for valid policy simulations. Parameter constancy and

invariance are of more general interest as well. Economic theory focuses
on the invariants of the economic process, as reflected by the continuing
debates on autonomy, "deep" or "structural" parameters, and the Lucas critique. Given the intimate link between parameter constancy and predictive
accuracy, valid forecasting also relies on constant parameters. Thus, many of
the applications in this volume employ recursive estimation and tests of parameter constancy and predictive accuracy. The articles in Part III specifically
analyze and develop tests of parameter constancy and predictive accuracy.

Cointegrated systems have specific implications for exogeneity, which
have led to a re-interpretation of exogeneity and to the design of additional
tests. So, a brief description of cointegration is useful.

The concept of *cointegration* is a central development in the econometric
literature over the last decade. Introduced by Granger (1981) and Engle
and Granger (1987), cointegration is a statistical property that may describe
the long-run behavior of economic time series. Importantly, cointegration
ties together several apparently disparate fields. First, cointegration links
the economic notion of a long-run relationship between economic variables
to a statistical model of those variables. If a long-run relationship exists,
the variables involved are "cointegrated". Second, the technical and previously somewhat obscure statistical theory on unit-root processes provides
[252]   the basis for statistical inference about the empirical existence of cointegration. Third, cointegration implies and is implied by the existence of an
error correction representation of the relevant variables. Thus, cointegration
establishes a firmer statistical and economic basis for the empirically successful error correction models (ECMs). Fourth, through that isomorphism with
error correction models, cointegration brings together short- and long-run
information in modeling the data. That unification resolves the "debate" on
whether to use levels or differences, with Box-Jenkins time-series models and
classical "structural" models both being special cases of ECMs. Fifth, via
the distributional theory of integrated processes, cointegration clarifies the
"spurious regressions" or "nonsense-correlations" problem associated with
trending time-series data.

Separately, cointegration and exogeneity have proved useful conceptual
and empirical tools. Analytical relationships exist *between* cointegration and
exogeneity, and have additional implications for statistical inference, forecasting, and policy analysis. Johansen (Chapter 5) and Hunter (Chapter 6)
focus on the possible lacks of various long-run feedbacks, which relate to weak
exogeneity and cointegrating exogeneity respectively. Other chapters examine the nature of those feedbacks through both system and single-equation
modeling.

We now turn to more detailed discussions of exogeneity (Section 2) and
cointegration (Section 3). Each section considers the analytical structure

of the associated concept, statistical inference, and policy implications, in that order. Examples en route help demonstrate the roles of exogeneity and cointegration. The issues in Sections 2 and 3 are discussed at greater length in Ericsson, Campos, and Tran (1990), itself summarizing David Hendry's empirical econometric methodology; see Hendry and Richard (1982, 1983), Hendry (1983), Spanos (1986), Hendry (1987, 1994), and Doornik and Hendry (1994).

2 Exogeneity

Whether a variable is exogenous depends upon whether that variable can be taken as "given" without losing information for the purpose at hand. The distinct purposes of statistical inference, forecasting, and policy analysis define the three concepts of weak, strong, and super exogeneity. Valid [253] exogeneity assumptions may permit simpler modeling strategies, reduce computational expense, and help isolate invariants of the economic mechanism. Invalid exogeneity assumptions may lead to inefficient or inconsistent inferences and result in misleading forecasts and policy simulations. Section 2.1 defines the exogeneity concepts and illustrates them with a static bivariate normal process (Example 1), the well-known cobweb model (Example 2), and a first-order vector autoregression (Example 3). Section 2.2 discusses tests of exogeneity and, in particular, tests of super exogeneity, since that concept is relevant for policy analysis. Section 2.3 comments on the policy implications of exogeneity. The examples here and in Section 3 generalize straightforwardly to linear multivariate dynamic processes.

2.1 Concepts and Structure

WEAK EXOGENEITY. The essential concept is weak exogeneity, which is required for efficient inference (i.e., estimation and hypothesis testing) in a conditional model.[1] Weak exogeneity can be explained with one of the simplest processes, the bivariate normal. In this first example, the bivariate normal density is factorized into its conditional and marginal densities. Analyzing the conditional density leads to the concepts *parameters of interest* and *variation free*, and so to weak exogeneity. Example 2 discusses these concepts in greater detail for the cobweb model.

Example 1: Joint, conditional, and marginal densities. Consider two variables, y_t and z_t, which are jointly normally distributed and serially independent:

---

[1] Weak exogeneity implies that inference about the parameters of interest can be conducted from the conditional density alone (rather than from the joint density) without loss of information. Here and below, the phrase "efficient inference" is used in the sense of being without loss of information.

$$\begin{bmatrix} y_t \\ z_t \end{bmatrix} \sim \mathsf{IN}(\mu, \Omega) \qquad t = 1, \ldots, T. \tag{1}$$

The subscript t denotes time, T is the total number of observations on $(y_t, z_t)'$, and the notation "$\sim \mathsf{IN}(\mu, \Omega)$" denotes "is distributed independently and normally, with mean μ and covariance matrix Ω". In an economic context, y_t and z_t might be money and an interest rate, or consumers' expenditure and income, or wages and prices. Let x_t be $(y_t, z_t)'$, and define ε_t as the "error" $x_t - \mathcal{E}(x_t)$, which is $x_t - \mu$, where $\mathcal{E}(\cdot)$ is the expectation operator. Then (1) becomes:

$$x_t = \mu + \varepsilon_t \qquad \varepsilon_t \sim \mathsf{IN}(0, \Omega). \tag{2}$$

Equation (2) is in "model form", rather than being written directly as a distribution, as in (1). Below, it will be helpful to express μ and Ω explicitly in terms of their scalar elements:

[254]

$$\mu = \begin{bmatrix} \mu_1 \\ \mu_2 \end{bmatrix} \tag{3a}$$

$$\Omega = \begin{bmatrix} \omega_{11} & \omega_{12} \\ \omega_{21} & \omega_{22} \end{bmatrix}. \tag{3b}$$

Without loss of generality, (1) can be factorized into the *conditional* density of y_t given z_t and the *marginal* density of z_t,[2] as follows:

$$y_t \mid z_t \sim \mathsf{IN}(a + bz_t, \sigma^2) \tag{4a}$$

$$z_t \sim \mathsf{IN}(\mu_2, \omega_{22}), \tag{4b}$$

where $b = \omega_{12}/\omega_{22}$, $a = \mu_1 - b\mu_2$, $\sigma^2 = \omega_{11} - \omega_{12}^2/\omega_{22}$, and the vertical bar $\mid$ is the conditioning operator. In model form, (4) is:

$$y_t = a + bz_t + \nu_{1t} \qquad \nu_{1t} \sim \mathsf{IN}(0, \sigma^2) \tag{5a}$$

$$z_t = \mu_2 + \varepsilon_{2t} \qquad \varepsilon_{2t} \sim \mathsf{IN}(0, \omega_{22}), \tag{5b}$$

where ν_{1t} $[= \varepsilon_{1t} - (\omega_{12}/\omega_{22})\varepsilon_{2t}]$ is the error in the conditional model for y_t given z_t, and the error ε_t is $(\varepsilon_{1t}, \varepsilon_{2t})'$. In the standard regression framework, (5a) would be obtained by conditioning y_t on z_t. Since (5a) is a conditional model, ν_{1t} is $y_t - \mathcal{E}(y_t \mid z_t)$. Thus, ν_{1t} contains only the part of y_t that is uncorrelated with z_t, and so is uncorrelated with ε_{2t}, in light of (5b). It then follows that $\mathcal{E}(z_t \cdot \nu_{1t}) = 0$ and $\mathcal{E}(\varepsilon_{2t} \cdot \nu_{1t}) = 0$.

---

[2] The word *marginal* is used here and elsewhere in its statistical sense. Its usage in statistics arises from summing a tabulated joint distribution function across its rows or down its columns and entering those sums in the margin, to obtain what is known as the marginal distribution; see Kendall and Stuart (1977, p. 22). *Marginal* as used here is not to be confused with its economic sense, as in "marginal versus average cost".

Symbolically, the relationship between (1) and (4) [or between (2) and (5)] is:

$$F_x(x_t; \theta) = F_{y|z}(y_t \mid z_t; \lambda_1) \cdot F_z(z_t; \lambda_2), \tag{6}$$

where $F_u(\cdot)$ denotes the density function for variable u. Thus, $F_x(x_t; \theta)$ is the joint density of x_t, $F_{y|z}(y_t \mid z_t; \lambda_1)$ is the conditional density of y_t given z_t, and $F_z(z_t; \lambda_2)$ is the marginal density of z_t. The parameter vector θ is the full set of parameters in the joint process; λ_1 and λ_2 are the parameters of the conditional and marginal models; and the respective parameter spaces are Θ, Λ_1, and Λ_2. Defining λ as $(\lambda_1', \lambda_2')'$ and denoting its parameter space as Λ, then there is a one-to-one function $g(\cdot)$ such that $\lambda = g(\theta)$. Above, $\theta = [\mu', \mathrm{vec}(\Omega)']'$, $\lambda_1 = (a, b, \sigma^2)'$, and $\lambda_2 = (\mu_2, \omega_{22})'$. The representation in (6) is important throughout this overview.

In (6), the joint density of x_t is factorized into the conditional density [255] of y_t given z_t and the marginal density of z_t. This factorization is *without* loss of generality. Even so, analyzing the conditional density $F_{y|z}(y_t \mid z_t; \lambda_1)$ while ignoring the corresponding marginal density $F_z(z_t; \lambda_2)$ is *with* loss of generality, and in general implies a loss of information about the conditional process being modeled. Analyzing the conditional model alone is the statistical formalization of taking z_t as given, so the remainder of this section considers the corresponding implications.

Modeling the conditional density (4a) by itself ignores some information about the conditional model's parameters (a, b, σ^2) when any of a, b, and σ^2 are linked to the marginal model's parameters (μ_2, ω_{22}), for example, by cross-equation restrictions. However, in spite of the definitions of a, b, and σ^2, such dependence may be absent. For instance, if ω_{12} took values in proportion to ω_{22} as (for example) ω_{22} varied across different regimes for z_t, then the value of ω_{22} (in λ_2) would be uninformative about b, which is ω_{12}/ω_{22}, and is in λ_1.

"Lack of dependence" between λ_1 and λ_2 is an overly strong condition for inference. Instead, a related concept, the *sequential cut* of a density function, is used. Specifically, the factorization (6) operates a sequential cut if and only if λ_1 and λ_2 are *variation free*, that is, (λ_1, λ_2) belong to $\Lambda_1 \times \Lambda_2$, the product of their individual parameter spaces. Thus, λ_1 and λ_2 are variation free if the parameter space Λ_1 is not a function of the parameter λ_2, and the parameter space Λ_2 is not a function of the parameter λ_1. Expressed slightly differently, knowledge about the value of one parameter provides no information on the other parameter's range of potential values. Thus, under weak exogeneity, permissible θ are always reconstructed correctly from separately selected values of λ_1 and λ_2. Example 2 below examines the concept *variation free* in greater detail.

That the parameters λ_1 and λ_2 are variation free is not enough to ensure valid inference about the parameters of interest, using the conditional model (4a) alone. For instance, if an investigator were interested in μ, both (4a) and (4b) would need to be estimated: μ cannot be retrieved from only (a, b, σ^2). Thus, the formal notion of *parameters of interest* (denoted ψ) is introduced. This leads to the definition of weak exogeneity.

> DEFINITION. The variable z_t is weakly exogenous over the sample period for the parameters of interest ψ if and only if there exists a reparameterization of θ as λ, with $\lambda = (\lambda_1', \lambda_2')'$ such that:
> (i) ψ is a function of λ_1 alone, and
> (ii) the factorization in (6) operates a sequential cut, that is,
> $$F_x(x_t; \theta) = F_{y|z}(y_t \mid z_t; \lambda_1) \cdot F_z(z_t; \lambda_2),$$
> where $\lambda \in \Lambda_1 \times \Lambda_2$.
> [Engle, Hendry, and Richard (1983, p. 282)]

[256]

If weak exogeneity holds, then efficient estimation and testing can be conducted by analyzing only the conditional model (4a), ignoring the information of the marginal process (4b). In economic analysis, there may be many variables in z_t but relatively few in y_t, so weak exogeneity can greatly reduce the modeling effort required.

Example 2: The cobweb model. The concepts *parameters of interest*, *variation free*, and *weak exogeneity* are illustrated clearly with the standard economic cobweb model. This model characterizes a market with lags in the production process, as might occur with agricultural commodities. See Tinbergen (1931) and Suits (1955) for pivotal contributions, and Henderson and Quandt (1971, pp. 142–145) for an exposition.

The cobweb model is obtained by a simple generalization of the static bivariate normal model in Example 1. Specifically, let the mean of z_t depend linearly upon y_{t-1}, the lagged value of y_t: Example 3 gives details. From (5a) and (5b), the resulting model is:

$$y_t = a + bz_t + \nu_{1t} \qquad \nu_{1t} \sim \mathsf{IN}(0, \sigma^2) \tag{7a}$$

$$z_t = ky_{t-1} + \varepsilon_{2t} \qquad \varepsilon_{2t} \sim \mathsf{IN}(0, \omega_{22}), \tag{7b}$$

where k is a parameter capturing the linear dependence of z_t on y_{t-1}. In the cobweb model, y_t and z_t are interpreted as the logs of price and quantity, respectively. Denoting those logs as p_t and q_t, and ignoring the constant a (for ease of exposition), (7a) and (7b) become:

$$p_t = bq_t + \nu_{1t} \qquad \nu_{1t} \sim \mathsf{IN}(0, \sigma^2) \tag{8a}$$

$$q_t = kp_{t-1} + \varepsilon_{2t} \qquad \varepsilon_{2t} \sim \mathsf{IN}(0, \omega_{22}). \tag{8b}$$

As before, $\mathcal{E}(q_t \cdot \nu_{1t}) = 0$ and $\mathcal{E}(\varepsilon_{2t} \cdot \nu_{1t}) = 0$.

The cobweb model (8) has the following interpretation and properties. The first equation, (8a), is derived from a demand equation: the price (p_t) clears the market for a given quantity (q_t) supplied. The value $1/b$ is the price elasticity of demand. The second equation, (8b), is a supply equation, capturing (for example) how much farmers decide to produce this year (q_t), depending upon the price they were able to obtain in the previous year (p_{t-1}). The value k is the price elasticity of supply. The stability of (8a) and (8b) as a system is sometimes of interest, and can be determined from the reduced form for p_t [e.g., by substituting (8b) into (8a)]:

$$p_t = \rho p_{t-1} + \varepsilon_{1t} \qquad \varepsilon_{1t} \sim \mathsf{IN}(0, \omega_{11}), \qquad (9)$$

[257]

where ρ is the root of (9), and is equal to $b \cdot k$. If $|\rho| < 1$, the market is dynamically stable. If $|\rho| = 1$, the market generates prices that oscillate without dampening; and if $|\rho| > 1$, the market is dynamically unstable.

Now, consider how parameters of interest and parameter spaces determine whether the quantity q_t in (8a) is weakly exogenous. Specifically, consider conditions (i) and (ii) for weak exogeneity individually, recognizing that both conditions must be satisfied for weak exogeneity to hold. In the notation from Example 1, the parameters of the conditional model (8a) are $\lambda_1 = (b, \sigma^2)'$, and the parameters of the marginal model (8b) are $\lambda_2 = (k, \omega_{22})'$.

Condition (i) for weak exogeneity requires that the parameters of interest ψ be a function of the conditional model's parameters λ_1 only. If the parameter of interest is the demand elasticity $(1/b)$, this condition is satisfied: b enters λ_1, and λ_1 alone. However, if the stability of the system is at issue and so the parameter of interest is the root ρ, condition (i) is violated. The parameter ρ requires knowledge of both b (in λ_1) and k (in λ_2) and so necessitates analysis of the full system. Thus, q_t is not weakly exogenous for the root ρ; but q_t may be weakly exogenous for the elasticity $1/b$, depending upon whether condition (ii) is satisfied. Choosing the parameters of interest is not an innocuous decision.

Condition (ii) for weak exogeneity requires that the parameters of the conditional and marginal models (λ_1 and λ_2) are variation free. The following three situations show how these parameters might or might not be so. For ease of exposition, ignore the presence of σ^2 and ω_{22} in λ_1 and λ_2, thereby allowing analysis of the parameter space Λ [now the parameter space of (b, k)] on a plane.

First, suppose that b and k are completely unrestricted real values. Their parameter space Λ is $\Re^2$, the complete real plane. For every value of k, the parameter b can take any value in the interval $(-\infty, +\infty)$, which is Λ_1. The value of the marginal model's parameter k does not affect the range of the conditional model's parameter b, and conversely, so b and k (i.e., λ_1 and λ_2) are variation free. Equivalently, the parameter space Λ is the product space

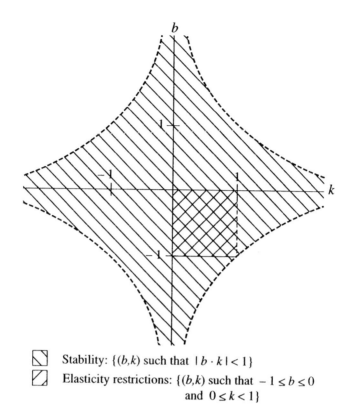

Stability: $\{(b,k)$ such that $|b \cdot k| < 1\}$
Elasticity restrictions: $\{(b,k)$ such that $-1 \leq b \leq 0$
and $0 \leq k < 1\}$

FIGURE 1. Possible parameter spaces of the cobweb model.

of Λ_1 and Λ_2, that is, $(-\infty, +\infty) \times (-\infty, +\infty)$, which is $\Re^2$. Thus, q_t is weakly exogenous for (for example) the elasticity $1/b$.

Second, suppose that b and k are restricted such that the system (8a)–(8b) is stable, that is, such that $|b \cdot k| < 1$. Their corresponding parameter space Λ appears in Figure 1, labelled "stability". Unlike the previous case, [258] the value of k does affect the range of b. For instance, if $k = 0.5$, then b must lie in the interval $(-2, +2)$, whereas if $k = 0.2$, then b lies in the interval $(-5, +5)$. Formally, Λ_1, which is the parameter space of b (or λ_1), depends upon the values of the marginal process's parameter k (or λ_2). Thus, λ_1 and λ_2 are not variation free.

[259]   Equally, the parameter space Λ is not $\Lambda_1 \times \Lambda_2$, the product of the spaces of b and k. For example, for $k = 0.2$, Λ_1 is $(-5, +5)$; and for $b = 1$, Λ_2 is $(-1, +1)$. However, the product space $\Lambda_1 \times \Lambda_2$, which is $(-5, +5) \times (-1, +1)$, is not the parameter space Λ for (b, k), which is defined by $|b \cdot k| < 1$. Put somewhat differently, the value of k is informative about the value of b, even

though k does not determine the specific value of b. Inference using the conditional density alone loses information about b from k in the marginal density, so q_t is not weakly exogenous for the elasticity $1/b$.

Third, suppose that (for example) economic theory or intuition suggests the following restrictions: that the supply elasticity k lies in the unit interval $[0,1)$ and that the demand elasticity $1/b$ is negative and is greater than or equal to unity in absolute value (implying that $-1 \leq b \leq 0$). The corresponding parameter space Λ appears in Figure 1, labelled "elasticity restrictions". The parameter b lies in the interval $[-1,0]$, regardless of the value of k; and k lies in the interval $[0,1)$, regardless of the value of b. The parameters *are* variation free: the product space $[-1,0] \times [0,1)$, which is $\Lambda_1 \times \Lambda_2$, is also the space in which (b,k) lies, that is, Λ. Thus, under the elasticity restrictions, q_t is weakly exogenous for the elasticity $1/b$. As with parameters of interest, the choice of parameter space is important in the determination of a variable's status as exogenous or endogenous.

To summarize, the parameter space and the parameters of interest are important concepts, both statistically and economically. Their choice is critical to the exogeneity status of a given variable. The introduction of dynamics in (7) above leads naturally to another concept of exogeneity, *strong exogeneity*.

STRONG EXOGENEITY. Strong exogeneity is the conjunction of weak exogeneity and Granger noncausality, and it insures valid conditional forecasting. Figure 2 shows the relationship between weak exogeneity, Granger noncausality, and strong exogeneity with a Venn diagram. Figure 2 also includes a set for the property of invariance, which helps define super exogeneity (discussed after strong exogeneity).

To discuss the concept of strong exogeneity, Example 1 is modified to include dynamics by reinterpreting (1) as the joint density of x_t, conditional on the past of x_t (denoted X_{t-1}). In general, X_{t-1} may affect the distribution of x_t through both μ and Ω, and in a rather arbitrary fashion. For simplicity, only *linear* dependence of μ on the *first* lag of x_t is considered. Thus, the mean μ in (1) is interpreted as the conditional mean of x_t given X_{t-1}. That is, $\mu = \pi_1 x_{t-1}$, where π_1 is a matrix of coefficients, and the constant term is ignored for simplicity.

Example 3: Joint, conditional, and marginal densities with lags. Under [260] this simplifying assumption about lags and linearity, (1) becomes a first-order vector autoregression (VAR) in model form:

$$x_t = \pi_1 x_{t-1} + \varepsilon_t \qquad \varepsilon_t \sim \text{IN}(0, \Omega). \qquad (10)$$

Equations (5a) and (5b) become conditional and marginal autoregressive distributed lag (AD) models:

$$y_t = b_0 z_t + b_1 z_{t-1} + b_2 y_{t-1} + \nu_{1t} \qquad \nu_{1t} \sim \text{IN}(0, \sigma^2) \qquad (11a)$$

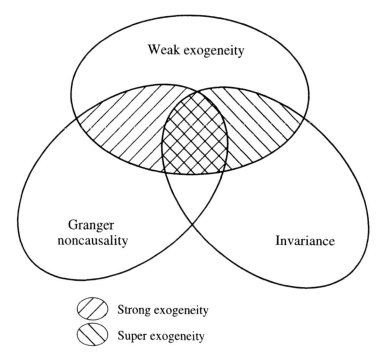

FIGURE 2.   The relationship between Granger noncausality, invariance, and three forms of exogeneity.

$$z_t = \pi_{22} z_{t-1} + \pi_{21} y_{t-1} + \varepsilon_{2t} \qquad \varepsilon_{2t} \sim \mathsf{IN}(0, \omega_{22}), \qquad (11\text{b})$$

[261]

where π_{ij} denotes the (i,j)th element of π_1, and (b_0, b_1, b_2) are derived from π_1 and Ω, paralleling the relation between b and (μ, Ω) in (4a). Specifically, $b_0 = \omega_{12}/\omega_{22}$, $b_1 = \pi_{12} - (\omega_{12}/\omega_{22})\pi_{22}$, and $b_2 = \pi_{11} - (\omega_{12}/\omega_{22})\pi_{21}$; see Engle, Hendry, and Richard (1983, p. 297).

Valid prediction of y from its conditional model (11a) requires more than weak exogeneity. With weak exogeneity alone, y_{t-1} influences z_t if $\pi_{21} \neq 0$ in the marginal model (11b), in which case z_t in the conditional model (11a) cannot be treated as "fixed" for prediction of y_t. The requisite additional restriction is that $\pi_{21} = 0$, or (in general) that y does not Granger-cause z.[3] Weak exogeneity plus Granger noncausality generates strong exogeneity. Strong exogeneity permits valid multi-step ahead prediction of y from (11a),

---

[3] Specifically, Granger noncausality means that only lagged values of z_t enter (11b) or its generalization. Equally, Granger noncausality means that lags of other variables (other than of z_t) do not enter the marginal model for z_t.

conditional on predictions of z generated from (11b) (with $\pi_{21} = 0$), where the predictions of z depend upon only their own lags. With $\pi_{21} \neq 0$, valid prediction of y must account for the feedback of y onto z in (11b), period by period: valid multi-step prediction therefore *requires* joint analysis of (11a) and (11b), violating the exogeneity of z_t in (11a).

Error correction models (and so cointegrated processes) are closely related to the autoregressive distributed lag model in (11a). By appropriately adding and subtracting y_{t-1} and z_{t-1} from (11a), that equation can be written as an ECM:

$$\Delta y_t = \gamma_1 \Delta z_t + \gamma_2 (y_{t-1} - \delta z_{t-1}) + \nu_{1t}, \qquad (12)$$

where $\gamma_1 = b_0$, $\gamma_2 = b_2 - 1$, and $\delta = -(b_0 + b_1)/(b_2 - 1)$.[4] Equation (12) involves no loss of generality relative to (11a), provided $b_2 \neq 1$. The term $\gamma_1 \Delta z_t$ is the immediate impact that a change in z_t has on y_t. The term $\gamma_2 (y_{t-1} - \delta z_{t-1})$ (with $\gamma_2 < 0$ required for dynamic stability) is the impact on Δy_t of having y_{t-1} out of line with δz_{t-1}: $y = \delta z$ is the long-run static solution to (12). Discrepancies between y_{t-1} and δz_{t-1} could arise from errors in agents' past decisions, with the presence of $\gamma_2 (y_{t-1} - \delta z_{t-1})$ reflecting their attempts to correct such errors: hence the name *error correction* model. Most of the papers in this volume develop conditional ECMs in the course of modeling.

Hendry, Pagan, and Sargan (1984, pp. 1040–1049) discuss the properties of ECMs in greater detail, and show that many classes of models common in empirical research are subsumed by the ECM. The ECM representation is [262] also central to the discussion of cointegration, as shown in Example 7 below.

SUPER EXOGENEITY. Super exogeneity is the conjunction of weak exogeneity and "invariance" (see Figure 2), and insures valid policy simulations. The concept of invariance can be motivated as follows.

Frequently, the reduced form (2) is empirically nonconstant, owing to (for example) OPEC shocks, changes in policy rules, and financial innovations. The factorization (6) may aim to isolate those nonconstancies into the subvector λ_2, leaving the parameters of the conditional model λ_1 invariant to the changes that have occurred. Thus, the concept of *invariance* is introduced. The parameter λ_1 is invariant to a class of interventions to the marginal process for z_t (i.e., to a set of changes in λ_2) if λ_1 is not a function of λ_2 for that class of interventions.[5] For invariance, lack of dependence between

---

[4] With the lag operator L defined as $Lx_t = x_{t-1}$, the difference operator Δ is $(1 - L)$; hence $\Delta x_t = x_t - x_{t-1}$. More generally, $\Delta_j^i x_t = (1 - L^j)^i x_t$. If i (or j) is undefined, it is taken to be unity.

[5] Engle, Hendry, and Richard (1983, p. 284) call this structural invariance, rather than invariance.

the parameters themselves matters, and not just lack of dependence between parameters and parameter spaces.

Policy analysis (or counterfactual analysis) often involves changing the marginal process of z_t. Valid analysis of the conditional model under such changes requires that the parameters λ_1 be *invariant* to those changes (or "interventions"). The relevant concept is super exogeneity, whereby z_t is weakly exogenous for the parameters of interest ψ, and λ_1 is invariant to the class of interventions to λ_2 under consideration (see Figure 2). Importantly, a variable is super exogenous with respect to a *specified* class of interventions (e.g., those that occurred within sample): the variable need not be super exogenous with respect to interventions outside that class, although it may be.

To illustrate the concept of super exogeneity, interpret y_t and z_t as money and an interest rate, (11a) as a money demand function, and (11b) as the Fed's interest rate reaction function (assuming that there is one). Then policy analysis of (11a) for money demanded at different levels of the interest rate is valid only if the parameters in the money demand function (λ_1) are invariant to the specified changes in the parameters of the interest rate reaction function (λ_2) that would generate those levels. That condition is equivalently that the interest rate is super exogenous for the parameters in the money demand function with respect to the changes in the reaction function under consideration.

[263]   PREDETERMINEDNESS AND STRICT EXOGENEITY. Before turning to tests of exogeneity (Section 2.2), the concepts of predeterminedness and strict exogeneity are considered briefly, as they often appear in discussions of exogeneity. Neither concept specifies parameters of interest; and that is a major drawback of each concept, given the preceding exposition. For instance, in the cobweb model, q_t is predetermined in the conditional model (8a), and OLS of (8a) is consistent for b. However, that conditional model is not sufficient to obtain the parameter of interest if the parameter of interest is the root ρ. Likewise, z_t is strictly exogenous in (5), but that conditional equation by itself is not sufficient to obtain μ_1. Neither predeterminedness nor strict exogeneity is sufficient for efficient statistical inference; lack of necessity can be shown as well. See Engle, Hendry, and Richard (1983) for details and examples, including an example with a dynamic simultaneous equations model.

2.2   Inference

Whether z_t is exogenous depends *inter alia* upon the process generating y_t and z_t, so exogeneity may be testable.

Even so, testing for weak exogeneity *per se* is often difficult because doing so involves modeling z_t, whereas a motivation for assuming weak exogeneity is to avoid modeling z_t. Also, weak exogeneity depends upon the parameters of interest, which are chosen by the investigator. Still, a few tests of weak exogeneity have been proposed, notably in the context of cointegration; see Chapter 5 and the discussion of Johansen (1992) in Section 3.2 below.

While strong exogeneity requires weak exogeneity, the former is refuted by finding Granger causality of y onto z. Thus, Granger noncausality, which is a necessary condition for strong exogeneity, generates an easily calculated (albeit incomplete) test of strong exogeneity.

Super exogeneity requires weak exogeneity of z_t for the parameters of interest ψ, and invariance of the conditional model's parameters λ_1 (on which ψ depends) to changes in the parameters of the marginal process (λ_2). Thus, two common tests for super exogeneity are as follows.

1. Establish the constancy of λ_1 and the nonconstancy of λ_2. With λ_1 constant and λ_2 not, then λ_1 must be invariant to λ_2, and so super exogeneity holds; see Hendry (1988) [Chapter 3].

2. Having established that the conditions in test 1 hold, further develop the marginal model for z_t until it is empirically constant. For instance, [264] by adding dummies and/or other variables, model the way in which λ_2 varies over time. Then test for the significance of those dummies and/or other variables when they are added to the conditional model. Their *insignificance* in the conditional model demonstrates invariance of the conditional model's parameters λ_1 to the changes in the marginal process; see Engle and Hendry (1993) [Chapter 4].

Tests of parameter constancy thus are central to tests of super exogeneity.

Parameter constancy is of more general interest as well. Economic theory focuses on the invariants of the economic process, as reflected by the continuing debates on autonomy, "deep" or "structural" parameters, and the Lucas critique. Given the intimate link between parameter constancy and predictive accuracy, valid forecasting also relies on constant parameters [Hendry (1979)]. Most estimation techniques require parameter constancy for valid inference, so parameter constancy is a central concept from a statistical perspective. Even models with time-varying parameters posit meta-parameters, which are assumed constant over time and whose empirical constancy can be tested. Recursive estimation is an incisive tool for investigating parameter constancy, both through the sequence of estimated coefficient values and through the associated Chow (1960) statistics for constancy.

Thus, the constancy of a model bears on its economic interpretability, on forecasting, and on policy analysis, the latter specifically via tests of super exogeneity. Because of the critical role of parameter constancy in economic analysis, many of the chapters in this volume employ recursive estimation and tests of parameter constancy and predictive accuracy. Furthermore, the chapters in Part III analyze and develop tests of parameter constancy and predictive accuracy themselves. See Section 4 below.

2.3 Policy Implications

Super exogeneity has several implications for policy analysis.

First, the empirical presence of super exogeneity immunizes the conditional model from the Lucas (1976) critique; see Hendry (1988), Engle and Hendry (1993), Ericsson and Hendry (1989), and Favero and Hendry (1992). For example, suppose that the conditional and marginal models represent agents' and policymakers' decision rules, respectively. Then, under super exogeneity, the agents' parameter vector λ_1 is invariant to changes in policymakers' rules (via λ_2), which is opposite to the implication of the Lucas critique.

[265]   Second, "inverting" the conditional model is invalid. For example, inverting a money demand equation to obtain a price equation is invalid. The bivariate normal distribution in (1) demonstrates how and why that is so.

In (4a) and (4b), the joint density (1) was factorized into the conditional density of y_t given z_t and the marginal density of z_t. Equation (1) also can be factorized into the conditional density of z_t given y_t and the marginal density of y_t:

$$z_t \mid y_t \sim \mathsf{IN}(c + dy_t, \tau^2) \tag{13a}$$

$$y_t \sim \mathsf{IN}(\mu_1, \omega_{11}), \tag{13b}$$

where $d = \omega_{21}/\omega_{11}$, $c = \mu_2 - d\mu_1$, and $\tau^2 = \omega_{22} - \omega_{21}^2/\omega_{11}$. The factorization in (13) is "opposite" to that in (4). In model form, (13) is:

$$z_t = c + dy_t + \nu_{2t} \qquad \nu_{2t} \sim \mathsf{IN}(0, \tau^2) \tag{14a}$$

$$y_t = \mu_1 + \varepsilon_{1t} \qquad \varepsilon_{1t} \sim \mathsf{IN}(0, \omega_{11}), \tag{14b}$$

where ν_{2t} is the error in the conditional model for z_t given y_t. Paralleling results for (5), $\mathcal{E}(\nu_{2t} \cdot y_t) = 0$ and $\mathcal{E}(\nu_{2t} \cdot \varepsilon_{1t}) = 0$. Symbolically, (13) is:

$$F_x(x_t; \theta) = F_{z|y}(z_t \mid y_t; \phi_1) \cdot F_y(y_t; \phi_2), \tag{15}$$

where the parameterization is $\phi \equiv (\phi_1', \phi_2')' = h(\theta)$, and $h(\cdot)$ is a one-to-one function. Thus, via $g(\cdot)$ and $h(\cdot)$, there is a one-to-one mapping between (λ_1', λ_2') and (ϕ_1', ϕ_2'). Specifically, the coefficient on y_t in (14a) is $d = b\omega_{22}/(\sigma^2 + b^2\omega_{22})$, which is not $1/b$ unless (5a) is nonstochastic (i.e., $\sigma^2 = 0$). Further, if z_t is super exogenous for b and σ^2, then d will vary as the marginal process for z_t varies (via ω_{22}) even though b remains constant. Inversion does not obtain the correct parameter for the inverted equation, and the parameter in the inverted model may be nonconstant even if the "uninverted" conditional model is constant.

Inversion may appear peculiar at first glance, but it is precisely what occurs when (for example) estimated money demand functions are "inverted" to obtain prices as a function of money (common among macro-economists) or to obtain interest rates as a function of money (common among macro-modelers). For example, suppose a conditional money demand function is estimated:

$$m = \kappa_1 p + \kappa_2 i - \kappa_3 R, \tag{16}$$

where m, p, and i are the logs of nominal money, the price level, and real income respectively, R is the interest rate, and the $\{\kappa_i\}$ are coefficients, all [266] assumed positive. The two inversions above correspond to

$$p = (1/\kappa_1)m - (\kappa_2/\kappa_1)i + (\kappa_3/\kappa_1)R \tag{17a}$$

and

$$R = (-1/\kappa_3)m + (\kappa_1/\kappa_3)p + (\kappa_2/\kappa_3)i, \tag{17b}$$

where $b = \kappa_1$ in the first instance and $b = -\kappa_3$ in the second. From the analytical relationship between d and b above, the *empirically estimated* coefficient on m in (17a) or (17b) need not be at all close to $1/b$, even for large samples. The nonconstancy of the inverted model can be demonstrated empirically as well, as in Hendry (1985) and Hendry and Ericsson (1991a, 1991b).

Third, super exogeneity can identify parameters, in the sense of uniqueness, because any (nontrivial) combination of the conditional and marginal equations would be nonconstant [Hendry (1987, p. 40)]. This contrasts with (for example) Cooley and Leroy (1981).

Fourth, Granger noncausality is neither necessary nor sufficient for policy analysis, in contrast to a common approach to exogeneity. Lagged y in (11b) may influence current z (e.g., the Fed might pay attention to lagged money in setting the interest rate), yet the conditional model (11a) (e.g., a money demand equation) would still be valid for policy analysis if z_t were super exogenous for λ_1. Granger noncausality is relevant for strong exogeneity, but that concept is for forecasting, not policy analysis.

We now turn to the concept of cointegration.

3   Cointegration

Cointegration formalizes in statistical terms the property of a long-run relation between "integrated" economic variables. In this section, integration and cointegration are illustrated by (10), first as a first-order scalar autoregression (Example 4), then as a higher-order vector autoregression (Example 5). Specifically, the first-order bivariate (vector) autoregression is used to illustrate cointegration (Example 6), the relationship between cointegration and error correction models (Example 7), and implications for weak exogeneity (Example 8). Then a first-order trivariate vector autoregression shows how two cointegrating vectors might arise (Example 9).

[267]

Section 3.1 describes integration and cointegration by means of the examples. Section 3.2 summarizes several techniques for testing the order of integration and the existence of cointegration. Section 3.3 draws upon Section 2 (on exogeneity) to discuss the implications of cointegration for policy analysis.

For the initial development of cointegration, see Granger (1981), Granger and Weiss (1983), the articles in Hendry (1986), and Engle and Granger (1987). For recent summaries and extensions, see Johansen (1988), Hylleberg and Mizon (1989), Dolado, Jenkinson, and Sosvilla-Rivero (1990), Johansen and Juselius (1990), Campbell and Perron (1991), Engle and Yoo (1991), Phillips (1991), Phillips and Loretan (1991), Ericsson, Campos, and Tran (1990), Banerjee, Dolado, Galbraith, and Hendry (1993), and Johansen (1991a, 1991b).

For the initial (and much earlier) development of error correction, see Phillips (1954, 1957), who *inter alia* discusses how error correction in policymakers' rules might help stabilize the economy. Important subsequent empirical and analytical contributions include Sargan (1964), Davidson, Hendry, Srba, and Yeo (1978), Salmon (1982), and Hendry, Pagan, and Sargan (1984).

3.1 Concepts and Structure

The essential concepts are integration and cointegration, which apply to individual time series and sets of time series, respectively. A variable is integrated if it requires differencing to make it stationary. Many economic time series appear to be integrated [Nelson and Plosser (1982)]. A set of integrated time series is cointegrated if some linear combination of those (nonstationary) series is stationary.

Example 4: Integration. For a scalar (rather than bivariate) x_t, (10) is a first-order autoregression,

$$x_t = \pi_1 x_{t-1} + \varepsilon_t, \qquad (18)$$

which can be rewritten as:

$$\Delta x_t = \pi x_{t-1} + \varepsilon_t, \qquad (19)$$

where $\pi = \pi_1 - 1$ by subtracting x_{t-1} from both sides of (18). If $\pi_1 = 1$ or equivalently $\pi = 0$, then x_t has a unit root and is said to be integrated of order one [denoted I(1)], meaning that x_t must be differenced once to achieve stationarity. In the simple case of (18), x_t is a random walk if it has a unit root. If $|\pi_1| < 1$, then x_t is stationary. For general autoregressive processes, (18) includes additional lags of x_t; thus (19) includes lags of Δx_t.

Example 5: Cointegration. Equation (18) can be generalized to represent a vector of variables [as in (10)] and to include higher-order lags of x_t. Together, these result in:

$$x_t = \sum_{i=1}^{\ell} \pi_i x_{t-i} + \varepsilon_t \qquad \varepsilon_t \sim \mathsf{IN}(0, \Omega), \qquad (20)$$

[268]

where ℓ is the maximum lag, and (20) may include a constant and dummies as well. In terms of the joint density in (1), the mean of x_t conditional on X_{t-1} is $\mu = \sum_{i=1}^{\ell} \pi_i x_{t-i}$.

Following Johansen (1988) and Johansen and Juselius (1990), (20) provides the basis for cointegration analysis. By adding and subtracting various lags of x_t, (20) can be rewritten as:

$$\Delta x_t = \pi x_{t-1} + \sum_{i=1}^{\ell-1} \Gamma_i \Delta x_{t-i} + \varepsilon_t, \qquad (21)$$

where the $\{\Gamma_i\}$ are:

$$\Gamma_i = -(\pi_{i+1} + \cdots + \pi_\ell) \qquad i = 1, \ldots, \ell - 1, \qquad (22)$$

and

$$\pi \equiv \left(\sum_{i=1}^{\ell} \pi_i \right) - I. \qquad (23)$$

Equation (20), and so (21), simplifies to (10) for $\ell = 1$.[6] As in (19), π in (21) could be zero. If so, Δx_t in (21) depends upon ε_t and lags of Δx_t alone, all of which are $\mathsf{I}(0)$; so x_t is $\mathsf{I}(1)$.[7] If π is nonzero and of full rank with all the roots of an associated polynomial being within the unit circle, then all the x_t are $\mathsf{I}(0)$, paralleling $|\pi| < 1$ in the univariate case. However, because π is a matrix in (21) rather than a scalar, π may be of less than full rank, but of rank greater than zero. If so, each of the variables in x_t can be $\mathsf{I}(1)$, even while some linear combinations of those variables are $\mathsf{I}(0)$. The variables in x_t are then said to be cointegrated.

To show how cointegration can occur, denote the dimension of x_t as $p \times 1$ and the polynomial $(\sum_{i=1}^{\ell} \pi_i z^i) - I_p$ as $\pi(z)$, where z is the argument of

---

[6] Johansen (1988), Johansen and Juselius (1990), and some others write (21) with the level of x entering at the ℓth lag rather than at the first lag. Doing so does not alter the coefficient on the lagged level (which is π) although it does change the coefficients on the lagged values of Δx_t. Since the analysis of cointegration concerns the properties of π alone, the choice of lag on x is irrelevant in this context.

[7] Here, we do not consider situations in which x_t is of an order of integration greater than unity.

the polynomial. Note that $\pi = \pi(1)$, from (23). The three possibilities for rank(π) are as follows.

[269]   1. rank$(\pi) = p$. For π to have full rank, none of the roots of $|\pi(z^{-1})| = 0$ can be unity. Provided $|\pi(z^{-1})| = 0$ has all its $\ell \cdot p$ roots strictly inside the unit circle, x_t is stationary because $\pi(L)$ can be inverted to give an infinite moving average representation of x_t.

   2. rank$(\pi) = 0$. Because $\pi = 0$, equation (21) is in differences only, and there are p unit roots in $|\pi(z^{-1})| = 0$.

   3. $0 < $ rank$(\pi) \equiv r < p$. In this case, π can be expressed as the outer product of two (full column rank) $p \times r$ matrices α and β:

$$\pi = \alpha\beta'; \tag{24}$$

and there are $p - r$ unit roots in $|\pi(z^{-1})| = 0.$[8]

In (24), β' is the matrix of cointegrating vectors, and α is the matrix of "weighting elements". Substituting (24) into (21) gives:

$$\Delta x_t = \alpha\beta' x_{t-1} + \sum_{i=1}^{\ell-1} \Gamma_i \Delta x_{t-i} + \varepsilon_t. \tag{25}$$

Each $1 \times p$ row β_i' in β' is an individual cointegrating vector, as is required for "balance" to make each cointegrating relation $\beta_i' x_{t-1}$ an I(0) process in (25). Each $1 \times r$ row α_j of α is the set of weights for the r cointegrating terms appearing in the jth equation. Thus, the rank r is also the number of cointegrating vectors in the system. While α and β themselves are not unique, β uniquely defines the cointegration space, and suitable normalizations for α and β are available.

In essence, $\alpha\beta' x_{t-1}$ in (25) contains all the long-run (levels) information on the process for x_t: the only other observables in (25) are current and lagged Δx_t. The vector $\beta' x_{t-1}$ measures the extent to which actual data deviate from the long-run relationship(s) among the variables in x_{t-1}.

Engle and Granger (1987) establish an isomorphism between cointegration and error correction models: models with valid ECMs entail cointegration and, conversely, cointegrated series imply an error correction representation for the econometric model. [For an exposition and extension, see Granger (1986).] To illustrate these and related issues, consider (20) as a first-order bivariate VAR.

[270]   *Example 6: A single cointegrating vector.* As a first-order bivariate VAR, (20) is:

---

[8] For example, for the first-order univariate model (18), $\pi(z)$ is $\pi_1 z - 1$, so the root of $|\pi(z^{-1})| = 0$ is π_1 itself. Possibilities 1 and 2 correspond to $|\pi_1| < 1$ and $\pi_1 = 1$, respectively; and possibility 3 is not possible because $p = 1$.

$$\Delta y_t = \pi_{(11)}y_{t-1} + \pi_{(12)}z_{t-1} + \varepsilon_{1t} \qquad (26a)$$

$$\Delta z_t = \pi_{(21)}y_{t-1} + \pi_{(22)}z_{t-1} + \varepsilon_{2t}, \qquad (26b)$$

when expressed as (21) with $\pi = \{\pi_{(ij)}\}$, and noting that $x_t = (y_t, z_t)'$.[9] If there is one cointegrating vector ($r = 1$), then α and β' are 2×1 and 1×2 vectors, which can be denoted $(\alpha_1, \alpha_2)'$ and (β_1, β_2), respectively. Without loss of generality, β can be normalized with $\beta_1 = 1$. For convenience, denote the normalized β' vector as $(1, -\delta)$. Thus, (26) can be rewritten as:

$$\Delta y_t = \alpha_1(y_{t-1} - \delta z_{t-1}) + \varepsilon_{1t} \qquad (27a)$$

$$\Delta z_t = \alpha_2(y_{t-1} - \delta z_{t-1}) + \varepsilon_{2t}, \qquad (27b)$$

where $\alpha_1 = \pi_{(11)}$, $\alpha_2 = \pi_{(21)}$, and $\delta = -\pi_{(12)}/\pi_{(11)} = -\pi_{(22)}/\pi_{(21)}$. The cointegrating relation $\beta'x_{t-1}$ is $(y_{t-1} - \delta z_{t-1})$. Equations (27a) and (27b) express the growth rate of each variable in terms of a past disequilibrium and a random error. If lags of Δx_t appear in (21) (i.e., $\ell > 1$), then lagged values of Δy_t and Δz_t will be present in (27a) and (27b).

Example 7: Cointegration and error correction models. Together, (27a) and (27b) correspond to the joint distribution of x_t conditional on its past (X_{t-1}), as described in Section 2. Equations (27a) and (27b) can be factorized into the conditional distribution of y_t given z_t and lags of both variables, and the marginal distribution of z_t (also given lags of both variables):

$$\Delta y_t = \gamma_1 \Delta z_t + \gamma_2(y_{t-1} - \delta z_{t-1}) + \nu_{1t} \qquad (28a)$$

$$\Delta z_t = \alpha_2(y_{t-1} - \delta z_{t-1}) + \varepsilon_{2t}, \qquad (28b)$$

where $\gamma_1 = \omega_{12}/\omega_{22}$ and $\gamma_2 = \alpha_1 - (\omega_{12}/\omega_{22})\alpha_2$. Equation (28a) is also the ECM in (12), and the marginal equation, (28b), is the same as (27b). ECMs imply and are implied by cointegration.

Example 8: Cointegration and weak exogeneity. The parameters in the conditional and marginal models (28a) and (28b) are $(\gamma_1, \gamma_2, \delta, \sigma^2)'$ and $(\alpha_2, \delta, \omega_{22})'$ respectively, and have been denoted λ_1 and λ_2 previously. For cointegrated variables, λ_1 and λ_2 are (in general) linked via δ and α_2. The parameter δ enters both λ_1 and λ_2 directly; α_2 enters λ_2 directly and λ_1 via γ_2, which is $\alpha_1 - (\omega_{12}/\omega_{22})\alpha_2$. Thus, z_t is not (in general) weakly exogenous [271] for the cointegrating vector β', or (hence) for δ.

Weak exogeneity of z_t for β' is obtained when $\alpha_2 = 0$, in which case (28) becomes:

---

[9] The notation $\pi_{(ij)}$ distinguishes this (i,j)th element of π from the (i,j)th element of π_1, which is denoted π_{ij} [as in (11b)].

$$\Delta y_t = \gamma_1 \Delta z_t + \gamma_2 (y_{t-1} - \delta z_{t-1}) + \nu_{1t} \qquad (29a)$$

$$\Delta z_t = \varepsilon_{2t}, \qquad (29b)$$

where $\gamma_2 = \alpha_1$, $\lambda_1 = (\gamma_1, \gamma_2, \delta, \sigma^2)'$, and $\lambda_2 = (\omega_{22})$. Then (29a) alone is sufficient for fully efficient inference about β', that is, about δ. Johansen's (1992) test for weak exogeneity is a test of $\alpha_2 = 0$; see Chapter 5.

Example 9: Two cointegrating vectors. Multiple cointegrating vectors for integrated processes exist between only three or more series. For exposional convenience, consider just three time series $x_t = (y_t, z_t, w_t)'$ with two cointegrating vectors:

$$\beta' = \begin{bmatrix} 1 & -\delta_1 & 0 \\ 0 & 1 & -\delta_2 \end{bmatrix}. \qquad (30)$$

The unit coefficients are normalizations and are without loss of generality. The zero restrictions are *with* loss of generality, and are included for ease of exposition only. From (21), the VAR representation of x_t is:

$$\Delta y_t = \alpha_{11}(y_{t-1} - \delta_1 z_{t-1}) + \alpha_{12}(z_{t-1} - \delta_2 w_{t-1}) + \varepsilon_{1t} \qquad (31a)$$

$$\Delta z_t = \alpha_{21}(y_{t-1} - \delta_1 z_{t-1}) + \alpha_{22}(z_{t-1} - \delta_2 w_{t-1}) + \varepsilon_{2t} \qquad (31b)$$

$$\Delta w_t = \alpha_{31}(y_{t-1} - \delta_1 z_{t-1}) + \alpha_{32}(z_{t-1} - \delta_2 w_{t-1}) + \varepsilon_{3t}, \qquad (31c)$$

where $\alpha = \{\alpha_{ij}\}$. In (31), much more complicated interactions may exist between disequilibria [i.e., $(y_{t-1} - \delta_1 z_{t-1})$ and $(z_{t-1} - \delta_2 w_{t-1})$] and the variables themselves than in (27). With $\ell > 1$, lags of Δy_t, Δz_t, and Δw_t enter (31a)–(31c), further enriching the dynamics.

Empirical analysis of data with multiple cointegrating vectors is harder than with a single vector, but some such studies already exist. Hendry and Mizon (1993) and Hendry and Doornik (1994) detect two cointegrating vectors between money, prices, income, and interest rates for the United Kingdom. One vector is a money demand function, and the other is a relation between inflation, the interest rate, and observed and potential income, where the last is proxied by a trend. Johansen and Juselius (1992) find both purchasing power parity and uncovered interest rate parity in data on the U.K. effective exchange rate, the U.K. wholesale price index, a trade-weighted foreign price index, and U.K. and Eurodollar interest rates.

3.2 Inference

[272] The presence of unit roots complicates inference because some associated limiting distributions are nonstandard. Dickey and Fuller (1979) have tabulated the critical values for the least squares estimator of π and its t ratio for the univariate process (19). The presence of lagged Δx_t does not affect their

limiting distributions under the null hypothesis of one unit root [Dickey and Fuller (1981)].

Numerous system-based test procedures have been proposed, with the conceptually most straightforward being that of Johansen (1988) and Johansen and Juselius (1990).

First, Johansen and Juselius develop a maximum likelihood-based testing procedure for determining the value of r, and tabulate the (asymptotic) critical values of the likelihood ratio (LR) statistic as a function of $p - r$. This statistic generalizes the Dickey-Fuller statistic to the multivariate context. Further, noting that rank(π) is the number of nonzero eigenvalues in a determinantal equation closely related to estimating π, the LR test ties back directly to π by testing how many of those eigenvalues are zero. Additionally, the cointegrating vectors in β' are a subset of the eigenvectors, being those associated with the nonzero eigenvalues. Two variants of the LR statistic exist, one using the maximal eigenvalue over a subset of smallest eigenvalues (the maximal eigenvalue statistic), the other using all eigenvalues in that subset (the trace statistic). These tests and α and β' are computed in several of the chapters below.

Second, Johansen and Juselius develop procedures for testing hypotheses about α and β', such as zero restrictions. Weak exogeneity corresponds to certain zero restrictions on α and so may be tested (as in Example 8 above). Conversely, weak exogeneity of z_t for the cointegrating vectors β is lost if one of those cointegrating vectors appears in both the conditional and marginal densities (i.e., it has nonzero weights in both). Johansen (1992) proposes an ingenious likelihood-based test of weak exogeneity pertaining to the cointegrating vectors. Conditional ECMs by themselves *assume* weak exogeneity, thereby excluding the same cointegrating vector from appearing in both the conditional and marginal processes. If weak exogeneity is valid, cointegration analysis can proceed on the conditional model without loss of information, and Johansen (1992) shows how to do so. Related tests of weak exogeneity have been developed by Boswijk (1991) and Urbain (1992).

The consequences of invalidly assuming weak exogeneity are also of issue. In deriving his statistic for testing weak exogeneity, Johansen (1992) shows how the asymptotic distributions of sub-system cointegration statistics vary, depending upon the presence or lack of weak exogeneity. Hendry (1995) also examines such effects, using asymptotics and Monte Carlo simulation.

> Granger causality does not seriously impede inference when weak exogeneity holds, so strong exogeneity is not necessary to sustain inference. However, the absence of weak exogeneity can have adverse effects on estimation in small samples, and on inference even asymptotically, in cointegrated processes even when the model

under analysis coincides with the conditional expectation. ...
The concept of weak exogeneity as the basis for inference with
no loss of relevant information seems to be at least as relevant
in I(1) processes as it has proved to be in stationary processes.
Hendry (1995, conclusion)

Empirically, tests of weak exogeneity must play a critical role in guiding the
development of models for cointegrated systems, as is readily apparent in
many chapters of this volume.

[273]   Prior to Johansen (1988), Engle and Granger (1987) proposed the use of,
and established the consistency of, unit-root tests in the context of cointegration. Specifically, Engle and Granger proposed testing whether an error
u_t (defined as $\beta' x_t$) is I(0) by testing whether an autoregression in u_t had its
roots within the unit circle. Test statistics include the Dickey-Fuller statistic and the Durbin-Watson statistic, using bounds in Sargan and Bhargava
(1983) for the latter. Engle and Granger proposed estimating β by least
squares in a static regression of the variables in x_t. Stock (1987), Phillips
(1987), and Phillips and Durlauf (1986) derived the asymptotic distribution
of that estimator, showing that it is "super-consistent", converging to β at
$O_p(T^{-1})$ rather than the usual $O_p(T^{-1/2})$.

Nevertheless, the computationally simple Engle-Granger technique suffers from several problems. Inference about β depends upon nuisance parameters; and, as Banerjee, Dolado, Hendry, and Smith (1986) demonstrate,
large finite sample biases can result when β is estimated by a static regression. Unit-root tests applied directly to u_t usually lack power relative to
Johansen's test because the latter conditions on the dynamics of the system,
whereas the former ignores much of that dynamics [Kremers, Ericsson, and
Dolado (1992)]. The number of cointegrating vectors is often of interest,
but the Engle-Granger approach lacks means to estimate that number. The
choice of normalization in regression affects the finite sample properties of the
Engle-Granger technique. Finally, many hypotheses of interest relate to the
complete conditional model specification and concern speeds of adjustment
and the constancy of β over time.

3.3   Policy Implications

Changes in policymaker's "rules" or reaction functions [such as (28b)] may
change the cointegration and/or exogeneity properties of the system. For
instance, if a policymaker reacts to the same cointegrating vector as appears
in the economic agents' conditional model [e.g., (28a)], weak exogeneity for
that cointegrating vector is lost. If a cointegrating vector appears in only
the reaction function [e.g., $\gamma_2 = 0$ and $\alpha_2 \neq 0$ in (28)], and the policymaker
decides to ignore that disequilibrium information (i.e., changing α_2 to zero),
that cointegrating vector disappears from the system. Nevertheless, growth

rate (short-run) effects might still be present: for higher-order VARs, lags of Δy_t and Δz_t could enter (28b) even if $\alpha_2 = 0$. More generally, changes in policymaker's rules may identify conditional models as structural by demonstrating the conditional models' invariance to switches in policy. Many of the tests developed and applied by the studies in this volume aim to address precisely these questions. [274]

4   An Overview of *Testing Exogeneity*

This section summarizes the remaining chapters in *Testing Exogeneity*.

Part I, "A Framework for Testing Exogeneity", provides the conceptual, analytical, and statistical background necessary for implementing and interpreting tests of exogeneity. Engle, Hendry, and Richard (1983) [Chapter 2] is the central reference on exogeneity as a concept. The authors define and distinguish between weak, strong, and super exogeneity, and show how these concepts differ from (and are more useful than) the "classical" concepts of strict exogeneity and pre-determinedness. Section 2 above has provided a non-technical introduction to Engle, Hendry, and Richard's work.

In the next two chapters, Hendry (1988) [Chapter 3] and Engle and Hendry (1993) [Chapter 4] propose and implement two tests of super exogeneity, one based on tests of constancy and the other based on tests of invariance. Super exogeneity is the concept relevant for valid conditioning when regimes change and so is of particular interest to economists. Both approaches provide means of testing the Lucas critique.

Chapter 3 develops procedures for discriminating between feedback and feedforward models, highlighting the role of changes in the marginal models for the expectations processes. Sufficient changes in the marginal processes permit distinguishing between feedback and feedforward models, which advocates testing the constancy of the proposed marginal models. Recursive estimation and testing seem useful tools for doing so. Empirically, Cuthbertson's (1988) expectations interpretation of a constant conditional model for U.K. M1 demand is rejected. Such conditional models still have a forward-looking interpretation, albeit one formulated in terms of data-based rather than model-based predictors; see Campos and Ericsson (1988) and Hendry and Ericsson (1991b).

Chapter 4 introduces a test of super exogeneity based on testing for invariance. Parameters in the conditional model are constant if the conditioning variables are super exogenous, whereas those parameters shift as the marginal processes change if super exogeneity does not hold. The test relies on modeling the changes in the marginal processes and evaluating whether the modeled changes affect the conditional model, above and beyond the effect that the conditioned variables themselves have. An empirical example of U.K. money demand finds prices and interest rates super exogenous in a conditional model; but when the inflation specification changes, super exogeneity fails, although standard specification tests do not reject. We are delighted to include in this chapter an analytical discussion of inversion (or "reverse regression"), which adds important insights to the testing of super exogeneity. This discussion appeared in an earlier version of Engle and Hendry's paper, but was deleted before the paper's publication in the *Journal of Econometrics*.

[275]   Johansen (Chapter 5) describes his (1992) test of weak exogeneity for cointegrating vectors, shows how cointegration analysis is feasible for series that are integrated of order two [I(2)], and applies both developments to U.K. money demand data; see Johansen (1991c). Nominal money and prices appear to be I(2), and they cointegrate as real money to become I(1). Real money in turn cointegrates with real total final expenditure (the scale variable), interest rates, and inflation to generate an I(0) linear combination. Prices, income, and interest rates appear weakly exogenous for the single cointegrating vector in the system, whereas money is clearly not exogenous.

Hunter (Chapter 6) describes his recent concept of "cointegrating exogeneity", which has implications for long-run forecasting of cointegrated variables. Cointegrating exogeneity is the condition that the long-run cointegrating relations between a set of variables are block triangular. Under cointegrating exogeneity, cointegrating relations between a subset of those variables may feed back onto all variables, but cointegrating relations between all variables do not feed back onto the subset. Thus, for long-run purposes, the subset of variables may be forecast without considering long-run relations involving the remaining variables. Cointegrating exogeneity is distinct from weak, strong, and super exogeneity, but is most closely akin to strong exogeneity because of the latter's implications for forecasting.

Hunter then tests for weak and cointegrating exogeneity empirically. He uses Johansen and Juselius's (1990) procedures for testing hypotheses about the cointegrating vectors and the weighting coefficients on the cointegrating relations (equivalently, the error correction coefficients). Certain zero restrictions on the weighting coefficients correspond to weak exogeneity, and other zero restrictions on both the weighting coefficients and the cointegrating vectors imply cointegrating exogeneity. As parametric restrictions, both exogeneity hypotheses may be tested. Hunter illustrates the tests of weak and cointegrating exogeneity with data on prices, interest rates, and the exchange rate for the United Kingdom. These data have been studied previously by Fisher, Tanna, Turner, Wallis, and Whitley (1990) and Johansen and Juselius (1992).

The articles in Part II, "Testing Exogeneity in Practice", apply the principles in Part I, with tests of exogeneity for models of wages and prices

(Juselius, Nymoen), money demand (Ahumada, Bårdsen), and expenditure (Hendry). These articles also develop and evaluate the specification of their models, as does Chapter 3 in Part I (for a model of U.K. money demand).

Beginning Part II, Juselius (Chapter 7) models the determination of prices in a small open economy, Denmark. Danish inflation may be influenced by deviations from several markets' long-run solutions: purchasing power parity (in the international goods market), uncovered interest rate parity (in the international assets market), domestic money demand (via a portfolio effect), and the real wage share (via the labor market). Too few observations are available to analyze all markets together; and, even if enough observations were available, system analysis of several cointegrating vectors jointly and subsequent system modeling of short-run dynamics appear very difficult in practice. Thus, Juselius analyzes each market separately to determine the corresponding cointegrating vectors. Then, she models inflation as an error correction mechanism, with all four cointegrating vectors entering as error correction terms. Foreign effects via purchasing power parity and interest rate parity dominate the long-run determination of Danish inflation; German inflation is an important short-run determinant. Tests of exogeneity show that the estimated error correction model is robust across changes in government party and substantial changes in government policy.

Ahumada (Chapter 8) models the demand for notes and coin in Argentina. She applies tests of cointegration to real money, inflation, and domestic expenditure, and finds a single cointegrating vector, which is interpretable as a money demand relation. Modeling from a general specification and simplifying, Ahumada obtains a parsimonious ECM that satisfies a battery of diagnostic tests. She applies both types of super exogeneity tests, and finds that prices, income, and interest rates appear super exogenous for the parameters of her money demand equation, in spite of dramatic changes in the processes for those variables.

Bårdsen (Chapter 9) models the demand for narrow money in Norway by applying recently developed techniques for testing cointegration and exogeneity. While the sample describes a period with increased financial deregulation, changing monetary policy, and an economy moving from industrial production to oil exportation, Bårdsen is able to obtain a valid conditional model with empirically constant parameters. Prices, real expenditure, and interest rates are super exogenous for the parameters of money demand, permitting valid monetary and fiscal policy simulations of this equation.

Nymoen (Chapter 10) models the relationship between wages, prices, and productivity in Finland. Theoretically and empirically, he distinguishes between two often-confused concepts: *real-wage flexibility* (i.e., the responsiveness of nominal wages to changes in the price level and productivity) and *hysteresis* (whereby real wages may be more or less responsive to other

[276] determinants, such as unemployment). This distinction resolves several conflicting results in the literature. System-based tests of cointegration help
identify the existence and extent of real-wage flexibility, with disequilibria
in wages inducing adjustments in all of wages, prices, and productivity. In
a conditional single-equation analysis, Nymoen develops an error correction
model that determines the extent of hysteresis present. Nymoen's model has
constant parameters, while the marginal models are clearly nonconstant.
That implies super exogeneity in his conditional model, as do Engle and
Hendry's (1993) recent tests of invariance. Finally, Nymoen's model encompasses numerous previous empirical models, while none of the latter can
encompass Nymoen's model.

Hendry (Chapter 11) models the demand for TV advertising expenditure
in the United Kingdom. Both the presence and amounts of advertising on
the various TV channels are regulated by the government, so the demand for
advertising expenditure has been a highly political issue. Cointegration analysis clarifies the long-run relationships in the data. Modeling the dynamics
of prices and quantities on quarterly data obtains a large (absolute) price
elasticity and strong within-year feedbacks between prices and quantities.
Previous estimated price elasticities were obtained from annual data and
were all small in absolute value. The within-year feedbacks in the quarterly
model imply simultaneity bias in the annual estimates, thereby explaining
the difference in price elasticities. Since the price elasticity directly affects
advertising revenues, which accrue to the commercial TV companies and to
a government agency, policy implications are immediate.

The four articles in Part III, "Extensions to Testing Procedures", develop
and extend tests of parameter constancy and predictive accuracy, which are
central to Hendry's (1988) procedure for testing super exogeneity. Empirically constant parameters also are an important element of an economically
interpretable model.

Ericsson (Chapter 12) begins with an exposition of the statistical criteria
for model evaluation and design, including various forecast-based criteria. Using Hendry and Richard's (1982, 1983) taxonomy for model criteria, Ericsson
resolves a debate between modelers emphasizing parameter constancy and
those running "horse races" based on mean square forecast errors (MSFEs).
Both parameter constancy and minimizing MSFE across a set of models are
necessary for good forecast performance, but neither (nor both) is sufficient.
Simple linear models illustrate how these criteria bear on forecasting. Hendry and Richard's taxonomy also leads to a new test statistic, forecast-model
encompassing, which Ericsson applies to two models of U.K. money demand.
Properties of several of the forecast-based tests are affected by the presence of
integrated and cointegrated variables. Ericsson's Table 2 categorizes numerous model evaluation and design criteria according to Hendry and Richard's

taxonomy. This table provides a useful reference, as many of those criteria are used elsewhere in this volume.

Granger and Deutsch (Chapter 13) develop tests from the conditional and unconditional forecasts of a model in which some of the conditioning variables (z_t in Section 2 above) are under policy control. If the conditional model is well-specified and policy "matters" in the conditional model, then the conditional forecasts should be more accurate than the unconditional ones. Specifically, Granger and Deutsch develop a test for whether or not the conditional MSFE is smaller than the unconditional MSFE. Since conditioning is the essence of exogeneity, Granger and Deutsch's test for that improvement in accuracy is an indirect test of valid exogeneity. In practice, if the inequality between the MSFEs does not hold, the conditional model is mis-specified, the policy considered is not influential in the conditional model, and/or (in finite samples) the test lacks power. Numerous related tests employing conditional and unconditional forecasts follow immediately. To illustrate these forecast-based tests, Granger and Deutsch examine Barro and Rush's natural rate/rational expectations model of unemployment, Goldfeld and Kane's and Dutkowsky's models of the demand for borrowed reserves, and Hendry and Ericsson's model of U.K. money demand.

Campos (Chapter 14) derives the confidence intervals for linear combinations of forecasts from general dynamic econometric models. From the associated formulae, tests of parameter constancy are developed, which are valuable in testing for super exogeneity. The forecast confidence intervals as well as the constancy of the associated model may be important inputs to the policymaking process. To demonstrate the techniques developed, confidence intervals and test statistics are calculated for models of an oil price and of the Venezuelan CPI. Several appendices detail how to implement the formulas for confidence intervals and tests in practice.

Hansen (Chapter 15) explains the basis for his recent, easily computable tests of parameter constancy as applied to linear models. His tests generalize Fisher's (1922) and Chow's (1960) split-sample (covariance) test by not requiring *a priori* knowledge of when a break (if any) appears in the sample. In empirical practice, the modeler rarely knows the precise dating of a break. Even when it is known, treating the break date as *given* may be invalid: the occurrence and size of the break may be determined in part by other economic factors, thereby making the break stochastic. For instance, the Great Depression and the OPEC oil price increases might have occurred at other times, and with severities differing from what actually happened. Hansen's applications include a univariate model of GNP and an error correction model of consumers' expenditure, both with U.S. data. [277]

Bibliography

(References marked with an asterisk * are included in this volume.)

Banerjee, A., J. J. Dolado, J. W. Galbraith, and D. F. Hendry (1993) *Cointegration, Error Correction, and the Econometric Analysis of Nonstationary Data*, Oxford, Oxford University Press; originally cited as (1991), forthcoming.

Banerjee, A., J. J. Dolado, D. F. Hendry, and G. W. Smith (1986) "Exploring Equilibrium Relationships in Econometrics through Static Models: Some Monte Carlo Evidence", *Oxford Bulletin of Economics and Statistics*, 48, 3, 253–277.

Barndorff-Nielsen, O. (1978) *Information and Exponential Families: In Statistical Theory*, Chichester, John Wiley.

Boswijk, H. P. (1991) "The LM-test for Weak Exogeneity in Error Correction Models", paper presented at the European Meeting of the Econometric Society, Cambridge, England, September.

Campbell, J. Y., and P. Perron (1991) "Pitfalls and Opportunities: What Macroeconomists Should Know About Unit Roots", in O. J. Blanchard and S. Fischer (eds.) *NBER Macroeconomics Annual 1991*, Cambridge, Massachusetts, MIT Press, 141–219 (with discussion); originally cited as (1991), Technical Working Paper No. 100, Cambridge, Massachusetts, National Bureau of Economic Research.

Campos, J., and N. R. Ericsson (1988) "Econometric Modeling of Consumers' Expenditure in Venezuela", International Finance Discussion Paper No. 325, Board of Governors of the Federal Reserve System, Washington, D.C., June.

Chow, G. C. (1960) "Tests of Equality Between Sets of Coefficients in Two Linear Regressions", *Econometrica*, 28, 3, 591–605.

Cooley, T. F., and S. F. LeRoy (1981) "Identification and Estimation of Money Demand", *American Economic Review*, 71, 5, 825–844.

Cuthbertson, K. (1988) "The Demand for M1: A Forward Looking Buffer Stock Model", *Oxford Economic Papers*, 40, 1, 110–131.

Davidson, J. E. H., D. F. Hendry, F. Srba, and S. Yeo (1978) "Econometric Modelling of the Aggregate Time-series Relationship Between Consumers' Expenditure and Income in the United Kingdom", *Economic Journal*, 88, 352, 661–692.

Dickey, D. A., and W. A. Fuller (1979) "Distribution of the Estimators for Autoregressive Time Series with a Unit Root", *Journal of the American Statistical Association*, 74, 366, 427–431.

Dickey, D. A., and W. A. Fuller (1981) "Likelihood Ratio Statistics for Auto-regressive Time Series with a Unit Root", *Econometrica*, 49, 4, 1057–1072.

Dolado, J. J., T. Jenkinson, and S. Sosvilla-Rivero (1990) "Cointegration and Unit Roots", *Journal of Economic Surveys*, 4, 3, 249–273.

Doornik, J. A., and D. F. Hendry (1994) *PcGive Professional 8.0: An Interactive Econometric Modelling System*, London, International Thomson Publishing; originally cited as D. F. Hendry (1989) *PC-GIVE: An Interactive Econometric Modelling System*, Version 6.0/6.01, Oxford, Institute of Economics and Statistics and Nuffield College, University of Oxford.

Engle, R. F., and C. W. J. Granger (1987) "Co-integration and Error Correction: Representation, Estimation, and Testing", *Econometrica*, 55, 2, 251–276.

*Engle, R. F., and D. F. Hendry (1993) "Testing Super Exogeneity and Invariance in Regression Models", *Journal of Econometrics*, 56, 1/2, 119–139; originally cited as (1989) "Testing Super Exogeneity and Invariance", Discussion Paper No. 89–51, Department of Economics, University of California at San Diego, La Jolla, California, forthcoming in the *Journal of Econometrics*.

*Engle, R. F., D. F. Hendry, and J.-F. Richard (1983) "Exogeneity", *Econometrica*, 51, 2, 277–304.

Engle, R. F., and B. S. Yoo (1991) "Cointegrated Economic Time Series: An Overview with New Results", Chapter 12 in R. F. Engle and C. W. J. Granger (eds.) *Long-run Economic Relationships: Readings in Cointegration*, Oxford, Oxford University Press, 237–266; originally cited as (1991) "Cointegrated Economic Time Series: A Survey with New Results", Discussion Paper 87–26R, Department of Economics, University of California at San Diego, La Jolla, California, forthcoming in R. F. Engle and C. W. J. Granger (eds.) *Long-run Economic Relationships: Readings in Cointegration*, Oxford, Oxford University Press.   [278]

Ericsson, N. R., J. Campos, and H.-A. Tran (1990) "PC-GIVE and David Hendry's Econometric Methodology", *Revista de Econometria*, 10, 1, 7–117; originally cited as (1991), International Finance Discussion Paper No. 406, Board of Governors of the Federal Reserve System, Washington, D.C., forthcoming in *Revista de Econometria*.

Ericsson, N. R., and D. F. Hendry (1989) "Encompassing and Rational Expectations: How Sequential Corroboration Can Imply Refutation", International Finance Discussion Paper No. 354, Board of Governors of the Federal Reserve System, Washington, D.C.

Favero, C., and D. F. Hendry (1992) "Testing the Lucas Critique: A Review",

Econometric Reviews, 11, 3, 265–306; originally cited as (1989), mimeo, Nuffield College, Oxford, forthcoming in *Econometric Reviews*.

Fisher, P. G., S. K. Tanna, D. S. Turner, K. F. Wallis, and J. D. Whitley (1990) "Econometric Evaluation of the Exchange Rate in Models of the UK Economy", *Economic Journal*, 100, 403, 1230–1244.

Fisher, R. A. (1922) "The Goodness of Fit of Regression Formulae, and the Distribution of Regression Coefficients", *Journal of the Royal Statistical Society*, 85, 4, 597–612.

Florens, J.-P., and M. Mouchart (1985a) "Conditioning in Dynamic Models", *Journal of Time Series Analysis*, 6, 1, 15–34.

Florens, J.-P., and M. Mouchart (1985b) "A Linear Theory for Noncausality", *Econometrica*, 53, 1, 157–175.

Granger, C. W. J. (1981) "Some Properties of Time Series Data and Their Use in Econometric Model Specification", *Journal of Econometrics*, 16, 1, 121–130.

Granger, C. W. J. (1986) "Developments in the Study of Cointegrated Economic Variables", *Oxford Bulletin of Economics and Statistics*, 48, 3, 213–228.

Granger, C. W. J., and A. A. Weiss (1983) "Time Series Analysis of Error-correction Models", in S. Karlin, T. Amemiya, and L. A. Goodman (eds.) *Studies in Econometrics, Time Series, and Multivariate Statistics: In Honor of Theodore W. Anderson*, New York, Academic Press, 255–278.

Henderson, J. M., and R. E. Quandt (1971) *Microeconomic Theory: A Mathematical Approach*, New York, McGraw-Hill, Second Edition.

Hendry, D. F. (1979) "Predictive Failure and Econometric Modelling in Macroeconomics: The Transactions Demand for Money", Chapter 9 in P. Ormerod (ed.) *Economic Modelling*, London, Heinemann Education Books, 217–242.

Hendry, D. F. (1983) "Econometric Modelling: The 'Consumption Function' in Retrospect", *Scottish Journal of Political Economy*, 30, 3, 193–220.

Hendry, D. F. (1985) "Monetary Economic Myth and Econometric Reality", *Oxford Review of Economic Policy*, 1, 1, 72–84.

Hendry, D. F. (ed.) (1986) *Economic Modelling with Cointegrated Variables*, *Oxford Bulletin of Economics and Statistics*, Special Issue, 48, 3.

Hendry, D. F. (1987) "Econometric Methodology: A Personal Perspective", Chapter 10 in T. F. Bewley (ed.) *Advances in Econometrics: Fifth World Congress*, Cambridge, Cambridge University Press, Volume 2, 29–48.

*Hendry, D. F. (1988) "The Encompassing Implications of Feedback versus Feedforward Mechanisms in Econometrics", *Oxford Economic Papers*,

40, 1, 132–149.

Hendry, D. F. (1994) *Dynamic Econometrics*, Oxford, Oxford University Press, in press; originally cited as (1990) *Lectures on Econometric Methodology* (D. F. Hendry, with D. Qin and C. Favero), forthcoming.

Hendry, D. F. (1995) "On the Interactions of Unit Roots and Exogeneity", *Econometric Reviews*, in press.

Hendry, D. F., and J. A. Doornik (1994) "Modelling Linear Dynamic Econometric Systems", *Scottish Journal of Political Economy*, 41, 1, 1–33.

Hendry, D. F., and N. R. Ericsson (1991a) "An Econometric Analysis of [279] U.K. Money Demand in *Monetary Trends in the United States and the United Kingdom* by Milton Friedman and Anna J. Schwartz", *American Economic Review*, 81, 1, 8–38.

Hendry, D. F., and N. R. Ericsson (1991b) "Modeling the Demand for Narrow Money in the United Kingdom and the United States", *European Economic Review*, 35, 4, 833–881.

Hendry, D. F., and G. E. Mizon (1993) "Evaluating Dynamic Econometric Models by Encompassing the VAR", in P. C. B. Phillips (ed.) *Models, Methods, and Applications of Econometrics*, Oxford, Basil Blackwell, 272–300; originally cited as (1989), mimeo, Nuffield College, Oxford, forthcoming in P. C. B. Phillips and V. B. Hall (eds.) *Models, Methods and Applications of Econometrics*.

Hendry, D. F., A. R. Pagan, and J. D. Sargan (1984) "Dynamic Specification", Chapter 18 in Z. Griliches and M. D. Intriligator (eds.) *Handbook of Econometrics*, Amsterdam, North-Holland, Volume 2, 1023–1100.

Hendry, D. F., and J.-F. Richard (1982) "On the Formulation of Empirical Models in Dynamic Econometrics", *Journal of Econometrics*, 20, 1, 3–33; reprinted as Chapter 14 in C. W. J. Granger (ed.) (1990) *Modelling Economic Series: Readings in Econometric Methodology*, Oxford, Oxford University Press, 304–334.

Hendry, D. F., and J.-F. Richard (1983) "The Econometric Analysis of Economic Time Series", *International Statistical Review*, 51, 2, 111–163 (with discussion).

Hylleberg, S., and G. E. Mizon (1989) "Cointegration and Error Correction Mechanisms", *Economic Journal*, 99, 395, Supplement, 113–125.

Johansen, S. (1988) "Statistical Analysis of Cointegration Vectors", *Journal of Economic Dynamics and Control*, 12, 2/3, 231–254.

Johansen, S. (1991a) "Estimating Systems of Trending Variables", invited lecture at the European Meeting of the Econometric Society, Cambridge, England, September; forthcoming in *Econometric Reviews*.

Johansen, S. (1991b) "Estimation and Hypothesis Testing of Cointegration Vectors in Gaussian Vector Autoregressive Models", *Econometrica*, 59, 6, 1551–1580.

Johansen, S. (1991c) "A Statistical Analysis of Cointegration for I(2) Variables", forthcoming in *Econometric Theory*; originally cited as (1991c), Research Report No. 77, Department of Statistics, University of Helsinki, Helsinki, Finland.

Johansen, S. (1992) "Cointegration in Partial Systems and the Efficiency of Single-equation Analysis", *Journal of Econometrics*, 52, 3, 389–402; originally cited as (1990), mimeo, Institute of Mathematical Statistics, University of Copenhagen, Copenhagen, Denmark, forthcoming in the *Journal of Econometrics*.

Johansen, S., and K. Juselius (1990) "Maximum Likelihood Estimation and Inference on Cointegration—With Applications to the Demand for Money", *Oxford Bulletin of Economics and Statistics*, 52, 2, 169–210.

Johansen, S., and K. Juselius (1992) "Testing Structural Hypotheses in a Multivariate Cointegration Analysis of the PPP and the UIP for UK", *Journal of Econometrics*, 53, 1/2/3, 211–244; originally cited as (1990b) "Some Structural Hypotheses in a Multivariate Cointegration Analysis of the Purchasing Power Parity and the Uncovered Interest Parity for UK", Preprint No. 1990:1, Institute of Mathematical Statistics, University of Copenhagen, Copenhagen, Denmark, forthcoming in the *Journal of Econometrics*.

Kendall, M., and A. Stuart (1977) *The Advanced Theory of Statistics: Distribution Theory*, London, Charles Griffin, Fourth Edition, Volume 1.

Koopmans, T. C. (1950) "When Is an Equation System Complete for Statistical Purposes?", Chapter 17 in T. C. Koopmans (ed.) *Statistical Inference in Dynamic Economic Models*, New York, John Wiley, 393–409.

Kremers, J. J. M., N. R. Ericsson, and J. J. Dolado (1992) "The Power of Cointegration Tests", *Oxford Bulletin of Economics and Statistics*, 54, 3, 325–348; originally cited as (1989), mimeo, Board of Governors of the Federal Reserve System, Washington, D.C., presented at the World Congress of the Econometric Society, Barcelona, Spain, August 1990, forthcoming in the *Oxford Bulletin of Economics and Statistics*, 54, 3.

Lucas, Jr., R. E. (1976) "Econometric Policy Evaluation: A Critique" in K. Brunner and A. H. Meltzer (eds.) *Carnegie-Rochester Conference Series on Public Policy: The Phillips Curve and Labor Markets*, Volume 1, *Journal of Monetary Economics*, Supplement, 19–46.

[280] Nelson, C. R., and C. I. Plosser (1982) "Trends and Random Walks in

Macroeconomic Time Series: Some Evidence and Implications", *Journal of Monetary Economics*, 10, 2, 139–162.

Phillips, A. W. (1954) "Stabilisation Policy in a Closed Economy", *Economic Journal*, 64, 254, 290–323.

Phillips, A. W. (1957) "Stabilisation Policy and the Time-forms of Lagged Responses", *Economic Journal*, 67, 266, 265–277.

Phillips, P. C. B. (1987) "Time Series Regression with a Unit Root", *Econometrica*, 55, 2, 277–301.

Phillips, P. C. B. (1991) "Optimal Inference in Cointegrated Systems", *Econometrica*, 59, 2, 283–306.

Phillips, P. C. B., and S. N. Durlauf (1986) "Multiple Time Series Regression with Integrated Processes", *Review of Economic Studies*, 53, 4, 473–495.

Phillips, P. C. B., and M. Loretan (1991) "Estimating Long-run Economic Equilibria", *Review of Economic Studies*, 58, 3, 407–436.

Richard, J.-F. (1980) "Models with Several Regimes and Changes in Exogeneity", *Review of Economic Studies*, 47, 1, 1–20.

Salmon, M. (1982) "Error Correction Mechanisms", *Economic Journal*, 92, 367, 615–629.

Sargan, J. D. (1964) "Wages and Prices in the United Kingdom: A Study in Econometric Methodology", in P. E. Hart, G. Mills, and J. K. Whitaker (eds.) *Econometric Analysis for National Economic Planning*, Colston Papers, Volume 16, London, Butterworths, 25–63 (with discussion); reprinted as Chapter 10 in D. F. Hendry and K. F. Wallis (eds.) (1984) *Econometrics and Quantitative Economics*, Oxford, Basil Blackwell, 275–314.

Sargan, J. D., and A. Bhargava (1983) "Testing Residuals from Least Squares Regression for Being Generated by the Gaussian Random Walk", *Econometrica*, 51, 1, 153–174.

Spanos, A. (1986) *Statistical Foundations of Econometric Modelling*, Cambridge, Cambridge University Press.

Stock, J. H. (1987) "Asymptotic Properties of Least Squares Estimators of Cointegrating Vectors", *Econometrica*, 55, 5, 1035–1056.

Suits, D. B. (1955) "An Econometric Model of the Watermelon Market", *American Journal of Agricultural Economics* (formerly the *Journal of Farm Economics*), 37, 2, 237–251.

Tinbergen, J. (1931) "Ein Schiffbauzyklus?", *Weltwirtschaftliches Archiv*, 34, 152–164; reprinted as "A Shipbuilding Cycle?", in L. H. Klaassen, L. M. Koyck, and H. J. Witteveen (eds.) (1959) *Jan Tinbergen: Selected Papers*, Amsterdam, North-Holland, 1–14.

Urbain J.-P. (1992) "On Weak Exogeneity in Error Correction Models", *Oxford Bulletin of Economics and Statistics*, 54, 2, 187–207; originally cited as (1991), paper presented at the European Meeting of the Econometric Society, Cambridge, England, September, forthcoming in the *Oxford Bulletin of Economics and Statistics*, 54, 2.

2

Exogeneity

ROBERT F. ENGLE, DAVID F. HENDRY, and
JEAN-FRANÇOIS RICHARD*

Abstract

Definitions are proposed for *weak* and *strong* exogeneity in terms
of the distribution of *observable* variables. The objectives of the paper
are to clarify the concepts involved, isolate the essential requirements
for a variable to be exogenous, and relate them to notions of predeterminedness, *strict* exogeneity and causality in order to facilitate
econometric modelling. Worlds of parameter change are considered
and exogeneity is related to structural invariance leading to a definition of *super* exogeneity. Throughout the paper, illustrative models
are used to exposit the analysis.

1 Introduction

Since "exogeneity" is fundamental to most empirical econometric modelling,
its conceptualization, its role in inference, and the testing of its validity have
been the subject of extensive discussion [see inter alia, Koopmans (1950),
Orcutt (1952), Marschak (1953), Phillips (1956), Sims (1972, 1977), Geweke

* This paper is an abbreviated and substantially rewritten version of CORE Discussion Paper 80–38 (and U.C.S.D. Discussion Paper 81–1). This was itself an extensive
revision of Warwick Discussion Paper No. 162, which was initially prepared during the
1979 Warwick Summer Workshop, with support from the Social Science Research Council. We are indebted to participants in the Workshop for useful discussions on several of
the ideas developed in the paper and to Mary Morgan for historical references. We also
greatly benefited from discussions with A. S. Deaton, J. P. Florens, S. Goldfeld, A. Holly,
M. Mouchart, R. Quandt, C. Sims, and A. Ullah. Three anonymous referees made many
constructive comments. Financial support from the Ford Foundation, the National Science Foundation, and the International Centre for Economics and Related Disciplines at
the London School of Economics is gratefully acknowledged.

Reprinted with permission from *Econometrica* (March 1983), 51, 2, 277–304.

(1978, 1982) and Richard (1980)]. Nevertheless, as perusal of the literature (and especially econometrics textbooks) quickly reveals, precise definitions of "exogeneity" are elusive and consequently, it is unclear exactly what is entailed for *inference* by the discovery that a certain variable is "exogenous" on any given definition. Moreover, the motivation underlying various "exogeneity" concepts has not always been stated explicitly so that their relationships to alternative notions of "causality" [see Wiener (1956), Strotz and Wold (1960), Granger (1969), and Zellner (1979)] remain ambiguous. This results in part because some definitions have been formulated for limited classes of models so that appropriate generalizations such as to non-linear or non-Gaussian situations are not straightforward, while others are formulated in terms involving unobservable disturbances from relationships which contain unknown parameters. Whether or not such disturbances satisfy orthogonality conditions with certain observables may be a matter of construction or may be a testable hypothesis and a clear distinction between these situations is essential.

In this paper, definitions are proposed for *weak* and *strong* exogeneity in terms of the distributions of observable variables,[1] thereby explicitly relating these concepts to the likelihood function and hence efficient estimation:[2] essentially, a variable z_t in a model is defined to be weakly exogenous for estimating a set of parameters λ if inference on λ conditional on z_t involves no loss of information. Heuristically, given that the joint density of random variables (y_t, z_t) always can be written as the product of y_t conditional on z_t times the marginal of z_t, the weak exogeneity of z_t entails that the precise specification of the latter density is irrelevant to the analysis, and, in particular that all parameters which appear in this marginal density are nuisance parameters. Such an approach builds on the important paper by Koopmans (1950) using recently developed concepts of statistical inference [see, e.g., Barndorff-Nielsen (1978) and Florens, Mouchart, and Rolin (1990)]. If in addition to being weakly exogenous, z_t is *not caused* in the sense of Granger (1969) by any of the endogenous variables in the system, then z_t is defined to be strongly exogenous.

The concept of exogeneity is then extended to the class of models where the mechanism generating z_t changes. Such changes could come about for a variety of reasons; one of the most interesting is the attempt by one agent

[278]

---

[1] The emphasis on observables does not preclude formulating theories in terms of unobservables (e.g., "permanent" components, expectations, disturbances, etc.), but these should be integrated out first in order to obtain an operational model to which our concepts may be applied.

[2] Throughout the paper, the term "efficient estimation" is used as a shorthand for "conducting inference without loss of relevant information", and does not entail any claims as to e.g., the efficiency of particular estimators in small samples.

to control the behavior of another. If all the parameters λ of the conditional model are invariant to any change in the marginal density of z_t, and z_t is weakly exogenous for λ, then z_t is said to be *super* exogenous. That is, changes in the values of z_t or its generating function will not affect the conditional relation between y_t and z_t. This aspect builds on the work of Frisch (1938), Marschak (1953), Hurwicz (1962), Sims (1977), and Richard (1980).

The paper is organized as follows: formal definitions of weak, strong, and super exogeneity are introduced in Section 2; and, to ensure an unambiguous discussion, the familiar notions of predeterminedness, strict exogeneity, and Granger noncausality are also defined. These are then discussed in the light of several examples in Section 3. The examples illustrate the relations between the concepts in familiar models showing the importance of each part of the new definitions and showing the incompleteness of the more conventional notions. Special attention is paid to the impact of serial correlation. The analysis is then applied to potentially incomplete dynamic simultaneous equations systems in Section 4. The conclusion restates the main themes and implications of the paper.

1.1 Notation

Let $x_t \in \Re^n$ be a vector of *observable* random variables generated at time t, on which observations ($t = 1, \ldots, T$) are available. Let X_t^1 denote the $t \times n$ matrix:

$$X_t^1 = (x_1, \ldots, x_t)' \tag{1}$$

and let X_0 represent the (possibly infinite) matrix of initial conditions. The analysis is conducted conditionally on X_0. For a discussion of marginalization with respect to initial conditions, see Engle, Hendry, and Richard (1980), [279] hereafter EHR. The information available at time t is given by

$$X_{t-1} = \begin{bmatrix} X_0 \\ X_{t-1}^1 \end{bmatrix}. \tag{2}$$

The process generating the T observations is assumed to be continuous with respect to some appropriate measure and is represented by the joint data density function $D(X_T^1 \mid X_0, \theta)$ where θ, in the interior of Θ, is an (identified) vector of unknown parameters. The likelihood function of θ, given the initial conditions X_0, is denoted by $L^0(\theta; X_T^1)$.

Below, $f_N^n(\cdot \mid \mu, \Sigma)$ denotes the n-dimensional normal density function with mean vector μ and covariance matrix Σ. The notation $x_t \sim \mathsf{IN}(\mu, \Sigma)$ reads as "the vectors $x_1, \ldots, x_T$ are identically independently normally distributed with common mean vector μ and covariance matrix Σ". C_n denotes the set of symmetric positive definite matrices.

The vector x_t is partitioned into

$$x_t = \begin{bmatrix} y_t \\ z_t \end{bmatrix}, \quad y_t \in \Re^p, \ z_t \in \Re^q, \ p + q = n. \tag{3}$$

The matrices X_0, X_t^1, and X_t are partitioned conformably:

$$X_0 = (Y_0 \ Z_0), \quad X_t^1 = (Y_t^1 \ Z_t^1), \quad X_t = (Y_t \ Z_t). \tag{4}$$

The expressions "$x_t \parallel y_t$" and "$x_t \parallel y_t \mid w_t$" read respectively as "$x_t$ and y_t are independent (in probability)" and "conditionally on w_t, x_t and y_t are independent". In our framework it is implicit that all such independence statements are *conditional* on θ. The operator $\sum$ denotes a summation which starts at $i = 1$ and is over all relevant lags.

2   Definitions

Often the objective of empirical econometrics is to model how the observation x_t is generated conditionally on the past, so we factorize the joint data density as

$$D(X_T^1 \mid X_0, \theta) = \prod_{t=1}^{T} D(x_t \mid X_{t-1}, \theta) \tag{5}$$

and focus attention on the conditional density functions $D(x_t \mid X_{t-1}, \theta)$. These are assumed to have a common functional form with a *finite*[3] dimensional parameter space Θ.

The following formal definitions must be introduced immediately to ensure an unambiguous discussion, but the examples presented below attempt to elucidate their content; the reader wishing a general view of the paper could proceed fairly rapidly to Section 3 and return to this section later.

[280]

2.1   Granger Noncausality

For the class of models defined by (5), conditioned throughout on X_0, Granger (1969) provides a definition of noncausality which can be restated as:

Definition 2.1 Y_{t-1}^1 *does not Granger cause* z_t *with respect to* X_{t-1} *if and only if*

$$D(z_t \mid X_{t-1}, \theta) = D(z_t \mid Z_{t-1}, Y_0, \theta), \tag{6}$$

i.e., if and only if

$$z_t \parallel Y_{t-1}^1 \mid Z_{t-1}, Y_0. \tag{7}$$

---

[3] It is assumed that the dimensionality of Θ is sufficiently small relative to nT that it makes sense to discuss, e.g., "efficient" estimation.

If condition (6) holds over the sample period, then the joint data density $D(X_T^1 \mid X_0, \theta)$ factorizes as

$$D(X_T^1 \mid X_0, \theta) = \left[\prod_{t=1}^{T} D(y_t \mid z_t, X_{t-1}, \theta)\right] \left[\prod_{t=1}^{T} D(z_t \mid Z_{t-1}, Y_0, \theta)\right] \quad (8)$$

where the last term is $D(Z_T^1 \mid X_0, \theta)$ and the middle term is therefore $D(Y_T^1 \mid Z_T^1, X_0, \theta)$.

Where no ambiguity is likely, condition (6) is stated below as "y does not Granger cause z". Note that the definition in Chamberlain (1982) is the same as 2.1.

2.2 Predeterminedness and Strict Exogeneity

Consider a set of $g \leq n$ behavioral relationships (whose exact interpretation is discussed in Section 4 below):

$$B^* x_t + \sum C^*(i) x_{t-i} = u_t \quad (9)$$

where B^* and $\{C^*(i)\}$ are $g \times n$ matrix functions of θ, with rank $B^* = g$ almost everywhere in Θ, and u_t is the corresponding "disturbance".

The following definitions are adapted from Koopmans and Hood (1953) — see also Christ (1966, Chapters IV.4, VI.4) and Sims (1977).

Definition 2.2 z_t is predetermined in (9) if and only if

$$z_t \parallel u_{t+i} \quad \text{for all } i \geq 0. \quad (10)$$

Definition 2.3 z_t is strictly exogenous[4] in (9) if and only if

$$z_t \parallel u_{t+i} \quad \text{for all } i. \quad (11)$$

The connections between strict exogeneity and Granger noncausality have [281] been discussed by several authors—and in particular by Sims (1977) and Geweke (1978)—for complete dynamic simultaneous equations models. This issue is reconsidered in Section 4. See also the discussion in Chamberlain (1982) and Florens and Mouchart (1982).

2.3 Parameters of Interest

Often a model user is not interested in all the parameters in θ, so that his (implicit) loss function depends only on some functions of θ, say:

$$f : \Theta \to \Psi; \quad \theta \to \psi = f(\theta). \quad (12)$$

These functions are called *parameters of interest*. Parameters may be of interest, e.g., because they are directly related to theories the model user

---

[4] We use the term "strictly exogenous" where some authors use "exogenous" to distinguish this concept from that introduced below.

wishes to test concerning the structure of the economy. Equally, in seeking empirical econometric relationships which are constant over the sample period and hopefully over the forecast period, parameters which are *structurally invariant* (see Section 2.6), are typically of interest.

Since models can be parameterized in infinitely many ways, parameters of interest need not coincide with those which are chosen to characterize the data density (e.g., the mean vector and the covariance matrix in a normal framework). Consider, therefore, an arbitrary one-to-one transformation or reparameterization:

$$h : \Theta \to \Lambda; \qquad \theta \to \lambda = h(\theta) \qquad (13)$$

together with a partition of λ into (λ_1, λ_2). Let Λ_i denote the set of admissible values of λ_i. The question of whether or not the parameters of interest are *functions* of λ_1 plays an essential role in our analysis: that is, whether there exists a function ϕ,

$$\phi : \Lambda_1 \to \Psi; \qquad \lambda_1 \to \psi = \phi(\lambda_1) \qquad (14)$$

such that

$$\text{for all } \lambda \in \Lambda, \qquad \psi = f[h^{-1}(\lambda)] \equiv \phi(\lambda_1). \qquad (15)$$

When (15) holds, λ_2 is often called a *nuisance* parameter.[5]

2.4   Sequential Cuts

Let $x_t \in \Re^n$ be partitioned as in (3) and let $\lambda = (\lambda_1, \lambda_2)$ be a reparameterization as in (13). The following definition is adapted from Florens, [282] Mouchart, and Rolin (1990), who generalized the notion of cut discussed (e.g.) by Barndorff-Nielsen (1978) to dynamic models:

Definition 2.4 $[(y_t \mid z_t; \lambda_1), (z_t; \lambda_2)]$ *operates a (classical) sequential cut on* $D(x_t \mid X_{t-1}, \lambda)$ *if and only if*

$$D(x_t \mid X_{t-1}, \lambda) = D(y_t \mid z_t, X_{t-1}, \lambda_1) D(z_t \mid X_{t-1}, \lambda_2) \qquad (16)$$

where λ_1 and λ_2 are variation free, i.e.,

$$(\lambda_1, \lambda_2) \in \Lambda_1 \times \Lambda_2. \qquad (17)$$

Since Λ_i denotes the set of admissible values of λ_i, condition (17) requires in effect that λ_1 and λ_2 should not be subject to "cross-restrictions", whether exact or inequality restrictions, since then the range of admissible values for λ_i would vary with λ_j $(i, j = 1, 2; j \neq i)$.

---

[5] The concept of *nuisance* parameter is, however, ambiguous. Whether or not a parameter is a *nuisance* parameter critically depends on which (re)parameterization is used. If, for example, $\theta = (\alpha, \beta)$ and β is the sole parameter of interest, then α is a nuisance parameter. In contrast, a reparameterization using (α, γ) where $\gamma = \beta/\alpha$ entails that β is not a function of γ alone, and so α is not a *nuisance* parameter.

2.5 Weak and Strong Exogeneity

The following definitions are adapted from Richard (1980). As in (12), ψ denotes the parameter of interest.

Definition 2.5 z_t is weakly exogenous *over the sample period for ψ if and only if there exists a reparameterization with $\lambda = (\lambda_1, \lambda_2)$ such that*

(i) ψ *is a function of λ_1 (as in (15)),*

(ii) $[(y_t \mid z_t; \lambda_1), (z_t; \lambda_2)]$ *operates a sequential cut.*

Definition 2.6 z_t is strongly exogenous *over the sample period for ψ if and only if it is weakly exogenous for ψ and in addition*

(iii) y *does not Granger cause z.*

When (ii) holds, $L^0(\lambda; X_T^1)$ factorizes as in

$$L^0(\lambda; X_T^1) = L_1^0(\lambda_1; X_T^1) L_2^0(\lambda_2; X_T^1), \tag{18}$$

where

$$L_1^0(\lambda_1; X_T^1) = \prod_{t=1}^{T} D(y_t \mid z_t, X_{t-1}, \lambda_1), \tag{19}$$

$$L_2^0(\lambda_2; X_T^1) = \prod_{t=1}^{T} D(z_t \mid X_{t-1}, \lambda_2), \tag{20}$$

and the two factors in (18) can be analyzed independently of each other [283] (which, irrespective of whether or not (i) holds may considerably reduce the computational burden). If in addition (i) holds, then all the sample information concerning the parameter of interest ψ can be obtained from the partial likelihood function $L_1^0(\lambda_1; X_T^1)$. If it were known (or assumed a priori) that z_t was weakly exogenous for ψ, then the marginal process $D(z_t \mid X_{t-1}, \lambda_2)$ would not even need to be specified. However, tests of the weak exogeneity of z_t for ψ, as described in Section 6.1 of EHR and Engle (1982), evidently require that the *joint* model $D(x_t \mid X_{t-1}, \lambda)$ be specified.

The factorization (18)–(20) does not entail that the conditional process generating $\{y_t \mid z_t\}$ and the marginal process generating $\{z_t\}$ can be separated from each other, i.e., for example, that z_t can be treated as "fixed" in the conditional model $D(y_t \mid z_t, X_{t-1}, \lambda_1)$ since lagged values of y_t may still affect the process generating z_t.[6] Factorizing the joint data density $D(X_T^1 \mid X_0, \lambda)$ requires an additional assumption and this is precisely the object of Granger

---

[6] It follows that, unless y does not Granger cause z, $L_1^0(\lambda_1; X_T^1)$ is not *sensu stricto* a likelihood function, although it is often implicitly treated as such in the econometric literature, but it is a valid basis for inferences about ψ, *provided z_t is weakly exogenous for ψ.*

noncausality. When both (ii) and (iii) hold we can factorize $D(X_T^1 \mid X_0, \lambda)$ as in

$$D(X_T^1 \mid X_0, \lambda) = D(Y_T^1 \mid Z_T^1, X_0, \lambda_1) D(Z_T^1 \mid X_0, \lambda_2), \qquad (21)$$

where

$$D(Y_T^1 \mid Z_T^1, X_0, \lambda_1) = \prod_{t=1}^{T} D(y_t \mid z_t, X_{t-1}, \lambda_1), \qquad (22)$$

$$D(Z_T^1 \mid X_0, \lambda_2) = \prod_{t=1}^{T} D(z_t \mid Z_{t-1}, Y_0, \lambda_2). \qquad (23)$$

It must be stressed that the definition of Granger noncausality, as given in (6) and (8), includes *no* assumption about the *parameters*. This is precisely why it must be completed by an assumption of weak exogeneity in order to entail a complete separation of the processes generating respectively $\{y_t \mid z_t\}$ and $\{z_t\}$.

2.6   *Structural Invariance and Super Exogeneity*

A closely related issue of statistical inference is parameter constancy. Over time, it is possible that some of the parameters of the joint distribution may change perhaps through changing tastes, technology, or institutions such as government policy making. For some classes of parameter change or "interventions" there may be parameters which remain constant and which can be estimated without difficulty even though interventions occur over the sample period. This is a familiar assumption about parameters in econometrics which is here called invariance. Just as weak exogeneity sustains conditional inference within a regime, we develop the relevant exogeneity concept for models subject to a particular class of regime changes.

[284]

Definition 2.7 *A parameter is* invariant *for a class of interventions if it remains constant under these interventions. A model is invariant for such interventions if all its parameters are.*

Definition 2.8 *A conditional model is* structurally invariant *if all its parameters are invariant for any change in the distribution of the conditioning variables.*[7]

Since weak exogeneity guarantees that the parameters of the conditional model and those of the marginal model are variation free, it offers a natural framework for analyzing the structural invariance of parameters of conditional models. However, by itself, weak exogeneity is neither necessary nor sufficient for structural invariance of a conditional model. Note, first, that

---

[7] The definition can always be restricted to a specific class of distribution changes. This will implicitly be the case in the examples which are discussed in Section 3.

the conditional model may be structurally invariant without its parameters providing an estimate of the parameters of interest. Conversely, weak exogeneity of the conditioning variables does not rule out the possibility that economic agents change their behavior in relation to interventions. That is, even though the parameters of interest and the nuisance parameters are variation free over any given regime, where a regime is characterized by a fixed distribution of the conditioning variables, their variations between regimes may be related. This will become clear in the examples.

The concept of structurally invariant conditional models characterizes the conditions which guarantee the appropriateness of "policy simulations" or other control exercises, since any change in the distribution of the conditioning variables has no effect on the conditional submodel and therefore on the conditional forecasts of the endogenous variables. This requirement is clearly very strong and its untested assumption has been criticized in conventional practice by Lucas (1976) and Sargent (1981).

To sustain conditional inference in processes subject to interventions, we define the concept of *super exogeneity*.

Definition 2.9 z_t is super exogenous *for ψ if z_t is weakly exogenous for ψ and the conditional model $D(y_t \mid z_t, X_{t-1}, \lambda_1)$ is structurally invariant.*

Note that Definition 2.9 relates explicitly to *conditional* submodels: since estimable models with invariant parameters but no weakly exogenous variables are easily formulated (see Example 3.2 below), super exogeneity is a sufficient but not a necessary condition for valid inference under interventions [see e.g. the discussion of feasible policy analyses under rational expectations in Wallis (1980) and the formulation in Sargent (1981)].

It is clear that any assertion concerning super exogeneity is refutable in [285] the data for past changes in $D(z_t \mid X_{t-1}, \lambda_2)$ by examining the behavior of the conditional model for invariance when the parameters of the exogenous process changed. For an example of this see Hendry (1979b). However, super exogeneity for all changes in the distribution of z_t must remain a conjecture until refuted, both because nothing precludes agents from simply changing their behavior at a certain instant and because only a limited range of interventions will have occurred in any given sample period [compare the notion of nonexcitation in Salmon and Wallis (1982)]. Such an approach is, of course, standard scientific practice. When derived from a well-articulated theory, a conditional submodel with z_t super exogenous seems to satisfy the requirement for Zellner causality of "predictability according to a law" [see Zellner (1979)].

2.7 Comments

The motivation for introducing the concept of weak exogeneity is that it provides a sufficient[8] condition for conducting inference conditionally on z_t without loss of relevant sample information. Our concept is a direct extension of Koopmans' (1950) discussion of exogeneity. He shows that an implicit static simultaneous equations system which has the properties: (a) the variables of the first block of equations do not enter the second block, (b) the disturbances between the two blocks are independent, and (c) the Jacobian of the transformation from the disturbances to the observables is nowhere zero, will have a likelihood function which factors into two components as in (18), a conditional and a marginal. The variables in the second block are labeled exogenous. Implicit in his analysis is the notion that the parameters of interest are all located in the first block and that this parameterization operates a cut. The failure to state precisely these components of the definition, leads to a lack of force in the definition as is illustrated in several of the examples in this paper. Koopmans then analyzes dynamic systems in the same framework leading to a notion of exogeneity which corresponds to our strong exogeneity and predeterminedness corresponding to that concept as defined above.

Koopmans presents sufficient conditions for the factorization of the likelihood but does not discuss the case where the factorization holds but his sufficient conditions do not. Our work therefore extends Koopmans' by making precise the assumptions about the parameters of interest and by putting the definitions squarely on the appropriate factorization of the likelihood. More recent literature has in fact stepped back from Koopmans' approach, employing definitions such as that of strict exogeneity in Section 2.2. As shown in Section 4, strict exogeneity, when applied to dynamic simultaneous [286] equations models includes condition (iii) of Definition 2.6 together with predeterminedness; condition (ii) of Definition 2.5 is not required explicitly but, at least for just identified models, is often satisfied by construction; condition (i) of Definition 2.5 is certainly absent which, in our view, is a major lacuna[9]

---

[8] It is also necessary for most purposes. However, since in (14) ψ need not depend on all the elements in λ_1 it might happen that ψ and λ_2 are variation free even though λ_1 and λ_2 are not, in which case neglecting the restrictions between λ_1 and λ_2 *might* entail no loss of efficiency for inference on ψ. More subtly, whether or not cuts are necessary to conduct inference based on partial models without loss of information obviously very much depends on how sample information is measured. See in particular the concepts of G- and M-ancillarity in Barndorff-Nielsen (1978).

[9] This criticism is hardly specific to the concept of exogeneity. For example, unless there are parameters of interest, it is meaningless to require that an estimator should be consistent since it is always possible to redefine the "parameters" such that any chosen convergent estimation method yields consistent estimates thereof [see, e.g., Hendry (1979a)].

since, unless it holds, strict exogeneity of z_t does not ensure that there is no loss of relevant sample information when conducting inference conditionally on z_t. On the other hand, if (i) and (ii) hold, then (iii) becomes irrelevant[10] since it no longer affects inference on the parameters of interest. This does not mean that condition (iii) has no merit on its own—a model user might express specific interest in detecting causal orderings and ψ should then be defined accordingly—but simply that it is misleading to emphasize Granger noncausality when discussing exogeneity. The two concepts serve different purposes: weak exogeneity validates conducting *inference* conditional on z_t while Granger noncausality validates *forecasting* z and then forecasting y *conditional* on the future z's. As is well known, the condition that y does not Granger cause z is neither necessary nor sufficient for the weak exogeneity of z. Obviously, if estimation is required before conditional predictions are made, then strong exogeneity which covers both Granger noncausality *and* weak exogeneity becomes the relevant concept.

Note that if $[(y_t \mid z_t; \lambda_1), (z_t; \lambda_2)]$ operates a sequential cut, then the information matrix, if it exists, is block-diagonal between λ_1 and λ_2. In fact for most of the examples discussed in this paper and in EHR the condition that the information matrix be block-diagonal appears to be equivalent to the condition that the parameterization should operate a sequential cut. However, at a more general level, the finding that the information matrix is block-diagonal between two sets of parameters, one of which contains all the parameters of interest, does not entail that the likelihood function factorize as in (18). Block-diagonality of the information matrix may reflect other features of the likelihood function. Therefore, it seems difficult to discuss exogeneity by means of information matrices without explicitly referring to reparameterizations in terms of conditional and marginal submodels. Further, information matrices are often difficult to obtain analytically especially in the presence of lagged endogenous variables.

Note also that some definitions seem designed to validate specific estimation methods such as ordinary least squares within a single equation framework. For example, Phillips (1956, Section IV) presents conditions justifying least squares estimation in dynamic systems, which if fulfilled would allow regressors to be treated as "given", despite the presence of Granger causal feedbacks. The concept of weak exogeneity is *not directly* related to validating specific estimation methods but concerns instead the conditions under which attention may be restricted to conditional submodels without loss of relevant sample information. Later selection of an *inappropriate* estimator [287]

---

[10] Evidently if one wished to test the conditions under which (ii) held then overidentifying restrictions such as the ones typically implied by Granger noncausality would affect the properties of the test.

may produce inefficiency (and inconsistency) even when weak exogeneity conditions are fulfilled.

Many existing definitions of exogeneity have been formulated in terms of orthogonality conditions between observed variables and (unobservable) disturbances in linear relationships within processes which are usually required to be Gaussian. Definitions 2.5 and 2.6 apply equally well to any joint density function and therefore encompass nonlinear and non-Gaussian processes and truncated or otherwise limited dependent variables. As such nonclassical models come into more use it is particularly important to have definitions of exogeneity which can be directly applied. See for example Gourieroux, Laffont, and Montfort (1980) or Maddala and Lee (1976). For a formulation tantamount to weak exogeneity in the context of conditional logit models, see McFadden (1979, Section 5.1). Exogeneity also has been discussed from the Bayesian point of view by Florens, Mouchart, and Rolin (1990). The issue then becomes whether or not the posterior density of the parameters of interest as derived from a conditional submodel coincides with that derived from the complete model. Such is the case if z_t is weakly exogenous and in addition λ_1 and λ_2 in Definition 2.5 are a priori independent. However the conditions are not necessary and it may be the case that, in the absence of a sequential cut, the prior density is such that the desired result is still achieved.

3 Examples

Many of the points made in the previous section can be illustrated with the simplest of all multivariate models, the bivariate normal. Because this is a static model, the concepts of weak and strong exogeneity coincide as do the concepts of predeterminedness and strict exogeneity. The central role of the choice of parameters of interest is seen directly.

Example 3.1 Let the data on y_t and z_t be generated by:

$$\begin{bmatrix} y_t \\ z_t \end{bmatrix} \sim \mathsf{IN}(\mu, \Omega), \quad \mu = (\mu_i), \quad \Omega = (\omega_{ij}), \quad i, j = 1, 2, \tag{24}$$

with the conditional distribution of y_t given z_t :

$$y_t \mid z_t \sim \mathsf{IN}(\alpha + \beta z_t, \sigma^2) \tag{25}$$

where $\beta = \omega_{12}/\omega_{22}$, $\alpha = \mu_1 - \beta\mu_2$, and $\sigma^2 = \omega_{11} - \omega_{12}^2/\omega_{22}$. Letting

$$u_{1t} = y_t - \mathcal{E}(y_t \mid z_t), \quad v_{2t} = z_t - \mathcal{E}(z_t), \tag{26}$$

the model is correspondingly reformulated as

$$y_t = \alpha + \beta z_t + u_{1t}, \quad u_{1t} \sim \mathsf{IN}(0, \sigma^2), \tag{27}$$

$$z_t = \mu_2 + v_{2t}, \quad v_{2t} \sim \mathsf{IN}(0, \omega_{22}), \tag{28}$$

where $\text{cov}(z_t, u_{1t}) = \text{cov}(v_{2t}, u_{1t}) = 0$ by construction. The parameters of the conditional model (27) are $(\alpha, \beta, \sigma^2)$ and those of the marginal model (28) are (μ_2, ω_{22}). They are in one-to-one correspondence with (μ, Ω) and are variation free since, for arbitrary choices of $(\alpha, \beta, \sigma^2)$ and (μ_2, ω_{22}) in their sets of admissible values which are respectively $\Re^2 \times \Re_+$ and $\Re \times \Re_+$, μ and Ω are given by [288]

$$\mu = \left[\begin{array}{c} \alpha + \beta\mu_2 \\ \mu_2 \end{array} \right], \qquad \Omega = \left[\begin{array}{cc} \sigma^2 + \beta^2\omega_{22} & \beta\omega_{22} \\ \beta\omega_{22} & \omega_{22} \end{array} \right], \qquad (29)$$

and the constraint that Ω be positive definite is automatically satisfied (see Lemma 5.1 in Drèze and Richard (1983) for a generalization of this result to multivariate regression models). It follows that z_t is weakly exogenous for $(\alpha, \beta, \sigma^2)$ or for any well-defined function thereof.

However, similar reasoning applies by symmetry to the factorization

$$z_t = \gamma + \delta y_t + u_{2t}, \qquad u_{2t} \sim \text{IN}(0, \tau^2), \qquad (30)$$

$$y_t = \mu_1 + v_{1t}, \qquad v_{1t} \sim \text{IN}(0, \omega_{11}), \qquad (31)$$

where $\delta = \omega_{12}/\omega_{11}$, $\gamma = \mu_2 - \delta\mu_1$, $\tau^2 = \omega_{22} - \omega_{12}^2/\omega_{11}$, and $\text{cov}(y_t, u_{2t}) = \text{cov}(v_{1t}, u_{2t}) = 0$ by construction. Therefore, y_t is weakly exogenous for (γ, δ, τ^2) or for any well-defined function thereof. In this example the choice of parameters of interest is the sole determinant of weak exogeneity which is, therefore, not directly testable.

Next, consider the concept of predeterminedness which is here equivalent to that of strict exogeneity. Regardless of the parameters of interest, z_t is predetermined in (27) by construction and so is y_t in (30). Which variable is predetermined depends upon the form of the equation, not upon the properties of the joint density function. Until some of the parameters are assumed to be more fundamental or structural (i.e., parameters of interest), the notion of predeterminedness has no force. When δ is the parameter of interest, z_t is predetermined in equation (27) but not weakly exogenous while y_t is weakly exogenous but not predetermined. Similar results hold in more complex models where the assumptions of exogeneity can be tested.

This example also illustrates the ambiguity in Koopmans' sufficient conditions as discussed in Section 2.7 since their application leads to the conclusion that z_t is exogenous in (27) and (28) while y_t is exogenous in (30) and (31), a conclusion which seems to misrepresent Koopmans' views about exogeneity.

Now consider the concepts of structural invariance and super exogeneity. Will the parameter β in (27) be invariant to an intervention which changes the variance of z? The answer depends upon the structure of the process. If β is truly a constant parameter (because, e.g., (27) is an autonomous behavioral equation) then ω_{12} will vary with ω_{22} since, given (26), $\omega_{12} = \beta\omega_{22}$. Alternatively it might be ω_{12} which is the fixed constant of nature in (24) and in this case β will not be invariant to changes in ω_{22}; z_t can be weakly exogenous for β within one regime with β a derived parameter which changes between regimes. By making β the parameter of interest, most investigators [289] are implicitly assuming that it will remain constant when the distribution of the exogenous variables changes; however, this is an assumption which may not be acceptable in the light of the Lucas (1976) critique. Similar arguments apply to α or σ^2. Therefore, if $(\alpha, \beta, \sigma^2)$ are invariant to any changes in the distribution of z_t or, more specifically in this restricted framework, to changes in μ_2 and ω_{22}, then z_t is super exogenous for $(\alpha, \beta, \sigma^2)$. If, on the other hand, β is invariant to such changes while α and σ^2 are not, e.g., because μ_1 and ω_{11} are invariant, then z_t might be weakly exogenous for β within each regime but is not super exogenous for β since the marginal process (28) now contains valuable information on the shifts of α and σ^2 between regimes.[11] It is clear from the above argument that weak exogeneity does not imply structural invariance. It is also clear that even if β is invariant to changes in the distribution of z or in fact the conditional model (27) is structurally invariant, the parameter of interest could be γ and therefore z_t would not be weakly exogenous, and thus not super exogenous either.

Finally, since weak exogeneity explicitly requires that all relevant sample information be processed, overidentifying restrictions are bound to play an essential role in a discussion of weak exogeneity assumptions.[12] This will be discussed further in Section 4 within the framework of dynamic simultaneous equations models. Example 3.2 illustrates the role of overidentifying restrictions in a simple structure.

Example 3.2 Consider the following two-equation overidentified model:

$$y_t = z_t\beta + \varepsilon_{1t}, \tag{32}$$

$$z_t = z_{t-1}\delta_1 + y_{t-1}\delta_2 + \varepsilon_{2t}, \tag{33}$$

$$\begin{bmatrix} \varepsilon_{1t} \\ \varepsilon_{2t} \end{bmatrix} \sim \mathsf{IN}(0, \Sigma), \quad \Sigma = \begin{bmatrix} \sigma_{11} & \sigma_{12} \\ \sigma_{12} & \sigma_{22} \end{bmatrix}. \tag{34}$$

---

[11] This illustrates the importance of incorporating in Definition 2.9 the requirement that the conditional model $D(y_t \mid z_t, X_{t-1}, \lambda_1)$ be structurally invariant even though ψ may depend only on a subvector of λ_1.

[12] An interesting example of the complexities arising from overidentification occurs if $\omega_{11} = 1$ in (24) a priori. Then the factorization (27) and (28) no longer operates a cut as a result of the overidentifying constraint $\sigma^2 + \beta^2\omega_{22} = 1$, while the factorization (30) and (31) still does. Further, β and σ^2 are well-defined functions of (γ, δ, τ^2) since $\beta = \delta/(\delta^2 + \tau^2)$ and $\sigma^2 = \tau^2/(\delta^2 + \tau^2)$ while α is not. Therefore, z_t is no longer weakly exogenous for (β, σ^2) while y_t now is! Neither of these two variables is weakly exogenous for α.

Equation (33) is a typical control rule for an agent attempting to control y. For example, this could be a governmental policy reaction function or a farmer's supply decision or a worker's rule for deciding whether to undertake training. These cobweb models have a long history in econometrics. The parameter of interest is assumed to be β.

The reduced form consists of (33) and

[290]

$$y_t = \beta\delta_1 z_{t-1} + \beta\delta_2 y_{t-1} + v_t \tag{35}$$

$$\begin{bmatrix} v_t \\ \varepsilon_{2t} \end{bmatrix} \sim \mathsf{IN}(0, \Omega), \quad \Omega = \begin{bmatrix} \sigma_{11} + 2\beta\sigma_{12} + \beta^2\sigma_{22} & \sigma_{12} + \beta\sigma_{22} \\ \sigma_{12} + \beta\sigma_{22} & \sigma_{22} \end{bmatrix}, \tag{36}$$

and the conditional density of y_t given z, is

$$D(y_t \mid z_t, X_{t-1}, \theta) = \mathsf{N}(bz_t + c_1 z_{t-1} + c_2 y_{t-1}, \sigma^2) \tag{37}$$

where

$$b = \beta + \frac{\sigma_{12}}{\sigma_{22}}, \quad c_i = -\delta_i \frac{\sigma_{12}}{\sigma_{22}}, \quad \sigma^2 = \sigma_{11} - \sigma_{12}^2/\sigma_{22}, \tag{38}$$

which can be written as the regression

$$y_t = bz_t + c_1 z_{t-1} + c_2 y_{t-1} + u_t, \quad u_t \sim \mathsf{IN}(0, \sigma^2). \tag{39}$$

The condition which is of first concern is the value of the parameter σ_{12}. If $\sigma_{12} = 0$, then z_t is predetermined in (32) and is weakly exogenous for β since (β, σ_{11}) and $(\delta_1, \delta_2, \sigma_{22})$ operates a cut. Even so, for $\delta_2 \neq 0$, y Granger causes z and therefore z is not strongly exogenous, nor is it strictly exogenous. However, the important criterion for efficient estimation is weak exogeneity, not strong exogeneity, and tests for Granger causality have no bearing on either the estimability of (32), or the choice of estimator.

If σ_{12} is not zero, then z_t is not weakly exogenous for β because this parameter cannot be recovered from only the parameters b, c_1, c_2, σ^2 of the conditional distribution (37). In (32) z_t is also not predetermined; however, in (39) it is, again showing the ambiguities in this concept. Whether or not a variable is predetermined depends on which equation is checked, and is not an intrinsic property of a variable.

The preceding results remain unchanged if $\delta_2 = 0$, in which case y does not Granger cause z, yet z_t is still not weakly exogenous for β when $\sigma_{12} \neq 0$. Granger noncausality is neither necessary nor sufficient for weak exogeneity, or for that matter, for predeterminedness.

Suppose instead that b is the parameter of interest and $\delta_2 \neq 0$. Then OLS on (39) will give a consistent estimate. This however will not be an efficient estimate since the parameters should satisfy the restriction

$$\delta_1 c_2 = \delta_2 c_1 \tag{40}$$

and consequently joint estimation of (39) and (33) would be more efficient. The parameterization (b, c_1, c_2, σ^2), $(\delta_1, \delta_2, \sigma_{22})$ does not operate a cut because the parameter sets are not variation free so z_t is not weakly exogenous for b. If, however, $\delta_2 = 0$ so that the system becomes just identified then z_t will be weakly exogenous for b as (b, c_1, σ^2), (δ_1, σ_{22}) operates a cut. In both cases, z_t is still predetermined in (39).

[291]   Which parameter "ought" to be the parameter of interest requires further information about the behavior of the system and its possible invariants. Usually, it seems desirable to choose as parameters of interest those parameters which are invariant to changes in the distribution of the weakly exogenous variables. Returning to the first case where β is the parameter of interest and $\sigma_{12} = 0$, the investigator might assume that (β, σ_{11}) would be invariant to changes in the distribution of z. If this were valid, z_t would be super exogenous, even though it is still Granger caused by y so it is not strongly exogenous nor strictly exogenous. Changes in the parameters of (33) or even of the distribution of z_t will not affect estimation of β nor will control of z affect the conditional relation between y_t and z_t given in (32). Conversely, if $\delta_2 = 0$, but $\sigma_{12} \neq 0$, then (b, c_1, σ^2) and (δ_1, σ_{22}) operates a cut, and z is strictly exogenous in (39) and strongly exogenous for b, yet that regression is by hypothesis not invariant to changes in either δ_1 or σ_{22}, cautioning against constructing cuts which do not isolate invariants.

The assumption of super exogeneity is testable if it is known that the parameters of the marginal distribution have changed over the sample period. A test for changes in β could be interpreted as a test for super exogeneity with respect to the particular interventions observed.

To clarify the question of structural invariance in this example, consider a derivation of the behavioral equation (32) based on the assumption that the agent chooses y to maximize his expected utility conditional on the information available to him. Let the utility function be

$$U(y, z; \beta) = -(y - z\beta)^2 \tag{41}$$

where β is a parameter which is by hypothesis completely unrelated to the distribution of z and hence is invariant to any changes in the δ's in equation (33). Allowing for a possible random error ν_t, arising from optimization, the decision rule is

$$y_t = \beta z_t^e + \nu_t \tag{42}$$

where z_t^e represents the agent's expectation of z_t conditionally on his information set I_t. In the perfect information case where z_t is contained in I_t, $z_t^e = z_t$ and (32) follows directly from (42). Hence β is structurally invariant and the assumption that $\sigma_{12} = \text{cov}(\nu_t, \varepsilon_{2t}) = 0$ is sufficient for the weak exogeneity of β and, consequently, for its super exogeneity. The imperfect information case raises more subtle issues since, as argued e.g. in Hendry and Richard (1983), z_t^e may not coincide with the expectation of z_t as derived from (33). In this example, however, we discuss only the rational expectations formulation originally proposed by Muth (1961) whereby it is assumed that z_t^e and $\mathcal{E}(z_t \,|\, \cdot)$ in (33) coincide. Hence (32) follows from (42) and

$$\varepsilon_{1t} = \nu_t - \beta\varepsilon_{2t} \tag{43}$$

so that $\sigma_{12} = \mathrm{cov}(\nu_t, \varepsilon_{2t}) - \beta\sigma_{22}$. Therefore, the conventional assumption that $\mathrm{cov}(\nu_t, \varepsilon_{2t}) = 0$ entails that $\sigma_{12} = -\beta\sigma_{22} \neq 0$ in which case z_t is neither weakly exogenous nor super exogenous for β even though β is invariant. On [292] the other hand, rational expectations per se does not exclude the possibility that $\sigma_{12} = 0$ (so that z_t remains weakly exogenous for β) since, e.g.,

$$\mathrm{cov}(\nu_t, \varepsilon_{2t}) = \sigma_{22}\beta \tag{44}$$

suffices.

Under the familiar assumptions, $\mathrm{cov}(\nu_t, \varepsilon_{2t}) = 0$, the conditional expectation (37), and the reduced form, (35), coincide. No current value of z belongs in the conditional expectation of y_t given (z_t, I_t). Nevertheless, z_t is not weakly exogenous for β because the parameter β cannot be recovered from the reduced form coefficients c_1 and c_2 alone. This illustrates that even when the current value fails to enter the conditional expectation, weak exogeneity need not hold.

If the c_i were the parameters of interest, then z_t would be weakly exogenous, but these reduced form parameters are not structurally invariant to changes in the δ's. The Lucas (1976) criticism applies directly to this equation regardless of whether y Granger causes z. The derivation and the noninvariance of these parameters suggests why they should not be the parameters of interest. Once again, testing for Granger causality has little to do with the Lucas criticism or the estimability or formulation of the parameters of interest. It is still possible to estimate β efficiently, for example by estimating (32) and (33) jointly as suggested by Wallis (1980), but this requires specifying and estimating both equations.[13] If there is a structural shift in the parameters of the second equation, this must also be allowed for in the joint estimation. This example shows the close relationship between weak exogeneity and structural invariance and points out how models derived from rational expectations behavior may or may not have weak exogeneity and structural invariance.

Example 3.3 This final example shows that with a slight extension of the linear Gaussian structure to include serial correlation, the concept of predeterminedness becomes even less useful.

---

[13] Depending on the model fomulation, instrumental variables estimation of (say) (32) alone is sometimes fully efficient.

Consider the model

$$y_t = \beta z_t + u_t, \tag{45}$$

$$u_t = \rho u_{t-1} + \varepsilon_{1t}, \tag{46}$$

$$z_t = \gamma y_{t-1} + \varepsilon_{2t}, \tag{47}$$

$$\begin{bmatrix} \varepsilon_{1t} \\ \varepsilon_{2t} \end{bmatrix} \sim \mathsf{IN}(0, \Sigma), \quad \Sigma = \begin{bmatrix} \sigma_{11} & \sigma_{12} \\ \sigma_{12} & \sigma_{22} \end{bmatrix}. \tag{48}$$

Although this model is unidentified in a rather subtle sense, this need not concern us here as all the special cases to be discussed will be identified. The issue is dealt with more fully in EHR.

[293]   The conditional expectation of y_t given z_t and X_{t-1} implies the regression

$$y_t = b z_t + c y_{t-1} + d z_{t-1} + \eta_t, \quad \eta_t \sim \mathsf{IN}(0, \sigma^2), \tag{49}$$

where

$$b = \beta + \sigma_{12}/\sigma_{22}, \quad c = \rho - \gamma \sigma_{12}/\sigma_{22}, \quad d = -\beta\rho, \quad \sigma^2 = \sigma_{11} - \sigma_{12}^2/\sigma_{22}. \tag{50}$$

The covariance between z_t and u_t is given by

$$\mathrm{cov}(z_t, u_t) = \left(\sigma_{12} + \sigma_{11} \frac{\gamma\rho}{1 - \rho^2} \right) / (1 - \gamma\rho\beta). \tag{51}$$

Note first that, as indicated by (51), the condition $\sigma_{12} = 0$ is *not* sufficient for the predeterminedness of z_t in (45). However, $\sigma_{12} = 0$ is sufficient for the weak exogeneity of z_t for the parameters β and ρ, as can be seen directly from (50) where the parameters of the conditional model (49) are subject to a common factor restriction but are variation free with those of the marginal model (47). Thus, the parameters of (49) could be estimated by imposing the restrictions through some form of autoregressive maximum likelihood method. Ordinary least squares estimation of β in (45) will be inconsistent whereas autoregressive least squares will be both consistent and asymptotically efficient. This example shows the advantages of formulating definitions in terms of expectations conditional on the past.

A second interesting property of this model occurs when $\sigma_{12} \neq 0$ but $\gamma = 0$. Again (51) shows that z_t is not predetermined in (45), but surprisingly, it is weakly exogenous for β and ρ. The three regression coefficients in (49) are now a nonsingular transformation of the three unknown parameters $(\beta, \rho, \sigma_{12}/\sigma_{22})$ and these operate a cut with respect to the remaining nuisance parameter σ_{22}. *Ordinary* least squares estimation of (49) provides efficient estimates of its parameters and the maximum likelihood estimate of β is $-d/c$. Both ordinary least squares and autoregressive least squares estimation of (45) would yield inconsistent estimates of β.

The case where

$$(1 - \rho^2)\sigma_{12} + \gamma\rho\sigma_{11} = 0 \qquad\qquad (52)$$

raises several important issues which are discussed in detail in EHR. In short, the condition (52) identifies the model but violates both conditions (i) and (ii) in Definition 2.5 so that z_t is not weakly exogenous for (β, ρ), neither is it for (b, c, d) in (49). In particular, the autoregressive least squares estimator of β in (45) and (46) is inconsistent even though, as a consequence of the predeterminedness of z_t in (45), the first step ordinary least squares estimators of β in (45) and ρ in (46) are consistent (but not efficient).

This concludes the discussion of the examples. It is hoped that these have shown the usefulness of the concepts of weak and strong exogeneity, structural invariance, and super exogeneity in analyzing familiar and possibly some unfamiliar situations. Further examples can be found in EHR including [294] a truncated latent variable model based upon Maddala and Lee (1976).

4 Application to Dynamic Simultaneous Equations Models

In this section we shall apply our analysis to dynamic simultaneous equations models (DSEM). As this is the arena in which notions of exogeneity are most heavily used and tested, it is important to relate our concepts to conventional wisdom. It will be shown that the conventional definitions must be supplemented with several conditions for the concepts to have force. However, when these conditions are added, then in standard textbook models, predeterminedness becomes equivalent to weak exogeneity and strict exogeneity becomes equivalent to strong exogeneity. Finally, our framework helps clarify the connections between such (modified) concepts and the notions of Wold causal orderings [see Strotz and Wold (1960)], "block recursive structures" [see Fisher (1966)], and "exogeneity tests" as in Wu (1973).

Following Richard (1980, 1984) the system of equations need not be complete and thus the analysis is directly a generalization of the conventional DSEM. Assuming normality and linearity of the conditional expectations $\phi_t = \mathcal{E}(x_t \mid X_{t-1}, \theta)$, let[14]

---

[14] Our framework explicitly requires that the distribution of the endogenous variables be completely specified. Normality (and linearity) assumptions are introduced here because they prove algebraically convenient. Other distributional assumptions could be considered at the cost of complicating the algebra. Furthermore, there exist distributions, such as the multivariate student distribution, for which there exist no cuts. Evidently weak exogeneity can always be achieved by construction, simply by specifying independently of each other a conditional and a marginal model, but is then no longer testable. More interestingly, conditions such as the ones which are derived below could be viewed as "approximate" or "local" exogeneity conditions under more general specifications. Given the recent upsurge of nonlinear non-Gaussian models in econometrics this is clearly an area which deserves further investigation.

$$D(x_t \mid X_{t-1}, \theta) = f_N^n(x_t \mid \sum \Pi(i) x_{t-i}, \Omega) \tag{53}$$

where $\{\Pi(i)\}$ and Ω are functions of a vector of unknown parameters $\theta \in \Theta$. *Define* the "innovations" or "reduced form disturbances" v_t by

$$v_t = x_t - \phi_t = x_t - \sum \Pi(i) x_{t-i}. \tag{54}$$

Then, ϕ_t being conditional on X_{t-1},

$$\mathrm{cov}(v_t, x_{t-i}) = 0 \quad \text{for all } i > 0, \tag{55}$$

and hence

$$\mathrm{cov}(v_t, v_{t-i}) = 0 \quad \text{for all } i > 0. \tag{56}$$

We define the dynamic multipliers $Q(i)$ by the recursion

$$Q(0) = I_n$$

and

$$Q(i) = \sum_{j=1}^{i} \Pi(j) Q(i-j), \quad \text{for all } i \geq 1, \tag{57}$$

[295] and note that

$$\mathrm{cov}(v_t, x_{t+i}) = Q(i)\Omega \quad \text{for all } i \geq 0. \tag{58}$$

Often the specification of θ is (partially) achieved by considering sets of behavioral relationships. Such relationships can correspond to optimizing behavior given expectations about future events, allow for adaptive responses and include mechanisms for correcting previous mistakes. In our framework, where attention is focused on the conditional densities $D(x_t \mid X_{t-1}, \theta)$ it is natural to specify these relationships in terms of the conditional expectations ϕ_t. Consider, therefore, a set of $g \leq n$ linear behavioral relationships of the form

$$B\phi_t + \sum C(i) x_{t-i} = 0 \tag{59}$$

where B and $\{C(i)\}$ are $g \times n$ matrix functions of a vector of "structural" coefficients $\delta \in \Delta$, with rank $B = g$ almost everywhere in Δ. The δ's are typically parameters of interest. We can also define a g-dimensional vector of unobservable "structural disturbances":

$$\varepsilon_t = Bx_t + \sum C(i) x_{t-i} \tag{60}$$

which also satisfy, by construction, the properties (55), (56).

Let Σ denote the covariance matrix of ε_t. In all generality Σ is also treated as a function of δ. From (53), (54), (59), and (60) we must have $\varepsilon_t = Bv_t$, and

$$B\Pi(i) + C(i) \equiv 0, \quad \text{for all } i \geq 1; \quad \Sigma = B\Omega B'. \tag{61}$$

The identities (61) define a correspondence between Δ and Θ or, equivalently, a function h from Δ to $P(\Theta)$, the set of all subsets of Θ. To any given $\delta \in \Delta$, h associates a subset of Θ which we denote by $h(\delta)$. In the rest of the paper it is assumed that:

(i) δ is *identified* in the sense that

$$\text{for all } \delta, \ \delta^* \in \Delta, \quad \delta \neq \delta^* \rightarrow h(\delta) \cap h(\delta^*) = \emptyset; \qquad (62)$$

(ii) all values in Θ are compatible with (61),

$$\Theta = \bigcup_{\delta \in \Delta} h(\delta), \qquad (63)$$

so that $\{h(\delta)\}$ is a partition of Θ.

Let s denote the number of nonzero columns in $\{\Pi(i)\}$ and C_n the set of $n \times n$ symmetric positive definite matrices. If $\Theta = \Re^{sn} \times C_n$, except for the set of zero Lebesgue measure, then the model (53) is *just identified*. It is *overidentified* if Θ is a strict subset of $\Re^{sn} \times C_n$.

When $g < n$, it often proves convenient to define an auxiliary parameter vector, say $\overline{\theta} \in \overline{\Theta}$ of the form $\overline{\theta} = (\delta, \theta_2)$ where θ_2 is a subvector of θ defined in such a way that $\overline{\Theta}$ and Θ are in one-to-one correspondence. If, in particular, $\{\Pi(i)\}$ and Ω are subject to no other constraints than those derived from the identities (61) as implicitly assumed in this section, then we can select for θ_2 the coefficients of $n - g$ unconstrained "reduced form" equations,[15] whereby [296]

$$\overline{\Theta} = \Delta \times \Theta_2, \quad \text{with} \quad \Theta_2 = \Re^{s(n-g)} \times C_{n-g}. \qquad (64)$$

The specification of many econometric models "allows for" serial correlation of the residuals, i.e., incorporates linear relationships of the form

$$B^* x_t + \sum C^*(i) x_{t-i} = u_t \sim \mathsf{N}(0, \Phi) \qquad (65)$$

where B^* and $\{C^*(i)\}$ are claimed to be parameters of interest (or well defined functions thereof) and u_t is seen as a g-dimensional "autonomous" process, subject to serial correlation. Note that if (65) is to be used to *derive* the distribution of x_t *from* that of u_t, then the system must be "complete", i.e., $g = n$.

Provided u_t has an autoregressive representation,

$$u_t = \sum R_i u_{t-i} + e_t, \quad \text{where} \quad e_t \sim \mathsf{IN}(0, \Sigma), \qquad (66)$$

---

[15] This is current practice in the literature on so-called limited information procedures. Non-Bayesian inference procedures based on likelihood principles are invariant with respect to the choice of these $n - g$ reduced form equations, provided they form a nonsingular set of equations together with the g structural relationships (59). Also, in a Bayesian framework there exist prior densities on θ such that the corresponding posterior densities on δ have similar invariance properties. For details, see e.g. Drèze and Richard (1983) for $g = 1$, or Richard (1984) for $g > 1$.

then (65) can be transformed to have serially uncorrelated "errors" [the new parameterization being subject to common factor restrictions as in Sargan (1980)] in which case the transformed model can be reinterpreted in terms of conditional expectations as in (53). More general specifications of u_t are not ruled out in principle, but might seriously complicate the analysis.

We can now unambiguously characterize and inter-relate the concepts of Granger noncausality, predeterminedness and strict exogeneity, as given in Definitions 2.1–2.3, for potentially overidentified and incomplete DSEM which have been transformed to have serially uncorrelated residuals. Since these concepts may apply only to a subset of the equation system (59), this is accordingly partitioned into the first $g_1 \leq p$ equations and the remaining $g_2 = g - g_1 \leq q$ equations—see e.g. Fisher (1966) on the notion of block recursive structures. We partition the Π's, Q's, and Ω conformably with the variables $x_t' = (y_t' \ z_t')$, B conformably with the variables and the equations and the C's and Σ conformably with the equations as:

$$\Pi(i) = \begin{bmatrix} \Pi_1(i) \\ \Pi_2(i) \end{bmatrix} = \begin{bmatrix} \Pi_{11}(i) & \Pi_{12}(i) \\ \Pi_{21}(i) & \Pi_{22}(i) \end{bmatrix},$$

$$Q(i) = \begin{bmatrix} Q_1(i) \\ Q_2(i) \end{bmatrix} = \begin{bmatrix} Q_{11}(i) & Q_{12}(i) \\ Q_{21}(i) & Q_{22}(i) \end{bmatrix},$$

$$\Omega = (\Omega_1 \ \Omega_2) = \begin{bmatrix} \Omega_{11} & \Omega_{12} \\ \Omega_{21} & \Omega_{22} \end{bmatrix}, \quad B = \begin{bmatrix} B_1 \\ B_2 \end{bmatrix} = \begin{bmatrix} B_{11} & B_{12} \\ B_{21} & B_{22} \end{bmatrix},$$

$$C(i) = \begin{bmatrix} C_1(i) \\ C_2(i) \end{bmatrix}, \quad \text{and} \quad \Sigma = \begin{bmatrix} \Sigma_{11} & \Sigma_{12} \\ \Sigma_{21} & \Sigma_{22} \end{bmatrix}. \tag{67}$$

[297]   **Theorem 4.1** *For the class of models defined by (53) plus (59):*

(i) *y does not Granger cause z if and only if*

$$Q_{21}(i) = 0 \quad \text{for all } i \geq 1;$$

(ii) *z_t is predetermined in the first g_1 equations of (59) if and only if*

$$B_1\Omega_2 = 0;$$

(iii) *z_t is strictly exogenous in the first g_1 equations of (59) if and only if*

$$B_1\Omega Q_2'(i) = 0 \quad \text{for all } i \geq 0.$$

(iv) *Conditions (i) and (ii) are sufficient for (iii). If $g_1 = p$, they are also necessary for (iii).*

(v) *If $B_{21} = 0$, $\Sigma_{12} = 0$, and rank $B_{22} = q \ (= g_2)$, then z_t is predetermined in the first g_1 equations of (59).*

Proof. The proof follows from the Definitions 2.1–2.3 together with (57), wherefrom it can be shown by recurrence that $(\Pi_{21}(i) = 0;\ i \geq 1)$ is equivalent to $(Q_{21}(i) = 0;\ i \geq 1)$. See EHR for more details. $\square$

In order to discuss weak exogeneity the parameters of interest must be defined. In the theorems below it will be assumed that the parameters of interest are all grouped together in the first g_1 equations. Thus it is not a cavalier matter which equations are put in the first group. For example, in a control problem, the first g_1 equations might describe the behavior of the economic agents given the controlled values of z_t, while the remaining g_2 equations describe the control rules which have been operative.

Factorizing the joint density (53) also requires the introduction of an appropriate reparameterization. This is the object of Lemma 4.2 which translates into our notation results which are otherwise well-known.

Lemma 4.2 *The joint density (53) factorizes into the product of the conditional density*

$$D(y_t \mid z_t, X_{t-1}, \lambda_1) = f_N^p \left(y_t \mid \Delta_{12} z_t + \sum \Pi_{1.2}(i) x_{t-i}, \Omega_{11.2} \right) \qquad (68)$$

and the marginal density

$$D(z_t \mid X_{t-1}, \lambda_2) = f_N^q \left(z_t \mid \sum \Pi_2(i) x_{t-i}, \Omega_{22} \right) \qquad (69)$$

with $\lambda_1 = (\Delta_{12}, \{\Pi_{1.2}(i)\}, \Omega_{11.2})$, $\lambda_2 = (\{\Pi_2(i)\}, \Omega_{22})$,

$$
\begin{aligned}
\Delta_{12} &= \Omega_{12}\Omega_{22}^{-1}, \\
\Omega_{11.2} &= \Omega_{11} - \Omega_{12}\Omega_{22}^{-1}\Omega_{21}, \ and \\
\Pi_{1.2}(i) &= \Pi_1(i) - \Delta_{12}\Pi_2(i).
\end{aligned}
\qquad (70)
$$

Proof. See e.g. Press (1972, Sections 3.4 and 3.5). $\square$

If the model (53) is *just identified*, then λ_1 and λ_2 are variation free with [298] respective domains of variation $\Lambda_1 = \Re^{p \times q} \times \{\Re^{p \times n}\} \times C_p$ and $\Lambda_2 = \{\Re^{q \times n}\} \times C_q$ and z_t is weakly exogenous for ψ if and only if ψ is a function of λ_1 only. However, in order to be operational within the framework of DSEM's, such a condition should be expressed in terms of the structural coefficients δ since these are themselves typically parameters of interest. Also, most applications involve overidentified models for which λ_1 and λ_2 are no longer variation free unless some additional conditions are satisfied. Thus, the object of Theorem 4.3 is to derive *general* conditions on δ for the weak exogeneity of z_t for ψ. By their nature, these conditions are *sufficient* and, as in Section 3, it is easy to construct examples in which they are *not necessary*. Consequently, insofar as so-called "exogeneity tests" are typically tests for such conditions, rejection on such a test does not necessarily entail that the weak exogeneity assumption is invalid (see e.g. Example 3.3 when $\sigma_{12} \neq 0$ and $\gamma = 0$).

Theorem 4.3 *For the DSEM in (53) plus (59) consider the following conditions:*

(i) $B_1\Omega_2 = 0$,

(ii) $B_{21} = 0$,

(iii) $(B_1, \{C_1(i)\}, \Sigma_{11})$ and $(B_2, \{C_2(i)\}, \Sigma_{22})$ are variation free,

(iv) ψ is a function of $(B_1, \{C_1(i)\}, \Sigma_{11})$,

(v) $\Sigma_{12} = 0$,

(vi) rank $B_{22} = q$,

(vii) $(B_2, \{C_2(i)\}, \Sigma_{22})$ are just identified parameters.

The following sets of conditions are sufficient for the weak exogeneity of z_t for ψ:

(a) (i)(ii)(iii)(iv),

(b) (ii)(iii)(iv)(v)(vi),

(c) (i)(iii)(iv)(vii).

Proof. The basic result (a) generalizes Theorem 3.1 in Richard (1980) in that it also covers cases where restrictions are imposed on Σ. The proof in Richard extends to the more general case since, under (i) and (ii), the identity $\Sigma = B\Omega B'$ separates into the two identities $\Sigma_{11} = B_{11}\Omega_{11.2}B'_{11}$ and $\Sigma_{22} = B_{22}\Omega_{22}B'_{22}$. Result (b) follows from (a) together with condition (ii) and (v) in Theorem 4.1. Result (c) follows by applying (a) to a system consisting of the first g_1 behavioral relationships and g_2 *unrestricted* reduced form equations whose parameters are in one-to-one correspondence with $(B_2, \{C_2(i)\}, \Sigma_{22})$ and variation free with $(B_1, \{C_1(i)\}, \Sigma_{11})$ following conditions (vii) and (iii). $\square$

[299]   The major differences in the sufficient conditions for weak exogeneity and for predeterminedness are conditions (iii) and (iv) of Theorem 4.3, which assure the model builder that there are no cross equation restrictions to the second block of equations and that there are no interesting parameters in that block.

To show the importance of these conditions in any definition, consider a set of $g \leq p < n$ just identified behavioral relationships, as given by (59) such that $B\Omega_2 \neq 0$. As is well known [see, for example, Strotz and Wold (1960)] the system (59) can be replaced by an observationally equivalent one in which z_t is predetermined, and hence is strictly exogenous if y does not Granger cause z. For example let

$$\overline{B} = \Phi(I_g : -\Omega_{12}\Omega_{22}^{-1}),\qquad(71)$$

$$\overline{C}(i) = -\overline{B}\Pi(i),\quad i \geq 1,\qquad(72)$$

where Φ is an arbitrary but known $g \times g$ nonsingular matrix so that $(\overline{B}, \{\overline{C}(i)\})$ are just-identified by construction. Such transformations, with $\Phi = I_2$, have been implicitly used in the Examples 3.1–3.3. Replacing (59) by

$$\overline{B}\phi_t + \sum \overline{C}(i)x_{t-i} = 0 \qquad (73)$$

leaves (53) unaffected, but now $\overline{B}\Omega_2 = 0$. Consequently, $(\overline{B}, \{\overline{C}(i)\})$ can be estimated consistently from the conditional model $D(y_t \mid z_t, X_{t-1}, \cdot)$ together with (73). These estimates would be efficient provided (59) were just-identified. However, it is essential to realize that, since $g \le p < n$, the parameters $(B, \{C(i)\})$ are typically not functions of $(\overline{B}, \{\overline{C}(i)\})$ alone and if the former are of interest, transforming (59) to (73) does not allow valid inference conditionally on z_t.

Thus, although at first sight, in normal DSEM weak exogeneity appears to be close to the notion of a Wold causal ordering, without the concept of parameters of interest the latter lacks force since there may be no cut which separates the parameters of interest and the nuisance parameters. Nevertheless, it must be stressed that Wold and Jureen (1955, p. 14) *explicitly* include the condition that "each equation in the system expresses a unilateral causal dependence" which, in the spirit of our use of sequential cuts, seems designed to exclude arbitrary transformations of the system (59); see also the distinction in Bentzel and Hansen (1955) between basic and derived models.

In Wu's (1973) analysis, where $g_1 = 1$, it is implicit that conditions (iii) and (vii) of Theorem 4.3 are satisfied, in which case the condition for predeterminedness ($B_1\Omega_2 = 0$) is indeed sufficient for the weak exogeneity of z_t for the parameters of the first behavioral equation (but not necessarily for other parameters of interest). It must be stressed, however, that if the remaining behavioral equations in the model under consideration are over-identified, then predeterminedness might no longer be sufficient on its own for the weak exogeneity of z_t. Therefore, even if the conditions (iii) and (iv) of Theorem 4.3 are incorporated in the definition of predeterminedness as is sometimes implicitly done, there would remain many situations where weak exogeneity and predeterminedness would still differ. Cases (a) and (b) in Theorem 4.3 provide *sufficient* conditions which are applicable to [300] more general cases than the one considered in Wu. Note, however, that condition (ii) in particular is not necessary and that case (c) could be made more general at the cost of some tedious notation as hinted by the following example.[16]

Example 4.4 *Consider a (complete) DSEM with $n = 3$, $p = g_1 = 1$, $q = g_2 = 2$, and*

$$B = \begin{bmatrix} 1 & b_1 & 0 \\ b_2 & 1 & 0 \\ 0 & b_3 & 1 \end{bmatrix} \quad C(1) = \begin{bmatrix} c_1 & 0 & 0 \\ 0 & c_2 & c_3 \\ 0 & c_4 & 0 \end{bmatrix} \quad C(i) = 0, \; i > 1.$$

---

[16] We are grateful to A. Holly for providing us with this example and, more generally, for pointing out several shortcomings in earlier drafts of this section.

The b's and c's are assumed to be variation free. The condition $B_1\Omega_2 = 0$, which is equivalent to $\sigma_{12} = b_2\sigma_{11}$ and $\sigma_{13} = 0$, is sufficient for the weak exogeneity of (y_{2t}, y_{3t}) for (b_1, c_1, σ_{11}) even though $B'_{21} = (b_2\ 0) \neq 0$ and the third behavioral relationship is overidentified (but does not contain y_{1t}!). Note that the predeterminedness of y_{2t} in the first behavioral relationship ($\sigma_{12} = b_2\sigma_{11}$) is sufficient for the *consistency* of OLS estimation of (b_1, c_1, σ_{11}) in that relationship but not for the weak exogeneity of (y_{2t}, y_{3t})—or y_{2t} alone—for (b_1, c_1, σ_{11}). In the absence of additional restrictions such as $\sigma_{13} = 0$ a more *efficient* estimator of (b_1, c_1, σ_{11}) is obtained e.g. by FIML estimation of the complete DSEM.

Note finally from Theorem 4.1 (v) and 4.3 (b) that the standard block-recursive model is sufficient for both (block) predeterminedness and (block) weak exogeneity (again assuming the parameterization satisfies (iii) and (iv)); this may help explain its importance in the development of the theory of simultaneous equations models.

5   Summary and Conclusions

Given the pervasive role of the concept of "exogeneity" in econometrics, it is essential to uniquely characterize the implications of claims that certain variables are "exogenous" according to particular definitions. Also, it is useful to have definitions which require minimal conditions and yet are applicable to as wide a class of relevant models as possible. Consequently, general and unambiguous definitions are proposed for *weak*, *strong*, and *super* exogeneity in terms of the joint densities of observable variables and the parameters of interest in given models, thus extending and formalizing the approach in Koopmans (1950). "Exogeneity" assertions are usually intended to allow the analysis of one set of variables without having to specify exactly how a second [301] related set is determined and such an analysis could comprise any or all of inference, forecasting, or policy. In each case, the conclusions are conditional on the validity of the relevant "exogeneity" claims (a comment germane to theoretical models also, although we only consider observable variables) and since different conditioning statements are required in these three cases, three distinct, but inter-related, concepts of exogeneity are necessary.

The joint density of the observed variables $x_t = (y'_t\ z'_t)'$, conditional on their past, always can be factorized as the conditional density of y_t given z_t times the marginal density of z_t. If: (a) the parameters λ_1 and λ_2 of these conditional and marginal densities are not subject to cross-restrictions (i.e., there is a cut) and, (b) the parameters of interest (denoted by ψ) can be uniquely determined from the parameters of the conditional model alone (i.e., $\psi = f(\lambda_1)$), then inference concerning ψ from the joint density will be equivalent to that from the conditional density so that the latter may be used without loss of relevant information. Under such conditions, z_t is *weakly* exogenous for ψ, and for purposes of *inference* about ψ, z_t may be treated "as if" it were determined outside the (conditional) model under study, making the analysis simpler and more robust.

Conditions (a) and (b) clearly are not sufficient to treat z_t as if it were fixed in repeated samples, since the definition of weak exogeneity is unspecific about relationships between z_t and y_{t-i} for $i \geq 1$. However, if: (c) y does not Granger cause z, then the data density of $X_t^1 = (x_1, \ldots, x_t)'$ factorizes into the conditional density of Y_t^1 given Z_t^1 times the marginal of Z_t^1 and hence $\{z_t\}$ may be treated as if it were fixed. If (a), (b), and (c) are satisfied, then z_t is *strongly exogenous* for ψ and forecasts could be made conditional on fixed future z's.

Nevertheless, strong exogeneity is insufficient to sustain conditional policy analysis since (a) does not preclude the possibility that while λ_1 and λ_2 are variation free within any *given* "regime", λ_1 might vary in response to a change in λ_2 between "regimes". The additional condition that: (d) λ_1 is invariant to changes in λ_2 (or more generally the conditional distribution is invariant to any change in the marginal distribution) is required to sustain conditional *policy* experiments for fixed λ_1, and z_t is *super exogenous* for ψ if (a), (b), and (d) are satisfied (so that (c) is not necessary either).

In fact, if the generating process of the conditioning variables is susceptible to changes over either sample or forecast periods, then the failure of (d) will invalidate inference and predictions based on the assertion that λ_1 is a constant parameter, whether or not z_t includes "policy variables". In worlds where policy parameters change, false super-exogeneity assumptions are liable to produce predictive failures in conditional models [see Lucas (1976)]. Control experiments which involve changes in λ_2 must first establish the super exogeneity of z_t for ψ under the class of interventions considered; we know of no sufficient conditions for establishing such results, but a necessary condition is that the conditional model does not experience predictive failure within sample [see Hendry (1979b)].

Even in constant parameter worlds (and certainly in worlds of parameter change), the new concepts are distinct from the more familiar notions of predeterminedness and strict exogeneity. Following precise definitions of these two concepts, it is shown through examples that their formulation in terms of [302] *unobservable* disturbances entails ambiguous implications for inference and that strict exogeneity is neither necessary nor sufficient for inference in conditional models without loss of relevant information. Moreover, models in which predeterminedness is obtained by construction need not have invariant parameters and since predeterminedness is necessary for strict exogeneity, establishing only the latter does not provide a valid basis for conditional prediction or conditional policy. The various concepts are compared and con trasted in detail in closed linear dynamic simultaneous equations systems, and the usefulness of (a) and (b) in clarifying the debate about Wold-causal-orderings is demonstrated.

It is natural to enquire about the testable implications of alternative exogeneity assumptions. Condition (d) is indirectly testable (as noted) via tests for parameter constancy, although as with all test procedures, rejection of the null does not indicate what alternative is relevant and non-rejection may simply reflect low power [so that there are advantages in specifying the regime shift process as in Richard (1980)]. Condition (c) is common to both strong and strict exogeneity notions and may be testable in the conditional model [see Sims (1972) and Geweke (1982)] but may also require specification of the marginal density of z_t as in Granger (1969). Also, predeterminedness tests have been the subject of a large literature [see inter alia Wu (1973)].

To test weak exogeneity, the conditional and marginal densities could be embedded in a joint density function, although the choice of the latter may or may not generate testable implications. It is somewhat paradoxical to estimate the parameters of a (potentially very complicated) marginal model just to test whether or not one needed to specify that model. Moreover, misspecifications in the marginal model may induce false rejection of the null of weak exogeneity. Nevertheless, Engle (1982, 1984) considers various weak exogeneity tests based on the Lagrange multiplier principle. Also, on a positive note, while both weak exogeneity and parameter constancy are conjectural features in a conditional modelling exercise, if the data generating process of z_t has changed, but the conditional model has not, then some credibility must attach to the latter since it was hazarded to potential rejection and survived.

Finally, we believe that the new concepts are not only general (being based explicitly on density functions and encompassing worlds of parameter change) and unambiguously characterized (thus clarifying a vital concept in econometrics) but also highlight interesting and novel aspects of familiar problems (as shown in the examples in Section 3).

[303]   Bibliography

(References marked with an asterisk * are included in this volume.)

Barndorff-Nielsen, O. (1978) *Information and Exponential Families in Statistical Theory*, New York, John Wiley and Sons.

Bentzel, R. and B. Hansen (1955) "On Recursiveness and Interdependency in Economic Models", *Review of Economic Studies*, 22, 153–168.

Chamberlain, G. (1982) "The General Equivalence of Granger and Sims Causality", *Econometrica*, 50, 569–582.

Christ, C. F. (1966) *Econometric Models and Methods*, New York, John Wiley and Sons.

Drèze, J. H., and J.-F. Richard (1983) "Bayesian Analysis of Simultaneous Equation Systems", Chapter 9 in Z. Griliches and M. D. Intriligator (eds.) *Handbook of Econometrics*, Volume 1, Amsterdam, North-Holland, 517–598; originally cited as forthcoming in the *Handbook of Econometrics*.

Engle, R. F. (1982) "A General Approach to Lagrange Multiplier Model Diagnostics", *Journal of Econometrics*, 20, 1, 83–104; originally cited as (1979) "A General Approach to the Construction of Model Diagnostics Based Upon the Lagrange Multiplier Principle", University of Warwick Discussion Paper 156, UCSD Discussion Paper 79–43.

Engle, R. F. (1984) "Wald, Likelihood Ratio, and Lagrange Multiplier Tests in Econometrics", Chapter 13 in Z. Griliches and M. D. Intriligator (eds.) *Handbook of Econometrics*, Volume 2, Amsterdam, North-Holland, 775–826; originally cited as forthcoming in the *Handbook of Econometrics*.

Engle, R. F., D. F. Hendry, and J.-F. Richard (1980) "Exogeneity, Causality and Structural Invariance in Econometric Modelling", CORE Discussion Paper 80–38, UCSD Discussion Paper 81–1.

Fisher, F. M. (1966) *The Identification Problem in Econometrics*, New York, McGraw-Hill.

Florens, J.-P., M. Mouchart, and J.-M. Rolin (1990) *Elements of Bayesian Statistics*, New York, Marcel Dekker, Chapter 6 ("Sequential Experiments"); originally cited as J.-P. Florens and M. Mouchart (1980) "Initial and Sequential Reduction of Bayesian Experiments", CORE Discussion Paper 8015, Université Catholique de Louvain, Louvain-la-Neuve, Belgium.

Florens, J.-P., and M. Mouchart (1982) "A Note on Non-Causality", *Econometrica*, 50, 583–592.

Frisch, R. (1938) "Autonomy of Economic Relations", paper read at the Cambridge Conference of the Econometric Society; reprinted in D. F. Hendry and M. S. Morgan (eds.) (1994) *Foundations of Econometric Analysis*, Cambridge, Cambridge University Press.

Geweke, J. (1978) "Testing the Exogeneity Specification in the Complete Dynamic Simultaneous Equations Model", *Journal of Econometrics*, 7, 163–185.

Geweke, J. (1982) "Causality, Exogeneity, and Inference", Chapter 7 in W. Hildenbrand (ed.) *Advances in Econometrics: Invited Papers for the Fourth World Congress of the Econometric Society*, Cambridge, Cambridge University Press, 209–235; originally cited as (1980) Invited paper, Fourth World Congress of the Econometric Society, Aix-en-Provence.

Gourieroux, C., J.-J. Laffont, and A. Montfort (1980) "Disequilibrium Econometrics in Simultaneous Equations Systems", *Econometrica*, 48, 75–96.

Granger, C. W. J. (1969) "Investigating Causal Relations by Econometric Models and Cross-Spectral Methods", *Econometrica*, 37, 424–438.

Hendry, D. F. (1979a) "The Behavior of Inconsistent Instrumental Variables Estimators in Dynamic Systems with Autocorrelated Errors", *Journal of Econometrics*, 9, 295–314.

Hendry, D. F. (1979b) "Predictive Failure and Econometric Modelling in Macroeconomics: The Transactions Demand for Money", Chapter 9 in P. Ormerod (ed.) *Economic Modelling*, London, Heinemann Educational Books, 217–242; originally cited as (1980).

Hendry, D. F., and J.-F. Richard (1983) "The Econometric Analysis of Economic Time Series", *International Statistical Review*, 51, 2, 111–163 (with discussion); originally cited as forthcoming in the *International Statistical Review*.

Hurwicz, L. (1962) "On the Structural Form of Interdependent Systems", in E. Nagel *et al.* (eds.) *Logic, Methodology and the Philosophy of Science*, Palo Alto, Stanford University Press.

Koopmans, T. C. (1950) "When is an Equation System Complete for Statistical Purposes?", in T. C. Koopmans (ed.) *Statistical Inference in Dynamic Economic Models*, New York, John Wiley and Sons.

Koopmans, T. C., and W. C. Hood (1953) "The Estimation of Simultaneous Linear Economic Relationships", in W. C. Hood and T. C. Koopmans (eds.) *Studies in Econometric Method*, New Haven, Yale University Press.

Lucas, R. E., Jr. (1976) "Econometric Policy Evaluation: A Critique", in K. Brunner and A. Meltzer (eds.) *Carnegie-Rochester Conferences on Public Policy*, Volume 1, supplementary series to the *Journal of Monetary Economics*, Amsterdam, North-Holland, 19–46.

McFadden, D. (1979) "Econometric Analysis of Discrete Data", Fisher-Schultz Lecture, European Meeting of the Econometric Society, Athens.

Maddala, G. S., and L. F. Lee (1976) "Recursive Models with Qualitative Endogenous Variables", *Annals of Economic and Social Measurement*, 5, 525–545.

[304] Marschak, J. (1953) "Economic Measurements for Policy and Prediction", in W. C. Hood and T. C. Koopmans (eds.) *Studies in Econometric Method*, New Haven, Yale University Press.

Muth, J. F. (1961) "Rational Expectations and the Theory of Price Movements", *Econometrica*, 29, 315–335.

Orcutt, G. H. (1952) "Toward a Partial Redirection of Econometrics", *Review of Economics and Statistics*, 34, 195–213.

Phillips, A. W. (1956) "Some Notes on the Estimation of Time-Forms of Reactions in Interdependent Dynamic Systems", *Economica*, 23, 99–113.

Press, S. J. (1972) *Applied Multivariate Analysis*, New York, Holt, Rinehard, and Winston.

Richard, J.-F. (1980) "Models with Several Regimes and Changes in Exogeneity", *Review of Economic Studies*, 47, 1–20.

Richard, J.-F. (1984) "Classical and Bayesian Inference in Incomplete Simultaneous Equation Models", Chapter 4 in D. F. Hendry and K. F. Wallis (eds.) *Econometrics and Quantitative Economics*, Oxford, Basil Blackwell, 61–102; originally cited as (1979) "Exogeneity, Inference and Prediction in So-called Incomplete Dynamic Simultaneous Equation Models", CORE Discussion Paper 7922, Université Catholique de Louvain, Louvain-la-Neuve, Belgium.

Rothenberg, T. J. (1973) *Efficient Estimation with A Priori Information*, Cowles Foundation Monograph 23, New Haven, Yale University Press.

Salmon, M., and K. F. Wallis (1982) "Model Validation and Forecast Comparisons: Theoretical and Practical Considerations", in G. C. Chow and P. Corsi (eds.) *Evaluating the Reliability of Macroeconomic Models*, London, John Wiley and Sons.

Sargan, J. D. (1961) "The Maximum Likelihood Estimation of Economic Relationships with Autoregressive Residuals", *Econometrica*, 29, 414–426.

Sargan, J. D. (1980) "Some Tests of Dynamic Specification for a Single Equation", *Econometrica*, 48, 879–897.

Sargent, T. J. (1981) "Interpreting Economic Time Series", *Journal of Political Economy*, 89, 213–248.

Sims, C. A. (1972) "Money, Income and Causality", *American Economic Review*, 62, 540–552.

Sims, C. A. (1977) "Exogeneity and Causal Ordering in Macroeconomic Models", in C. A. Sims (ed.) *New Methods in Business Cycle Research: Proceedings from a Conference*, Minneapolis, Federal Reserve Bank of Minneapolis.

Strotz, R. H., and H. O. A. Wold (1960) "Recursive Versus Non-Recursive Systems: An Attempt at a Synthesis", *Econometrica*, 28, 417–421.

Wallis, K. F. (1980) "Econometric Implications of the Rational Expectations Hypothesis", *Econometrica*, 48, 49–73.

Wiener, N. (1956) "The Theory of Prediction", in E. F. Beckenback (ed.) *Modern Mathematics for Engineers*, New York, McGraw-Hill.

Wold, H. O. A., and L. Jureen (1955) *Demand Analysis—A Study in Econometrics*, New York, John Wiley and Sons.

Wu, D. M. (1973) "Alternative Tests of Independence between Stochastic Regressors and Disturbances", *Econometrica*, 41, 733–750.

Zellner, A. (1979) "Causality and Econometrics", in K. Brunner and A. H. Meltzer (eds.) *Three Aspects of Policy and Policymaking*, Amsterdam, North-Holland.

3

The Encompassing Implications of Feedback versus Feedforward Mechanisms in Econometrics

DAVID F. HENDRY*

Abstract

This paper develops procedures for discriminating between feedback and feedforward models, highlighting the role of changes in the marginal models for the expectations processes. For sufficient change in the marginal processes, the combination of encompassing and super exogeneity allows discrimination between feedback and feedforward models. Thus, prior to advocating expectations processes, it is important to test the constancy of the proposed marginal models; and recursive estimation and testing seem useful tools for doing so. Empirically, an expectations interpretation of a constant conditional model for U.K. M1 demand is rejected.

1 Introduction

In many areas of applied economics, alternative modelling strategies based on expectations mechanisms and on feedback rules have been tried. The former approach (emphasising the role of feedforward mechanisms) derives its force from the dependence of much economic theory on inter-temporal optimization. Thus, formal theory-models tend to incorporate both expectations

* The author is grateful to the ESRC for finance under grant B00220012 for research on "The Roles of Expectational Variables and Feedback Mechanisms in Econometric Models". Helpful comments from Juan Dolado, Neil Ericsson, John Muellbauer, Adrian Neale, Steve Nickell, and two anonymous referees of this Journal are gratefully acknowledged.

Reprinted from *Oxford Economic Papers* (March 1988), 40, 1, 132–149, by permission of Oxford University Press.

about future outcomes and feedbacks as determinants of current plans. Unfortunately, empirical models of aggregate variables at (say) a quarterly frequency are far removed from theories of representative agents' decision rules with undefined time periods. Thus, there are legitimate grounds to doubt the translation from the (micro) theory to the (macro) data model. Conversely, feedback-only models (which eschew expectations interpretations) can be justified as being simplified rules-of-thumb which representative agents may adopt in complex environments. Despite such theoretical justifications, their widespread use probably rests more on the pragmatic grounds of empirical success as simple models which have relatively constant parameters. Consequently, if expectations formation is in fact an important aspect of economic behaviour, such models must always be open to potential parameter change whenever expectations processes alter.

Two questions about models based on these rival economic hypotheses seem particularly apposite:

(i) Can either hypothesis account for the results obtained by the other?

(ii) Does either hypothesis isolate the actual invariants of the economic process?

The first question concerns the issue of encompassing [see Davidson, Hendry, Srba, and Yeo (1978), Mizon (1984), Mizon and Richard (1986), Hendry and Richard (1982, 1989)]. The encompassing approach examines the implications which each hypothesis entails for the other, treating each in turn as the data generation process. If either incorrectly predicts the presence or absence of salient features of the other, then its status as a valid representation of the data generation process (DGP) is cast into doubt. Denoting any two hypotheses by H_1 and H_2, a failure by H_i to encompass H_j $(i \neq j)$ reveals H_j to contain specific data information excluded from H_i.

[133]   The second question raises the issue of *super exogeneity* [see Lucas (1976), Engle, Hendry, and Richard (1983), and Engle and Hendry (1993)]. Two facets of a model are involved in super exogeneity, namely the weak exogeneity of the conditioning information for the parameters of interest, and the invariance of those parameters to changes in the marginal distributions of the conditioning variables. Both facets are pertinent to ascertaining the roles of expectations and conditional variables in any given econometric model. We will focus below on the invariance aspect since the Lucas critique that optimal decision rules for economic agents depend on policy rules [see Lucas (1976, p. 41)] and the assumption of rational expectations [see Muth (1961) and Wallis (1980)] each link the parameters of structural models to those of other processes; Hendry and Neale (1988) discuss the issue of weak exogeneity in a related context. In Section 2, formal representations of the expectations (feedforward) and conditional (feedback) alternatives are analysed

assuming a data generation process which exhibits parameter change in the marginal models for the variables entering the behavioural equation. Since each hypothesis entails views about the other which confound behavioural parameters with the parameters of the marginal models, *if the marginal models exhibit enough change at least one hypothesis can be rejected on non-constancy grounds.* Thus, a symmetric analysis results from examining the encompassing implications of super exogeneity in a changing world: for expectations hypotheses the Lucas critique is potentially refutable as well as confirmable. The issue of how to discover the relevant model is *not* discussed, only the evaluation of each hypothesis once it has been formulated.

In Section 3, the analysis is applied to models of the demand for narrow money in the U.K. and contrasts the equations in Hendry (1985) and Cuthbertson (1988). The latter seeks to reinterpret the former as being an approximation to a "forward-looking" equation in which expectations are formed autoregressively. The constancy of the marginal expectations models was not tested by Cuthbertson, however, and the evidence provided here shows that in fact constancy does *not* hold across the sample either on Cuthbertson's data, or for analogue equations fitted to the data used by Hendry (1985). Given the analysis in Section 2, that finding precludes precisely the interpretation which Cuthbertson wishes to make, since the constancy of the conditional model is inconsistent with its being an approximation to an expectations model when the expectations equations used are *not* constant *de facto*.

2 Discriminating Feedback and Feedforward Representations

Consider the following behavioural model of a variable y_t hypothesised to depend on a vector x_t in the linear form:

$$E(y_t \mid I) = \beta_t' E(x_t \mid I). \qquad (1)$$

It is assumed that (1) correctly characterises the behaviour of the relevant [134] economic agents for some specification of the information set I, and that $\beta_t = \beta \; \forall t$ for that choice of I. The rival hypotheses about expectations and conditioning are expressed as follows:

$$H_c : \{x_t\} \in I \qquad \text{(conditional/feedback)}$$

$$H_e : \{z_{t-1}\} \in I \qquad \text{(expectational/feedforward)},$$

where H_c entails the conditional irrelevance of z_{t-1} given x_t, whereas H_e entails the invalidity of conditioning on x_t. Throughout, it will be assumed that *one* of the two hypotheses is correct, in that it coincides with the equation actually generating $\{y_t\}$, and that such an equation is *congruent* in the sense of Hendry (1985, 1987), i.e., has an error which is a homoscedastic innovation against the relevant I, has valid conditional variables, constant parameters, is data admissible and is consistent with the associated economic theory. Finally, β is the primary parameter of interest under both hypotheses, despite requiring distinctly different models to define it. Indeed, under H_c (meaning "when H_c is the DGP"):

$$F(y_t \mid x_t) = \beta' x_t, \tag{2}$$

whereas under H_e :

$$E(y_t \mid z_{t-1}) = \beta' E(x_t \mid z_{t-1}). \tag{3}$$

To avoid confusion, and allow for the possibility that either hypothesis may be incorrect, we re-express these as:

$$E_c(y_t \mid x_t) = \gamma' x_t \tag{4}$$

and

$$E_e(y_t \mid z_{t-1}) = \delta' E_e(x_t \mid z_{t-1}), \tag{5}$$

where E_i denotes expectations under H_i and hence E_i coincides with E when H_i coincides with the DGP (and the associated parameter coincides with β). Writing the hypotheses as models:

$$H_c : y_t = \gamma' x_t + \nu_t \quad \text{where} \quad E_c(x_t \nu_t) = 0 \tag{6}$$

and

$$H_e : y_t = \delta' E_e(x_t \mid z_{t-1}) + \varepsilon_t \quad \text{where} \quad E_e(z_{t-1} \varepsilon_t) = 0. \tag{7}$$

While the above formulation tries to capture the distinction between conditional and expectational hypotheses, a number of clarifying comments are essential. Firstly, mixed cases involving both conditioning and expectations will occur in practice [see e.g. Nickell (1985)], as will situations in which it is invalid to condition on contemporaneous variables due to (say) simultaneity, or in which contemporaneous variables represent the effects of expectations about future events but are strictly exogenous. Extensions of the present [135] encompassing framework to handle such complications are possible (e.g., allowing some of the elements of x_t and z_{t-1} to be in common), but attention is restricted to the simplest case here to clarify the logic of the approach. Secondly, the above analysis treated the models as deriving from rival economic hypotheses, but in statistical terms, H_c and H_e are complicated composite hypotheses which are not as yet fully specified. Rather, it would be preferable to commence the analysis with the joint density function of (y_t, x_t, z_t) conditional on past information (denoted $Y_{t-1}, X_{t-1}, Z_{t-1}$) and examine the validity of alternative reductions due to conditioning and marginalising. In fact, since the relationship between x_t and z_{t-1} is crucial to the present analysis it should be viewed as arising from the underlying joint density and *not* as an "auxiliary model". Specifically:

$$E(x_t \mid z_{t-1}) = \Pi_t z_{t-1}, \tag{8}$$

or in model form:

$$x_t = \Pi_t Z_{t-1} + w_t \quad \text{with} \quad w_t \sim \mathsf{ID}(0, \Omega_t) \tag{9}$$

(meaning Independently Distributed with mean zero and covariance matrix Ω_t).

Thirdly, while (6) and (7) appear to be incommensurate by using different probability spaces, they are comparable due to the requirement of congruency such that one of E_c and E_e must then coincide with E. Thus, we can explore the encompassing predictions of each hypothesis for the other, denoting encompassing by $\mathcal{E}$.

(A) *Encompassing Predictions of H_c $\mathcal{E}$ H_e*

When (6)+(9) correctly characterise the sequential process generating (y_t, x_t) conditional on $(Y_{t-1}, X_{t-1}, Z_{t-1})$ then the following implications hold:

(i) Conditional on x_t, y_t is independent of z_{t-1}. This is derived from:

$$E_c(\nu_t \mid z_{t-1}) = 0 \quad \Rightarrow \quad E_c(y_t \mid x_t, z_{t-1}) = \gamma' x_t, \tag{10}$$

and hence if:

$$y_t = \lambda_1' x_t + \lambda_2' z_{t-1} + \eta_t, \tag{11}$$

then $\lambda_1 = \gamma$ and $\lambda_2 = 0$ [see Hendry and Neale (1988) for the relationship of these implications on λ_i to Hausman (1978) specification tests and Mizon and Richard (1986) simplification encompassing tests respectively].

(ii) The conditional model sustains an expectations interpretation. From (6):

$$E_c(y_t \mid z_{t-1}) = \gamma' E_c(x_t \mid z_{t-1}). \tag{12}$$

Moreover, from (7),   [136]

$$E_e(y_t \mid z_{t-1}) = \delta' E_e(x_t \mid z_{t-1}), \tag{13}$$

so that both hypotheses anticipate a constant linear relationship between $E_i(y_t \mid z_{t-1})$ and $E_i(x_t \mid z_{t-1})$ (i.e., both expect constancy in instrumental variables estimation relating y_t to x_t using z_{t-1} as instruments).

(iii) If (Π_t, Ω_t) in (9) are indeed nonconstant, then the projection of y_t onto z_{t-1} *only* (the reduced form) is also nonconstant:

$$E_c(y_t \mid z_{t-1}) = \gamma' \Pi_t z_{t-1} = \gamma_t^{*\prime} z_{t-1}, \tag{14}$$

and the error variance is nonconstant since:

$$y_t - E_c(y_t \mid z_{t-1}) = \nu_t + \gamma' w_t = \xi_t \tag{15}$$

with $E_c(\xi_t^2) - \upsilon_\nu^2 + \gamma' \Omega_t \gamma$.

(iv) The reduced form (assuming either constant or nonconstant parameters) should fit worse than the behavioural model (6): this follows from (15) since $\gamma' \Omega_t \gamma \geq 0$.

(v) The behavioural model (6) should be constant: this holds by assumption but is stated for completeness.

(B) *Encompassing Predictions of H_e & H_c*

When (7)+(9) correctly characterise the DGP, a different set of implications holds:

(i) Conditional on z_{t-1}, y_t may or may not be independent of x_t. This can be derived from (7)–(9):

$$E_e(\varepsilon_t \mid x_t, z_{t-1}) = \mu_{1t}' x_t + \mu_{2t}' z_{t-1}, \tag{16}$$

where both $\mu_{it} = 0$ if $E_e(x_t \varepsilon_t) = \omega_t = 0 \ \forall t$. The inchoate nature of the "simple-general" analysis is again revealed by the need to introduce at this late stage an auxiliary assumption about the status of x_t under H_e, which would have arisen at the outset when considering the joint density of (y_t, x_t, z_t).

(ii) The conditional model cannot be constant if (Π_t, Ω_t) are sufficiently variable (which is the Lucas critique in the expectations context). To establish this result, consider:

$$E_e(y_t \mid x_t) = \alpha_t' x_t, \tag{17}$$

where

$$\alpha_t = [E_e(x_t x_t')]^{-1} E_e(x_t y_t)$$
$$= [\Pi_t E_e(z_{t-1} z_{t-1}') \Pi_t' + \Omega_t]^{-1} [\Pi_t E_e(z_{t-1} z_{t-1}') \Pi_t' \delta + \omega_t]$$
$$= \delta + [\Pi_t M_{tt} \Pi_t' + \Omega_t]^{-1} [\omega_t - \Omega_t \delta] \tag{18}$$

[137] if $M_{tt} = E_e(z_{t-1} z_{t-1}')$. While there exist conditions under which α_t would be constant (for example, $M_{tt} = M \ \forall t$, $\Pi_t = h(t)\Pi$, $\Omega_t = h(t)^2 \Omega$ and $\omega_t = 0$), if Π_t and Ω_t are varying independently, then α_t must also

vary. Thus, x_t cannot be super exogenous for δ under H_e even though x_t does not even enter (7).

(iii) As with A(iii), the projection of y_t onto z_{t-1} is nonconstant, but with parameter vector $\delta'\Pi_t = \delta_t^*$.

(iv) A less clear-cut outcome can be obtained for the error variance ranking since:

$$y_t - E_e(y_t \mid z_{t-1}) = \varepsilon_t, \tag{19}$$

whereas:

$$y_t - E_e(y_t \mid x_t) = (\delta - \alpha_t)'x_t + \varepsilon_t - \delta'w_t = \zeta_t \tag{20}$$

and

$$E_e(\zeta_t^2) = (\delta - \alpha_t)'\Pi_t M_{tt}\Pi_t'(\delta - \alpha_t) + \sigma_\varepsilon^2 + \alpha_t'\Omega_t\alpha_t - 2\alpha_t'\omega_t.$$

If y_t conditional on z_{t-1} is independent of x_t, then $E_e(\zeta_t^2) > \sigma_\varepsilon^2$, reversing the ranking of A(iv).

(v) The behavioural model (7) should be constant, again by assumption. Consequently the regression of y_t on $\hat{x}_t$ (where $\hat{x}_t$ is the projection of x_t onto z_{t-1}) will be constant.

(C) Incomplete Information

Prior to drawing together the two sets of encompassing predictions in (A) and (B) above, we briefly consider the empirically relevant case in which z_{t-1} is in fact only a subset of the information on which agents base their expectations of x_t and the actual DGP is:

$$x_t = \Psi_1 z_{t-1} + \Psi_2 z_{t-1}^* + u_t \quad \text{with} \quad u_t \sim \text{IID}(0, \Sigma). \tag{21}$$

Notice that (21) embodies the extreme assumption that if the econometrician could observe z_{t-1}^*, then the parameterisation would be constant (nonconstant Ψ's simply replicate the implications of the previous analysis). However, the crucial point is that given (9), the relationship between z_t^* and z_t could not be constant, and we must have:

$$z_t^* = \Phi_t z_t + a_t \quad \text{(say)} \quad \text{with} \quad a_t \sim \text{ID}(0, A_t) \quad \text{so that}$$

$$\Pi_t = (\Psi_1 + \Psi_2\Phi_t) \quad \text{and} \quad \Omega_t = \Sigma + \Psi_2 A_t \Psi_2'. \tag{22}$$

Excepting a coincidental cancellation due to equivalent variations in the parameters and error variances with the second moments of (z_t, z_t^*), the regression of y_t on x_t still cannot be constant. In effect, in a generalised notation, the analogues of Π, Ω, and ω in (18) are now constant but from (22) the generalisation of M_{tt} cannot be.

We can now combine the conclusions of (A) and (B) for the case of relevance to the empirical section of the paper.

[138]   If:

$$E(y_t \mid x_t) = \gamma' x_t \tag{23}$$

has γ constant, and

$$E(y_t \mid z_{t-1}) - \delta' E(x_t \mid z_{t-1}) \tag{24}$$

has δ constant, but

$$E(x_t \mid z_{t-1}) = \Pi_t z_{t-1} \tag{25}$$

does not have Π_t constant, then (excepting coincidental cancellation, the nature of which has testable implications in turn)

$$H_e \not\subseteq H_c.$$

Moreover, from (C), if the preceding result holds for a subset of the correct information, it will continue to hold on an extended information set which makes the marginal model of x_t constant. Conversely, the assertion that $H_e \; \& \; H_c$ can be refuted by showing (23)–(25) for any subset of the relevant information set.

As claimed in the introduction, the Lucas critique for a super exogeneity violation due to agents forming expectations is potentially refutable; and once refuted, cannot be rescued by an appeal to having used only limited information. Clearly, the critique is also confirmable by the refutation of any of A(i), A(iv), or especially A(v). Thus, a symmetric situation exists precisely because in the Lucas critique, if the assumptions hold (behavioural and other parameters are confounded and the latter vary), then the conclusion must also hold (the compound parameters must vary); refutation follows if the conclusion does not hold. As argued in Hendry and Neale (1988), tests of A(i) and A(iv) or B(i) and B(iv) are likely to lack power in a general to simple modelling approach, since many potential candidates for the role of z_{t-1} variables will have been pre-tested for inclusion in the conditional/expectational models. However, variance encompassing tests may be able to detect A(iv) versus B(iv). Since A(ii) = B(v) and A(iii) = B(iii) are in common, no discrimination is feasible by testing these, although rejection here would invalidate a common assumption of both hypotheses. These considerations prompted the focus on A(v) versus B(ii). The power of the present proposal is unknown, and clearly depends on the extent of nonconstancy in (Π_t, Ω_t), but since predictive failure is pandemic in economics, some discrimination seems likely. In statistical terms, formal tests could be derived from the respective restrictions entailed on a vector autoregressive representation (VAR) but such are non-operational until the variations in (Π_t, Ω_t) can be modelled.

3 An Application to U.K. Money Demand

Cuthbertson (1988) has advanced an expectations interpretation for the M1 model proposed in Hendry (1979) and developed in Trundle (1982) and Hendry (1985). Cuthbertson espouses a forward-looking theory of M1 demand which leads to a dynamic specification like that of Hendry (1985) *but* with the use of marginal models for the formation of expectations on prices, incomes, and interest rates. Estimates for the whole sample period are reported by Cuthbertson and the constancy of his δ was, but of his Π was not, [139] tested. The final model fits somewhat worse than that in Hendry (1985), but not greatly so, and Cuthbertson attributes this to the former being "data based". The results in Hendry (1985) and in the update to data ending in 1985 reported in Hendry (1986) are consistent with γ being constant, and Cuthbertson does not challenge that claim. The evidence in Cuthbertson is consistent with δ being constant and since all the instruments are lagged, that constancy by itself is not inconsistent with γ being constant and a conditional model being valid. The issue is whether the "forward model ... provides an alternative *interpretation* of conventional error feedback equations" Cuthbertson (1988, p. 125, italics added). To examine that claim, we investigate the constancy of the marginal models for the claimed expectations formation processes which Cuthbertson uses. The data sets used are those of Cuthbertson (1988)[1] (which is quarterly seasonally unadjusted) and of Hendry (1986) (quarterly seasonally adjusted). In the former, the income variable is real personal disposable income (RPDI), whereas in the latter the income variable is real Total Final Expenditure (TFE); the Price measures are the relevant implicit deflators. TFE seems a more appropriate scale variable for total M1 demand than RPDI, although the results for the whole sample period for equations (26)–(28) below are little different from those reported by Cuthbertson, beyond the anticipated differences in the lag lengths of variables due to seasonal adjustment.

Since constancy is the key issue, the natural estimators to adopt are recursive generalisations of least squares (RLS) and instrumental variables (RIV) [see e.g. Brown, Durbin, and Evans (1975), Phillips (1977), Harvey (1981), and Hendry and Neale (1987)]. Given an initialisation sample of $n > k$ observations for k explanatory variables (larger if instruments are used), each equation is updated an observation at a time so that the entire track of coefficient estimates is available when the full sample T is reached. The estimates were calculated using PC-GIVE which provides graphs of the output

---

[1] Kindly provided by him to the author.

together with the appropriate metric based on $\pm 2 \cdot \text{SE}_t$ where SE_t is the estimated standard error of the coefficient at sample size t, for $t = n, \ldots, T$.
Similarly, the 1-step residuals $\hat{v}_t$ together with $0 \pm 2\hat{\sigma}_t$ ($\hat{\sigma}_t$ is the equation
standard error at sample size t) can be graphed. From the sequence of inno-
vations, various Chow-tests can be constructed [see e.g. McAleer and Fisher
(1982)] including those for every single 1-step ahead forecast, an increasingly
long horizon $(n+1, n+2, n+3, \ldots, T)$ or a decreasing horizon. In PC-GIVE,
the resulting statistics are scaled by their nominal "one-off test" 5% critical
values to correct for changes in degrees of freedom, so that a 5% value becomes a horizontal straight line on the graph. These tools provide incisive
methods for examining the constancy or otherwise of the empirical models
under consideration.

We first consider the results for the data set used in Hendry (1986) and
denote the estimates in Cuthbertson (1988) by (C.x) for equation x. The
[140]   equivalent equation to (C.19) is (26) below (using the same notation except
that lower case denotes logs, noting that income is measured by TFE and
not GNP as in Hendry (1985) or RPDI as in Cuthbertson):

$$\widehat{\Delta(m-p)}_t = \underset{[0.006]}{0.030} + \underset{[0.13]}{0.33}\,\Delta y_{t-1} - \underset{[0.24]}{0.79}\,\Delta p_t$$

$$- \underset{[0.08]}{0.34}\,\Delta(m-p)_{t-1} - \underset{[0.10]}{0.71}\,R_t - \underset{[0.01]}{0.10}\,(m-p-y)_{t-2}$$

$$(26)$$

RLS   1964(iii)–1979(iv) $R^2 = 0.70$ $\hat{\sigma} = 1.38\%$ $dw = 1.9$
LM4F $= 0.10$ CH$(12, 56) = 0.37$ HF$(12) = 5.1$.

[*Author's note*: The data are nominal M1 (M), real total final expenditure
(Y) and its deflator (P), and the three-month local authority interest rate
(R), all for the United Kingdom. The difference operator is denoted by
Δ.] In (26), [·] denote heteroscedastic consistent standard errors [see White
(1980)], LM4F is the Lagrange Multiplier test for fourth order residual autocorrelation (distributed as $F(4, T - k - 4)$ on the null), CH$(\ell, T - k - \ell)$ is
the Chow test for parameter constancy (distributed as $F(\ell, T - k - \ell)$ on the
null), and HF(12) is a measure of *ex ante* forecast accuracy (asymptotically
distributed as $\chi^2(12)$ on the null of constant parameters).

Judging by the degrees of freedom of the CH statistic, the sample size
reported in Cuthbertson is before creating lags whereas that in (26) is after.
The estimates are very similar to (C.19) although the CH and LM4F tests are
"better" here. Within sample, (26) is remarkably constant as shown in Fig-
ure 1 (using $n = 16$) since $\hat{\sigma}_t$ *falls* slightly from 1971–79 after a slight initial
rise. Figure 2 shows the sequence of 1-step ahead forecasts over 1980(i)–
1982(iv) together with ± 2 forecast standard error bars. Re-estimating (26)
by RIV with Δp_t and R_t as endogenous produces a similar story; Figure 3

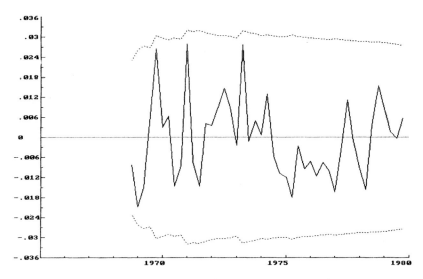

FIGURE 1. One-step residuals ($—$) for the $\Delta(m - p)$ model with $0 \pm 2\hat{\sigma}_t$ ($\cdots$) for 1968(4)–1979(4).

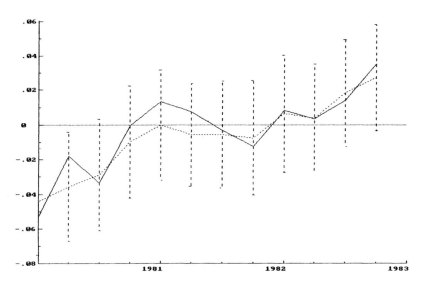

FIGURE 2. Actual values ($—$) and forecasts ($\cdots$) over 1980(1)–1982(4) for $\Delta(m - p)$, with ± 2 forecast standard errors (vertical dashed bars).

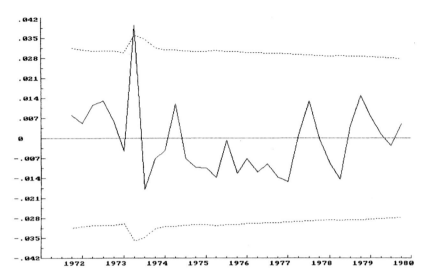

FIGURE 3. RIV one-step residuals (—) of the $\Delta(m - p)$ model
with $0 \pm 2\hat{\sigma}_t$ ($\cdots$) for 1971(4)–1979(4).

shows $\hat{\sigma}_t$ and the 1-step residuals, using R_{t-1}, R_{t-2}, Δp_{t-1}, and Δp_{t-2} as
[141]   instruments.[2] In both RLS and RIV, the individual coefficient estimates are
constant and for the former, *none* of the increasing or decreasing sequences
of Chow-tests is significant at the 5% level: only the graphs of the $\hat{\sigma}_t$ are
reported as these seem the closest to providing sufficient summary statistics
of a large volume of output.

[142]   At this stage, therefore, granting the constancy of Cuthbertson's model,
apparently both feedback and expectations representations of the money
demand equation are constant. Although the solved form equivalent to (14)
fits worse than the RIV estimates of (26), and the Sargan (1964) test for
instrument validity yields $\chi^2(2) = 0.2$, these anomalous findings for H_e could
be dismissed as arising either from the data-selection origins of (26) (which
probably excluded lags on R and Δp precisely because they were irrelevant,
albeit over a shorter sample period) or from incomplete information on I.

Next we record the whole-sample equations equivalent to the autoregressions in Table 1 of Cuthbertson:

---

[2] These are the main explanatory variables from the autoregressions for R_t and Δp_t,
selected given the programme constraint of 11 variables in the RIV option of PC-GIVE.

$$\widehat{\Delta p_t} = \underset{[0.0018]}{0.0024} + \underset{[0.07]}{0.92\,\Delta p_{t-1}} - \underset{[0.12]}{0.20\,\Delta^2 p_{t-4}} + \underset{[0.005]}{0.018\,D793_t} \quad (27)$$

OLS   1964(iii)–1979(iv) $R^2 = 0.81$ $\hat\sigma = 0.69\%$ $dw = 1.9$
LM4F = 0.17   CH(12, 58) = 1.04   HF(12) = 13.7,

(where D793 is a +1/–1 dummy variable for the last two in-sample data points)

$$\widehat{\Delta y_t} = \underset{[0.003]}{0.012} - \underset{[0.065]}{0.14}\left(\textstyle\sum_{i=1}^5 \Delta y_{t-i}\right) - \underset{[0.007]}{0.004\,D793_t} \quad (28)$$

OLS   1964(iii)–1979(iv) $R^2 = 0.06$ $\hat\sigma = 1.56\%$ $dw = 2.1$
LM4F = 0.18   CH(12, 59) = 1.06   HF(12) = 16.8,

$$\widehat{R_t} = \underset{[0.13]}{1.29\,R_{t-1}} - \underset{[0.13]}{0.29\,R_{t-2}} \quad (29)$$

OLS   1964(iii)–1979(iv) $R^2 = 0.98$ $\hat\sigma = 0.013$ $dw = 1.9$
LM4F = 0.34   CH(12, 60) = 1.07   HF(12) = 13.6.

Note that the σ values in these equations correspond to diagonal elements of Ω from Section 2. Also, (29) is isomorphic to the common-factor representation in Cuthbertson but R^2 does not allow for a mean; and if the unit root is imposed, $R^2 = 0.09$ for ΔR_t. Thus, all of (26)–(29) are closely similar to Cuthbertson's results, but none of (27), (28), or (29) offers any real hope of actually predicting *changes* in Δp_t, y_t, or R_t. A further test is apparent from (27): if the dummy variable D793 really is necessary for the expectations model of Δp_t, then under H_e it should be an omitted variable from (26), and it certainly was *not* pretested in selecting (26)! Adding it to (26) yields $F(1, 55) = 0.12$, so another anomaly for H_e occurs.

We turn now to the recursive estimation tests.[3] Figure 4 shows the graphs of $(\hat v_t, 0 \pm 2\hat\sigma_t)$ for Δp_t from (27) within sample, and Figure 5 shows the sequence of estimates of the coefficient of Δp_{t-1}. Constancy of coefficients [143] and of error variances is rejected. Similar for (28), where the equivalent graphs for the Δy_t model are shown in Figures 6 and 7: again constancy is untenable (actually, so is normality for (27) and (28) making inference depend on an asymptotic justification and hence being somewhat hazardous in the present small sample but revealing the dangers of casual testing). Finally, for R_t, the worst results of all obtain for $\hat\sigma_t$ as shown in Figure 8, although the coefficients of R_{t-1}, R_{t-2} correspond throughout to roughly the model $\Delta R_t = 0.3\Delta R_{t-1}$. Thus, the only nonconstant parameter is σ_t

---

[3] The presence of D793 makes this awkward but two solutions were tried: (a) estimating up to 1979(ii) only; and (b) imposing the whole sample estimate of D793 (e.g., by subtracting $0.018 \cdot D793_t$ from Δp_t for (27)). Unsurprisingly, very similar results were obtained and only approach (b) is quoted below.

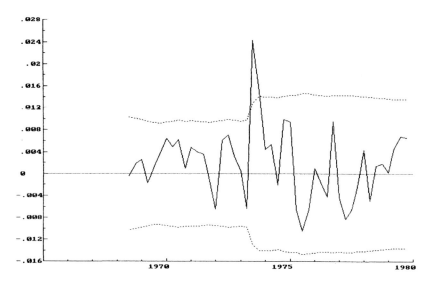

FIGURE 4. One-step residuals (—) from the Δp model (27) with $D793$ corrected, and $0 \pm 2\hat{\sigma}_t$ (···).

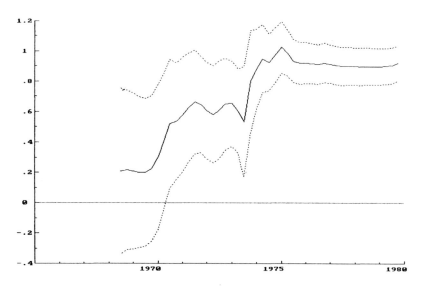

FIGURE 5. Recursive estimates (—) of the coefficient of Δp_{t-1} in (27), with ± 2 estimated standard errors (···).

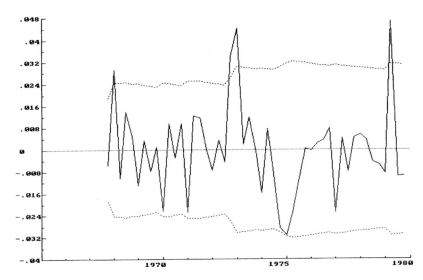

FIGURE 6. One-step residuals (—) from the Δy model (28), with $0 \pm 2\hat{\sigma}_t$ ($\cdots$).

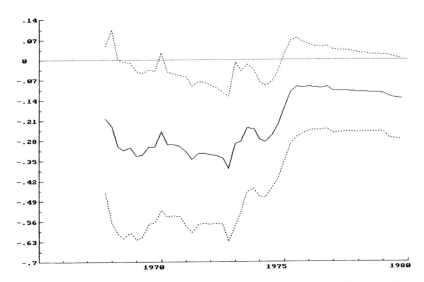

FIGURE 7.   Recursive estimates (—) of the coefficient of $\left(\sum_{i=1}^{5} \Delta y_{t-i}\right)$ in (28), with ± 2 estimated standard errors ($\cdots$).

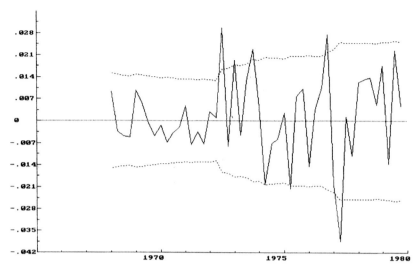

FIGURE 8. One-step residuals (—) of the ΔR model in (29), with
$0 \pm 2\hat{\sigma}_t \ (\cdots)$, for 1968(1)–1979(4).

[144]   but that is sufficient in view of (18). Figure 9 shows the fitted and actual
values of this differenced model—it is difficult to imagine agents bothering to
use such a model to allocate *transactions* balances. The decreasing horizon
Chow-test sequence for R_t is shown as Figure 10, cutting the 5% significance
line in 1977 *from above*.

It is clear that the autoregressive forecasting equations are not constant
and hence given that the conditional equation is constant, all the anomalies
vanish: H_e is false. The model in (26) does not have the "forward looking
interpretation" claimed by Cuthbertson.

[145]   Notwithstanding the theoretical analysis in 2(C) above, could that interpretation be rescued in practice by generalizing the model for the contemporaneous variables? Certainly, scalar autoregressions are simplistic models, and a test of the unrestricted fourth order scalar autoregressions for
$(\Delta m_t, \Delta p_t, \Delta y_t, R_t)$ against a general fourth order vector autoregression[4]
(both including D793) yields the likelihood ratio test $\chi^2(48) = 112$, strongly
[146]   rejecting the former. Indeed, the equation standard errors on the VAR are
(1.53%, 0.49%, 1.15%, 0.010). Unfortunately, a forecast test for the VAR
over 1980(i)–1982(iv), taking account of the coefficient variance matrix as in

---

[4] It is unclear why Cuthbertson excluded lagged money from his VAR.

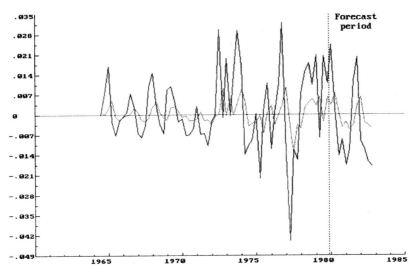

FIGURE 9. Actual (—), fitted (· · ·), and forecast (· · ·) values of ΔR for 1964(3)–1982(4).

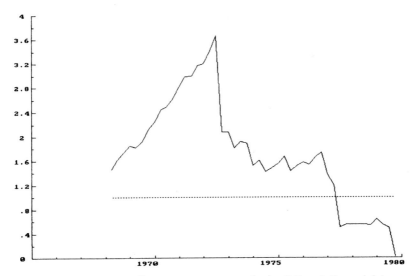

FIGURE 10. The Chow test sequence (—) of the ΔR model in (29) for 1968(2)–1979(4), normalized by one-off 5% critical values (· · ·).

Calzolari (1981), yields $F(48, 45) = 2.0$ again rejecting constancy.[5] Ignoring
the coefficient variances and degrees of freedom generates $\chi^2(48) = 252$ highlighting the *ex ante* inaccuracy of even *1-step* forecasts! Thus, empirically
VAR forecasts as expectations proxies offer no solace either.

The empirical findings in (26)–(29) have several further implications.
From (29), ΔR_t is essentially *ex ante* unpredictable so it would be surprising
if conditioning on this policy determined variable in (26) induced a problem. Moreover, the current value of Δy_t does not enter the model in (26)
and while there are similar specifications in which it does do so, it too is
close to being *ex ante* unpredictable from (28). The weak exogeneity of R_t
and y_t, does not seem implausible in a financial system in which agents are
free to determine their transactions balances and the authorities determine
interest rates (albeit in an effort to control monetary growth). Strong exogeneity is not needed for inference or for parameter constancy but relative
to the restricted information set in use here, is empirically invalid. Super
exogeneity is the key issue, however, and given the analysis in Section 2,
that receives considerable support from the constancy of (26) confronting
the nonconstancy of the VAR.

The final issue is the absence of a role for expectations about Δp_t, since
it seems surprising that agents should ignore the predictability of inflation
in adjusting their M1 balances. Reconsider the coefficient values in (26):
[147] if the dependent variable is rewritten as Δm_t, then the coefficient of Δp_t
becomes 0.20 [0.21] and so is "insignificant". Alternatively, retaining Δm_t
as the regressand and *deleting* Δp_t altogether yields:

$$\widehat{\Delta m_t} = \underset{[0.005]}{0.027} + \underset{[0.13]}{0.32}\,\Delta y_{t-1} - \underset{[0.08]}{0.35}\,\Delta(m-p)_{t-1}$$

$$- \underset{[0.07]}{0.64}\,R_t - \underset{[0.01]}{0.11}\,(m-p-y)_{t-2} \qquad (30)$$

RLS   1964(iii)–1979(iv) $R^2 = 0.59$ $\hat\sigma = 1.37\%$ $dw = 1.8$
LM4F $= 0.27$ CH$(12, 57) = 0.39$ HF$(12) = 4.92$.

Extending the sample up to 1985(ii) yields $\hat\sigma = 1.33\%$. This evidence is
consistent with nominal short-run adjustment, but real long-run adjustment
rather like a "bands" model in the class discussed by Milbourne (1983) [also
see Miller and Orr (1966) and Akerlof (1973)]. For 1-step ahead adjustment,
Δp_t does not enter the money demand model despite the costs that inflation
imposes on money holdings. A possible explanation is that *changes* in Δp_t
are hard to predict (see (27)) and that as more nominal money is required to
support the higher level of nominal transactions resulting from inflation, the

---

[5] This was calculated using the author's program PC-FIML [see Hendry and Srba
(1980)].

large negative coefficient on Δp_t in (26) represents a compromise between these conflicting effects.

Turning now to the data set used by Cuthbertson, very similar results were obtained. Within-sample constancy was rejected for all of the scalar autoregressions (which now included seasonal shift dummies) and for the restricted VARs (with or without modelling $\Delta(m - p)$). Some of the unrestricted VAR equations were constant *within* sample, but all of the marginal models were rejected out of sample over the period 1980(1)–1983(4), with the restricted VAR suffering the worst (Forecast $F(54, 64) = 3.47$). Since the model for $(m - p)_t$ performs well (as Cuthbertson reports), the attempted "expectations reinterpretation" is again rejected. However, the results do *not* imply that the parameters in (26) are super exogenous to all possible changes in the marginal processes, merely that they did not vary as anticipated from the feedforward hypothesis.

4 Conclusion

A statistical theory-model to discriminate between rival pure feedback and feedforward models was presented and the role of changes in the marginal models for the expectations processes was highlighted. The analysis reveals that for sufficient change in the marginal processes, it is feasible to tell the model types apart despite their similarities. In the particular example of M1 demand the expectations interpretation of the conditional model was rejected, perhaps because no predicted contemporaneous variables actually enter the money demand function. Further studies on other variables will reveal whether or not the method proposed above has power more generally. [148] Nevertheless, prior to advocating expectations processes, it is important to test the constancy of the proposed marginal models, and the recursive estimation and testing approach adopted above seems a useful tool for doing so.

Bibliography

(References marked with an asterisk * are included in this volume.)

Akerlof, G. A. (1973) "The Demand for Money: A General Equilibrium Inventory-theoretic Approach", *Review of Economic Studies*, 40, 115–130.

Brown, R. L., J. Durbin, and J. M. Evans (1975) "Techniques for Testing the Constancy of Regression Relationships over Time" (with discussion), *Journal of the Royal Statistical Society, Series B*, 37, 149–192.

Calzolari, G. (1981) "A Note on the Variance of Ex Post Forecasts in Econometric Models", *Econometrica*, 49, 1593–1596.

Cuthbertson, K. (1988) "The Demand for M1: A Forward Looking Buffer Stock Model", *Oxford Economic Papers*, 40, 110–131.

Davidson, J. E. H., D. F. Hendry, F. Srba, and S. Yeo (1978) "Econometric Modelling of the Aggregate Time Series Relationship Between Consumers' Expenditure and Income in the United Kingdom", *Economic Journal*, 88, 661–692.

*Engle, R. F., and D. F. Hendry (1993) "Testing Super Exogeneity and Invariance in Regression Models", *Journal of Econometrics*, 56, 1/2, 119–139; originally cited as (1986) "Testing Super Exogeneity and Invariance", mimeo, Nuffield College, Oxford.

*Engle, R. F., D. F. Hendry, and J.-F. Richard (1983) "Exogeneity", *Econometrica*, 51, 277–304.

Harvey, A. C. (1981) *Econometric Analysis of Time Series*, London, Philip Allan.

Hausman, J. (1978) "Specification Tests in Econometrics", *Econometrica*, 46, 1251–1272.

Hendry, D. F. (1979) "Predictive Failure and Econometric Modelling in Macro-economics: The Transactions Demand for Money", Chapter 9 in P. Ormeród (ed.) *Economic Modelling*, London, Heinemann Education Books, 217–242.

Hendry, D. F. (1985) "Monetary Economic Myth and Econometric Reality", *Oxford Review of Economic Policy*, 1, 1, 72–84.

Hendry, D. F. (1986) "On the Credibility of Econometric Evidence", Walras-Bowley Lecture, North American Meeting of the Econometric Society, 1986.

Hendry, D. F. (1987) "Econometric Methodology: A Personal Perspective", Chapter 10 in T. F. Bewley (ed.) *Advances in Econometrics: Fifth World Congress*, Cambridge, Cambridge University Press, Volume 2, 29–48.

Hendry, D. F., and A. J. Neale (1987) "Monte Carlo Experimentation using PC-NAIVE", in T. B. Fomby and G. F. Rhodes, Jr. (eds.) *Advances in Econometrics*, Greenwich, Connecticut, JAI Press, Volume 6, 91–125.

Hendry, D. F., and A. J. Neale (1988) "Interpreting Long-run Equilibrium Solutions in Conventional Macro Models: A Comment", *Economic Journal*, 98, 392, 808–817; originally cited as (1988), forthcoming in *Economic Journal*.

Hendry, D. F., and J.-F. Richard (1982) "On the Formulation of Empirical Models in Dynamic Econometrics", *Journal of Econometrics*, 20, 3–33.

Hendry, D. F., and J.-F. Richard (1989) "Recent Developments in the Theory of Encompassing", Chapter 12 in B. Cornet and H. Tulkens (eds.)

Contributions to Operations Research and Economics: The Twentieth Anniversary of CORE, Cambridge, Massachusetts, MIT Press, 393–440; originally cited as (1987).

Hendry, D. F., and F. Srba (1980) "AUTOREG: A Computer Program Library for Dynamic Econometric Models with Autoregressive Errors", *Journal of Econometrics*, 12, 85–102.

Lucas, R. E., Jr. (1976) "Econometric Policy Evaluation: A Critique", in K. Brunner and A. H. Meltzer (eds.) *The Phillips Curve and Labor Markets, Carnegie-Rochester Conference Series on Public Policy*, Volume 1, Amsterdam, North-Holland, 19–46.

McAleer, M., and G. Fisher (1982) "Testing Separate Regression Models Subject to Specification Error", *Journal of Econometrics*, 19, 125–145; originally cited as (1982), Working Papers in Economics and Econometrics No. 67, Faculty of Economics, Australian National University.

Milbourne, R. (1983) "Optimal Money Holding under Uncertainty", *International Economic Review*, 24, 685–698.   [149]

Miller, M. H., and D. Orr (1966) "A Model of the Demand for Money by Firms", *Quarterly Journal of Economics*, 80, 735–750.

Mizon, G. E. (1984) "The Encompassing Approach in Econometrics", in D. F. Hendry and K. F. Wallis (eds.), *Econometrics and Quantitative Economics*, Oxford, Basil Blackwell, 135–172.

Mizon, G. E., and J.-F. Richard (1986) "The Encompassing Principle and Its Application to Non-nested Hypothesis Tests", *Econometrica*, 54, 657–678.

Muth, J. F. (1961) "Rational Expectations and the Theory of Price Movements", *Econometrica*, 29, 315–335.

Nickell, S. J. (1985) "Error Correction, Partial Adjustment and All That: An Expository Note", *Oxford Bulletin of Economics and Statistics*, 47, 119–130.

Phillips, G. D. A. (1977) "Recursions for the Two-stage Least Squares Estimators", *Journal of Econometrics*, 6, 65–77.

Sargan, J. D. (1964) "Wages and Prices in the United Kingdom: A Study in Econometric Methodology", in P. E. Hart, G. Mills, and J. K. Whitaker (eds.) *Econometric Analysis for National Economic Planning*, Butterworths, London.

Trundle, J. (1982) "The Demand for M1 in the U.K.", mimeo, Bank of England, London.

Wallis, K. F. (1980) "Econometric Implications of the Rational Expectations Hypothesis", *Econometrica*, 48, 49–73.

White, H. (1980) "A Heteroskedasticity-consistent Covariance Matrix Esti-
    mator and a Direct Test for Heteroskedasticity", *Econometrica*, 48, 4,
    817–838.

4

Testing Super Exogeneity and Invariance in Regression Models

ROBERT F. ENGLE and DAVID F. HENDRY*

Abstract

This paper introduces tests of super exogeneity and invariance. Under the null hypothesis the conditional model exhibits parameter constancy, while under the alternative, shifts in the process of the independent variables induce shifts in the conditional model. The test is sensitive to particular types of parameter nonconstancy, especially with changing variances and covariances. We relate the test to rational expectations models and the Lucas critique. An empirical example of money demand finds prices and interest rates super exogenous in a conditional model, but when the inflation specification changes, super exogeneity fails although standard specification tests do not.

1 Introduction

Well-specified econometric models should have parameters which are both constant over the historical period used to fit the model and are anticipated to remain constant in the future, thereby allowing *ex ante* forecasting under various scenarios. For example, parameters which measure "tastes and technology" are sometimes considered to be invariant to changes in policy rules or to shifts in the distributions of other variables taken as given in the model under scrutiny. Conversely, casually-specified regression models may

* Support for this research from the National Science Foundation and from the U.K. Economic and Social Research Council through grants B00220012 and R231184 is gratefully acknowledged. We are indebted to Neil R. Ericsson, Carlo Favero, Andreas Fischer, Adrian J. Neale, and Jean-François Richard for helpful comments on an earlier draft.

Reprinted with permission from the *Journal of Econometrics* (March 1993), 56, 1/2, 119–139.

93

be potentially prone to "structural breaks" when regimes alter as argued by Lucas (1976). In both cases, tests of claims about invariance or its absence are obviously of interest.

[120]   Empirical evidence on the constancy of parameters over the historical period is typically marshalled by specification tests of the Chow (1960) form or simply by testing for interactions with dummy variables. However, these commonly-used procedures are unsatisfactory if there is no guidance on the number or dates of the breaks which are tested: if incorrect dates are chosen, the test will lack power, and if too many versions are tested, the test size will be far above its nominal value. In contrast, there are almost no procedures to test whether parameters are likely to remain constant in the future or whether they are invariant to changes in regime. This paper presents tests specifically designed to ascertain whether or not parameters have changed *in response* to changes in regime during the historical period. Thus, the tests are closely related to parameter constancy tests, but the causes, periods, and magnitudes of changes to be tested are determined by the economic situation and the historical evidence for regime changes embodied in the conditioning variables. A rejection of the constant parameter conditional model clearly indicates a problem with the hypothesized model, however it is, as always, incorrect to conclude that the alternative model is correct. For example, nonlinearities or non-normality could be responsible for the rejection and a clever investigator would be advised to test for these directly.

Three distinct concepts are involved when formulating such tests for conditional models: *exogeneity*, *constancy*, and *invariance*, and so we first briefly review these three notions as well as the composite property of *super exogeneity* in Section 2. In Section 3, the basic formulation of our analysis and relevant definitions are provided. In Section 4, the role of expectations and the Lucas Critique are explored for formulating alternatives. In Section 5, tests are proposed for invariance of behavioral parameters and super exogeneity of conditioning variables in regression models under various states of nature determined by the degree of nonconstancy in the process generating the observables. Section 6 provides some empirical examples of the proposed tests, and Section 7 concludes the paper.

2   Exogeneity, Constancy, Invariance, and Super Exogeneity

The joint distribution of y_t and x_t conditional on the sigma field, $\mathcal{F}_t$, consisting of the past of both series and the current and past values of other valid conditioning variables, can be written

$$D_{\mathcal{J}}(y_t, x_t \mid \mathcal{F}_t; \lambda_t) = D_C(y_t \mid x_t, \mathcal{F}_t; \lambda_{1t})D_{\mathcal{M}}(x_t \mid \mathcal{F}_t; \lambda_{2t}),$$

where $D_{\mathcal{J}}$, D_C, and $D_{\mathcal{M}}$ refer respectively to the joint density, the conditional density of y given x, and the marginal density of x. The parameters are then labeled correspondingly λ_t, λ_{1t}, and λ_{2t}. This expression recognizes that [121] these parameters may not be constant over time.

Engle, Hendry, and Richard (1983) define a variable x_t as *weakly exogenous* for a set of parameters of interest θ if:

(a) θ is a function of the parameters λ_{1t} *alone*, and

(b) λ_{1t} and the parameters λ_{2t} of the marginal model for x_t are variation free.

Consequently, if x_t is *weakly exogenous* for θ, there is no loss of information about θ from neglecting to model the process determining x_t. In other words, even perfect knowledge of λ_{2t} could not improve the estimate of λ_{1t} over any period during which they are both constant. If, in addition, y_t fails to Granger cause x_t, then x_t is defined as *strongly exogenous* for θ.

Next, *constancy* of the "basic" or "meta" parameters is an essential property of most econometric models. We will be concerned in particular with the constancy of the parameters of the conditional model, λ_{1t}. Good empirical practice checks this assumption, but there is much evidence that parameter variation is common even in final models. See, for example, Judd and Scadding (1982) on U.S. M1 models and Hendry (1979) on "predictive failure".

Thirdly, the parameters λ_1 are said to be *invariant* if changes in λ_2 do not imply changes in λ_1. This concept differs from the notion of "free variation" used for weak exogeneity and a simple example will illustrate the point. Suppose λ_{1t} and λ_{2t} are both scalars and are related by

$$\lambda_{1t} = \phi\lambda_{2t},$$

where ϕ is an unknown scalar. Over periods of constant λ_{2t} there is no information in λ_2 which would be helpful in estimating λ_1, so they are variation free, however λ_1 clearly is not invariant with respect to λ_2. If instead, the relation were

$$\lambda_1 = \phi_t\lambda_{2t}, \qquad \forall t,$$

invariance would be satisfied.

The idea of *invariance* has a long history which includes important contributions from Frisch (1938) (reprinted in 1948) and Haavelmo (1944), both of whom discussed the concept in terms of *autonomy*—the extent to which one relationship remained the same when others altered. In particular, they sought to distinguish the *structural* equations of an economy from the *confluent* relationships induced by the interdependent nature of economic behavior [also see Marschak (1953) and Hurwicz (1962); Aldrich (1989) provides a history]. From a theory perspective, Lucas (1976) criticized invariance claims

in "conventional macro-economic models" on the grounds that agents' expectational mechanisms would alter as policies changed, so that conditional
[122] policy simulations would yield misleading inferences in models where the invariant behavioral parameters were not separately estimated from the changing parameters of the expectations processes. Thus, only careful theoretical analysis (such as that now claimed to be associated with "rational expectations econometrics") could reveal which parameters were potential invariants (sometimes referred to as "deep" or "structural" parameters).

In response to such critiques, the theoretical underpinnings of many models have been strengthened, more rigorous testing procedures have been adopted, "time-varying parameter" processes[1] have been investigated, and so on. Nevertheless, a formal analysis of invariance testing still seems to be lacking. For example, although constancy and invariance are different concepts, tests for the former are sometimes interpreted as tests of the latter. In principle, parameters could vary (over time, say, due to seasonality) but be invariant to policy changes, or be constant over historical interventions but vary with some other alteration in the "input topology" [see Salmon and Wallis (1982)]. Moreover, the power of constancy tests might be low for investigating invariance claims.

Finally, Engle, Hendry, and Richard (1983) defined x_t as *super exogenous* for θ if x_t is weakly exogenous for θ and λ_1 is invariant to changes in λ_2. Thus, tests of super exogeneity may be tests of weak exogeneity or tests of invariance or both. As will be seen below, both aspects enter the general formulation. Indeed, tests for invariance raise a number of technical complications due to the need to formulate the alternative model which details how and why the parameters vary. The test must discern whether there has been a shift in regime and, if so, how big a change in parameters would thereby be expected.

3   Formulating Super Exogeneity and Invariance Hypotheses

The null hypothesis to be tested in most cases is a linear regression equation which is hypothesized to represent the constant conditional mean of a random variable y_t given another random variable x_t, as well as other information. The tests developed in this paper require careful formulation of the alternative hypotheses which are to be viewed as failures of weak exogeneity, invariance, or super exogeneity.

Consider the joint distribution of two random variables y_t and x_t conditional on an information set $\mathcal{F}_t$ which includes the past of y and x and the current and past of other valid conditioning variables $z_t : \mathcal{F}_t = (Y_{t-1}^1, X_{t-1}^1, Z_t^1)$.

---

[1] However, such processes are not very aptly named since they merely shift which parameters are assumed constant.

We assume throughout that the data generation process of (y_t, x_t) is a conditional normal distribution (so regressions are linear), given by   [123]

$$\begin{pmatrix} y_t \\ x_t \end{pmatrix} \Big| \mathcal{F}_t \sim \mathsf{N}\left[\begin{pmatrix} \mu_t^y \\ \mu_t^x \end{pmatrix}, \begin{pmatrix} \sigma_t^{yy} & \sigma_t^{yx} \\ \sigma_t^{yx} & \sigma_t^{xx} \end{pmatrix}\right] = \mathsf{N}(\mu_t, \Sigma_t), \qquad (1)$$

where $\mathsf{N}(\alpha, \Omega)$ denotes a normal distribution with mean α and variance matrix Ω. Each of the means and covariances in (1) potentially depends upon the information set $\mathcal{F}_t$, although any particular moments could be constant in practice. The means μ_t^y and μ_t^x are the conditional expectations of y_t and x_t given $\mathcal{F}_t$: $\mu_t^y = E(y_t \,|\, \mathcal{F}_t)$ and $\mu_t^x = E(x_t \,|\, \mathcal{F}_t)$. Finally, Σ_t is the possibly nonconstant error covariance matrix: $\sigma_t^{xx} = E[(x_t - \mu_t^x)^2 \,|\, \mathcal{F}_t)$, etc.

The conditional model of interest to the econometrician concerns the relationship between y_t and x_t. From (1), this is in fact given by

$$y_t \,|\, x_t, \mathcal{F}_t \sim \mathsf{N}[\delta_t(x_t - \mu_t^x) + \mu_t^y, \; \omega_t], \qquad (2)$$

where $\delta_t = \sigma_t^{yx}/\sigma_t^{xx}$ is the regression coefficient of y_t on x_t conditional on $\mathcal{F}_t$, and $\omega_t = \sigma_t^{yy} - (\sigma_t^{yx})^2/\sigma_t^{xx}$ denotes the conditional variance. The analysis generalizes to x_t being a vector, with suitable notation for equation (7) below, but the bivariate case will suffice to highlight the principles involved.

The parameters of interest in the analysis are β and γ in the theoretical behavioral relationship:

$$\mu_t^y = \beta_t(\lambda_{2t})\mu_t^x + z_t'\gamma, \qquad (3)$$

which equation relates the conditional means of y_t and x_t to the set of variables $z_t \in \mathcal{F}_t$. However, we have allowed for the possibility that the "parameter" β might vary with changes in the parameters of the marginal density of x_t which are denoted by λ_{2t}, and that the form of this relation may itself be time-varying. In expression (1) it appears that these parameters coincide with μ_t^x and σ_t^{xx}, however more general shifts can easily be considered. Well-known examples of (3) in which β is often taken as constant and invariant are the Permanent Income Hypothesis, where μ_t^y and μ_t^x denote permanent consumption and permanent income, or money demand models in which μ_t^y and μ_t^x become planned money holdings and expected income and z_t characterizes interest rates. In this paper, we maintain the assumption that γ does not vary with λ_{2t}, since otherwise z_t would merely be reclassified as part of an extended vector x_t.

The issue of central concern in this paper is when an econometrician can formulate and estimate the empirical model corresponding to (3) as the regression equation:

$$y_t = \beta x_t + z_t'\gamma + \varepsilon_t \quad \text{where} \quad \varepsilon_t \sim \mathsf{IN}[0, \omega].$$

That step entails exogeneity, constancy, and invariance assumptions which   [124] are open to empirical evaluation, and we first analyze these three assumptions and their implications.

Substituting (3) into (2) and rearranging yields

$$y_t \mid x_t, \mathcal{F}_t \sim \mathsf{N}[\beta_t(\lambda_{2t})x_t + z_t'\gamma + \{\delta_t - \beta_t(\lambda_{2t})\}(x_t - \mu_t^x),\ \omega_t]. \qquad (4)$$

As discussed in Section 1, three conditions are needed to sustain regression analysis of $y_t \mid x_t, \mathcal{F}_t$:

(a) *Weak exogeneity* of x_t for the parameters of interest. This requires that μ_t^x and σ_t^{xx} do not enter the conditional model. Thus, a necessary condition for the weak exogeneity of x_t for (β, γ) is $\delta_t = \beta_t(\lambda_{2t})$.

(b) *Constancy* of the regression coefficients. The coefficient of x_t in (4) is simply δ_t, so a necessary condition is that $\delta_t = \delta,\ \forall t$. From the definition of δ_t, the ratio of the error covariance to the variance of x_t must be constant over t, and therefore $\omega_t = \omega,\ \forall t$, if $\sigma_t^{yy} = \omega + \delta\sigma_t^{xx}$; otherwise, (5) below would have a heteroscedastic innovation process. We maintain homoscedasticity for simplicity, although generalizations to heteroscedastic processes can be carried out.

(c) *Invariance* of β to the potential changes in λ_{2t}. This requires that $\beta_t(\lambda_{2t}) = \beta_t,\ \forall t$, where the set of parameters β_t may vary over time without depending on variations in λ_{2t}.

Together, these three restrictions entail that $\delta = \beta$. Individually, they constitute necessary conditions to validate constant parameter, invariant conditional models. The conjunction of (a) and (c) ensures that x_t is super exogenous for β, but it is unclear how one might proceed if δ_t nevertheless varied in unknown ways (while maintaining equality to β_t). Consequently, we require all three conditions to hold in practice for the parameters of interest in conditional models. For example, if (a) fails, then generally *both* weak exogeneity and constancy will fail because the mean and variance of x_t appear in the conditional model: hence, changes in μ_t^x and σ_t^{xx} will affect the parameters of the conditional model. Conversely, it is possible that over the historical sample, $D(y_t, x_t \mid \mathcal{F}_t)$ is weakly stationary, so δ is constant and x_t is weakly exogenous for (β, γ) but an intervention alters β post-sample. Thus, (a) and (b) alone do not entail (c).

If (a), (b), and (c) hold, then the conditional distribution (4) becomes

$$y_t \mid x_t, \mathcal{F}_t \sim \mathsf{N}(\beta x_t + z_t'\gamma,\ \omega), \qquad (5)$$

and hence yields the conventional constant parameter regression model. Rewriting (1), given (5), reveals that for this particular model (5) is the condition for the structural error, ε_t, and the reduced form error, η_t, to be uncorrelated in the equations:

$$y_t - x_t\beta - z_t'\gamma = \varepsilon_t \sim \mathsf{IN}[0, \omega], \qquad x_t - \mu_t^x = \eta_t \sim \mathsf{IN}[0, \sigma_t^{xx}]. \qquad (6)$$

As noted, $E[\varepsilon_t \eta_t] \neq 0$ may imply nonconstancy as well as invalid exogeneity.

A broad alternative model for a general test of super exogeneity must recognize that, in addition, the behavioral model in (3) may not have constant parameters because β may be affected by λ_{2t}. Specifically, we consider how variations in the *moments* of x might influence β, but maintain that this is a time-invariant relationship. This would allow a class of tests of Lucas Critique assertions to be conducted for historical interventions associated with $\{x_t\}$, together with both constancy tests [of (b) above] and exogeneity tests [of (a)]. Thus, we allow $\beta(\lambda_{2t})$ in (3) to be a function of (μ_t^x, σ_t^{xx}) and approximate $\beta(\cdot)\mu_t^x$ by

$$\beta(\mu_t^x, \sigma_t^{xx})\mu_t^x = \beta_0 \mu_t^x + \beta_1(\mu_t^x)^2 + \beta_2 \sigma_t^{xx} + \beta_3 \sigma_t^{xx}\mu_t^x, \tag{7}$$

assuming $\mu_t^x \neq 0$, $\forall t$. Higher-order expansions could be used if they were thought likely to matter. Given (7), (3) then becomes

$$\mu_t^y = \beta_0 \mu_t^x + z_t'\gamma + \beta_1(\mu_t^x)^2 + \beta_2 \sigma_t^{xx} + \beta_3 \mu_t^x \sigma_t^{xx}, \tag{8}$$

since the term linear in μ_t^x is incorporated through β_0. Under the null of invariance, $\beta_1 = \beta_2 = \beta_3 = 0$ and so $\beta_0 = \beta$.

Substituting (8) into (2) yields

$$y_t \,|\, x_t, \mathcal{F}_t \ \sim \ \mathsf{N}[x_t\beta_0 + z_t'\gamma + (\delta_t - \beta_0)(x_t - \mu_t^x)$$
$$+\beta_1(\mu_t^x)^2 + \beta_2 \sigma_t^{xx} + \beta_3 \mu_t^x \sigma_t^{xx}, \ \omega], \tag{9}$$

so that super exogeneity can fail through the moments of x_t appearing directly in the regression of y_t on x_t even if $\delta_t = \delta$.

An alternative representation is the restricted reduced form, which could remain valid even when x is not weakly exogenous for β. Substituting into (8) and (1) directly:

$$y_t \,|\, \mathcal{F}_t \ \sim \ \mathsf{N}[\mu_t^x\beta_0 + z_t'\gamma + \beta_1(\mu_t^x)^2 + \beta_2 \sigma_t^{xx} + \beta_3 \mu_t^x \sigma_t^{xx}, \ \sigma_t^{yy}],$$

which is operational when an expression for the reduced form of x is available such as $\mu_t^x = \pi_x' Z_t$ for a set of instruments Z_t. In this context, the invariance of the parameter β can be tested without the weak exogeneity assumption. [126] Using 2SLS or FIML to estimate the parameters with x_t replacing μ_t^x, it is simple to test various portions of the hypothesis $\beta_1 = \beta_2 = \beta_3 = 0$. In this case, there is no contemporaneous conditioning but it is still possible and interesting to test the hypothesis of invariance.

4 Future Expectations, Invariance, and the Lucas Critique

Many econometric models derive from economic theories involving expectations. Such models can often be written in precisely the form of (5), except that their parameters are no longer invariant to the process of the forcing variables as was so effectively pointed out by Lucas (1976). Thus tests of backward-looking models are typically conjectured to suffer from parameter nonconstancy and noninvariance. Here we develop a specific class of maintained hypotheses against which such models can be tested. Thus the Lucas Critique can be used to formulate particular alternatives to a backward-looking conditional model. If we fail to reject such a null hypothesis, we find no evidence in support of the Lucas Critique. Interestingly however, in this case [as pointed out by Favero and Hendry (1992) in a survey of related work] the power of such a test can be established, and if it is high, we have strong evidence against the Lucas Critique.

The analysis of the previous section can be interpreted in an expectations framework. If μ_t^x represents an expectation formed about x_t, then (9) allows for the usual possibility that $\delta \neq \beta$ (assuming that δ is constant) as well as covering situations when δ is not constant and β varies with changes in the expectations process.

More generally, consider a model in which $\mathcal{F}_t$ denotes information available at the start of planning period t, μ_t^y is the planned value of y_t, and the plan depends on the expectation held about $\{x_{t+i}; i = 1, \ldots, N\}$. Thus, in place of (3), we have the distributed lead model:

$$\mu_t^y = \beta(\lambda_{2t})E[x_t \mid \mathcal{F}_t] + \rho_1 E[x_{t+1} \mid \mathcal{F}_t] + \cdots + \rho_N E[x_{t+N} \mid \mathcal{F}_t] + z_t'\gamma, \quad (3^*)$$

where we have taken N to be finite and will focus on the case $N = 1$ as this highlights the main analytical issues. The potential variation of ρ_i with respect to λ_{2t} would lead to extended versions of the tests described below.

To develop a maintained hypothesis, a model of x_t is postulated where

$$x_{t+1} = E[x_{t+1} \mid \mathcal{F}_t] + \nu_{t+1} = \varphi_t'Z_t + \nu_{t+1}, \quad (10)$$

[127] when $Z_t \in \mathcal{F}_t$, and φ_t potentially varies over time. Substituting (10) into (3^*) for $N = 1$, and the result into (2), yields the appropriate generalization of (4):

$$y_t \mid x_t, \mathcal{F}_t \sim \mathsf{N}\left[\beta(\lambda_{2t})x_t + z_t'\gamma + \{\delta_t - \beta(\lambda_{2t})\}(x_t - \mu_t^x) + \rho_1\varphi_t'Z_t, \omega\right]. \quad (11)$$

Clearly, x_t is not weakly exogenous for β even if $\delta_t = \beta(\lambda_{2t})$ since the parameter φ_t appears directly in the conditional density but must be estimated from the marginal density of x_t. The presence of the future expectation introduces a possibly time-varying function of the current information set into the regression. Such a regression model will typically appear to be nonconstant unless φ and Z have very simple forms, and will not be invariant to the process generating x_t which is incorporated in φ_t and Z_t.

To formulate a general alternative to super exogeneity in this type of rational expectations model, we allow for failures of invariance, and substitute (7) into (11) to get

$$y_t \mid x_t, \mathcal{F}_t \sim \mathsf{N}\left[x_t\beta_0 + z_t'\gamma + (\delta_t - \beta_0)(x_t - \mu_t^x) \right.$$
$$\left. +\beta_1(\mu_t^x)^2 + \beta_2\sigma_t^{xx} + \beta_3\mu_t^x\sigma_t^{xx} + \rho_1\varphi_t'Z_t, \ \omega\right]. \qquad (12)$$

Hence, (5) will be the estimated model if $\delta_t = \beta_0$, $\beta_1 = \beta_2 = \beta_3 = 0$, and $\rho_1 = 0$. Then tests of these restrictions will comprise a super exogeneity test in the expectations context. These assumptions guarantee the weak exogeneity of x_t for β_0 and the invariance of the conditional model to variations in the generating process of x_t. Of course, to carry out this test in practice (as discussed in the next section), it is necessary to specify and estimate parameters such as φ_t as well as μ_t^x.

Super exogeneity can hold only if there are no future expectations in the behavioral model. However, it may still be of interest to test models in which x_t is not weakly exogenous for β for failures of invariance. By replacing $\varphi_t'Z_t$ in (11) with x_{t+1} and assuming that $\delta_t = \beta(\lambda_{2t})$, possibly because $x_t \in \mathcal{F}_t$, the model has the familiar errors-in-variables form of rational expectations model popularized by McCallum (1976):

$$y_t = \beta(\lambda_{2t})x_t + \rho_1x_{t+1} + \gamma'z_t + \varepsilon_t - \beta(\lambda_{2t})v_{t+1},$$

which requires estimation with instruments (Z_t, z_t) in order to achieve consistency even when $\beta(\lambda_{2t}) = \beta$. To test for invariance of β, (7) above can still be used but only after estimating with instrumental variables rather than by least squares, as in the last example of the previous section.

The ability of these tests to detect failures of super exogeneity, partic- [128] ularly through the expectations mechanism, is intimately connected to the complexities of the marginal process of the conditioning variable. For example, if $\varphi_t = \varphi$ and $Z_t = z_t$, then the restriction $\rho_1 = 0$ is not testable. Thus, the power of the testing procedures can be ascertained by examining the marginal processes for changing parameters and additional causal variables.

The argument of this section can be generalized to multiple future leads. Formulating the multi-step predictors as $E_tx_{t+i} = \varphi_{it}'Z_t$ yields the conditional model:

$$y_t \mid x_t, \mathcal{F}_t \sim \mathsf{N}[x_t\beta_0 + z_t'\gamma + (\delta_t - \beta_0)(x_t - \mu_t^x)$$
$$+\beta_1(\mu_t^x)^2 + \beta_2\sigma_t^{xx} + \beta_3\mu_t^x\sigma_t^{xx} + \sum_{i=1}^{N}\rho_i\varphi_{it}'Z_t, \ \omega], \qquad (13)$$

where each of the expectations terms could be tested separately, except that for most forcing variables x only a small subset would be linearly independent.

The most widely-used model of forward expectations is the present discounted value (PDV) model which has been used to explain stock prices as a function of dividends, long rates as a function of short rates, and consumption as a function of income. In each case, it is typically assumed that a conditional model is mis-specified, and it is assumed that the model is invariant with constant discount factors. We consider in somewhat more detail the testing of the present discounted value model.

Consider the example where y_t is an end-of-period stock price, x_t is its dividend, and as before, $\mathcal{F}_t$ is the sigma field including past values of y and x as well as current values of valid conditioning variables. The PDV model is

$$E[y_t \mid \mathcal{F}_{t+1}] = y_t = \beta \sum_{i=1}^{\infty} \theta^i E[x_{t+i} \mid \mathcal{F}_{t+1}], \quad \theta = 1/(1+r),$$

which can be rewritten as the backward-looking model

$$E[y_t + \beta x_t \mid \mathcal{F}_t] = (1+r)y_{t-1}$$

or

$$\mu_t^y = -\beta \mu_t^x + (1+r)y_{t-1},$$

where it is desired to ascertain whether $\beta = 1$. This is now in the form of (3) and can be examined for super exogeneity of x_t. From (9), $z_t = y_{t-1}$, $\gamma = (1+r)$, and the test would require $\beta_1 = \beta_2 = \beta_3 = 0$, $\delta_t = \beta_0$. There is nothing in the theory which would suggest that the weak exogeneity component of this hypothesis would be true. Hence, we expect to reject the null hypothesis of super exogeneity as we expect that this truly is a forward-looking system. Estimates of β_0 above 1 indicate excess sensitivity of prices to dividends, but these are easily confused by the natural simultaneity between y and x.

To test whether β is invariant to λ_{2t} and equal to 1 without assuming weak exogeneity, one must either use instrumental variables or estimate the reduced form. In this context, one can test interesting hypotheses about the expectations mechanism. For example, suppose the PDV model is only geometric for higher leads, so that

$$y_t = \beta \sum_{i=1}^{\infty} \theta^i E[x_{t+i} \mid \mathcal{F}_{t+1}] + \sum_{i=1}^{I} \psi_i E[x_{t+i} \mid \mathcal{F}_{t+1}],$$

and we wish to test that $\psi_i = 0, \forall i$. Rewriting this model gives

$$y_t = (1+r)y_{t-1} + [-\beta - (1+r)\psi_1]x_t$$

$$+ \sum_{i=1}^{I} \{\psi_i E[x_{t+i} \mid \mathcal{F}_{t+1}] - (1+r)\psi_{i+1} E[x_{t+i} \mid \mathcal{F}_t]\},$$

where $\psi_{I+1} \equiv 0$, and computing the reduced form by taking expectations conditional on $\mathcal{F}_t$ gives

[129]

$$E[y_t \,|\, \mathcal{F}_t] \;=\; (1+r)y_{t-1} + [-\beta - (1+r)\psi_1]\mu_t^x$$

$$+ \sum_{i=1}^{I} \{\psi_i - (1+r)\psi_{i+1}\}\, E[x_{t+i} \,|\, \mathcal{F}_t],$$

which is of the form of (13) and can be used to test hypotheses on the expectations mechanism by testing for invariance in the relation between y and x when the process of x changes.

5   Tests for Super Exogeneity

A variety of tests for super exogeneity will be proposed; tests for invariance in models without weakly exogenous conditioning variables only need modification along the lines sketched above. In each case, the null hypothesis will be that x_t is super exogenous for β in the regression:

$$y_t = x_t\beta + z_t'\gamma + \varepsilon_t. \tag{5*}$$

Different tests will be sensitive to different alternatives, and we separately [130] consider worlds where Σ_t is constant and where it varies over time (whether under the null or alternative).

5.1 Σ_t Is Constant

Assuming temporarily that $\beta_i = 0$, $(i = 1, 2, 3)$, this case is the classical issue of testing for weak exogeneity. Wu (1973) and Hausman (1978) proposed tests and Engle (1982a) established their optimality through showing them to be Lagrange Multiplier tests. To construct a test, μ_t^x must be parameterized. Suppose there is a set of instruments Z_t, including z_t, which describe the mean of x through

$$x_t = Z_t'\pi_x + \eta_t. \tag{14}$$

The construction of Z_t is assumed to allow for and define regime shifts. Some of the variables in Z_t may be lagged x's and y's or dichotomous variables interacting with other observable variables. This specification, therefore, gives wide scope to specifying changes in policy regime, expectations formation, or states of nature.

If $E[\varepsilon_t\eta_t] \neq 0$, then there will be simultaneous equations bias. The LM test for weak exogeneity is to test the estimate of $\{\eta_t\}$ given from (14) as $x_t - Z_t'\hat{\pi}_x = x_t - \hat{x}_t = \hat{\eta}_t$ for its presence in the model (5). Notice that in equation (4) with δ and β constant, their difference is zero if η_t has a zero coefficient. The t-statistic on $\hat{\eta}_t$ is a simple and intuitive form of the test. Since $x_t = \hat{x}_t + \hat{\eta}_t$, an equivalent form would be the t-statistic on $\hat{x}_t$. If $\hat{\eta}_t$ belongs in the regression but is excluded, then other diagnostic tests may have some power. In particular, parameter constancy tests have been used in this case, although their power is crucially dependent on changes having occurred in the underlying data process. Indeed, constancy tests are an example of one choice of Z corresponding to using (0,1) dummy variables. However, for an H-period constancy test, H dummies are required and the lack of a constructive alternative either for the break period or for the cause of the break suggests that they will lack power relative to a directed test of the form proposed here. Moreover, a failure to reject may simply reflect a constant within-sample process for x and so throw no light on invariance.

In the common case where one is unwilling or unable to specify the entire set Z, it may still be possible to perform the test. Partition Z into (z, Z_1, Z_2) where Z_1 and Z_2 are excluded from (5) on *a priori* grounds (rather than merely because of insignificant coefficients in pre-tests) and Z_1 is observed. Z_1 might be dummies for shifts in regimes which, under super exogeneity, ought not to enter (5). A test of super exogeneity would then be whether [131] Z_1 enters (5). A test for any linear combination of Z_1 would also be such a test and, from (4), the linear combination most closely approximating μ_t^x should be most powerful. The test can be constructed as before: regress x_t on (z_t, Z_{1t}) and test $\hat{x}_t$ (or equivalently $\hat{\eta}_t$) in equation (5).

An alternative interpretation of these tests is insightful. Under the null that $E[\varepsilon_t \eta_t] = 0$, the restricted reduced form for y_t derived from the two-equation system (5) and (14) is

$$y_t = \beta \pi_x' Z_t + \gamma' z_t + \varepsilon_t + \beta \eta_t = \pi_y' Z_t + u_t \quad \text{(say)}. \quad (15)$$

The unrestricted reduced form is simply the regression of y_t on Z_t. Thus, one can equivalently test whether the former encompasses the latter [for discussions of encompassing, see Hendry and Richard (1982), Mizon (1984), Mizon and Richard (1986), and Hendry and Richard (1989)]. One degree of freedom tests [see Cox (1961), Pesaran (1974), and Ericsson (1983)] evaluate variance encompassing which corresponds to testing: $\sigma_u^2 = \sigma_\varepsilon^2 + \beta^2 \sigma_\eta^2$, where σ_u^2 is estimated from the unrestricted reduced form. Providing that $E[\varepsilon_t \eta_t] = 0$, *variance encompassing* will indeed ensue. Tests based on this approach are reported in Favero (1989). *Parameter encompassing* tests will have ℓ degrees of freedom for ℓ restrictions on π_y, and as shown in Mizon (1984), these tests are equivalent to the test of independence of instruments and errors in Sargan (1964).

If we now allow $\beta_i \neq 0$ $(i = 1, 2, 3)$ but retain $\Sigma_t = \Sigma$, then we have $\hat{x}_t$ entering the regression through its square as well as its level. Thus one would perform an F-test on $\hat{x}_t$ and $\hat{x}_t^2$. If we further allow the possibility of future expectations, then we must form multi-step predictors of future x. Letting $\hat{x}_{ti}$ be the estimated forecast of x_{t+i} using information available at time t, the test procedure would perform a joint test on $\hat{x}_t$, $\hat{x}_t^2$, $\hat{x}_{t1}, \ldots, \hat{x}_{tN}$.

5.2 Σ_t Varying

In this more general case, the coefficient of x_t is potentially varying as shown in (9). Note that if, for example, σ_t^{xx} is constant within regimes, but not between, then one might find weak exogeneity within each regime but no super exogeneity. Charemza and Kiraly (1986) suggest recursive analogues of the tests in Section 5.1 above to detect such cases.

To develop formal testing procedures, expand $\sigma_t^{yx}/\sigma_t^{xx} = \delta_t = \delta_0 + \delta_1 \sigma_t^{xx}$ so that (9) can be written in testable form as:

$$y_t = x_t \beta_0 + z_t'\gamma + (\delta_0 - \beta_0)\hat{\eta}_t + \delta_1 \sigma_t^{xx}\hat{\eta}_t + \beta_1 \hat{x}_t^2 + \beta_2 \sigma_t^{xx} + \beta_3 \hat{x}_t \sigma_t^{xx} + \varepsilon_t, \quad (16)$$

where again $x_t = Z_t'\hat{\pi}_x + \hat{\eta}_t = \hat{x}_t + \hat{\eta}_t$. If we suppose that σ_t^{xx} has distinct [132] values over different but clearly defined regimes, then the three separate hypotheses described in Section 2 are susceptible to test:

(a) *Weak exogeneity of x_t for β_0.* This entails a zero effect from $\hat{\eta}_t$ as in Section 5.1.

(b) *Constancy of δ entails $\delta_1 = 0$.* Given (15), constancy tests should be conducted for the coefficients of $\hat{\eta}_t$ and $\hat{x}_t$, or equivalently for x_t and $\hat{\eta}_t$.

(c) *Invariance of β.* This entails that $\beta_i = 0$ $(i = 1, 2, 3)$ in (15) taking σ_t^{xx} to be given by disjoint values.

Depending on how rich a maintained hypothesis is desired, the statistic could jointly test for the significance of all the terms involving δ and β. Notice, however, that $z_t'\gamma$ will *not* have changing coefficients in the present formulation.

From the reduced form regression $x_t = Z_t'\pi_x + \eta_t$, it is possible to draw inferences about σ_t^{xx}. A heteroscedasticity function could be fit which specifies $\text{var}(\eta_t \mid \mathcal{F}_t) = Z_t'\kappa$. Even simpler might be the ARCH model of Engle (1982b) which allows a flexible form of conditional heteroscedasticity:

$$\text{var}(\eta_t \mid \mathcal{F}_t) = \kappa_0 + \sum \kappa_i \eta_{t-i}^2, \quad (17)$$

so that Z_t corresponds to lagged values of η_t^2. Estimation of (14) with (17) will improve the efficiency of the estimates in (14) and provide an estimated series $\hat{\sigma}_t^{xx}$ to use with $\hat{x}_t$ in testing (16). Moreover, both $\{\hat{\sigma}_t^{xx}\}$ and $\{\hat{\eta}_t^2 - \hat{\sigma}_t^{xx}\}$ could be included to check on the impact of systematic versus unanticipated error variance changes.

Throughout this section it has been assumed that $\omega_t = \sigma_t^{yy} - (\sigma_t^{xy})^2/\sigma_t^{xx}$ is constant under both the null and the alternative. While this is surely true under the null, there may be power lost by failing to define an expression for ω_t as a function of σ_t^{xx}. There does not seem to be any natural such expression, however, and so we maintain $\omega_t = \omega$ throughout, letting σ_t^{yy}

adjust. This assumption is itself testable empirically, or might suggest the use of robust standard errors for the various tests as in White (1980).

6   An Empirical Illustration

The example selected relates to testing the super exogeneity of the parameters of the money demand function in Hendry (1988). This is a particularly appropriate example because considerable debate has addressed parameter constancy and exogeneity assumptions in this context. For example, a long sequence of predictive failures in U.S. M1 is documented by Judd and Scadding (1982) and reviewed and interpreted by Baba, Hendry, and Starr (1992). In addition, the exogeneity assumptions implicit in money demand [133] models have been criticized by Cooley and Leroy (1981) and Hendry and Ericsson (1991) among others. The issue is that if the money stock M is taken as a policy variable whose value depends only on past information, then at least one of the interest rate, R, real income, Y, or the price level, P, must be endogenous. If the last of these is selected as endogenous, models of real money should be formulated with P as the dependent variable potentially allowing conditioning on M. Instead, some studies condition on P, taking M as the dependent variable [see, e.g., H.M. Treasury (1980)]. Since both M and P cannot be weakly exogenous for the parameters of the money demand function, and in most cases, both cannot have constant parameterizations, both conditional models cannot be invariant to the monetary rule. In short, the exogeneity assumptions are usually very important.

The measure of money is quarterly M1 in the United Kingdom over the period 1963–1982, the precise dates depending on the lag lengths of the various models. The income measure is Total Final Expenditure, the price measure is the implicit deflator of TFE, and the interest rate is the three-month Local Authority bill rate. Lower-case letters denote logarithms of capitals. The original model takes the form:[2]

$$
\begin{aligned}
\Delta[m-p]_t = {} & - \underset{(0.144)}{0.854}\,\Delta p_t - \underset{(0.001)}{0.007}\,R_t - \underset{(0.091)}{0.354}\,\Delta[m-p]_{t-1} \\
& + \underset{(0.104)}{0.280}\,\Delta y_{t-1} - \underset{(0.011)}{0.105}\,ECM_{t-2} + \underset{(0.006)}{0.031} \quad (18)
\end{aligned}
$$

$T = 1965(2)\text{--}1982(4)$ $R^2 = 0.732$ $\sigma = 1.31\%$ $DW = 1.90$

Mean $= -0.00293$ SD $= 0.0244$ $\chi^2(2) = 1.87$ AR $1 - 5\ F[5, 60] = 0.35$

ARCH 4 $F[4, 57] = 0.02$ $X_i^2\ F[10, 54] = 1.62$ RESET $F[1, 64] = 0.43$.

In (18), Δ denotes a first difference, $ECM_t = (m - p - y)_t$, and R^2, σ, DW, Mean, and SD, respectively, denote the squared multiple correlation coefficient, the residual standard deviation, the Durbin-Watson statistic, the

---

[2] All of the calculations were undertaken using PC-GIVE 6.0 [see Hendry (1989)].

mean quarterly growth rate of real money, and its unconditional standard deviation. Also, AR $1-5$ F-test (with degrees of freedom shown) is a Lagrange multiplier test for residual autocorrelation; ARCH 4 F-test checks for residual heteroscedasticity of the ARCH form; X_i^2, again in F-form, is the test suggested by White (1980); $\chi^2(2)$ is the Jarque-Bera (1980) normality statistic; and the RESET test is due to Ramsey (1969). None of these diagnostic checks is significant, nor is *any* recursively computed "break point" [134] Chow test, so (18) also appears to be constant over the sample period. Note that $(\cdot)$ and $[\cdot]$ beneath coefficients denote conventional and heteroscedastic consistent standard errors, respectively.

There have been several potential regime shifts over the sample period, including the Competition and Credit Control Regulations of 1971, the shift from fixed to floating exchange rates in that year, the oil crisis in late 1973, the change in the Value Added Tax rate from 8% to 15% in 1979, and the tight monetary policy introduced by the Thatcher Government after 1979. Dummy variables were created for step changes [e.g., $D73(4)$ denoting starting year and quarter] or impulses [e.g., $D^*69(1/2)$ denoting the $+1$, -1 periods]. Level and interactive combinations of these dummy variables were tried for the impact of these potential shift events in the marginal models for p_t and R_t and any first round significant effects were retained. The resulting models took the form:

$$\Delta p_t = \underset{(0.004)}{0.009\ D79(3)_t} - \underset{(0.008)}{0.051\ D73(4)_t} - \underset{(0.008)}{0.055\ D73(4)_t p_{t-1}}$$

$$+ \underset{(0.108)}{0.488\ D73(4)_t \Delta p_{t-1}} + \underset{(0.005)}{0.030\ p_{t-1}} + \underset{(0.006)}{0.022\ \Delta D79(3)}$$

$$+ \underset{(0.008)}{0.056}\ , \tag{19}$$

$T = 1963(3)\text{--}1982(4)$ $R^2 = 0.870$ $\sigma = 0.549\%$ $DW = 2.01$
Mean $= 0.0234$ SD $= 0.0146$ $\chi^2(2) = 0.43$ AR $1-5$ $F[5,66] = 0.91$
ARCH 4 $F[4,63] = 0.20$ X_i^2 $F[9,61] = 0.94$ RESET $F[1,70] = 0.03$,

and

$$\Delta R_t = -\underset{(0.060)}{0.202\ R_{t-1}} + \underset{(0.106)}{0.408\ \Delta R_{t-1}} + \underset{(1.19)}{3.07\ \Delta D73(4)_t}$$

$$+ \underset{(0.444)}{1.496} + \underset{(0.424)}{0.897\ D73(4)_{t-1}}, \tag{20}$$

$T = 1963(3)\text{--}1982(4)$ $R^2 = 0.277$ $\sigma = 1.148$ $DW = 2.07$
Mean $= 0.0727$ SD $= 1.314$ $\chi^2(2) = 3.12$ AR $1-5$ $F[5,68] = 0.90$
ARCH 4 $F[4,65] = 3.63$ X_i^2 $F[6,66] = 1.46$ RESET $F[1,72] = 0.50$.

In (19) and (20), the "oil-crisis" dummy is significant in several forms, but [135] the dummy for the VAT increase to 15% in 1979 is important only in the Δp_t equation. Both equations pass the diagnostic checks for residual autocorrelation, residual heteroscedasticity, normality, and the RESET test. However, residual ARCH is significant for ΔR_t, and is modelled below. Overall, (19) and (20) seem reasonable marginal models for the analogues of μ_t^x, especially since the standard errors (σ) are about $\frac{1}{2}\%$ and one point, respectively, and there is strong evidence of structural breaks in the linear projections alone. However, the presence of many dummies precluded recursive constancy tests.

Equation (20) suggests that R_t is integrated of order zero denoted I(0) [see Granger (1986) and Engle and Granger (1987)] and that the oil crisis raised interest rates considerably, both in the short run and the long run (by about 4.5 points). However, it is much harder to interpret (19): certainly, the VAT change raised inflation substantially, but whether or not the oil crisis did so depends on both the prevailing price level and inflation rate. Despite this problem of interpretation, both equations strongly reflect important regime effects compared to conventional autoregressive representations, which is the key requirement for the illustrations of this section.

From these two models, $\hat{\eta}(\Delta p)_t$, $\hat{\eta}(R)_t$, $\hat{x}(\Delta p)_t$, and $\hat{x}(R)_t$ were calculated and then measures of σ_t^{xx} were constructed: for Δp_t, a three-period moving average of $\hat{\eta}_t^2(\Delta p)$ was tried despite the insignificance of the ARCH test [denoted $V(\Delta p)$]; for R, a two-period ARCH error denoted $A(R)$ was estimated [$F[2,69] = 6.1$ in (20)] as was the deviation of $\hat{\eta}_t^2(R)$ from $A(R)$ [denoted $Dev(R)$]. All of these constructed variables were then included in the money demand function, which had conditioned on both Δp_t and R_t; in addition, the subgroups of variables which were most promising for rejecting invariance were included. However, no combination proved significant, and (21) reports the estimates when all five test constructs were added:

$$\Delta[m-p]_t = \underset{[0.155]}{-0.754\,\Delta p_t} - \underset{[0.001]}{0.006\,R_t} - \underset{[0.105]}{0.259\,\Delta[m-p]_{t-1}}$$

$$+ \underset{[0.137]}{0.310\,\Delta y_{t-1}} - \underset{[0.014]}{0.100\,ECM_{t-2}} + \underset{[0.008]}{0.026}$$

$$- \underset{[0.283]}{0.392\,\hat{\eta}(\Delta p)_t} + \underset{[70.4]}{43.1\,V(\Delta p)_t} - \underset{[0.002]}{0.002\,\hat{\eta}(R)_t}$$

$$- \underset{[0.002]}{0.003\,A(R)_t} - \underset{[0.001]}{0.001\,Dev(R)_t} \tag{21}$$

[136]

$T = 1965(2)\text{--}1982(4)$ $R^2 = 0.750$ $\sigma = 1.32\%$ $DW = 1.95$

Mean $= -0.00293$ SD $= 0.0244$ $\chi^2(2) = 0.50$ AR $1-5\ F[5,56] = 0.60$

ARCH 4 $F[4,53] = 0.89$ $X_i^2\ F[16,44] = 0.57$ RESET $F[1,60] = 0.09$

F-Test [for adding $\hat{\eta}(\Delta p)_t, V(\Delta p)_t, \hat{\eta}(R)_t, A(R)_t, Dev(R)_t$] $: F[5,60] = 0.85$.

Thus, the evidence is consistent with the super exogeneity of Δp_t and R_t in the original M1 model.

A natural issue is the power of this class of tests, and to investigate that, two variants of the basic model were evaluated. The first omitted Δp_t and hence imposed price homogeneity at all lags rather than just in the long run, and the second replaced Δp_t by Δp_{t-1} as a solved form, with the possible interpretation of an extrapolative predictor of inflation. In both cases, strong rejection was obtained as seen below:

$$
\begin{aligned}
\Delta[m-p]_t = &- \underset{[0.001]}{0.006}\, R_t - \underset{[0.111]}{0.056}\, \Delta[m-p]_{t-1} + \underset{[0.151]}{0.269}\, \Delta y_{t-1} \\
&+ \underset{[0.008]}{0.022} - \underset{[0.015]}{0.080}\, ECM_{t-2} \\
&- \underset{[0.391]}{1.157}\, \hat{\eta}(\Delta p)_t - \underset{[73.6]}{77.0}\, V(\Delta p)_t - \underset{[0.002]}{0.002}\, \hat{\eta}(R)_t \\
&- \underset{[0.002]}{0.005}\, A(R)_t - \underset{[0.001]}{0.001}\, Dev(R)_t
\end{aligned}
\tag{22}
$$

$R^2 = 0.679 \quad \sigma = 1.48\% \quad DW = 1.97 \quad \chi^2(2) = 0.50 \quad \text{RESET } F[1,60] = 0.09$
$\text{AR } 1-5\ F[5,56] = 0.60 \quad \text{ARCH } 4\ F[4,53] = 0.89 \quad X_i^2\ F[16,44] = 0.57$
$F\text{-test [for adding } \hat{\eta}(\Delta p)_t, V(\Delta p)_t, \hat{\eta}(R)_t, A(R)_t, Dev(R)_t] : F[5,61] = 3.47,$

and

$$
\begin{aligned}
\Delta[m-p]_t = &- \underset{[0.001]}{0.007}\, R_t - \underset{[0.128]}{0.295}\, \Delta[m-p]_{t-1} + \underset{[0.144]}{0.236}\, \Delta y_{t-1} \\
&- \underset{[0.014]}{0.103}\, ECM_{t-2} + \underset{[0.008]}{0.026} - \underset{[0.317]}{1.093}\, \hat{\eta}(\Delta p)_t \\
&- \underset{[67.1]}{17.1}\, V(\Delta p)_t - \underset{[0.002]}{0.002}\, \hat{\eta}(R)_t - \underset{[0.002]}{0.003}\, A(R)_t \\
&- \underset{[0.001]}{0.001}\, Dev(R)_t - \underset{[0.145]}{0.648}\, \Delta p_{t-1}
\end{aligned}
\tag{23}
$$

$R^2 = 0.735 \quad \sigma = 1.36\% \quad DW = 1.87 \quad \chi^2(2) = 2.34 \quad \text{RESET } F[1,59] = 0.07 \quad [137]$
$\text{AR } 1-5\ F[5,55] = 0.34 \quad \text{ARCH } 4\ F[4,52] = 0.30 \quad X_i^2\ F[18,41] = 0.59$
$F\text{-Test [for adding } \hat{\eta}(\Delta p)_t, V(\Delta p)_t, \hat{\eta}(R)_t, A(R)_t, Dev(R)_t] : F[5,60] = 2.99.$

In particular, both the weak exogeneity component of inflation and the anticipated error variance of interest rates are significant in the two misspecified models, even though (23) without the test variables is almost as well-fitting as the selected equation. Thus, the test procedure has some power and the nonrejection of (21) is consistent with its previously established constancy over more than five years after first selection.

Interestingly, (23) without the test variables is constant over the sample period as judged by recursive "break point" Chow tests: there is no split sample point commencing in 1965(2) and ending in 1982(4) where rejection would have been obtained at even the 5% level for a single test. Thus, this mis-specification would not have been detected by any of the other tests reported here.

Finally, we consider the "inversion" of (19) to determine inflation as a function of an assumed exogenous money stock and the arguments of the money demand function. If the money demand equation is invariant and constant, then the inverted equation will not be. The Chow statistics for a structural break are computed for each point in the sample period. Although the critical values of the maxima of these are the subject of continuing research, the contrast with earlier models is marked since constancy would have been rejected at the 0.1% level by any investigator testing almost anywhere within sample, despite the constancy of (19). [*Editors' note: the appendix to this chapter provides a parallel analytical example.*]

7   Conclusion

The main result of this paper is that hypotheses of invariance and super exogeneity of regression parameters can be tested directly and the proposed tests seem to have power to detect incorrect assertions. In an example where a previously established model was tested, nonrejection was obtained, whereas rejection occurred in two mis-specified variants of that model. Further examples are provided in Favero (1989) who uses super exogeneity, cointegration, and encompassing tests to distinguish between approximate and exact models of the expectations theory of the term structure of interest rates. Recursive analogues of the tests in Section 3 would facilitate joint investigation of constancy and invariance, especially in the context of expectations-based equations.

[*Editors' note: The following material appeared in an earlier version of this paper but was deleted before publication in the* Journal of Econometrics. *It adds insights to the testing of super exogeneity and so has been reincluded.*]

Appendix.   The Reverse Regression

If x_t is weakly exogenous for (β, γ), then y_t cannot be so. This is shown by Engle, Hendry, and Richard (1983) in the bivariate normal model. Here we examine the conditions under which parameter constancy in the model for y given x is compatible with parameter constancy in the reverse regression. The reverse regression for (18) illustrates how nonconstancy can result.

Let $w_t' = (y_t \ x_t)$ and reconsider the conditional process in (1) written explicitly as:

$$w_t \mid Z_t \sim \mathsf{N}[\Pi_t Z_t, \Sigma_t] \qquad \text{where} \qquad \Sigma_t = \begin{pmatrix} \sigma_t^{yy} & \sigma_t^{xy} \\ \sigma_t^{xy} & \sigma_t^{xx} \end{pmatrix}. \qquad \text{(A.1)}$$

We now investigate the consequences when the process in (A.1) is generated by:

$$y_t = \beta x_t + \gamma^{*\prime} Z_t + \varepsilon_t \qquad \text{where} \qquad \varepsilon_t \sim \mathsf{IN}[0, \omega]$$

$$x_t = \Pi'_{xt} Z_t + \eta_t \qquad \text{with} \qquad \eta_t \sim \mathsf{IN}[0, \sigma_t^{xx}], \qquad \text{(A.2)}$$

where γ^* denotes γ augmented by zeros, so (A.2) parameterizes (6), consistent with the null hypothesis that x_t is super exogenous for β. Comparing (A.2) and (A.1) entails:

$$\beta = (\sigma_t^{xx})^{-1} \sigma_t^{xy} \quad \forall t \qquad \text{so} \qquad \sigma_t^{xy} = \beta \sigma_t^{xx}.$$

Also, $\gamma^* + \beta \Pi'_{xt} = \Pi'_{yt}$. Finally, $\sigma_t^{yy} = \omega + \beta^2 \sigma_t^{xx}$ and therefore:

$$\Sigma_t = \begin{pmatrix} \omega + \beta^2 \sigma_t^{xx} & \beta \sigma_t^{xx} \\ \beta \sigma_t^{xx} & \sigma_t^{xx} \end{pmatrix}.$$

At first sight, inverting the first equation of (A.2) seems innocuous, since we have:

$$x_t = \frac{1}{\beta} y_t - \frac{1}{\beta} \gamma^{*\prime} Z_t - \frac{1}{\beta} \varepsilon_t. \qquad \text{(A.3)}$$

However, since $E[y_t \varepsilon_t] = \omega \neq 0$, (A.3) is *not* the inverse conditional regression, which is instead given by:[3]

$$E[x_t \mid y_t, Z_t] = \sigma_t^{xy}(\sigma_t^{yy})^{-1} y_t + (\Pi_{xt} - \sigma_t^{xy}(\sigma_t^{yy})^{-1}\Pi_{yt})' Z_t$$

$$= \frac{\beta \sigma_t^{xx}}{(\omega + \beta^2 \sigma_t^{xx})} y_t + \alpha'_t Z_t. \qquad \text{(A.4)}$$

(The actual moments are derived below.) The last expression *cannot* be constant when β and γ are constant unless both σ_t^{xx} and Π_{xt} are constant. Therefore, the reverse regression does not deliver invariants since its parameters vary when σ_t^{xx} and Π_{xt} alter. We conclude that:

> If a given conditional model has *both* invariant parameters and invariant error variances across regimes, and if the conditioning process also varies across the regimes, then the reverse regression cannot have invariant parameters. Thus, it should fail either or both constancy and invariance tests.

---

[3] An alternative, suggested by Andreas Fischer, which corresponds to letting γ^* be unconstrained, is to condition unrestrictedly on Z_t to clarify that the nonconstancy is due to conditioning incorrectly on y_t and not to dynamic mis-specification in the reverse regression. In practice, (A.3) seems the more usual interpretation.

For example, if a money demand equation conditional on prices has constant regression parameters (as might be claimed) and the price process has varied over time (as indeed it has) *then* it is invalid to "invert" the former to determine prices in the sense that (a) the resultant *regression* could not have constant parameters and (b) the derived equation would not correctly predict the price response (due to confounding the error and inverted regressor effects). We illustrate these consequences of reverse regression with the U.K. M1 model from Section 6.

Using recursive least squares, Hendry (1988) shows that (18) is constant over its sample, whereas marginal equations for Δp, Δy, and R are nonconstant over the same sample. From the analysis above, that combination of constancy and nonconstancy implies the nonconstancy of the reverse regression for (18). To perform that reverse regression, we first add Δp_t to both sides of (18) (without loss of generality), thereby transforming the equation into one of Δm_t regressed on Δp_t and other variables. Then, Δm_t and Δp_t are swapped to make Δp_t the dependent variable. The resulting equation is (A.5).

$$\Delta p_t = \underset{(0.105)}{0.106}\ \Delta m_t + \underset{(0.001)}{0.002}\ R_t - \underset{(0.085)}{0.118}\ \Delta[m-p]_{t-1}$$
$$- \underset{(0.093)}{0.018}\ \Delta y_{t-1} - \underset{(0.015)}{0.003}\ ECM_{t-2} - \underset{(0.006)}{0.002} \tag{A.5}$$

$$T = 1965(2)\text{--}1982(4) \quad R^2 = 0.456 \quad \sigma = 1.12\% \quad DW = 0.73$$
$$\chi^2(2) = 1.83 \quad AR\ 1-5\ F[5,60] = 17.76 \quad ARCH\ 4\ F[4,57] = 4.45$$
$$X_i^2\ F[10,54] = 1.52 \quad RESET\ F[1,64] = 0.00$$

Every coefficient except for the one on R_t is statistically insignificant in (A.5), contrasting with the highly significant coefficients in (18). In (A.5), the estimated coefficient on Δm_t is 0.106, far from its implied "inverted" value of 6.85 from (18) (i.e., $1/[1-0.854]$). That discrepancy indicates the importance of (18) as a regression equation rather than a deterministic relation, in line with a nonzero ω in (A.4).

Nonconstancy of (A.5) is easily detected. Figure 1 plots the one-step residuals and plus-or-minus twice the corresponding equation standard errors. The estimated equation standard error trebles over the subsample. Figure 2 records the "break-point" Chow (1960) statistics for the sequence {1969(3)–1982(4), 1969(4)–1982(4), ..., 1982(3)–1982(4), 1982(4)}. All but the last eight of the Chow statistics are significant at their one-off 0.1% critical values, and all but the last four are significant at their one-off 1% critical values. Hansen's (1992) test against coefficient nonconstancy with an unknown break point is significant at the 5% level for Δm_t, at the 1% level for R_t, ECM_{t-2}, and the constant, and at the 1% level for the coefficients

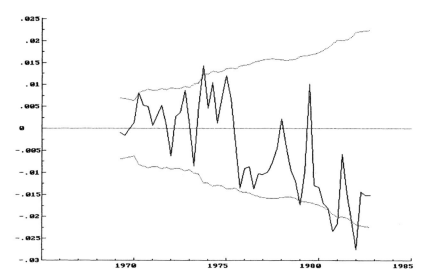

FIGURE 1. One-step residuals (—) from the reverse regression,
with 0 ± 2 estimated equation standard errors ($\cdots$).

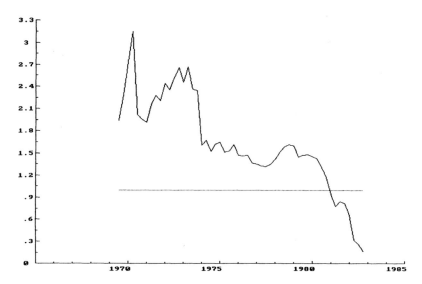

FIGURE 2. Break-point F statistics (—) for the reverse regression, normalized by their one-off 0.1% critical values ($\cdots$).

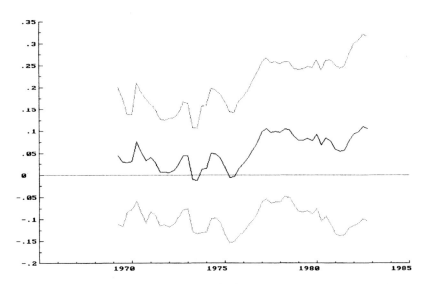

FIGURE 3. Recursive estimates (—) of the coefficient on Δm_t for the reverse regression, with ± 2 estimated standard errors ($\cdots$).

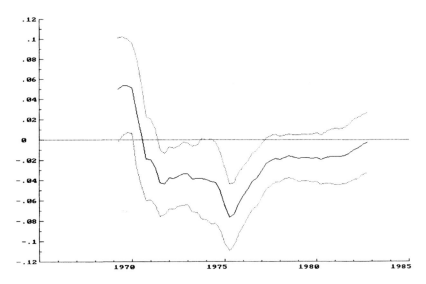

FIGURE 4. Recursive estimates (—) of the coefficient on ECM_{t-2} for the reverse regression, with ± 2 estimated standard errors ($\cdots$).

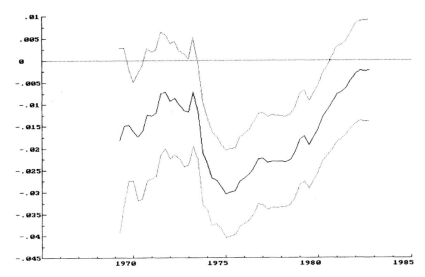

FIGURE 5. Recursive estimates (—) of the coefficient on the constant for the reverse regression, with ± 2 estimated standard errors $(\cdots)$.

and equation error variance jointly. Figures 3, 4, and 5 plot the recursive estimates and standard error bands for coefficients on three central variables: the current growth rate of nominal money $[\Delta m_t]$, the error correction term $[ECM_{t-2}]$, and the constant. The estimated standard errors increase markedly for the coefficient on Δm_t (rather than decrease), and the estimated coefficients for both ECM_{t-2} and the constant move outside previously estimated 95% confidence intervals. Reverse regression has induced nonconstancy of the estimated coefficients.

The moments of the process in (A.1) are now derived for use in (A.4).

$$E[w_t \mid Z_t] = \Pi_t Z_t, \qquad\qquad\qquad (A.6)$$

$$E[(w_t - \Pi_t Z_t) \mid Z_t] = E[\nu_t] = 0, \qquad\qquad (A.7)$$

$$E[\nu_t \nu_t' \mid Z_t] = \Sigma_t, \qquad\qquad\qquad (A.8)$$

and

$$E[w_t w_t' \mid Z_t] = \Pi_t M_{zz} \Pi_t' + \Sigma_t \qquad\qquad (A.9)$$

for

$$E[Z_t Z_t'] = M_{zz} \quad (\forall t) \qquad\qquad\qquad (A.10)$$

where:[4]

$$\Pi_t = \begin{pmatrix} (\gamma + \beta\Pi_{xt})' \\ \Pi'_{xt} \end{pmatrix}, \tag{A.11}$$

$$\Sigma_t = \begin{pmatrix} \omega + \beta^2 \sigma_t^{xx} \beta \sigma_t^{xx} \\ \beta\sigma_t^{xx} \quad \sigma_t^{xx} \end{pmatrix}, \tag{A.12}$$

and

$$E[w_t Z_t'] = \Pi_t M_{zz}. \tag{A.13}$$

From these moments, therefore, the following formulae can be obtained directly:

$$M_{xxt} = \Pi'_{xt} M_{zz} \Pi_{xt} + \sigma_t^{xx},$$

$$M_{yyt} = \Pi'_{yt} M_{zz} \Pi_{yt} + \sigma_t^{yy}$$

$$= \beta^2 M_{xxt} + \gamma' M_{zz}\gamma + 2\beta\Pi'_{xt} M_{zz}\gamma + \omega,$$

$$M_{yxt} = \Pi'_{xt} M_{zz}\gamma + \beta M_{xxt},$$

$$M_{xzt} = \Pi'_{xt} M_{zz}, \text{ and}$$

$$M_{yzt} = (\beta\Pi'_{xt} + \gamma') M_{zz}. \tag{A.14}$$

As in equation (A.4), let:

$$E[x_t \mid y_t, Z_t] = \lambda_t y_t + \alpha'_t Z_t, \tag{A.15}$$

then equation (A.15) can be estimated by:

(i) partialling the effects of Z_t from y_t, which implies that $\nu_t = y_t - \Pi'_{yt} Z_t$ is left; and

(ii) regressing x_t on ν_t, which implies a coefficient of $(\sigma_t^{yy})^{-1}\sigma_t^{xy}$ [as in (A.4)].

Thus, the resulting coefficient is indeed nonconstant if Σ varies. In the converse regression of y_t on (x_t, Z_t), the first stage removes $\Pi'_{xt} Z_t$ from x_t, leaving η_t; and the second delivers $\beta = (\sigma_t^{xx})^{-1}\sigma_t^{xy}$ as required.

---

[4] If lagged values of w_t occur in Z_t then clearly M_{zz} cannot be constant but an extended version of the analysis delivers the analogous result after the relevant lags have been explicitly incorporated into the formulation to leave the constant-moment process in Z.

Bibliography

(References marked with an asterisk * are included in this volume.)

Aldrich, J. (1989) "Autonomy", *Oxford Economic Papers*, 41, 15–34.

Baba, Y., D. F. Hendry, and R. M. Starr (1992) "The Demand for M1 in the U.S.A., 1960–1988", *Review of Economic Studies*, 59, 1, 25–61.

Charemza, W., and J. Kiraly (1986) "A Simple Test for Conditional Super Exogeneity", Mimeo, University of Birmingham, Birmingham.

Chow, G. C. (1960) "Tests of Equality Between Sets of Coefficients in Two Linear Regressions", *Econometrica*, 28, 591–605. [138]

Cooley, T., and S. LeRoy (1981) "Identification and Estimation of Money Demand", *American Economic Review*, 71, 825–844.

Cox, D. R. (1961) "Tests of Separate Families of Hypotheses", in *Proceedings of the Fourth Berkeley Symposium on Mathematical Statistics and Probability*, Volume 1, Berkeley, University of California Press, 105–123.

Engle, R. F. (1982a) "A General Approach to Lagrange Multiplier Model Diagnostics", *Journal of Econometrics*, 20, 83–104.

Engle, R. F. (1982b) "Autoregressive Conditional Heteroscedasticity, with Estimates of the Variance of United Kingdom Inflation", *Econometrica*, 50, 987–1007.

Engle, R. F., and C. W. J. Granger (1987) "Cointegration and Error Correction: Representation, Estimation, and Testing", *Econometrica*, 55, 251–276.

*Engle, R. F., D. F. Hendry, and J.-F. Richard (1983) "Exogeneity", *Econometrica*, 51, 277–304.

Ericsson, N. R. (1983) "Asymptotic Properties of Instrumental Variables Statistics For Testing Non-nested Hypotheses", *Review of Economic Studies*, 50, 287–303.

Favero, C. (1989) "Testing for Super Exogeneity: The Case of the Term Structure of Interest Rates", Discussion Paper 67, Oxford Institute of Economics and Statistics, Oxford.

Favero, C., and D. F. Hendry (1992) "Testing the Lucas Critique: A Review", *Econometric Reviews*, 11, 3, 265–306; originally cited as (1990) forthcoming.

Friedman, M., and A. J. Schwartz (1982) *Monetary Trends in the United States and the United Kingdom: Their Relation to Income, Prices and Interest Rates, 1867–1975*, Chicago, University of Chicago Press.

Frisch, R. (1938) "Statistical *versus* Theoretical Relations in Economic Macrodynamics", in *Autonomy of Economic Relations*, Memorandum published in 1948, University of Oslo, Oslo; reprinted in D. F. Hendry and M. S. Morgan (eds.) (1994) *Foundations of Econometric Analysis*, Cambridge, Cambridge University Press.

Granger, C. W. J. (1986) "Developments in the Study of Cointegrated Economic Variables", *Oxford Bulletin of Economics and Statistics*, 48, 213–228.

Haavelmo, T. (1944) "The Probability Approach in Econometrics", *Econometrica*, 12, Supplement, 1–118.

*Hansen, B. E. (1992) "Testing for Parameter Instability in Linear Models", *Journal of Policy Modeling*, 14, 4, 517–533.

Hausman, J. (1978) "Specification Tests in Econometrics", *Econometrica*, 46, 1251–1271.

Hendry, D. F. (1979) "Predictive Failure and Econometric Modelling in Macroeconomics: The Transactions Demand for Money", Chapter 9 in P. Ormerod (ed.) *Modelling the Economy*, London, Heinemann Educational Books.

*Hendry, D. F. (1988) "The Encompassing Implications of Feedback *versus* Feedforward Mechanisms in Econometrics", *Oxford Economic Papers*, 40, 132–149.

Hendry, D. F. (1989) *PC-GIVE: An Interactive Econometric Modelling System*, Oxford, Institute of Economics and Statistics.

Hendry, D. F., and N. R. Ericsson (1991) "An Econometric Analysis of U.K. Money Demand in *Monetary Trends in the United States and the United Kingdom* by Milton Friedman and Anna J. Schwartz", *American Economic Review*, 81, 8–38.

Hendry, D. F., and A. J. Neale (1988) "Interpreting Long-run Equilibrium Solutions in Conventional Macro Models: A Comment", *Economic Journal*, 98, 808–817.

Hendry, D. F., and J.-F. Richard (1982) "On the Formulation of Empirical Models in Dynamic Econometrics", *Journal of Econometrics*, 20, 3–33.

Hendry, D. F., and J.-F. Richard (1989) "Recent Developments in the Theory of Encompassing", in B. Cornet and H. Tulkens (eds.) *Contributions to Operations Research and Econometrics, The Twentieth Anniversary of CORE*, Cambridge, MIT Press.

H. M. Treasury (1980) "Background to the Government's Economic Policy", London, Her Majesty's Stationery Office.

Hurwicz, L. (1962) "On the Structural Form of Interdependent Systems", in E. Nagel *et al.* (eds.) *Logic, Methodology and the Philosophy of Science*, Palo Alto, Stanford University Press.

Jarque, C. M., and A. K. Bera (1980) "Efficient Tests for Normality, Homo-scedasticity and Serial Independence of Regression Residuals", *Economics Letters*, 6, 3, 255–259.

Judd, J., and J. Scadding (1982) "The Search for a Stable Money Demand Function: A Survey of the Post-1973 Literature", *Journal of Economic Literature*, 20, 993–1023.

Lucas, R. E., Jr. (1976) "Econometric Policy Evaluation: A Critique", in K. Brunner and A. H. Meltzer (eds.) *The Phillips Curve and Labor Markets*, Amsterdam, North-Holland, 19–46.

Marschak, J. (1953) "Economic Measurements for Policy and Prediction", in Wm. C. Hood and T. C. Koopmans (eds.) *Studies in Econometric Method*, New Haven, Yale University Press. [139]

McCallum, B. T. (1976) "Rational Expectations and the Estimation of Econometric Models: An Alternative Procedure", *International Economic Review*, 17, 484–490.

Mizon, G. E. (1984) "The Encompassing Approach in Econometrics", in D. F. Hendry and K. F. Wallis (eds.) *Econometrics and Quantitative Economics*, Oxford, Basil Blackwell, 135–172.

Mizon, G. E., and J.-F. Richard (1986) "The Encompassing Principle and its Application to Non-nested Hypothesis Tests", *Econometrica*, 54, 657–678.

Pesaran, M. H. (1974) "On the General Problem of Model Selection", *Review of Economic Studies*, 41, 153–171.

Ramsey, J. B. (1969) "Tests for Specification Errors in Classical Linear Least Squares Regression Analysis", *Journal of the Royal Statistical Society*, B, 31, 350–371.

Salmon, M., and K. F. Wallis (1982) "Model Validation and Forecast Comparisons: Theoretical and Practical Considerations", Chapter 12 in G. C. Chow and P. Corsi (eds.) *Evaluating the Reliability of Macro-economic Models*, New York, John Wiley.

Sargan, J. D. (1964) "Wages and Prices in the United Kingdom: A Study in Econometric Methodology", in P. E. Hart, G. Mills, and J. K. Whitaker (eds.) *Econometric Analysis for National Economic Planning*, London, Butterworths (reprinted in Hendry and Wallis, *op. cit.*).

White, H. (1980) "A Heteroskedastic-consistent Covariance Matrix Estimator and a Direct Test for Heteroskedasticity", *Econometrica*, 48, 817–838.

Wu, D. (1973) "Alternative Tests of Independence Between Stochastic Regressors and Disturbances", *Econometrica*, 41, 733–750.

5

Testing Weak Exogeneity and the Order of Cointegration in U.K. Money Demand Data

SØREN JOHANSEN*

Abstract

This paper discusses autoregressive models allowing for processes integrated of order 2, and the various types of cointegration that can occur. A statistical analysis of such models that allows for the determination of the order of integration and the cointegrating ranks is outlined. The notion of weak exogeneity is discussed for I(1) processes. The results are illustrated by the U.K. money data of Hendry and Ericsson (1991).

1 Introduction

Many macro-variables show trending behavior over time. In econometrics this phenomenon is modeled by nonstationary time series, and this paper discusses autoregressive Gaussian models for p-dimensional systems of economic variables. Such a time series X_t is called I(1) if the difference $\Delta X_t = X_t - X_{t-1}$ is stationary while X_t is nonstationary. For a p-dimensional system of I(1) processes, it can occur that a linear combination $\nu' X_t$ is stationary. If this

* This paper was written while the author was visiting the Department of Statistics, University of Helsinki. The visit was supported by the Danish Social Sciences Research Council account number 14–5793.

I have benefited from discussions with Katarina Juselius and Paolo Paruolo on various aspects of the paper. The calculations are performed in RATS and checked by Paolo Paruolo by means of GAUSS.

Reprinted with permission from the *Journal of Policy Modeling* (June 1992), 14, 3, 313–334.

is the case, the variables are called cointegrated, the stationary relation is a cointegrating relation, and ν is the cointegrating vector. An alternative formulation is that the common nonstationary forces, the so-called common trends, can be eliminated by considering the linear combination $\nu'X_t$.

Some time series, such as the log of prices (p), have the property that even the inflation rate Δp is nonstationary, whereas the second difference $\Delta^2 p$ is stationary. Such a variable is called I(2), and we shall show by a statistical analysis how one can analyze processes that may be I(2).

[314]

For I(2) variables various types of cointegration can occur. First, linear combinations of I(2) variables may be I(1) or even I(0), but it is also possible that there are linear I(1) combinations that cointegrate with the difference of the process, which is an I(1) process.

The concept of cointegration was introduced by Granger (1981) and is used in econometrics to discuss long-run economic relations. This definition allows the question of existence of long-run economic relations to be discussed from a statistical point of view, which is what we shall do in this article.

A very important consequence of the basic definition of cointegration as a statistical concept is that the cointegrating properties of a multivariate time series can be analyzed from the reduced form of the model, even if they gain their importance only when interpreted in a suitable structural model.

It was shown in Johansen (1988), Johansen and Juselius (1990), and Ahn and Reinsel (1990) how one can make inference on the number of cointegrating relations and how one can test hypotheses about the coefficients of the cointegrating relations, such that economic questions and hypotheses can be tested against the data.

There are in particular two questions that we shall be concerned with in this article, namely, the order of integration of the variables and the concept of weak exogeneity.

The statistical analysis of a system of variables is somewhat involved and is sometimes replaced by the analysis of a partial system, thereby reducing the dimensionality of the system whose properties need to be modeled explicitly. The concept of weak exogeneity [see Engle, Hendry, and Richard (1983)] was introduced to justify considering some variables as given (exogenous) in the analysis of other (endogenous) variables. It is important to emphasize that weak exogeneity is also a statistical concept and as such can be tested against the data.

With this background the purpose of the present article is to show by example how one can test for weak exogeneity and investigate the order of nonstationarity of the processes.

2   Error Correction Models, Cointegration, and the I(1) Analysis

This section contains a reformulation of the vector autoregressive (VAR) model as a reduced form error correction model and a discussion of the hypothesis of cointegration and its consequences for the process formulated [315] as a representation theorem for I(1) variables. The statistical analysis based on the likelihood function is described, and the results are illustrated by means of the money demand data for the United Kingdom. We show how the cointegrating rank can be determined and how some hypotheses on the coefficients of the long-run relations can be tested.

2.1   The Reduced Form Error Correction Model and the Representation of I(1) Processes

The p-dimensional vector autoregressive process X_t is defined by the equations

$$X_t = \sum_{i=1}^{k} \Pi_i X_{t-i} + \mu + \varepsilon_t, \qquad t = 1, \ldots, T, \tag{1}$$

where $X_{-k+1}, \ldots, X_0$ are fixed and $\{\varepsilon_t, t = 1, 2, \ldots\}$ is a sequence of independent Gaussian variables with mean zero and covariance matrix Ω. The parameters are the $p \times p$ matrices $\Pi_1, \ldots, \Pi_k$, the covariance matrix Ω, together with the p-dimensional vector μ. The model can be written as a reduced form error correction model

$$\Delta X_t = \Pi X_{t-1} + \sum_{i=1}^{k-1} \Gamma_i \Delta X_{t-i} + \mu + \varepsilon_t, \qquad t = 1, \ldots, T, \tag{2}$$

where

$$\Pi = \sum_{i=1}^{k} \Pi_i - I,$$

$$\Gamma_i = -\sum_{j=i+1}^{k} \Pi_j, \qquad i = 1, \ldots, k-1;$$

or, in anticipation of the later analysis of the I(2) model, we can write it as

$$\Delta^2 X_t = \Pi X_{t-2} + \Gamma \Delta X_{t-1} + \sum_{i=1}^{k-2} \Gamma_i^* \Delta^2 X_{t-i} + \mu + \varepsilon_t, \qquad t = 1, \ldots, T, \tag{3}$$

where

$$\Gamma = \sum_{i=1}^{k-1} \Gamma_i - I + \Pi,$$

$$\Gamma_i^* = - \sum_{j=i+1}^{k-2} \Gamma_j, \qquad i = 1, \dots, k-2.$$

The advantage of this reformulation is that the hypothesis of cointegration can be formulated entirely as a restriction on the matrix Π, leaving the other parameters unrestricted.

For $r = 0, 1, \dots, p$, the hypothesis of at most r cointegrating vectors is defined as the reduced rank condition

$$H_r : \Pi = \alpha\beta', \tag{4}$$

where α and β are $p \times r$ matrices. Thus H_0 specifies that $\Pi = 0$, and H_p that Π is unrestricted. If $\mathrm{rank}(\alpha) = \mathrm{rank}(\beta) = r$, and if

$$\mathrm{rank}\{\alpha_\perp' \Gamma \beta_\perp\} = p - r, \tag{5}$$

then the process X_t generated by model (1), or equivalently (2), is nonstationary but the differences are stationary; that is, X_t is an I(1) process. We [316] have used the notation $\alpha_\perp$ for a $p \times (p-r)$ matrix of full rank such that $\alpha'\alpha_\perp = 0$, and hence $\mathrm{rank}(\alpha, \alpha_\perp) = p$. In the case $r = 0$, that is, when r, α, and β are all zero, we define $\alpha_\perp = \beta_\perp = I$. In this case, (2) becomes a model for ΔX_t, and the full rank condition (5) reduces to the requirement that ΔX_t be an invertible stationary process that excludes cointegration between levels.

Later we multiply the equations by the full rank matrix $(\alpha, \alpha_\perp)$ and transform the variables by means of the full rank matrix $(\beta, \beta_\perp)$. It is a property of the system (1) with conditions (4) and (5) that the linear combinations $\beta'X_t$, the cointegrating relations, are stationary. The fundamental paper by Engle and Granger (1987) contains the basic definitions and results for this type of nonstationary process, which can be summarized in Granger's representation theorem, which describes the solution of equation (1) under conditions (4) and (5):

$$X_t = C \sum_{i=1}^{t} \varepsilon_i + C_1(L)\varepsilon_t + \tau_0 + \tau_1 t,$$

where $C = -\beta_\perp(\alpha_\perp' \Gamma \beta_\perp)^{-1}\alpha_\perp'$ so that $\beta'C = C\alpha = 0$. The trend is determined by $\tau_1 = C\mu$, so that the trend vanishes if $\alpha_\perp'\mu = 0$.

2.2   The Statistical Analysis of the I(1) Model

The statistical analysis of model (2) under the restriction of reduced rank of the matrix Π can be performed by reduced rank regression as introduced by

Anderson (1951). See also Johansen (1988) for the application to nonstation-ary processes and Ahn and Reinsel (1988) for the application to stationary processes. The variables ΔX_t and X_{t-1} are regressed on the lagged val-ues $\Delta X_{t-1}, \ldots, \Delta X_{t-k+1}$ and 1 to form residuals R_{0t} and R_{1t}, and residual product moment matrices

$$S_{ij} = T^{-1} \sum_{t=1}^{T} R_{it} R_{jt}', \qquad i, j = 0, 1.$$

The cointegrating relations are then estimated as the eigenvectors corre-sponding to the r largest eigenvalues of the equation

$$|\lambda S_{11} - S_{10} S_{00}^{-1} S_{01}| = 0. \tag{6}$$

The likelihood ratio test statistic of the hypothesis H_r in H_p is given by the so-called trace statistic:

$$Q_r = -T \sum_{i=r+1}^{p} \ln(1 - \hat{\lambda}_i). \tag{7}$$

Under the assumption that the number of cointegrating relations is r and that the coefficient $\alpha_\perp' \mu \neq 0$, such that there is a linear trend in the data, the limit distribution, which only depends on the degrees of freedom $p - r$, [317] is nonstandard and tabulated by simulation in Johansen and Juselius (1990, Table A1). The hypothesis H_r^* that the trend is absent ($\alpha_\perp' \mu = 0$) can be analyzed by another reduced rank regression, and the test statistic Q_r^* of H_r^* in H_p has under H_r^* a limit distribution given by Table A3 in Johansen and Juselius (1990).

2.3   An Illustration of the I(1) Analysis by the U.K. Money Demand Data

To illustrate the results of the I(1) analysis, we analyze the data on the U.K. money demand given in Hendry and Ericsson (1991) and discussed in Er-icsson, Campos, and Tran (1990) and Hendry and Mizon (1993). The data consists of four variables: the measure of money M is nominal money M1. The income measure is denoted by INC and is given by constant price total final expenditure (TFE) at 1985 prices. The price measure P is the implicit deflator of TFE, and as a measure of the opportunity cost of holding money we use R^*. Here R^* is defined as the 3-month local authority interest rate ($R3$) less the learning adjusted retail sight-deposit interest rate (Rra). The data are quarterly seasonally adjusted from 1963(1) to 1989(2), and the first six observations are used as initial values in order to fit an autoregressive model with five lags. This leaves a total of 100 effective observations. The data are carefully discussed in the preceding references and the present ana-lysis is a supplement to the previous analysis with respect to the question of weak exogeneity and the question of the order of integration of the variables.

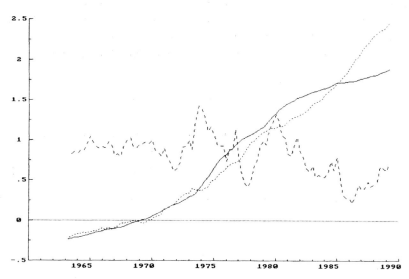

FIGURE 1.   Graphs of the series m_t $(\cdots)$ and p_t $(-)$, together with the disequilibrium error $(- - -)$ given by $coint_t = m_t - 1.04p_t - 0.95inc_t + 7.46R_t + 4.75\Delta p_t$.

The data are transformed logarithmically into m_t, inc_t, and p_t, whereas the interest rate R_t^* is not transformed. Figure 1 shows the nonstationarity of the variables m and p, and Figure 2 shows the differences of m and p. The results of the initial cointegration analysis from model (2) with five lags reproduce the results in Ericsson, Campos, and Tran (1990). The determination of the cointegrating rank is made difficult by the many hypotheses that can be formulated and by the nonstandard limit distributions. As mentioned in Section 2.2, the limit distribution of Q_r [see (7)] depends on the presence or absence of the trend. The distribution of Q_r, if in fact the trend is absent, is given by Table A2 in Johansen and Juselius (1990) and has broader tails than that given by Table A1. Thus if one wants to make sure that the size of the test based upon Q_r has the correct value for all parameter points in H_r, one should apply the quantiles in Table A2. This procedure increases the quantiles considerably for small degrees of freedom, and instead another [318] procedure based on an idea of Pantula (1989) is suggested [see Johansen (1992b)]. The idea is to use not one test statistic to reject H_r but two, namely Q_r compared to its quantile c_r given by Table A1 and Q_r^* compared to its quantile c_r^* given by Table A3. Hence H_r is rejected if $H_0, \ldots, H_{r-1}$ are rejected and if further $Q_r^* > c_r^*$ and $Q_r > c_r$. This procedure guarantees that

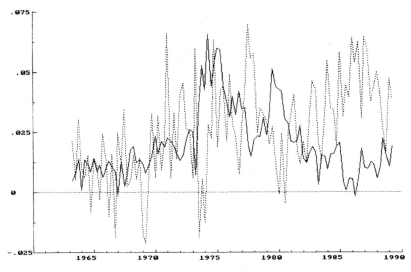

FIGURE 2. Graphs of the series Δm_t ($\cdots$) and Δp_t (—).

the asymptotic size of the test is correct for all parameter values in $H_r \backslash H_r^*$.

In the example we have concluded on the basis of Figure 1 that a trend is needed to describe the data. Thus we have accepted that Q_r^* is larger than its quantile, and the rest of the analysis only requires the quantiles as given by Table A1. The cointegrating rank can be formally estimated as the smallest r that is not rejected at a given level of significance. In the present example (see Table 1), we can clearly reject $r = 0$, since the test statistic is 77.54 and the quantile is only 47.18. The hypothesis H_1 of $r \le 1$ is a borderline case since the statistic 30.50 corresponds roughly to the 95% quantile in the asymptotic distribution. The hypothesis H_2 can be accepted. If we decide [319] to accept H_1, we can work with $r = 1$ in the following, and we shall, but the evidence for a choice between $r = 1$ and $r = 2$ is not very strong. When it is decided that $r = 1$, the estimate of β is given as the first column of the eigenvectors in Table 1, and the estimate of α is the first column of the adjustment coefficients in Table 1. Note that if we had chosen $r = 2$, the estimates of α and β are given as the first two columns. Thus it is quite easy, once the eigenvalue problem has been solved, to do the analysis for various values of r.

The solution of the eigenvalue problem (6) constructs the eigenvectors as new regressors in model (2). They are normalized such that the eigenvalues λ_i measure the size of the adjustment coefficients: $\lambda_i = \alpha_i' S_{00}^{-1} \alpha_i$. Thus the test that $r = 1$ is really a test that $\lambda_2 = \lambda_3 = \lambda_4 = 0$, whereas $\lambda_1 > 0$, or

TABLE 1.
The Cointegration Analysis of the U.K. Money Demand Data

Eigenvalues	0.375	0.166	0.115	0.002
Hypotheses	$r = 0$	$r \leq 1$	$r \leq 2$	$r \leq 3$
Trace statistics	77.54	30.50	12.35	0.15
95% Quantiles	47.18	29.51	15.20	3.96
	Eigenvectors β			
m	1.00	1.22	-0.61	1.17
p	-1.04	1.00	0.35	-1.05
inc	-0.95	-9.82	1.00	-0.70
R^*	7.46	-8.11	-3.06	1.00
	Adjustment coefficients α			
Δm	-0.150	-0.007	-0.006	-0.001
Δp	0.030	-0.008	0.006	0.001
Δinc	0.008	0.001	0.053	-0.001
ΔR^*	0.031	0.001	0.031	0.003

The variables are m, p, inc, and R^*.

equivalently that the α's in the last three columns are insignificantly small.

It is quite clear that the first cointegrating relation, the first column of the eigenvectors, shows homogeneity of the price and income variables. This can be formulated as a test on the coefficients β of the form $K'\beta = 0$ where K contains the two vectors $(1,1,0,0)$ and $(1,0,1,0)$. This type of hypothesis was analyzed in Johansen and Juselius (1990), where it was shown that under such a restriction the statistical analysis was still given by a reduced rank regression and that the test statistic was a comparison of the eigenvalues from (6) by means of the statistic

$$T \sum_{i=1}^{r} \ln \left(\frac{1 - \tilde{\lambda}_i}{1 - \hat{\lambda}_i} \right) = 1.02,$$

which in this case is asymptotically χ^2 with two degrees of freedom. Here $\hat{\lambda}_i$ ($\tilde{\lambda}_i$) is calculated without (with) the restrictions on β. Since $\chi^2_{95\%}(2) = 5.99$, the test statistic is seen not to be significant and the analysis of the full system can be summarized from the point of view of the long-run relation by

$$m_t^{lr} = p_t + inc_t - 7.01 R_t^*,$$

which represents the optimal estimate of the long-run economic relation between the variables, provided model (2) with condition (4) and $r = 1$ is maintained. The coefficients in the relation are found as the first column of the eigenvectors estimated under the restriction $K'\beta = 0$.

3 Partial Systems and Weak Exogeneity

This section contains a discussion of the concepts of weak exogeneity and partial or conditional models. The hypothesis of weak exogeneity for the [321] long-run parameters is formulated as a parametric restriction on the adjustment coefficients, and the procedure is illustrated by the U.K. money demand data.

3.1 Weak Exogeneity and the Efficiency of Partial Models

An advantage of the vector autoregressive formulation is that one can formulate a partial system as a conditional model and discuss its properties. That is, despite one's interest in modeling only the equations of some of the variables given the others, the stochastic properties of the conditioning variables are well defined in the VAR model.

Consider therefore the autoregressive model (2) under the hypothesis of cointegration H_r [see (4)]. Let the process X_t be decomposed into the variables Y_t and Z_t of dimension p_y and p_z, respectively, where $p = p_y + p_z$, and let $\alpha, \Gamma_1, \ldots, \Gamma_{k-1}, \mu, \varepsilon_t$, and Ω be decomposed correspondingly. Model (2) can be decomposed into the conditional model for Y_t given Z_t:

$$\Delta Y_t = \omega \Delta Z_t + (\alpha_y - \omega \alpha_z)\beta' X_{t-1} + \sum_{i=1}^{k-1}(\Gamma_{yi} - \omega \Gamma_{zi})\Delta X_{t-i}$$
$$+ \mu_y - \omega \mu_z + \varepsilon_{yt} - \omega \varepsilon_{zt}, \tag{8}$$

and the marginal model of Z_t

$$\Delta Z_t = \alpha_z \beta' X_{t-1} + \sum_{i=1}^{k-1}\Gamma_{zi}\Delta X_{t-i} + \mu_z + \varepsilon_{zt}, \tag{9}$$

where $\omega = \Omega_{yz}\Omega_{zz}^{-1}$.

Note that all the cointegrating relations $\beta' X_{t-1}$ enter into the marginal as well as the conditional model, and that the conditional model has new adjustment coefficients $\alpha_y - \omega \alpha_z$ depending on the covariance matrix of the errors and all the adjustment coefficients. In general the parameters of the marginal and the conditional system are interrelated, which means that full system analysis is needed to draw efficient inference about the parameters.

There is, however, a very special case in which the partial model (8) contains as much information as the full system about the cointegrating relations and the adjustment coefficients, and where analysis of the partial model is efficient. This is when Z_t is weakly exogenous for α and β [see Engle, Hendry, and Richard (1983)].

The variable Z_t is said to be weakly exogenous for the parameters of interest, if

Condition 1 The parameters of interest are functions of the parameters in the conditional model.

[322] **Condition 2** The parameters in the conditional model and the parameters in the marginal model are variation free; that is, they do not have any joint restrictions.

It can be shown that if we define the parameters of interest in model (2) to be all the parameters of β, then weak exogeneity of Z_t with respect to β is equivalent to the condition that $\alpha_z = 0$. That is, the rows of α corresponding to the z equations are zero and the models (8) and (9) reduce to

$$\Delta Y_t = \omega \Delta Z_t + \alpha_y \beta' X_{t-1} + \sum_{i=1}^{k-1}(\Gamma_{yi} - \omega\Gamma_{zi})\Delta X_{t-i}$$
$$+ \mu_y - \omega\mu_z + \varepsilon_{yt} - \omega\varepsilon_{zt}, \tag{10}$$

and

$$\Delta Z_t = \sum_{i=1}^{k-1}\Gamma_{zi}\Delta X_{t-i} + \mu_z + \varepsilon_{zt}. \tag{11}$$

In this case β and the remaining adjustment coefficients α_y enter only in the partial model (10), and the properties of the Gaussian distribution show that the parameters in the models (10) and (11) are variation free. See Johansen and Juselius (1990) for a discussion of the results and Johansen (1992a) and Boswijk (1990) for a fuller discussion of partial systems. Note that equation (11) contains ΔZ_{t-i} as well as ΔY_{t-i}. If also the coefficients of ΔY_{t-i} are zero, or in other words Y_t does not Granger cause Z_t, then Z_t is said to be strongly exogenous for β. Thus weak exogeneity means that ΔZ_t does not react to disequilibrium errors but may still react to lagged changes of Y_t, and strong exogeneity implies that ΔZ_t does not react to the lagged Y_t, whether Y is in changes or levels.

It should be pointed out that the notion of weak exogeneity depends on an explicit choice of parameters of interest. If, for instance, $p_y = 1$, and if we define the parameters of interest to be the cointegrating vector in the conditional model $\beta'_y = (\alpha_y - \omega\alpha_z)\beta'$, then Condition 1 is certainly satisfied. If we then decompose β into β_y and β_z and write $\alpha_z\beta' = \alpha_{zy}\beta'_y + \alpha_{zz}\beta'_z$, then the parameters of the conditional and marginal models become variation free only if $\alpha_{zy} = 0$. Thus for this choice of parameters of interest, Z_t is weakly exogenous if $\alpha_{zy} = 0$. This situation occurs in the analysis of Hendry and Mizon (1993).

The statistical analysis of (10) consists of a reduced rank regression if $p_y > r$ and an ordinary regression if $p_y = r$. In particular, if $p_y = r = 1$, the analysis of (10) reduces to the well-known single-equation analysis. It is seen that this analysis is efficient if the remaining variables are weakly exogenous for β and if there is only one cointegrating relation.

Modeling and analyzing the partial system with $p_y = r$ are therefore simpler and easier to interpret, but the usefulness is limited by the fact that   [323] more assumptions need to be made. Thus, for instance, one has to assume weak exogeneity and $p_y = r$, which are easy to assume but difficult to check efficiently without a full system analysis.

Thus the hypothesis of weak exogeneity of Z_t for α and β is formulated as

$$H : \alpha_z = 0.$$

This hypothesis is a linear restriction on α and is discussed in Johansen and Juselius (1990), where it is shown that under the hypothesis H the maximum likelihood estimation of the parameters could be performed by reduced rank regression, and that the test of H in H_r consists in comparing the eigenvalues $\hat{\lambda}_i$ ($\tilde{\lambda}_i$) calculated without (with) the restriction. The test statistic is

$$T \sum_{i=1}^{r} \ln \left(\frac{1 - \tilde{\lambda}_i}{1 - \hat{\lambda}_i} \right), \tag{12}$$

which is asymptotically distributed as $\chi^2(rp_z)$.

The test requires that the partial model be embedded in the full model and in fact comes from an analysis of the full model. For the present example, where only four variables enter the system, the analysis of the full model is relatively simple. For systems with 25 variables the full system analysis is more difficult, and it is advisable to make a simplified analysis by assuming that $p_y \geq r$ and analyze the partial model by reduced rank regression. The weak exogeneity can then be tested by an F test in the marginal model (11), as the hypothesis that the coefficients to the added regressor $\hat{\beta}' X_{t-1}$ equal zero [see Johansen (1992a)].

3.2   An Illustration of the Test for Weak Exogeneity

In Table 2, we have calculated the statistic (12) to test the weak exogeneity of each of the variables m, p, inc, and R^*, in the hope that one can justify the analysis of a single equation. It is seen that we can safely assume that inc and R^* are weakly exogenous for the long-run parameters, but it seems   [324] that the equation for p may contain information about the cointegrating relation and a single-equation analysis is going to miss this. The test of the hypothesis that p, inc, and R^* are all weakly exogenous for the long-run parameters, that is, that $\alpha_p = \alpha_{inc} = \alpha_{R^*} = 0$, can be performed by

TABLE 2. The Likelihood Ratio Statistics for Testing Weak
Exogeneity of Each of the Variables with Respect to β

m	p	inc	R^*
24.82	4.21	0.11	1.89

The asymptotic distribution is $\chi^2(1)$, for which the 95% quantile is 3.84.

the same procedure, and it is found that the test statistic is 4.85, which
should be compared with a $\chi^2_{95\%}(3) = 7.81$. This is clearly not significant,
and it follows that by testing all hypotheses simultaneously one can hide the
information in the second equation. There is, however, no strong evidence
against weak exogeneity of (p, inc, R^*) but the individual tests indicate that
there may be some information in the equation for p, and as a consequence it
may not be efficient to analyze a single equation to estimate the parameters
in β.

The purpose of reporting the single equation for Δm_t given Δp_t, Δinc_t,
ΔR_t^*, and the lags of all variables is to obtain a single equation describing
the dynamics of money. This single equation can of course be derived from
the full system and is given by (8) for $Y_t = m_t$ and $Z_t = (p_t, inc_t, R_t^*)'$.
For a given value of $\beta = \hat{\beta}$, the equation can then be further reduced by
conventional F tests to decrease the number of parameters needed in the
equation. See Ericsson, Campos, and Tran (1990) or Hendry and Mizon
(1993) for details.

It should be emphasized that the difficulty with the single-equation approach lies in the estimation of β. The estimator of β is consistent, but
the asymptotic distribution of the estimator does not permit the use of the
usual χ^2 distribution, unless there is weak exogeneity. This problem is also
discussed in Phillips (1991).

Thus it is advisable to keep the full system analysis for inference on β,
and once the relevant hypotheses on β have been tested, one can go to the
single-equation estimation, in which one can interpret and make the usual
inference on the remaining parameters, keeping β fixed.

4   Formulation and Analysis of a Model for I(2) Variables

Section 4 contains results for I(2) processes that parallel the results for I(1)
processes. We formulate conditions on the parameters of the VAR model for
the process to be I(2) and discuss the various types of cointegration that can
occur. The properties of the process are summarized in a representation for
I(2) processes. A statistical analysis, which consists of an analysis of model
(2) with reduced rank of Π, followed by a reduced rank regression of an

equation derived for the differenced data, is suggested. The money demand [325] data are used to illustrate the determination of the cointegrating ranks, and the long-run economic relation is estimated for the I(2) system.

4.1 Cointegration in the I(2) Model and the Representation of I(2) Processes

Consider again model (2) under the condition of reduced rank (4). If condition (5) fails and the matrix $\alpha'_\perp \Gamma \beta_\perp$ has reduced rank:

$$\alpha'_\perp \Gamma \beta_\perp = \varphi \eta', \tag{13}$$

where φ and η are $(p - r) \times s$ of rank s, and if a further full rank condition is satisfied, then the process X_t is I(2). In the special case $r = 0$, so that $\alpha = \beta = 0$ and $\alpha_\perp = \beta_\perp = I$, condition (13) reduces to the condition that the impact matrix for the process ΔX_t has reduced rank, allowing ΔX_t to be I(1) and hence X_t to be I(2). In any case one obtains [see Johansen (1992c)] that the properties of the process can be summarized by the representation

$$X_t = C_2 \sum_{j=1}^{t} \sum_{i=1}^{j} \varepsilon_i + C_1 \sum_{i=1}^{t} \varepsilon_i + C_2(L)\varepsilon_t + \tau_0 + \tau_1 t + \frac{1}{2}\tau_2 t(t+1).$$

The matrices C_2 and C_1 determine the cointegration properties of the process, and since $\beta' C_2 = 0$ but $\beta' C_1 \neq 0$, it is seen that $\beta' X_t$ is not stationary in general, but only I(1). To make it stationary, one needs to bring in the differences in the form $\eta'_\perp \beta'_\perp \Delta X_t$, and it can be shown that

$$\beta' X_t + \kappa \beta_\perp^{2\prime} \Delta X_t \tag{14}$$

is a stationary process, where $\beta_\perp^2 = \beta_\perp \eta_\perp$, and $\kappa = (\alpha'\alpha)^{-1}\alpha'\Gamma\beta_\perp^2(\beta_\perp^{2\prime}\beta_\perp^2)^{-1}$. The vectors $\beta_\perp^1 = \beta_\perp(\beta'_\perp\beta_\perp)^{-1}\eta$ determine other combinations that reduce the order from 2 to 1, but they do not cointegrate with the differences. Similarly we define $\alpha_\perp^1 = \alpha'_\perp(\alpha'_\perp\alpha_\perp)^{-1}\varphi$, and $\alpha_\perp^2 = \alpha_\perp\varphi_\perp$. With this notation we can express

$$C_2 = \beta_\perp^2 \tau \alpha_\perp^{2\prime}, \tag{15}$$

for some $(p - r) \times (p - r)$ matrix τ of full rank.

Thus the p components of X_t are split into three sets of dimensions r, s, and $p - r - s$, respectively. The $p \times (r + s)$ matrix $(\beta, \beta_\perp^1)$ represents all the possible cointegrating relations, in the sense that $(\beta, \beta_\perp^1)'X_t$ is either I(1) or I(0), whereas $\beta_\perp^{2\prime}X_t$ is an I(2) process that does not cointegrate. The process $\beta_\perp^{1\prime}X_t$ is an I(1) process that does not cointegrate, and finally $\beta' X_t$ cointegrates with the I(1) process $\beta_\perp^{2\prime}\Delta X_t$ and hence is in general an I(1) [326] process. Finally if ξ is a matrix such that $\xi'\kappa = 0$, then $\xi'\beta'X_t$ is stationary [see (14)]. The expression (15) for C_2 in terms of $\beta_\perp^2$ and $\alpha_\perp^2$ shows that the cumulated shocks $\sum_{j=1}^{t}\sum_{i=1}^{j}\varepsilon_i$ enter the variables through the linear combinations α_1^2, and that they are distributed among the variables through the coefficients β_1^2. This interpretation will be useful in the discussion of the example.

4.2   The Statistical Analysis of the I(2) Model

The hypothesis $H_{r,s}$ is defined by conditions (4) and (13) with α and β of full rank r and φ and η of dimensions $(p-r) \times s$. The likelihood function is easily described for the I(2) model because of the Gaussian errors. The analysis, however, does not lead to explicit solutions. The problem is, of course, how to estimate the parameters α and β at the same time as the matrices φ and η since the second reduced rank condition (13) involves all parameters.

Instead, another procedure is suggested; it consists of first analyzing model (2), that is, the VAR model, with reduced rank of Π, but without the restriction (13), and then performing another reduced rank regression on a derived equation for the differenced process. The following procedure turns out to yield valid inference [see Johansen (1995)].

(A) Perform a reduced rank regression of ΔX_t on X_{t-1} corrected for ΔX_{t-1}, $\ldots, \Delta X_{t-k+1}$ and 1. This determines $\hat{r}$, $\hat{\alpha}$, and $\hat{\beta}$.

(B) Perform a reduced rank regression of $\hat{\alpha}_\perp' \Delta^2 X_t$ on $\hat{\beta}_\perp' \Delta X_{t-1}$ corrected for $\Delta^2 X_{t-1}, \ldots, \Delta^2 X_{t-k+2}$, 1, and $\hat{\beta}' \Delta X_{t-1}$. This determines $\hat{s}$, $\hat{\varphi}$, and $\hat{\eta}$.[1]

To see that this analysis is relevant, consider the equation given by (3) but multiplied by $\alpha_\perp'$:

$$\alpha_\perp' \Delta^2 X_t = \alpha_\perp' \Gamma \Delta X_{t-1} + \sum_{1}^{k-2} \Gamma_i^* \Delta^2 X_{t-i} + \alpha_\perp' \mu + \alpha_\perp' \varepsilon_t. \qquad (16)$$

This is now a reduced form error correction model for the differences.

The decomposition

$$\alpha_\perp' \Gamma = \alpha_\perp' \Gamma \{\beta(\beta'\beta)^{-1}\beta' + \beta_\perp(\beta_\perp'\beta_\perp)^{-1}\beta_\perp'\}$$

$$= \alpha_\perp' \Gamma \beta(\beta'\beta)^{-1}\beta' + \varphi\eta'(\beta_\perp'\beta_\perp)^{-1}\beta_\perp'$$

introduces the second reduced rank condition (13) explicitly into the equation and shows that if we know α and β we can estimate equation (16) by the reduced rank regression discussed.

Equation (16) can interpreted as an analysis of the common trends. Granger defines $\alpha_\perp' X_t$ as the common trends since the equation for $\alpha_\perp$ does not contain any term corresponding to the disequilibrium error. Thus the second step in the analysis is a reduced rank analysis of the common trends.

---

[1] It can easily be seen that the first step in the analysis is equivalent to a reduced rank regression of $\Delta^2 X_t$ on X_{t-2} corrected for $\Delta^2 X_{t-1}, \ldots, \Delta^2 X_{t-k+2}$, 1, and ΔX_{t-1}.

[*Author's note: This interpretation of $\alpha'_\perp X_t$ as a common trend is now known to be incorrect, since $\alpha'_\perp X_t$ can be stationary.*]

The reduced rank analysis of (16) reduces to the solution of an eigenvalue problem like (6), giving eigenvalues ρ_i, $i = 1, \ldots, p - r$. The test statistic for the hypothesis $H_{r,s}$ in H_r is given by

$$Q_{r,s} = -T \sum_{i=s+1}^{p-r} \ln(1 - \rho_i). \qquad (17)$$

It can be shown [see Johansen (1995)] that the estimators of β and φ are asymptotically mixed Gaussian, allowing for usual χ^2 inference, and that $Q_{r,s}$ has the same limit distribution as Q_r, but with $p - r - s$ degrees of freedom. Thus both Q_r and $Q_{r,s}$ have a distribution determined by the deficiency of the matrix being tested for reduced rank.

Another important consequence of the limit results is that the tests performed on the coefficients α and β in the I(1) analysis remain valid in the I(2) analysis, but of course the parameters and hence the hypotheses have a different interpretation. Thus the test that m, p, and inc have coefficients proportional to $(1, -1, -1)$ still holds in the presence of I(2) variables, but for a relation that is I(1). One can also test $\alpha_z = 0$ by a χ^2 test, but the restriction (13) ruins the variation independence of the parameters, and hence the interpretation of the hypothesis as a hypothesis of weak exogeneity is not valid. Thus the formal properties of the test remain valid, but the interpretation has changed in the I(2) model.

4.3   An Illustrative Example

The nominal variables p_t and m_t might well be I(2) instead of I(1) processes. Graphs of the data in differences (see Figure 2) show that indeed the differences could be described by an I(1) process, and we shall here show how one can analyze this phenomenon by means of the methods of Johansen (1995).

By repeated application of reduced rank regression we can estimate all [328] parameters in the I(2) model. We also demonstrate how to determine the ranks r and s.

For the U.K. data we find the results in Table 3, where the test statistics $Q_{r,s}$ and Q_r are given as functions of the degrees of freedom $p - r$ and $p - r - s$ to facilitate the comparison with the quantiles.

The value of r is determined by reading the Q_r column from top to bottom and comparing the observed value with the quantile for $p - r$ degrees of freedom from Table A1 in Johansen and Juselius (1990) derived under the assumption that there is a linear trend in the data. Once the value of $\hat{r}$ has been determined, one reads the table from left to right in the row with $r = \hat{r}$ and compares with the quantiles with $p - r - s$ degrees of freedom

TABLE 3.
The Results of the I(2) Analysis of the U.K. Money Demand Data

r	$Q_{r,s}$				Q_r	$tr(95\%)$	$p-r$
0	108.46	57.97	14.68	4.39	77.54	47.18	4
	$s=0$	$s=1$	$s=2$	$s=3$			
1		62.32	12.20	4.07	30.50	29.51	3
		$s=0$	$s=1$	$s=2$			
2			24.89	5.76	12.35	15.20	2
			$s=0$	$s=1$			
3				0.29	0.15	3.96	1
				$s=0$			
$tr(95\%)$	47.18	29.51	15.20	3.96			
$p-r-s$	4	3	2	1	0		

from before, but now listed in the second row from the bottom for ease of reference. This again requires that we accept a constant term in model (16).

Thus the determination of r is exactly as in the I(1) analysis, where we have chosen $\hat{r} = 1$. Reading the row $r = 1$ from left to right, we first test the hypothesis $H_{1,0}$ that $s = 0$ by the test statistic 62.32 as compared to the quantile 29.51. Thus $H_{1,0}$ is rejected. Next compare the test statistic $Q_{1,1} = 12.20$ with the quantile 15.20. This hypothesis is accepted, indicating that $s = 1$ and that the number of I(2) components is $p-r-s = 2$. Since this is a borderline case, we choose also to compare $Q_{1,2} = 4.07$ with its quantile 3.96, which is also a borderline case. Thus there seem to be I(2) variables in the system, but exactly how many is not so clear.

The choice of the 95 percent quantile is quite arbitrary, and the actual distribution of the test statistics is probably not very well approximated by the asymptotic distribution. From economic reasoning it seems plausible [329] that there is no more than one common I(2) variable that drives the other variables, namely one that measures the nominal growth, and this hypothesis is supported by the above analysis of the data and by the graphs that show that only Δp_t and Δm_t can best be described by I(1) processes and $m - p$ by an I(1) process.

We have thus continued the analysis of the data with $r = 1$, $s = 2$, and hence $p-r-s = 1$. We first give the results for the estimates of the matrix Γ in the I(1) model and the I(2) model in Table 4. The estimates of Γ in

TABLE 4.
Γ Estimated from the I(1) Model and from the I(2) Model

		Γ Estimated from the I(1) Model		
m	−2.078	0.974	−0.112	−0.397
p	0.319	−0.224	0.297	0.100
inc	0.486	−0.619	−1.861	0.327
R^*	0.384	−0.129	0.603	−1.069
		Γ Estimated from the I(2) Model		
m	−2.037	1.032	−0.105	−0.379
p	0.373	−0.148	0.306	0.123
inc	0.500	−0.600	−1.859	0.333
R^*	0.395	−0.114	0.605	−1.065

the two models are very similar, because the reduced rank hypothesis (13) restricts a $(p - r) \times (p - r) = 3 \times 3$ matrix to have rank $s = 2$. This really loses only one degree of freedom; thus the difference between the I(1) model and the I(2) model corresponds to only one parameter restriction. Hence the estimates are rather similar.

If we proceed with the assumption of $r = 1$, $s = 2$, and $p - r - s = 1$, then there is one common I(2) trend that drives all the variables. The vector $\beta' X_t$ is in this case just one linear combination, and it is I(1) and not stationary. It can be made stationary by including the differences [see (14)] with coefficients proportional to the vector $\beta_\perp^2 = \beta_\perp \eta_\perp$. Normalized on m_t, the stationary relation becomes

$$m_t - 1.04 p_t - 0.95 inc_t + 7.46 R_t^* + 2.33 \Delta m_t$$
$$+ 2.71 \Delta p_t - 0.30 \Delta inc_t + 0.03 \Delta R_t^*. \qquad (18)$$

It must be emphasized that since $(\beta, \beta_\perp^1)' \Delta X_t$ is stationary, there are many different relations between $\beta' X_t$ and ΔX_t that are stationary. We shall derive another later; see (19) and (20). The interpretation of the vectors in Table 5 is not so easy. First, the vector β is taken from Table 1 with the corresponding adjustment coefficient α. The vector no longer represents a stationary [330] relation. To make it stationary, it has to be corrected for the differences by means of $\beta_\perp^{2\prime} \Delta X_t$ [see (14)]. The adjustment coefficients α are interpreted as the strength of the adjustment to the disequilibrium error defined by (14). The vectors $\beta_\perp^1$ represent I(1) variables that do not cointegrate, and the last column, $\beta_\perp^2$, represents an I(2) variable, the changes of which can be used to make $\beta' X_t$ stationary as described.

TABLE 5. Estimates of Various Matrices

The Estimates of the Cointegrating Vectors β and the
Supplementary Vectors $\beta_\perp^1 = \beta_\perp(\beta_\perp'\beta_\perp)^{-1}\eta$ and $\beta_\perp^2 = \beta_\perp\eta_\perp$

	β	$\beta_\perp^1$		$\beta_\perp^2$
m	1.00	0.88	8.24	−0.97
p	−1.04	−1.46	−7.41	−1.13
inc	−0.95	−6.52	−3.17	0.12
R^*	7.46	−1.15	−2.54	−0.01

The Estimates of the Adjustment Coefficients α and the
Supplementary Vectors $\alpha_\perp^1 = \alpha_\perp(\alpha_\perp'\alpha_\perp)^{-1}\varphi$ and $\alpha_\perp^2 = \alpha_\perp\varphi_\perp$

	α	$\alpha_\perp^1$		$\alpha_\perp^2$
Δm	−0.150	−0.010	0.005	0.046
Δp	0.030	−0.042	0.000	0.253
Δinc	0.008	0.270	0.008	0.034
ΔR^*	0.031	−0.076	0.022	−0.026

The parameters $\alpha_\perp^2 = \alpha_\perp\varphi_\perp$ are of special interest since the common $\mathsf{I}(2)$ trend is given by $\alpha_\perp^{2\prime}X_t$, which in this case is practically equal to the price variable. Thus the price is chosen as the variable that does not react to the disequilibrium error, and in this sense it is the common driving $\mathsf{I}(2)$ force. The coefficients of $\beta_\perp^2$ from Table 5 show that the $\mathsf{I}(2)$ variables are mainly to be found in the variables m and p [see the expression (15) for the coefficients C_2 of the twice cumulated shocks]. Since the first two coefficients of $\beta_\perp^2$ are approximately equal, the common $\mathsf{I}(2)$ trend can be eliminated by taking the difference $m - p$.

In view of this analysis it seems that by introducing the variable $m_t - p_t$ one can eliminate the $\mathsf{I}(2)$ component and then work with the inflation rate $infl_t = \Delta p_t$ instead of p_t. With the variables $(m_t - p_t, infl_t, inc_t, R_t^*)$ we can repeat the $\mathsf{I}(1)$ analysis and find first the results summarized in Table 6.

[331]   It is seen from Table 6 that again there is just one cointegrating vector in the data. The coefficients are about the same as for the first eigenvector of Table 5, but this time with the coefficient of 7.22 to $infl_t$. Thus it is seen that the inflation rate and the interest rate suffice to reduce the variable

TABLE 6.

The I(1) Cointegration Analysis of the U.K. Money Demand Data

Eigenvalues	0.386	0.128	0.050	0.009
Hypotheses	$r = 0$	$r \leq 1$	$r \leq 2$	$r \leq 3$
Trace statistics	68.58	19.83	6.09	0.95
95% Quantiles	47.18	29.51	15.20	3.96

Eigenvectors β				
$m - p$	1.00	-0.08	-1.26	1.33
$infl$	7.22	1.00	16.07	6.56
inc	-1.08	-0.04	1.00	-0.13
R^*	7.16	-0.79	-7.00	1.00

Adjustment coefficients α				
$\Delta(m - p)$	-0.183	-0.034	0.002	-0.003
$\Delta infl$	0.023	-0.046	-0.005	0.003
Δinc	0.000	0.227	-0.007	-0.001
ΔR^*	0.034	0.139	0.002	0.007

Tests for weak exogeneity with respect to (α, β)

$m - p$	$infl$	inc	R^*
34.54	3.42	0.00	2.25

The 95% quantile of the asymptotic $\chi^2(1)$ distribution is 3.84.

The variables are $m - p$, Δp, inc, and R^*.

$(m - p - y)_t$ to stationarity. For this interpretation to hold we need to check that the reduction did in fact remove the I(2) components. Hence the I(2) analysis is performed for the new system and the results are reported in Table 7. From Table 7 it follows that for $r = 1$, the values $s = 0$, 1, and 2 are rejected, corresponding to the choice of $s = p - r = 3$, in which case the matrix in (13) has full rank, such that there are no I(2) variables.

Thus it seems that the I(2) analysis can be avoided by introducing real variables rather than nominal values. It is interesting to compare the cointegrating relation derived from this second system, as given by the first column in Table 6, with the relation (18) derived as stationary from the I(2) analysis. In equation (14) we have used a vector proportional to $\beta_\perp^2$ in order to achieve stationarity. In reality we can use any vector not orthogonal to $\beta_\perp^2$, that is, any vector not in the space spanned by β and $\beta_\perp^1$. The reason for this is, of

TABLE 7. The I(2) Analysis of the U.K. Money Demand Data

r	$Q_{r,s}$				Q_r	$tr(95\%)$	$p-r$
0	133.53	80.62	39.71	8.30	68.58	47.18	4
	$s=0$	$s=1$	$s=2$	$s=3$			
1		85.16	37.77	6.38	19.83	29.51	3
		$s=0$	$s=1$	$s=2$			
2			33.40	1.24	6.09	15.20	2
			$s=0$	$s=1$			
3				10.03	0.95	3.96	1
				$s=0$			
$tr(95\%)$	47.18	29.51	15.20	3.96			
$p-r-s$	4	3	2	1	0		

The variables are $m-p$, $infl$, inc, and R^*.

course, that the vectors $\beta'\Delta X_t$ and $\beta_\perp^{1'}\Delta X_t$ are already stationary and can be added to (18) without changing the stationarity of the relation. Any vector v can be decomposed into the directions β, $\beta_\perp^1$, and $\beta_\perp^2$, and only the projection in the direction $\beta_\perp^2$ is needed. This projection is given by $\beta_\perp^2(\beta_\perp^{2'}\beta_\perp^2)^{-1}\beta_\perp^{2'}v$, which shows that we can replace the vector $\beta_\perp^2 = (2.33, 2.71, -0.30, 0.03)$ by the vector $(\beta_\perp^{2'}\beta_\perp^2)(\beta_\perp^{2'}v)^{-1}v$. As an example we can express the relation (18) as a relation between levels and Δp by considering $v = (0, 1, 0, 0)$. This gives

[332]

$$m_t - 1.04p_t - 0.95inc_t + 7.46R_t^* + 4.75\Delta p_t. \qquad (19)$$

This result from the I(2) analysis of m, p, inc, and R^* is plotted in Figure 1 and can then be compared with the result from the preceding I(1) analysis of the reduced system, which gives

$$m_t - p_t - 1.08inc_t + 7.16R_t^* + 7.22\Delta p_t. \qquad (20)$$

These equations are derived from different models, and the differences in the coefficients reflect the statistical variability of the estimates.

It should be pointed out that a sudden jump in an otherwise stationary variable can be mistakenly considered as an indication of a general persistence of the shocks to the variable, that is, as an indication that the variables are I(1). Thus one should be careful about drawing overly strong conclusions from these various ways of looking at the data. What is demonstrated here is that the tools now exist for a statistical analysis, and they have to be combined by careful inspection of residuals, constancy over time of the estimated parameters, and so forth.

5   Conclusion   [333]

We have illustrated two statistical methods by an analysis of U.K. money demand. The test of weak exogeneity of the variables p_t, inc_t, and R_t^* requires that the full data vector can be described by an autoregressive model. If this is the case, a simple test can be performed. The test is required for the simpler analysis of a single-equation regression to be efficient. Weak exogeneity is devised to avoid investigating a full system, yet the test requires the modeling of a full system. If one can apply a VAR model for this, the easiest is, of course, to analyze the full system.

After this has been done, one can derive the conditional model that one would like to interpret, in the present case the model for Δm_t conditional on p_t, inc_t, and R_t^* together with the lags of all variables in levels. This last reduction does not require weak exogeneity. Weak exogeneity is only relevant if one wants to apply the conditional model for the estimation of the long-run parameters.

The presence of $I(2)$ components makes the analysis more difficult, not so much because the method becomes much more complicated, but because the interpretation becomes more difficult: what was stationary before is now just $I(1)$, and the differences of the process have to be invoked to produce a stationary relation. The $I(2)$ analysis, however, allows one to identify the common $I(2)$ trends that drive the economy and that lend themselves to an economic interpretation. The challenge of the $I(2)$ analysis is that it seems to allow more economic questions to be asked and interpreted.

It is important to note that, if one wants to describe this data by an $I(2)$ model, different choices of the dimensions r and s are consistent with the data. The values chosen are chosen partly on the basis of the statistical analysis and partly on the basis of what is economically reasonable. We have fitted five lags to a four-dimensional series, to produce 94 parameters and 400 observations. The $I(2)$ model rests on only one restriction of these parameters, and it is important to check the extent to which the conclusions depend on the choice of model.

The present analysis is meant as a first illustration of a new technique, where the details have yet to be worked out, and it will take some time until we understand where these methods can be applied with success.

Bibliography

(References marked with an asterisk * are included in this volume.)

Ahn, S. K., and G. C. Reinsel (1988) "Nested Reduced-rank Autoregressive Models for Multiple Time Series", *Journal of the American Statistical Association*, 83, 849–856.

[334] Ahn, S. K., and G. C. Reinsel (1990) "Estimation for Partially Nonstationary Multivariate Autoregressive Models", *Journal of the American Statistical Association*, 85, 815–823.

Anderson, T. W. (1951) "Estimating Linear Restrictions on Regression Coefficients for Multivariate Normal Distributions", *Annals of Mathematical Statistics*, 22, 327–351.

Boswijk, H. P. (1990) "On the Scope of Conditional Dynamic Modeling of Cointegrated Variables", *Tinbergen Institute Research Bulletin*, 2, 97–111.

Engle, R. F., and C. W. J. Granger (1987) "Co-integration and Error Correction: Representation, Estimation, and Testing", *Econometrica*, 55, 2, 251–276.

*Engle, R. F., D. F. Hendry, and J.-F. Richard (1983) "Exogeneity", *Econometrica*, 51, 2, 277–304.

Ericsson, N. R., J. Campos, and H.-A. Tran (1990) "PC-GIVE and David Hendry's Econometric Methodology", *Revista de Econometria*, 10, 1, 7–117; originally cited as (1991), International Finance Discussion Paper No. 406, Board of Governors of the Federal Reserve System, Washington, D.C., forthcoming in *Revista de Econometria*.

Granger, C. W. J. (1981) "Some Properties of Time Series Data and Their Use in Econometric Model Specification", *Journal of Econometrics*, 16, 121–130.

Hendry, D. F., and N. R. Ericsson (1991) "Modeling the Demand for Narrow Money in the United Kingdom and the United States", *European Economic Review*, 35, 833–881.

Hendry, D. F., and G. E. Mizon (1993) "Evaluating Dynamic Econometric Models by Encompassing the VAR", in P. C. B. Phillips (ed.) *Models, Methods, and Applications of Econometrics*, Oxford, Basil Blackwell, 272–300; originally cited as (1990), Discussion Paper, University of Oxford.

Johansen, S. (1988) "Statistical Analysis of Cointegration Vectors", *Journal of Economic Dynamics and Control*, 12, 231–254.

Johansen, S. (1992a) "Cointegration in Partial Systems and the Efficiency of Single-equation Analysis", *Journal of Econometrics*, 52, 3, 389–402;

originally cited as (1992b), forthcoming in *Journal of Econometrics*.

Johansen, S. (1992b) "Determination of Cointegration Rank in the Presence of a Linear Trend", *Oxford Bulletin of Economics and Statistics*, 54, 3, 383–397; originally cited as (1991a), forthcoming in *Oxford Bulletin of Economics and Statistics*.

Johansen, S. (1992c) "A Representation of Vector Autoregressive Processes Integrated of Order 2", *Econometric Theory*, 8, 2, 188–202; originally cited as (1992a).

Johansen, S. (1995) "A Statistical Analysis of Cointegration for I(2) Variables", *Econometric Theory*, in press; originally cited as (1991b).

Johansen, S., and K. Juselius (1990) "Maximum Likelihood Estimation and Inference on Cointegration—With Applications to the Demand for Money", *Oxford Bulletin of Economics and Statistics*, 52, 2, 169–210.

Pantula, S. G. (1989) "Testing for Unit Roots in Time Series Data", *Econometric Theory*, 5, 2, 256–271.

Phillips, P. C. B. (1991) "Optimal Inference in Cointegrated Systems", *Econometrica*, 59, 2, 283–306.

6

Tests of Cointegrating Exogeneity for PPP and Uncovered Interest Rate Parity in the United Kingdom

JOHN HUNTER*

Abstract

In this article we try to determine whether the purchasing power parity and uncovered interest rate arbitrage conditions are satisfied by data on the U.K. exchange rate. This study compares the notions of cointegrating exogeneity and weak exogeneity, and then tests these hypotheses.

1 Introduction

In this article we test for cointegration and exogeneity in an empirical model of the exchange rate. The two cointegrating relationships dealt with are purchasing power parity (PPP) and uncovered interest rate parity (UIP). We have used the data analyzed by Fisher, Tanna, Turner, Wallis, and Whitley (1990) and Johansen and Juselius (1992) to determine the role of cointegration. Johansen and Juselius find partial confirmation of the PPP and UIP hypotheses for a system that includes U.K. and foreign prices (p_1 and p_2), a U.K. effective exchange rate (e_{12}, the value of the basket in terms of pounds sterling), the U.K. Treasury bill rate (i_1), and the eurodollar rate

---

* I would like to thank Neil Ericsson, David Hendry, Denis Sargan, and two anonymous referees for their comments. I have also benefited from detailed discussion with Rocco Mosconi and Paul Fisher. I would also like to thank Rocco for the use of his program and Paul for a complete data set.

Reprinted with permission from the *Journal of Policy Modeling* (August 1992), 14, 4, 453–463.

(i_2) as endogenous variables, and the world price of oil (p_o) as an exogenous variable. We complement their results by testing for cointegration and exogeneity without assuming the exogeneity of oil prices.

In Section 2 we briefly discuss the economic theory. In Section 3, we use the notion of cointegrating exogeneity, due to Hunter (1990), to partition [454] the cointegrating variables into vectors of endogenous and (potentially) exogenous cointegrated variables. Then we describe the restrictions required for both cointegrating exogeneity and weak exogeneity. In Section 4, we estimate an exchange rate system and test the long-run parameter matrix for the restrictions associated with cointegration and exogeneity. Conclusions are presented in Section 5.

2   Theoretical Specifications of the Exchange Rate

Johansen and Juselius (1992) consider two long-run hypotheses, purchasing power parity:

$$p_1 - p_2 = e_{12}, \tag{1}$$

and uncovered interest rate parity:

$$i_1 - i_2 = \Delta e_{12}. \tag{2}$$

PPP is the logical conclusion of the law of one price applied to international trade relationships. The UIP model has been formulated in the context of rational expectations by Baillie, Lippens, and MacMahon (1983), and it has an older Keynesian tradition associated with the opening up of the ISLM model.

3   Conditional Models and Testing for Cointegration and Exogeneity

In this section we formulate a vector autoregression (VAR) and relate it to an error correction model. The conditions for cointegration are specified in terms of the levels parameters in the error correction model. Cointegration imposes a restriction on the matrix of long-run parameters, implying that questions about the nature of exogeneity need to be discussed in this context. At the end of this section, we look at cointegrating exogeneity and the restrictions on the long-run parameters associated with cointegrating and weak exogeneity.

We take the g-variable, kth-order VAR in levels with Gaussian errors:

$$A(L)x_t = \mu + \Psi D_t + \varepsilon_t \quad \varepsilon_t \sim \mathsf{NIID}(0, \Sigma) \quad t = 1, \ldots, n, \tag{3}$$

where $A(L) = I - A_1 L - A_2 L^2 - \cdots - A_k L^k$, D_t are centered dummies, and

$x'_t = [p_{ot} \; p_{1t} \; p_{2t} \; e_{12t} \; i_{1t} \; i_{2t}].$[1] Economic series that are l(1) individually, form
l(0) relationships under cointegration [Granger (1983); Engle and Granger   [455]
(1987)]. In that case, (3) has an error correction form in terms of stationary
variables:

$$\Gamma(L)\Delta x_t = \Pi x_{t-1} + \mu + \Psi D_t + \varepsilon_t, \qquad (4)$$

where $\Gamma(L) = I - \Gamma_1 L - \Gamma_2 L^2 - \cdots - \Gamma_{k-1} L^{k-1}$, and Πx_{t-1} is a set of nonzero
stationary linear combinations of x_{t-1}. The hypothesis of r cointegrating
vectors is:

$$H_1(r) : \Pi = \alpha\beta',$$

where $\text{rank}(\Pi) = \text{rank}(\alpha) = \text{rank}(\beta) = r$ and $0 \leq r \leq g$. Johansen (1988)
and Johansen and Juselius (1990) present tests of the rank of Π to determine
r. We can test further restrictions on Π to determine whether the variables
are cointegrating exogenous and/or weakly exogenous.

Engle, Hendry, and Richard (1983) distinguish between a number of concepts of exogeneity: strict, strong, weak, and super. The cointegration literature has mainly dealt with the weak exogeneity of a variable z_t for β
[Johansen (1992)]. Weak exogeneity is defined in terms of specific parameters of interest and formulated in terms of the distribution of observable
variables. The joint density of x_t in (3) can be partitioned into a conditional
density of y_t, given z_t, and a marginal density of z_t [Engle, Hendry, and
Richard (1983)]:

$$D(x_t|X_{t-1}, \phi) = D_{y|z}(y_t|z_t, X_{t-1}, \phi_1) \cdot D_z(z_t|X_{t-1}, \phi_2),$$

where $x'_t = [y'_t, z'_t]$ and $X_t = (X_0, x_1, x_2, \ldots, x_t)$. Weak exogeneity requires
that the parameters of interest depend on only the parameters of the conditional density of y_t (ϕ_1) and that there is a sequential cut of the parameter spaces for ϕ_1 and ϕ_2 [Florens, Mouchart, and Rolin (1990)]. If so,
the marginal density for z_t can be ignored without loss of information when
conducting statistical inference about the parameters of interest. Strong
exogeneity combines weak exogeneity with Granger noncausality, so that the
marginal density for z_t becomes $D_z(z_t|Z_{t-1}, \phi_2)$. Super exogeneity requires
weak exogeneity and that the parameters of the conditional process for y_t be
invariant to changes in the process for z_t.

Cointegrating exogeneity [Hunter (1990)] is a long-run notion of exogeneity that implies that the long-run relations are block triangular. We
partition Π to separate the cointegrating vectors into those related to the
exogenous variables z_t alone and those related to both y_t and z_t:

---

[1] In contrast to Johansen and Juselius (1992), we add p_o to p_1 and p_2 in the VAR,
because it is convenient for testing.

$$\Pi = \begin{bmatrix} \Pi_{11} & \Pi_{12} \\ \Pi_{21} & \Pi_{22} \end{bmatrix} = \begin{bmatrix} \alpha_1 \\ \alpha_2 \end{bmatrix} \begin{bmatrix} \beta_1 \\ \beta_2 \end{bmatrix}' = \begin{bmatrix} \alpha_1\beta_1' & \alpha_1\beta_2' \\ \alpha_2\beta_1' & \alpha_2\beta_2' \end{bmatrix},$$

[456]   where α_1 is $g_1 \times r$, α_2 is $g_2 \times r$, β_1' is $r \times g_1$, and β_2' is $r \times g_2$. Cointegrating exogeneity is defined by the condition that $\Pi_{21} = \alpha_2\beta_1' = 0$. It follows from a result by Mosconi and Giannini (1992) that under this hypothesis the model can be parameterized as follows:

$$\alpha = \begin{bmatrix} \alpha_{11} & \alpha_{12} \\ 0 & \alpha_{22} \end{bmatrix} \qquad \beta = \begin{bmatrix} \beta_{11} & 0 \\ \beta_{21} & \beta_{22} \end{bmatrix},$$

such that

$$\Pi = \begin{bmatrix} \alpha_{11}\beta_{11}' & \alpha_{11}\beta_{21}' + \alpha_{12}\beta_{22}' \\ 0 & \alpha_{22}\beta_{22}' \end{bmatrix},$$

where $\alpha_i = [\alpha_{i1}\ \alpha_{i2}]$, $\beta_i = [\beta_{i1}\ \beta_{i2}]$, α_{ij} $(g_i \times r_j)$, and β_{ij}' $(r_j \times g_i)$. Here, we have assumed that Mosconi and Giannini's r^* $(\equiv r - r_1 - r_2)$ equals zero.

Under the assumption that $\mathrm{rank}(\Pi) = \mathrm{rank}(\beta) = \mathrm{rank}(\alpha) = r$, the necessary and sufficient conditions for z_t to be cointegrating exogenous for $[\beta_{11}'\ \beta_{21}']$ is:

$$\Pi_{21} = 0, \tag{i}$$

where the normalization above on α and β is adopted. Then the following vectors, η_{1t} and η_{2t}, define r_1 and r_2 vectors of stationary variables:

$$\eta_{1t} = [\beta_{11}'\ \beta_{21}']x_t \sim \mathrm{I}(0),$$

$$\eta_{2t} = \beta_{22}'z_t \sim \mathrm{I}(0).$$

A variable z_t is weakly exogenous for the full cointegrating vector β when:

$$\alpha_{21} = 0 \quad \text{and} \quad \alpha_{22} = 0 \tag{ii}$$

[Johansen (1992)]. Such weak exogeneity implies that all the cointegrating vectors enter only the conditional model. The variable z_t is both cointegrating exogenous and weakly exogenous for the first r_1 cointegrating vectors $[\beta_{11}'\ \beta_{21}']$ when two restrictions hold: (i) above, and

$$\alpha_{12} = 0. \tag{iii}$$

Cointegrating exogeneity means no long-term feedback of y onto z (because $\Pi_{21} = 0$), and so implies a "weak" form of Granger noncausality. Thus, cointegrating exogeneity parallels strong exogeneity. The latter permits valid forecasts of y from the conditional model, given forecasts of z from the marginal model. Cointegrating exogeneity permits valid *long-run* forecasts of y, given the forecasts of z.

[457]   Unlike strong exogeneity, cointegrating exogeneity does not require a sequential cut between the parameters of the conditional model and those of

the marginal model, and so cointegrating exogeneity does not require weak exogeneity. That has two implications: for statistical inference and for policy analysis. First, joint estimation of the process for y and z may be necessary to obtain the parameters in the conditional model of y (used for forecasting y). Specifically, joint estimation may be required to obtain the cointegrating vectors entering the conditional model. Second, under cointegrating exogeneity, the parameters of the conditional model need not be structurally invariant to changes in the parameters of the marginal process, so cointegrating exogeneity by itself does not sustain valid counterfactual analysis. Rather, the focus of cointegrating exogeneity is long-run forecasting, given knowledge of the cointegrating vectors.

4   A VAR Model of the U.K. Exchange Rate with Tests of Cointegration and Exogeneity

We re-estimate the model of Johansen and Juselius (1992) and compare it with a model that does not impose two restrictions: that the oil price is weakly exogenous for the cointegrating vectors β, and that the oil price does not enter β. We then use this "extended" model to test the hypotheses of weak and cointegrating exogeneity.

The model of Johansen and Juselius (1992) is equivalent to a six variable VAR(2) in (3) that sets to zero both the long-run coefficients of the price of oil and the long-run coefficients in the oil equation, that is,

$$\Pi = \left[\begin{array}{c} 0 \\ - - - - \\ 0 \mid \Pi_{JJ} \end{array} \right]. \tag{5}$$

The matrix Π_{JJ} is estimated over the period 1972(3)–1987(2) and it appears in Table 1. Estimating without the zero restrictions in (5), we obtain Table 2. We refer to the VAR without (5) imposed as the *extended* VAR.[2]

Johansen and Juselius test for and find two cointegrating vectors: [458]

$$\eta_t = \left[\begin{array}{cccccc} 0 & 1.0 & -0.91 & -0.93 & -3.38 & -1.89 \\ 0 & 0.03 & -0.03 & -0.10 & 1.0 & -0.94 \end{array} \right] \left[\begin{array}{c} p_{ot} \\ p_{1t} \\ p_{2t} \\ e_{12t} \\ i_{1t} \\ i_{2t} \end{array} \right].$$

The first cointegrating vector is essentially $(p_1 - p_2 - e_{12})$, augmented by

---

[2] Both Johansen and Juselius's VAR and an extended VAR show some misspecification in terms of non-normality and nonconstancy. Additionally, some variables (e.g., prices) may be I(2), affecting inference [Johansen (1995)]. Nonetheless we will proceed, for illustrative purposes.

John Hunter

TABLE 1. The Π_{JJ} Matrix for Johansen and Juselius's Model

	p_1	p_2	e_{12}	i_1	i_2
p_1	−0.081	0.077	0.063	0.233	0.08
p_2	−0.007	−0.021	0.007	0.038	0.06
e_{12}	−0.041	0.147	−0.168	−0.591	−0.11
i_1	0.008	−0.009	−0.005	−0.351	0.11
i_2	0.097	−0.158	−0.054	0.079	−0.48

Note: $\ln L = 744.82$; $n = 60$.

TABLE 2. The Π Matrix for the VAR(2) with Oil Prices

	p_o	p_1	p_2	e_{12}	i_1	i_2
p_o	−0.224	−0.547	0.599	0.925	1.292	4.787
p_1	−0.002	−0.09	0.087	0.078	0.253	0.155
p_2	−0.011	−0.046	0.020	0.071	0.127	0.393
e_{12}	0.004	−0.039	0.144	−0.172	−0.596	−0.133
i_1	−0.002	0.002	−0.002	0.006	−0.336	0.171
i_2	0.011	0.087	−0.147	−0.037	0.103	−0.398

Note: $\ln L = 767.01$; $n = 60$.

TABLE 3. Cointegration Tests for the Extended VAR(2)

i	λ_i	$-n\ln(1-\lambda_i)$	$\lambda_{\max}(0.95)$	$-n\Sigma\ln(1-\lambda_i)$	$\lambda_{\text{trace}}(0.95)$
1	0.083	5.18	8.08	5.18	8.08
2	0.128	8.22	14.6	13.41	17.84
3	0.161	10.52	21.28	23.93	31.25
4	0.289	20.44	27.34	44.37	48.41
5	0.335	24.48	33.26	68.86	69.98
6	0.571	50.82*	39.43	119.69*	95.18

Normalized eigenvectors $\beta_{\cdot i}$ for $i = 1, 2$[a]

	$\beta_{\cdot 1}$	$\beta_{\cdot 2}$	$\nu_{\cdot 3}$	$\nu_{\cdot 4}$	$\nu_{\cdot 5}$	$\nu_{\cdot 6}$
p_o	−0.113	0.024	0.043	−0.167	0.386	−0.016
p_1	−0.914	−0.063	1.000	1.000	1.000	1.000
p_2	0.931	−0.001	−1.364	−1.342	−3.221	−1.416
e_{12}	1.000	0.029	−2.234	0.33	1.243	−0.481
i_1	2.039	1.000	−1.786	0.498	−2.52	2.31
i_2	3.964	−0.671	−3.926	0.355	1.949	0.808

[a] As r = 2, $\nu_{\cdot i}$ are not considered to be proper eigenvectors [Johansen and Juselius (1992)].

* Significant at the 5 percent level.

two interest rates. The second is close to $(i_1 - i_2)$, the UIP hypothesis. Johansen and Juselius undertake a number of additional tests that confirm that imposing the unit coefficients of the PPP and UIP hypotheses does not affect the results, though PPP on its own does not define a valid cointegrating vector.

We now look at the results of the Johansen procedure for the extended VAR. First we obtain tests of cointegration, as shown in Table 3.[3] The trace and max tests imply that $r = 1$ or possibly $r = 2$; to follow Johansen and Juselius (1992) we select $r = 2$. The first two vectors in β' are approximately [459]

$$\begin{bmatrix} 0.11 & 1.0 & -1.0 & -1.0 & -2.0 & -4.0 \\ 0.0 & 0.0 & 0.0 & 0.0 & 1.0 & -1.0 \end{bmatrix}.$$

The first row vector gives the PPP hypotheses, augmented by interest rates

[3] The computer program PCFIML [Hendry (1989)] was used and the results were then confirmed by Johansen and Juselius's own procedure, written by Henrik Hansen [Juselius (1991)].

and the oil price, while the second row is the UIP condition. The results seem to agree with those of both Fisher, Tanna, Turner, Wallis, and Whitley (1990) and Johansen and Juselius (1992), for whom the PPP relationship requires the interest rates for stationarity.

We consider the tests of restrictions on α and β presented in Johansen and Juselius (1990, 1992) and Mosconi and Giannini (1992).[4]

$$H_{4\beta} : \beta = H_{4\beta}\varphi, \qquad H_{4\beta} \ (g \times s), \ \varphi \ (s \times r) \text{ where } r \leq s \leq g.$$

$$H_{6\beta} : \beta = (H_{6\beta}\varphi_1, \psi_2), \quad H_{6\beta} \ (g \times s), \ \varphi_1 \ (s \times r_1), \ \psi_2 \ (g \times r_2)$$
$$\text{and } r \leq s \leq g, \ r = r_1 + r_2.$$

$$H_{7\beta} : \beta = (\psi_1, H_{7\beta}\varphi_2), \quad H_{7\beta} \ (g \times s), \ \varphi_2 \ (s \times r_2), \ \psi_1 \ (g \times r_1)$$
$$\text{and } r \leq s \leq g, \ r = r_1 + r_2.$$

$$H_{4\alpha} : \alpha = H_{4\alpha}\vartheta, \qquad H_{4\alpha} \ (g \times s), \ \vartheta \ (s \times r) \text{ where } r \leq s \leq g.$$

$$H_{6\alpha} : \alpha = (H_{6\alpha}\vartheta_1, \kappa_2), \quad H_{6\alpha} \ (g \times s), \ \vartheta_1 \ (s \times r_1), \ \kappa_2 \ (g \times r_2)$$
$$\text{and } r \leq s \leq g, \ r = r_1 + r_2.$$

$$H_{7\alpha} : \alpha = (\kappa_1, H_{7\alpha}\vartheta_2), \quad H_{7\alpha} \ (g \times s), \ \vartheta_2 \ (s \times r_2), \ \kappa_1 \ (g \times r_1)$$
$$\text{and } r \leq s \leq g, \ r = r_1 + r_2.$$

[460] Johansen and Juselius (1990) show that these hypotheses can be tested by a likelihood ratio test that is asymptotically distributed χ^2 under the null. The distributional assumptions are valid for the correct choice of r, which is why we restate the λ_{trace} test at the start of Table 4. Then we test (a) whether p_o can be excluded from the VAR to validate the Johansen and Juselius model:

$$\alpha = H_{4.1\alpha}\vartheta = \begin{bmatrix} 0\ 0\ 0\ 0\ 0 \\ -\ -\ -\ - \\ I_5 \end{bmatrix} \vartheta \quad \text{and} \quad \beta = H_{4.1\beta}\varphi = \begin{bmatrix} 0\ 0\ 0\ 0\ 0 \\ -\ -\ -\ - \\ I_5 \end{bmatrix} \varphi, \quad \text{(a)}$$

where φ is defined above for $H_{4\beta}$, ϑ is an equivalent term for $H_{4\alpha}$, j in $H_{i.j\alpha}$ indexes the particular hypothesis tested, and the same applies for $H_{i.j\beta}$. See Table 4.

The second block of Table 4 contains tests for (b) cointegrating exogeneity of i_1 and i_2, (c) PPP and UIP, (d) cointegrating exogeneity of e_{12}, (e) block diagonality of α, (f) weak exogeneity of i_1 and e_{12} for β, and (g) weak exogeneity of i_2 for β. The normalized β and α matrices under (b), (c), (d), and (e) are:

---

[4] Rocco Mosconi has written a program that tests the hypotheses on the subspaces of α and β [Mosconi and Giannini (1992)].

TABLE 4. Tests of Cointegration and Exogeneity

Hypothesis[a,b]		Null[c]	d.f.[d]	Statistic (95% level)
$r = 2$	(C)	$r \leq 1$	–	68.86 (69.98)
(a) $H_{4.1\alpha} + H_{4.1\beta}\|r = 2$		$\alpha_{1j} = 0, \beta_{1j} = 0, j = 1,2$	4	23.83** (9.49)
(i) (b) $H_{7.1\beta} + H_{6.1\alpha}\|r = 2$ (CE)		$\alpha_{51} = 0, \alpha_{61} = 0, \beta_{j2} = 0, j = 1,\ldots,4$	6	7.82 (12.59)
(c) $H_{6.1\beta} + H_{7.2\beta}\|$(b)		$\beta_{21} - \beta_{31} - \beta_{41} = 0, \beta_{52} - \beta_{62} = 0$	3	2.01 (7.82)
(d) $H_{6.2\alpha}\|$(c)	(CE)	$\alpha_{41} = 0$	1	0.44 (3.84)
(iii) (e) $H_{7.1\alpha}\|$(d)	(Diag-onal α)	$\alpha_{j2} = 0, j = 1,2,3$	3	4.05 (7.82)
(b)+(c)+(d)+(e)		(joint null for the tests above)	13	14.32 (22.36)
(f) $H_{7.2\alpha}\|$(d)	(WE)	$\alpha_{42} = 0, \alpha_{52} = 0$	2	3.07 (5.99)
(g) $H_{7.3\alpha}\|$(d)	(WE)	$\alpha_{62} = 0$	1	8.52** (3.84)
(PPP) $H_{4.2\beta}\|r = 2$		$\beta_{2j} - \beta_{3j} - \beta_{4j} = 0, j = 1,2$	6	2.69 (12.59)
(UIP) $H_{4.3\beta}\|r = 2$		$\beta_{5j} - \beta_{6j} = 0, j = 1,2$	4	26.00** (9.49)
(ii) $H_{4.2\alpha}\|r = 2$	(WE)	$\alpha_{4j} = 0, \alpha_{5j} = 0, \alpha_{6j} = 0, j = 1,2$	6	13.65* (12.59)
(ii) $H_{4.3\alpha}\|r = 2$	(WE)	$\alpha_{5j} = 0, \alpha_{6j} = 0, j = 1,2$	4	10.52* (9.49)
(ii) $H_{4.4\alpha}\|r = 2$	(WE)	$\alpha_{4j} = 0, \alpha_{5j} = 0, j = 1,2$	4	4.04 (9.49)
$H_{7.1\alpha} + H_{6.2\alpha}\|r = 2$	(Diag-onal α)	$\alpha_{j2} = 0, j = 1,2,3, \alpha_{i1} = 0, i = 4,5,6$	6	3.96 (12.59)

[a] C = cointegration; CE = cointegrating exogeneity; WE = weak exogeneity.
[b] Conditions (i)–(iii) are discussed in Section 3.
[c] α_{ij} and β_{ij} define single elements of α and β.
[d] All asymptotic distributions are χ^2 with degrees of freedom (d.f.) as indicated, except for the first, which is distributed as $-n\Sigma \ln(1 - \lambda_i)$.
* Significant at the 5 percent level; **significant at the 1 percent level.

$$\beta = \begin{bmatrix} 0.12 & 0 \\ 1 & 0 \\ -1 & 0 \\ 1 & 0 \\ 3.47 & 1 \\ 3.40 & -1 \end{bmatrix} \quad \text{and} \quad \alpha = \begin{bmatrix} -0.996 & 0.0 \\ -0.062 & 0.0 \\ -0.097 & 0.0 \\ 0.0 & -0.216 \\ 0.0 & -0.134 \\ 0.0 & 0.287 \end{bmatrix}.$$

The tests are undertaken sequentially and Table 4 provides exact definitions of the null hypotheses. For example, the test for cointegrating exogencity of i_1 and i_2 uses the following hypotheses to specify the necessary and sufficient condition in (i):

$$\begin{bmatrix} \alpha_{11} \\ \alpha_{21} \end{bmatrix} = \begin{bmatrix} I_4 \\ \hline 0\,0\,0\,0 \\ 0\,0\,0\,0 \end{bmatrix} \vartheta_1 \quad \text{and} \quad \begin{bmatrix} \beta_{12} \\ \beta_{22} \end{bmatrix} = \begin{bmatrix} 0 & 0 \\ 0 & 0 \\ 0 & 0 \\ 0 & 0 \\ 1 & 0 \\ 0 & 1 \end{bmatrix} \varphi_2, \qquad \text{(b)}$$

where φ_2 is defined above for $H_{7\beta}$ and ϑ_1 is an equivalent term for $H_{6\alpha}$. We formulate similar hypotheses to carry out (c)–(g) and the other tests in Table 4. Having partitioned α and β into two subspaces, we impose the unit coefficient restriction for PPP on $\beta_{.1}$ and that for UIP on $\beta_{.2}$ ($\beta_{.i}$ is defined by Table 3). The second restriction is of particular interest as Johansen and Juselius find that UIP does not hold for the whole space of β.

Cointegrating exogeneity for i_1 and i_2 having been imposed, cointegrating exogeneity of e_{12} requires only one restriction on α_{21}, diagonal α implies condition (ii), and weak exogeneity involves additional zero restrictions on α_{22}. At the end of Table 4, we repeat Johansen and Juselius's tests of PPP and UIP for β; we test for weak exogeneity (WE) of (e_{12}, i_1, i_2), (i_1, i_2), and (e_{12}, i_1); and we test for diagonal α.

[462]   From Table 4, hypotheses (b)–(f) appear satisfied. However, (a) is rejected, meaning that Johansen and Juselius's restriction on Π in (5) appears invalid. Even so, this rejection is tentative because the test used depends upon the extended model having Gaussian errors; and that assumption appears invalid (see footnote 2). Hypothesis (g) is also rejected, implying that i_2 is not weakly exogenous. Satisfaction of (b) and (d) means that the conditions for cointegrating exogeneity of i_1, i_2, and e_{12} for $\beta_{.1}$ are satisfied. The test of weak exogeneity of e_{12} and i_1 for β cannot be rejected, conditional upon (b)–(e). However, the joint tests of weak exogeneity for (e_{12}, i_1, i_2) and (i_1, i_2) are significant while that for (i_1, e_{12}) is not. The PPP restriction and block diagonal α are met with or without cointegrating exogeneity being imposed, but UIP holds only for $\beta_{.2}$. The model imposing (b)–(e) satisfies all of the associated restrictions, but it does not impose weak exogeneity of

e_{12} and i_1 for β. Given the variables used, it seems odd that the exchange rate and the U.K. interest rate are weakly exogenous, especially as the α coefficients for e_{12} and i_2 are of a very similar magnitude.

5   Conclusion

Our evidence supports a UIP hypothesis and a PPP relationship augmented by both interest rates and the price of oil. Further, the interest rates and the exchange rate appear to be cointegrating exogenous for the augmented PPP relation. The Treasury bill rate and the exchange rate appear to be weakly exogenous for both the UIP and the augmented PPP relations, implying that no variables in levels enter the marginal equations for the Treasury bill rate and the exchange rate. Thus, these two variables are described by generalized random walks, and the UIP condition (for example) does not affect them in the long run. These results should be treated with some care, as Johansen (1992) has provided evidence that the price series are $I(2)$; and specification tests suggest that the extended VAR may be mis-specified.

Appendix.   The Data

P_o is a measure of the real oil price provided by H.M. Treasury.

P_1 is the U.K. output price for manufacturing excluding food, drink, and tobacco [OECD Main Economic Indicators (1988)].

P_2 is output prices for the six leading industrial countries (OECD).

E_{12} is the inverse of the sterling exchange rate index, rebased to 1980 = 100 [CSO Economic Trends (1988), 1975 = 100].

I_1 is the U.K. treasury bill rate average for the quarter (Bank of England [463] Quarterly Bulletin, various editions).

I_2 is the 3-month eurodollar rate average for the quarter (Bank of England Quarterly Bulletin, various editions).

The series used are all based on 1980 = 100. All data are quarterly and are in logarithms, which are indicated by lower case.

Bibliography

(References marked with an asterisk * are included in this volume.)

Baillie, R. T., R. E. Lippens, and P. C. MacMahon (1983) "Testing Rational Expectations and Efficiency in the Foreign Exchange Market", *Economet- rica*, 51, 3, 553–563; originally cited as (1981) Discussion Paper, Series A, Department of Economics, University of Birmingham, Birmingham, England.

Engle, R. F., and C. W. J. Granger (1987) "Co-integration and Error Correction: Representation, Estimation, and Testing", *Econometrica*, 55, 251–276.

*Engle, R. F., D. F. Hendry, and J.-F. Richard (1983) "Exogeneity", *Econometrica*, 51, 277–304.

Fisher, P. G., S. K. Tanna, D. S. Turner, K. F. Wallis, and J. D. Whitley (1990) "Econometric Evaluation of the Exchange Rate in Models of the UK Economy", *Economic Journal*, 100, 403, 1024–1056.

Florens, J.-P., M. Mouchart, and J.-M. Rolin (1990) "Sequential Experiments", Chapter 6 in *Elements of Bayesian Statistics*, New York, Marcel Dekker; originally cited as J.-P. Florens and M. Mouchart (1980) "Initial and Sequential Reduction of Bayesian Experiments", CORE Discussion Paper 8015, Université Catholique de Louvain, Louvain-la-Neuve, Belgium.

Granger, C. W. J. (1983) "Cointegrated Variables and Error-correcting Models", Discussion Paper 83–13, Department of Economics, University of California at San Diego, La Jolla, California.

Hendry, D. F. (1989) *PC-GIVE: An Interactive Econometric Modelling System*, Oxford, England, Institute of Economics and Statistics and Nuffield College, Oxford University.

Hunter, J. (1990) "Cointegrating Exogeneity", *Economics Letters*, 34, 33–35.

Johansen, S. (1988) "Statistical Analysis of Cointegrating Vectors", *Journal of Economic Dynamics and Control*, 12, 231–254.

Johansen, S. (1992) "Cointegration in Partial Systems and the Efficiency of Single-equation Analysis", *Journal of Econometrics*, 52, 3, 389–402.

Johansen, S. (1995) "A Statistical Analysis of Cointegration for I(2) Variables", *Econometric Theory*, in press; originally cited as (1991) Report No. 77, Department of Statistics, University of Helsinki, Helsinki, Finland, forthcoming in *Econometric Theory*.

Johansen, S., and K. Juselius (1990) "Maximum Likelihood Estimation and Inference on Cointegration—With Applications to the Demand for Money", *Oxford Bulletin of Economics and Statistics*, 52, 169–210.

Johansen, S., and K. Juselius (1992) "Testing Structural Hypotheses in a Multivariate Cointegration Analysis of the PPP and the UIP for UK", *Journal of Econometrics*, 53, 211–244; originally cited as (1991) "Some Structural Hypotheses in a Multivariate Cointegration Analysis of the Purchasing Power Parity and the Uncovered Interest Parity for UK", forthcoming in the *Journal of Econometrics*.

Juselius, K. (1991) *CATS in RATS: A Manual to Cointegration Analysis*, Copenhagen, Denmark, Institute of Economics, University of Copenhagen; originally cited as (1991) *Cointegration Analysis of Time Series, The RATS Manual*, Doan Associates.

Mosconi, R., and C. Giannini (1992) "Non-causality in Cointegrated Systems: Representation, Estimation, and Testing", *Oxford Bulletin of Economics and Statistics*, 54, 3, 399–417; originally cited as C. Giannini and R. Mosconi (1990) "Non-causality and Neutrality in Cointegrated Systems: Representation, Estimation, and Testing", Discussion Paper No. 90–002, Department of Economics, Politecnico di Milano, Milan, Italy.

Part II

TESTING EXOGENEITY IN PRACTICE

7

Domestic and Foreign Effects on Prices in an Open Economy: The Case of Denmark

KATARINA JUSELIUS*

Abstract

Domestic price determination in Denmark is investigated using three kinds of macro-economic explanations: (1) internal labor market theories describing the relation between price and wage inflation, (2) pure monetarist theories describing the effect of excess money on the inflation rate, and (3) external theories describing the foreign transmission effects on a small open economy. The empirical analysis makes use of the multivariate cointegration model, which is based on the joint analysis of long- and short-run behavior. The deviations from derived underlying steady states in each sector were found to be the main determinants of the inflation rate. Among these, the domestic effects were small compared to the foreign effects. The empirical results strongly favored a backward-looking behavioral model in terms of structurally stable parameters as opposed to a forward-looking expectations model. The results stand up as quite strong evidence against the Lucas critique.

* This article was prepared as a part of a Nordic research project with financial support from the Nordic Council for Cooperation in the Social Sciences. It was presented at the EC^2 conference in Amsterdam, December 1990, at the Nordic workshop on multivariate cointegration in Ål, Norway, 1990, at the Economics Department, University of Lund, and at the workshop on cointegration in Berlin, 1991. Comments and suggestions from participants in these meetings are gratefully acknowledged. A special thanks for valuable comments and useful suggestions goes to the editor and to Søren Johansen.

Reprinted with permission from the *Journal of Policy Modeling* (August 1992), 14, 4, 401–428.

1 Introduction

The empirical purpose of this article is to investigate domestic and international transmission effects on prices in Denmark. It illustrates possible causes of inflation in a small open economy and the way inflation is affected by the increasing economic integration within the European Economic Community. The basic idea is that consumer price inflation can be associated with domestic wage inflation, that is, nominal wages above the underlying steady-state level; with monetary inflation, that is, excess money; and with imported inflation. To derive observational variables for these three theoretical concepts, we will use some recent econometric contributions to the analysis of [402] nonstationary time series, namely, the analysis of multivariate cointegration [Johansen (1988), Johansen (1989), Johansen and Juselius (1990)]. An important feature of the multivariate cointegration model is that it is based on a fully specified statistical model. This has the important advantage of using all information in the chosen data set, thereby increasing estimation efficiency. The explicit distinction between stationarity and nonstationarity provides a natural framework for the joint analysis of long- and short-run behavior. The information given by the nonstationarity in the data is used to derive the deviations from the underlying steady-states in each sector. The econometric approach is to analyze each sector separately and then use the derived disequilibrium states as the basic explanatory variables to consumer price inflation. This econometric procedure makes it possible to investigate complicated interactions of several markets in the determination of a single variable.

The sample period, 1974(1)–1987(3), is in many respects ideal for the investigation of the causes of inflation. The first part, 1974–1982, coincided with a long period of Social Democratic rule, and the second part, 1983–1987, with the present Conservative government. The latter announced as one of its main political objectives the lowering of the high inflation rate that had plagued the 1970s. Somewhat simplistically one can say that the economic policy pursued by the Social Democratic government was more influenced by Keynesian ideas, whereas the Conservative government showed an increasing political belief in the monetarist explanation of macro-economics. An important part of the latter school is the belief that excessive growth in the money supply is the main cause of price inflation. Thus the sample covers two different political regimes with different weights placed on inflation control. It also covers the effects of the two major oil price shocks in 1973 and 1979, and finally it covers a major change in the Danish economy in connection with the abolishment of foreign capital control in 1983. Thus we think that the data are informative enough to provide some answers about what have been the main causes of price inflation in Denmark.

The organization of the article is as follows. In Section 2 the economic background is briefly discussed. In Section 3 the analysis of cointegration is discussed in terms of the full information maximum likelihood procedure. In Section 4 long-run analysis is performed for three different systems of equations, describing first the labor sector, next the money sector, and finally the foreign sector. In Section 5 a structural model for the determination of the Danish inflation rate is estimated using the derived long-run results. Considerable attention is given to parameter parsimony and structural stability. The latter issue turns out to be of particular importance at the beginning [403] of 1983, when Denmark abandoned (most of) the control regulations for international capital movements, with resulting structural changes in some of the marginal processes. In Section 6 the main results are summarized.

2   Economic Background

Macro-economic theory suggests several alternative ways of approaching the problem of inflation. Basic concepts in this context are (1) the short-run Phillips curve, which basically describes short-run supply side effects usually associated with cost push, (2) the demand pressure curve, and (3) the long-run Phillips curve, which relates unemployment with wage and price inflation. The long-run effects are usually associated with demand pull effects when aggregate demand is above the full employment level.

The basic argument of the monetarist school is that the cause of inflation lies in excessive monetary growth, and thus that the desired inflation rate should be obtained by controlling the money supply. One important implication of the monetarist view is that the long-run Phillips curve is vertical at the natural rate of unemployment, and therefore that there are no offsetting gains between wage and price inflation and unemployment. Against this stands the belief that there is a negative association between wage inflation and unemployment, implying off-setting gains between these two.

In an open economy we have to add the external effects that influence the economy via changes in the balance of payments. The interesting question is through which transmission channels inflation is imported and how strongly it is transmitted. Here we will distinguish between the effects of disequilibrium in the goods and the capital markets.

The analysis of this article will account for all three effects. In this sense it is similar to the approach suggested by Surrey (1989), who investigated the determination of the U.K. inflation rate by distinguishing between the same kinds of explanations:

> (1) pure monetarist theories, in which expansions of the (appropriately defined) supply of money at a rate greater than warranted by the growth of real productive potential is a necessary

and sufficient condition for there to be inflation;

(2) internal theories, which may usefully be divided into (i) labor market theories and (ii) excess demand theories. The first of these two appeals to the notion of the wage, as the price of labour, influenced by excess demand/supply of labor reflected in unemployment and in turn forming the major part of unit costs. The second connotes pure excess demand inflation (in a closed economy) but may be difficult to distinguish in practice from the first;

[404]   (3) external theories, which can be split into (i) theories involving the transmission of inflation of import prices in foreign currency terms into general domestic inflation, and (ii) inflation following from depreciation of the exchange rate, which causes inflation of (home-currency) import costs independently of changes in foreign-currency price movements.

The way we approach the empirical problem, however, is different. Surrey analyzes the inflation effects using the differences of the variables (his differencing is motivated by the nonstationarity of the data), thereby losing all information in the data on long-run behavior. By contrast, we will use the nonstationarity property to derive what we believe are the crucial determinants to price inflation. Another difference compared with Surrey's approach is that each sector is analyzed as a system of interrelated equations; this has the important advantage of using all information in the chosen data set. Finally the explicit distinction between short- and long-run effects provides a richer picture of the dynamics of the complicated mechanisms generating the nominal growth in the economy. Since many diverging views of existing theories are in fact related to different assumptions on some key parameters, the values of which might be different depending on the interval over which the total impact is calculated, this distinction is probably crucial. Whether a certain policy measure in the end will decrease the inflation rate and/or aggregate real income is debatable, and more information on relative adjustment paths is very much needed.

3   The Analysis of Long-run Relations

In this section we discuss the basic concepts of the multivariate cointegration model and the way this approach facilitates the estimation and testing of economically interesting long-run relations. This is done by first estimating the cointegration space [Johansen and Juselius (1990)] and then testing more specific hypotheses of economic interest within this space [Johansen and Juselius (1992)].

As a first tentative description of the data generating process we will consider the vector autoregressive model with Gaussian errors

$$x_t = A_1 x_{t-1} + \cdots + A_k x_{t-k} + \mu + \psi D_t + \varepsilon_t, \qquad t = 1, \ldots, T, \qquad (1)$$

where x_t is a $p \times 1$ vector of stochastic variables, $x_{-k+1}, \ldots, x_0$ are fixed, $\varepsilon_1, \ldots, \varepsilon_T$ are $\mathsf{NIID}_p(0, \Sigma)$, and D_t are centered seasonal dummies. If the stochastic specification is found to be data-consistent, model (1) can be considered a first approximation to the unknown data generating process. Thus it provides a basic statistical model within which economically interesting [405] questions can be asked and tested. By reparameterizing (1) in the error correction form, we can directly distinguish between the effects related to the short- and long-run variation in the data:

$$\Delta x_t = \Gamma_1 \Delta x_{t-1} + \cdots + \Gamma_{k-1} \Delta x_{t-k+1} + \Pi x_{t-k} + \mu + \psi D_t + \varepsilon_t,$$
$$t = 1, \ldots, T. \qquad (2)$$

The model specification (2) describes a generally formulated reduced-form model in which the short-run dynamics, given by $\Gamma_1, \ldots, \Gamma_{k-1}$, are likely to be heavily over-parameterized. Therefore, the estimates of these matrices are usually not very interesting as such but serve the purpose of correcting for the variation in x_t related to the short run. This is actually quite important, since a satisfactory description of the short-run variation is often needed for efficient inference on the long-run structure. Kremers, Ericsson, and Dolado (1992) have shown that this is particularly so when the short-run effects are essentially different from the long-run effects.

Assuming that x_t is $\mathsf{I}(1)$, then (2) contains a mixture of stationary and nonstationary components. To resolve this problem we need the hypothesis of reduced rank of the Π matrix:

$$H_0 : \Pi = \alpha \beta', \qquad (3)$$

where α and β are $p \times r$ matrices. The likelihood ratio test for the determination of the rank r is discussed in Johansen (1992b). In general, tests of the hypothesis $r \leq q$ use the likelihood ratio test statistics:

$$Q_r = -T \sum_{i=q+1}^{p} \ln(1 - \hat{\lambda}_i). \qquad (4)$$

The distribution of the test statistic, which is a nonstandard multivariate Dickey-Fuller type distribution, has been tabulated by simulation for the asymptotic case in Johansen and Juselius (1990).

Given the rank r, the process Δx_t is stationary, x_t is nonstationary, and $\beta' x_t$ is stationary. The last property gives the reason why we can interpret the relations $\beta' x_t$ as potential candidates for economic long-run relations. To be interesting, however, the linear weights should be interpretable in terms of economically interesting parameters. This requirement is not necessarily fulfilled for the estimated vectors $\beta_i' x_t$, which are based on the chosen normalization $\beta' S_{kk} \beta = I$, where S_{kk} is the conditional covariance matrix of x_t [see Johansen and Juselius (1990) for further details]. The testing of structural hypotheses is, therefore, a very crucial part of the analysis, in particular when there is more than one cointegrating vector. In that case, [406] only the cointegration space is uniquely determined, but not the individual vectors [see Johansen and Juselius (1992)].

The structural hypotheses are formulated as tests about the cointegration space. This means that we can ask questions whether some hypothetical relations can be assumed to lie in the stationary part of the space spanned by the nonstationary variables. In an economic sense this usually implies testing whether the deviations from a hypothetical underlying steady state are stationary. This type of hypothesis usually has been tested by some of the univariate Dickey-Fuller type procedures. Note, however, that the testing here will be done in the multivariate framework. Since a multivariate model is likely to give substantially lower residual variance than a univariate model, these tests are likely to be more efficient than the corresponding univariate tests. Note also that our tests are fundamentally different from the corresponding univariate tests by formulating the null of stationarity instead of nonstationarity. Intuitively one would expect an economically well-founded relation to hold in the long run. Therefore, it seems more reasonable to choose stationarity as the null hypothesis.

To summarize, the formulation (2) with the hypothesis of cointegration (3) allows the precise formulation of a number of interesting economic hypotheses on the long-run behavior in such a way that they can be tested in a well-defined statistical framework.

However, a drawback of the analysis of the multivariate cointegration model in the present stage is that the difficulties of interpreting the cointegration space grow when more variables are added to the vector autoregressive (VAR) system. In practice, it may be advisable to start by choosing only the most basic variables assumed to be relevant to the phenomenon of interest and then investigate the dynamic structure between these variables. This can be related to a discussion in Haavelmo (1944, p. 22) about the question of simplicity in the formulation of economic laws:

> However, both types of relations (i.e. causal relationships versus relations of the mutual dependence type) have, I think their place in economic theory; and moreover they are not necessarily opposed to each other, because a system of relations of the mutual dependence type for the economy *as a whole* may be built up from *open* systems of causal relations within the various *sectors*

of the economy. ... Our hope ... is that it may be possible to establish constant and relatively *simple* relations between dependent variables, y, and a relatively *small* number of independent variables, x. [italics in original]

An advantage of taking a statistically well-defined model such as (2) as a starting point is that it provides a framework within which the validity of structurally more interesting models can be tested, for instance, by means of the concept of encompassing [Hendry and Mizon (1993)]. Restrictions imposed on the short- and long-run parameters should be data-consistent with the general model; adding more information to the empirical analysis should imply variance encompassing [Hendry (1988)]; conditioning on some of the marginal processes should be associated with weak exogeneity requirements [Engle, Hendry, and Richard (1983); Johansen (1992a)]; and so on.

[407]

In the following empirical analysis we will demonstrate the practical value of the concepts discussed previously in an analysis of domestic and foreign effects on price inflation.

4   The Analysis of the Long-run Structure

In this section we will investigate the long-run structure of the data in terms of stationary cointegration relations, which will be interpreted as deviations from steady-state relations.[1] The purpose is to find out how disequilibria in the domestic labor sector, monetary sector, and foreign sector affect the rate of inflation as measured by the official price index. The procedure is illustrated in Figure 1.

4.1   The Analysis of Wage Inflation

Domestic wage inflation is usually related to the notion of excess demand in the economy. That is, when aggregate demand is above the full employment level, nominal wages are correspondingly bid up. Though "excess demand" is theoretically well defined, its empirical counterpart is not easily established. Before the stagflation period in the seventies, the unemployment rate was often considered a reasonable proxy for excess demand. Recent experiences have clearly indicated that this is not a good choice. The utilization rate has also been suggested, although the measurement of this variable has often proved problematic. The basic objective of this subsection is to identify a stable long-run wage relation by means of the concept of cointegration and then to use the deviations from this relation as a measure of excess demand pressure in the economy. If nominal wages are above the steady-state level, one would expect a corresponding upward pressure on prices.

---

[1] The calculations have been performed by the computer package CATS in RATS [Juselius (1991b)].

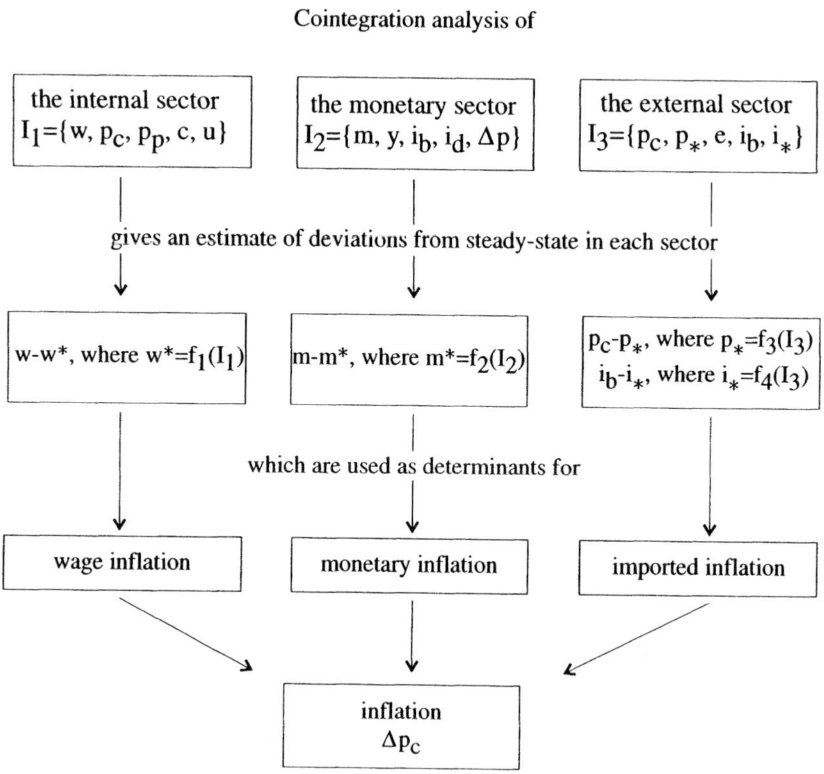

Cointegration analysis of

| the internal sector $I_1=\{w, p_c, p_p, c, u\}$ | the monetary sector $I_2=\{m, y, i_b, i_d, \Delta p\}$ | the external sector $I_3=\{p_c, p_*, e, i_b, i_*\}$ |

gives an estimate of deviations from steady-state in each sector

| $w-w^*$, where $w^*=f_1(I_1)$ | $m-m^*$, where $m^*=f_2(I_2)$ | p_c-p_*, where $p_*=f_3(I_3)$ i_b-i_*, where $i_*=f_4(I_3)$ |

which are used as determinants for

| wage inflation | monetary inflation | imported inflation |

| inflation Δp_c |

FIGURE 1. The basic scheme for the empirical analysis.

In general, we assume that the interplay between demand and supply for labor determines the level of the long-run real wage but that in the short run [408] the actual outcome has to be related to the specific type of collective wage bargaining situation of the Danish labor market. See, for instance, Andersen and Risager (1990) for a recent analysis of a wage-bargaining model for Denmark. We expect producers to follow mark-up pricing, implying that nominal wage claims above the productivity level are passed through to prices. For the labor unions we expect the long-run acceptable nominal wage W_t to be related to the level of consumer price costs P_{ct}, the level of productivity C_t, and the level of unemployment U_t, whereas the affordable wage of the producers is related to the level of producer cost prices P_{pt} and the productivity level. The choice of observed variables reflects a desire to keep the system manageable: only the most important variables expected to determine the long-run wage relation are considered in the first stage. The

TABLE 1.

The Cointegration Analysis of the Domestic Labor Market
for the Sample Period 1974(1)–1987(3)

$\hat{\lambda}_i$	0.566	0.498	0.381	0.201	0.091
Q_r	123.10	78.93	42.39	16.96	5.05
95% critical value	69.98	48.41	31.26	17.84	8.08

TABLE 2.

Estimated Cointegration Vectors and Corresponding Weights

	$\hat{\beta}_1$	$\hat{\beta}_2$	$\hat{\beta}_3$	$\hat{\alpha}_1$	$\hat{\alpha}_2$	$\hat{\alpha}_3$
w	−0.24	−0.01	1.00	−0.23	−0.03	−0.04
p_c	0.00	1.00	−1.16	−0.17	0.06	0.06
p_p	0.15	−1.41	0.06	−0.05	0.04	−0.10
c	1.00	1.74	−0.37	−0.61	−0.14	0.06
u	−0.43	−3.36	2.58	−0.04	0.03	−0.03

cointegration results in Tables 1 and 2 are based on a vector autoregression of the observed variables $z'_t = [w_t, p_{ct}, p_{pt}, c_t, u_t]$, where lower-case letters indicate logarithms. Since there have been several exogenous shocks to the price level during the sample period, there is also a need to include some dummy variables to account for the corresponding short-run effects. The [409] most important of these shocks are three increases in the value added tax rate, four periods of price control, two cases of special commodity taxes, and one year when the value added tax was partly abolished.[2]

The final VAR model had a lag order $k = 2$, a constant term, seasonal dummies, and four intervention dummies. The appropriateness of this specification was tested with the Box-Pierce test for residual autocorrelation, the

---

[2] These interventions have been accounted for by including the following four dummy variables, $Dvat$, $Dprstop$, $Dcotax$, and $D75(4)$, defined in the Appendix. If these interventions are not properly accounted for, they strongly affect the residual variance of the model and thus make inference less efficient. Actually, with inclusion of the dummy variables the residual standard deviation decreased substantially, and not only in the price equation, as can be seen from the comparison of the estimated residual standard deviations:

	Δw	Δp_c	Δp_p	Δc	Δu
Without dummies	0.0063	0.0085	0.0131	0.0178	0.0029
With dummies	0.0061	0.0052	0.0124	0.0166	0.0024

Jarque-Bera test for normality, and the ARCH test for homoscedasticity.
Generally the tests indicated that this model specification was a satisfactory
approximation to the unknown data generation process (DGP). Only in the
nominal wage equation was there some indication of residual autocorrelation.
Because the residual autocorrelations disappeared when the first year, 1974,
was omitted from the sample, it seems plausible that this is related to the
huge fluctuations after the first oil crisis. The likelihood ratio test statistic
(4) for the determination of the cointegration rank is given in Table 1; in
light of those results, we chose the rank to be equal to 3. This implies three
stationary relations, the estimates of which are given in Table 2, together
with the corresponding weights. An investigation of the individual α and β
vectors shows that a direct interpretation is not straightforward. The reason
for this was briefly discussed in Section 3. Nevertheless, heuristically the first
β vector is primarily reflecting a positive relationship between productivity
and unemployment, suggesting that producers react by firing the less productive part of the work force when facing too high prices or, alternatively,
[410]   too low productivity. The second cointegration vector seems to suggest a
positive association between the unemployment rate and the wedge between
consumer and producer prices, consistent with the previous interpretation.
The third vector suggests a real consumer wages relation with negative unemployment effects.

This raises a number of testable questions. Is real consumer wage around
the productivity trend stationary and/or is the profit share stationary? If
the answer is negative, we can ask whether a linear combination of real
consumer wage and unemployment rate and/or of profit share and price
wedge is stationary. To give a visual impression of this, we have drawn the
graphs of real consumer wage around productivity trend w_c and the profit
share w_p in Figure 2a, and the wedge between consumer prices and producer
prices $p_c - p_p$ and the unemployment rate u in Figure 2b.

The difference between the relative growth paths of the real consumer and
producer wages in the seventies and the eighties is quite striking. Also, in
the former period consumer prices seem to have grown relatively more than
producer prices, whereas in the eighties they grow at similar rates. Looking
at the unemployment rate, it is obvious that the general unemployment level
is lower in the seventies than in the eighties; the question arises whether
this is related to the relative decline in producer prices. It seems likely
that producers have reduced the level of producer prices by firing the least
productive part of the labor force, thereby increasing productivity but at
the cost of increasing unemployment. This can be investigated by asking
whether the growth in the price wedge is compensated by the growth in the
unemployment rate such that a linear combination between them becomes
stationary. In particular we will investigate whether real wages around the

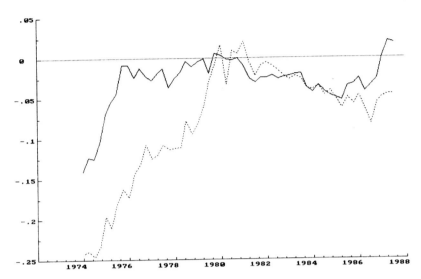

FIGURE 2a.   Consumer wages w_c (—) and producer wages w_p (···).

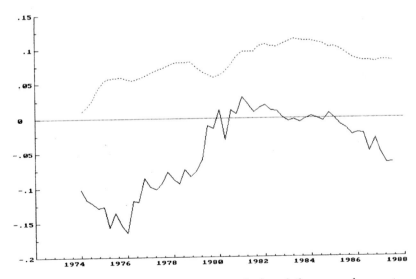

FIGURE 2b. The price wedge $p_c - p_p$ (—) and the unemployment rate u (···).

TABLE 3. Testing Various Structural Hypotheses

Hypothesis	Likelihood ratio (df)	p
$H^1 : (1, 0, -1, -1, 0) \in Sp(\beta)$	8.32 (2)	0.016
$H^2 : (1, -1, 0, -1, 0) \in Sp(\beta)$	10.02 (2)	0.007
$H^3 : (0, 0, 0, 0, 1) \in Sp(\beta)$	9.32 (2)	0.009
$H^4 : (1, -1, 0, -1, a) \in Sp(\beta)$	2.26 (1)	0.132
$H^5 : (1, -1, 0, 0, b) \in Sp(\beta)$	7.01 (1)	0.019
$H^6 : (1, -c, -(1 - c), -1, \ 0) \in Sp(\beta)$	2.87 (1)	0.090
$H^7 : (0, 1, -1, 0, d) \in Sp(\beta)$	4.27 (1)	0.038

productivity trend and the unemployment rate are stationary processes and, if stationarity is rejected, whether they cointegrate or not. The hypotheses and the test outcomes are given in Table 3.

The first hypothesis is about the stationarity of the profit share (H^1), followed by the stationarity of real consumer wages (H^2) and the unemployment rate (H^3), respectively. The likelihood ratio tests, which are asymptotically distributed as χ^2 with the appropriate degrees of freedom given in parentheses, indicate that stationarity has to be rejected for all three cases. [411]

The hypothesis H^4 is concerned with the question whether real consumer wage around the productivity trend cointegrates with the unemployment rate. The hypothesis H^5 is testing whether real consumer wage cointegrates with the unemployment rate as such. This is motivated by the fact that the productivity variable, being measured as output per worker hour, has been strongly affected by the level of unemployment at least during this sample period. The hypothesis H^6 tests whether the profit share cointegrates with price wedge, and the last hypothesis investigates whether the price wedge cointegrates with the unemployment rate as suggested by the second cointegration vector. Of these hypotheses H^4 can be accepted with a p value of 0.132 and an estimate of $a = 1.69$. This result implies that nominal wages follow consumer price index, wage earners get their share of the productivity growth, and the level of unemployment has a negative effect on nominal wage claims. Since the coefficients are plausible, we choose $w = p + c - 1.69u$ as an acceptable long-run wage equation. Altogether the empirical analysis gives some evidence against the monetarist assumption of a vertical long-run Phillips curve. Hypothesis H^6 can also be accepted with $c = 0.43$, indicating that the profit share cointegrates with the price wedge. Combining this result with the evidence that the price wedge and the unemployment rate show similar developments, one can conclude that an acceptable profit share [412]

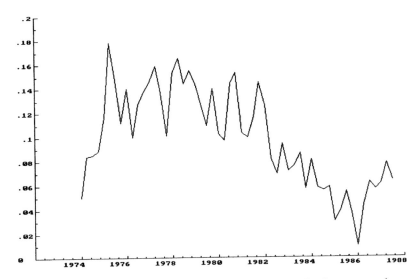

FIGURE 3. Deviations of nominal wages from the long-run relation, $ecm(w)$.

is maintained at the cost of increased unemployment. This, on the other hand, tends to put a damper on further nominal wage claims, thus giving some support to the assumption that demand and supply forces have a role to play in the labor market.

The steady-state deviations are graphed in Figure 3. In the beginning of the period one can see the influence of the first oil crisis when nominal wages were below the steady-state level as determined by nominal consumer prices. From about 1983 the nominal wages relative to the steady-state values exhibit a downward-sloping development, which turns upwards only in the last year of the sample. In Section 5 we will investigate how the deviations from this estimated long-run wage relation affects consumer prices under the a priori hypothesis that positive deviations increase price inflation.

4.2 The Analysis of Monetary Inflation   [413]

We will now analyze the effect on prices associated with an inflationary monetary policy. Related to this is the question of monetary growth in excess of the growth in real productive factors and the way this affects the inflation rate. It is crucial in this context to identify a long-run aggregate demand-for-money relation and estimate the parameters of this relation. This analysis has been extensively discussed in Juselius (1994); therefore, we only repro-

174   Katarina Juselius

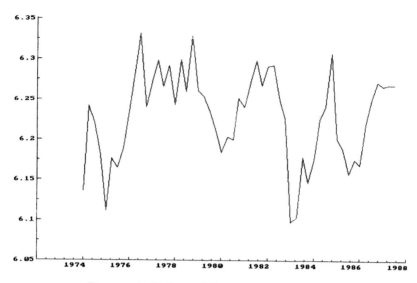

FIGURE 4. Estimated "excess money", $ecm(m)$.

duce some of the main results needed for this article. From estimating a
five-dimensional vector autoregression of the vector $z' = (m, y, i_b, i_d, \Delta p)$,
the following long-run demand was found: $m^* = y - 4.7i_b + 3.4i_d$, where m is
real money holdings, y is real domestic demand, i_b is the Danish bond rate,
and i_d is the Danish deposit rate. The long-run money demand is strongly
interest-elastic, a result that is more in line with a Keynesian interpretation.
From the analysis of the adjustment coefficients $\hat{\alpha}_{ij}$, it was found that excess
money, defined as $m_t - m_t^*$, had an important impact on the changes in real
money holdings, possibly some weak impact on the bond rate, but no impact
on the inflation rate as measured by the changes in the implicit price deflator
for domestic demand. The latter observation was quite surprising, considering the crucial role in macro-economics of the assumption of inflationary
expectations associated with exogenous changes in money stock. In Section 5 we will investigate this further on a more extensive information set. It
[414] is still possible that excess money can be found to be statistically significant
for the inflation rate when we account for a larger set of ceteris paribus assumptions by including determinants from the internal and external sectors,
respectively.

The graph of $m_t - m_t^*$ is given in Figure 4. The economy seems to have
been below the steady-state level of money holdings at the beginning and
end of the sample. The drastic fall in excess money at about 1983 can
be explained by the huge drop in the Danish bond rate, which accordingly

resulted in a higher level of desired money holdings.

4.3   The Analysis of Imported Inflation

As mentioned in the Introduction, the external theories of the inflation rate
can be split into theories involving the transmission from input prices in foreign currency and inflation following from depreciation of the exchange rate.
In this section we are mainly interested in a combination of the two questions, namely whether there is a long-run tendency for the Danish prices to
follow the foreign prices measured in a common currency. This is essentially
the question whether the purchasing power parity holds in the long run or
equivalently whether the real exchange rate is stationary. If this is the case,
Danish prices are affected by changes in the exchange rate as well as changes
in foreign prices, and the next question is whether the adjustment is primarily in exchange rates or in prices. For the sample period under investigation,
Denmark was a member of the "exchange snake" and later a member of [415]
the European Monetary System (EMS), which replaced the snake. In this
system, the exchange rates have been restricted to move within the ranges
specified by the rules of the EMS, except when explicitly agreed otherwise.
In a sense this regime is a mixture of the pure floating and fixed exchange
rates. Therefore, one would expect to find some tendency of prices to adjust
when the purchasing power parity is violated.

Since the determination of exchange rates can be assumed to take place
in both the goods and the capital markets, we need to account for the interaction between them to understand the external effects on prices. It is,
therefore, crucial to start with an information set that can describe the joint
determination in both markets. This is reflected in the fact that both prices
and interest rates are included in the vector $z'_t = (p_c, p_*, e, i_b, i_*)_t$, where p_c
is the Danish consumer price index, i_b is the Danish bond rate, a subscript
"*" indicates Germany, and e is the exchange rate between Denmark and
Germany. We have chosen Germany to represent the foreign influence since
it is by far the most important trading country for Denmark.

The empirical results of the cointegration analysis is described in more
detail in Juselius (1991a), and we reproduce only the main results here. We
found that the deviation from purchasing power parity ppp $(= p_c - p_* - e)$
was stationary, although with a very slow mean reversion, consistent with the
assumption of costly arbitrage in the goods market. Including the interest
rates in the long-run relation increased the mean reversion rate considerably,
indicating that the interaction between the goods and the asset markets
is indeed important. We also found that the adjustment primarily took
place in the exchange rates rather than in the prices, consistent with the
notion of sticky nominal prices. The interest rate differential was found to be
stationary, and the interaction between the asset and the goods markets was

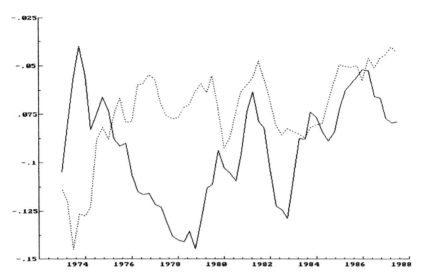

FIGURE 5.   The negative of the interest rate differential $-(i_b - i_*)$ (—), and deviations from purchasing power parity $ecm(ppp)$ ($\cdots$).

strongly supported by the data. To illustrate this we have drawn the graphs of the real exchange rate and the negative of the interest rate differential in Figure 5.

5   The Analysis of the Short-run Structure

In this section we turn to a more careful analysis of the short-run effects, with the purpose of imposing more economic structure and at the same [416]   time obtaining parsimony.[3] The procedure we have followed is to start with the conditional expectation of current inflation given two information sets, $E(\Delta p_{ct}|I_a, I_b)$:

$$I_a = \{ecm(w)_{t-1}, \ ecm(m)_{t-1}, \ ecm(ppp)_{t-1}, \ (i_b - i_*)_{t-1}\}$$

$$I_b = \{\Delta p_{ct-1}, \ \Delta p_{*t-j}, \ \Delta i_{bt-j}, \ \Delta i_{*t-j}, \ \Delta e_{t-j}, \ \Delta w_{t-j}, \ \Delta c_{t-j},$$
$$u_{t-j}, \ \Delta e_{\$t}, \ D_t; \ j = 0, 1\}.$$

I_a is assumed to contain the basic variables of interest in the form of deviations from long-run steady-state relations derived in the sectoral cointe-

---

[3] The calculations were performed by the computer package PC-GIVE Version 6.0 [Hendry (1989)].

TABLE 4. The Estimates of the Preferred Model
for the Sample Period 1974(3)–1987(3)

$$
\widehat{\Delta p_{ct}} = \underset{(0.12)}{0.51} \ \Delta p_{*t} + \underset{(0.08)}{0.27} \ \Delta i_{*t-1} + \underset{(0.07)}{0.10} \ \Delta w_{t-1}
$$

$$
- \underset{(0.03)}{0.18} \ ecm(ppp)_{t-1} + \underset{(0.01)}{0.07} \ ecm(m)_{t-1}
$$

$$
- \underset{(0.03)}{0.11} \ ecm(uip)_{t-1} + \underset{(0.02)}{0.04} \ ecm(w)_{t-1}
$$

$$
+ \underset{(0.002)}{0.010} + \underset{(0.003)}{0.021} \ Dcotax_t
$$

$$
+ \underset{(0.001)}{0.006} \ Dvat_t - \underset{(0.003)}{0.005} \ Dprstop_t + \underset{(0.004)}{0.022} \ D75(4)_t
$$

$R^2 = 0.88$	$\sigma_\varepsilon = 0.0043$	$\eta_1(4) = 3.61$
$\eta_2(4, 37) = 0.68$	$ARCH_1(4) = 1.8$	$ARCH_2(4, 34) = 0.58$
$Norm(2) = 0.58$	$Hetero(20, 20) = 0.90$	$RESET(1, 41) = 2.33$

η_1 and η_2 are Lagrange multiplier tests for autocorrelation distributed as $\chi^2(f)$ and $F(f_1, f_2)$, respectively. $ARCH_1$ and $ARCH_2$ are tests for autoregressive conditional heteroscedasticity distributed as $\chi^2(f)$ and $F(f_1, f_2)$, respectively. $Norm$ is the Jarque-Bera test for normality distributed as $\chi^2(2)$, and $RESET$ is the first-order test statistic for heteroscedasticity suggested by Ramsey (1969) distributed as $F(1, f_1)$. See, for instance, Hendry (1989) for a more extended discussion.

Omitted variables F tests $F(1, 40)$ for adding:

$D83(1) = 0.28 \ (0.60) \qquad \Delta i_{bt} = 0.03 \ (0.85) \qquad \Delta e_{\$t} = 2.72 \ (0.11)$

$\Delta c_{t-1} = 0.06 \ (0.81) \qquad \Delta u_{t-1} = 0.25 \ (0.61) \qquad \Delta m_{t-1} = 0.03 \ (0.85).$

gration analyses, and I_b is a broadly defined set of possible determinants to the short-run variations in the inflation rate. D_t is a vector of the four intervention dummies, $Dvat$, $Dprstop$, $Dcotax$, and $D75(4)$. All variables are described in the Appendix. As a first step, the inflation rate was regressed on the variables in I_a and I_b. This gives us a very broadly specified model within which parameter restrictions, mostly zero restrictions, can be tested.

In simplifying, the coefficients on Δe_t and $(i_b - i_*)_{t-1}$ became almost equal with opposite sign. Thus changes in German exchange rates seem to affect the domestic price inflation only to the extent that these changes exceed the interest rate parity. As a consequence, we introduced the restricted variable $ecm(uip)_{t-1} = (i_b - i_*)_{t-1} - \Delta e_t$, that is, the deviation of the lagged uncovered interest rate parity when the expected change in interest rates is replaced by the actual change. The graph of this variable is given in Figure 6 and our

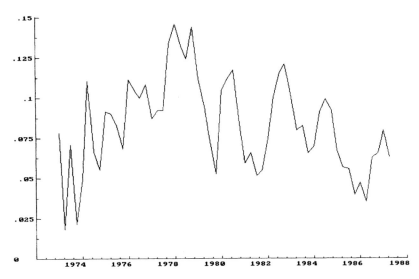

FIGURE 6.   Deviations from uncovered interest rate parity,
ecm(uip).

final (parsimonious) specification is in Table 4.

[417]   The model estimates appear constant when recursively estimated over 1981(3)–1987(3); see the graphs in Figures 7a–7f, which plot the recursive estimates (—) and the estimates plus-or-minus twice their recursively estimated standard errors (···).[4] This is a very strong empirical result against the Lucas critique, which in short claims that conditional behavioral models cannot have constant parameters in an economy subject to policy changes and with agents having forward-looking expectations. Favero and Hendry
[418] (1992) have shown that if the conditional (feedback) model has constant parameters while the marginal model(s) have nonconstant parameters, then the forward-looking expectations hypothesis cannot be true. They conclude, "a high degree of constancy in a contingent plan equation is required to claim an inconsistency with the joint existence of an expectations interpretation and nonconstant expectations formation process".

---

[4] *Editors' note*: Owing to program limitations, PC-GIVE 6.0 restricts recursive estimation to equations with no more than ten regressors. The equation in Table 4 has twelve, so some regression coefficients were set to their full-sample values when Figures 7a–7f were produced for initial publication in the *Journal of Policy Modeling*. PcGive 8.0, which was used to reproduce these graphs for this volume, does not have such a stringent limitation, so all coefficients were estimated recursively. The original figures differ from their reproductions only slightly.

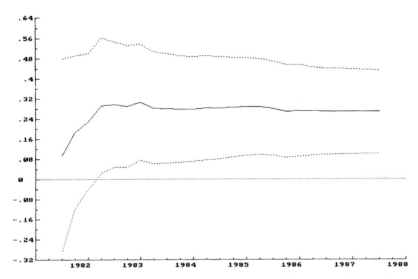

FIGURE 7a. Recursive estimates of the coefficient on Δi_{*t-1} in the preferred model.

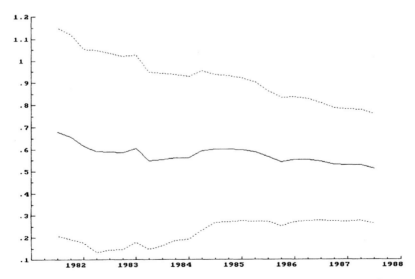

FIGURE 7b. Recursive estimates of the coefficient on Δp_{*t} in the preferred model.

Katarina Juselius

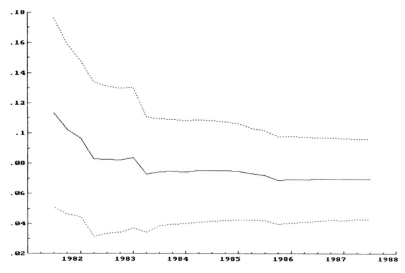

FIGURE 7c. Recursive estimates of the coefficient on $ecm(m)_{t-1}$ in the preferred model.

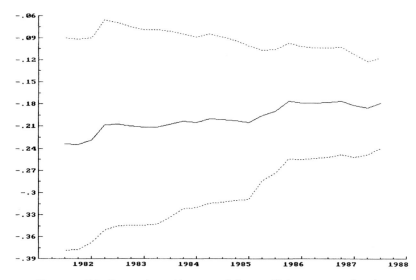

FIGURE 7d. Recursive estimates of the coefficient on $ecm(ppp)_{t-1}$ in the preferred model.

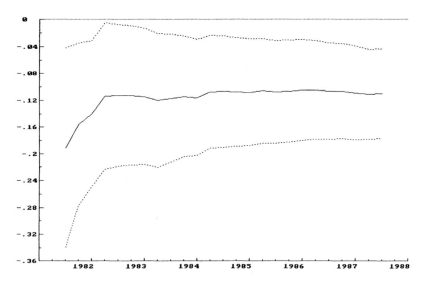

FIGURE 7e. Recursive estimates of the coefficient on $ecm(uip)_{t-1}$ in the preferred model.

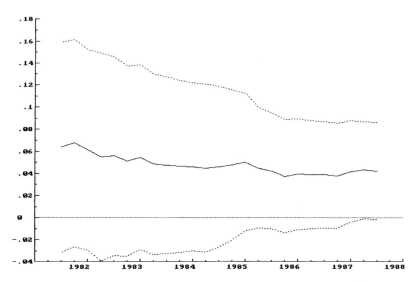

FIGURE 7f. Recursive estimates of the coefficient on $ecm(w)_{t-1}$ in the preferred model.

In our case, the parameters of the marginal model for Δe were clearly non-constant, especially in connection with the abolishment of the capital control at about 1983, when some of the parameters exhibited substantial changes [see Juselius (1992) for further details on the empirical results]. Therefore, our data provide a powerful design for testing the relevance of feedback versus feedforward models to describe the aggregate price-setting behavior of the Danish economy. The conclusion is that they strongly support a feedback model. Also, the model in Table 4 is nonconstant if $ecm(w)_{t-1}$ and Δe_t are deleted, illustrating the important association between "correct specification" and parameter stability.

In terms of diagnostic test statistics, the estimated model performs satisfactorily. There is no indication of residual autocorrelation; the normality and homoscedasticity of the residuals are clearly accepted. The estimated standard error of regression is very low indeed, 0.0043, meaning that within the sample, the model explains the changes in price inflation very precisely, considering the substantial fluctuations in the sample, in particular those related to the two oil crises and the two political regimes. This is illustrated by the graphs of actual and fitted inflation rates and the residuals in Figure 8a and 8b.

Omitted variable F tests are given at the bottom of the table for some of the more interesting variables. To increase readability, these are only given for single variables. Joint tests have been performed, and do not change any of the results qualitatively.

The estimated coefficients are generally highly significant; and the coefficients have the "right" expected sign, with the exception of the coefficient on Δi_{*t-1}, which is $+0.27$. Also, a priori, one would have expected the inflation rate to be positively correlated with changes in the Danish interest rate instead of the German rate. However, as can be inferred from the insignificant F test in Table 4, the change in the Danish bond rate had no explanatory power. If we assume that the producers follow markup pricing and that the interest rate measures the cost of capital, we can interpret the result as an indication of how strongly the Danish industry has used the German capital market for loan taking. Another noteworthy observation is [422] that the estimated coefficient on the German inflation is very large: about half of German inflation feeds into Danish inflation within a quarter.

It is quite interesting to investigate the external transmission effects as a result of being out of equilibrium in the goods and the capital markets. The first effect is estimated by the speed of adjustment coefficient to the long-run purchasing power parity between Denmark and Germany. The estimate of this turned out to be -0.18, which seems to indicate that prices do adjust, contrary to the hypothesis of nominal price stickiness. Considering the restrictions implied by the snake and later by the EMS, this outcome is

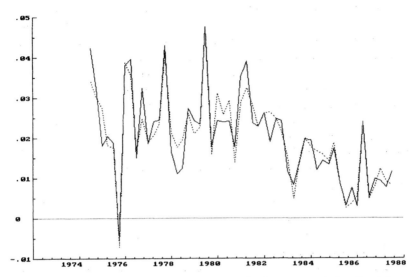

FIGURE 8a. Actual (—) and fitted (···) values of the Danish inflation rate.

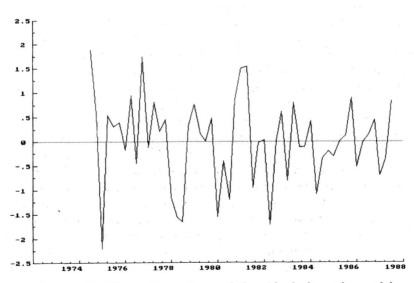

FIGURE 8b. The corrsponding scaled residuals from the model of the Danish inflation rate.

not unreasonable. The second effect is related to disequilibria in the capital market and measured by the deviation of the lagged interest rate differential $(i_b - i_*)_{t-1}$ from Δe_t, the coefficient of which is estimated as -0.11 and is highly significant. It is also interesting to notice that prices seem to adjust in a backward looking manner to this determinant.

Among the domestic labor variables, prices adjust to lagged nominal wages with a coefficient of 0.10, which is not even significant at standard significance levels. The deviations of nominal wages from the steady-state wage relation have a small, 0.04, but significant effect on price inflation. This gives some empirical support to the hypothesis that producers pass nominal wage claims above productivity growth through to prices. Taken together, these results indicate that the domestic part of Danish cost push inflation is not very dominant.

The effect of excess money is positive as expected with a small, 0.07, but highly significant coefficient. This is contrary to the results in Juselius (1994) but can easily be explained: the latter analysis was based on a smaller information set and consequently on a different set of conditioning variables. It illustrates how the economic interpretation of the estimated coefficients is generally not invariant to different sets of conditioning variables.

The effect of the various interventions are described by the estimated coefficients of the dummy variables. The *Dvat* variable has a coefficient that indicates that approximately 60 percent of an increase in the value added tax (VAT) transmits to consumer prices. The price control variable has a coefficient of -0.005, indicating that the effect of imposing price control has been an average decrease in prices of 0.5 percent. The imposed commodity taxes raised the computed price index by an average of 2.2 percent.

Interestingly, the F test for inclusion of the dummy variable $D83(1)$ gave a completely insignificant result, meaning that there is no additional so-called Schlüter (the prime minister of the Conservative government) effect [424] on the inflation rate. This is quite remarkable, considering the substantial decrease in the level of the inflation rate during the period from 1983 onward (compare Figure 8). As mentioned, this coincides with the year when the Conservative government took over after a long era of Social Democratic governments. The change of political government also meant a change in economic policy more in the direction of the monetarist school. Therefore, one can argue that testing the null hypothesis of no shift in the level of the inflation rate from 1983 to the end of the sample is actually a strong test of the economic relevance of the included determinants in our model. Since the null was clearly accepted, we consider this result additional support for the interpretation that the preferred model is structurally robust as a behavioral model and therefore can be considered as a candidate for policy simulations, independent of the political regime.

Finally, the estimate of the constant term is highly significant and the quarterly estimate of 0.010 indicates that on a yearly basis the Danish inflation rate has grown with an additional four percent, after all other effects have been accounted for. One likely explanation for this extra national inflation is the fact that backward-looking behavior in a linear growth model implies that the target is never reached [see Nickell (1985)]. Since there is strong linear growth in the nominal variables of our model, the Nickell result would predict a gap between the actual inflation and the target inflation, related to the magnitude of the linear growth in this sector. Another possible explanation is that excess domestic demand, which we have not been able to estimate so far, is an important omitted determinant for consumer price inflation. Against the latter explanation is the fact that excess domestic demand can hardly be approximated by a constant term. Therefore, we find the first explanation more plausible. If it is true, it certainly would have some important policy implications.

To conclude, external effects dominate the determination of consumer price inflation. This is clearly quite interesting from a policy point of view, since Denmark is the only Scandinavian member of the European Economic Community (EEC) and consequently can be assumed to be more directly influenced by the price development within these countries, of which Germany is probably the most influential. Another important result is the rather high "autonomous" part of the Danish consumer price inflation accounted for by the constant term of the model.

6 Summary

The domestic price determination in Denmark was investigated in terms of three kinds of macro-economic explanations: (1) internal labor market [425] theories describing domestic wage setting and the relation between price and wage inflation, (2) pure monetarist theories describing the effect of excess money on the inflation rate, and (3) external theories describing the foreign transmission effects on a small open economy. The sample included two different political regimes with different political weights on inflation control, the effects of the two major oil price shocks in 1973 and 1979, and the abolishment of foreign capital controls in 1983.

In the empirical analysis, we used recent contributions in cointegration analysis, which provide a natural framework for the joint analysis of long- and short-run behavior. The long-run behavior of each sector was analyzed in a system of interrelated equations, and the deviations from the estimated steady-state relations were included as determinants in the final structural model for the inflation rate.

In the long-run analysis of the domestic labor market, we tested various hypotheses in a three-dimensional cointegration space. The stationarity of the real wage around the productivity trend was rejected, as was the stationarity of the unemployment rate, whereas the hypothesis that these two cointegrate was accepted. The estimated vector was interpreted as a long-run wage relation in which nominal wages follow consumer prices and productivity growth, with offsetting unemployment effects. We found some empirical evidence that producers pass nominal wage claims above productivity changes through to prices, although the effects of wage inflation on price inflation were generally small. The question whether excess money affects price inflation, when excess money is measured as a stationary cointegration relation among real money stock, aggregate domestic demand, the bond rate, and the deposit interest rate, was investigated jointly with the determinants for wage inflation and imported inflation. Excess money seems to have an effect, but only a marginal one compared with the other effects.

In the external sector, the stationarity of the real exchange rate and the interest rate differential was investigated in a system of Danish and German prices, exchange rates, and interest rates. The result gave empirical support for purchasing power parity between the countries as well as for interest rate parity. These results were used to investigate the external transmission effects on price inflation as a result of being out of equilibrium in the goods and capital markets. We found that both prices and exchange rates adjust to deviations from the purchasing power parity but that the direct effect on prices from changes in exchange rates is transmitted via deviations from the lagged uncovered interest rate parity. The empirical results strongly favored [426] a backward-looking behavioral model when the alternative hypothesis is a model based on forward-looking expectations.

Another important result was the rather high "autonomous" part of the Danish consumer price inflation, which was interpreted to be the result of the backward-looking adjustment behavior implied by the model.

Since the estimates for the preferred model suggest that the domestic influence on the consumer price level is modest compared to the external influence, it would be of some interest to analyze the pattern of common stochastic (and deterministic) trends in the external sector. Such an analysis was performed in Juselius (1991a), where it was found that the German price variable seemed to play the role of the main driving force in this five-dimensional system. This is an observation consistent with the findings in Surrey (1989), suggesting that commodity prices within the industrial countries are basically determined by some common international commodity price level. Considering the dominant role of Germany within the EEC, it seems reasonable to assume that German commodity prices are indicative in a broader context of the European price level.

Appendix.   Definitions of the Variables

The Domestic Labor Sector

w_t	log of the nominal wage/hour in manufacturing
p_{ct}	log of the consumer price index
p_{pt}	log of the producer price index
c_t	Index measuring productivity as the log of output/hour in private industry
u_t	log of the unemployment rate
$ecm(w)_t$	$w_t - p_{ct} - c_t + 1.69u_t$
$Dvat_t$	3.0 for $t = 1977(4)$
	2.25 for $t = 1978(4)$
	1.75 for $t = 1980(3)$
	0 otherwise
$Dprstop_t$	1 for $t = 1978(4)$
	1 for $t = 1979(1)$
	1 for $t = 1979(4)$
	1 for $t = 1980(1)$
	0 otherwise
$Dcotax_t$	1 for $t = 1979(3)$
	1 for $t = 1986(2)$
	0 otherwise
$D75(4)_t$	−1 for $t = 1975(4)$
	0.5 for $t = 1976(1)$
	0.5 for $t = 1976(2)$
	0 otherwise
$D83(1)_t$	1 for $t = 1983(1)$–$1987(3)$
	0 otherwise

[427]

The Monetary Sector

m_t	$nm_t - p_{yt}$
nm_t	log of the nominal money stock measured as deposits in private banks
p_{yt}	log of the implicit deflator of aggregate demand (y_t)
i_{bt}	Danish bond interest rate
i_{dt}	Danish deposit interest rate
$ecm(m)_t$	$m_t - y_t + 4.7i_{bt} - 3.4i_{dt}$

The External Sector

p_{ct}	log of the consumer price index in Denmark
p_{*t}	log of the consumer price index in West Germany
e_t	log of the exchange rate between Denmark and West Germany in Dkr/Dmk
i_{bt}	Danish bond rate
i_{*t}	German 3-month Treasury bill rate
$e_{\$t}$	log of the exchange rate between Denmark and the United States in Dkr/\$
$ecm(ppp)_t$	$p_{ct} - p_{*t} - e_t$
$ecm(uip)_{t-1}$	$(i_b - i_*)_{t-1} - \Delta e_t$

Bibliography

(References marked with an asterisk * are included in this volume.)

Andersen, T. M., and O. Risager (1990) "A Wage-bargaining Model for Denmark", in Calmfors (ed.) *Wage Formation and Macroeconomic Policy in the Nordic Countries*, Oxford, Oxford University Press.

Aukrust, O. (1977) "Inflation in the Open Economy: A Norwegian Model", in L. B. Krause and W. S. Salant (eds.) *Worldwide Inflation: Theory and Recent Experience*, Washington, D.C., Brookings Institution.

*Engle, R. F., D. F. Hendry, and J.-F. Richard (1983) "Exogeneity", *Econometrica*, 51, 2, 277–304.

Favero, C., and D. F. Hendry (1992) "Testing the Lucas Critique: A Review", *Econometric Reviews*, 11, 3, 265–306; originally cited as (1992), Discussion Paper No. 220, Department of Economics, Queen Mary and Westfield College, London, forthcoming in *Econometric Reviews*.

Haavelmo, T. (1944) "The Probability Approach in Econometrics", *Econometrica*, 13, Supplement, 1–118.

Hendry, D. F. (1987) "Econometric Methodology: A Personal Perspective", Chapter 10 in T. F. Bewley (ed.) *Advances in Econometrics*, Volume 2, Cambridge, Cambridge University Press.

[428] Hendry, D. F. (1988) "Encompassing", *National Economic Review*, 125, 88–92.

Hendry, D. F. (1989) *PC-GIVE: An Interactive Econometric Modelling System*, Version 6.0/6.01, Oxford, University of Oxford, Institute of Economics and Statistics and Nuffield College.

Hendry, D. F., and G. E. Mizon (1993) "Evaluating Dynamic Econometric Models by Encompassing the VAR", in P. C. B. Phillips (ed.) *Mod-

els, Methods, and Applications of Econometrics, Oxford, Basil Blackwell, 272–300; originally cited as (1992), in *Models, Methods, and Applications of Econometrics*.

Johansen, S. (1988) "Statistical Analysis of Cointegration Vectors", *Journal of Economic Dynamics and Control*, 12, 231–254.

Johansen, S. (1989) "Likelihood Based Inference on Cointegration, Theory and Applications", Lecture notes, Institute of Mathematical Statistics, University of Copenhagen, Copenhagen, Denmark.

Johansen, S. (1991) "Estimation and Hypothesis Testing of Cointegration Vectors in Gaussian Vector Autoregressive Models", *Econometrica*, 59, 1551–1580.

Johansen, S. (1992a) "Cointegration in Partial Systems and the Efficiency of Single Equation Analysis", *Journal of Econometrics*, 52, 389–402.

Johansen, S. (1992b) "Determination of Cointegration Rank in the Presence of a Linear Trend", *Oxford Bulletin of Economics and Statistics*, 54, 3, 383–397.

Johansen, S., and K. Juselius (1990) "Maximum Likelihood Estimation and Inference on Cointegration—With Applications to the Demand for Money", *Oxford Bulletin of Economics and Statistics*, 52, 169–210.

Johansen, S., and K. Juselius (1992) "Testing Structural Hypotheses in a Multivariate Cointegration Analysis of the PPP and the UIP for UK", *Journal of Econometrics*, 53, 211–244; originally cited as (1992), forthcoming in *Journal of Econometrics*.

Juselius, K. (1991a) "Long-run Relations in a Well Defined Statistical Model for the Data Generating Process: Cointegration Analysis of the PPP and UIP Relations Between Denmark and Germany", in J. Gruber (ed.) *Econometric Decision Models: New Methods of Modelling and Applications*, Berlin, Springer-Verlag.

Juselius, K. (1991b) *CATS in RATS. A Manual to Cointegration Analysis*, Copenhagen, Denmark, Institute of Economics, University of Copenhagen; originally cited as (1991c).

Juselius, K. (1992) "On the Empirical Verification of the Purchasing Power Parity and the Uncovered Interest Rate Parity", *Nationaløkonomisk Tidsskrift*, 130, 1, 57–66; originally cited as (1991b) "The Determination of Exchange Rates and Interest Rates in an Open Economy: The Case of Denmark", Discussion Paper, Institute of Economics, University of Copenhagen, Copenhagen, Denmark.

Juselius, K. (1994) "On the Duality Between Long-run Relations and Common Trends in the I(1) versus I(2) Model: An Application to Aggregate

Money Holdings", *Econometric Reviews*, 13, 2, 151–178; originally cited as (1992), forthcoming in *Econometric Reviews*.

Kremers, J. J. M., N. R. Ericsson, and J. J. Dolado (1992) "The Power of Cointegration Tests", *Oxford Bulletin of Economics and Statistics*, 54, 3, 325–348.

Nickell, S. J. (1985) "Error Correction, Partial Adjustment, and All That: An Expository Note", *Oxford Bulletin of Economics and Statistics*, 47, 119–130.

Ramsey, J. B. (1969) "Tests for Specification Errors in Classical Linear Least-squares Regression Analysis", *Journal of the Royal Statistical Society, Series B*, 31, 2, 350–371.

Rowlatt, P. A. (1988) "Analysis of the Recent Path of UK Inflation", *Oxford Bulletin of Economics and Statistics*, 50, 335–360.

Surrey, M. J. C. (1989) "Money, Commodity Prices, and Inflation: Some Simple Tests", *Oxford Bulletin of Economics and Statistics*, 51, 219–239.

8

A Dynamic Model of the Demand for Currency: Argentina 1977–1988

HILDEGART AHUMADA*

Abstract

This work models money in the complex, highly inflationary environment of Argentina (1977–1988). First, cointegration techniques proposed by Engle and Granger (1987) and extended by Johansen (1988) are applied and show that real cash balances, income, and inflation are cointegrated. Second, data information are used to specify the dynamics of this relationship, following the "general-to-specific" methodology developed by Hendry *et al*. The model selected appears to be a satisfactory representation of money demand, including being empirically constant over 1985–1988, during which there were major policy changes. However, constant, well-specified inflation or interest rate equations cannot be obtained by inverting the money demand equation, given the results found when testing for super exogeneity.

1 Introduction

This work models real cash balances in the complex highly inflationary environment of Argentina (1977–1988). First, the paper analyzes the long-run determinants using an information set which includes interest rates, domestic prices, and transactions volumes. Cointegration techniques, proposed by Engle and Granger (1987) and extended by Johansen (1988), are applied

* The author wishes to acknowledge useful comments from an anonymous referee and is greatly indebted to Neil Ericsson for his encouragement and valuable help in improving an earlier version. Remaining errors and the views expressed in the paper are solely the responsibility of the author.

Reprinted with permission from the *Journal of Policy Modeling* (June 1992), 14, 3, 335–361.

to evaluate the long-run hypothesis that real money, real income, and the inflation rate are cointegrated. Second, data information are used to specify the dynamics of the model following the "general-to-specific" methodology developed by Hendry *et al.*

[336]   The selected model incorporates a linear error correction term and an asymmetric effect of inflation. It has a suitable economic interpretation and satisfies a range of statistical criteria, so it is considered a tentative approximation to the underlying data generating process of real cash balances. For policy purposes it should be noted that the model remains constant up to the outbreak of hyperinflation. Notwithstanding its constancy, the model is not useful to derive a model for inflation or the interest rate by inversion.

The next section summarizes money-demand theory and the Argentine institutions and data. Section 3 describes cointegration techniques and their relation to error correction models. The long-run hypothesis via cointegration techniques are investigated in Section 4. Section 5 reports results of modeling short-run dynamics, and Section 6 discusses the model obtained. Section 7 concentrates on exogeneity issues. Finally, conclusions are stated in Section 8.

2   Theory, Institutions, and Data

The basic model of the demand for money includes transactions (Y) and the opportunity cost of holding real cash balances as explanatory variables. Total final domestic expenditure (GDP plus imports minus exports) in real terms is used for Y, since it has proven to be more useful than other definitions. Both inflation (π) and interest rates (R) may help measure the opportunity cost.[1]

Although usual theories of the demand for money include interest rates, several problems are found empirically for Argentina. For instance, in periods of regulated interest rates, no records exist for the differential paid in the black market, which probably has varied with the levels of restrictions. Friedman (1956) and Cagan (1956) stress the importance of the effect of inflation on real cash balances when inflation is high. However, whether inflation dominates the interest rate at high inflation rates is an empirical issue. In the long run, nevertheless, inflation and interest rates are supposed to move together, in a relationship similar to that of the Fisher hypothesis. At high inflation rates, deviations between them seem to be negligible in the long run, although substantial deviations may occur in the short run.

---

[1] See the appendix for data definitions and sources. Unless otherwise indicated, capital letters denote the generic names while logs of the scalars are in lower case. The price index (P) is CPI and $\pi = (p_t - p_{t-1})$. The interest rate is the rate on savings and the interest rate enters the model as $r = \ln(1 + R)$.

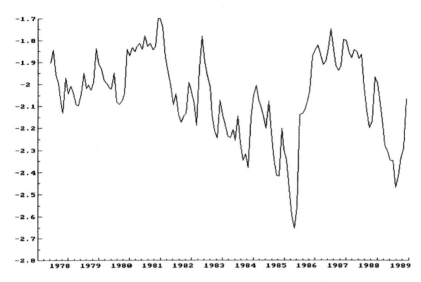

FIGURE 1. Real cash balances $(m - p)_t$.

In the last decade, the Argentine economic authorities tried different strategies to moderate inflation. These attempts included price controls, fixed interest rates, and fixed exchange rates, alternated with tough monetary policies which derived mainly from high compulsory reserve requirements, aimed at increasing the spread of domestic over foreign asset returns. As a consequence, it is sometimes believed that data may not always reflect [337] the underlying behavior of monetary variables and that it is not possible to find constant econometric relationships even over a few years. The model developed in Sections 4–7 provides evidence against these views.

Before modeling the data, we should consider its basic statistical properties. Figure 1 shows monthly real cash balances (or "money") from 1977 to 1988. That spans the period from the monetary reform that ended the system of nationalized deposits until the appearance of hyperinflation at the beginning of 1989. Real holdings of money, $m - p$, declined during the early 1980s, but increased sharply after the reform of June 1985, the Austral Plan. That reform included a combination of orthodox and heterodox policies and is associated with the main recuperation of real cash money holdings in the sample period. It was followed by a new demonetization period with partial recoveries in 1987 and 1988 until August 1988, when the "Primavera" plan was launched.

Figure 2 charts real money with inflation, in which the former has been transformed to a pseudo-velocity measure $[-(m-p-\frac{1}{2}y)]$. The figure suggests a close relation between them. Also, $-(m - p - \frac{1}{2}y)$ looks very similar to the inversion of $m - p$ in Figure 1, implying that transactions are not moving much relative to $m - p$. The transaction's behavior can be observed in Figure 3. Both transactions and real balances also show seasonal behavior; that of money holdings is mainly associated with the two complementary payments received in July and December by all wage earners.

[338]

3 Dynamic Specification: Cointegration and Error Correction Mechanisms

This section discusses the relation of the dynamic error correction (EC) model to the "general-to-specific" modeling approach and to cointegration.

A common practice in applied econometrics has been to estimate regressions in differences of the variables to avoid the spurious correlation problem of trending series discussed by Granger and Newbold (1977). However, this kind of dynamic model is unable to display long-run behavior, e.g., to solve for the levels of the variables when these grow at constant rates. For that reason, among others, other authors have attained stationarity through error correction models, which not only encompass models in differences, but also have a suitable economic interpretation. For the first versions, see Phillips (1957) and Sargan (1964), and for more recent versions, see Davidson, Hendry, Srba, and Yeo (1978) and Hendry and Mizon (1978), among others.

[339]

For a linear single-equation model with two variables, x and y, and one-lag, the EC representation is:

$$\Delta y_t = \beta_0 + \beta_1 \Delta x_t - (1 - \beta_3)(y - Ax)_{t-1} + e_t \quad e_t \sim \mathsf{N}(0, \sigma_e^2). \quad (1)$$

In practice x and y often are logs of the underlying economic series, denoted X and Y. The rate of growth of Y_t depends not only on that of X_t (short-run impact), but also on the past disequilibrium $(y - Ax)_{t-1}$. If the long-run equilibrium is static ($t = t - 1$ and $\Delta y = \Delta x = 0$), then (1) implies $Y = K \cdot X^A$, where $\ln K = \beta_0/(1 - \beta_3)$ (which simplifies to proportionality for $A = 1$).

For steady-state growth with $\Delta y = \Delta x = \tau$, (1) implies $Y = K'X^A$, where $\ln K' = [\beta_0 + (\beta_1 - 1)\tau]/(1 - \beta_3)$. The economic relevance of a model like (1) follows because many economic theories suggest long-run proportionality, e.g., the permanent income hypothesis and the quantity theory of money. Furthermore, (1) can be derived from a certain kind of optimizing behavior, with agents responding to their past disequilibrium. For instance, growth in Y_t will be greater than β_1 times the growth in X_t if Y_{t-1} was less than its long-run desired value. Thus, this representation is more general than that of differences models while still obtaining stationarity in the variables

[340]

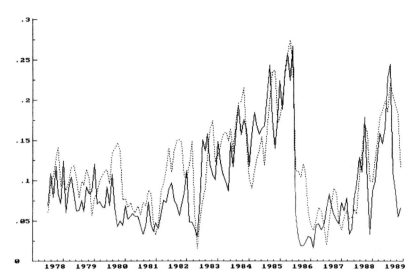

FIGURE 2. The inflation rate π_t (—) and the pseudo-velocity, $-(m - p - \frac{1}{2}y)_t$ ($\cdots$), matched by ranges.

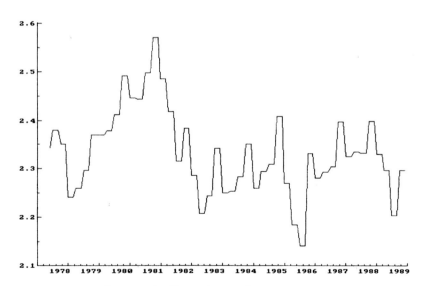

FIGURE 3. The volume of transactions y_t.

included. For a comparison with other dynamic specifications, see Hendry, Pagan, and Sargan (1984).

In the "general to specific" approach to modeling, equation (1) is equivalent to the unrestricted dynamic regression of y on x:

$$y_t = \beta_0 + \beta_1 x_t + \beta_2 x_{t-1} + \beta_3 y_{t-1} + e_t, \tag{2}$$

where $A = (\beta_1 + \beta_2)/(1 - \beta_3)$. If X and Y are proportional in the long run, then $A = 1$ or, equivalently, $\beta_1 + \beta_2 + \beta_3 = 1$.

The study of long-run relationships between economic time series variables has been developed further through the cointegration concept proposed by Engle and Granger (1987).[2] The basic idea is that individual economic time-series variables wander considerably, but certain linear combinations of the series do not move too far apart from each other. Economic forces tend to bring those series into line, e.g., as hypothesized by some economic theory. The series in such a relationship are said to be cointegrated.

More formally, if y_t and x_t are both $I(1)$, then it is possible that a linear combination of them,

$$u_t = y_t - Ax_t, \tag{3}$$

is $I(0)$. If so, y and x are cointegrated with a cointegration vector $(1 : -A)'$. The error u_t measures the disequilibrium present between y_t and x_t. Since it is $I(0)$, u_{t-1} can be used as a regressor in a representation that includes Δy_t as dependent variable, which is also $I(0)$ [Hendry (1986)].

Two properties of cointegration should be emphasized. First, Engle and Granger (1987) show that cointegrated series have an EC representation and that EC mechanisms imply cointegrated variables. Second, Stock (1987) shows that when variables are cointegrated, ordinary least squares (OLS) estimates of cointegration parameters converge to their true values more rapidly than with stationary variables. Thus, Engle and Granger (1987) suggest a two-step estimation approach for dynamic specification, each step requiring only OLS. In the first step, A is estimated by regressing y_t on x_t. In the second step, u_{t-1} (using $\hat{A}$) is included as a regressor to explain Δy_t as part of the systematic dynamics. As a test of cointegration, they propose
[341]   evaluating whether u_t is $I(0)$ after testing that x and y are $I(1)$. Several tests can be used, the most common being the (possibly augmented) Dickey-Fuller (DF) statistic and the Cointegrating Regression Durbin-Watson statistic (CRDW) [Dickey and Fuller (1979, 1981) and Sargan and Bhargava (1983)]. However, the long-run parameter A estimated from the static regression can be severely biased in finite samples, as Banerjee, Dolado, Hendry, and Smith (1986) demonstrate. In particular, when R^2 is small in the cointegrating

---

[2] See also the special issue on cointegration of the *Oxford Bulletin of Economics and Statistics* (1986).

TABLE 1.
Tests of the Order of Integration of Individual Variables

Alternative	Statistic	$m - p$	y	π	r
I(0)	dw	0.23	0.22	0.40	0.18
	$ADF(3)$	-2.7	-2.6	-3.3	-2.5
I(1)	dw	1.72	2.00	2.27	1.70
	$ADF(3)$	-7.9	-6.3	-7.9	-6.9

dw and ADF are the Durbin-Watson and argumented Dickey-Fuller statistics
[Sargan and Bhargava (1983) and Dickey and Fuller (1979, 1981)]. The first
column lists the alternative hypothesis, I(j), where the null hypothesis is I($j+1$)
($j = 0, 1$).

TABLE 2.
Cointegration Results: Eigenvalues and Related Test Statistics

		Maximal eigenvalue		Eigenvalue trace	
	Eigenvalue	Statistic	95% critical value	Statistic	95% critical value
1	0.030	4.07	8.08	4.07	8.08
2	0.051	6.96	14.60	11.02	17.84
3	0.150	21.51*	21.28	32.53*	31.26

The statistics are defined in Johansen (1988) and Johansen and Juselius (1990), and
critical values are taken from the latter's Table A2.
* Significant at the 95% critical value.

TABLE 3.
Cointegration Results: Normalized α and β' Matrices

Variable	α (weighting matrix)			β' (cointegration vectors)		
$m - p$	-0.234	-0.026	-0.034	1.000	2.776	-0.482
π	-0.001	-0.032	0.026	-0.129	1.000	1.048
y	0.069	-0.051	-0.007	0.112	-3.020	1.000

regression, static and dynamic estimates can differ, and the authors suggest full dynamic modeling as an alternative.

An improved procedure for testing cointegration, allowing for more than one cointegration vector, is that suggested in Johansen (1988) and generalized in Johansen and Juselius (1990). Based on the unrestricted estimation of a system, parameterized in terms of levels and differences, they propose Likelihood Ratio statistics for testing the number of cointegration vectors. The coefficient matrix for levels contains information about long-run relationships between the variables in the data vector. Since its rank is the number of nonzero eigenvalues in a determinental equation closely related to estimating the system, the number of cointegrating vectors is determined by testing how many of those eigenvalues are nonzero. The cointegrating vectors (denoted β') are shown to be a subset of the associated eigenvectors. Furthermore, the associated weighting coefficients (denoted α) can be useful to evaluate weak exogeneity, because it is lost if a cointegration vector appears in the conditional and marginal models [Johansen (1992)].

In Section 4, both Engle-Granger and Johansen techniques are applied to testing a long-run hypothesis about the demand for money in the Argentine case. Section 5 presents the results of modeling that function by using the "general-to-simple" approach.[3]

4 Long-run Behavior

Given the basic economic model of the demand for money and the variables' behavior, real money balances are hypothesized to be cointegrated with the volume of real transactions and the opportunity cost of holding money, defined as π. Cointegration has been tested with two different measures of opportunity cost: r and π. The second is preferred in terms of the stability of the long-run parameters, and so is the only one presented below.

From Table 1, all variables appear to be I(1). Inflation may be an exception, as its statistics are very sensitive to the sample period chosen. Even so, π is considered to be I(1), having the same order of integration as that of r.[4]

[342]

The static Engle-Granger cointegration regression is:

---

[3] Hendry's (1989) PC-GIVE was used for estimation.

[4] ADF statistics for this set of variables are very sensitive to the sample size, the inclusion or exclusion of a constant or trend, and the model of seasonality (deterministic or autoregressive). However, the estimation of the unrestricted model suggests that the assumed order of integration is appropriate.

$$m - p = -3.1 + 0.53y - 2.3\pi \qquad (4)$$

$T = 139\ [1977(6)\text{--}1988(12)] \qquad R^2 = 0.62 \qquad CRDW = 0.68$

$DF = -5.3 \qquad ADF(13) = -4.0.$

All the statistics reject the hypothesis of non-cointegration at the critical values provided by Engle and Yoo (1987) for the three-variable case. The low R^2 may imply bias in estimating the long-run parameters.

To analyze cointegration of these series further, the system-based procedure from Johansen (1988) and Johansen and Juselius (1990) is applied to $m - p$, π, and y with six lags, a constant, and seasonal dummies. Table 2 lists the eigenvalues from the smallest (closest to a unit root) to the largest [343] (most stationary) and the LR statistics based on the maximal eigenvalue and on the eigenvalue trace. Table 3 presents the normalized weighting matrix, α, and the matrix of cointegrating vectors, β'.

Both statistics in Table 2 indicate that there is one cointegration vector. Furthermore, the cointegration vector (row 1 of β' in Table 3) has a coefficient close to 0.5 on transactions and a coefficient on inflation of -2.78, similar to those obtained by the static regression (4). Note that this remarkable similarity may be due to the large variation of the data involved. Also note that the cointegration vectors estimated by both procedures are very close to the square-root law of the Baumol-Tobin model.

From the weighting values in Table 3, the cointegrating vector enters the money equation with a coefficient of -0.23 while the money-demand cointegrating vector does not appear to enter the equations for π or y. That is necessary for π and y to be weakly exogenous in a conditional money-demand equation [Johansen (1992)].

5   Short-run Dynamics and the Hypothesis of Asymmetry

Asymmetric effects of inflation on real cash balances have been hypothesized for Argentina. In empirical studies, that hypothesis has been tested using a ratchet effect based upon the maximum of past π. This ratchet reinforces the asymmetric effect of π in a Cagan equation, as in Piterman (1988) and Melnick (1990). Ahumada (1989) discusses some problems of this empirical measure. In particular, the assumption of irreversibility associated with it ensures the ratchet's role in the long-run relationship. From the above cointegration analysis, it seems possible empirically to ignore this hysteresis effect in the long-run relationship. This does not preclude asymmetric effects in the short run, and therefore, separate effects for rising and falling inflation are included as regressors in modeling short-run dynamics.

To model dynamics and the long run jointly, an unrestricted autoregres- [344] sive distributed lag of $m - p$ on y, π, and r is estimated with seven successive lags, seasonal lags (12 and 13), and monthly dummies. Furthermore, a dummy variable (denoted by WD, equal to 1 for April and May of 1982) is included in the unrestricted regression to take into account the jump in the demand for currency during the war conflict over the Malvinas. No significant loss of information is found in restricting the model to three lags and four seasonal dummies (SD) for July, August, November, and December. Also, long-run price homogeneity is not rejected when tested by including p_{t-1} in the latter regression; its coefficient is not significant. Table 4 presents the autoregressive distributed lag for $m - p$ where $\Delta\pi_t^+$, $\Delta\pi_t^-$, and their lags are included along with π_t. The terms $\Delta\pi_t^+$ and $\Delta\pi_t^-$ denote $\max(0, \Delta\pi_t)$ and $\min(0, \Delta\pi_t)$. This parameterization is a generalization of including π_t and its lags, with the latter imposing coefficient equality on $\Delta\pi_{t-j}^+$ and $\Delta\pi_{t-j}^-$.

The solved long-run solution to Table 4 is:

$$
\begin{aligned}
m - p = \; & - \underset{(1.1)}{2.7} + \underset{(0.45)}{0.35}\, y - \underset{(1.9)}{2.7}\, \pi + \underset{(2.2)}{0.54}\, r \\
& + \underset{(0.8)}{1.8}\, WD + \textstyle\sum \gamma_s SD_s.
\end{aligned}
\tag{5}
$$

This confirms the results of the last section but with a wider information set. The coefficient of π is similar to that in (4), whereas that of r is positive. That supports the view of a long-run relationship between real balances, transactions, and π alone. The long-run coefficient of y is similar to the Baumol-Tobin elasticity obtained in (4), albeit with a large standard error.

Substantial sequential reduction from Table 4 results in the following restricted conditional model:

$$
\begin{aligned}
\Delta(\widehat{m - p})_t = \; & \underset{(0.04)}{0.13}\, \Delta(m-p)_{t-1} + \underset{(0.07)}{0.32}\, \Delta_2 y_{t-1} - \underset{(0.12)}{0.78}\, \Delta_2 r_t \\
& - \underset{(0.19)}{1.20}\, \Delta\pi_t^+ - \underset{(0.15)}{0.53}\, \Delta\pi_t^- \\
& - \underset{(0.03)}{0.14}\, [m - p - \tfrac{1}{2}y - (-3 - 2.3\pi)]_{t-1} \\
& + \underset{(0.02)}{0.20}\, WD + \textstyle\sum \gamma_s SD_s - \underset{(0.0055)}{0.0050}
\end{aligned}
\tag{6}
$$

$T = 136$ [1977(9)–1988(12)] $R^2 = 0.87$ $\sigma = 3.4\%$ $BP\ \chi^2(13) = 15.9$
$AR\ F(7, 117) = 0.52$ $ARCH\ F(7, 110) = 1.46$ $RESET\ F(1, 123) = 0.76$
$NORM\ \chi^2(2) = 4.6$ $X_i^2\ F(16, 107) = 1.98$ $ENC\ F(19, 104) = 0.96,$

where σ is the estimated standard deviation of residuals; standard errors are in parentheses; $BP\ \chi^2(q)$ is the Box-Pierce (1970) statistic for qth-order autocorrelation; $AR\ F(q,\ T - K - q)$ is the LM statistic for qth-order autocorrelation [Harvey (1981)]; $ARCH\ F(q,\ T - K - 2q)$ is the LM statistic for

TABLE 4.
Autoregressive Distributed Lag Representation for $(m - p)$

| Variable | \multicolumn{5}{c}{Lag j (or index)} |
	0	1	2	3	$\Sigma_{j=0}^3$
$(m - p)_{t-j}$	-1	0.918	-0.095	0.063	-0.114
	$(-)$	(0.083)	(0.123)	(0.077)	(0.046)
π_{t-j}	-0.305				-0.305
	(0.203)				(0.203)
$\Delta\pi_{t-j}^+$	-0.805	-0.337	-0.248		-1.390
	(0.302)	(0.294)	(0.269)		(0.580)
$\Delta\pi_{t-j}^-$	-0.310	0.195	-0.159		-0.274
	(0.234)	(0.208)	(0.168)		(0.415)
r_{t-j}	-0.790	-0.029	0.519	0.361	0.061
	(0.177)	(0.266)	(0.289)	(0.244)	(0.236)
y_{t-j}	0.087	0.349	-0.102	-0.294	0.040
	(0.140)	(0.181)	(0.184)	(0.132)	(0.058)
SD_{t-j}		0.016	0.100	-0.060	
		(0.017)	(0.017)	(0.018)	
SD_{t-j-4}	-0.019	-0.005	-0.034	0.149	
	(0.020)	(0.020)	(0.021)	(0.021)	
SD_{t-j-8}	0.020	0.037	-0.008	-0.005	
	(0.023)	(0.024)	(0.019)	(0.017)	
WD	0.207				
	(0.030)				
Constant	-0.310				
	(0.192)				

$T = 135$ [1977(10)–1988(12)] $R^2 = 0.975$ $\sigma = 3.48\%$ $BP\ \chi^2(16) = 17.8$
$AR\ F(7,97) = 1.31$ $ARCH\ F(7,90) = 1.88$
$RESET\ F(1,103) = 0.17$ $NORM\ \chi^2(2) = 4.2$ $X_i^2\ F(36,67) = 0.71$.
See the text below (6) for a description of the statistics.

qth-order ARCH [Engle (1982)]; *RESET* $F(q, T - K - q)$ is Ramsey's (1969) statistic; *NORM* $\chi^2(2)$ is Jarque and Bera's (1980) statistic; X_i^2 $F(q, T - K - q - 1)$ is the statistic for heteroscedasticity quadratic in regressors [White (1980) and Nicholls and Pagan (1983)]; and *ENC* $F(q, T - K - q)$ evaluates q-parameter restrictions relative to Table 4 [Johnston (1963)]. Equation (6) has much simpler dynamics than Table 4. Equation (6) also imposes the Baumol-Tobin long-run income elasticity of one half, and imposes the long-run inflation elasticity of -2.3 from (4). The next section discusses the properties of equation (6).

[345]
6   Evaluation

[346]
Equation (6) has a clear economic interpretation. Real holdings of currency are determined by transactions and inflation in the long run. In the short run, agents increase (decrease) their money holdings by 14 percent of the past month's excess demand (supply).

Notwithstanding that disequilibrium effect, inflation has an asymmetric effect on real money, the effect depending on whether inflation is rising or falling, since both $\Delta\pi^+$ and $\Delta\pi^-$ enter (6). The coefficient on $\Delta\pi$ is -1.2 when π increases and -0.53 when it falls. The effect of $\Delta\pi^+$ and $\Delta\pi^-$ also can be interpreted as a part of a forward-looking model of inflation, in which these variables are data-based predictors of π_{t+1} [Campos and Ericsson (1988) and Hendry and Ericsson (1991b)]. Furthermore, money holdings depend on contemporaneous changes in the interest rate and lagged changes in transactions.

From the diagnostic statistics, the residual of the estimated equation appears to be white noise (BP χ^2, AR F), homoscedastic ($ARCH$ F; White's standard errors of coefficients are also similar to those OLS estimated), and an innovation (ENC F).[5],[6] The LM statistic based on the squares of regressors (X_i^2 F) indicates some mis-specification, perhaps the need for a nonlinear error correction. A cubic relationship was tried and the derived regressor $(u_{t-1} - 0.14)u_{t-1}^2$ was included in the model. This error correction response is similar to that found for the United Kingdom [Hendry and Ericsson (1991a)]. Although this representation reduces the LM statistic to $F(16, 107) = 1.32$, it exhibits parameter instability for the period of increasing monetization after the economic plan known as "Primavera". The instability seems to be derived from the real money responses to excess demand, which is increasing

---

[5] For the different criteria and information sets for model design and evaluation see Hendry and Richard (1982), Hendry (1983), and Hendry (1989).

[6] The possibility of an additional effect, that of the exchange rate, was evaluated using an LM statistic for omitted variables. However, the exchange rate does not appear to play a significant role (for log differences with three lags $F(4, 119) = 1.17$ and for a 3-month moving average of them, $F(4, 116) = 0.90$).

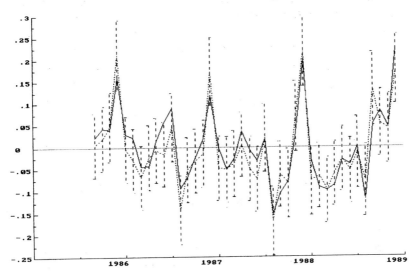

FIGURE 4. Equation (6): actual values (—) and one-step-ahead forecasts ($\cdots$) of $\Delta(m-p)_t$, with ± 2 forecast standard errors (vertical dashed bars).

in that cubic function (although it may be appropriate for the cases of excess supply, above a certain level). Even so, the linear error correction model is preferred, given its much better predictive performance in the last 3 years.

Parameter constancy is evaluated over three periods, which include the main attempts at economic stabilization. First, for the last 40 months [1985(9)–1988(12)], the Chow and forecast χ^2 statistics are $CHOW$ $F(40, 84) = 0.77$ and $\chi_f^2(40)/40 = 0.95$. These statistics indicate that the null hypothesis of parameter constancy cannot be rejected. Figure 4 charts the one-step prediction for this subsample.

An earlier, overlapping sample, 1985(6)–1988(9), includes the introduction of the Austral Plan in June 1985. The corresponding statistics become $CHOW$ $F(40, 81) = 1.11$ and $\chi_f^2(40)/40 = 1.39$. Although the overall statistics are insignificant, the forecasted change in real cash balances for June 1985 is somewhat higher than two times the forecast standard error, with a t ratio of 2.69. The reform took place on June 15, when a price freeze and a compulsory (downwards) renegotiation of interest rates were implemented. The reported consumer price index and interest rate statistics registered an abrupt change only a month later. Thus, this shock appears to reflect a measurement (timing) error rather than any change in the behavior assumed by

[347]

(6). Finally, for the "Primavera" plan in August 1988, these statistics are $CHOW\ F(5,119) = 1.32$ and $\chi_f^2(5)/5 = 1.72$ over 1988(8)–1988(12).

Parameter constancy is also confirmed by recursive estimation. Figures 5–9 show recursive estimates of the main coefficients in (6) for the period in which the mentioned reforms took place.[7] These coefficient estimates are well inside the ex ante standard errors, and the estimates become

[348] more precise after the Austral plan, which introduced new information. In addition, from Figure 10, none of the break-point Chow statistics for the sequence [1985(1)–1988(12), 1985(2)–1988(12), ..., 1985(6)–1988(12), ..., 1988(11)–1988(12), 1988(12)] are significant at the 5 percent level. The evaluation just performed is critical for testing exogeneity, as discussed in the next section.

7 Exogeneity

Weak exogeneity of the current-dated regressors in (6) is required for its analysis as a single equation to be efficient [Engle, Hendry, and Richard (1983)]. System estimates with Johansen's techniques in Section 4 support that weak exogeneity, because the money-demand cointegrating vector does not appear to enter the equations for π or y.

Moreover, weak exogeneity can be tested as an implication of super exogeneity, requiring constant parameters in the conditional money-demand model across different economic regimes. The above statistics suggest a partial proof in that direction, although the nonconstancy of the marginal processes for inflation and the interest rate (those variables which enter with-

[349] out lags) should also be tested. If the marginal processes of current dated variables change while the conditional model remains constant, then super exogeneity holds. In this case, the Lucas critique does not apply for the relevant class of interventions [Hendry (1988)]. A very appealing aspect of testing super exogeneity is that only a simple marginal model needs to be nonconstant. Here, univariate autoregressive (AR) models for inflation and interest rates are estimated to show their nonconstancy.

The following models are obtained by simplifying AR(13) models with seasonal dummies:[8]

---

[7] For computational reasons, the dependent variable for the recursive estimations is $(\Delta m - p - 0.2\ WD)$ and the (insignificant) constant term is set equal to zero.

[8] For inflation, only four seasonal dummies (for January, March, June, and August) were retained.

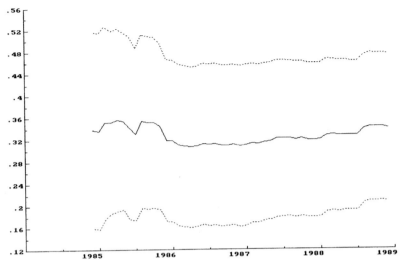

FIGURE 5. Equation (6): recursive estimates (—) of the coefficient on $\Delta_2 y_{t-1}$ for a model of $\Delta(m - p)_t$, with ± 2 estimated standard errors ($\cdots$).

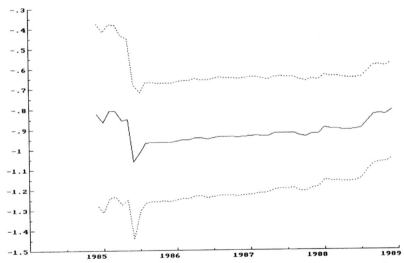

FIGURE 6. Equation (6): recursive estimates (—) of the coefficient on $\Delta_2 r_t$ for a model of $\Delta(m - p)_t$, with ± 2 estimated standard errors ($\cdots$).

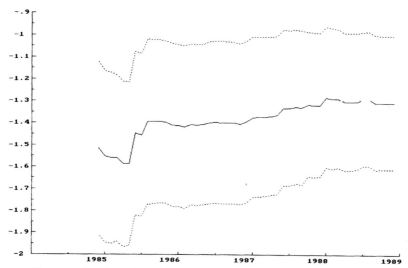

FIGURE 7. Equation (6): recursive estimates (—) of the coefficient on $\Delta \pi_t^+$ for a model of $\Delta(m-p)_t$, with ± 2 estimated standard errors $(\cdots)$.

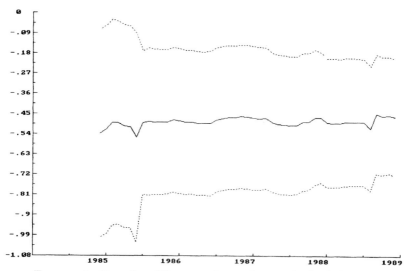

FIGURE 8. Equation (6): recursive estimates (—) of the coefficient on π_t^- for a model of $\Delta(m-p)_t$, with ± 2 estimated standard errors $(\cdots)$.

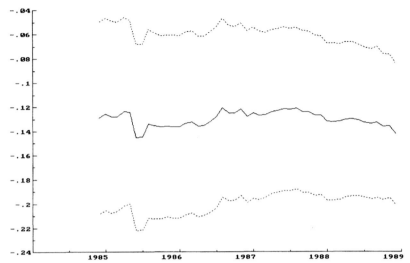

FIGURE 9. Equation (6): recursive estimates (—) of the coefficient on the error correction term $[(m - p - \frac{1}{2}y) - (-3 - 2.3\pi)]_{t-1}$ for a model of $\Delta(m-p)_t$, with ± 2 estimated standard errors ($\cdots$).

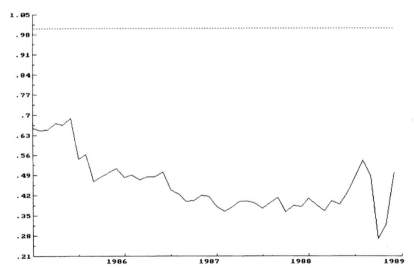

FIGURE 10. Equation (6): the sequence of break-point Chow statistics (—) for a model of $\Delta(m - p)_t$, with the statistics scaled by their one-off 5% critical values ($\cdots$).

$$\widehat{\Delta \pi_t} = -\underset{(0.05)}{0.17} \pi_{t-1} + \underset{(0.008)}{0.008} + \sum \delta_s SD_s \tag{7}$$

$T = 136\ [1977(9)\text{--}1988(12)]$ $R^2 = 0.22$ $\sigma = 3.3\%$ $BP\ \chi^2(13) = 14.3$
$AR\ F(7, 123) = 0.79$ $ARCH\ F(7, 116) = 0.24$
$RESET\ F(1, 129) = 11.5$ $NORM\ \chi^2(2) = 173.5$ $X_i^2\ F(6, 123) = 7.5,$

[350]
$$\widehat{\Delta r_t} = -\underset{(0.03)}{0.12} r_{t-2} + \underset{(0.004)}{0.011} \tag{8}$$

$T = 136\ [1977(9)\text{--}1988(12)]$ $R^2 = 0.76$ $\sigma = 2.0\%$ $BP\ \chi^2(13) = 8.88$
$AR\ F(7, 127) = 0.79$ $ARCH\ F(7, 120) = 4.0$
$RESET\ F(1, 133) = 15.3$ $NORM\ \chi^2(2) = 290.5$ $X_i^2\ F(2, 131) = 61.7.$

Figures 11 and 12 show the sequence of break-point Chow statistics for (7) and (8): constancy of the marginal processes is rejected.

Engle and Hendry (1993) propose how to use determinants of nonconstancies in the marginal process to test super exogeneity. If inflation and interest rates are super exogenous in the conditional model (6), then the determinants of the marginal processes' nonconstancies should be statistically insignificant if added to (6). To capture the nonconstancies of these models, several zero-one dummies are included in (7) and (8). The expanded models
[351] are:

$$\widehat{\Delta \pi_t} = -\underset{(0.04)}{0.07} \pi_{t-1} + \underset{(0.005)}{0.003} + \sum \delta_s SD_s - \underset{(0.03)}{0.19}\ D85(7)$$
$$+ \underset{(0.03)}{0.07}\ D87(10) - \underset{(0.02)}{0.06}\ D87(11,12)$$
$$+ \underset{(0.03)}{0.07}\ D88(7) - \underset{(0.03)}{0.12}\ D88(9) \tag{9}$$

$T = 136\ [1977(9)\text{--}1988(12)]$ $R^2 = 0.57$ $\sigma = 2.4\%$ $BP\ \chi^2(13) = 21.5$
$AR\ F(7, 118) = 2.66$ $ARCH\ F(7, 111) = 0.70$
$RESET\ F(1, 124) = 1.93$ $NORM\ \chi^2(2) = 1.95$ $X_i^2\ F(11, 113) = 1.32,$

$$\widehat{\Delta r_t} = \underset{(0.001)}{0.003} - \underset{(0.01)}{0.11}\ D85(6) - \underset{(0.01)}{0.11}\ D85(7) - \underset{(0.01)}{0.09}\ D88(8) \tag{10}$$

$T = 136\ [1977(9)\text{--}1988(12)]$ $R^2 = 0.55$ $\sigma = 1.4\%$ $BP\ \chi^2(13) = 18.0$
$AR\ F(7, 125) = 0.95$ $ARCH\ F(7, 118) = 5.33$
$RESET\ F(1, 131) = 0.00$ $NORM\ \chi^2(2) = 27.5$ $X_i^2\ F(3, 128) = 0.88.$

The dummies are for the observations indicated by their names. Two observations should be made: (i) most of the dummies are near or during the two main economic reforms of 1985 and 1988, and (ii) adding the dummies, the

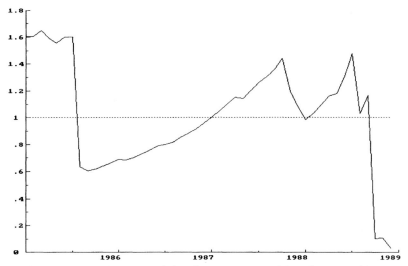

FIGURE 11. Equation (7): the sequence of break-point Chow statistics (—) for a time-series model of $\Delta \pi_t$, with the statistics scaled by their one-off 5% critical values ($\cdots$).

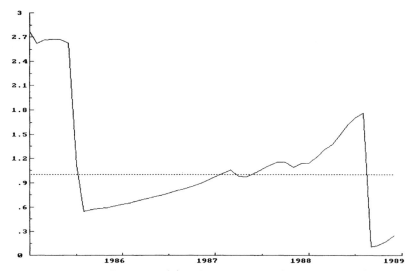

FIGURE 12. Equation (8): the sequence of break-point Chow statistics (—) for a time-series model of Δr_t, with the statistics scaled by their one-off 5% critical values ($\cdots$).

[352] coefficients of π_{t-1} and r_{t-2} in (7) and (8) become insignificant; even so, π_{t-1}
is still in (9) because deleting it induces residual autocorrelation.

Two tests of super exogeneity are conducted, one adding the dummies of
equation (9) and (10) to (6), and the other adding functions of their residuals
to (6). First, adding the dummies, (6) becomes:

$$\Delta(\widehat{m-p})_t = \underset{(0.04)}{0.15} \Delta(m-p)_{t-1} + \underset{(0.07)}{0.31} \Delta_2 y_{t-1}$$

$$- \underset{(0.16)}{0.64} \Delta_2 r_t - \underset{(0.22)}{1.34} \Delta\pi_t^+ - \underset{(0.21)}{0.56} \Delta\pi_t^-$$

$$- \underset{(0.03)}{0.12} [m - p - \tfrac{1}{2}y + 3 + 2.3\pi]_{t-1} + \underset{(0.03)}{0.20} WD$$

$$+ \sum \gamma_s SD_s + \underset{(0.07)}{0.05} D85(7) + \underset{(0.04)}{0.02} D87(10)$$

$$- \underset{(0.03)}{0.02} D87(11,12) + \underset{(0.04)}{0.01} D88(7)$$

$$- \underset{(0.06)}{0.04} D88(9) + \underset{(0.04)}{0.12} D85(6) - \underset{(0.04)}{0.03} D88(8) \quad (11)$$

$$T = 136 \; [1977(9)-1988(12)] \qquad R^2 = 0.89 \qquad \sigma = 3.4\% \qquad BP \; \chi^2(13) = 21.5$$
$$ENC \; F(7,117) = 2.09.$$

[353] All dummies are insignificant except for that of June 1985. As discussed
in the previous section, this observation appears to be mis-measured, rather
than indicating a regime shift. Also, adding functions of the residuals of (9)
and (10) to (6),[9] it becomes:

$$\Delta(\widehat{m-p})_t = \underset{(0.04)}{0.14} \Delta(m-p)_{t-1} + \underset{(0.08)}{0.39} \Delta_2 y_{t-1}$$

$$- \underset{(0.17)}{1.08} \Delta_2 r_t - \underset{(0.33)}{1.09} \Delta\pi_t^+ - \underset{(0.10)}{0.27} \Delta\pi_t^-$$

$$- \underset{(0.03)}{0.14} [m - p - \tfrac{1}{2}y + 3 + 2.3\pi]_{t-1} + \underset{(0.03)}{0.20} WD$$

$$+ \underset{(0.29)}{0.80} u_r - \underset{(0.92)}{0.66} u_r^2 - \underset{(0.07)}{0.12} ARCH \; u_r$$

$$- \underset{(0.24)}{0.17} u_\pi - \underset{(0.66)}{0.57} dev_{12}u_r + \underset{(0.53)}{0.08} dev_{12}u_\pi$$

$$+ \sum \gamma_s SD_s \qquad\qquad\qquad\qquad (12)$$

[354] $T = 124 \; [1978(9)-1988(12)] \qquad R^2 = 0.88 \qquad \sigma = 3.5\% \qquad BP \; \chi^2(13) = 12.4$
$ENC \; F(6,106) = 1.61.$

---

[9] Note that (12) is estimated for a different sample size in order to obtain dev_{12}.

The residuals of (9) and (10) are u_r and u_π; $dev_{12}u_r$ and $dev_{12}u_\pi$ are 12-month moving standard deviations of u_r and u_π; u_r^2 and $ARCH\ u_r$ are the squares and the predicted ARCH model of u_r. Although the functions of residuals are not jointly significant at the 5 percent level, the super exogeneity of the interest rate is tentative because u_r and its ARCH predictions appear significant as a pair [their F statistic is $F(2, 110) = 4.04$].

In any case, (6) cannot be used to determine inflation (or the interest rate) even when (6) is identified as a constant money demand function. Super exogeneity is not invariant to renormalization, and one implication is that an inverted money demand equation may be nonconstant [Hendry and Ericsson (1991b)]. Estimation of price and interest rate equations inverted from (6) provides additional empirical evidence of super exogeneity.

Before inverting (6), note that (6) is equivalent to an equation in which nominal growth of money Δm is the dependent variable, since $\Delta(m - p)_t = \Delta m_t - \pi_t$. Then, (6) can be re-estimated as an inverted equation for π_t or [355] $\Delta \pi_t$, with Δm_t and π_{t-1} as additional regressors in (6). However, (6) assumes a different behavior for rising and falling inflation, so the inversion of that equation for $\Delta \pi_t$ should also allow for different coefficients, depending on whether $\Delta \pi$ is positive or negative. Thus, multiplicative dummies for negative values of $\Delta \pi$ are introduced. After eliminating insignificant variables, the resulting equation[10] is:

$$
\begin{aligned}
\widehat{\Delta \pi_t} = & - \underset{(0.03)}{0.05} \Delta_2 y_{t-1} + \underset{(0.09)}{0.12} \Delta_2 r_t + \underset{(0.04)}{0.06} \pi_{t-1} \\
& - \underset{(0.02)}{0.01} \Delta m_t + \underset{(0.02)}{0.03} \Delta m_{t-1} \\
& - \underset{(0.02)}{0.02} [m - p - \tfrac{1}{2}y + 3 + 2.3\pi]_{t-1} + \underset{(0.004)}{0.02} \\
& - \underset{(0.006)}{0.01}\ (\Delta \pi < 0) + \underset{(0.011)}{0.38}\ \Delta_2 r_t(\Delta \pi < 0) \\
& - \underset{(0.05)}{0.38}\ \pi_{t-1}(\Delta \pi < 0) \hspace{4cm} (13)
\end{aligned}
$$

$T = 136\ [1977(9)-1988(12)]$ $R^2 = 0.80$ $\sigma = 1.7\%$ $BP\ \chi^2(13) = 8.4$ [356]
$AR\ F(7, 119) = 0.15$ $ARCH\ F(7, 112) = 1.0$ $RESET\ F(1, 125) = 9.8$
$NORM\ \chi^2(2) = 20.5$ $X_i^2\ F(17, 108) = 1.27$ $ENC\ F(16, 110) = 0.73.$

The sequence of break-point Chow statistics appears in Figure 13.   Equation (13) appears only barely nonconstant for a few break points. However, the RESET and normality tests indicate mis-specification, which may invalidate the Chow statistic.

Inverting (6) for the interest rate obtains:

---

[10] All seasonal dummies were initially included.

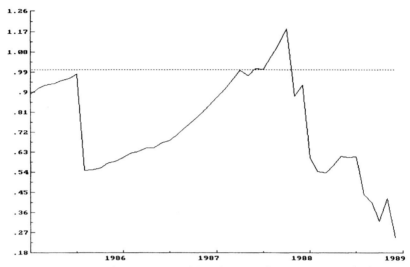

FIGURE 13. The sequence of break-point Chow statistics (—) for
the inverted money-demand model (13) explaining $\Delta \pi_t$, with the
statistics scaled by their one-off 5% critical values ($\cdots$).

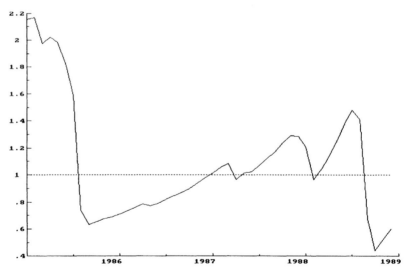

FIGURE 14. The sequence of break-point Chow statistics (—)
for the inverted money-demand model (14) explaining $\Delta_2 r_t$, with
the statistics scaled by their one-off 5% critical values ($\cdots$).

$$\widehat{\Delta_2 r_t} = \underset{(0.05)}{-\ 0.31}\ \Delta(m-p)_t - \underset{(0.03)}{0.04}\ \Delta(m-p)_{t-1} + \underset{(0.05)}{0.20}\ \Delta_2 y_{t-1}$$

$$\underset{(0.40)}{-\ 0.39}\ \Delta\pi_t^+ - \underset{(0.09)}{0.31}\ \Delta\pi_t^-$$

$$\underset{(0.02)}{-\ 0.01}\ [m-p-\tfrac{1}{2}y+3+2.3\pi]_{t-1}$$

$$\underset{(0.02)}{-\ 0.08}\ WD + \underset{(0.003)}{0.01} + \sum \gamma_s SD_s \qquad (14)$$

$T = 136\ [1977(9)–1988(12)] \qquad R^2 = 0.56 \qquad \sigma = 3.3\% \qquad BP\ \chi^2(13) = 20.3\ [357]$
$AR\ F(7,117) = 2.5 \qquad ARCH\ F(7,110) = 0.91$
$RESET\ F(1,123) = 24.6 \qquad NORM\ \chi^2(2) = 8.0 \qquad X_t^2\ F(16,107) = 1.84.$

The sequence of break-point Chow statistics in Figure 14 indicates nonconstancy.[11]

The mis-specification of the above equations has a clear policy implication. While the demand for cash balances appears constant over the period examined, it is not possible to invert that demand function to obtain a constant, well-specified equation for inflation or the interest rate.

8 Summary and Conclusions

In the 1980s, Argentine inflation reached unprecedented rates. Several combinations of different policies characterized the period pursuing stability in [358] inflation. As a consequence, it is sometimes believed that real money cash holdings could not be a stable function.

This study models private holdings of currency and finds a relationship that remains stable over major policy changes from July 1985 to December 1988. The model focuses on just a few variables that reflect opportunity costs and transactions. Long-run properties are analyzed by cointegration techniques, following which short-run dynamics are modeled. The resulting model appears to be a satisfactory representation of the data generating process of money holdings.

This article discusses exogeneity issues and applies several tests. The conditional model of real cash balances appears constant, so the empirically nonconstant univariate marginal models for inflation and the interest rate imply the super exogeneity of those variables in the conditional model. Engle and Hendry's variable-addition test is less conclusive.

Since super exogeneity is not invariant to renormalization, a constant money demand equation inverted for inflation or the interest rate may be

---

[11] Equation (14) was estimated with seasonal dummies for July, August, November, and December. WD and one seasonal (for November) were excluded for recursive estimation.

nonconstant. That seems to be the case in Argentina. The constant relationship found for money holdings cannot be used to derive models of inflation or the interest rate.

This analysis is restricted to the narrowest definition of money (private holdings of currency), which contrasts with traditional transactions demand measures such as M1.[12] As a caveat to this study, changes in the Argentine tax on writing checks might induce a substitution for currency.[13] However, in Argentina, owners of current accounts are mainly firms and economic agents of the highest levels of income, and they have access to a wider range of assets to avoid the inflationary tax when inflation is increasing. That suggests different demand functions for currency and current accounts, and would justify the more disaggregated approach in this article.

Appendix.   Data Definitions and Sources

M Money: the monthly average of daily private holdings of currency (Central Bank of Argentina [BCRA]).

P Prices: general level of consumer prices (National Institute of Statistics and Census [INDEC]).

[359] R Interest rate: a series specially constructed for the free market (before October 1987), as the average of different term deposits (on the basis of information from the BCRA).

Y Real aggregate transactions: domestic expenditure (total GDP plus imports minus exports), 1970 prices, all on a monthly basis corresponding to repeated quarterly values (BCRA).

Several unrestricted estimations previously were tried using different definitions for the explanatory variables [Ahumada (1987, 1989)].

Bibliography

(References marked with an asterisk * are included in this volume.)

Ahumada, H. (1987) "Econometría Dinámica: Una Aplicación a la Demanda de Billetes y Monedas en Poder del Público", *Económica*, La Plata, Argentina, jul-dic., 159–184.

Ahumada, H. (1989) "Saldos Monetarios Reales e Inflación: Pruebas de Efectos Asimétricos Irreversibles Usando Técnicas de Co-integración", *Anales de la Asociación Argentina de Economía Política*, 24e Reunión, Rosario, Volume 1.

---

[12] Available data for private holdings of current accounts (monthly average of daily data) are too short to estimate dynamic models for M1.

[13] A variable reflecting a negative return for current accounts based on this tax was tried unsuccessfully in the unrestricted equations.

Banerjee, A., J. J. Dolado, D. F. Hendry, and G. W. Smith (1986) "Exploring Equilibrium Relationships in Econometrics through Static Models: Some Monte Carlo Evidence", *Oxford Bulletin of Economics and Statistics*, 48, 3, 253–277.

Box, G. E. P., and D. A. Pierce (1970) "Distribution of Residual Auto-correlations in ARIMA Time Series Models", *Journal of the American Statistical Association*, 65, 1509–1526.

Cagan, P. (1956) "The Monetary Dynamics of Hyperinflation", in M. Friedman (ed.) *Studies in the Quantity Theory of Money*, Chicago, University of Chicago Press.

Campos, J., and N. R. Ericsson (1988) "Econometric Modeling of Consumers' Expenditure in Venezuela", International Finance Discussion Paper No. 325, Board of Governors of the Federal Reserve System, Washington, D.C., June.

Chow, G. C. (1960) "Tests of Equality Between Sets of Coefficients in Two Linear Regressions", *Econometrica*, 28, 591–605.

Davidson, J. E. H., D. F. Hendry, F. Srba, and S. Yeo (1978) "Econometric Modelling of the Aggregate Time Series Relationship Between Consumers' Expenditure and Income in the United Kingdom", *Economic Journal*, 88, 661–692.

Dickey, D. A., and W. A. Fuller (1979) "Distributions of the Estimators for Autoregressive Time Series with a Unit Root", *Journal of the American Statistical Association*, 74, 427–431.

Engle, R. F. (1982) "Autoregressive Conditional Heteroscedasticity with Estimates of the Variance of United Kingdom Inflation", *Econometrica*, 50, 987–1007.

*Engle, R. F., and D. F. Hendry (1993) "Testing Super Exogeneity and Invariance in Regression Models", *Journal of Econometrics*, 56, 1/2, 119–139; originally cited as (1989) "Testing Super Exogeneity and Invariance", Department of Economics Discussion Paper 89–51, University of California at San Diego, La Jolla, California.

*Engle, R. F., D. F. Hendry, and J.-F. Richard (1983) "Exogeneity", *Econometrica*, 51, 277–304.

Engle, R. F., and C. W. J. Granger (1987) "Co-integration and Error Correction: Representation, Estimation, and Testing", *Econometrica*, 55, 251–277.

Engle, R. F., and B. S. Yoo (1987) "Forecasting and Testing in Cointegrated Systems", *Journal of Econometrics*, 35, 143–159.

Friedman, M. (1956) "The Quantity Theory of Money—A Restatement", in M. Friedman (ed.) *Studies in the Quantity Theory of Money*, Chicago, University of Chicago Press, 3–21.

Granger, C. W. J., and P. Newbold (1977) *Forecasting Economic Time Series*, New York, Academic Press.

Hall, S. G. (1986) "An Application of the Granger and Engle Two-step Estimation Procedure to United Kingdom Aggregate Wage Data", *Oxford Bulletin of Economics and Statistics*, 48, 3, 228–240.

[360] Harvey, A. C. (1981) *The Econometric Analysis of Time Series*, Oxford, Philip Allan.

Hendry, D. F. (1983) "Econometric Modelling: The 'Consumption Function' in Retrospect", *Scottish Journal of Political Economy*, 30, 3, 193–220.

Hendry, D. F. (1986) "Econometric Modelling with Cointegrated Variables: An Overview", *Oxford Bulletin of Economics and Statistics*, 48, 3, 201–212.

*Hendry, D. F. (1988) "The Encompassing Implications of Feedback versus Feedforward Mechanisms in Econometrics", *Oxford Economic Papers*, 40, 1, 132–149.

Hendry, D. F. (1989) *PC-GIVE: An Interactive Econometric Modelling System*, Version 6.0/6.1, Oxford, Institute of Economics and Statistics and Nuffield College.

Hendry, D. F., and N. R. Ericsson (1991a) "An Econometric Analysis of U. K. Money Demand in *Monetary Trends in the United States and the United Kingdom* by Milton Friedman and Anna J. Schwartz", *American Economic Review*, 81, 1, 8–38.

Hendry, D. F., and N. R. Ericsson (1991b) "Modeling the Demand for Narrow Money in the United Kingdom and the United States", *European Economic Review*, 35, 4, 833–881.

Hendry, D. F., and G. E. Mizon (1978) "Serial Correlation as a Convenient Simplification, not a Nuisance: A Comment on a Study of the Demand for Money by the Bank of England", *Economic Journal*, 88, 549–563.

Hendry, D. F., and J.-F. Richard (1982) "On the Formulation of Empirical Models in Dynamic Econometrics", *Journal of Econometrics*, 20, 1, 3–33.

Hendry, D. F., A. R. Pagan, and J. D. Sargan (1984) "Dynamic Specification", Chapter 18 in Z. Griliches and M. D. Intriligator (eds.) *Handbook of Econometrics*, Amsterdam, North-Holland, Volume 2, 1023–1100.

Jarque, C. M., and A. K. Bera (1980) "Efficient Tests for Normality, Homoscedasticity, and Serial Independence of Regression Residuals", *Economics Letters*, 6, 255–259.

Jenkinson, T. J. (1986) "Testing Neo-classical Theories of Labour Demand: An Application of Co-integration Techniques", *Oxford Bulletin of Economics and Statistics*, 48, 3, 241–249.

Johansen, S. (1988) "Statistical Analysis of Cointegration Vectors", *Journal of Economic Dynamics and Control*, 12, 2/3, 231–254.

Johansen, S. (1992) "Cointegration in Partial Systems and the Efficiency of Single-equation Analysis", *Journal of Econometrics*, 52, 3, 389–402; originally cited as (1990), Institute of Mathematical Statistics, University of Copenhagen, Copenhagen, Denmark.

Johansen, S., and K. Juselius (1990) "Maximum Likelihood Estimation and Inference on Cointegration—With Applications to the Demand for Money", *Oxford Bulletin of Economics and Statistics*, 52, 2, 169–210.

Johnston, J. (1963) *Econometric Methods*, New York, McGraw Hill.

Melnick, R. (1990) "The Demand for Money in Argentina 1978–1987: Before and After the Austral Program", *Journal of Business and Economic Statistics*, 8, 4, 427–434; originally cited as (1988) "The Demand for Money in Argentina 1978–1987", Research Department, Bank of Israel, Tel Aviv, Israel.

Mizon, G. E., and D. F. Hendry (1980) "An Empirical Application and Monte Carlo Analysis of Tests of Dynamic Specification", *Review of Economic Studies*, 47, 290–323.

Nicholls, D. F., and A. R. Pagan (1983) "Heteroscedasticity in Models with Lagged Dependent Variables", *Econometrica*, 51, 1233–1242.

Phillips, A. W. (1957) "Stabilization Policy and the Time-forms of Lagged Responses", *Economic Journal*, 67, 265–277.

Piterman, S. (1988) "The Irreversibility of the Relationship Between Inflation and Real Balances", *Bank of Israel Review*, 60, 72–80.

Ramsey, J. B. (1969) "Tests for Specification Errors in Classical Linear Least-squares Regression Analysis", *Journal of the Royal Statistical Society, Series B*, 31, 350–371.

Sargan, J. D. (1964) "Wages and Prices in the United Kingdom: A Study in Econometric Methodology" in P. E. Hart, G. Mills, and J. K. Whitaker (eds.) *Econometric Analysis for National Economic Planning*, Colston Papers, Volume 16, London, Butterworths, 25–63 (with discussion).

Sargan, J. D., and A. Bhargava (1983) "Testing Residuals from Least Squares [361] Regression for Being Generated by the Gaussian Random Walk", *Econometrica*, 51, 153–174.

Stock, J. H. (1987) "Asymptotic Properties of Least Squares Estimators of Cointegrating Vectors", *Econometrica*, 55, 5, 1035–1056.

Tobin, J. (1958) "Liquidity Preference as Behavior Toward Risk", *Review of Economic Studies*, 25, 65–86.

White, H. (1980) "A Heteroskedasticity-consistent Covariance Matrix Estimator and a Direct Test for Heteroskedasticity", *Econometrica*, 48, 817–838.

9

Dynamic Modeling of the Demand for Narrow Money in Norway

GUNNAR BÅRDSEN*

Abstract

The role and stability of the demand for money are recurring issues in applied econometrics. Does a constant long-run demand for money function exist? If so, is money exogenous, and hence a policy variable, or endogenous?

The notion of cointegration provides a tool for identifying long-run relationships, to be embedded in dynamic error correction models with constant parameters, while the assumed exogeneity status of variables for the parameters of interest can be assessed by recently developed tests.

This paper derives a demand function for narrow money in Norway by applying these tools, starting out with a vector autoregressive representation that includes money (M1), prices, real expenditure, and several interest rates.

* This is a substantially revised version of "Dynamic Modelling and the Demand for Narrow Money in Norway", Discussion Paper 07/90, Norwegian School of Economics and Business Administration, Bergen.

I would like to thank in particular Neil R. Ericsson, Jan Tore Klovland, and Ragnar Nymoen for their extensive comments on various versions of the paper. The latter two also provided most of the data series used. I would also like to thank Peter Burridge, Øyvind Eitrheim, Paul G. Fisher, David F. Hendry, Eilev S. Jansen, Søren Johansen, Katarina Juselius, Bjørn Naug, Erling Steigum, and a referee for helpful comments on earlier versions. Thanks also to Birger Strøm of the Central Bureau of Statistics for excellent service. Financial support from the Norwegian Research Council for Science and the Humanities is gratefully acknowledged.

Reprinted with permission from the *Journal of Policy Modeling* (June 1992), 14, 3, 363–393.

Given a sample riddled with financial deregulation, changing monetary policy, and an economy switching its basis from industrial production towards oil exportation, one should not be surprised to find an unstable demand for money function. A conditional model with constant parameters is nevertheless established. Finally, tests for weak and super exogeneity are conducted. Prices, real expenditure, and interest rates are super exogenous for the parameters of the demand for money. This means that simulation experiments can be conducted for the effects of monetary and fiscal policy on the demand for money.

1   Motivation

[364]

It is a widely held view that demand functions for narrow money with constant parameters do not exist; they are fragile econometric constructs, blown away by the changing policy regimes and financial innovations sweeping across the desks of econometricians at frequent intervals—especially during the last decade or so.[1]

Norway is an excellent testing field in this respect. Not only has the basis of the economy changed from industrial production to include a large oil exporting sector from the early 1970s on, but the monetary environment has been subject to numerous changes during the last twenty years. The changes relevant for the demand for money can be summarized as follows:

1. While direct regulation had prevailed in the early part of the period considered here, the determination of interest rates was gradually left to market forces from the early 1980s.

2. Targets for monetary policy changed from interest rates and credit volume to the exchange rate in 1986.

3. A system of direct and selective controls of credit volume was replaced by a market-oriented policy in 1983.

The net result of these changes was a surge in bank lending, as well as in interest rates, creating demand pressure and fueling inflation. The resulting pressure on the exchange rate caused a 10 percent devaluation in May 1986. The "over-reaction" from the private sector prompted a tight monetary policy in the form of higher required reserve ratios from the start of 1986 until credit regulations were totally abolished in 1988.

The story of credit market deregulation is told in Table 1.[2] All the regulations were in force at the end of 1983. Note in particular the reintroductions of loan controls and loan guarantee limits in 1986(1).

---

[1] See Goldfeld and Sichel (1990) for international evidence on instability.

[2] Bårdsen and Klovland (1990) investigate the cointegration properties of money, credit, and income in Norway.

TABLE 1. Credit Market Regulations in Norway, 1983–1989

Type of Regulation	Dates when abolished (A) or reintroduced (R)				
	Banks	Finance company	Loan association	Life insurance	Non-life-insurance
Direct loan controls[a]	A1984(1) R1986(1) A1987(3)	A1988(3)	A1988(3)		A1988(3)
Primary reserve requirement	A1987(2)	A1987(3)		A1987(2)	
Bond investment quota[b]	A1984(1)			A1985(1)	
Loan guarantee limits	A1984(3) R1986(1) A1988(3)	A1984(3) R1986(1) A1988(3)	A1984(3) R1986(1) A1988(3)	A1984(3) R1986(1) A1988(3)	A1984(3) R1986(1) A1988(3)
Max. interest rate on loans	A1985(3)			A1985(3)	

Note: If no date is specified, no regulation applies. In all other cases the regulation was in operation at the end of 1983. The information is compiled from *Annual Reports of the Norges Bank* 1984–1988 and various issues of *Penger og Kreditt* in the same period. The table is taken from Bårdsen and Klovland (1990).

[a] Credit extended by the finance companies in the form of factoring and leasing contracts was exempted as from 1984(4). The regulations concerning mortgage loan associations only applied to loans to households and selected industries.

[b] The dates refer to the point in time when the required percentage of growth was set equal to zero, viz., net additions to the bond portfolio were no longer required. The regulation was completely removed in 1985(1) for banks and in 1985(3) for life insurance companies.

The effect of a deregulation of credit rationing on money demand is uncertain.[3] During the regime of rationing, only a small number of liquid assets held by households could be converted quickly into money. Without rationing, many more assets—including human capital—could be converted quickly. Therefore, larger precautionary money balances supposedly were held in the earlier period. Also, when considering loan applications, banks took previous saving into consideration, thus effectively reducing the demand for narrow money.

[365]

---

[3] Goldfeld and Sichel (1990) identify financial deregulation as a source of narrow money demand functions breaking down.

Everything said so far suggests an unstable demand for money function for Norway, and this is indeed the conclusion reached by Fair (1987).

The present study presents a model of demand for narrow money in Norway with constant parameters estimated on data spanning the regime shifts described.

Section 2 discusses the choice of variables, and presents the data and the econometric implementation of the demand function. Section 3 gives a brief methodological background for the estimation of the model in Section 4, while Section 5 investigates weak and super exogeneity and derives the consequences in the form of endogenous money and invariance of the parameters with respect to changes in the processes for prices, income, and interest rates. Section 6 summarizes this study.

[366]

2   Choosing the Variables

A long-run money demand function sufficiently general to include most theoretical specifications is:

$$M = f(\ P,\quad X,\quad RD1,\quad R\ ),\qquad\qquad (1)$$
$$ +\quad\ +\quad\ +\quad\ -$$

where M is demand for money; P is the price level; X is a measure of the volume of transactions, income, and/or wealth; $RD1$ is the own yield of holding money; and R is the vector of alternative costs to holding money. The expected signs of the coefficients, conditional on the demand equation, are given below the variables. Whether a demand for money function is specified in real or nominal terms is irrelevant as long as prices are allowed to enter the specification.

The choice of scale variable in a money demand function is usually between income, expenditure, or wealth. Klovland (1990) finds a long-run wealth effect and a short-run influence from income in his study of Norwegian $M2$ over 1968–1989.

The scale variable preferred in the present study is a measure of total final expenditure, or real absorption—i.e., real gross domestic expenditure, investment in ships and off-shore industry excluded; its implicit deflator is taken to be the price variable. The choice makes sense in modeling narrow money, since the impact from the oil sector would be more relevant using a broader definition of the money stock.

Narrow money has been interest-bearing in Norway during the sample period and neglecting this fact would imply a potential mis-specification. The own yield is represented by the interest rate on demand deposits.

In regard to the opportunity cost of money holding, the literature is at least as diverse as for scale variables. In this study several interest rates are included, while the real-wage rate as a measure of the brokerage fee—following Laidler (1985, p. 68)—was discarded at an early stage. The long-term bond yield is available together with the average rate on time deposits from banks. But considering Norway's position as a small open economy, an interest rate reflecting international influence is required—as stressed by Hamburger (1977). A natural candidate is the 3-month Eurokrone rate. Although a surrogate measure for the earlier part of the period, the variable represents both a shadow price on credit in domestic markets as well as a covered yield on foreign assets.

Applied econometrics implies a choice of functional form. Here log-linearity is taken as a basis for an error correction model—building upon [367] the work of Hendry (1979, 1985, 1988) and Hendry and Ericsson (1991).

These assumptions specify equation (1) as:

$$M = P^{\beta_1} \cdot X^{\beta_2} \cdot \exp\{\beta_3 RD1 + \beta_4 RD2 + \beta_5 RL + \beta_6 RS\}, \qquad (2)$$

so the long-run function to be estimated is:

$$m = \beta_1 p + \beta_2 x + \beta_3 RD1 + \beta_4 RD2 + \beta_5 RL + \beta_6 RS, \qquad (3)$$

where M is narrow money, P is the deflator of gross domestic expenditure X, X is real gross domestic expenditure, $RD1$ is the interest rate on demand deposits, $RD2$ is the interest rate on time deposits, RL is the long-term private bond yield, and RS is the 3-month Eurokrone rate.[4]

Here and below, lower-case letters of the regressors denote natural logarithms of the corresponding upper-case variables. The choice of interest rates in levels follows Trundle (1982).

The task at hand is amply illustrated in Figure 1, where the behavior of the inverse velocity, in logarithmic scale, is shown over time. The constant long-run relationship between money and income (in other words, cointegration) falls totally apart after 1983. But such a changing trend is also evident [368] for the interest rates in Figure 2. The own rate in particular starts growing toward the end of the sample period. Although narrow money has had a positive own yield throughout the sample period, the importance of the variable is clearly increasing after the credit deregulation. Consequently, money demand functions omitting this variable are likely to suffer a breakdown after 1983.

This preliminary examination suggests that the relationship between real money and real expenditure has to be augmented with other variables in order to obtain long-run money demand stability. The interest rates are natural candidates for this, and the own yield in particular.

---

[4] Detailed definitions of the data are given in the appendix.

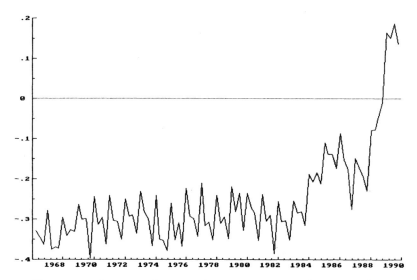

FIGURE 1. Inverse velocity in logarithmic scale: $(m - p - x)$.

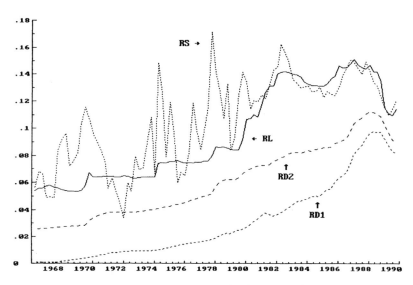

FIGURE 2. The interest rates RS $(\cdots)$, RL $(—)$, $RD2$ $(- - -)$, and $RD1$ (- - -).

3 Econometric Approach

3.1 Systems Cointegration Analysis

Following Hendry and Mizon (1993), the starting point of estimation is a congruent statistical system of unrestricted reduced forms:

$$z_t = \sum_{j=1}^{p} \Pi_j z_{t-j} + \Phi D_t + v_t \qquad v_t \sim \mathsf{IN}(0, \Omega), \tag{4}$$

where z_t is a $(n \times 1)$ vector of $\mathsf{I}(1)$ and/or $\mathsf{I}(0)$ variables and D_t represents deterministic components.[5]

Utilizing $\Delta z_t \equiv z_t - z_{t-1}$, a convenient reparameterization of (4) is: [369]

$$\Delta z_t = \sum_{i=1}^{p-1} \Pi_i^* \Delta z_{t-j} + \Pi^* z_{t-p} + \Phi D_t + v_t, \tag{5}$$

with

$$\Pi_i^* = \sum_{j=1}^{i} \Pi_j - I,$$

$$\Pi^* = \sum_{j=1}^{p} \Pi_j - I. \tag{6}$$

This is the vector autoregression (VAR) approach that Johansen (1988) and Johansen and Juselius (1990) used to investigate the cointegration properties of the system. Since v_t is stationary, the rank ρ of the "long-run" matrix Π^* determines how many linear combinations of z_t are stationary. If $\rho = n$, all z_t are stationary, while if $\rho = 0$ so that $\Pi^* = 0$, Δz_t is stationary and all linear combinations of z_t are $\mathsf{I}(1)$. For $0 < \rho < n$, there exist ρ cointegrating vectors, meaning ρ stationary linear combinations of z_t. In that case, Π^* can be factored as $\alpha \beta'$ with both α and β being $(n \times \rho)$ matrices. The cointegrating vectors of β are the error correction mechanisms in the system, while α contains the adjustment parameters.[6] Johansen and Juselius (1990) provide a full procedure for estimation and testing within this framework.

3.2 Exogeneity Concepts

For $z_t' = (y_t, x_t')$, the joint distribution of (4) can be factorized into a conditional distribution for y_t given x_t and a marginal distribution for x_t. If

---

[5] The notation $\mathsf{I}(1)$ means "integrated of order 1". Introductions to integration, and cointegration, which is encountered later on, can be found in Hendry (1986) and Granger (1986).

[6] This result is known as Granger's Representation Theorem. Engle and Granger (1987) give the original result, while an extended version can be found in Hylleberg and Mizon (1989).

the parameters of interest are only functions of the parameters of the conditional distribution, and if the parameters of the conditional and marginal distributions are variation free, then the variables are weakly exogenous for the parameters of interest.[7,8] Further, if x_t is weakly exogenous for the parameters of interest and there is no feedback from y_t to x_t, then x_t is strongly exogenous for the parameters of interest. And finally, if x_t is weakly exogenous for the parameters of interest and they are invariant to changes in

[370] the parameters of the marginal distribution for x_t, then x_t is super exogenous for the parameters of interest, to the class of changes occurring in the sample. A test of weak exogeneity for the elements of β is due to Johansen (1992a) and illustrated in Johansen (1992b). Weak exogeneity for all the conditional parameters can be tested via the tests of super exogeneity of Engle and Hendry (1993) presented in Section 5.

3.3   Conditional Model Analysis

As a conditional model, the first equation of (4) becomes the dynamic linear regression model:

$$y_t = \delta_0' x_t + \sum_{j=1}^{p}(\gamma_j y_{t-j} + \delta_j' x_{t-j}) + \varphi' d_t + u_t. \tag{7}$$

Some general considerations about dynamic specification, of equal validity in the individual equations in the systems analyzed above, can be illustrated by means of (7). The conditional model representation of the first equation of (5) is:

$$\Delta y_t = \delta_0' \Delta x_t + \sum_{i=1}^{p-1}(\gamma_i^* \Delta y_{t-i} + \delta_i^{*'} \Delta x_{t-i})$$
$$+ \gamma_p^* y_{t-p} + \delta_p^{*'} x_{t-p} + \varphi' d_t + u_t, \tag{8}$$

where

$$\gamma_i^* = \sum_{j=1}^{i} \gamma_j - 1,$$
$$\delta_i^* = \sum_{j=0}^{i} \delta_j. \tag{9}$$

Equation (9) shows that the short-run dynamics of (8) have a clear interpretation as the adjustment towards equilibrium; the parameters are implicit interim multipliers [see also Hylleberg and Mizon (1989)]. But (8) is also an error correction model:

---

[7] See Engle, Hendry, and Richard (1983) for the original exposition.

[8] Loosely speaking, "variation free" means that the parameters of the two distributions are free to take any value independently of each other.

$$\Delta y_t \;=\; \delta_0' \Delta x_t + \sum_{i=1}^{p-1} (\gamma_i^* \Delta y_{t-i} + \delta_i^{*\prime} \Delta x_{t-i})$$

$$+ \;\alpha\beta'[y_{t-p}, x_{t-p}']' + \varphi' d_t + u_t, \tag{10}$$

where $\alpha = \gamma_p^*$, and estimates of the elements in the cointegrating vector are:[9]

$$\hat{\beta}_k = -\hat{\delta}_{kp}^*/\hat{\gamma}_p^*. \tag{11}$$

[371]

The large sample variance of $\hat{\beta}_k$ can be estimated by:

$$\widehat{\mathrm{var}(\hat{\beta}_k)} = (\hat{\gamma}_p^*)^{-2}[(\hat{\beta}_k)^2 \widehat{\mathrm{var}(\hat{\gamma}_p^*)} + \widehat{\mathrm{var}(\hat{\delta}_{kp}^*)} + 2\hat{\beta}_k \widehat{\mathrm{cov}(\hat{\gamma}_p^*, \hat{\delta}_{kp}^*)}]. \tag{12}$$

Equation (8) has two advantages over (7). First, it shows both the long-run solution of the model and the adjustment towards long-run equilibrium. And second, it may be a more efficient starting point for conducting a specification search for a parsimonious model under the null hypothesis of an error correction representation of the data generation process. But (8) and (10) can be inconvenient to use in the early stages of a simplification search since a natural first step is to restrict lag lengths, which means testing $\delta_{kp}^* = \delta_{k(p-1)}^*$, say, and could consequently lead to a lot of reformulations.

The testing of lag lengths is easier with the error correction term on the first lag, as in the usual exposition of error correction models. Rewrite (8) as:

$$\Delta y_t \;=\; \delta_0' \Delta x_t + \sum_{i=1}^{p-1} (\gamma_i^\dagger \Delta y_{t-i} + \delta_i^{\dagger\prime} \Delta x_{t-i})$$

$$+ \;\gamma_p^* y_{t-1} + \delta_p^{*\prime} x_{t-1} + \varphi' d_t + u_t, \tag{13}$$

with

$$\gamma_i^\dagger = - \sum_{j=i+1}^{p} \gamma_j - 1,$$

$$\delta_i^\dagger = - \sum_{j=i+1}^{p} \delta_j, \qquad i = 1, \dots, p-1. \tag{14}$$

See also Harvey (1990, p. 281).

The consequence of moving the levels terms around in the unrestricted error correction model is clear from (9) and (14). In general, if the levels terms are on lag i, the coefficients of the differenced variables are increasing partial sums of the parameters of the dynamic linear regression model until lag $i-1$. From lag i onwards, the coefficients of the differenced variables

---

[9] This is the nonlinear least squares estimator investigated by Stock (1987). An independent derivation can be found in Bårdsen (1989) together with the variance formula given below. See also Johansen and Juselius (1990) and Johansen (1992a).

are decreasing partial sums multiplied by -1. The longest sum runs from lag $i + 1$ to the final lag, while the shortest is the final lag. Consequently, in form (13), sequential testing of maximum lag orders is straightforward. The disadvantage of this parameterization is that all the lagged short-run dynamics change sign compared to (8), so the implicit interim multiplier interpretation is lost.

[372]   Standard inference theory assumes weakly stationary data series, but can be valid even if the series in (4) and (7) are I(1). The first condition for this to hold, from Sims, Stock, and Watson (1990), is formulated by Stock and West (1988, p. 86) as: "... the usual testing procedures are asymptotically valid if a regression can be rewritten so that the coefficients of interest are on stationary, zero mean regressors". The second result needed is due to Park and Phillips (1989, p. 117). Their Theorem 5.3 ensures asymptotically normally distributed parameter estimates if the regressors are cointegrated.

The distribution of the cointegrating vectors is the final uncertainty. Phillips (1988, 1991), Phillips and Loretan (1991), and Johansen (1992a) investigate inference in models such as (8). Their results show that the limit distribution of the long-run coefficients is a mixture of normals. A pilot simulation study in Bårdsen (1990) indicated that the normal distribution could be used for inference. Both the conditional and the VAR approach will be utilized in the next section.

4   Modeling the Demand for Narrow Money in Norway

4.1   Systems Cointegration Analysis

Some tests of the individual time series properties are reported in Bårdsen (1990). It appears that all series are I(1), with the exception of RS, which could be stationary around a trend. The next step is to establish the cointegration properties of the system. To achieve this, we start out with the vector autoregression approach of Johansen (1988) and Johansen and Juselius (1990).[10]

The results of the Johansen procedure are in Table 2. It seems clear that at least two, possibly five, cointegrating vectors are present. The first eigenvector normalized with respect to m looks like a money demand function, with long-run homogeneity with respect to prices as a reasonable restriction. Normalized on m, the first eigenvector is:

$$m = 0.810p + 1.374x + 6.553RD1 - 1.544RD2 - 0.995RL - 0.097RS.$$

The corresponding adjustment coefficients are:

---

[10] The estimation was carried out by RATS programs generously supplied by Katarina Juselius, RATS procedures written by the author, and PC-GIVE 6.0.

TABLE 2. The Johansen Procedure:
A VAR with Five Lags, a Constant, and Seasonal Dummies
(The sample is 1967(3)–1989(4), 90 observations.)

Test type	The test statistics (Testing the number of cointegrating vectors)						
	$\rho = 0$	$\rho \leq 1$	$\rho \leq 2$	$\rho \leq 3$	$\rho \leq 4$	$\rho \leq 5$	$\rho \leq 6$
Trace	211.040*	147.187*	88.920*	56.833*	34.479*	15.000	2.556
$\lambda_{\max}$	63.853*	58.267*	32.087	22.354	19.479	12.444	2.556

The eigenvectors, β

m	1.000	−0.653	1.260	−0.012	0.034	0.066	0.329
p	−0.805	1.000	−2.805	−1.083	0.005	−0.388	1.133
x	−1.374	−6.816	1.000	2.128	−0.078	0.253	−2.061
$RD1$	−6.553	−67.551	0.312	1.000	−0.289	−0.321	10.737
$RD2$	1.544	194.563	7.255	−6.097	1.000	1.986	−19.163
RL	0.995	−58.492	2.696	2.275	−0.454	−1.000	−4.606
RS	0.097	14.552	3.281	2.368	−0.388	0.196	1.000

The adjustment coefficients, α

m	−0.225	0.005	−0.028	0.017	−0.383	0.039	−0.026
p	−0.018	0.002	0.017	0.053	0.045	0.076	0.009
x	0.429	−0.005	−0.045	0.012	0.095	−0.203	−0.020
$RD1$	0.014	0.000	0.002	−0.003	−0.017	−0.008	−0.001
$RD2$	0.014	0.000	0.001	0.002	−0.029	−0.017	0.000
RL	0.052	0.005	0.002	0.002	0.056	−0.069	−0.002
RS	−0.062	−0.009	−0.002	0.018	0.593	−0.511	−0.007

The eigenvalues

0.508	0.477	0.230	0.220	0.195	0.129	0.028

Diagnostic statistics

	Normality $\chi^2(2)$	AR 1–5 $F(5, 46)$	ARCH 4 $F(4, 43)$
m	1.433	0.677	0.564
p	1.050	1.593	0.340
x	5.285	2.453*	0.335
$RD1$	0.011	2.422*	1.010
$RD2$	0.839	3.087*	0.518
RL	14.356*	0.762	0.366
RS	48.247*	0.597	0.012

A test statistic marked with an asterisk means that the relevant H_0 is rejected at the 5% level. The critical values for the cointegration tests are taken from Osterwald-Lenum (1992).

m: -0.225 p: -0.018 x: 0.429 $RD1$: 0.014

$RD2$: 0.014 RL: 0.052 RS: -0.062.

Note the large coefficient on the own yield, $RD1$. It seems like this cointegrating vector also enters the expenditure equation, thereby violating weak
exogeneity. We shall return to this issue in Section 5.

[373]   "Normality $\chi^2(2)$" refers to the Jarque-Bera (1980) test for normality
of the residuals, with a correction for degrees of freedom. The "AR 1–$df1$
$F(df1, df2)$" is the test for autocorrelation performed by testing the significance of augmenting the original model by $df1$ lagged residuals. The F
[374]   form of the test is used, as recommended by Kiviet (1986). "ARCH $df1$
$F(df1, df2)$" refers to the test for ARCH errors introduced by Engle (1982).
A more detailed account of these tests and the ones used later on can be
found in Hendry (1989), Spanos (1986), and Godfrey (1988).

These mis-specification tests clearly reveal that the assumption of congruency is violated. Several of the equations exhibit autocorrelation, while
the equations of the interest rates have non-normal residuals. This is not
surprising, given the many shocks to the system in the form of changing
policy regimes and financial innovation described in Section 1. These shocks
can have altered the processes driving the variables.

Estimation with multivariate recursive least squares facilitates such stability analysis. Figures 3–6 provide a graphical account of "break-point" F
tests: Chow tests where the equations of the VAR at each period are tested
for stability against the end period of 1989(4).[11] The horizontal line $(\cdots)$
represents the critical values at the 5 percent level. The test sequence fails to
reject parameter stability of the money equation throughout the estimation
period while the models for the interest rates are highly nonconstant.

[376]   Since the money demand equation passes all the diagnostics, I choose
to condition on the other variables instead of trying to model the shocks
within the system, assuming those variables are weakly exogenous for the
parameters of the money demand equation. The apparent nonconstancy
of the marginal models will form the basis of tests of the validity of the
assumption of weak exogeneity in Section 5.

4.2   Conditional Model Analysis

Table 3 displays the result from estimating the general model in the form

---

[11] Only three lags of RS are used in these calculations, owing to the limitation of 40
variables in PC-FIML 6.0. [*Editors' note*: PcFiml 8.0, which was used to reproduce these
graphs, does not have such a stringent limitation. At the author's request, 5 lags on all
variables (including RS) were included in the VAR to generate Figures 3–6. Recursive
estimation was initialized with a sample size of 47 rather than 45, owing to the increased
number of parameters estimated. These graphs and the ones appearing in the original
publication are very similar.]

FIGURE 3. Break-point F statistics (—) for m in the VAR, normalized by their one-off 5% critical values ($\cdots$).

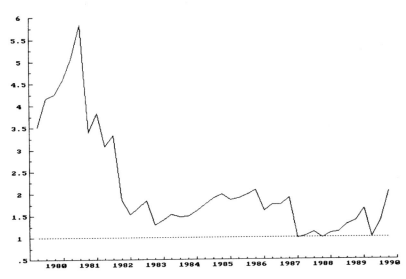

FIGURE 4. Break-point F statistics (—) for $RD1$ in the VAR, normalized by their one-off 5% critical values ($\cdots$).

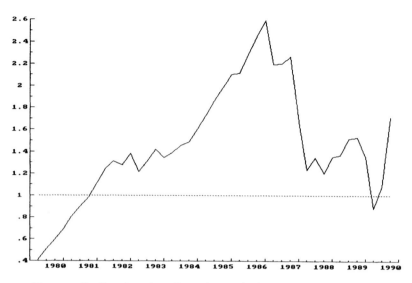

FIGURE 5. Break-point F statistics (—) for $RD2$ in the VAR, normalized by their one-off 5% critical values ($\cdots$).

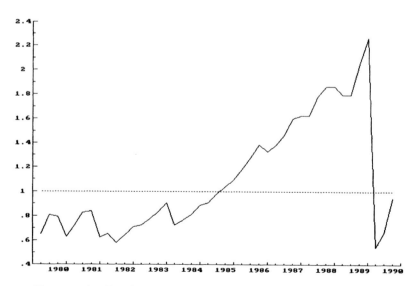

FIGURE 6. Break-point F statistics (—) for RL in the VAR, normalized by their one-off 5% critical values ($\cdots$).

TABLE 3. The General Model: Ordinary Least Squares Estimates
of the General Model in the Form of (13)

Lags	Differences: $(\gamma_i^\dagger, \delta_i^\dagger)$					Levels: (γ_p^*, δ_p^*)
	0	1	2	3	4	1
m	—	-0.036 (0.136)	0.261 (0.142)	0.386 (0.146)	0.544 (0.136)	-0.360 (0.096)
p	0.615 (0.257)	-0.066 (0.263)	-0.363 (0.236)	-0.231 (0.276)	-0.207 (0.287)	0.335 (0.125)
x	0.376 (0.126)	-0.076 (0.209)	-0.134 (0.200)	-0.029 (0.194)	-0.077 (0.153)	0.356 (0.187)
$RD1$	1.884 (2.518)	1.175 (2.770)	-1.918 (2.999)	-2.944 (2.742)	0.046 (2.996)	1.249 (0.904)
$RD2$	-3.279 (3.053)	-3.159 (3.256)	1.678 (3.239)	-1.197 (3.267)	-2.644 (3.271)	1.194 (1.651)
RL	-1.002 (0.833)	0.224 (0.672)	-0.477 (0.724)	0.367 (0.757)	0.279 (0.836)	-0.841 (0.519)
RS	-0.099 (0.132)	-0.323 (0.178)	-0.143 (0.178)	-0.204 (0.149)	-0.022 (0.132)	0.178 (0.195)
d	-0.081 (1.700)	-0.031 (0.030)	-0.037 (0.024)	-0.022 (0.024)	—	—

Long run solution

$m = 0.931\,p + 0.989\,x + 3.470\,RD1 + 3.317\,RD2 - 2.336\,RL + 0.496\,RS$
$\quad\;\,(0.257)\quad(0.390)\quad(1.979)\qquad(4.808)\qquad(1.485)\qquad(0.576)$

Diagnostics

$R^2 = 0.97$ $\sigma = 0.0147$ $dw = 1.95$ $RSS = 0.0097$
$Normality\ \chi^2(2) = 0.41$ $AR\ 1\text{--}5\ F(5,40) = 2.35$
$ARCH\ 4\ F(4,37) = 0.58$ $RESET\ F(1,44) = 0.05$

Test of lag lengths

$H_0 : \gamma_4^\dagger = \delta_4^\dagger = 0$ $F(7,45) = 2.60^*$.

The sample is 1967(3) to 1989(4); 90 observations, 45 parameters.

of (13). "*RESET* $F(1, df2)$" is Ramsey's test for correct specification—performed by testing the relevance of adding the squared predicted values to the original model. The model is well determined according to the diagnostics, although there is some sign of autocorrelation.

The next step is to test and impose restrictions on the elements of cointegrating vector, which from (3) are:

$$m = \beta_1 p + \beta_2 x + \beta_3 RD1 + \beta_4 RD2 + \beta_5 RL + \beta_6 RS. \qquad (15)$$

A natural question at this point is what the testing sequence should be. A purely statistical answer would probably be to impose all the restrictions and use an F test. The strategy followed is a pragmatic mixture of statistical
[377] criteria and economic theory. First, homogeneity of real money with respect to real income is tested together with the exclusion of $RD2$ and RS in the long-run solution, and then the remaining long-run coefficients are estimated and imposed. The restrictions on the cointegrating vector are all easily accepted, as Table 4 shows. In the long run, real money is homogeneous in real income. There appear to be considerable differences in the liquidity, and riskiness, between money and bonds, since a percentage point change in the own yield must be offset by at least a change of three percentage points in RL, the alternative yield on bonds, if no portfolio adjustment is to take place.
[378]   Next, the error correction mechanism is moved back to the longest lag in order to preserve the interim multiplier interpretation, and this restricted model is the starting point of the "general-to-specific" search.[12] The building of the short-run dynamics to obtain a parsimonious model with interpretable parameters is the most difficult part. The general approach is that of Hendry and Richard (1982, 1983), but the most important guidelines used are parsimony, robustness, and economic interpretation. I have also opted for short lags and simple restrictions. The strive for parsimony has for instance resulted in the exclusion of seasonal dummies, since they are unnecessary—a striking result with seasonally unadjusted data.[13]
[379]   These considerations have reduced Table 3 to (16):

$$\widehat{\Delta m_t} = \underset{(0.146)}{0.540}\,\Delta p_t + \underset{(0.025)}{0.264}\,\Delta x_t - \underset{(0.024)}{0.058}\,\Delta(m-p-x)_{t-1}$$

$$- \underset{(1.295)}{3.919}\,\Delta(RD2-RD1)_t - \underset{(0.047)}{0.117}\,RS_t$$

$$- \underset{(0.004)}{0.290}\,(m-p-x-4.7RD1+1.5RL)_{t-5} - \underset{(0.011)}{0.044} \qquad (16)$$

---

[12] I did try a simplification search with the error correction mechanism on the first lag, but it proved less successful.

[13] The F test for adding three seasonal dummies yields $F(3,80) = 0.608$.

TABLE 4.
Testing Long-run Restrictions on the Model from Table 3

The long-run solution
$$m = \beta_1 p + \beta_2 x + \beta_3 RD1 + \beta_4 RD2 + \beta_5 RL + \beta_6 RS$$

Panel A
Testing $\beta_1 = \beta_2 = 1$ and $\beta_4 = \beta_6 = 0$: $F(4, 45) = 0.28$

Long-run solution

$$
\begin{aligned}
(m - p - x) = \quad &- \underset{(0.257)}{0.069}\ p \ - \underset{(0.390)}{0.011}\ x \ + \underset{(1.980)}{3.470}\ RD1 \\
&+ \underset{(4.808)}{3.317}\ RD2 \ - \underset{(1.485)}{2.336}\ RL \ + \underset{(0.576)}{0.496}\ RS
\end{aligned}
$$

Panel B
Restricting $\beta_1 = \beta_2 = 1$ and $\beta_4 = \beta_6 = 0$

Long-run solution

$$
(m - p - x) = \ + \underset{(0.712)}{4.719}\ RD1 \ - \underset{(0.408)}{1.520}\ RL
$$

Diagnostics: 41 parameters

$R^2 = 0.73 \quad \sigma = 0.0142 \quad dw = 1.93 \quad RSS = 0.0099$
$Normality \ \chi^2(2) = 0.90 \quad AR \ 1\text{--}5 \ F(5, 44) = 1.99$
$ARCH \ 4 \ F(4, 41) = 0.44 \quad RESET \ F(1, 48) = 0.01$

Panel C
Testing: $m = p + x + 4.7RD1 - 1.5RL$: $F(6, 45) = 0.19$

Long-run solution

$$
\begin{aligned}
(m - p - x - 4.7RD1 + 1.5RL) = \quad &- \underset{(0.476)}{0.069}\ p \ - \underset{(0.390)}{0.011}\ x \ - \underset{(1.980)}{1.230}\ RD1 \\
&+ \underset{(4.808)}{3.317}\ RD2 \ - \underset{(1.484)}{0.836}\ RL \ + \underset{(0.576)}{0.496}\ RS
\end{aligned}
$$

The sample is 1967(3)–1989(4), 90 observations.

$R^2 = 0.60$ $\sigma = 0.0134$ $dw = 2.29$ $RSS = 0.0150$
Normality $\chi^2(2) = 2.87$ *AR* 1–5 $F(5,78) = 1.72$ *ARCH* 4 $F(4,75) = 1.66$
Hetero $F(12,70) = 0.44$ *RESET* $F(1,82) = 1.66$ *Form* $F(27,55) = 0.88$.

"*Hetero* $F(df1, df2)$" is White's test for heteroscedasticity and tests the joint significance in a regression of the squared residuals on the regressors and their squares. The validity of the chosen functional form is assessed through the "*Form* $F(df1, df2)$" test due to White (1980): the squared residuals are regressed against all the squares and cross products of the regressors.

Whether one estimates real or nominal demand for money, provided inflation is included in both cases, is a matter of indifference. The two specifications are numerically and analytically equivalent. I will therefore continue to use the nominal version in the following.

According to (16), the demand for nominal money growth per quarter depends negatively upon the money market rate and the quarterly change in the spread between own yield and the alternative yield on time deposits.[14] There is an immediate positive effect from growth of prices and real expenditure, while there is a smaller adjustment to changes in the money-income ratio in the previous quarter. Finally there is the adjustment to deviations from the long-run desired relation between real money, real income, the own yield, and the maximum alternative yield for long-term investments. At least three times as large a yield on bonds over money is required before it is considered worthwhile to adjust the portfolio in the long run. So in the short run, agents speculate in the money market and change their money holdings between demand and savings deposits, while in the long run the portfolio is adjusted between money and bonds.

The "break-point" F tests, from recursive least squares estimation, in Figure 7 fail to reject parameter nonconstancy over the estimation period. [381] And the standard error of the equation is virtually unchanged from 1976 on, as Figure 8 demonstrates. Consequently the model suggests that no structural change in agent behavior has taken place as a result of the credit liberalization. But this matter can be more thoroughly investigated by means of testing the invariance of the parameters.

5   Testing Exogeneity

The exogeneity status of the regressors in demand for money studies are always controversial. While Cooley and LeRoy (1981) argue that simultaneity is important, Laidler (1985) takes the opposite view. Bias due to failure of weak exogeneity is seldom significant when tested for [see, for example,

---

[14] The presence of RS is a bit puzzling, considering the results of Table 4. One explanation could be that RS is stationary.

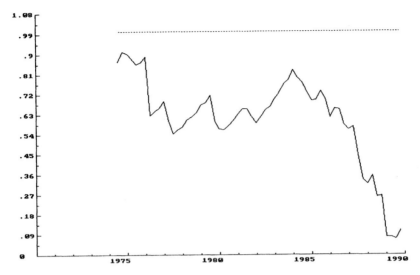

FIGURE 7. Break-point F statistics (—) for the money demand equation, normalized by their one-off 5% critical values ($\cdots$).

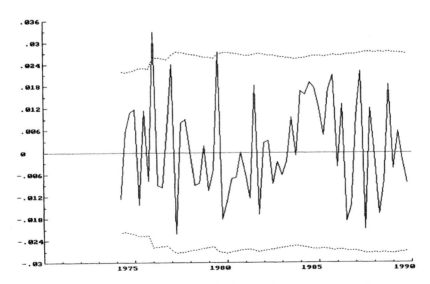

FIGURE 8. One-step residuals (—) from the money demand equation, with $0 \pm 2\hat{\sigma}_t$ ($\cdots$).

Poloz (1980), Gregory and McAleer (1981), and Klovland (1983, 1990)]. But exogeneity has wider implications.

So far, prices, expenditure, and interest rates have been taken to be weakly exogenous; therefore, they can be conditioned upon for statistical analysis of the parameters of the demand equation. This is intuitively reasonable in the case of a small open economy with a fixed exchange rate. If this assumption is valid and the parameters are invariant to the class of interventions occurring during the sample period, the variables are super exogenous with respect to the parameters—see Engle, Hendry, and Richard (1983). This means that policy analysis can be performed by suitably changing the processes driving these variables. There are two ways to investigate this question, which are explained below.[15]

5.1   Testing Constancy of Marginal Models

If the conditional model has constant parameters, as shown, but the marginal models have nonconstant parameters, then the conditional model parameters could not depend upon the marginal model parameters. This is the test of Hendry (1988). The following marginal models were estimated from univariate fifth-order autoregressive processes:[16]

[382]

$$\widehat{\Delta p_t} = \underset{(0.098)}{0.361} \Delta p_{t-1} + \underset{(0.060)}{0.135} \Delta(p_{t-2} + p_{t-4})$$

$$+ \underset{(0.007)}{0.030} [VAT(p) + Freeze]_t + \underset{(0.003)}{0.006}$$

$$+ \underset{(0.003)}{0.006} Q_{t-1} - \underset{(0.003)}{0.004} Q_{t-2} - \underset{(0.003)}{0.001} Q_{t-3} \qquad (17)$$

$R^2 = 0.39$ $\sigma = 0.0093$ $dw = 1.86$ $RSS = 0.0071$
Normality $\chi^2(2) = 0.22$ *AR* $1\text{-}5$ $F(5,78) = 0.21$ *ARCH* 4 $F(4,75) = 0.37$
Hetero $F(8,74) = 0.63$ *RESET* $F(1,82) = 0.32$ *Form* $F(16,66) = 0.32$,

$$\widehat{\Delta x_t} = - \underset{(0.065)}{0.228} \Delta_3\Delta x_{t-1} + \underset{(0.014)}{0.071} [VAT(x) - 0.5Freeze]_t$$

$$- \underset{(0.008)}{0.094} + \underset{(0.019)}{0.120} Q_{t-1} + \underset{(0.006)}{0.121} Q_{t-2} + \underset{(0.008)}{0.176} Q_{t-3} \qquad (18)$$

$R^2 = 0.95$ $\sigma = 0.0177$ $dw = 1.83$ $RSS = 0.0263$
Normality $\chi^2(2) = 1.43$ *AR* $1\text{-}5$ $F(5,79) = 1.33$ *ARCH* 4 $F(4,76) = 0.58$
Hetero $F(7,76) = 1.33$ *RESET* $F(1,83) = 0.68$ *Form* $F(11,72) = 0.93$,

---

[15] The approach adopted in this section owes a lot to Hendry and Ericsson (1991).
[16] The variable $\Delta(RD2 - RD1)$ is multiplied by 100 in the following.

$$\Delta(\widehat{RD2 - RD1})_t \;=\; \begin{array}{l} 0.597 \; \Delta(RD2 - RD1)_{t-1} \\ (0.094) \end{array}$$

$$\begin{array}{ll} -\; 0.184 \; \Delta^2(RD2 - RD1)_{t-2} \; - & 0.008 \\ (0.098) & (0.010) \end{array} \qquad (19)$$

$R^2 = 0.32 \quad \sigma = 0.0971 \quad dw = 2.00 \quad RSS = 0.8199$

Normality $\chi^2(2) = 87.96 \quad AR\ 1\text{–}5\ F(5, 82) = 3.26 \quad ARCH\ 4\ F(4, 79) = 0.15$

Hetero $F(4, 82) = 0.12 \quad RESET\ F(1, 86) = 0.01 \quad Form\ F(5, 81) = 0.10,$

$$\widehat{RS}_t \;=\; \begin{array}{l} 0.672 \; RS_{t-1} \; + \\ (0.086) \end{array} \begin{array}{l} 0.176 \; RS_{t-3} \; - \\ (0.084) \end{array} \begin{array}{l} 0.010 \\ (0.008) \end{array}$$

$$\begin{array}{lll} +\; 0.011 \; Q_{t-1} \; + & 0.005 \; Q_{t-2} \; + & 0.012 \; Q_{t-3} \\ (0.005) & (0.005) & (0.005) \end{array} \qquad (20)$$

$R^2 = 0.69 \quad \sigma = 0.0179 \quad dw = 1.95 \quad RSS = 0.0270$

Normality $\chi^2(2) = 25.49 \quad AR\ 1\text{–}5\ F(5, 79) = 0.46 \quad ARCH\ 4\ F(4, 76) = 0.96$

Hetero $F(7, 76) = 0.70 \quad RESET\ F(1, 83) = 0.18 \quad Form\ F(14, 69) = 0.85.$

The dummy $VAT(p)$ is unity in 1970(1) and models the effect of the introduction of VAT on inflation, while $VAT(x)$ is 1 in 1969(4) and -1 in 1970(1) to capture the effect of the pre-announced introduction of VAT in 1970(1) on expenditure demand. The *Freeze* dummy is unity in 1980(2) to represent the lifting of the wage and price freeze from 1979(1) to 1980(1).

Figures 9–12 give sequential F tests for the constancy of the parameters of the marginal models. The "Forecast" test for RS in Figure 12 evaluates model stability against an early period [1972(3)], while the "break-point" tests in Figures 9–11 use the end of the sample [1989(4)] as the evaluation point. Constancy is easily rejected for all the models, implying the super exogeneity of the variables of the conditional model for the class of interventions [385] occurring during the sample period.

5.2   Testing Invariance

A different class of tests of weak and super exogeneity have been developed by Engle and Hendry (1993). If the marginal processes are constant, we can use Wu-Hausman tests for independence between the conditioning variables and the residuals. It implies testing the significance of the residuals from the marginal model, or reduced form, in the conditional model. And if the marginal processes have changed over the sample period, a test of invariance is to model the interventions in the marginal models, and test for the significance of this model part in the conditional model. If the parameters of the conditional model are invariant to the changes in the marginal processes, including these changes should add no explanatory power.

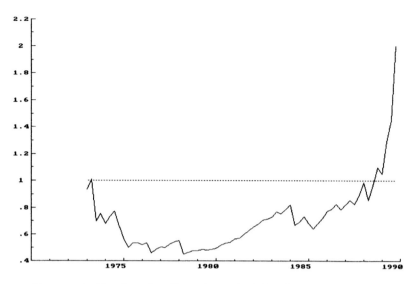

FIGURE 9. Break-point F statistics (—) for the simple marginal model for Δp, normalized by their one-off 5% critical values ($\cdots$).

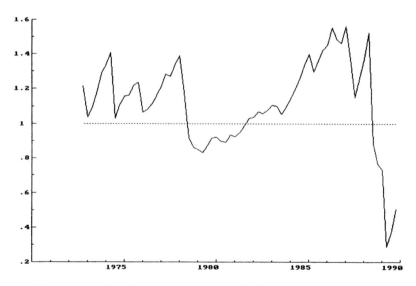

FIGURE 10. Break-point F statistics (—) for the simple marginal model for Δx, normalized by their one-off 5% critical values ($\cdots$).

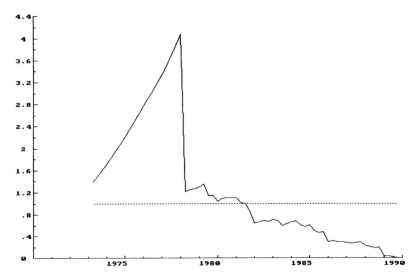

FIGURE 11. Break-point F statistics (—) for the simple marginal model for $\Delta(RD2-RD1)$, normalized by their one-off 5% critical values ($\cdots$).

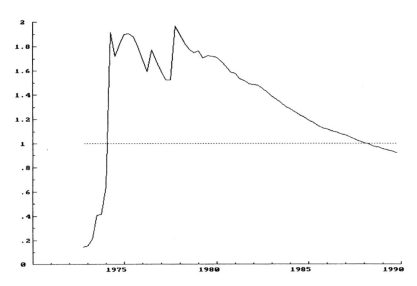

FIGURE 12. Forecast F statistics (—) for the simple marginal model for RS, normalized by their one-off 5% critical values ($\cdots$).

We know by now that well-specified marginal models are unavailable from the information set used so far. The set is therefore augmented with the following instruments: $REUR$, the Eurodollar rate; RBN, the marginal lending rate of the central bank; $pimp$, the price of imports; imp, the volume of imports of the main trading partners of Norway weighted by the weights of the official currency basket; cg, real public expenditure; and ig, real public investment.

With this information, the following marginal models are obtained:

$$\widehat{\Delta p_t} = \underset{(0.042)}{0.326}\ \Delta(pimp - p)_{t-3} + \underset{(0.011)}{0.071}\ \Delta x_{t-2}$$

$$+ \underset{(0.014)}{0.105}\ \Delta x_{t-3} + \underset{(0.184)}{0.337}\ \Delta RL_{t-3}$$

$$- \underset{(0.031)}{0.243}\ [p - 0.35(m + x) - 1.7RL - 0.18pimp]_{t-4}$$

$$+ \underset{(0.004)}{0.031}\ [VAT(p) + 0.5Freeze + D76(2)]_t - \underset{(0.266)}{2.055} \qquad (21)$$

$R^2 = 0.71 \quad \sigma = 0.0065 \quad dw = 2.03 \quad RSS = 0.0035$
Normality $\chi^2(2) = 0.37 \quad AR\ 1\text{-}5\ F(5,78) = 1.02 \quad ARCH\ 4\ F(4,75) = 0.45$
Hetero $F(12,70) = 0.60 \quad RESET\ F(1,82) = 0.96 \quad Form\ F(23,59) = 0.50,$

[386]

$$\widehat{\Delta x_t} = -\underset{(0.065)}{0.364}\ \Delta x_{t-1} + \underset{(0.016)}{0.067}\ \Delta ig_t + \underset{(0.041)}{0.147}\ \Delta imp_t$$

$$- \underset{(0.008)}{0.053}\ [x - 1.5(cg - ig + imp) + 20RD2]_{t-2}$$

$$+ \underset{(0.006)}{0.069}\ [VAT(x)_t + 0.5(D78(1)_t + D78(1)_{t-1} - Freeze)]$$

$$+ \underset{(0.038)}{0.145} + \underset{(0.014)}{0.085}\ Q_{t-1} + \underset{(0.004)}{0.107}\ Q_{t-2} + \underset{(0.008)}{0.143}\ Q_{t-3} \qquad (22)$$

$R^2 = 0.98 \quad \sigma = 0.0124 \quad dw = 2.12 \quad RSS = 0.0124$
Normality $\chi^2(2) = 1.77 \quad AR\ 1\text{-}5\ F(5,76) = 0.64 \quad ARCH\ 4\ F(4,73) = 0.36$
Hetero $F(13,67) = 0.65 \quad RESET\ F(1,80) = 0.13 \quad Form\ F(24,56) = 0.85,$

$$\Delta(\widehat{RD2 - RD1})_t = \underset{(0.024)}{0.067} + \underset{(0.066)}{0.498}\ \Delta(RD2 - RD1)_{t-1}$$

$$- \underset{(0.068)}{0.202}\ \Delta^2(RD2 - RD1)_{t-2}$$

$$- \underset{(0.235)}{0.839}\ RS_{t-1} - \underset{(0.930)}{3.857}\ \Delta RBN_{t-1}$$

$$+ \underset{(0.058)}{0.548}\ [D78(1) + 0.5(D69(4) + D81(4))]_t \qquad (23)$$

$R^2 = 0.68$ $\sigma = 0.0667$ $dw = 2.21$ $RSS = 0.3741$
Normality $\chi^2(2) = 2.81$ AR 1–5 $F(5,79) = 0.31$ ARCH 4 $F(4,76) = 2.70$
Hetero $F(10,73) = 0.86$ RESET $F(1,83) = 0.26$ Form $F(18,65) = 0.90$,

$$
\widehat{RS}_t = \underset{(0.005)}{0.012} + \underset{(0.074)}{0.485}\ RS_{t-1} + \underset{(0.162)}{1.056}\ RBN_t - \underset{(0.169)}{0.673}\ RBN_{t-1}
$$
$$
+ \underset{(0.044)}{0.099}\ REUR_t + \underset{(0.010)}{0.069}\ [D77(4) + 0.5D74(1,2)]_t
$$

$$(24)$$

$R^2 = 0.87$ $\sigma = 0.0119$ $dw = 1.99$ $RSS = 0.0118$
Normality $\chi^2(2) = 0.21$ AR 1–5 $F(5,79) = 0.57$ ARCH 4 $F(4,76) = 0.55$
Hetero $F(10,73) = 1.05$ RESET $F(1,83) = 4.30$ Form $F(17,66) = 1.45$.

The dummy $D74(1,2)$ takes the value -1 in 1974(1) and 1 in 1974(2). The rest are unity at the date indicated and zero elsewhere.

The "break-point" tests corresponding to the equations are shown in Figures 13–16. Only the equation for $\Delta(RD2 - RD1)$ has nonconstant parameters, which is not surprising, in that the data generating process was [389] one of political regulation over most of the sample.

From the results of the Johansen procedure, one could anticipate that the error correction term of the money demand equation would have some explanatory power in the expenditure equation. However, this is not the case.

Testing for invariance is performed by adding the auxiliary variables in (21)–(24) to the conditional model to see if they affect the parameters of the model. The F statistics for adding the intervention variables for Δp, Δx, $\Delta(RD2 - RD1)$, and RS are: $F(3,80) = 0.82$, $F(4,79) = 1.59$, $F(2,81) = 0.15$, and $F(4,79) = 1.56$. None of the determinants of nonconstancy are significant, and the joint test that the parameters of the variables are all zero is also accepted: $F(13,70) = 1.25$.[17]

For the case of $\Delta(RD2 - RD1)$, the residuals from (23), or functions of them, could also represent interventions. For the other variables, the test for the significance of the residuals is the Wu-Hausman test for weak exogeneity. The F statistic for adding the residuals from (21)–(24) to the money demand equation yields $F(4,79) = 1.56$, which is not significant. Consequently, prices, real expenditure, and interest rates can all be considered super exogenous for the parameters of the demand for narrow money in Norway.

---

[17] As noted by Engle and Hendry (1993) and Hendry and Ericsson (1991), these tests appear to have considerable power. Mis-specifying (16) by using lagged inflation and testing the inclusion of the intervention variables of inflation resulted in $F(3,80) = 4.24$, which has a p value of 0.0078.

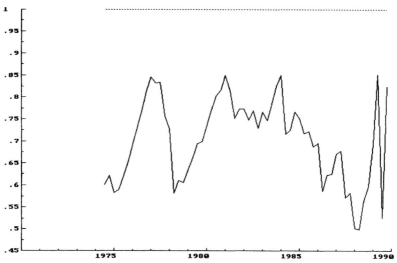

FIGURE 13. Break-point F statistics (—) for the augmented marginal model for Δp, normalized by their one-off 5% critical values ($\cdots$).

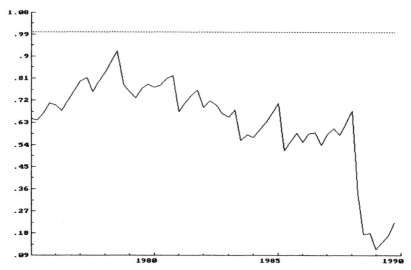

FIGURE 14. Break-point F statistics (—) for the augmented marginal model for Δx, normalized by their one-off 5% critical values ($\cdots$).

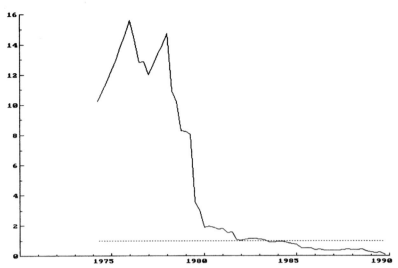

FIGURE 15. Break-point F statistics (—) for the augmented marginal model for $\Delta(RD2 - RD1)$, normalized by their one-off 5% critical values ($\cdots$).

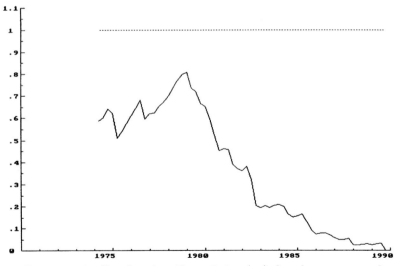

FIGURE 16. Break-point F statistics (—) for the augmented marginal model for RS, normalized by their one-off 5% critical values ($\cdots$).

6   Concluding Remarks

Given a sample riddled with changing policy regimes, the paper illustrates one way to go from a general statistical model to an interpretable and parsimonious representation of a demand for money function with constant parameters.

The empirical model especially highlights the role of the own yield and the rate of return of alternative assets. In the long run, the own rate and the alternative yield on bonds reflect the considerable differences in the riskiness and liquidity factors between money and bonds. In the short run, agents respond to changes in the alternative yield represented by time deposits and the money market rate. The implications of the analysis are that money is endogenously determined by prices, real expenditure, and interest rates, and that these determinants can be varied for a wide class of policy analyses.

Appendix.   The Data

[390]

All data are seasonally unadjusted.

- M Coins and currency notes and demand deposits held by the domestic nonbank public. The bank deposits included in this aggregate comprise deposits in domestic and foreign currency with domestic commercial and savings banks and postal institutions, excluding all deposits held by nonresidents. The data are rescaled to take account of a widening in the definition of demand deposits in 1987(1) and a break in the official data in 1987(2). Quarterly average of end-of-month data. Source: Bank of Norway.

- X Real gross domestic expenditure, excluding investment in the following sectors: petroleum and natural gas, pipeline transport, oil platforms, and ships. Sources: Various issues of *Quarterly National Accounts*.

- P Implicit deflator of X. Source: as for X.

- $RD1$ Average interest rate paid on banks' demand deposits. Quarterly data prior to 1978 are obtained by interpolation between end-of-year figures. Between 1978(1) and 1985(3) the series is a weighted average of lowest (weight $= 1/3$) and highest (weight $= 2/3$) interest rates paid on demand deposits by commercial and savings banks. From 1985(4), properly averaged data are compiled by the Bank of Norway. End-of-quarter estimates averaged over periods t and $t - 1$. Sources: Various issues of *Credit Market Statistics* and *Economic Bulletin of Norges Bank*.

- $RD2$ Average interest rate paid on banks' total deposits denominated in domestic currency (Norwegian Krone, NKr). Methods of calculation and sources as for $RD1$.

RL   Yield to average life of long-term bonds (more than six years to expected maturity date) issued by private mortgage loan associations. Quarterly average of end-of-month data. Source: Yield calculations based on bond prices quoted at the Oslo Stock Exchange.

RS   Three-month Eurocurrency interest rate on NKr computed from the covered interest parity relationship using middle quotations on spot and three-month forward exchange rates (NKr against $US) and the three-month Eurodollar interest rate. Quarterly average of end-of-month data. Source: Data on exchange rates and the Eurodollar interest rate [391] obtained from *International Financial Statistics* tapes and some private banks; from 1988(1), interest data as quoted in *Economic Bulletin of Norges Bank*.

Bibliography

(References marked with an asterisk * are included in this volume.)

Bårdsen, G. (1989) "Estimation of Long Run Coefficients in Error Correction Models", *Oxford Bulletin of Economics and Statistics*, 51, 345–350.

Bårdsen, G. (1990) "Dynamic Modelling and the Demand for Narrow Money in Norway", Discussion Paper 07/90, Norwegian School of Economics and Business Administration, Bergen, Norway.

Bårdsen, G., and J. T. Klovland (1990) "Finding the Right Nominal Anchor: The Cointegration of Money, Credit and Nominal Income in Norway", Warwick Economic Research Papers No. 350, Department of Economics, University of Warwick, Warwick, England.

Cooley, T. F., and S. F. LeRoy (1981) "Identification and Estimation of Money Demand", *American Economic Review*, 71, 825–844.

Engle, R. F. (1982) "Autoregressive Conditional Heteroscedasticity with Estimates of the Variance of United Kingdom Inflation", *Econometrica*, 50, 987–1007.

Engle, R. F., and C. W. J. Granger (1987) "Co-integration and Error Correction: Representation, Estimation, and Testing", *Econometrica*, 55, 251–276.

*Engle, R. F., and D. F. Hendry (1993) "Testing Super Exogeneity and Invariance in Regression Models", *Journal of Econometrics*, 56, 1/2, 119–139; originally cited as (1990), Applied Economics Discussion Paper No. 100, Institute of Economics and Statistics, Oxford, England.

*Engle, R. F., D. F. Hendry, and J.-F. Richard (1983) "Exogeneity", *Econometrica*, 51, 277–304.

Fair, R. C. (1987) "International Evidence on the Demand for Money", *Review of Economics and Statistics*, 69, 473–480.

Godfrey, L. (1988) *Misspecification Tests in Econometrics*, Cambridge, Cambridge University Press.

Goldfeld, S. M., and D. E. Sichel (1990) "The Demand for Money", in B. M. Friedman and F. H. Hahn (eds.) *Handbook of Monetary Economics*, Volume 1, Amsterdam, North-Holland.

Granger, C. W. J. (1986) "Developments in the Study of Cointegrated Economic Variables", *Oxford Bulletin of Economics and Statistics*, 48, 213–228.

Gregory, A. W., and M. McAleer (1981) "Simultaneity and the Demand for Money in Canada: Comments and Extensions", *Canadian Journal of Economics*, 14, 488–496.

Hamburger, M. J. (1977) "The Demand for Money in an Open Economy, Germany and the United Kingdom", *Journal of Monetary Economics*, 3, 25–40.

Harvey A. C. (1990) *The Econometric Analysis of Time Series*, Second Edition, London, Philip Allan.

Hendry, D. F. (1979) "Predictive Failure and Econometric Modelling in Macroeconomics: The Transactions Demand for Money", in P. Ormerod (ed.) *Modelling the Economy*, London, Heinemann Educational Books.

Hendry, D. F. (1985) "Monetary Economic Myth and Econometric Reality", *Oxford Review of Economic Policy*, 1, 72–84.

Hendry, D. F. (1986) "Econometric Modelling with Cointegrated Variables: An Overview", *Oxford Bulletin of Economics and Statistics*, 48, 201–213.

*Hendry, D. F. (1988) "The Encompassing Implications of Feedback versus Feedforward Mechanisms in Econometrics", *Oxford Economic Papers*, 40, 132–149.

[392] Hendry, D. F. (1989) *PC-GIVE: An Interactive Econometric Modelling System*, Oxford, University of Oxford, Institute of Economics and Statistics and Nuffield College.

Hendry, D. F., and N. R. Ericsson (1991) "Modeling the Demand for Narrow Money in the United Kingdom and the United States", *European Economic Review*, 35, 833–881.

Hendry, D. F., and G. E. Mizon (1993) "Evaluating Dynamic Econometric Models by Encompassing the VAR", in P. C. B. Phillips (ed.) *Models, Methods, and Applications of Econometrics*, Oxford, Basil Blackwell, 272–300; originally cited as (1990), Applied Economics Discussion Paper No. 102, Institute of Economics and Statistics, Oxford, England.

Hendry, D. F., and J.-F. Richard (1982) "On the Formulation of Empirical Models in Dynamic Econometrics", *Journal of Econometrics*, 20, 3–33.

Hendry, D. F., and J.-F. Richard (1983) "The Econometric Analysis of Economic Time Series", *International Statistical Review*, 51, 111–163.

Hylleberg, S., and G. Mizon (1989) "Cointegration and Error Correction Mechanisms", *Economic Journal*, 99 (Conference 1989), 113–125.

Jarque, C. M., and A. K. Bera (1980) "Efficient Tests for Normality, Homoscedasticity, and Serial Independence of Regression Residuals", *Economics Letters*, 6, 255–259.

Johansen, S. (1988) "Statistical Analysis of Cointegration Vectors", *Journal of Economic Dynamics and Control*, 12, 231–254.

Johansen, S. (1992a) "Cointegration in Partial Systems and the Efficiency of Single-equation Analysis", *Journal of Econometrics*, 52, 3, 389–402; originally cited as (1990), Mimeo, Institute of Mathematical Statistics, University of Copenhagen, Copenhagen, Denmark.

*Johansen, S. (1992b) "Testing Weak Exogeneity and the Order of Cointegration in UK Money Demand Data", *Journal of Policy Modeling*, 14, 3, 313–334.

Johansen, S., and K. Juselius (1990) "Maximum Likelihood Estimation and Inference on Cointegration—With Applications to the Demand for Money", *Oxford Bulletin of Economics and Statistics*, 52, 169–210.

Kiviet, J. (1986) "On the Rigour of Some Specification Tests for Modelling Dynamic Relationships", *Review of Economic Studies*, 53, 241–262.

Klovland, J. T. (1983) "The Demand for Money in Secular Perspective: The Case of Norway, 1867–1980", *European Economic Review*, 21, 193–218.

Klovland, J. T. (1990) "Wealth and the Demand for Money in Norway 1968–1989", Discussion Paper No. 01/90, Norwegian School of Economics and Business Administration, Bergen, Norway.

Laidler, D. E. W. (1985) *The Demand for Money: Theories, Evidence, and Problems*, Third Edition, New York, Harper and Row.

Osterwald-Lenum, M. (1992) "A Note with Quantiles of the Asymptotic Distribution of the Maximum Likelihood Cointegration Rank Test Statistics", *Oxford Bulletin of Economics and Statistics*, 54, 3, 461–472; originally cited as (1990) "Recalculated and Extended Tables of the Asymptotic Distribution of Some Important Maximum Likelihood Cointegration Test Statistics", Mimeo, University of Copenhagen, Copenhagen, Denmark.

Park, J. Y., and P. C. B. Phillips (1989) "Statistical Inference in Regressions with Integrated Processes: Part 2", *Econometric Theory*, 5, 95–131.

Phillips, P. C. B. (1988) "Reflections on Econometric Methodology", *Economic Record*, 64, 344–359.

Phillips, P. C. B. (1991) "Optimal Inference in Cointegrated Systems", *Econometrica*, 59, 238–306.

Phillips, P. C. B., and M. Loretan (1991) "Estimating Long Run Economic Equilibria", *Review of Economic Studies*, 58, 407–436.

Poloz, S. S. (1980) "Simultaneity and the Demand for Money in Canada", *Canadian Journal of Economics*, 13, 407–420.

Sims, C. A., J. H. Stock, and M. W. Watson (1990) "Inference in Linear Time Series Models with Some Unit Roots", *Econometrica*, 58, 113–144.

Spanos, A. (1986) *Statistical Foundations of Econometric Modelling*, Cambridge, Cambridge University Press.

Stock, J. H. (1987) "Asymptotic Properties of Least Squares Estimators of Cointegrating Vectors", *Econometrica*, 55, 1035–1056.

[393] Stock, J. H., and K. D. West (1988) "Integrated Regressors and Tests of the Permanent-Income Hypothesis," *Journal of Monetary Economics*, 21, 88–95.

Trundle, J. M. (1982) "The Demand for M1 in the UK", Bank of England Discussion Paper, London, England.

White, H. (1980) "A Heteroskedasticity-consistent Covariance Matrix Estimator and a Direct Test for Heteroskedasticity", *Econometrica*, 48, 1–48.

10

Finnish Manufacturing Wages 1960–1987: Real-wage Flexibility and Hysteresis

RAGNAR NYMOEN*

Abstract

We show that when real-wage flexibility is defined in terms of cointegration of the product real-wage and productivity, the wage formation system in Finnish manufacturing maintains considerable real-wage flexibility. We develop an empirical error correction model of wages and show that the responsiveness of wages to changes in unemployment is much less important in explaining real-wage flexibility than existing studies suggest. For example, we find hysteresis effects, which are usually associated with real-wage rigidity rather than flexibility. This puzzle is resolved by pointing out that theoretically hysteresis is only a necessary condition for rigidity. Empirically, strong equilibriating mechanisms, including labor market policies, have induced considerable wage flexibility even in the presence of hysteresis. Our conclusions are substantiated by tests of parameter invariance and encompassing.

* I am grateful to Neil R. Ericsson and an anonymous referee for their substantive comments and advice on earlier drafts. Thanks also to L. Calmfors, R. Hammersland, T. Mellingsæter, and E. Nesset. The usual disclaimer applies. Alan Manning gave me access to the "OECD-data" used in the section on encompassing. All numerical results were obtained with PC-GIVE Version 6.1 [Hendry (1989)].

Reprinted with permission from the *Journal of Policy Modeling* (August 1992), 14, 4, 429–451.

1   Introduction

In policy discussions and in economic analysis, wage flexibility is often confounded with wage responsiveness to unemployment. One aim of our analysis
is to demonstrate some advantages of treating wage responsiveness and wage
flexibility as conceptually different. We define real-wage flexibility in terms
of cointegration of three variables: nominal wage costs, output price, and
average labor productivity. Product real-wages are "flexible" when the wage
share is a stationary stochastic variable. Wage responsiveness to unemployment, on the other hand, is defined in terms of the sign structure of the
[430]   distributed lag between nominal wages and unemployment. Wage hysteresis
is an extreme form of low responsiveness: that is, shocks to unemployment
have only a temporary wage-reducing effect. In our framework, hysteresis is
one potentially important source of wage rigidity but does not in itself imply
rigidity.

There is a puzzle over Finnish real-wage adjustment, since existing studies find hysteresis effects although considerable flexibility is evident in the
real-wage data. We show that hysteresis may coexist with real-wage flexibility, so no conflict need exist. However, if hysteresis is present, then other
forces must be at work to maintain wage flexibility. An aim of the article
is to identify these equilibrating mechanisms. For example, we find that a
reversion toward less accommodative labor market policies has contributed
significantly to the observed wage adjustment.

The rest of the article is organized as follows. The conceptual distinction
between wage responsiveness to unemployment and real-wage flexibility is
established in Section 2. Thus, in Section 3, we estimate the degree of wage
flexibility in Finland, using a multivariate cointegration framework. One important result is that flexibility in real wages affects not only nominal wage
formation but also price and productivity adjustments. However, nominal
wage adjustment remains an important source of real-wage flexibility. For
example, policy initiatives to increase flexibility usually aim to influence wage
bargaining outcomes, rather than price formation or productivity growth. In
Sections 4 and 5 we therefore focus on nominal wage adjustment. We review
the findings of existing studies in Section 4 and present our new study in
Section 5. Section 5 also features tests of exogeneity and parameter invariance, and so of the Lucas critique, and shows the encompassing properties
of our results with respect to the existing studies. Section 6 contains our
conclusions and a brief discussion.

2   Real-wage Flexibility and Hysteresis in Wage Equations

To establish the distinction between real-wage flexibility and hysteresis, consider the following *stylized* wage equation:

$$\Delta w_t = \delta_0 + \delta_1 U_t + \delta_2 U_{t-1} + \delta_3 (wc - q - y)_{t-1} + \delta_4 (p - q)_{t-1} + \varepsilon_t, \quad (1)$$

where the δ_i's are constants, ε_t is a residual, and the variables are:

w money wage per hour,

wc wage costs per hour,

U rate of unemployment,

q producer price index, [431]

p consumer price index, and

y productivity index.

Lower-case letters are used for variables measured in logarithms. If $\delta_4 = 0$, so that the relative price $(p - q)_{t-1}$ drops out, (1) implies that the development of the wage level is governed by firm-side variables (productivity and product price), and by labor market fluctuations (i.e., U_t and U_{t-1}). More generally, $\delta_4 \geq 0$, which means that worker-side interests may influence the wage outcome, that is, through the consumption price.

In the spirit of Layard, Nickell, and Jackman (1991), we define *wage hysteresis* as a situation in which the negative impact of a shock to unemployment on wages is larger in the short run than in the long run. A necessary requirement is clearly that $\delta_1 < 0$ and $\delta_2 > 0$. A stronger form of wage hysteresis occurs when there is no long-run response to unemployment: that is, $\delta_1 + \delta_2 = 0$ [Blanchard and Summers (1986)].

In (1), assume that the real-wage $(wc-q)_t$ and productivity y_t are nonstationary variables, which become stationary after a single differencing; that is, they are I(1) variables [see Granger (1981) and Engle and Granger (1987)]. In this (realistic) case, the seriousness of real-wage rigidity can be described in terms of a *wage gap*, defined as:

$$\omega_t = (wc - q)_t - \theta y_t,$$

for a constant θ. If the real wage does not drift too far from productivity over time, $\omega_t \sim$ I(0): that is, there is wage flexibility in a very substantial sense. Conversely, real-wage rigidity can be defined by $\omega_t \sim$ I(1) for all θ. Since the wage gap is a linear combination of I(1) terms, real-wage flexibility is a proposition about *cointegration* between real wages and productivity.

In the following, y_t is measured by average labor productivity. It is then natural to set $\theta = 1$ so that the wage gap ω_t is defined in terms of the observed wage share. Now consider the situation when the lagged wage share in (1) is stationary. $\delta_3 < 0$ then reflects that flexibility partly explains nominal wage adjustments (which we assume to be stationary).[1] Note that

---

[1] In principle we can have $\omega_t \sim$ I(0) even with $\delta_3 = 0$, since both prices and productivity can adjust to ω_{t-1}.

this situation with error correction in wages may, or may not, coexist with
hysteresis. Conversely, there may be rigidity, but without strong hysteresis:
one possibility is that the wage share cointegrates with $(p - q)_t$ and that U_t
is stationary.[2]

[432]   In the earlier literature, the notions of wage flexibility and wage responsiveness to unemployment are often confounded. Grubb, Jackman, and Layard (1983, p. 11) define real-wage rigidity by "the inverse of the long-run
coefficient on unemployment in the wage equation", thus equating low wage
responsiveness with wage rigidity. Bruno and Sachs (1985) define the wage
gap as the difference between the observed wage and the full employment
wage, but they do not test for the impact of this term in their wage equations. In the influential paper by Blanchard and Summers (1986), there is
no clear distinction between hysteresis and real-wage rigidity.

In one sense, stationarity of the wage share is a weak definition of flexibility. For example, two economies can display considerable differences in their
adjustments to shocks, even though $\omega_t \sim \mathrm{I}(0)$ in both economies. However,
for the same reason that $\omega_t \sim \mathrm{I}(0)$ is a weak condition of wage flexibility,
nonstationary ω_t is a sign of serious rigidity. In (1), such rigidity arises if
$(p - q)_t \sim \mathrm{I}(1)$ and $\delta_3 < 0$ and $\delta_4 > 0$; that is, the wage cointegrates with
a nonstationary relative price. When there is drift in the relative price,
long-run effects of consumer prices result in wage rigidity.

3   Finnish Wage Formation: Evidence of Real-wage Flexibility

Finland provides an interesting example of real-wage adjustment since, like
Norway and Sweden, Finland has been relatively successful in maintaining
high employment, but notably without the help of oil fortunes (Norway) or
extremely centralized wage-setting institutions (Sweden). [See, e.g., Calmfors and Driffill (1988) and Calmfors and Nymoen (1990)].

The log of the wage-share series is shown in Figure 1. That the graph
crosses the zero line on several occasions suggests that the wage-share formulation achieves cointegration between nominal wage costs (WC_t), value-
added price (Q_t), and average labor productivity (Y_t).

A formal test can be based on the cointegration analysis developed by
Johansen (1988) and Johansen and Juselius (1990). To outline the Johansen
procedure, let X_t denote a vector of variables of interest. In our case $X_t =$
$(wc_t, q_t, y_t)'$, the logs of wage costs, product price, and productivity. The
vector autoregressive representation (VAR) (or reduced form) of the system

---

[2] In this case we would have $\delta_3 < 0$ as in the $\omega_t \sim \mathrm{I}(0)$ case, and $\delta_1 + \delta_2 < 0$, but also
$\delta_4 > 0$ as opposed to $\delta_4 = 0$.

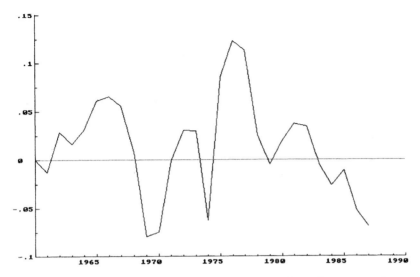

FIGURE 1. Log of the manufacturing wage share $(wc - q - y)_t$.

can be written in the following interim multiplier form [e.g., Hylleberg and Mizon (1989)]:

$$\Delta X_t = \sum_{i=1}^{k-1} \Pi_i \Delta X_{t-i} - \Pi_k X_{t-k} + \mu + V_t \qquad V_t \sim \mathsf{IID}(0, \Omega). \qquad (2)$$

All the Π matrices are 3×3 in our case and the constant term μ is 3×1. [433] Π_i $(i = 1, \ldots, k-1)$ give the interim-multiplier structure. The cointegration analysis focuses on the matrix of level coefficients Π_k:

$$\Pi_k = \alpha \beta'. \qquad (3)$$

$\beta' X_{t-k}$ are linear combinations of the $\mathsf{I}(1)$ series X_{t-k}. Only stationary linear combinations can explain the $\mathsf{I}(0)$ series ΔX_t. Hence, in large samples, the columns of α should be zero except those columns corresponding to the stationary linear combinations.

Our sample period is 1960–1987. The order of the VAR is set to 2, since a first-order process did not suffice to produce even approximately white-noise residuals.[3] This leaves us with 26 observations, which are admittedly few for this kind of analysis. Nevertheless, the results in Table 1 lend themselves easily to interpretation. In part (a) of the table we list the hypothesized number

---

[3] With the VAR of order 3 the cointegration statistic becomes only marginally significant. The estimated relationship in (4) is affected very little, though.

TABLE 1. Results of the Cointegration Analysis

Eigenvalues	0.02	0.28	0.56

(a) Cointegration test statistics

r	1	2	3
max statistic	0.52	8.65	21.12
5% critical value	(7.71)	(13.97)	(19.74)
trace statistic	0.52	9.17	30.29
5% critical value	(7.71)	(16.84)	(29.30)

(b) Cointegration coefficients (β's)

	β_1	β_2	β_3
wc	1.0	−0.001	−0.61
q	−1.16	1.0	0.54
y	−0.68	1.73	1.0

(c) Error correction coefficients (α's)

Δwc	−0.18	−0.10	−0.01
Δq	−0.54	−0.09	−0.02
Δy	0.18	−0.02	0.02

Notes: The VAR is second-order in (wc_t, q_t, y_t), augmented by an unrestricted constant, estimated on annual data for 1962–1987. r denotes the number of unit roots. See Johansen (1988) for definition of the statistics "max" and "trace", and Eitrheim (1990) for critical values (in parentheses).

[434] (r) of unit roots in the levels lag polynomial for the system in (2) and the corresponding canonical correlations. The "trace" and "max" statistics test if there are r unit roots in that polynomial. Rejection implies at least $3-r+1$ cointegrating vectors. The statistics reject three unit roots in (2), given the critical values from Johansen and Juselius (1990) and Eitrheim (1990). Thus, we infer one cointegrating relation, consistent with our economic theory.

In part (b) of Table 1, the cointegrating vector β_1, corresponding to the highest eigenvalue, is normalized with respect to wage cost. Considering the limited number of observations, the relationship

$$\widehat{wc}_t = 1.16q_t + 0.68y_t \qquad (4)$$

comes close to a wage-share formulation.

Since the choice of normalization is arbitrary, (4) is not interpretable as a "wage equation". In fact, part (c) of Table 1 indicates that a disequilibrium in wages, prices, and productivity induces adjustment in all of prices, productivity, and wages. Nevertheless, a well-specified dynamic wage equation will be helpful to understanding the mechanisms underlying the observed real-wage flexibility.

4 Nominal Wage Adjustments: Existing Evidence

As a prelude to our own study of Finnish nominal wage formation in Section 5, this section reviews the results of pre-existing studies of wage responsiveness to unemployment. The works of Newell and Symons (1985, 1988), Bean, Layard, and Nickell (1986), Grubb (1986), and Alogoskoufis and Manning (1988) are examples of broad comparative studies that include equations for Finland. Saikkonen and Teräsvirta (1985) and Eriksson, Suvanto, and Vartia (1990) are the most accessible recent Finnish studies.   [435]

These studies show little agreement on the strength of wage responsiveness to unemployment. Table 2 shows that Newell and Symons (1985) (N-S '85) report a 0.5 percent immediate effect on wages of a one-percentage-point reduction in unemployment. In contrast, Alogoskoufis and Manning's (A-M) (1988) estimate is a 4.4 percent wage increase. The estimates of the long-run effects vary even more.[4]

The available studies are in more agreement on the relevance of hysteresis effects. The two studies that include a second-year effect of unemployment both find a sign switch for the estimated coefficients. In addition, Eriksson, Suvanto, and Vartia include unemployment rates for different durations. In their results, increased long-term unemployment does not depress wages.   [436]

However, the existing studies disagree on other forms of wage adjustment. For example, the models estimated by Newell and Symons show significant error correction with respect to firm-side fundamentals, whereas A-M find no error correction. A new study of Finnish wage formation should be able to sort out why such conflicting evidence exists, and in which direction the reassessed evidence weighs.

5 Nominal Wage Adjustment: New Evidence

In this section we present the results of our own empirical study. In Section 5.1 we present the framework for the empirical model. We use an error

---

[4] Note that with the exception of the two papers by Finnish authors, all the studies use virtually the same data set: Grubb (1984) or updates of it.

TABLE 2.

Models of the Wage–Unemployment Relationship in Finland

Model[a]	w_{t-1}	U_t	U_{t-1}	$U(LR)$	$\hat{\sigma}$	Period	Method[b]
N-S '85	0.75	−0.46	0.23	−0.92	1.8%	1955–81	3SLS
N-S '88	0.69	−0.91	—	−2.93	1.7%	1955–83	IV
B-L-N	0.30	−2.10	—	−3.00	—	1953–83	FIML
G	0.64	−1.84	—	−2.87	4.96%	1952–83	OLS
A-M	0.99	−4.4	2.38	−202.4	—	1952–85	IV
E	—	—	—	−0.87	1.7%	—	IV
S-T	0.99	−2.1	−4.69	−254.55	1.0%	1962–79	FIML

Note: w_{t-1} gives the coefficient of the lagged wage level (in logs), when w_t is the dependent variable. U_t gives the first-year effect of the unemployment term: the percentage effect on w of a one-percentage-point increase in U. U_{t-1} gives the second-year effect. $U(LR)$ gives the estimated long-run effect.

[a] Authors of models compared:

    A-M   Alogoskoufis and Manning (1988, Table 5),

    N-S '85   Newell and Symons (1985, Table 6)

        (effect of U_{t-2} recorded in U_{t-1} column),

    N-S '88   Newell and Symons (1988, Table A.1),

    B-L-N   Bean, Layard, and Nickell (1986, Table 3),

    G   Grubb (1986, Appendix, Table 1),

    E   Eriksson, Suvanto, and Vartia (1990, Table 3, column 3), and

    S-T   Saikkonen and Teräsvirta (1985, Equation (3)).

[b] Methods: Full information maximum likelihood (FIML), instrumental variables (IV), ordinary least squares (OLS), three-stage least squares (3SLS).

correction model that is general enough to accommodate the salient features of the existing studies. Section 5.2 gives the results for our empirical model, and Sections 5.3 and 5.4 discuss the invariance and encompassing properties of that model. The series being explained (Δw) is given in Figure 2.

[437]

5.1 Framework

We start with the following equation:

$$
\begin{aligned}
\Delta w_t = {} & \gamma_0 + \gamma_{ec}(wc - q - y)_{t-1} + \gamma_{q0}\Delta q_t + \gamma_{q1}\Delta q_{t-1} + \gamma_{y0}\Delta y_t \\
& + \gamma_{y1}\Delta y_{t-1} + \gamma_{pt0}\Delta pt_t + \gamma_{pt1}\Delta pt_{t-1} + \gamma_{p0}\Delta p_t \\
& + \gamma_{p1}\Delta p_{t-1} + \gamma_{a0}\Delta at_t + \gamma_{a1}\Delta at_{t-1} + \gamma_u(SU\% - LU\%)_t \\
& + \gamma_r rpr_t + \nu_t.
\end{aligned}
\tag{5}
$$

Compared to (1), we have substituted U_t and U_{t-1} by the more specific

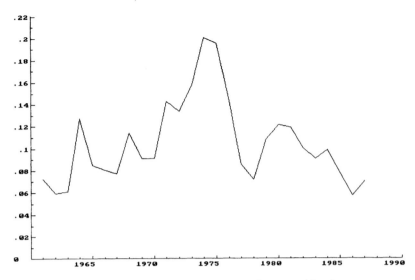

FIGURE 2. Growth in nominal wages (Δw_t).

hypothesis $(SU\% - LU\%)_t$, where $SU\%$ and $LU\%$ are the short- and long-term unemployment percentages. After a negative shock, $SU\%_t$ usually rises sharply, resulting in wage moderation. After a while $LU\%_t$ rises, while $SU\%_t$ starts to fall. If the long-term unemployed exert little downward wage pressure, these dynamics imply a sharper short-run than long-run response with respect to unemployment, that is, a hysteresis effect [Nickell (1987)].[5]

Whereas (1) has deliberately simple dynamics, (5) allows for short-run effects of consumer prices (Δp_t), producer prices (Δq_t), productivity (Δy_t), and income and payroll tax rates (Δat_t and Δpt_t). Δp_t in particular may be important because of formal and informal "cost-of-living" indexing of wage bargains [Eriksson, Suvanto, and Vartia (1990)].

Finally, an additional employee-side variable is included: the replacement ratio (rpr_t), which is the ratio between unemployment benefits and normal work income. The replacement ratio can affect wages through several channels. The "physiology of equity" can produce a balancing of remuneration of workers who have enjoyed different fortunes in the labor market, that is, if the jobless belong to the reference group of wage setters.[6] In a bargaining

---

[5] Restricting $SU\%$ and $LU\%$ in this way is supported by the data. When (5) is estimated (see Table 3), the F statistic for the restriction is $F(1, 11) = 0.15$. For (6) the F statistic is $F(1, 19) = 0.07$.

[6] See Carruth and Oswald (1989, Chapter 5) for a discussion of the "physiological law of equity" and wage formation.

TABLE 3. OLS Estimation of Equation (5)

	lag i			
Variable	0		1	
$(wc - q - y)_{t-i}$			−0.3097	(0.060)
Δy_{t-i}	0.305	(0.134)	0.2077	(0.137)
Δq_{t-i}	0.001	(0.068)	−0.1313	(0.083)
Δpt_{t-i}	−0.9189	(0.397)	−0.6734	(0.43)
Δp_{t-i}	1.036	(0.121)	0.1093	(0.118)
Δat_{t-i}	−0.0023	(0.114)	0.0166	(0.103)
$(SU\% - LU\%)_{t-i}$	−0.00816	(0.003)		
rpr_{t-i}	0.1138	(0.016)		
constant	−0.4272	(0.071)		

Note: $T = 26$ (1962–1987) $k = 14$ $R^2 = 0.9798$ $\hat{\sigma} = 0.79\%$ $dw = 2.78$
$F_{AR1-1}(1, 11) = 3.50$ $F_{AR1-2}(2, 10) = 1.75$ $F_{ARCH1-1}(1, 10) = 0.01$
$\chi^2_N(2) = 1.62$.

Statistics: T is the number of observations; k is the number of regressors; R^2 is the squared multiple correlation coefficient; $\hat{\sigma}$ is the standard error of the regression; and dw is the Durbin-Watson statistic. $F_{ARCH1-q}(q, T - k - 2q)$ is the qth-order ARCH test [Engle (1982)]; $F_{ARi-j}(q, T - k - q)$ is the statistic for testing ith- to jth-order autocorrelation, $q = j - i + 1$ [Harvey (1981, p. 173)]; $\chi^2_N(2)$ is the statistic for testing zero skewness and excess kurtosis ("normality") [Jarque and Bera (1980)].

Δw is the left-hand side variable. Standard errors are in parentheses.

framework, workers who currently have a job will reduce their wage claims as a response to cuts in benefits, because by doing so they can reduce the risk of losing their regular income and being exposed to the lower benefits level.

We interpret both $(SU\% - LU\%)_t$ and rpr_t as I(0) variables. Besides
[438] the lagged wage share, these are the only level terms. Adding an I(1) term, notably the relative price $(p - q)_t$, would result in an unbalanced equation.[7]

5.2 Estimation and Interpretation

Ordinary least squares (OLS) estimation of (5) over 1962–1987 gives the results in Table 3. The lagged wage share is significant, so the observed

---

[7] For $(p - q)_t$ the Durbin-Watson (dw) statistic is 0.24, and the simple and augmented (first-order) Dickey-Fuller tests give −1.20 and −1.30, respectively. Approximate critical values are 0.77 for dw and −3.00 for the two Dickey-Fuller tests [Sargan and Bhargava (1983), Fuller (1976)].

wage flexibility cannot be attributed entirely to wage responsiveness to unemployment. Other salient features of Table 3 include the highly significant
coefficient of the replacement ratio and the huge short-run effect of consumer
prices. It is intriguing that full short-run indexing to consumer prices goes
together with no long-run indexing. However, several recent studies have
found less pass-through of worker-side variables in the long run than in the
short run, for example, Rowlatt (1987) for U.K. data and Nymoen (1989,
1991a) for Norwegian data. Finally, there is strong backward shifting of payroll taxes. In contrast, we find no effect of income taxes. This asymmetry
between the two tax variables is found in several separate studies of wage [439]
formation in the Nordic countries [see, e.g., the country studies in Calmfors
(1990) and Calmfors and Nymoen (1990)].

The diagnostic tests do not reveal mis-specification; hence we take Table 3
as the starting point for designing a model of wage growth. Four classes of
simplifications are apparent from Table 3. First, the impact effects of both
consumer prices and the payroll-tax rate are near unity, so the left-hand side
variable can be transformed to $\Delta(w + pt) - \Delta p$. Second, the productivity
terms can be replaced by a single term $\Delta_2 y_t$, that can be seen as a way of
smoothing productivity growth to extract changes that are more permanent.
Third, after deletion of the impact effect of producer prices, Δq_{t-1} and Δp_{t-1}
can be expressed as $(\Delta p - \Delta q)_{t-1}$; that is, the lagged growth in the relative
price has a positive effect. It is less clear what to make of the change in
lagged payroll tax, but we chose to join Δpt_{t-1} to $(\Delta p - \Delta q)_{t-1}$. Finally,
since they are insignificant, the income-tax terms are deleted. The simplified
equation is shown in (6). Eight restrictions have been imposed, with a joint
F statistic of $F(8, 12) = 0.40.$[8]

---

[8] IV estimation, with $\Delta_2 y_t$, rpr_t, and $(SU\% - LU\%)_t$ as endogenous variables, gives

$$\widehat{\Delta w_t} - \Delta p_t + \Delta pt_t = \begin{array}{l} - \ 0.415 \\ (0.039) \end{array} \begin{array}{l} - \ 0.0072 \ (SU\% - LU\%)_t \\ (0.003\ ) \end{array}$$

$$+ \ \begin{array}{l} 0.1635 \ \Delta(p - q - pt)_{t-1} \\ (0.051\ ) \end{array} + \ \begin{array}{l} 0.207 \ \Delta_2 y_t \\ (0.057) \end{array}$$

$$+ \ \begin{array}{l} 0.112 \ rpr_t \\ (0.01\ ) \end{array} - \ \begin{array}{l} 0.331 \ (wc - q - y)_{t-1}. \\ (0.040) \end{array}$$

Instruments: $(SU\% - LU\%)_{t-1}$, $AMS\%_t$, Δpi_t, Δpi_{t-1}, Δy_{t-1}, rpr_{t-1}, $(mol-p)_{t-1}$,
$(pi - p)_{t-1}$. $AMS\%$ is the number of persons on labor market programs as a percentage
of the labor force; pi is (log of) the import price index; mol is (log of) an $M1$ money
measure. The chi-square test of instrument validity [Sargan (1964)] yields $\chi^2(5) = 7.50$.

$$\widehat{\Delta w_t} - \Delta p_t + \Delta pt_t = -\ \underset{(0.0363)}{0.419} \ -\ \underset{(0.0022)}{0.0073}\ (SU\% - LU\%)_t$$

$$+\ \underset{(0.05\ )}{0.160}\ \Delta(p - q - pt)_{t-1}\ +\ \underset{(0.048)}{0.228}\ \Delta_2 y_t$$

$$+\ \underset{(0.009)}{0.112}\ rpr_t\ -\ \underset{(0.037)}{0.328}\ (wc - q - y)_{t-1}\qquad (6)$$

$T \doteq 26\ (1962\text{–}1987)\qquad k = 6\qquad \hat{o} = 0.69\%\qquad dw - 2.63$

$F_{AR1-1}(1,19) = 3.51\qquad F_{AR1-2}(2,18) = 2.28\qquad F_{ARCH1-1}(1,18) = 0.01$

$\chi_N^2(2) = 0.92.$

[440] Equation (6) implies relatively moderate responsiveness to unemployment. The impact effect of a one-percentage-point reduction in short-term unemployment is a 0.73 percent increase in wage growth. The long-run effect for the wage level is 2.2 percent. If long-term unemployment adjusts, the long-run effect will be smaller; that is, the equation will display a wage-hysteresis effect. The result with open unemployment U instead of $SU\% - LU\%$ corroborates this interpretation: the coefficient of U_t is $\{-0.007\ (0.003)\}$ and of U_{t-1} $\{0.005\ (0.003)\}$.

The highly significant rpr_t variable is interesting from a policy perspective. Given the development of the replacement ratio in Figure 3, it suggests that a less accommodative policy stance has contributed significantly to wage moderation, particularly over the period 1972–1984.

The main equilibrating mechanism is via firm-side variables. Accordingly, automatic stabilization or error correction is an intrinsic feature of the wage-setting system. Second, the tightening of unemployment insurance schemes, resulting in a lower replacement ratio, has depressed wage growth, thus adding to real-wage flexibility. Compared with these two effects, responsiveness to labor market fluctuations appears to be of secondary importance.

[441]
5.3 Stability and Invariance

Within-sample parameter stability and invariance are desirable properties of empirical models. Stability and parameter invariance reflect a relationship's autonomy in the face of policy interventions and regime shifts [Engle, Hendry, and Richard (1983) and Engle and Hendry (1993)]. Failure to achieve either leaves the model unsuitable for policy analysis. For example, our claim that de-accommodation has contributed to wage adjustment is unfounded if the coefficient of rpr_t fluctuates with interventions in that variable. In this section we test the stability and invariance of (6).

First, we demonstrate the stability of the conditional model (6). Consider

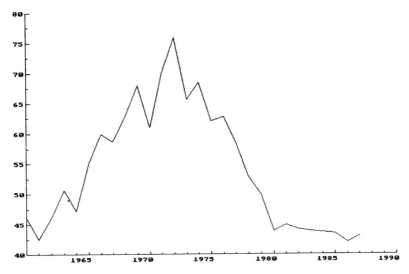

FIGURE 3. Unemployment benefits as a percentage of ordinary labor income: the replacement ratio (RPR_t).

Figure 4, which shows the one-step residuals and the corresponding standard errors; that is, $\{\hat{y}_t - \hat{\beta}_t' X_t\}$ and $\{0 \pm 2\hat{\sigma}_t\}$ in standard notation. The figure shows that $\hat{\sigma}$ is constant over the sample. Stability is also evident from the sequence of one-step-ahead Chow tests shown in Figure 5 [Chow (1960)]. None of the tests are significant. A caveat here is that the Chow test can have low power for poorly fitting models. However, with a standard error of 0.69 percent, this model compares favorably with existing models (compare Table 2). Of the individual coefficients, we focus on those of the labor market term and the unemployment insurance term, since they are most relevant from a policy perspective. Figures 6 and 7 show the recursively estimated [442] coefficients and their estimated standard errors. Both coefficients appear constant, given the estimated uncertainty.

In the spirit of Engle and Hendry (1993), we develop autoregressive models of the marginal processes for the replacement ratio rpr and the unemployment differential $SU\% - LU\%$. These models are not constant, so we introduce various dummies to obtain constancy. We first present the "augmented" models with evidence on the simpler models' nonconstancy. Then we use the dummies to test for invariance in the conditional model (6).

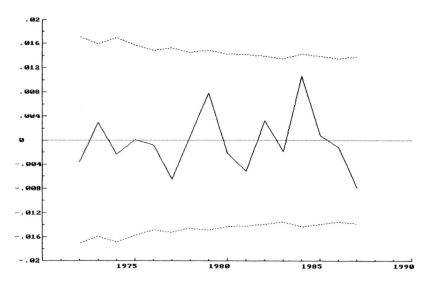

FIGURE 4. Equation (6): one-step residuals (—), with corresponding calculated equation standard errors as $0 \pm 2\hat{\sigma}_t$ ($\cdots$).

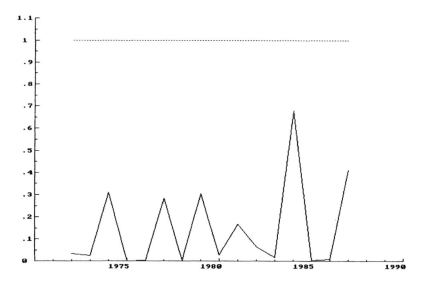

FIGURE 5. Equation (6): the sequence of one-step-ahead Chow statistics (—) over 1972–1987, with the statistics scaled by their one-off 5% critical values ($\cdots$).

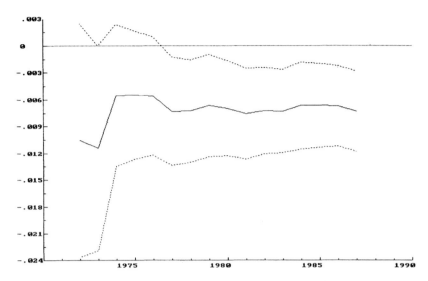

FIGURE 6. Equation (6): recursive estimates (—) of the coefficient of $(SU\% - LU\%)_t$, with ± 2 estimated standard errors $(\cdots)$.

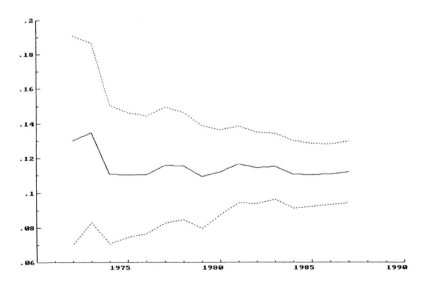

FIGURE 7. Equation (6): recursive estimates (—) of the coefficient of rpr_t, with ± 2 estimated standard errors $(\cdots)$.

$$\widehat{rpr}_t = \underset{(0.26)}{1.00} + \underset{(0.06)}{0.75}\ rpr_{t-1} - \underset{(0.54)}{0.84}\ \Delta at_t$$

$$- \underset{(0.016)}{0.086}\ [I_{64} - I_{69} - I_{71} - I_{72} + ST_{75} + I_{80}] \qquad (7a)$$

$T = 27\ (1961\text{--}1987) \qquad k = 4 \qquad R^2 = 0.92 \qquad \hat{\sigma} = 5.44\% \qquad dw = 1.95$

$F_{AR1-2}(2, 21) = 0.79 \qquad \chi^2_N(2) = 5.98 \qquad F_{ARCH1-1}(1, 21) = 0.09.$

[443]

$$(SU\% \widehat{- LU\%})_t = \underset{(0.088)}{0.236} + \underset{(0.043)}{0.791}\ (SU\% - LU\%)_{t-1}$$

$$- \underset{(0.363)}{1.048}\ [\Delta(mol - p)_{t-1} - \Delta(wc - q)_{t-1}]$$

$$- \underset{(0.007)}{0.095}\ \Delta AMUN\%_t$$

$$+ \underset{(0.078)}{0.548}\ [I_{68} + I_{74} - I_{78} + I_{80}] \qquad (7b)$$

$T = 26\ (1962\text{--}1987) \qquad k = 5 \qquad R^2 = 0.96 \qquad \hat{\sigma} = 0.144 \qquad dw = 1.46$

$F_{AR1-1}(1, 20) = 1.55 \qquad F_{AR1-2}(2, 19) = 0.76 \qquad F_{ARCH1-1}(1, 19) = 0.42$

$\chi^2_N(2) = 1.47.$

Equations (7a) and (7b) show *stable* marginal models of rpr_t and $(SU\% - LU\%)_t$, conditional on a set of intervention dummies. Equation (7a) is basically autoregressive, but with the change in the income-tax rate as an exogenous variable: until 1984 unemployment insurance was untaxed income [Eriksson, Suvanto, and Vartia (1990)]. In (7b), unemployment depends on a demand factor $([mol - p]_{t-1})$, wage costs $([wc - q]_{t-1})$, and a labor market policy term $AMUN\%_t$ (coverage of labor market programs). These equations appear constant when estimated recursively. In contrast, Figures 8 and 9 show the one-step-ahead Chow tests when the dummies for the rele-
[444] vant years in the 1973–1987 period are dropped. Considerable nonconstancy is evident. Thus the dummies covering the 1973–1987 period can be seen as proxying *determinants* of the nonconstancies in the unemployment and insurance processes.

If the parameters of the wage equation are invariant to the nonconstancies of the marginal processes, variables that are helpful in explaining the nonconstancies should be unimportant in the constant parameter conditional model. This is the basis for Engle and Hendry's (1993) test of invariance and super exogeneity. Adding the four relevant dummies (i.e., I_{74}, ST_{75}, I_{78}, and I_{80}) to (6) gives $F(4, 16) = 0.12$. Hence we cannot reject the null hypothesis that the errors of (6) are innovations relative to the enlarged information set.

In economic terms, our model is consistent with wage setters reacting to observed changes in unemployment, rather than to the projections about

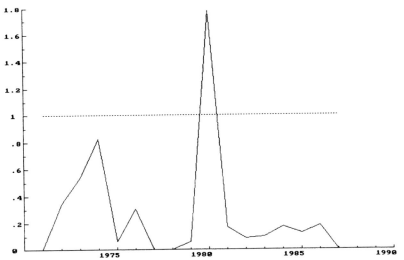

FIGURE 8. Modified (7a): the sequence of one-step-ahead Chow statistics (—) over 1971–1987, with the statistics scaled by their one-off 5% critical values (···).

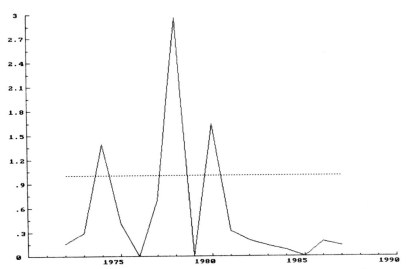

FIGURE 9. Modified (7b): the sequence of one-step-ahead Chow statistics (—) over 1972–1987, with the statistics scaled by their one-off 5% critical values (···).

unemployment on the basis of an expectations model. Consequently the Lucas critique is refuted for the model estimated here.

5.4   Comparison with Existing Studies: Encompassing

Encompassing stresses the importance of formal and informal comparison of empirical models with pre-existing formulations [Davidson, Hendry, Srba, and Yeo (1978); Mizon and Richard (1986); and Hendry and Richard (1989)]. Failure to encompass means that rival formulations contain specific informa-[446] tion about the economic phenomenon in question that is not captured by the current model. Hence encompassing can help test one's own model against other models' information sets.

The pre-existing studies of greatest interest to us are summarized in Table 2. Because of difficulties in the replication, one study [Bean, Layard, and Nickell (1986) (B-L-N)] is not considered in the formal encompassing tests [Nymoen (1991b)]. The Saikkonen and Teräsvirta (1985) (S-T) article uses quarterly data and is also left out of the following. This leaves us with four models: Alogoskoufis and Manning (1988) (A-M), Grubb (1986) (G), Newell and Symons (1988) (N-S '88),[9] and Eriksson, Suvanto, and Vartia (1990) (E).

Table 4 summarizes the results of pairwise model comparison.[10] Our equation (6) encompasses each of the rival models, whereas the others do not encompass (6).[11]

The other models often fail the pairwise test: A-M is rejected against N-S '88, which in turn does not encompass A-M. Our model implies this outcome. N-S '88 neglects short-run price indexation, unlike A-M. On the other hand, the levels terms in A-M do not cointegrate, while N-S '88 uses a product real-wage and productivity formulation similar to our model (6). [See Nymoen (1991b)].

6   Conclusion and Discussion

Three findings stand out. First, we find strong evidence of real-wage flexibility, in the sense that product real wages fluctuate around the productivity trend. Second, even though real-wage flexibility is a salient feature of the data, the degree of wage responsiveness is low. This is intriguing, since wage

---

[9] This is an update of the 1986 paper of the same name.

[10] Note that even if a model survives all pairwise encompassing tests, parsimonious encompassing does not follow. Parsimonious encompassing tests against the fully nesting model, which is impractical here.

[11] There is one minor caveat: we encompass the "OECD data equations" for a shorter sample than was used in the estimation of these models. The reason is that an important variable in our study, the replacement ratio (*rpr*), could not be calculated for the years 1950–1960.

TABLE 4. Pairwise Encompassing Tests (F and χ^2 Values)
for Alternative Models of Finnish Manufacturing Wages
(Estimated regression standard errors $\hat{\sigma}$ appear along the diagonal.)

Encompassing Model	Model To Be Encompassed				
	(6)	A-M	N-S '88	G	E[a]
Equation (6)	0.69%	0.44 $F(4,13)$	1.58 $F(6,9)$	1.8 $F(5,10)$	0.61 $F(6,14)$
A-M	70.0 $\chi^2(6)$	2.7%	58.38 $\chi^2(6)$	41.8 $\chi^2(3)$	27.1 $\chi^2(6)$
N-S '88	9.3 $F(7,8)$	4.36 $F(5,20)$	1.2%	0.2 $F(3,20)$	2.49 $F(6,14)$
G	47.6 $F(8,9)$	22.1 $F(5,23)$	17.4 $F(6,18)$	5.08%	0.43 $F(6,16)$
E	42.3 $F(7,11)$	17.9 $F(7,12)$	14.7 $F(7,10)$	10.6 $F(6,11)$	3.2%

Notes: See the note to Table 2 for references on the models. All the tests are based on the author's replication of the original models; see Nymoen (1991b). Instrumental variables $\hat{\sigma}$ values and χ^2 tests are given for A-M.

The estimation period varies across the models. Ideally, a model i should explain the properties of a model j, given the data and sample period of model j. In the construction of the table this principle was followed whenever practically possible. The most serious caveat applies to line 1, that is, our model (6): we encompass, for example, A-M for the period 1962–1985, while the A-M sample is 1952–1985.

[a] E was estimated for private sector wages, rather than for manufacturing sector wages. However, E includes variables that may be important also for manufacturing wages, such as union density and regular working time; hence we include E among the models to be encompassed by the manufacturing sector models. To make the table complete, we also report the encompassing properties of E.

hysteresis is commonly viewed as a possible cause of real-wage rigidity. The explanation of this puzzle is that unemployment is only one of the factors shaping the real-wage adjustment process. Other important factors such as the unemployment insurance system affect real wages through the nominal wage adjustment process. In addition, the cointegration analysis indicates that strong equilibrating forces are at work through both productivity and price adjustments.

[448]   Third, policy affected the wage–unemployment relationship. Looking at such indicators as the replacement ratio and the share of the unemployed who are allocated to labor market programs, employment policies have become less accommodative over time. On the basis of our results, we cannot rule out that these policy changes have induced an element of hysteresis, for example, by allowing the long-term unemployment percentage to rise. Even so, adoption of a less accommodative policy stance seems to have exerted strong downward pressure on wages.

Existing models of Finnish wage formation disagree about real-wage responsiveness to changes in unemployment. Our model implies low responsiveness, and it encompasses alternative models with high estimated responsiveness. Consequently, existing studies seem to have overstated the importance of the unemployment variable in explaining real-wage fluctuations.

Neither a full understanding of the process generating wage flexibility nor an assessment of the net benefits of the de-accommodation policies in Finland can be given in a single-equation context. However, it is our contention that the equation for wage growth developed here could prove a useful building block in such a model.

Appendix.   Data Definitions

All variables are from the databank of the Nordic Wage Formation Project [Calmfors (1990)]. Some series have been extrapolated to allow full sample estimation. This is noted explicitly below. Some series are constructed from the original databank variables; this is also noted below.

AMS% The number of persons on labor market programs as a percentage of the labor force.

AMUN% The number of persons on labor market programs as a percentage of total unemployment, that is, programs plus open unemployment.

AT (1 − average income tax rate).

LU% The number of long-term unemployed (> 6 months) as a percentage of the labor force. The series is extrapolated back to 1962 by assuming that LU% is constant at 0.2 percent in the years from 1962–1967. Given the stability of the overall unemployment rate in that period, this assumption is reasonable.

MO1 Narrow money (M1) holdings (1960 = 100).

P Consumer price index (1960 = 100).

[449]   PI Import price index (1960 = 100).

PT (1 + payroll tax rate).

PW Product real-wage index in manufacturing (1960 = 100).

Q Value added price index in manufacturing, defined as $(P/RP)\cdot 100$.

RP Relative consumer price index $(1960 = 100)$.

RPR Replacement ratio. In the databank this series begins in 1964. The series is extrapolated back to 1960 by using the formula $\Delta RPR/RPR_{t-1} = \Delta \ln(RB) - \Delta \ln(CW) - \Delta \ln(HA)$, where RB is real benefits, HA is average hours in manufacturing, and CW is W/P.

$SU\%$ The number of short-term unemployed (< 6 months) as a percentage of the labor force.

U Unemployment percentage.

UD Trade union members as a percent of the total labor force.

W Money wage index in manufacturing $(1960 = 100)$.

WC Wage cost per man-hour, defined as $PW \cdot Q$ $(1960 = 100)$.

Y Value added per man-hour in manufacturing $(1960 = 100)$.

I_{YEAR} and ST_{YEAR} denote impulse and step dummies, respectively. $YEAR$ (e.g., 68) is an abbreviation denoting the first year with a nonzero value (i.e., "1").

Unemployment equation: I_{68} corresponds to a sharp downturn that hit the Finnish wood and paper industry particularly hard. I_{74} is an OPEC–I dummy, and I_{78} partly captures the lagged effect on $LU\%$. I_{80} is an OPEC–II dummy.

Replacement-ratio equation: as an almost autonomous variable, the replacement ratio needs several dummies. Specifically, ST_{75} captures the fall in rpr_t from the mid-seventies, after adoption of a less accommodating policy stance. This policy change is also apparent in the $AMUN\%$ variable [see Calmfors and Nymoen (1990)].

Bibliography

(References marked with an asterisk * are included in this volume.)

Alogoskoufis, G. S. and A. Manning (1988) "On the Persistence of Unemployment", *Economic Policy*, 7, 429–469.

Bean, C. R., P. R. G. Layard, and S. J. Nickell (1986) "The Rise in Unemployment: A Multi-country Study", in C. R. Bean, P. R. G. Layard, and S. J Nickell (eds.) *The Rise in Unemployment*, Oxford, Basil Blackwell.

Blanchard, O. J., and L. Summers (1986) "Hysteresis and the European Unemployment Problem", *NBER Macro-economics Annual*, Cambridge, MIT Press.   [450]

Bruno, M., and J. D. Sachs (1985) *Economics of Worldwide Stagflation*, Oxford, Basil Blackwell.

Calmfors, L. (1990) "Wage Formation and Macroeconomic Policy in the Nordic Countries: A Summary", Chapter 1 in L. Calmfors (ed.) *Wage Formation and Macroeconomic Policy in the Nordic Countries*, Oxford, SNS and Oxford University Press.

Calmfors, L., and J. Driffill (1988) "Bargaining Structure, Corporatism and Macroeconomic Performance", *Economic Policy*, 6, 13–61.

Calmfors, L., and R. Nymoen (1990) "Real Wage Adjustment and Employment Policies in the Nordic Countries", *Economic Policy*, 11, 397–448.

Carruth, A. A., and A. J. Oswald (1989) *Pay Determination and Industrial Prosperity*, Oxford, Oxford University Press.

Chow, C. G. (1960) "Tests of Equality Between Sets of Coefficients in Two Linear Regressions", *Econometrica*, 28, 591–605.

Davidson, J. E. H., D. F. Hendry, F. Srba, and S. Yeo (1978) "Econometric Modelling of the Aggregate Time-series Relationship Between Consumers' Expenditure and Income in the United Kingdom", *Economic Journal*, 88, 661–692.

Eitrheim, O. (1990) "Testing Long-run Relationships Between Economic Time Series Using Likelihood-based Inference on Cointegration", Arbeidsnotat 1990/5, Research Department, Central Bank of Norway, Oslo, Norway.

Engle, R. F. (1982) "Autoregressive Conditional Heteroscedasticity with Estimates of the Variance of United Kingdom Inflation", *Econometrica*, 50, 982–1008.

Engle, R. F., and C. W. J. Granger (1987) "Co-integration and Error Correction: Representation, Estimation, and Testing", *Econometrica*, 55, 251–276.

*Engle, R. F., and D. F. Hendry (1993) "Testing Super Exogeneity and Invariance in Regression Models", *Journal of Econometrics*, 56, 1/2, 119–139; originally cited as (1989) "Testing Super Exogeneity and Invariance", Discussion Paper 89/51, Economics Department, University of California at San Diego, La Jolla, California, forthcoming in the *Journal of Econometrics*.

*Engle, R. F., D. F. Hendry, and J-F. Richard (1983) "Exogeneity", *Econometrica*, 51, 277–304.

Eriksson, T., A. Suvanto, and P. Vartia (1990) "Wage Formation in Finland", Chapter 4 in L. Calmfors (ed.) *Wage Formation and Macroeconomic Policy in the Nordic Countries*, Oxford, SNS and Oxford University Press.

Fuller, W. A. (1976) *Introduction to Statistical Time Series*, New York, John Wiley.

Granger, C. W. J. (1981) "Some Properties of Time Series Data and Their Use in Econometric Model Specification", *Journal of Econometrics*, 16, 121–130.

Grubb, D. (1984) "The O.E.C.D. Data Set", Working Paper No. 615, Centre for Labour Economics, London School of Economics, London, England.

Grubb, D. (1986) "Topics in the OECD Phillips Curve", *Economic Journal*, 96, 55–79.

Grubb, D., R. Jackman, and R. Layard (1983) "Wage Rigidity in OECD Countries", *European Economic Review*, 21, 11–39.

Harvey, A. (1981) *The Econometric Analysis of Time Series*, London, Philip Allan.

Hendry, D. F. (1989) *PC-GIVE: An Interactive Econometric Modelling System*, Version 6.0/6.1, Oxford, Institute of Economics and Statistics and Nuffield College.

Hendry, D. F., and J-F. Richard (1989) "Recent Developments in the Theory of Encompassing", Chapter 12 in B. Cornet and H. Tulkens (eds.) *Contributions to Operations Research and Economics: The Twentieth Anniversary of CORE*, Cambridge, Massachusetts, MIT Press, 393–440.

Hylleberg, S., and G. E. Mizon (1989) "Co-integration and Error Correction Mechanisms", *Economic Journal*, 99 (Conference 1989), 113–125.

Jarque, C. M., and A. K. Bera (1980) "Efficient Tests for Normality, Homoscedasticity, and Serial Independence of Regression Residuals", *Economics Letters*, 6, 255–259.

Johansen, S. (1988) "Statistical Analysis of Cointegrating Vectors", *Journal of Economic Dynamics and Control*, 12, 231–254. [451]

Johansen, S., and K. Juselius (1990) "Maximum Likelihood Estimation and Inference on Cointegration—With Applications to the Demand for Money", *Oxford Bulletin of Economics and Statistics*, 52, 169–210.

Layard, P. R. G., and S. J. Nickell (1986) "Unemployment in Britain", in C. R. Bean, P. R. G. Layard, and S. J. Nickell (eds.) *The Rise in Unemployment*, Oxford, Basil Blackwell.

Layard, P. R. G., S. J. Nickell, and R. Jackman (1991) *Unemployment*, Oxford, Oxford University Press, Chapter 8.

Mizon, G. E., and J.-F. Richard (1986) "The Encompassing Principle and Its Application to Testing Non-nested Hypotheses", *Econometrica*, 54, 657–678.

Newell, A., and J. Symons (1985) "Wages and Employment in the OECD Countries", Discussion Paper No. 219, Centre for Labour Economics, London School of Economics, London, England.

Newell, A., and J. Symons (1986) "The Phillips Curve is a Real Wage Equation", Discussion Paper No. 246, Centre for Labour Economics, London School of Economics, London, England.

Newell, A., and J. Symons (1988) "The Phillips Curve is a Real Wage Equation", Discussion Paper No. 1038, Centre for Labour Economics, London School of Economics, London, England.

Nickell, S. J. (1987) "Why Is Wage Inflation in Britain So High?", *Oxford Bulletin of Economics and Statistics*, 49, 103–128.

Nymoen, R. (1989) "Modelling Wages in the Small Open Economy: An Error Correction Model of Norwegian Manufacturing Wages", *Oxford Bulletin of Economics and Statistics*, 51, 239–258.

Nymoen, R. (1991a) "A Small Linear Model of Wage- and Price-inflation in the Norwegian Economy", *Journal of Applied Econometrics*, 6, 255–269.

Nymoen, R. (1991b) "Finnish Manufacturing Wages 1960–1987: Real-wage Flexibility and Hysteresis", Arbeidsnotat 1991/5, Norges Bank, Oslo, Norway.

Rowlatt, P. A. (1987) "A Model of Wage Bargaining", *Oxford Bulletin of Economics and Statistics*, 59, 347–371.

Rødseth, A., and S. Holden (1990) "Wage Setting in Norway", Chapter 5 in L. Calmfors (ed.) *Wage Formation and Macroeconomic Policy in the Nordic Countries*, Oxford, SNS and Oxford University Press.

Saikkonen P., and T. Teräsvirta (1985) "Modelling the Dynamic Relationship Between Wages and Prices in Finland", *Scandinavian Journal of Economics*, 87, 102–119.

Sargan, J. D. (1964) "Wages and Prices in the United Kingdom: A Study in Econometric Methodology", in P. E. Hart, G. Mills, and J. K. Whitaker (eds.) *Econometric Analysis for National Economic Planning*, London, Butterworths.

Sargan, J. D., and A. Bhargava (1983) "Testing Residuals from Least Squares Regression for Being Generated by a Gaussian Random Walk", *Econometrica*, 51, 153–174.

11

An Econometric Analysis of TV Advertising Expenditure in the United Kingdom

DAVID F. HENDRY*

Abstract

Previous econometric studies of the supply of and demand for TV advertising time in the United Kingdom using annual data found negative price elasticities of demand of less than unity in absolute value. Here, a dynamic, constant-parameter, econometric system for both the real price of TV advertising time and the number of commercial home minutes broadcast is estimated from quarterly data and finds a long-run price elasticity of about −2. The model explains the previous findings as due to the high degree of contemporaneous interdependence between price and quantity on annual data, which arises from within-year feedbacks.

1   Introduction

Previous econometric assessments of the determinants of the supply of and demand for TV advertising time in the United Kingdom include the studies by Budd (1985), Cave and Swann (1985), and NERA (1985), all of which

* This paper was originally written for National Economic Research Associates (NERA). The statistical calculations were undertaken using PC-GIVE 6.0 [see Hendry (1989)]. I am grateful to Neil Barnard, Martin Cave, Phillipa Marks, John Muellbauer, Penelope Rowlatt, and an anonymous referee of this journal for helpful comments on the material reported below. I am also indebted to Neil Ericsson for considerable help in preparing the revised version of the article.

Reprinted with permission from the *Journal of Policy Modeling* (June 1992), 14, 3, 281–311.

were submissions to the Peacock Committee on financing the BBC. The main empirical conclusion of those three studies—and of several others reported in Peacock (1986)—was that the price elasticity of demand for TV advertising time was negative but less than unity in absolute value, and consequently total revenue would fall if advertising was extended to the BBC, or indeed to further commercial television channels. The evidence presented was based on studies of advertising revenue, the average price of advertising time, and the volume of advertising time supplied, so the communality of the findings adduced considerable support for the hypothesis that the price elasticity was [282] less than unity, and indeed was close to (minus) one-half. Nevertheless, it is the contention of this article, on both theoretical and empirical grounds, that their joint conclusion is incorrect.

A dynamic econometric model explaining both the real price of TV advertising time and the number of commercial home minutes broadcast is developed below. Unlike most previous studies, which used annual data over 1961–1984, the present analysis uses a time series of quarterly observations covering the period 1973–1986. The model accounts for the data evidence on price and quantity, is constant over the sample, and has a long-run price elasticity of about −2. Moreover, the dynamic structure of the model provides a possible explanation for the earlier studies' finding of an elasticity of less than unity in terms of the high degree of interdependence between price and quantity on annual data, which could be avoided on quarterly data. Furthermore, the choice of which variables to analyze and which to treat as given, or exogenous, proves important. This study is a follow-up to a previous report undertaken on a subsample of the present data in which preliminary versions of the equations reported below were developed; see Hendry (1987c).

The major conclusions that follow from this research are the following:

1. The price elasticity of demand for TV advertising time is negative and considerably in excess of unity in absolute value.

2. As a consequence, an extension of available advertising time should raise total revenue even though the average price will fall.

3. Previous studies obtained a smaller elasticity because the data frequency was too low to allow demand and supply effects to be disentangled from the available information.

The structure of the analysis is as follows. Section 2 describes the institutional background to television broadcasting in the United Kingdom and Section 3 sets out the economic theoretic framework underlying the supply of and demand for TV advertising time. Section 4 discusses the econometric methodology and Section 5 describes the quarterly and annual time-series data analyzed. In Section 6, the quarterly data set is investigated by the approach described in Section 4. A constant-parameter model based on Section 3 is developed in which the price elasticity is greater than unity in absolute value. In Section 7, the methodology is applied to the annual time series and replicates the Peacock submissions' claim that the price elasticity appears to be less than unity. A reconciliation of the conflicting evidence is presented in Section 8 in terms of within-year feedbacks between price and [283] quantity, such that the annual elasticity estimates are biased downwards. The feedbacks may represent an actual supply response of quantity to price, or they may be a proxy for other omitted and unmodeled influences, but in either case they are better circumvented in the quarterly data model. Section 9 concludes the article.

2 Institutional Background

Television broadcasting in the United Kingdom is controlled by two authorities—the British Broadcasting Corporation (BBC) and the Independent Broadcasting Authority (IBA). The former had a monopoly until 1954, when the Independent Television Authority (ITA) was created to oversee commercial television. The ITA later became the IBA when commercial radio was introduced. Under its charter, the BBC is not allowed to advertise; it raises its revenue from a license fee levied annually on all owners of television and radio sets. This finances two TV channels called BBC1 and BBC2.

The commercial companies raise most of their revenue by selling advertising time, presently on two channels called ITV and Channel 4. The former was created in 1954 and the latter in the last quarter of 1982. The IBA controls the sale of broadcasting franchises, there being fifteen regional franchises at present. The IBA earns income from a levy on the profits of the franchisees and from the sale of (total) broadcasting air time to those companies, and it pays any surplus to the central government.

The maximum number of minutes of advertising time on each commercial channel is strictly regulated. No more than seven minutes of advertising time is allowed in any clock hour, with a maximum of six minutes per hour averaged over a day's programs. Presently, commercial TV companies are not broadcasting 24 hours per day. The quality and accuracy of advertising is also strictly regulated by the IBA.

Advertising time is sold by ITV for both commercial channels by several methods. A rate card is published and some slots are sold at those prices or in packages, but others are sold by a pre-empt auction. This occurs sequentially over time up to a fixed number of hours before broadcasting, during which advertisers make offers for such slots, with the current highest bid replacing earlier offers. ITV is expected to sell all available advertising space. Around 90% of the commercial companies' total revenue is derived from advertising, the remainder coming from the sale of programs. Channel 4 receives a fixed

[284]   percentage of the revenue, currently 16%. Acts of Parliament embody the relevant legislation.

A public inquiry into financing the BBC was undertaken in 1985 under the chairmanship of Alan Peacock, generating the Peacock (1986) report. This study found against introducing advertising on the BBC channels. Part of the evidence to the Peacock committee took the form of econometric models of the annual demand for TV advertising time, and these obtained negative price elasticities with an absolute value of less than unity. Such evidence suggested that total revenue would fall if advertising time were extended, and was one of several factors influencing the policy decision to retain the noncommercial status of the BBC channels. Part of the motivation for the present study is to reconsider and evaluate that econometric evidence on a recently collected quarterly data set.

3   An Economic Model of TV Advertising Demand

The general theoretical framework is that of supply and demand analysis, specialized to the case of TV advertising time, taking account of the oligopolistic nature of that industry [see *inter alia* Bowman (1977), NERA (1986), and Cave and Swann (1986)]. Advertising is an investment in future sales and thus is a derived demand that depends on final product demands, the price effectiveness of advertising, and the relative attractiveness of alternative advertising media. The demand is for commercial home minutes (H), which is the product of the number of commercial minutes (M) broadcast and the audience size (A), usually referred to as audience reach. Some slots are bought with a guaranteed reach, but most require the purchaser to take the risk, based on past information about program popularity.

The supply of advertising time units depends on the intensity of advertising allowed per hour and the number of allowable hours per day, both of which are controlled by regulation. It also depends on the number of companies broadcasting adverts and the total hours of TV broadcasting time (B). Most models are for the supply of and demand for H, the relevant measure of effective advertising time.

The ITV companies influence M by their choice of B, subject to regulations, and also determine their total expenditure (E_x) on TV program production, which is a major determinant of A. Since $H = M \cdot A$, both M and A are analyzed below. The price per unit of H (P_a) is assumed to adjust quickly to clear the market for given supply and demand conditions,

[285]   and is always well above the marginal cost of broadcasting. Thus, E_x and B are chosen to maximize net revenue, taking account of the demand for advertising time.

The demand function takes the following form:

$$H^d = \eta(P_a/P, \ \Delta p, \ d, \ s^d, \ P_c/P, \ f^d), \tag{1}$$

where P is a general price index (such as the retail price index), Δp is the rate of inflation (i.e., $\Delta \ln P_t = p_t - p_{t-1}$, using lower-case letters to denote logarithms), d is a vector of commodity and service demands for which advertising is deemed worthwhile (e.g., consumer durables C_d, holidays, etc.), s^d is a vector of special demand factors (such as the proportion of color televisions $[C_{ol}]$, which affects the attractiveness of adverts, and seasonal variation), P_c is a price index of competitive advertising media (such as newspapers, hoardings [billboards], and mail shots [mailings]), and f^d is a vector of enabling demand variables (including such factors as industrial and commercial company profits π, or their liquidity). Thus, (1) schematically reflects functional dependencies but ignores dynamic feedbacks, adjustment processes, habit factors, and expectations, all of which need to be modeled empirically.

The supply of advertising time in terms of commercial home minutes depends on the choice of B and E_x, given the demand function in (1), which is assumed to be known to the monopoly ITV supplier. The determination of H is via its components M and A, where it is assumed that

$$M^s = \tau B = \mu(\tau, \ P_a/P, \ s^s, \ C_{ol}, \ N, \ A), \tag{2}$$

where τ is the proportion of broadcast time allocated to advertising, given the maximum fixed by regulation, s^s is a vector of supply side factors such as strikes by ITV employees, and N is the number of commercial channels. A is expected to have a positive effect on B.

Next, audience reach depends on viewing habits, program popularity, the competitive quality of BBC television programs, the number of TV receivers, the number of hours of broadcasting, time of day, weather, season of the year, and so on, and is determined by

$$A = \phi(N, \ C_{ol}, \ f^s, \ M), \tag{3}$$

where f^s denotes the above enabling factors. M has a negative effect on A by lowering the attractiveness of commercial broadcasts through advertisers' interruptions. Solving for M from (2) and (3) yields

$$M^s = \lambda(\tau, \ P_a/P, \ s^s, \ C_{ol}, \ N, \ f^s). \tag{4} \quad [286]$$

Finally, $H^s = M^s \cdot A$.

The price of advertising time affects the supply of H through the absolute and the relative popularity of television viewing on the ITV companies, as well as by influencing the incentive to broadcast the maximum allowable time. Since increasing M lowers A, H^s could increase or decrease with P_a/P. The number of commercial channels might also respond to price pressures

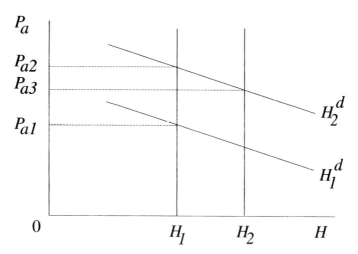

FIGURE 1. The change in the unit price caused by a change in demand for advertising time.

and M certainly does through longer hours of broadcast, greater regional coverage, and more minutes per hour up to the maximum.

On the assumption that the real price P_a/P adjusts rapidly to equilibrate H^d and H^s through the pre-empt auction of the available time slots, then

$$\Delta[p_a - p] = \psi(h^d - h^s), \tag{5}$$

where $\psi(\cdot)$ is a sign-preserving monotonic function and lower case denotes logarithms. Market clearing at every instant corresponds to taking $\psi(\cdot)$ as a constant coefficient that is so large that (5) can be rewritten as

$$h^d - h^s = \psi^{-1}\Delta[p_a - p] \approx 0. \tag{6}$$

In the short run, M is relatively unresponsive to price changes and can be regarded as almost fixed. Hence, overshooting can occur (as in housing markets), since a demand shock must result in enough of a price change to ensure that H^s is absorbed by the market in each period. Figure 1 illustrates the effect of a change from H_1^d to H_2^d on price, which moves from P_{a1} to P_{a2}. Over a longer time horizon, hours of broadcasting and the number of TV channels can change on the supply side, and producers of commodities and services can adjust their planned advertising budget levels, allocations, and pricing decisions, so the final outcome is P_{a3}. Thus, in this market, the short-run price response will generally exceed the long-run value. For an example of such a mechanism at work in the housing market, see Hendry (1984). These hypotheses are considered empirically below.

The main implication of the above analysis is that the demand equation is a price-determining equation, given H, consonant with the sequential bid mechanism for sales of available advertising slots. Consequently, the price equation can be interpreted as (5) having eliminated H^d using (1), or as the inverse of (1) given H:

$$\frac{P_a}{P} = \eta^*(H,\ \Delta p,\ d,\ s^d,\ P_c/P,\ f^d). \tag{7}$$

[287]

Nevertheless, as will be seen in the next section, that argument is not sufficient to justify treating H as weakly exogenous in the price equation. The complete economic model is given by dynamic versions of equations (3), (4), and (7).

A major institutional change occurred over the historical period under analysis with the creation of Channel 4 in late 1982. Because the data are an aggregate over all commercial television companies, the impact of Channel 4 must be explicitly modeled. Denote ITV and Channel 4 by subscripts 1 and 4, respectively, with prices P_{a1t} and P_{a4t}, outputs H_{1t} and H_{4t}, and net revenues R_{1t} and R_{4t}, respectively. Then total net revenue R_t is given by

$$\begin{aligned} R_t &= R_{1t} + R_{4t} \\ &= P_{a1t} \cdot H_{1t} + P_{a4t} \cdot H_{4t}, \end{aligned} \tag{8}$$

where $H_t = H_{1t} + H_{4t}$. Channel 4 may have raised total TV audience viewing, but part of the rise in H_{4t} is matched by a fall in H_{1t} to the extent that it attracts audiences away from ITV. Since M_t must rise considerably because

$$M_t = M_{1t} + M_{4t} = M_{1t}\left(1 + \frac{M_{4t}}{M_{1t}}\right),$$

the average audience reach must fall substantially, with

$$A_t = \frac{H_t}{M_t} = \frac{H_t}{M_{1t} + M_{4t}} = \frac{H_t/M_{1t}}{1 + M_{4t}/M_{1t}}. \tag{9}$$

The fall in A_t reflects the share of Channel 4 in commercial minutes broadcast.

The average observed TV advertising price is given by

$$P_{at} = \frac{R_t}{H_t} = P_{a1t}\left\{1 - \left(1 - \frac{P_{a4t}}{P_{a1t}}\right)\left(\frac{H_{4t}}{H_t}\right)\right\}. \tag{10}$$

Prior to the creation of Channel 4, $H_{4t} = 0$ and $P_{at} = P_{a1t}$; thereafter [288] if $P_{a4t} < P_{a1t}$, as seems natural for a new channel seeking to establish itself, then P_{at} will be observed to fall while H_t rises. Eventually, H_{4t}/H_t and P_{a4t}/P_{a1t} will both reach new equilibria and the adjustment effect will disappear. Even so, the effect on the observed value of P_{at} will vanish only if $P_{a4t}/P_{a1t} = 1$. Thus, both adjustment and long-run outcomes must be modeled. In the empirical analysis, the effect of creating Channel 4 is handled by a dummy variable D_{c4t}, which is zero until 1982(3), 0.5 in 1982(4), and unity thereafter. The same dummy is used in all equations and is anticipated to have a small negative effect on P_a/P, a large positive effect on M that is roughly equal in magnitude and opposite in sign to that on A, and a small, probably positive, effect on H.

Finally, an industrial dispute between the ITV companies and their employees led to a severe curtailment of commercial broadcasting in 1979(3)–1979(4), ending in November of that year. This is modeled by a dummy variable D_s with the values of -0.75 in 1979(3) and -0.25 in 1979(4), proportional to the number of months of strike-affected broadcasting. This is anticipated to have a large positive effect on M and H, and a smaller positive effect on A, perhaps with delayed effects, due to loss of loyalty, in later periods. If the demand–supply model is correctly formulated, the quantity effects should fully determine the price outcome, so that the dummy ought to have a negligible effect on the price, given H.

4 Background to the Econometrics

Since the economic mechanism is too complicated to be modeled exactly, all economic models must be simplifications, and hence false. Even so, some models are both a better characterization of reality and distinctly more useful than others. This section describes the modeling process and the evaluation of empirical models from the available evidence.

For a single economy such as the United Kingdom over a specific epoch like the last quarter century, all models of that economy derive from a common mechanism, called the data generation process (DGP). Given the measurement system whereby the data are defined, constructed, and recorded, empirical models represent reductions of that DGP. Since the dependent variable in an empirical model is observed, the disturbance, or unexplained component of the model, is a derived, not an autonomous, process that is defined by the specification of the model and its associated estimation procedure; see [289] Hendry and Richard (1982). Thus, the disturbance is susceptible to being re-designed by model re-specification to achieve certain objectives such as random errors or to satisfy certain criteria such as consistency with a given theoretical viewpoint. Readers unfamiliar with the econometric approach, which is important for understanding and evaluating the results obtained, could consult Spanos (1986), Hendry (1987a, 1987b), Hendry, Neale, and Srba (1988), Hendry and Ericsson (1991), and Hendry and Mizon (1993).

The statistical system is defined by the variables of interest, their status (modeled or not), their degree of integration, data transformations, the history of the process, and the sample period. Let $\{x_t\}$ denote the complete vector of variables under analysis, and for a sample period of size T, let $X_T^1 = (x_1 \ldots x_T)$. The statistical generating mechanism is $\mathsf{D}_X(X_T^1 \mid X_0, \theta)$

where $\mathsf{D}_X(\cdot)$ is the joint data density function, X_0 denotes the initial conditions, and $\theta \in \Theta \subseteq \Re^q$ is the parameter vector in a q-dimensional parameter space Θ. This is called the Haavelmo distribution after Haavelmo (1944), and is first sequentially factorized as

$$\mathsf{D}_X(X_T^1 \mid X_0, \theta) = \prod_{t=1}^{T} \mathsf{D}_X(x_t \mid X_{t-1}, \theta), \qquad (11)$$

where θ allows for any necessary transients such as dummy variables, and $X_{t-1} = (X_0 : X_{t-1}^1)$.

Let $x_t' = (y_t' : z_t')$ and $X_T^1 = (Y_T^1 : Z_T^1)$ where y_t is the $n \times 1$ vector of endogenous variables (here m_t, a_t, $[p_a - p]_t$, and h_t), and z_t is the $k \times 1$ vector of conditioning variables (here c_t, $[c_d - c]_t$, Δp_t, $[\pi - p]_t$, c_{olt}, and the dummies). Since z_t comprises aggregate variables with large effects on y_t, whereas TV advertising is under half of a percent of GNP, z_t is assumed to be weakly exogenous for the parameters of interest in the advertising model. If so, analyzing the conditional distribution of y_t, given z_t and the history of the process, involves no loss of information relative to analyzing the joint distribution of x_t. From (11),

$$\prod_{t=1}^{T} \mathsf{D}_X(x_t \mid X_{t-1}, \theta) = \prod_{t=1}^{T} \mathsf{D}_{Y|Z}(y_t \mid z_t, X_{t-1}, \lambda_1) \mathsf{D}_Z(z_t \mid X_{t-1}, \lambda_2), \qquad (12)$$

where $\lambda = f(\theta)$. Then z_t is weakly exogenous for λ_1 if the parameters of interest ϕ are a function of λ_1 alone and λ_1 and λ_2 are variation free: see Engle, Hendry, and Richard (1983).

We restrict attention to log-linear systems with data generated by a log-normal distribution, so that conditional models are also log-linear. The system formulation is therefore complete when the degrees and roots of every [290] lag polynomial are specified. Let $\mathsf{N}(\mu, \Omega)$ denote a normal distribution with mean μ and variance matrix Ω; then

$$y_t \mid z_t, X_{t-1} \sim \mathsf{N}(P_0 z_t + \textstyle\sum_{i=1}^s P_i x_{t-i}, \ \Omega), \qquad (13)$$

so that the longest lag is s periods, and the conditional system of n linear equations is

$$y_t = \sum_{j=0}^{s} \delta_{1j} z_{t-j} + \sum_{i=1}^{s} \delta_{2i} y_{t-i} + \nu_t \qquad \nu_t \sim \mathsf{IN}(0, \Omega), \qquad (14)$$

with $P_0 = \delta_{10}$ and $P_i = (\delta_{1i} : \delta_{2i})$ for $i = 1, \ldots, s$. Some of the variables in y_t are linked by an identity ($h_t \equiv m_t + a_t$) but otherwise Ω is symmetric, positive definite, and unrestricted. Thus, (14) is the unrestricted, conditional dynamic system once s is specified, with the derived error process ν_t. Let $\Phi = (\delta_{10} \ldots \delta_{1s}; \delta_{21} \ldots \delta_{2s})$. Then Φ and Ω are the variation-free parameters of interest in the conditional distribution, although they are not the parameters of interest in the overall analysis.

The system in (14) should be a congruent representation of the data, since it will be the specification against which all other simplifications are tested. Congruency requires the following:

1. $\{\nu_t\}$ is a homoscedastic innovation process against X_{t-1}, which depends on the specification of the lag structure [see Hendry, Pagan, and Sargan (1984)];

2. z_t is weakly exogenous for (Φ, Ω) [see Engle, Hendry, and Richard (1983)]; and

3. (Φ, Ω) is constant $\forall t$.

Tests can be constructed for residual autocorrelation, dynamic mis-specification, weak exogeneity, normality, further lagged nonmodeled variables, cross-equation independence, and constancy. Once a congruent system has been established, a theory-based model thereof can be constructed.

Many economic time series appear to be nonstationary, which affects the statistical distributions of estimators and tests. Conventionally, large-sample approximations to distributions in econometrics have been predicated on weak stationarity in the DGP such that $\sqrt{T}(\hat{\gamma} - \gamma)$ tends to a normal distribution for an estimator $\hat{\gamma}$ of a parameter vector γ [see e.g., White (1984)]. In practice, two important forms of nonstationarity arise when the autoregressive representation in (11) has unit roots, which induces integrated series [Dickey and Fuller (1979, 1981)], or when there are regime shifts, which induces nonconstancy in the system. We briefly consider these in turn.

[291] The degree of integration of $\{x_t\}$ is denoted by I(d) where d usually equals unity, but depends on the properties of the complete system. Differencing d times to create $\Delta^d x_t$ will produce an I(0), or nonintegrated, series. Cointegration occurs if some linear combinations of the x_t are I(0), denoted by $\beta' x_t \sim$ I(0) [see Granger and Weiss (1983), Engle and Granger (1987), and Hendry (1986)]. If $\beta' x_t$ is a cointegrated combination, then there exists an error correction representation and conversely: this is one aspect of the Granger representation theorem [see Granger (1986)]. The number of cointegrating vectors equals the rank of β and is denoted κ, which is usually unknown and has to be determined from the data at the level of the joint density.

Reconsider the system in (11) written in linear form as

$$\Delta x_t = \sum_{i=1}^{s-1} \Pi_i \Delta x_{t-i} + \delta x_{t-s} + v_t$$

$$= \Psi g_t + \delta x_{t-s} + v_t, \tag{15}$$

where $g_t = (\Delta x'_{t-1}, \ldots, \Delta x'_{t-s+1})'$, $\Psi = (\Pi_1, \ldots, \Pi_{s-1})$, and $v_t \sim \mathsf{IN}(0, \Upsilon)$. Equation (15) corresponds to $\mathsf{D}_X(x_t \mid X_{t-1}^{t-s}, \theta)$ re-parameterized into levels and differences, so that θ now comprises (Ψ, δ, Υ).

The next step is determining the number of cointegrating vectors $0 \leq \kappa \leq n + k$. Underestimating κ entails omitting empirically relevant error correction mechanisms (ECMs), whereas overestimating κ leads to the distributions of statistics being nonstandard so that incorrect inferences will result from using conventional critical values in tests. A test for κ cointegrating vectors can be based on the maximum likelihood approach proposed by Johansen (1988). The test is equivalent to testing whether $\delta = \alpha\beta'$, where β and α are $N \times \kappa$ when $N = (n + k)$, and hence the test is for δ having a reduced rank. Once κ is known, estimation of β and α follows. Here, the dimensionality of x_t, with $n + k = 9$, makes such an analysis unattractive, especially as z_t seems likely to be weakly exogenous for (Φ, Ω) (λ_1 in (12)), so that a conditional analysis is feasible from the outset. Cointegration was investigated for the n-equation subsystem and was also established for the three equations of interest in the N-variable system, since almost no lagged endogenous variables were needed in order to induce an innovation error.

Turning to the issue of regime shifts, if the parameters λ_1 of $\mathsf{D}_{Y|Z}(y_t \mid z_t, X_{t-1}, \lambda_1)$ depend on those of $\mathsf{D}_Z(z_t \mid X_{t-1}, \lambda_2)$, then the former will not be invariant to changes in the latter and super exogeneity will be violated. Consequently, if λ_2 changes, (14) will change because of invalid conditioning even if it is otherwise correctly specified [see Lucas (1976) and Engle and Hendry (1993), who propose tests for super exogeneity].

Many empirical econometric equations manifest nonconstancies, and it [292] is essential to uncover the reasons for predictive failure if scientific progress in modeling is to result: if behavioral equations involve parameters that are functions of policy rules, then the appropriate econometric model is very different from that required if apparent breaks are due to model misspecification. Several routes are open to resolving such debates: for example, by finding *de facto* constant equations, or by establishing that variations are due to policy changes. The former method depends on discovering constant parameterizations, so it is a function of the flair of the investigator, and need not result in any given instance. The latter, however, is open to direct testing, as in Engle and Hendry (1993). Either way, prior to policy scenarios being asserted, tests for historical invariance should be conducted.

Assuming success at doing so, we proceed to formulate a constant parameter conditional model of the system with the variables transformed to $\mathsf{I}(0)$ in terms of differences and ECMs. All linear structural models of (14) can be obtained by pre-multiplying by a nonsingular matrix B, which generates

$$By_t = \sum_{i=0}^{s} B\delta_{1i}z_{t-i} + \sum_{j=1}^{s} B\delta_{2j}y_{t-j} + B\nu_t. \tag{16}$$

Let $B_j = B\delta_{2j}$ for $j = 1, \ldots, s$ and $C_i = B\delta_{1i}$ for $i = 0, \ldots, s$ with $u_t = B\nu_t$; then

$$\sum_{j=0}^{s} B_j y_{t-j} + \sum_{i=0}^{s} C_i z_{t-i} = u_t \qquad u_t \sim \mathsf{IN}(0, \Sigma), \tag{17}$$

with $\Sigma = B\Omega B'$ and $B_0 = B$. Let $C = (B_1 \ldots B_s; C_0 \ldots C_s)$, with $A = (B : C)$ and $X = (Y : W)$, the matrices of all the coefficients and all of the observations, respectively. The diagonal of B_0 is normalized at unity to ensure a unique scaling in every equation. Since identities are present, the corresponding elements of $\{u_t\}$ are precisely zero, and the model is written as

$$AX' = \begin{bmatrix} A_1 \\ A_2 \end{bmatrix} X' = \begin{bmatrix} U_1' \\ 0 \end{bmatrix}, \tag{18}$$

where $n = n_1 + n_2$, for n_1 stochastic equations and n_2 identities. The elements of A_2 are known and do not need estimation.

The *model* is defined by the mapping between the unknown coefficients in the matrix A and the parameters of interest ϕ: without some restrictions, the coefficients in A will not be identified. Such restrictions are given by the theory model in Section 3 and are written as $A(\phi)$. Once ϕ is defined, the validity of the over-identifying restrictions can be tested against the congruent statistical system previously established. Such an approach avoids the [293] problems of going from the simple to the general: see Sims (1980), Hendry, Neale, and Srba (1988), and Hendry and Mizon (1993). For the *model* to be a valid, congruent representation of the data, given that the *system* already is, the model must parsimoniously encompass the system: see Mizon and Richard (1986) and Hendry and Richard (1989). This can be checked by a likelihood ratio test for over-identifying restrictions. The concentrated likelihood function $\mathcal{L}_1$ for the system (14) is

$$\mathcal{L}_1(\hat{\Phi}, \hat{\Omega}) = K_0 - \frac{1}{2}T \ln |T^{-1}\hat{V}_1'\hat{V}_1|, \tag{19}$$

where K_0 is a constant, and $\hat{V}_1$ denotes the matrix of residuals for the n_1 stochastic equations, excluding identities. The concentrated likelihood function for the complete model in (18) is

$$\mathcal{L}_0(\hat{\phi}, \hat{\Sigma}) = K_0 - \frac{1}{2}T \ln \left| \hat{A}_1 \left(\frac{X'X}{T} \right) \hat{A}_1' \right| + T \ln \left| |\hat{B}| \right|, \tag{20}$$

where $\hat{A}_1$ and $\hat{B}$ are the relevant full information maximum likelihood (FIML) estimates. For $\mathsf{I}(0)$ variables, the test is computed as

$$\xi(J - n_1^2) = 2(\mathcal{L}_1 - \mathcal{L}_0) \underset{a}{\sim} \chi^2(J - n_1^2), \qquad (21)$$

for J a priori restrictions on A. If $\xi(\cdot)$ is significant, then the model fails to encompass the system, in which case, that implementation of the underlying theory should be rejected. Several models could be consistent with the identification restrictions, even if all are highly over-identified, so that satisfying the test in (21) is insufficient to justify a model when the system is not rigorously tested for congruency.

The primary parameters of interest in this study are the impact and long-run price and income elasticities of demand for TV advertising time. These are well defined in the theoretical model and can be learned from the empirical evidence when the demand curve is identifiable. This seems possible on the quarterly data where h_t is predetermined and seems to be weakly exogenous for that equation's parameters. On the annual data, there is considerable simultaneity, and none of the variables in y_t can be treated as given in any of the other equations.

5   The Data

Two data sets are examined below.[1] The first comprises quarterly, seasonally unadjusted observations over the period 1973(1)–1986(4), and the second comprises annual data over the sample 1963–1984. The following variables' names are common to the two data sets.

R Net advertising revenue of the ITV companies (from the *Advertising* [294]
   Statistics Yearbook [ASY] 1987)

M Commercial minutes (based on transmission time from *Trends in Television*)

H Commercial home minutes (calculated as $H = 1.15R/P_a$ to include 15% agency charges)

P_a Price index of TV advertising time (*ASY*, various issues)

P Retail price index (*Economic Trends [ET]*, various issues)

C Real consumers' expenditure in 1980 prices (*ET*, Annual Supplement, 1988)

C_d Real consumers' expenditure on durables in 1980 prices (*ET*, Annual Supplement, 1988)

Π Gross trading profits of industrial and commercial companies (ICC) before providing for depreciation and stock appreciation (*ET*, Annual Supplement, 1988)

---

[1] I am indebted to NERA for providing the data.

C_{ol} Proportion of television licenses for colored TVs (*Annual Abstract of Statistics*)

Usable data on P_c could not be obtained. From these basic variables, audience reach A was calculated as H/M. In addition, real (or constant price) values are denoted by R/P, P_a/P, and Π/P. All variables were transformed to logs and these transformed variables are denoted by lower-case letters so that $\ln(P_a/P)_t = [p_a - p]_t$. Any necessary lags and differences were created and are shown as (say) $[p_a - p]_{t-1}$ and $\Delta[p_a - p]_t$, respectively. Estimated equations included dummy variables for the first three quarters of each year (denoted Q_i, where Q_i is unity in the ith quarter and zero otherwise) as well as a constant term, and two other special effects dummies, constructed as:

D_s Dummy for the strike in 1979(3)–1979(4) having values: $-3/4$, $-1/4$;

D_{c4} Step-shift dummy for the commencement of Channel 4, being zero prior to 1982(4), 0.5 in 1982(4), and unity thereafter.

This last variable is a crude approximation of both the impact and the long-run consequences of introducing Channel 4, but no additional empirical adjustments could be determined.

The data series on the relevant advertising variables undoubtedly contain significant measurement errors due to the method of compilation and construction, but the within-year totals of the quarterly data equaled the annual data for overlapping years, so this is unlikely to induce major differences between the two data sets. The data were also checked against other sources [such as Budd (1985) and Peacock (1986)] and other data (such as
[295] TV advertising expenditure, which includes the cost of making commercials: see ASY), both of which yielded a reasonable match.

Figure 2 shows the quarterly time series for $[p_a - p]_t$ and h_t; the large effect of the 1979 strike on h_t and its seasonal variation are obvious, and the rise in the real price of TV advertising time from 1976 is noticeable (about 5% per annum as against just over 1% for h_t). Figure 3 records the quarterly data on m_t and a_t; again, the strike effect on the former is clear, as is the impact of Channel 4 in 1982 on both variables. Furthermore, a_t shows a slight downward trend around marked seasonal variation, which appears to attenuate following the creation of Channel 4. Figure 4 shows the annual data
[296] on $[p_a - p]_t$ and h_t over 1962–1984; the former is almost U-shaped, whereas the latter reveals an upward strong trend till the early 1970s. Figures 5 and 6 record the quarterly time series of c_t and $[c_d - c]_t$, and $[\pi - p]_t$ and Δp_t for reference. The first two show considerable seasonal variation around upward trends, whereas the last two move in opposite directions over the sample as a whole. Note that Π is a gross measure and hence is always positive, and that $[\pi - p]_t$ is the best measure of the business cycle in this data set. (Data in the figures are mean-adjusted, where necessary.)

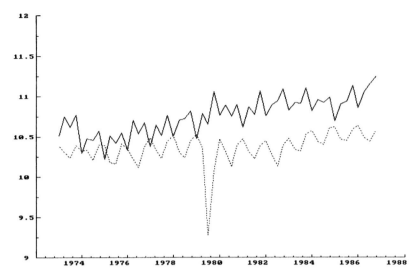

FIGURE 2. Quarterly time series of the real price of TV advertising $[p_a - p]_t$ (—) and commercial home minutes h_t ($\cdots$).

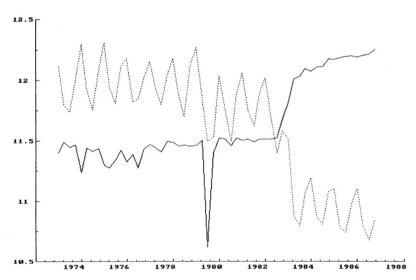

FIGURE 3. Quarterly time series of commercial minutes m_t (—) and audience reach a_t ($\cdots$).

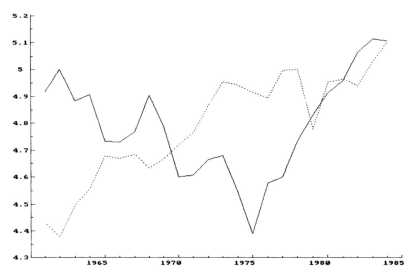

FIGURE 4. Annual time series of the real price of TV advertis-
ing $[\mathsf{p}_a - \mathsf{p}]_t$ (—) and commercial home minutes h_t ($\cdots$). For an
expanation of the use of sans serif font, see p. 299.

6   Quarterly Data Modeling

There were too many variables relative to the sample size to merit an unconditional analysis of x_t, and many of the variables were anyway determined at
the aggregate level such that a prior assumption of weak exogeneity seemed
sensible, as discussed in Section 4. The starting point was to study the
marginal joint density of the y_t variables in a vector autoregressive system
(VAR) to investigate their degrees of integration and cointegration. Because
of the importance of the trend, seasonals, 1979 strike, and the introduction
of Channel 4, all the variables were corrected by prior regression on these
dummies. Then y_t comprised $[p_a - p]_t$, m_t, and a_t. Two lags were used in
the equivalent of (15), and the resulting VAR was constant on recursive tests
over the last 25 observations.

There were two significant eigenvalues in the Johansen (1988) approach,
corresponding to transformed normalized eigenvectors of $(0.3, -0.2, 1)$ and
$(1, 0.6, 0.4)$. The first suggests that, adjusted for Channel 4, a_t is stationary,
which matches the graph of the adjusted variable, and the second entails that
the long-run price elasticity is about -2.5 with roughly equal effects from m_t

[297]

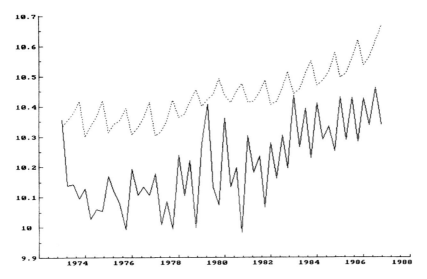

FIGURE 5. Quarterly time series of real consumers' expenditure c_t ($\cdots$) and the ratio of durable expenditure to total expenditure $[c_d - c]_t$ (—).

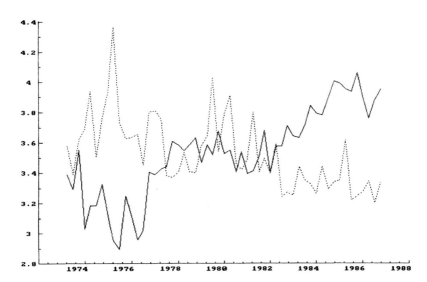

FIGURE 6. Quarterly time series of real ICC profits $[\pi - p]_t$ (—) and the rate of inflation Δp_t ($\cdots$).

and a_t. This second cointegrating vector had α coefficients of -0.4 and -0.2 for $[p_a - p]$ and m, respectively, which are relatively large and cast doubt on any weak exogeneity claims for conditioning on h in the price equation.

The next step was to analyze the joint density of the y_t, given the z_t, and reduce that system to an interpretable model based on the economic analysis sketched in Section 2, so the remaining analysis of M, A, H, and P_a/P is conducted conditionally on all the other variables. Short lags were found for most reactions, consistent with relatively rapid market clearing, and with the preceding evidence on integration and cointegration.

[298] The conditional empirical analysis commenced from an unrestricted linear dynamic system like (14) with two lags on every stochastic variable and one lag on the special effects dummies, plus a constant, seasonal dummies, and a trend, estimated from the sample 1973(4)–1986(4). Given the paucity of degrees of freedom, lagged variables with F statistics in the system of less than 0.5 were eliminated, and the resulting system was re-estimated. The stochastic dependent variables were Δm_t, Δa_t, and $\Delta[p_a - p]_t$, with Δh_t and the four levels being determined by identities. The stochastic regressors consisted of c_t, c_{t-1}, $[c_d - c]_t$, $[c_d - c]_{t-2}$, Δp_t, Δp_{t-2}, $[\pi - p]_t$, $[\pi - p]_{t-1}$, $[\pi - p]_{t-2}$, c_{olt}, c_{olt-1}, m_{t-1}, a_{t-1}, $[p_a - p]_{t-1}$, and $[p_a - p]_{t-2}$, which, with the dummies, made 24 explanatory system variables, almost all of which played a role in at least one equation of the system. The lagged level of the dependent variable was negative and highly significant in every equation, so that there was no problem of a lack of cointegration.

The constant and seasonals were fixed at their implicit full-sample values by partialing them out of the system, so that recursive estimators could be used to evaluate constancy. With 31 initial observations there were 22 test data points, and no equation revealed any evidence of nonconstancy over that sample. Furthermore, the residuals on all three equations satisfied a check for normality [based on Jarque and Bera's (1980) test], and the residual correlograms were reasonably flat. The residual standard deviations, adjusted for degrees of freedom, were $\hat{\sigma}_m = 0.035$; $\hat{\sigma}_a = 0.032$; and $\hat{\sigma}_{(p_a-p)} = 0.068$; the only non-negligible residual cross-correlation was -0.37 between the Δm_t and Δa_t equations. On the basis of this evidence, the system was judged to be adequately congruent and the analysis progressed to building a model of the system formulated in the light of the theory in Section 2.

Two approaches were adopted. First, single equation estimates of unrestricted dynamic relationships like (3), (4), and (7), reflecting the determinants schematically recorded in Section 2 but allowing up to two lags on every variable, were estimated over the sample of 1973(4)–1986(4). These equations were sequentially simplified to obtain parsimonious baseline relationships, which were also subjected to tests for constancy; homoscedastic, normal, innovations; functional form; dynamic specification; and possible omitted variables. These tests are only valid under the maintained hypothesis that any contemporaneous elements of y_t present in a given equation are weakly exogenous for its parameters. However, even using least squares, the only current dated element of y_t that appeared as a significant regressor in another equation was Δm_t in the Δa_t equation. The selected equations [299] were not rejected on any of the tests.

Second, taking the single equation estimates as a framework, a simultaneous model of the system like (17) was developed for three stochastic equations and five identities. The resulting model, with T equal to the 53 observations from 1973(4) to 1986(4), estimated by FIML yielded the following:

$$
\begin{aligned}
\widehat{\Delta m_t} = \quad &\underset{(1.02)}{5.82} \; - \; \underset{(0.08)}{1.01} \; m_{t-1} \; + \; \underset{(0.03)}{0.21} \; [\pi - p]_t \; - \; \underset{(0.05)}{0.19} \; [p_a - p]_{t-1} \\[4pt]
&+ \; \underset{(0.05)}{0.11} \; D_{c4t} \; + \; \underset{(0.06)}{0.31} \; D_{c4t-1} \; - \; \underset{(0.06)}{0.22} \; C_{olt} \; + \; \underset{(0.04)}{1.13} \; D_{st} \\[4pt]
&- \; \underset{(0.10)}{0.17} \; D_{st-1} \; + \; \underset{(0.23)}{0.45} \; c_t \; + \; \underset{(0.002)}{0.010} \; t \\[4pt]
&+ \; \underset{(0.03)}{0.05} \; Q_{1t} \; + \; \underset{(0.02)}{0.01} \; Q_{2t} \; + \; \underset{(0.02)}{0.01} \; Q_{3t} \tag{22}
\end{aligned}
$$

$$R(\Delta m, \widehat{\Delta m}) = 0.986 \qquad \hat{\sigma}_m = 0.029 \qquad \hat{\omega}_m = 0.029,$$

$$
\begin{aligned}
\widehat{\Delta a_t} = \quad &\underset{(0.99)}{3.06} \; - \; \underset{(0.09)}{0.68} \; \Delta m_t \; - \; \underset{(0.09)}{0.58} \; m_{t-1} \; + \; \underset{(0.04)}{0.14} \; \Delta[\pi - p]_t \\[4pt]
&+ \; \underset{(0.03)}{0.15} \; [\pi - p]_{t-2} \; - \; \underset{(0.07)}{0.86} \; a_{t-1} \; + \; \underset{(0.10)}{0.91} \; D_{st} \\[4pt]
&+ \; \underset{(0.04)}{0.08} \; D_{c4t} \; - \; \underset{(0.03)}{0.19} \; [p_a - p]_{t-2} \\[4pt]
&+ \; \underset{(0.02)}{0.06} \; Q_{1t} \; - \; \underset{(0.02)}{0.12} \; Q_{2t} \; - \; \underset{(0.01)}{0.22} \; Q_{3t} \tag{23}
\end{aligned}
$$

$$R(\Delta a, \widehat{\Delta a}) = 0.984 \qquad \hat{\sigma}_a = 0.024 \qquad \hat{\omega}_a = 0.025,$$

$$
\begin{aligned}
\widehat{\Delta[p_a - p]_t} = \quad &- \; \underset{(3.73)}{9.76} \; - \; \underset{(0.09)}{0.57} \; [p_a - p]_{t-1} \; - \; \underset{(0.05)}{0.23} \; h_{t-1} \\[4pt]
&+ \; \underset{(0.04)}{0.11} \; C_{olt-1} \; - \; \underset{(0.60)}{1.56} \; \Delta p_t \\[4pt]
&+ \; \underset{(0.29)}{0.57} \; c_{t-1} \; + \; \underset{(0.12)}{0.34} \; [c_d - c]_t \\[4pt]
&- \; \underset{(0.03)}{0.41} \; Q_{1t} \; + \; \underset{(0.04)}{0.05} \; Q_{2t} \; - \; \underset{(0.03)}{0.18} \; Q_{3t} \tag{24}
\end{aligned}
$$

$$R(\Delta[p_a - p], \widehat{\Delta[p_a - p]}) = 0.972 \qquad \hat{\sigma}_{(p_a-p)} = 0.052 \qquad \hat{\omega}_{(p_a-p)} = 0.052,$$

where $R(\cdot,\cdot)$ is the correlation coefficient and $\hat{\sigma}$ and $\hat{\omega}$ are diagonal elements of $\hat{\Sigma}$ and $\hat{\Omega}$.

These results are closely similar to the ordinary least squares (OLS) estimates noted above, which is unsurprising, given the lack of simultaneity. However, the standard errors, shown in parentheses below coefficient estimates, are not adjusted for degrees of freedom. Figures 7–10 show the plots of the outcomes, fitted values, and one-step forecasts for the corresponding subsample estimates where 12 observations are retained. As can be seen, the fits are close, and other than a slight underprediction of m_t, so are the [300] forecasts. Since the system has already been tested, the primary diagnostic checks on this model are that it parsimoniously encompasses the system (so that the over-identifying restrictions are valid) and that the structural model retains constant parameters, which was evaluated by the forecast test over the last twelve observations. Neither test is significant, and both the coefficient estimates and $\hat{\sigma}$ values have essentially the same values in the extended and shorter periods. Specifically, for the former,

$$\xi(35) = 45.5;$$

and for the latter,

$$F(36, 29) = 1.00.$$

The estimated structural and reduced form residual covariance matrices, Σ and Ω, respectively, expressed in terms of the correlations were

	$\hat{\Sigma}$		$\hat{\Omega}$		
	Δa_t	$\Delta[p_a - p]_t$	Δm_t	Δa_t	$\Delta[p_a - p]_t$
Δm_t	0.40	−0.03		−0.42	−0.03
Δa_t		−0.16			−0.14
Δh_t			0.64	0.42	−0.15

Equation (22) describes the determination of broadcast time as varying over the business cycle due to the highly significant positive coefficient on $[\pi - p]_t$; responding negatively to the real price of TV advertising time [301] $[p_a - p]_{t-1}$ as allowed from (3) and (4); growing with real income, as measured [302] by c_t and the trend; but, rather surprisingly, falling with the increasing proportion of colored TVs. There is no evidence of seasonal variation, but a large fall is measured during the 1979 strike, with a slight swing back one quarter later. The sum of the estimated coefficients of D_{c4} at 0.42 entails that Channel 4 increased total commercial minutes by about 50%, a coefficient of 0.69 being needed for a doubling. This suggests that the dummy has not overestimated the impact. Finally, in a levels formulation, the coefficient

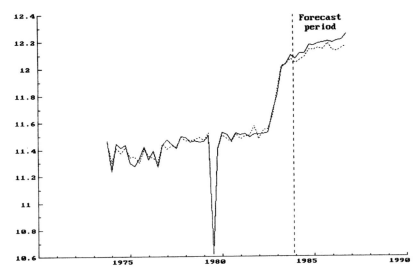

FIGURE 7. Actual (—), fitted (···), and forecast (···) values for commercial minutes m_t from the FIML estimates.

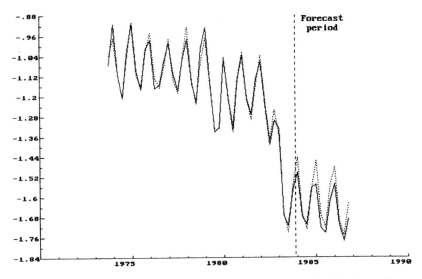

FIGURE 8. Actual (—), fitted (···), and forecast (···) values for audience reach a_t from the FIML estimates.

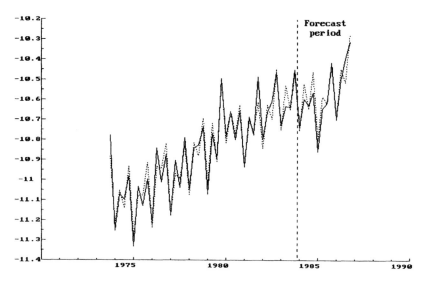

FIGURE 9. Actual (—), fitted (···), and forecast (···) values for
the real price of TV advertising $[p_a - p]_t$ from the FIML estimates.

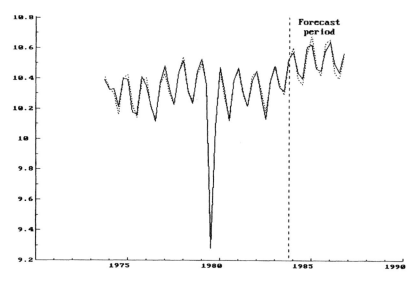

FIGURE 10. Actual (—), fitted (···), and forecast (···) values for
commercial home minutes h_t from the FIML estimates.

of the lagged dependent variable would be zero, so that all adjustment is completed within a quarter. Nevertheless, no contemporaneous effects from other elements of y_t could be established. At just under 3%, the residual standard deviation seems reasonable.

Next, (23) attributes much of the variation in measured audience reach to seasonal factors and the dummy for the 1979 strike. There is a large negative impact from m_t but otherwise a small increase of about 8% from Channel 4 (perhaps previous BBC viewers). There are positive effects from current and past real ICC profits, but no impact from real income or color. The effect of the real price of TV advertising time $[p_a - p]_{t-2}$ is again negative, but this must be a data proxy rather than a structural effect. Finally, lag responses are also very rapid, 86% of any disequilibrium being removed each quarter. The residual standard deviation of 2.5% seems reasonable.

Together, these two equations characterize the supply of commercial home minutes, which is their sum and has the following solved equation:

$$
\begin{aligned}
\widehat{\Delta h_t} = \ & 4.80 + 0.10\ m_{t-1} + 0.24\ [\pi - p]_t - 0.14\ [\pi - p]_{t-1} \\
& (\dots) \quad (0.04) \qquad\quad (0.04) \qquad\qquad (0.04) \\[4pt]
& + 0.15\ [\pi - p]_{t-2} - 0.06\ [p_a - p]_{t-1} - 0.19\ [p_a - p]_{t-2} \\
& \ \ (0.03) \qquad\qquad\ (0.03) \qquad\qquad\ \ (0.03) \\[4pt]
& - 0.04\ D_{c4t} + 0.10\ D_{c4t-1} - 0.07\ C_{olt} \\
& \ \ (0.04) \qquad\ \ (0.04) \qquad\qquad (0.03) \\[4pt]
& + 1.27\ D_{st} - 0.05\ D_{st-1} + 0.14\ c_t + 0.14\ a_{t-1} \\
& \ \ (0.04) \qquad (0.03) \qquad\quad (0.09) \qquad (0.07) \\[4pt]
& - 1.0\ h_{t-1} + 0.003\ t + 0.08 Q_{1t} - 0.12 Q_{2t} - 0.22 Q_{3t}, \quad (25) \\
& \ (-) \qquad\quad (0.001) \qquad (\dots) \qquad\quad (\dots) \qquad\quad (\dots)
\end{aligned}
$$

$R(\Delta h, \widehat{\Delta h}) = 0.995 \quad \hat{\omega}_h = 0.029.$

This is naturally a composite of both (22) and (23): (...) denotes that the relevant standard error was not calculated by the program, but the missing numbers are likely to be close to those in (23). Overall, Channel 4 has a small positive effect on h, whereas $[p_a - p]$ has a distinct negative effect. To check the results in (25), a reduced structural model of h and $[p_a - p]$ was [303] constructed, and produced closely similar estimates, with $\hat{\sigma}_h = 0.028$ and the same value of $R(\cdot)$: the standard errors of the seasonals were as in (23).

Finally, equation (24) represents the demand side. There are positive influences from both real consumers' expenditure and from the proportion spent on durables: in the long run, the former has a near unit elasticity effect on the real price. Inflation captures a short-run lack of homogeneity, with an annualized long-run effect of about –0.7. Color TV increased the real price by about 20% in the long run, but neither dummy variable D_s nor D_{c4} is estimated to have any effect on $[p_a - p]$ beyond that already captured by h: if added, their t values were -0.35 and -1.8, respectively, and the coefficient of h_{t-1} fell. Moreover, on this data set, h_t is irrelevant in the $[p_a-p]$ equation and only h_{t-1} enters. Most importantly, the impact price elasticity is estimated as $-1/0.23 \approx -4.3$ in the short run and $-0.57/0.23 \approx -2.4$ in the long run. An approximate standard error for the elasticity of -2.4, based on the formula for the variance of a ratio, is 0.6, yielding a 95% confidence interval of -2.4 ± 1.2. Although this derived statistic is relatively uncertain, the absolute value of the point elasticity is significantly larger than unity. Moreover, the initial over-reaction described in Section 2 appears to occur. If h_{t-1} is split into its two components a_{t-1} and m_{t-1}, they enter with nearly equal coefficients, confirming the restriction that commercial home minutes is the determinant of price.

To summarize, the equations pass all of the mis-specification tests, and the model's restrictions are accepted as valid despite the lack of correction for degrees of freedom. The long-run price elasticity is estimated at -2.4. The results are close to those obtained with least squares, since there is little evidence of simultaneity (see $\hat{\Sigma}$ above). To investigate the potential effects of measurement errors that might bias downwards the coefficient of h_{t-1} and hence bias upwards the long-run elasticity estimate, that variable was treated as endogenous in an instrumental variables estimation using only the macro variables as instruments, but the coefficient did not increase.

Finally, the model was transformed to an $I(0)$ representation in terms of first differences and cointegration combinations based on the long-run solution of the system. Re-estimation replicated the results recorded above, with somewhat smaller standard errors owing to the parameter restrictions, but these outcomes are not reported, since it is unclear that all of the variables are $I(1)$.

The main remaining problem is the marked conflict with the evidence presented to the Peacock Committee, where most estimates of the long-run price elasticity were around minus one half. To reach sensible policy [304] decisions, it is essential to determine which model is the best representation of the DGP, and hence which is the best estimate of the "true" long-run elasticity. We turn next to modeling the annual data both to replicate earlier findings and to test the models that were used.

7 Interpreting Previous Annual Data Results

Figure 8.2 on p. 72 of the Peacock (1986) report summarizes the bulk of earlier estimates of price and income elasticities, noting that Budd's (1985) study lies in the "Newspaper Society" circle, although it is not marked in the Peacock figure. Despite the wide range of values that have been obtained, the most reliable estimates cluster around an income elasticity of 2 and a price elasticity of -0.5, where reliable is a subjective judgment based on the reported testing. Because of revisions and slight changes in coverage, the actual data series used here differ from those analyzed previously, making it impossible to precisely replicate regression estimates reported by others. However, all of the essential features of the earlier annual models of Budd, Cave and Swann, and NERA could be reproduced on the present data set. We now note these features. To distinguish quarterly and annually measured variables of the same name, sans serif symbols are used for the latter.

1. Budd (1985) regressed h_t on $[p_a - p]_t$ and obtained an insignificant price elasticity of $-1/3$. Owing to the implausible exogeneity assumption that quantity does, and price does not, respond to demand changes, this evidence is suspect and is easily explained by the correlation being due to a price response with an incorrect direction of regression. Budd (1986) abandoned his earlier approach in favor of the NERA (1985) view and modeled $[p_a - p]_t$ as depending on h_t and c_t *inter alia*. He still obtained a price elasticity of less than unity (around $-1/2$ now), and the best fitting equation had a residual standard error of about 5% of P_a/P. This second finding, therefore, precludes explaining the low price elasticity in terms of invalid exogeneity alone.

2. Cave and Swann (1986) considered several models, including regressing advertising revenue on price and other variables, to find a similar price response to Budd's. Again the exogeneity assumption is unjustifiable, since their model is equivalent to that of Budd (1985) in taking price as given and quantity as the adjusting variate.

3. NERA (1986) regressed revenue on quantity, controlling for consumers' expenditure, ICC profits relative to GNP, the growth of color TVs, and dynamic responses. Again, a price elasticity of less than unity was found despite the more sensible exogeneity assumption.

This third study was the basis adopted for developing an annual model. [305] Data were not available on the split of h_t into m_t and a_t. First, an unrestricted dynamic system was estimated, linking $[p_a - p]_t$ and h_t to c_t, $[\pi - p]_t$, Δp_t, GNP_t, C_{olt}, D_{st}, and D_{c4t}, with one lag on every variable, and a constant. This system revealed the following.

(a) GNP_t mattered only if the restricted form $[\pi - GNP - p]$ was used [as in NERA (1986)] and did not enter the equation if unrestricted.

(b) Lags did not matter for most variables, suggesting that adjustment was essentially completed within a year.

(c) A constant-parameter system with innovation errors could be developed, although the small sample size mitigates against diagnostic tests having much power.

(d) A model of that system had an apparent price elasticity of less than unity.

The annual model like (17) finally selected from FIML estimation over 1962–1984 was the following:

$$\widehat{\Delta h_t} = -\underset{(1.3)}{11.1} + \underset{(0.08)}{0.32}\, C_{olt} - \underset{(0.08)}{0.71}\, h_{t-1} + \underset{(0.04)}{0.21}\, [\pi - p]_t$$
$$+ \underset{(0.13)}{1.3}\, c_t + \underset{(0.02)}{0.27}\, D_{st} - \underset{(0.06)}{0.21}\, [p_a - p]_t \tag{26}$$

$$R(h,\hat{h}) = 0.994 \qquad \hat{\sigma}_h = 0.022 \qquad \hat{\omega}_h = 0.032,$$

$$\widehat{\Delta[p_a - p]_t} = -\underset{(3.4)}{15.1} - \underset{(0.09)}{0.88}\, [p_a - p]_{t-1} - \underset{(0.20)}{1.21}\, h_t$$
$$+ \underset{(0.11)}{0.71}\, C_{olt} - \underset{(0.23)}{1.70}\, \Delta p_t + \underset{(0.07)}{0.30}\, [\pi - p]_t$$
$$+ \underset{(0.38)}{1.93}\, c_{t-1} + \underset{(0.05)}{0.23}\, D_{st} \tag{27}$$

$$R([p_a - p],[\widehat{p_a - p}]) = 0.939 \qquad \hat{\sigma}_{(p_a - p)} = 0.026 \qquad \hat{\omega}_{(p_a - p)} = 0.054.$$

The main features are the close goodness-of-fits of the structural equations, at 2.2% of H and 2.6% of P_a/P; the much poorer fits of the reduced forms, which are close to those of the quarterly data system; the joint dependence of h_t and $[p_a - p]_t$; the need to include the strike dummy in the $[p_a - p]$ equation, which is suggestive of an incorrect price elasticity estimate; and the long-run price elasticity of $-0.88/1.21 = -0.7$ from the $[p_a - p]$ equation, which reproduces the earlier annual findings of an elasticity distinctly less than unity. The likelihood ratio test of over-identifying restrictions yielded $\xi(3) = 10.4$, which is acceptable for such a small sample size. However, the likelihood function is very badly behaved for the parameters of the endogenous variables, as Figure 11 shows for the coefficient of h_t in the $[p_a - p]_t$ [306] equation. [*Author's note*: The figure shown here differs somewhat from the one in the original paper, but the qualitative results remain the same.] All of these items point towards problems with the annual data model.

The near absence of lags entails that the contemporaneous correlation of -0.85 between $[p_a - p]_t$ and h_t dominates the estimation of the price elasticity, yet is open to interpretation as being due to (unspecified) third factors. Much of the "explanatory" power in (27) is dependent on the contemporaneous value of commercial home minutes. Two points of note are that the dummy for Channel 4 was insignificant if added to the system, and that if profits were deleted in (27), the coefficient of h_t became -1.03.

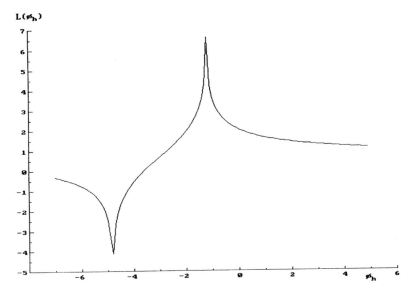

FIGURE 11. The likelihood function $\mathcal{L}(\phi_h)$ for the coefficient ϕ_h of h_t in the $[p_a - p]_t$ equation on annual data by FIML estimation.

The conclusion of this section is that the implications of previous annual results can be confirmed in a tested congruent model of the annual data, leaving a clear conflict with the quarterly data findings, which must be reconciled if either model is to have any credibility.

8   Reconciling the Results

The conflict in the evidence between the two data sets is marked. To analyze this, we refer to the discussion in Section 4. There it is argued that empirical models are derived reductions of the DGP, with properties determined by the specific reductions selected and by the method of estimation. The conflicting models have a common method of estimation, and while their sample periods are only partly overlapping, the evidence that both are constant within sample suggests that the explanation for the conflict cannot be the shorter historical record for the quarterly model. Since precisely the same variables could have entered each equation—but did not do so—and the annualized observations from the quarterly data set are identical to the [307] equivalent annual observations, the explanation must lie with the choice of data frequency.

The cross-correlations of the residuals from the structural models of $[p_a - p]$ and h reveal very different annual and quarterly outcomes, with a correlation of -0.85 in the annual data as against only -0.16 in the quarterly. From (22)–(24), none of h_t, m_t, or a_t are strongly exogenous for the parameters of the $[p_a - p]_t$ equation on quarterly data and hence cannot be weakly exogenous on annual data models. That entails that quantity is endogenous in the annual model, an implication that is consistent with the system modeling of h_t in (26). Such a finding precludes least squares estimates, but as shown in (26) and (27), FIML estimates with both h_t and $[p_a - p]_t$ treated as endogenous replicate the low-elasticity problem.

It is possible that the quarterly allocation by the TV companies' accounts of items that are essentially annual induces large, but nonsystematic, measurement errors relative to the annual data. However, that explanation would not account for the different lag structures and dependencies on different variables, except by chance cross-correlated errors of measurement. Thus, time aggregation and induced "identification" difficulties seem to be the culprit.

To analyze that conjecture, express the quarterly model as

$$
\begin{aligned}
y_t &= \Gamma y_{t-1} + \Lambda z_t + \varepsilon_t \\
&= (I - \Gamma L)^{-1} \Lambda z_t + u_t,
\end{aligned} \tag{28}
$$

where L denotes the lag operator, so that

$$
u_t = \Gamma u_{t-1} + \varepsilon_t \qquad \varepsilon_t \sim \mathsf{IN}(0, \Sigma). \tag{29}
$$

The annual data are sums of successive groups of four values of the quarterly data. We approximate the error covariance matrix of the annual data by that of u_t, namely

$$
E(u_t u_t') = \Psi = \Gamma \Psi \Gamma' + \Sigma. \tag{30}
$$

As there will be a negligible dependence between $\sum_{i=1}^{4} u_{t-i}$ and $\sum_{i=1}^{4} u_{t-i-4}$, Ψ should capture the main features of the contemporaneous residual covariance matrix for annual data. From the quarterly structural estimates for the joint model of the key variables h_t and $[p_a - p]_t$ expressed as in (28), we have

$$
\Gamma = \begin{bmatrix} 0.12 & -0.25 \\ -0.23 & 0.44 \end{bmatrix} \quad \text{and} \quad \Sigma = 10^{-3} \begin{bmatrix} 0.78 & -0.23 \\ -0.23 & 2.60 \end{bmatrix} \tag{31}
$$

so that

[308]

$$
\Psi = 10^{-3} \begin{bmatrix} 1.05 & -0.70 \\ -0.70 & 3.47 \end{bmatrix}. \tag{32}
$$

Consequently, this long-run covariance matrix generates a correlation of -0.37. Thus, the predicted value from the quarterly model is closer to that actually found on the annual data, although still much too small. Furthermore, the large degradation in fit from the structural errors to the reduced form errors in the annual model matches the result in (32) and so supports the hypothesis that time aggregation has biased upwards the coefficient of h in the price equation.

The final supporting evidence for that claim comes from a comparison of the solved long-run coefficients on both data frequencies. From (14), in static equilibrium we have

$$\left(I - \sum_{i=1}^{s} \delta_{2i}\right) y = \left(\sum_{j=0}^{s} \delta_{1j}\right) z, \tag{33}$$

or

$$G_0 y = G_1 z$$

so that

$$y = G_0^{-1} G_1 z.$$

The matrix G_0 represents the long-run endogenous inter-dependencies and $G_0^{-1} G_1$ are the long-run multipliers. Empirically, for the two unrestricted systems we find the following.

	G_0 Annual		G_0 Quarterly	
	h	$[p_a - p]$	h	$[p_a - p]$
h	−0.75	−0.14	−0.96	−0.25
$[p_a - p]$	−0.32	−0.70	−0.45	−0.73

These matrices are similar, and both show a "price elasticity" derived from the $[p_a - p]$ equation of well above unity in absolute value (and larger on the annual data), whereas that from the h equations is around −0.25.

To summarize the remaining long-run multipliers, the results are reported for h, $[p_a - p]$, and for real net revenue, which is defined by $r = h + [p_a - p]$, for variables in common:

	$G_0^{-1} G_1$ Annual					$G_0^{-1} G_1$ Quarterly				
	C_{ol}	c	$\pi - p$	$\dot{p}$	D_s	C_{ol}	c	$\pi - p$	$\dot{p}$	D_s
h	0.4	2.0	0.3	0.9	0.5	−0.0	0.1	0.3	0.1	0.4
$[p_a - p]$	0.3	−0.4	−0.1	−3.2	−0.4	0.2	1.2	−0.1	−0.7	−0.2
r	0.7	1.6	0.2	−2.3	0.1	0.2	1.3	0.2	−0.6	0.2

where $\dot{p}$ denotes annual inflation and D_s is calibrated to an annual rate. The quarterly estimates seem more plausible overall, especially for the expenditure elasticities. Thus, we conclude that the annual data do not provide [309] adequate information to determine the parameters of interest in the system and that the evidence favors a price elasticity exceeding unity in absolute value.

9 Conclusions

The summary of the main findings was stated in Section 1 and in the previous paragraph. The statistical analysis described in the body of the text shows that the volume of commercial home minutes broadcast responds negatively to prices and this correlation is sufficiently large to seriously bias any least squares outcome. It may represent a supply reaction, or reflect data correlations due to omitted variables rather than causative factors, but either effect violates weak exogeneity in annual data regressions of price on quantity.

Without good over-identifying information on the annual data, such a bias will prejudice inference even if system methods are used, so it may be difficult to disentangle the demand price elasticity from the annual evidence. The finer dynamic responses of the quarterly data make the elasticity estimates presented above more reliable.

On theoretical grounds, the elasticity estimates are also more reasonable, since it is hard to imagine industrial and commercial companies cutting budgets for TV advertising because advertising time has expanded. If the price elasticity lies between minus unity and zero, the IBA companies should reduce broadcasting time to increase profits. There is no evidence that their monopoly supplier ITV has attempted to do so. Rather, the extension of commercial broadcasting to TV–AM in late 1983 indicates a desire to expand broadcasting hours, and hence commercial minutes of advertising.

One potentially important excluded variable in the present study is the price of competitive media. There seems to be no good "representative" price index for other forms of advertising in the United Kingdom, and this is a serious lacuna in almost all studies to date. However, its omission will bias results towards too small an estimated elasticity, not too large. For example, consider the comparative responsiveness of a garage's gasoline sales as a function of: (a) absolute prices; and (b) the price relative to other garages. Thus, the estimates quoted herein may yet prove too low.

The model also suggests that expanding commercial minutes of broadcasting by introducing additional commercial channels will reduce audience reach almost in proportion, without much effect on the price or on total commercial home minutes. This implication does not apply to converting [310]   existing BBC channels to advertising, since that would greatly increase the total number of viewers. Conversely, the attractiveness of watching TV is estimated to fall because of the disturbing intrusion of adverts. Although the empirical economic evidence here is counter to that presented to the Peacock Committee, in that revenue seems almost certain to rise with expanded commercial broadcasting, that conclusion alone does not entail revising their recommendation on financing the BBC [see Ehrenberg (1986)]. However, it may entail a more favourable reaction to possible future commercial channels.

Bibliography

(References marked with an asterisk * are included in this volume.)

Bowman, G. W. (1977) "Demand and Supply of Network Television Advertising", *Bell Journal of Economics*, 258–267.

Budd, A. (1985) "The Impact on ITV Revenue of Extending Advertising to the BBC", London Business School, London.

Budd, A. (1986) "Channel Four Post Peacock: The Financial Implications of Recommendation 14", London Business School, London.

Cave, M., and P. Swann (1986) "The Effects on Advertising Revenues of Allowing Advertising on BBC Television", in A. Peacock (ed.) *Report of the Committee on Financing the BBC*, London, Her Majesty's Stationery Office, 178–186.

Dickey, D. A., and W. A. Fuller (1979) "Distribution of the Estimators for Autoregressive Time Series with a Unit Root", *Journal of American Statistical Association*, 74, 427–431.

Dickey, D. A., and W. A. Fuller (1981) "Likelihood Ratio Statistics for Autoregressive Time Series with a Unit Root", *Econometrica*, 49, 1057–1072.

Ehrenberg, A. S. C. (1986) *Advertisers or Viewers Paying?*, London, ADMAP Publications Ltd.

Engle, R. F. (1982) "Autoregressive Conditional Heteroscedasticity with Estimates of the Variance of United Kingdom Inflation", *Econometrica*, 50, 987–1007.

Engle, R. F., and C. W. J. Granger (1987) "Co-integration and Error Correction: Representation, Estimation, and Testing", *Econometrica*, 55, 251–276.

*Engle, R. F., and D. F. Hendry (1993) "Testing Super Exogeneity and Invariance in Regression Models", *Journal of Econometrics*, 56, 1/2, 119–139; originally cited as (1989) "Testing Super Exogeneity and Invariance", forthcoming in *Journal of Econometrics*.

*Engle, R. F., D. F. Hendry, and J.-F. Richard (1983) "Exogeneity", *Econometrica*, 51, 277–304.

Granger, C. W. J. (1986) "Developments in the Study of Cointegrated Economic Variables", *Oxford Bulletin of Economics and Statistics*, 48, 213–228.

Granger, C. W. J., and A. A. Weiss (1983) "Time Series Analysis of Error Correction Models", in S. Karlin, T. Amemiya, and L. A. Goodman (eds.) *Studies in Econometrics, Time Series, and Multivariate Statistics*, New York, Academic Press, 255–278.

Haavelmo, T, (1944) "The Probability Approach in Econometrics", *Econometrica*, 12, Supplement, 1–118.

Hendry, D. F. (1984) "Econometric Modelling of House Prices in the United Kingdom", in D. F. Hendry and K. F. Wallis (eds.) *Econometrics and Quantitative Economics*, Oxford, Basil Blackwell, 135–172.

Hendry, D. F. (ed.) (1986) *Econometric Modelling with Cointegrated Variables, Oxford Bulletin of Economics and Statistics*, Special Issue, 48, 3.

Hendry, D. F. (1987a) "Econometrics in Action", *Empirica*, 2/87, 135–156.

Hendry, D. F. (1987b) "Econometric Methodology: A Personal Perspective", Chapter 10 in T. F. Bewley (ed.) *Advances in Econometrics*, Cambridge, Cambridge University Press, Volume 2, 29–48.

[311] Hendry, D. F. (1987c) "A Reassessment of the Econometric Research on TV Advertising Revenue", report, London, National Economic Research Associates.

Hendry, D. F. (1989) *PC-GIVE: An Interactive Econometric Modelling System*, Version 6.0/6.01, Oxford, Institute of Economics and Statistics and Nuffield College, University of Oxford.

Hendry D. F., and N. R. Ericsson (1991) "An Econometric Analysis of U.K. Money Demand in *Monetary Trends in the United States and the United Kingdom* by Milton Friedman and Anna J. Schwartz", *American Economic Review*, 81, 8–38.

Hendry, D. F., and G. E. Mizon (1993) "Evaluating Dynamic Econometric Models by Encompassing the VAR", in P. C. B. Phillips (ed.) *Models, Methods, and Applications of Econometrics*, Oxford, Basil Blackwell, 272–300; originally cited as (1990), forthcoming in *Models, Methods, and Applications of Econometrics*.

Hendry, D. F., A. J. Neale, and F. Srba (1988) "Econometric Analysis of Small Linear Systems using PC-FIML", *Journal of Econometrics*, 38, 203–226.

Hendry, D. F., A. R. Pagan, and J. D. Sargan (1984) "Dynamic Specification", Chapter 18 in Z. Griliches and M. D. Intriligator (eds.) *Handbook of Econometrics*, Amsterdam, North-Holland, Volume 2, 1023–1100.

Hendry, D. F., and J.-F. Richard (1982) "On the Formulation of Empirical Models in Dynamic Econometrics", *Journal of Econometrics*, 20, 3–33.

Hendry, D. F., and J.-F. Richard (1989) "Recent Developments in the Theory of Encompassing", Chapter 12 in B. Cornet and H. Tulkens (eds.) *Contributions to Operations Research and Economics: The Twentieth Anniversary of CORE*, Cambridge, Massachusetts, MIT Press, 393–440.

Jarque, C. M., and A. K. Bera (1980) "Efficient Tests for Normality, Homoscedasticity, and Serial Independence of Regression Residuals", *Economics Letters*, 6, 255–259.

Johansen, S. (1988) "Statistical Analysis of Cointegration Vectors", *Journal of Economic Dynamics and Control*, 12, 231–254.

Lucas, R. E., Jr. (1976) "Econometric Policy Evaluation: A Critique", in K. Brunner and A. H. Meltzer (eds.) *The Phillips Curve and Labor Markets*, Amsterdam, North-Holland, 19–46.

Mizon, G. E., and J.-F. Richard (1986) "The Encompassing Principle and Its Application to Non-nested Hypothesis Tests", *Econometrica*, 54, 657–678.

National Economic Research Associates (NERA) (1986) "The Effects on ITV and Other Media of the Introduction of Advertising on the BBC in Various Amounts", in A. Peacock (ed.) *Report of the Committee on Financing the BBC*, London, Her Majesty's Stationery Office, 186–188.

Peacock, A. (1986) *Report of the Committee on Financing the BBC*, London, Her Majesty's Stationery Office.

Sims, C. A. (1980) "Macroeconomics and Reality", *Econometrica*, 48, 1–48.

Spanos, A. (1986) *Statistical Foundations of Econometric Modelling*, Cambridge, Cambridge University Press.

White, H. (1984) *Asymptotic Theory for Econometricians*, London, Academic Press.

Part III

EXTENSIONS TO TESTING PROCEDURES

12

Parameter Constancy, Mean Square Forecast Errors, and Measuring Forecast Performance: An Exposition, Extensions, and Illustration

NEIL R. ERICSSON*

Abstract

Parameter constancy and a model's mean square forecast error are two commonly used measures of forecast performance. By explicit consideration of the information sets involved, this paper clarifies the roles that each plays in analyzing a model's forecast accuracy. Both criteria are necessary for "good" forecast performance, but neither (nor both) is sufficient. Further, these criteria fit into a general

* The author is a staff economist in the Division of International Finance, Federal Reserve Board. The views expressed in this paper are solely the responsibility of the author and should not be interpreted as reflecting those of the Board of Governors of the Federal Reserve System or other members of its staff.

I am grateful to Julia Campos, Frank Diebold, Hali Edison, David Hendry, David Howard, Ross Levine, Jaime Marquez, Doug McManus, and Garry Schinasi for useful comments and discussions, and to Hong-Anh Tran for invaluable research assistance. I am particularly indebted to Edison, Schinasi, and P. A. V. B. Swamy, whose empirical papers on modeling and forecasting exchange rates motivated this paper; see Edison (1985), Edison and Klovland (1987), Edison (1991), Schinasi and Swamy (1989), and Swamy and Schinasi (1989). All numerical results were obtained using PC-GIVE Version 6.01 [Hendry (1989)].

Reprinted with permission from the *Journal of Policy Modeling* (August 1992), 14, 4, 465–495.

taxonomy of model evaluation statistics, and the information set corresponding to a model's mean square forecast error leads to a new test
statistic, forecast-model encompassing. Two models of U.K. money
demand illustrate the various measures of forecast accuracy.

1 Introduction

Parameter constancy and the mean square forecast error (MSFE) are two
commonly used measures of the forecast performance of empirical macromodels. Parameter constancy has long been viewed as a desirable economic
and statistical property, and it is closely linked to the issue of predictive failure [Chow (1960), Hendry (1979)]. Further, parameter constancy can imply
[466] super exogeneity, which is necessary to sustain counterfactual policy simulations of an econometric model [Hendry (1988)]. Lack of parameter constancy
can induce apparent unit roots, posing potential difficulties when testing for
cointegration [Hendry and Neale (1991)]. The MSFE is a common criterion
for evaluating the performance of alternative macromodels; see Fair (1986)
for a general discussion and Meese and Rogoff (1983) for a classic example
with models of the exchange rate.

Sometimes, the literature has viewed these two forecast criteria as competing rather than complementary. Thus, this paper aims to clarify the roles
of parameter constancy and the MSFE in evaluating the forecast accuracy
of a model.

Section 2 works through some simple examples to show that (i) parameter constancy is neither necessary nor sufficient for minimizing MSFE
across a given set of models, and (ii) both criteria together are necessary
but not sufficient to obtain the best forecasting model, even on only the
data available from the given set of models. Section 3 explains why, showing
that parameter constancy and minimizing MSFE are criteria that evaluate a
given model (respectively) against that model's own data and against other
models' data. Both are reasonable criteria, but other criteria are also important for determining the forecast adequacy of an empirical model. Section 4
introduces a new model evaluation criterion, "forecast-model" encompassing, and the corresponding test statistic. Further, Section 4 shows that
minimum MSFE, forecast encompassing, and forecast-model encompassing
parallel variance dominance, variance encompassing, and parameter encompassing, respectively. Section 5 discusses several implications for forecasting
integrated and cointegrated variables. Section 6 comments briefly on the
role of time-varying coefficient models in forecasting. Section 7 illustrates
the various forecast-based criteria with an application to two models of narrow money demand in the United Kingdom.

Before turning to the heart of the paper, three remarks may be helpful.
First, the results in this paper are quite general. To illustrate the central

concepts, however, simple, static, Gaussian models are used as examples throughout. See Hendry and Richard (1982) for a framework in which more general results may be obtained. Second, to abstract from sampling issues, results are often presented as "asymptotic". This in no way invalidates the results, but simply permits a clearer exposition. Third, the concept of an "adequate forecasting model" is intentionally left vague. Roughly, such a model efficiently uses the information available for creating forecasts. It is defined in part by its negation. For instance, a model is *in*adequate for forecasting if its forecast errors are predictable, a situation including both parameter nonconstancy and lack of forecast encompassing (as will be [467] seen below). For Gaussian processes, minimum MSFE is a condition for forecast adequacy, but Section 2 shows that it is not sufficient because the corresponding errors may still be predictable.

2   Parameter Constancy and Minimizing MSFE

This section shows that (i) parameter constancy is neither necessary nor sufficient for minimizing MSFE across a given set of models, and (ii) both criteria together are necessary (but not sufficient) to obtain the best forecasting model on the data available. Four "propositions" establish (i) and (ii), which are illustrated by some simple examples. The analytical form of the MSFE and of Chow's (1960) "prediction interval" statistic clarifies the absence of relationship between minimizing MSFE over a set of models and obtaining parameter constancy for an individual model.

To show the *lack* of connection between parameter constancy and minimizing MSFE, consider the following simple process in which the dependent variable y_t is linearly dependent upon three regressors, each of which is normally and independently distributed.

Models and the data generation process. Suppose that the data $(y_t, t = 1, \ldots, T + n)$ are generated by:

$$y_t = \beta_1 x_{1t} + \beta_2 x_{2t} + \beta_3 x_{3t} + \varepsilon_t \qquad \varepsilon_t \sim \mathsf{NID}(0, \sigma^2), \qquad (1a)$$

and the x_{it}'s are normally and independently distributed (NID):

$$x_{it} \sim \mathsf{NID}(0, \omega_{ii}) \qquad i = 1, 2, 3, \qquad (1b)$$

where ω_{ii}, the variance of x_{it}, may change over time. The double index on ω_{ii} denotes that the variance is the ith diagonal element from the (diagonal) contemporaneous covariance matrix (Ω) of the $\{x_{it}\}$. Together (1a) and (1b) are referred to as the data generation process (DGP). To exclude trivial cases, σ^2 and all ω_{ii}'s are positive and all β_i's are nonzero.

The econometrician does not know the DGP, and estimates the following (mis-specified) models by OLS over a subsample $[1, T]$ and evaluates their forecast performance over n periods $[T + 1, T + n]$.

$$M_1 : y_t = \alpha_1 x_{1t} + \qquad\qquad u_{1t} \qquad u_{1t} \sim \mathsf{NID}(0, \sigma_1^2) \qquad (2a)$$

$$M_2 : y_t = \gamma_1 x_{1t} + \gamma_2 x_{2t} + \qquad u_{2t} \qquad u_{2t} \sim \mathsf{NID}(0, \sigma_2^2) \qquad (2b)$$

$$M_3 : y_t = \delta_1 x_{1t} + \qquad \delta_3 x_{3t} + u_{3t} \qquad u_{3t} \sim \mathsf{NID}(0, \sigma_3^2) \qquad (2c)$$

[468] The sets of coefficients $\{\alpha_1\}$, $\{\gamma_1, \gamma_2\}$, and $\{\delta_1, \delta_3\}$ are used to distinguish the models' coefficients from the underlying coefficients of the DGP, i.e., $\{\beta_1, \beta_2, \beta_3\}$. For convenience, $\hat{y}_{ij}$ denotes the prediction of y in period j, using the parameter estimates from model M_i estimated over $[1, T]$. For example, $\hat{y}_{2j}$ is:

$$\hat{y}_{2j} = \hat{\gamma}_{1T} x_{1j} + \hat{\gamma}_{2T} x_{2j} \qquad j = T+1, \ldots, T+n, \qquad (3)$$

where $\hat{\gamma}_{1T}$ and $\hat{\gamma}_{2T}$ are the coefficients γ_1 and γ_2, estimated over $[1, T]$.

The MSFE for the ith model is:

$$MSFE_i = \mathcal{E}\left[\sum_{j=T+1}^{T+n} (y_j - \hat{y}_{ij})^2 / n \right] \qquad i = 1, 2, 3, \qquad (4a)$$

where the expectation $\mathcal{E}[\cdot]$ is over $\{\varepsilon_j\}$. For the models discussed in this paper, each term in the summation in (4a) has the same expectation, so $MSFE_i = \mathcal{E}[(y_j - \hat{y}_{ij})^2]$, independent of j, for $j = T+1, \ldots, T+n$.

In practice, the MSFE is estimated by the sample average of the squared forecast errors:

$$\widehat{MSFE}_i = \sum_{j=T+1}^{T+n} (y_j - \hat{y}_{ij})^2 / n \qquad i = 1, 2, 3, \qquad (4b)$$

for the ith model. Most of the discussion in this paper is in terms of the underlying population moments, i.e., the MSFE, thereby abstracting from the additional complication of the sampling distribution of (4b).[1]

Parameter constancy may be evaluated by any of a number of statistics, with Chow's (1960, pp. 594–595) "prediction interval" statistic being one of the more common.[2] The Chow statistic can be written as:

---

[1] Note that the estimation and forecast periods do not overlap. By contrast, (e.g.) dynamic simulation uses overlapping (usually identical) estimation and "forecast" periods. Mean square forecast errors from such simulations may have quite different properties from those discussed herein. See Hendry and Richard (1982), Chong and Hendry (1986), and Pagan (1989) on the role of dynamic simulation in model comparison.

[2] Chow (1960) also discusses a parameter constancy test statistic based on the analysis of covariance, in which estimates of the coefficients over the two subsamples are compared for equality; see Fisher (1922) for its original development. This statistic is distributed as $F(k_i, T+n-2k_i)$ under the null hypothesis, with classical assumptions about the regressors and disturbances. This covariance test statistic is sometimes (and confusingly) referred to as the "Chow statistic" although Chow (1960, p. 592) was well aware of its presence in the literature. In the current paper, the phrase "Chow statistic" refers exclusively to

[469]

$$\text{CHOW}_i\,(n, T - k_i) = \frac{\left(Y_{T+1}^{T+n} - \hat{Y}_{T+1}^{T+n}\right)' \left[\text{Var}\left(Y_{T+1}^{T+n} - \hat{Y}_{T+1}^{T+n}\right)\right]^{-1} \left(Y_{T+1}^{T+n} - \hat{Y}_{T+1}^{T+n}\right)/n}{\{\hat{\sigma}_{iT}^2/\sigma_{iT}^2\}}$$

$$= \left\{\sum_{j=T+1}^{T+n} (y_j - \hat{y}_{ij})^2 /n\right\} /\hat{\sigma}_{iT}^2 + O_p\left(T^{-1}\right)$$

$$= \widehat{MSFE}_i/\hat{\sigma}_{iT}^2 + O_p\left(T^{-1}\right), \tag{5}$$

where $Y_{T+1}^{T+n} = (y_{T+1} \dots y_{T+n})'$, $\hat{Y}_{T+1}^{T+n}$ is the forecast of Y_{T+1}^{T+n} by model M_i, $\hat{\sigma}_{iT}^2$ is the estimated equation error variance for model M_i over $[1, T]$, k_i is the number of regressors in model M_i, and $O_p(T^{-1})$ denotes a term of order T^{-1} in probability. As (5) clarifies, the Chow statistic in effect tests whether each of the forecast errors of a given model has zero mean, i.e., $\mathcal{E}(y_j - \hat{y}_{ij}) = 0$ for $j = T+1, \dots, T+n$. It does so by comparing the mean square forecast error against the estimated error variance over the estimation subsample. Under the null hypothesis, and with fixed regressors and normal disturbances, the Chow statistic is distributed as $F(n, T - k_i)$. "Significant" Chow statistics are often referred to as "predictive failure" [Hendry (1979)].[3]

To simplify the analysis even further, suppose that T is large enough so the uncertainty in estimating the model parameters can be ignored when considering the characteristics of the MSFE and the Chow statistic. This assumption and virtually all assumptions in (1)–(2) are for expositional purposes only, and most of the results below obtain under more general conditions (e.g., nonlinearity; autocorrelated, multicollinear, endogenous regressors; more or fewer regressors relative to those in the models here; nonnormality of the errors and/or regressors).

Examples 1 and 2 consider two situations, one in which all population data moments are constant and the other in which some of them change over time.

Example 1 *Constant population data moments. This is equivalent to having* $(\omega_{ii}, \beta_i, i = 1, 2, 3)$ *and* σ^2 *constant in (1).*

Chow's prediction interval statistic (5). Wilson (1978) discusses conditions under which each of the Chow (prediction interval) statistic and the covariance statistic is uniformly most powerful. Fisher (1970) and Dufour (1980) present intuitive derivations of the two statistics.

[3] The first term on the last line of (5) is $1/n$ times Hendry's (1979) χ^2 statistic for testing the *numerical* accuracy of the forecasts. Chow's statistic tests their *statistical* accuracy by accounting for the uncertainty arising from estimating (rather than knowing) the regression coefficients. This affects only the finite sample distribution of the statistic: Hendry's and Chow's statistics *are* asymptotically equivalent. Because coefficient uncertainty is ignored for the most part in this paper, the equivalency proves useful, given the simpler form of Hendry's statistic.

[470] All models (i.e., M_1, M_2, M_3) will have constant parameters because the
corresponding (OLS) estimators are functions of the sample data moments,
with the sample data moments being constant in expectation (by assumption). For the DGP in (1), OLS for each model in (2) is unbiased for the
relevant subset of $\{\beta_1, \beta_2, \beta_3\}$, and is so only because the regressors are uncorrelated with each other and are static. That property does *not* generalize;
however, even with correlated regressors, for example, constant population
data moments are sufficient for parameter constancy.

From (1) and (2), it follows directly that the mean square forecast errors
for M_1, M_2, and M_3 are:

$$MSFE_1 = \sigma^2 + \beta_2^2 \omega_{22} + \beta_3^2 \omega_{33} \tag{6a}$$

$$MSFE_2 = \sigma^2 + \phantom{\beta_2^2 \omega_{22} +} \beta_3^2 \omega_{33} \tag{6b}$$

$$MSFE_3 = \sigma^2 + \beta_2^2 \omega_{22}. \tag{6c}$$

Clearly, M_1 has the largest MSFE; the ranking of M_2 and M_3 depends upon
the relative magnitudes of $\beta_2^2 \omega_{22}$ and $\beta_3^2 \omega_{33}$. This indeterminacy leads to the
first proposition.

Proposition 1 *If a model has (empirically) constant parameters, it can have
either a smaller or a larger MSFE than some other model.*

That is, parameter constancy is not sufficient for obtaining the smallest
MSFE among a set of models.

Nonconstant population data moments help demonstrate the lack of necessity.

Example 2 *Nonconstant population data moments. Suppose that the vari-
ance of x_{2t} increases from ω_{22} to ω_{22}^* at time $T + 1$ and remains at ω_{22}^*
thereafter.*

For models M_1 and M_3, the increase from ω_{22} to ω_{22}^* implies a forecast error
variance larger than the estimation subsample error variance, so the Chow
statistic will indicate parameter nonconstancy. If regressors are correlated,
either or both models may have coefficient nonconstancy, apparent, for example, through graphs of the recursively estimated coefficients.

The mean square forecast errors for the models are:

$$MSFE_1 = \sigma^2 + \beta_2^2 \omega_{22}^* + \beta_3^2 \omega_{33} \tag{7a}$$

$$MSFE_2 = \sigma^2 + \phantom{\beta_2^2 \omega_{22}^* +} \beta_3^2 \omega_{33} \tag{7b}$$

$$MSFE_3 = \sigma^2 + \beta_2^2 \omega_{22}^*. \tag{7c}$$

[471] Again, M_1 has the largest MSFE, but the ranking of those for M_2 and M_3
could be the same as (or different from) the ranking of (6), depending upon

TABLE 1. Models for the Discussion of MSFE and Parameter Constancy

Model	Equation		$MSFE_i$		Constancy[a]
M_1	$y_t = \alpha_1 x_{1t} +$	u_{1t}	$\sigma^2 +$	$\beta_2^2 \omega_{22}^* + \beta_3^2 \omega_{33}$	No
M_2	$y_t = \gamma_1 x_{1t} + \gamma_2 x_{2t} +$	u_{2t}	$\sigma^2 +$	$\beta_3^2 \omega_{33}$	Yes
M_3	$y_t = \delta_1 x_{1t} + \quad \delta_3 x_{3t} + u_{3t}$		$\sigma^2 +$	$\beta_2^2 \omega_{22}^*$	No
M_4	$y_t = \quad \tau_2 x_{2t} +$	u_{4t}	$\sigma^2 + \beta_1^2 \omega_{11} +$	$\beta_3^2 \omega_{33}$	Yes
M_5	$y_t = \pi_1 x_{1t} + \pi_2 x_{2t} + \pi_3 x_{3t} + u_{5t}$		σ^2		Yes
DGP	$y_t = \beta_1 x_{1t} + \beta_2 x_{2t} + \beta_3 x_{3t} + \varepsilon_t$		σ^2		Yes

[a] Model constancy is evaluated under the condition that the variance of x_{2t} changes at time $T + 1$, i.e., that $\omega_{22}^* \neq \omega_{22}$. Hence, models excluding x_{2t} are nonconstant.

ω_{22}^*. Further, whether or not a model exhibits parameter nonconstancy has little to do with its ranking by MSFE. For instance, M_3 can have a smaller *or* larger MSFE than M_2, depending upon the values of $\beta_2^2 \omega_{22}^*$ and $\beta_3^2 \omega_{33}$, but M_3 exhibits parameter nonconstancy whereas M_2 does not. This indeterminacy implies another proposition.

Proposition 2 *If a model has (empirically) nonconstant parameters, it can have either a smaller or larger MSFE than some other model.*

That is, parameter constancy is not necessary for obtaining the smallest MSFE among a set of models.

Whether the parameters of the "other" model are constant or not makes no difference to either Proposition 1 or Proposition 2, and this provides a different view on the lack of necessity and sufficiency.

Proposition 3 *For both Propositions 1 and 2, the constancy or otherwise of the "other" model is immaterial.*

For instance, consider a fourth model:

$$M_4 : y_t = \tau_2 x_{2t} + u_{4t} \qquad u_{4t} \sim \mathsf{NID}(0, \sigma_4^2), \tag{8a}$$

which has MSFE:

$$MSFE_4 = \sigma^2 + \beta_1^2 \omega_{11} + \beta_3^2 \omega_{33}. \tag{8b}$$

Model M_4 has constant parameters, but its MSFE may be smaller or larger than that for M_1 (which has nonconstant parameters), depending upon the relative variances of the regressors. Hence, parameter constancy is neither necessary nor sufficient for minimizing MSFE across a given set of models. Table 1 summarizes the properties of these models; Figure 1 provides a schematic of their relationships in terms of MSFE. [Arrows denote direction of *decreasing* MSFE. The ranking of MSFE is indeterminate for each of the

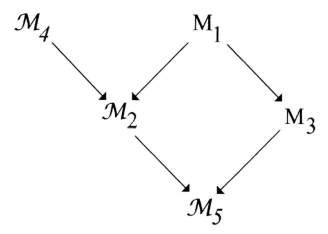

FIGURE 1. The ranking of $MSFE_i$ across models.

following pairs of models: $(\mathcal{M}_2, M_3)$, $(M_3, \mathcal{M}_4)$, and $(M_1, \mathcal{M}_4)$. Models in $\mathcal{SCRIPT}$ are always constant. Models in Roman are nonconstant if $\omega_{22}^* \neq \omega_{22}$, and are constant otherwise.]

The ranking of models by MSFE can change across subsamples as well. For instance, the ranking of the models above depends upon the variances of the regressors, and those need not remain constant over subsamples. Unless a model is well specified in a very general sense, i.e., "congruent" with the evidence [see, for example, Hendry (1987), Campos and Ericsson (1988), and White (1989)], there is no guarantee whatsoever that an observed ranking in mean square forecast error will obtain over different sample periods.

[473]   Finally, consider the relationship between the properties of parameter constancy and minimizing MSFE, and an adequate forecasting model.

Proposition 4 *Individually and jointly, parameter constancy and minimizing MSFE are necessary but not sufficient to ensure an adequate forecasting model.*

Necessity is shown by considering the implications of lacking either property. Specifically, forecast errors from a nonconstant model contain a predictable element: for instance, by imposing an incorrect coefficient on the variable with nonconstant moments. For example, M_3 imposes a zero coefficient on x_{2t}. Also, a model that does not minimize MSFE, does not do so because it makes inefficient use of the information available for forecasting. A model that has constant parameters and does minimize MSFE across a set of models meets a necessary condition for being an adequate forecasting model. That condition is only necessary, however, and is not sufficient.

[474]   Lack of sufficiency can be shown, as follows. For the DGP and models

above, model M_2 has constant parameters and, if $\beta_2^2 \omega_{22}^*$ is larger than $\beta_3^2 \omega_{33}$, M_2 minimizes MSFE among the models M_1, M_2, M_3, and M_4. However, the forecast errors for M_2 are:

$$\hat{u}_{2j} = y_j - \hat{y}_{2j} = \beta_3 x_{3j} + \varepsilon_j \qquad j = T+1, \ldots, T+n, \tag{9}$$

and so are predictable on the data sets available to the models M_1, M_2, M_3, and M_4. The regressor x_{3j} is valuable in forecasting y_j, and M_2 ignores that information, but M_3 does not. Technically speaking, the forecast error $\hat{u}_{2j}$ is not an innovation with respect to the information set generated by models M_1, M_2, M_3, and M_4.

This analysis clarifies why minimizing MSFE is *not* enough for obtaining a good forecasting model. Although model M_2 minimizes MSFE over the set of models M_1, M_2, M_4, and (if $\beta_3^2 \omega_{33} < \beta_2^2 \omega_{22}^*$) M_3, the forecast errors of each model may be (in part) predictable from some other model's data.

Conversely, it is possible to create a model from the data of those four models that uniformly dominates M_1, M_3, M_4, *and* M_2 in MSFE, and that has constant parameters. One such model, denoted M_5, is:

$$M_5 : y_t = \pi_1 x_{1t} + \pi_2 x_{2t} + \pi_3 x_{3t} + u_{5t} \qquad u_{5t} \sim \mathsf{NID}(0, \sigma_5^2), \tag{10a}$$

with MSFE:

$$MSFE_5 = \sigma^2. \tag{10b}$$

Model M_5 has a smaller MSFE than even M_2 and has constant coefficients. Model M_5 happens to be the DGP and happens to nest M_1, M_2, M_3, and M_4, but neither property is necessary for it to "dominate" the other models in terms of MSFE. Rather, model M_5 dominates M_1, M_2, M_3, and M_4 because the forecast errors of any one of those four models are in part predictable from the regressors used in M_5, but not conversely. Note also that ε_j itself may be in part predictable on a larger information set, in which case the corresponding model's MSFE would be smaller than σ^2 in (10b). Hendry (1986) discusses some of these issues in the related context of n-step ahead *ex ante* forecasts from macromodels.

If a model M_x minimizes the MSFE over a set of models $\{M_i\}$, that shows that the other models are worse in a specific sense. It does *not* show that M_x is a good forecasting model, *even on only the data available in the models $\{M_i\}$*. Even jointly, parameter constancy and minimum MSFE do not ensure efficient forecasting from the information available. Hence, there exists a need for more powerful tools in evaluating the forecast performance of models. The key to designing those tools is the information set against which models are being evaluated when MSFEs are compared. In Section 3, [475] information sets resolve the logical status of parameter constancy vis-à-vis minimum MSFE. In Section 4, information sets define a taxonomy for test criteria, with parameter constancy and minimum MSFE being members of that taxonomy.

3 Information Sets

Information sets help clarify both why the MSFE and parameter constancy are sensible criteria for evaluating how "well" a model forecasts, and why having constant parameters and minimizing MSFE over a set of models are not in general sufficient conditions for obtaining an adequate forecasting model. The MSFE and tests of parameter constancy evaluate a given model against different sources of information, being either other models' MSFEs or the given model's fit over the estimation subsample. The former is obvious; the latter follows from (5), the equation for the Chow statistic. Expressed somewhat differently, the Chow statistic evaluates a given model over different subsamples of that model's data, whereas minimizing MSFE evaluates several models over a given subsample but across the models' different datasets. The informational content of an alternative model's data and of the data of one's own model need not be (and generally are not) equivalent, so tests based on those information sets need not give similar results.

4 The Roles of Parameter Constancy and MSFE in Empirical Modeling

This section discusses how parameter constancy and minimizing MSFE fit into a general framework for evaluating (and designing) empirical models. That framework is based on the information sets against which models are evaluated and designed. It clarifies the relationship of parameter constancy and minimizing MSFE to other test statistics. It also results in a new test statistic, forecast-model encompassing, which is a more general and more stringent criteria for evaluating forecast performance than minimizing MSFE.

How well- or poorly designed an empirical economic model is depends upon its ability (or lack thereof) to capture salient features of the data and to deliver reliable inference on economic issues (e.g., coefficient estimates, predictions, and policy effects). Many statistics exist for evaluating such properties of a model; they relate to goodness-of-fit, absence of residual autocorrelation and heteroscedasticity, valid exogeneity, predictive ability, [476] parameter constancy, the statistical and economic interpretation of estimated coefficients, the validity of *a priori* restrictions, and the ability of a model to account for properties of alternative models. These test statistics can serve as criteria both for evaluating existing specifications and for designing new ones. Table 2 summarizes the statistics, which are arranged by the type of information generating testable null hypotheses:

TABLE 2. Evaluation/Design Criteria

Information Set	Null Hypothesis	Alternative Hypothesis	References
(A) own model's data			
(A1) relative past	innovation errors	first-order residual autocorrelation	Durbin and Watson (1950, 1951)
"	"	qth-order residual autocorrelation	Box and Pierce (1970); Godfrey (1978), Harvey (1981, p. 173)
"	"	invalid parameter restrictions	Johnston (1963, p. 126)
"	"	qth-order ARCH	Engle (1982)
"	"	heteroscedasticity quadratic in regressors	White (1980, p. 825), Nicholls and Pagan (1983)
"	"	qth-order RESET	Ramsey (1969)
"	normality of the errors	skewness and excess kurtosis	Jarque and Bera (1980)
(A2) relative present	weakly exogenous regressors	invalid conditioning	Sargan (1958, 1980), Engle, Hendry, and Richard (1983)
(A3) relative future	constant parameters, adequate forecasts	parameter nonconstancy, predictive failure	Fisher (1922), Chow (1960), Brown, Durbin, and Evans (1975), Hendry (1979)
(B) measurement system	data admissibility	"impossible" predictions of observables	—
(C) economic theory	theory consistency; cointegration	"implausible" coefficients, predictions; no cointegration	Engle and Granger (1987)
(D) alternative models' data			
(D1) relative past	variance dominance	poor fit relative to an alternative model	Hendry and Richard (1982)
"	variance encompassing	inexplicable observed error variance	Cox (1961, 1962), Pesaran (1974), Hendry (1983)
"	parameter encompassing	significant additional variables	Johnston (1963, p. 126), Mizon and Richard (1986)
(D2) relative present	exogeneity encompassing	inexplicable valid conditioning	Hendry (1988)
(D3) relative future	MSFE dominance	poor forecasts relative to those of alternative models	Granger (1989), Granger and Deutsch (1992)
"	forecast encompassing	informative forecasts from alternative models	Chong and Hendry (1986)
"	forecast-model encompassing	regressors from alternative models valuable for forecasting	(this paper)

(A) the data of one's own model,
(B) the measurement system of the data,
(C) economic theory, and
(D) the data of alternative models.

For details, see Spanos (1986), Hendry and Richard (1982), Ericsson and Hendry (1985), Hendry (1987), and Ericsson, Campos, and Tran (1990).

Parameter constancy belongs to category (A3) in Table 2 (the relative future of the data of one's own model) and is at the heart of model design, both statistically and economically. Most estimation techniques require parameter constancy for valid inference, and those that seem not to do so still posit "meta-parameters" assumed constant over time. Because economic systems appear far from constant empirically, and the coefficients of derived ("non-structural" or "reduced form") equations may alter when any of the underlying parameters or data correlations change, it is important to identify empirical models that have reasonably constant parameters and that remain interpretable when some change occurs.[4] That puts a premium on good theory. Conversely, empirical models with constant parameterizations in spite of "structural change" elsewhere in the economy may provide the seeds of fruitful research in economic theory. Parameter constancy typically is evaluated by comparing parameter estimates of a given model obtained from different subsamples of data. Recursive estimation of an equation provides an incisive tool for investigating parameter constancy, both through the sequence of estimated coefficient values and via the associated Chow statistics; see, for example, Dufour (1982).

Minimizing MSFE, like parameter constancy, focuses on the "relative future", but on that of alternative models' data rather than on the data of one's own model. Thus, MSFE dominance belongs to category (D3). Because the structure of (D3) parallels that of (D1) (the relative past of alternative models' data), (D1) is briefly discussed to elucidate the connections between the two. Also, for reasons which will be apparent shortly, the criterion of minimizing MSFE will be referred to as *MSFE dominance*.

[477]

Parameter encompassing, variance encompassing, and variance dominance. Consider the following two alternative non-nested linear models, both claiming to explain y_t.

$$M_1 : y_t = \delta_1' z_{1t} + \nu_{1t} \qquad \nu_{1t} \sim \mathsf{NID}(0, \sigma_1^2) \tag{11a}$$

$$M_2 : y_t = \delta_2' z_{2t} + \nu_{2t} \qquad \nu_{2t} \sim \mathsf{NID}(0, \sigma_2^2) \tag{11b}$$

---

[4] See Goldfeld and Sichel (1990) for a discussion of the nonconstancy of many estimated money-demand equations. That nonconstancy implies nonconstancy in one or more of the equations of the underlying data generation process.

The notation is distinct from that in Section 2 above. In (11a) and (11b), δ_1 and δ_2 are $k_1 \times 1$ and $k_2 \times 1$ vectors of unknown parameters. The vectors z_{1t} and z_{2t} are of k_1 and k_2 regressors respectively, with each vector having at least some variables that are not in common with those in the other vector. For simplicity, assume that none are in common. To ensure the feasibility of the parameter-encompassing and forecast-model encompassing statistics, assume that $T > k_1 + k_2$ and $n > \max(k_1, k_2)$.

As alternative models, (11a) entails the irrelevance of z_{2t} in explaining y_t, given z_{1t}; and vice versa for (11b). In any event, the variables y_t, z_{1t}, and z_{2t} are generated by *some* process, and, under the simplifying (but inessential) assumption of joint normality, z_{1t} and z_{2t} can be linked using:

$$z_{1t} = \Pi z_{2t} + \zeta_{1t}, \tag{12}$$

where Π is defined by $\mathcal{E}(z_{2t}\zeta'_{1t}) = 0$, and (again for expositional simplicity) $\mathcal{E}(\zeta_{1t}\zeta'_{1t}) = \Omega$. Substituting (12) into (11a) obtains:

$$
\begin{aligned}
y_t &= \delta'_1 z_{1t} &+& \quad \nu_{1t} \\
&= (\delta'_1 \Pi) z_{2t} &+& \quad (\nu_{1t} + \delta'_1 \zeta_{1t}) \\
&= (\delta'_2) z_{2t} &+& \quad \nu_{2t}.
\end{aligned}
\tag{13}
$$

In (13), the parameter δ_2 and the error ν_{2t} are derived from (11a) and (12), being $\Pi'\delta_1$ and $\nu_{1t} + \delta'_1\zeta_{1t}$ respectively. Consequently, (13) is what model (11a) predicts model (11b) should find, and it implies several hypotheses, including:

$$\mathsf{H}_a : \delta_2 = \Pi'\delta_1 \tag{14a}$$

and

$$\mathsf{H}_b : \sigma_2^2 = \sigma_1^2 + \delta'_1 \Omega \delta_1. \tag{14b}$$

These hypotheses are called *parameter encompassing* and *variance encom-* [480] *passing*, respectively, and the positive definiteness of Ω in the latter implies *variance dominance*:

$$\mathsf{H}_c : \sigma_1^2 < \sigma_2^2. \tag{14c}$$

H_a, H_b, and H_c are implications of omitted variable bias in (11b), assuming that (11a) plus (12) are the DGP. These three hypotheses, albeit in reverse order, generate the evaluation criteria for (D1) on Table 2 [see Hendry (1983) and Mizon and Richard (1986)].

Parameter encompassing by (11a) of (11b) may be tested using the formula in (14a) or by testing whether z_{2t} is irrelevant if added to (11a). To see the latter, let δ_2 be unconstrained, and define the $k_2 \times 1$ vector γ as $\delta_2 - \Pi'\delta_1$. H_a is equivalent to $\gamma = 0$. By substitution of $\delta_2 = \Pi'\delta_1 + \gamma$ in (13),

$$y_t = \delta'_1 z_{1t} + \gamma' z_{2t} + \nu_{1t}. \tag{15}$$

Thus, H_a is equivalent to claiming that z_{2t} has no power in explaining y_t, given z_{1t} (or in explaining the residuals from (11a)). In practice, it is simplest to estimate δ_1 and γ jointly in (15) and test $\gamma = 0$ with the standard F-statistic.

Variance encompassing may be tested either by using (14b) or by testing the insignificance in (11a) of the *fitted* values from (11b). That is, hypothesis H_b can be tested by jointly estimating δ_1 and α in:

$$y_t = \delta_1' z_{1t} + \alpha \hat{y}_{2t} + \nu_{1t}, \tag{16}$$

and testing that $\alpha = 0$ (where $\hat{y}_{2t} = \hat{\delta}_{2T}' z_{2t}$). Testing $\alpha = 0$ is equivalent to testing $\sigma_2^2 = \sigma_1^2 + \delta_1' \Omega \delta_1$; see Davidson and MacKinnon (1981, p. 789), Hendry (1983), and Mizon and Richard (1986). Equally, H_b is equivalent to claiming that a certain linear combination of z_{2t}, namely $\hat{y}_{2t}$, has no power in explaining the residuals from (11a). Because (16) is testing for the insignificance of that certain linear combination, rather than of any linear combination (as in (15)), the test of $\alpha = 0$ is a narrower test than that of $\gamma = 0$. The t-statistic on α in (16) is Davidson and MacKinnon's (1981) P statistic: it is asymptotically $N(0,1)$ when M_1 is true and is asymptotically equivalent to Cox's (1961) statistic for testing non-nested hypotheses, as applied to linear regression models by Pesaran (1974).

The logic of the hypotheses in (14) is as follows: variance dominance [481] is necessary, but not sufficient, for variance encompassing, which in turn is necessary, but not sufficient, for parameter encompassing. Conversely, if $\gamma = 0$ in (15), then α also must be zero in (16), from which it follows that σ_1^2 is less than σ_2^2 because z_{1t} is not an exact linear transformation of z_{2t}.

In light of the preceding analysis, it readily follows that MSFE dominance parallels variance dominance, and that two other forecast criteria (forecast encompassing and the new forecast-model encompassing) parallel variance encompassing and parameter encompassing. The remainder of this section explores those connections between (D1) and (D3) in Table 2.

Forecast-model encompassing, forecast encompassing, and MSFE dominance. Assume that the two alternative models, (11a) and (11b), have been estimated over the sample period $[1, T]$ and are being used to forecast over $[T + 1, T + n]$. The forecasts from the two models are:

$$\hat{y}_{1j} = \delta_1' z_{1j} \tag{17a}$$

$$\hat{y}_{2j} = \delta_2' z_{2j} \qquad j = T + 1, \ldots, T + n, \tag{17b}$$

ignoring (again) the uncertainty arising from estimating coefficients over $[1, T]$. As with (13) above, under M_1,

$$
\begin{aligned}
y_j &= \delta_1' z_{1j} &+& \ \nu_{1j} \\
&= (\delta_1' \Pi) z_{2j} &+& \ (\nu_{1j} + \delta_1' \zeta_{1j}) \\
&= (\delta_2') z_{2j} &+& \ [(y_j - \hat{y}_{1j}) + \delta_1' \zeta_{1j}] \\
&= \hat{y}_{2j} &+& \ (y_j - \hat{y}_{2j}),
\end{aligned}
\tag{18}
$$

where the last line follows from (17b) and the equality $y_j = y_j$. Equation (18) implies two testable hypotheses:

$$
\mathsf{H}_a^* : \delta_2 = \Pi' \delta_1
\tag{19a}
$$

and

$$
\mathsf{H}_b^* : \mathcal{E} \left(y_j - \hat{y}_{2j} \right)^2 = \mathcal{E} \left(y_j - \hat{y}_{1j} \right)^2 + \delta_1' \Omega^* \delta_1,
\tag{19b}
$$

where an asterisk * denotes the corresponding hypothesis or matrix over the *forecast* period. The second hypothesis may be written as:

$$
\mathsf{H}_b^* : \ MSFE_2 = MSFE_1 + \delta_1' \Omega^* \delta_1,
\tag{19c}
$$

and implies:

$$
\mathsf{H}_c^* : \ MSFE_1 < MSFE_2.
\tag{19d}
$$

[482]

These three hypotheses H_a^*, H_b^*, and H_c^* are called *forecast-model encompassing*, *forecast encompassing*, and *MSFE dominance*. Forecast encompassing could be called MSFE encompassing as well; see Chong and Hendry (1986). From (19d), it follows that an adequate forecasting model must minimize MSFE (asymptotically), but doing so is a necessary (and not sufficient) condition for obtaining an adequate forecasting model, as discussed in Section 2. The design of tests of H_a^* and H_b^* parallels those of H_a and H_b.

Forecast-model encompassing by (11a) of (11b) may be tested using the formula in (19a) or by testing whether z_{2j} is irrelevant in explaining the forecast errors from (17a). As with parameter encompassing, let $\gamma = \delta_2 - \Pi' \delta_1$. By substitution in (18),

$$
y_j = \delta_1' z_{1j} + \gamma' z_{2j} + \nu_{1j} \qquad j = T+1, \dots, T+n,
\tag{20a}
$$

or

$$
y_j - \hat{y}_{1j} = \gamma' z_{2j} + \nu_{1j}.
\tag{20b}
$$

H_a^* is equivalent to $\gamma = 0$ and so to claiming that z_{2j} has no power in explaining the forecast errors from (17a). For large T, fixed z_{ij}'s, and normal ν_{1j}, it is straightforward to show that the standard F-statistic testing $\gamma = 0$ in (20b) is distributed as $F(k_2, n - k_2)$ under M_1; for stochastic (weakly exogenous) z_{ij}'s, it is distributed as $F(k_2, n - k_2)$ for large n. See the Appendix for details.

An exact test of forecast-model encompassing also exists. It can be motivated most easily by recognizing why the F-statistic for $\gamma = 0$ in (20b) does not have a simple exact distribution: the statistic conditions upon the *estimated* value of δ_1, thereby ignoring the uncertainty inherent in the corresponding estimator of δ_1. The solution is simple: estimate δ_1 and γ jointly. To do so, consider the following model:

$$y_t = \delta_1' z_{1t} + \gamma' z_{2t}^* + \nu_{1t} \qquad t = 1, \ldots, T + n, \tag{21}$$

where the *entire* data sample $[1, T + n]$ is used, and z_{2t}^* is zero over $[1, T]$ and equal to z_{2t} over $[T + 1, T + n]$. The F-statistic for $\gamma = 0$ in (21) is exactly distributed as $F(k_2, T + n - k_1 - k_2)$ under M_1 for fixed z_{ij}'s and normal ν_{1j}, asymptotically so for stochastic (weakly exogenous) z_{ij}'s. Instrumental [483] variable and recursive generalizations of the test statistics for $\gamma = 0$ in (20b) and (21) follow naturally.[5]

Forecast encompassing by (11a) of (11b) may be tested either by using (19c) directly or by testing for the insignificance of the *forecast* values given by (17b) in explaining the forecast errors from (17a). Thus, H_b^* can be tested by estimating α in:

$$y_j - \hat{y}_{1j} = \alpha \hat{y}_{2j} + \nu_{1j} \qquad j = T + 1, \ldots, T + n, \tag{22}$$

and testing that $\alpha = 0$. That is equivalent to testing that $MSFE_2 = MSFE_1 + \delta_1' \Omega^* \delta_1$, following the logic used for variance encompassing. Noting that $\hat{y}_{1j} = \delta_1' z_{1j}$, (22) is similar to (16), the principal difference being that the time period is $[T + 1, T + n]$ rather than $[1, T]$. Chong and Hendry (1986) have shown that, for large T *and* n, the t-statistic on α is $N(0, 1)$.[6]

The logic of the hypotheses in (19) is as follows: MSFE dominance is necessary, but not sufficient, for forecast encompassing, which in turn is necessary, but not sufficient, for forecast-model encompassing. Conversely, if $\gamma = 0$ in (20b), then α [in (22)] must be zero because $\hat{y}_{2j} = \delta_2' z_{2j}$. If $\alpha = 0$, then $MSFE_1$ is less than $MSFE_2$ because z_{1j} is not an exact linear transformation of z_{2j}.

Forecast-type encompassing and parameter constancy. As illustrated in Section 2, even if the "structural" relationship has constant parameters

---

[5] The structure of (21) also leads to two classes of forecast-based encompassing tests, one which assumes constancy between the estimation and forecast samples, and one which does not.

[6] An extensive literature has developed on the combination or "pooling" of forecasts, i.e., where some (usually linear) combination of forecasts from different models is taken to obtain a new forecast. In comparison with any of the individual model forecasts, that new forecast may have better properties, usually being a smaller MSFE. Given the discussion in the text above, finding such a pooled forecast is *prima facie* evidence of all individual models being mis-specified, and may well indicate that a single model can be constructed that has a smaller MSFE than even the pooled forecast. See Clemen (1989) for a review and bibliography on combining forecasts, and Granger (1989, pp. 187–191) and Diebold (1989) for recent analyses.

[e.g., (π_i, σ_5^2) in (10a), or (δ_1, σ_1^2) in (11a)], nonconstant population data moments have implications for the empirical constancy (or lack thereof) of mis-specified models. Nonconstant population data moments also have implications for forecast-type encompassing tests. For instance, if the (reduced-form) variance matrix Ω changes, $MSFE_2$ in H_b^* will alter as that new matrix [i.e., Ω^* in (19c)] does. Likewise, if the Π matrix changes, because M_2 [484] (falsely) assumes δ_2 is constant, M_2 will have systematic forecast errors that are a function of the changing Π matrix. These "predictions" about model behavior suggest a more general encompassing strategy, including predicting problems in alternative models of which their proponents are unaware. Corroborating such phenomena adds credibility to the claim that the successful model reasonably represents the data generation process, whereas disconfirmation clarifies that it does not.

5   Forecasting with Integrated and Cointegrated Variables

This section describes a certain lack of invariance present in the forecast-encompassing statistics, and illustrates that lack of invariance with a cointegrated process. The forecast-encompassing statistic is then modified to produce an "invariant" test statistic, which tests "forecast-differential encompassing". See Lu and Mizon (1991) for a related discussion.

The forecast errors $y_j - \hat{y}_{1j}$ and $y_j - \hat{y}_{2j}$ are invariant to nonsingular linear transformations of the corresponding models' data, $(y_j, z'_{1j})'$ and $(y_j, z'_{2j})'$. The forecasts themselves, however, are *not* invariant to such transformations, and so neither is the forecast-encompassing test statistic from (22). Specifically, suppose that both z_{1j} and z_{2j} include the lagged dependent variable y_{j-1}, in which case models M_1 and M_2 may be written without loss of generality with either y_j or Δy_j as the dependent variable, where Δ is the first-difference operator. In the first case, with y_j, the auxiliary equation for the forecast-encompassing statistic is (22) as written. In the second case, $\widehat{\Delta y_{2j}}$ replaces $\hat{y}_{2j}$ as the right-hand side variable in (22). In both cases, the t-statistic on α is asymptotically $N(0,1)$ under the null hypothesis of M_1 being correctly specified. However, the two t-statistics are not necessarily equivalent under mis-specification of M_1. This is most apparent when y_j is an integrated process.

To illustrate, suppose that y_j, z_{1j}, and z_{2j} are each $I(1)$ processes, and that each model (M_1 and M_2) represents a cointegrating relationship. This could arise if, e.g., z_{1j} and z_{2j} involved different lag structures of the same underlying variables. From Granger (1986), the forecast errors $y_j - \hat{y}_{1j}$ and $y_j - \hat{y}_{2j}$ are each $I(0)$, whereas the forecasts $\hat{y}_{1j}$ and $\hat{y}_{2j}$ are $I(1)$. Thus, in order for (22) to be "balanced" in terms of orders of integration, α must be zero. Surprisingly, α must be zero even if M_1 is mis-specified and M_2 is the

[485] correct model. That is, the forecast-encompassing test may have no power
when the dependent variable is $I(1)$.[7,8]

For y_j, z_{1j}, and z_{2j} with the properties specified, both M_1 and M_2 have
error correction representations. In the error correction representation, the
dependent variable is Δy_j, rather than y_j. The corresponding forecast errors remain unchanged numerically, but the right-hand side variable in (22)
becomes $\widehat{\Delta y}_{2j}$, an $I(0)$ variable, in contrast to $\hat{y}_{2j}$, which is $I(1)$. Balance is
unaffected by the value of α in the regression with $\widehat{\Delta y}_{2j}$, so the corresponding
forecast-encompassing test appears more promising for good power proper-
ties than the test based on (22) with $\hat{y}_{2j}$ on the right-hand side. This feature
supports formulating forecast models "in $I(0)$ space" as error correction models, rather than "in $I(1)$ space" in terms of the original [$I(1)$] levels variables.

It may be desirable to have a forecast-encompassing test that is invariant to nonsingular linear transformations of the data. Such a test may be
constructed as follows. As (22) stands, the coefficient on $\hat{y}_{1j}$ is constrained
to be unity, while the coefficient on $\hat{y}_{2j}$ is estimated unrestrictedly. Instead,
both coefficients could be estimated, with their sum constrained to be unity.
The resulting equation can be written as:

$$y_j - \hat{y}_{1j} = \alpha^* \left(\hat{y}_{2j} - \hat{y}_{1j} \right) + \nu_{1j} \qquad j = T+1, \ldots, T+n, \qquad (23)$$

where α^* is estimated unrestrictedly, and $\alpha^* = 0$ is tested. This equation
would parallel Davidson and MacKinnon's (1981) J statistic if the coefficients
in $\hat{y}_{1j}$ were estimated jointly with α^*.

The test from (23) has two important features. First, because the right-
hand side variable is the differential between the two forecasts [$(\hat{y}_{2j} - \hat{y}_{1j})$]
rather than either forecast alone, the right-hand side variable is unaffected
by nonsingular linear transformations of the models' data. Thus, the test
of $\alpha^* = 0$ is invariant to such transformations. Second, for integrated
y_j, z_{1j}, and z_{2j} with both models cointegrated, the right-hand side variable
$(\hat{y}_{2j} - \hat{y}_{1j})$ is $I(0)$, preserving balance. This follows because $\hat{y}_{1j}$ and $\hat{y}_{2j}$ must
each cointegrate with y_j (with unit coefficients), and so $\hat{y}_{1j}$ cointegrates with
$\hat{y}_{2j}$ (also with unit coefficients). The t-statistic on α^* will be called the
forecast-differential encompassing statistic, noting the form of the right-hand
side variable.

[486]   As a practical matter, any of a model's forecast errors, its forecasts, or the

---

[7] I am grateful to Stephen Hall for bringing to my attention (via David Hendry) the
apparently low power empirically of Chong and Hendry's forecast-encompassing test with
$I(1)$ forecasted variables. Also, see Hendry (1989, pp. 95–97) on implications of nonsingular
linear transformations of a linear model's data.

[8] Either or both of models M_1 and M_2 might lack cointegration, in which case the
distributions of the forecast-based test statistics may change. We do not consider such
cases here.

forecast differential $(\hat{y}_{2j} - \hat{y}_{1j})$ may have a nonzero mean. Thus, the power of the tests from (22) and (23) can be affected by the inclusion of a constant term in the auxiliary regression. Under the null of correct specification, the constant term should have a zero coefficient, so it is appropriate to test that α (or α^*) and the constant term's coefficient are jointly zero.

Before applying several of the above tests to a pair of empirical models, we briefly consider the class of models with time-varying coefficients.

6   Forecasting and Models with Time-varying Coefficients

Time-varying coefficient (TVC) models have been proposed as a means of improving forecast performance. The results above can clarify when that may (or may not) be so.

First, if the data are generated with time-varying coefficients and a correctly specified TVC model is estimated and used for forecasting, then the TVC forecasts will minimize MSFE, and (in general) fixed-coefficient models will have a higher MSFE. Evidence that the TVC model satisfied the evaluation criteria listed on Table 2 would be necessary for the model to be credible as representing the data process.

Second, sometimes an estimated TVC model is recognized as being misspecified, but it is claimed that the TVC model will forecast better than fixed-coefficient models because the former accounts (in part, at least) for observed parameter nonconstancy in the latter [see, for example, Chow (1984)]. For general parameter nonconstancy, however, a TVC model need not minimize MSFE relative to a fixed-coefficient model, even asymptotically and even if the TVC model nests the fixed-coefficient model. An example suffices.

Suppose that the data are generated as:

$$y_t = \delta_{1t}' z_{1t} + \nu_{1t} \qquad \nu_{1t} \sim \mathsf{NID}(0, \sigma_1^2), \tag{24}$$

where z_{1t} is stationary, distributed as $\mathsf{N}(0, \Psi_{11})$; and $\delta_{1t} = \delta - \theta$ $(\theta \neq 0)$ for the first half of the estimation period, $\delta_{1t} = \delta + \theta$ for the second half of the estimation period, and $\delta_{1t} = \delta$ for the forecast period, which is the single observation $T + 1$ (for expository convenience). The fixed-coefficient model is (24) but assumes that δ_{1t} is constant. The TVC model specifies (e.g.) that $(\delta_{1t} - \bar{\delta}) = \phi(\delta_{1t-1} - \bar{\delta}) + \xi_t$ where ξ_t is assumed to be (e.g.) white noise, $|\phi| < 1$, and $\bar{\delta}$ is the unconditional mean of δ_{1t} [see, for example, Swamy and [487] Tinsley (1980) and Chow (1984)].

The fixed-coefficient model, although manifesting parameter nonconstancy in sample, has $\mathcal{E}(\hat{\delta}_{1T}) \approx \delta$, and so has a MSFE of approximately σ_1^2. The TVC estimate $\tilde{\delta}_{1T}$ is approximately $\delta + \theta$ because the TVC estimator places more weight on recent data than on older data. Here, the TVC model does so by obtaining estimates of $\bar{\delta}$ and ϕ which are approximately δ and unity respectively. For the forecast observation $T + 1$, the TVC model uses the prediction $\tilde{\delta}'_{1,T+1}z_{1,T+1}$, which is approximately $\tilde{\delta}'_{1,T}z_{1,T+1}$ or $(\delta + \theta)'z_{1,T+1}$. Thus, the TVC model has MSFE of approximately $\sigma_1^2 + \theta'\Psi_{11}\theta$, which is greater than σ_1^2.

7 An Empirical Illustration: Models of Narrow Money Demand in the United Kingdom

This section calculates the MSFE and forecast-type encompassing statistics for two models of U.K. money demand from Hendry and Ericsson (1991). The first model is an error correction model, the second is a partial adjustment model, and the forecast period is the 1980s.

Hendry and Ericsson (1991) develop a constant, parsimonious, error correction model of narrow money in the United Kingdom for the period 1964(3)–1989(2). Estimating their equation through 1979 and forecasting over the 1980s obtains the following:

$$
\widehat{\Delta(m-p)}_t = -\underset{(0.20)}{0.80}\,\Delta p_t - \underset{(0.07)}{0.20}\,\Delta(m-p-y)_{t-1}
$$

$$
-\underset{(0.10)}{0.63}\,R_t^* - \underset{(0.013)}{0.102}\,(m-p-y)_{t-1} + \underset{(0.007)}{0.021} \qquad (25)
$$

$T = 62\ [1964(3)\text{–}1979(4)] + 38$ forecasts $\quad R^2 = 0.69 \quad \hat{\sigma} = 1.389\%$.

The data are nominal M_1 (M), 1985 price total final expenditure (Y), the corresponding deflator (P), and a (learning-adjusted) net interest rate (R^*). Lower case denotes logarithms, and standard errors are in parentheses. Hendry and Ericsson (1991) describe the data in their appendix and discuss the statistical and economic merits of (25) in their Section 4.

Hendry and Ericsson (1991) also estimate a partial adjustment model for real narrow money with an autoregressive error, in the spirit of Goldfeld [488] (1973). Contrasting with results on U.S. data, the partial adjustment model appears reasonably constant during the missing money period: the Chow statistic is $F[12, 29] = 1.89$ [p-value $= 0.079$] for forecasts over 1973(1)–1975(4). When estimated through 1979 and forecast over the 1980s, the estimates for the partial adjustment model are as follows:

$$
\widehat{(m-p)}_t = \underset{(0.024)}{0.955}\,(m-p)_{t-1} + \underset{(0.020)}{0.087}\,y_t
$$

$$
-\underset{(0.07)}{0.78}\,R_t^* - \underset{(0.42)}{0.43} - \underset{(0.13)}{0.31}\,\hat{u}_{t-1} \qquad (26)
$$

$T = 62\ [1964(3)\text{–}1979(4)] + 38$ forecasts $\quad \hat{\sigma} = 1.572\%$.

The coefficient on $\hat{u}_{t-1}$ is the estimated parameter of the (modeled) first-order autoregressive disturbance.

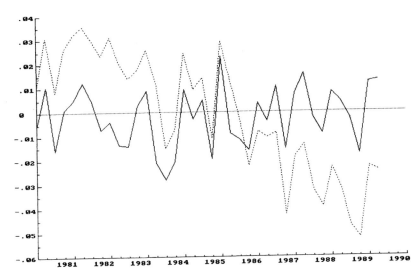

FIGURE 2. Forecast errors from two models of narrow money demand in the United Kingdom: equation (25) [the error correction model] (—) and equation (26) [the partial adjustment model] (···).

For money-demand equations, the 1980s are of particular interest to forecast, as Goldfeld and Sichel (1990, p. 300) note: "..., in the 1980s, U.S. money demand functions, whether or not fixed up to explain the 1970s, generally exhibited extended periods of under-prediction as observed velocity fell markedly." In the United Kingdom, velocity fell by twice the percentage drop in the United States. Somewhat surprisingly, neither model fails the Chow test, as seen in Table 3.

Figure 2 graphs the forecast errors from (25) and (26). Visually, the errors from (25) appear uncorrelated with near zero mean, whereas those from (26) are highly autocorrelated, trending from large and positive in 1980 to large and negative in 1989. These series are the dependent variables in the auxiliary regressions for calculating the forecast-type encompassing test statistics. The particular type of test determines the "independent" variables in those auxiliary regressions. Figures 3 and 4 present those variables for the forecast-encompassing tests. Figure 3 graphs the forecasts of $\Delta(m - p)_t$ from (25) and (26), whereas Figure 4 graphs the forecasts of $(m - p)_t$ from (25) and (26). For reference, Figures 3 and 4 also include the series being forecast. The initial under-prediction and subsequent over-prediction by (26)

TABLE 3. Chow, Encompassing, and Related Statistics

Statistic	Null hypothesis (i.e., hypothesized encompassing model)[a,b]			
	Error correction: (25)		Partial adjustment: (26)	
	no constant	constant	no constant	constant
Chow statistic	0.73 [0.84] F[38,57]		0.81 [0.75] F[38,57]	
$\hat{\sigma}$	1.389%		1.572%	
Root MSFE	1.232%		2.507%	
Forecast encompassing[c] Variable forecast is: $\Delta(m-p)_t$	0.00 [0.96] F[1,37]	0.70 [0.50] F[2,36]	4.22 [0.047] F[1,37]	3.78 [0.032] F[2,36]
Variable forecast is: $(m-p)_t$	1.12 [0.30] F[1,37]	1.21 [0.31] F[2,36]	0.09 [0.77] F[1,37]	63.14 [0.000] F[2,36]
Forecast-differential encompassing	2.27 [0.14] F[1,37]	1.65 [0.21] F[2,36]	125.54 [0.000] F[1,37]	63.35 [0.000] F[2,36]
Forecast-model encompassing	0.85 [0.53] F[5,33]		29.38 [0.000] F[5,33]	
Forecast-model encompassing[d] ("exact")	0.37 [0.87] F[5,90]		3.27 [0.009] F[5,90]	

[a] The three entries for a given statistic and equation are: the value of the statistic, the right-hand tail probability associated with that statistic, and the statistic's distribution under the null hypothesis of that equation being correctly specified. The estimation period is 1964(3)–1979(4) [$T = 62$]; the forecast period is 1980(1)–1989(2) [$n = 38$].
[b] The phrases "constant" and "no constant" denote whether or not a constant term is included in the auxiliary regression, i.e., in (22) or (23).
[c] Quantitatively similar results obtain for the following pairs of variables forecast: Δm_t and m_t, and $\Delta(m-p-y)_t$ and $(m-p-y)_t$.
[d] The full-sample ($T = 100$) values of $\hat{u}_{t-1}$ in (26) are used to calculate the "exact" forecast-model emcompassing test statistic.

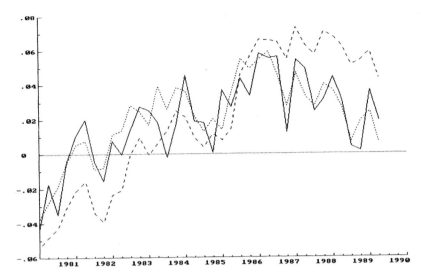

FIGURE 3. Actual values of the growth rate of real money in the United Kingdom $[\Delta(m-p)_t]$ (—) and the forecast values thereof from equations (25) $(\cdots)$ and (26) $(- - -)$.

is clear in both graphs although, from the Chow statistic, these deviations are not statistically detectable *as a structural break*. Even so, the forecast-type encompassing test statistics detect the systematic (and hence predictable) nature of (26)'s forecast errors.

Specifically, as shown in Table 3, equation (26) fails all forecast-type encompassing tests, except for the forecast-encompassing test with $(m-p)_t$ as the forecast variable and no constant term included in (22). That single lack of failure is due to the approximately zero mean of (26)'s forecast errors and the large nonzero mean of $(m-p)_t$: see Figures 2 and 4, respectively. Inclusion of a constant term results in rejection at the 0.1% level, with the (upwardly) trending $(m-p)_t$ "explaining" the (downwardly) trending forecast errors. [490]

Equation (25) dominates (26) substantially in terms of MSFE. Additionally, (25) encompasses (26) according to all forecast-based encompassing tests.

The results for (25) and (26) show how two models may be empirically constant, yet (at least) one may be inadequate for forecasting. This parallels Proposition 1. In evaluating models of the U.S. trade balance, Marquez and Ericsson (1993) find an empirically nonconstant model that obtains the

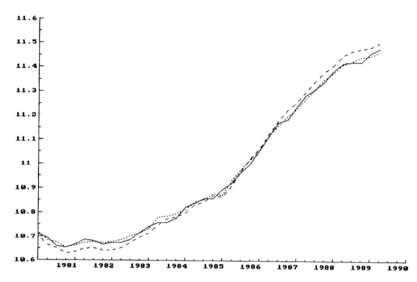

FIGURE 4. Actual values of the logarithm of real money in the
United Kingdom $[(m - p)_t]$ (—) and the forecast values thereof
from equations (25) ($\cdots$) and (26) ($- - -$).

minimum MSFE with respect to all other models considered. That parallels
Proposition 2.

8 Summary

[491]
Parameter constancy and minimizing the mean square forecast error are sensible criteria that evaluate empirical models against two different information sets, the data of one's own model and the data of alternative models. MSFE dominance is a necessary condition for two more general criteria for evaluating forecast performance: forecast encompassing and forecast-model encompassing. Parameter constancy, MSFE dominance, and the two types of forecast encompassing fit into a general taxonomy of model evaluation criteria. Satisfying *all* those evaluation criteria (and not just those of parameter constancy and MSFE dominance) are in general necessary for obtaining an adequate forecasting model. Two models for money demand in the United Kingdom help illustrate the concepts developed.

Appendix.   Distributions of Statistics for Testing Forecast-model Encompassing

The basis for the forecast-model encompassing test statistic is the auxiliary regression in (20b):

$$y_j - \hat{y}_{1j} = \gamma' z_{2j} + \nu_{1j} \qquad j = T + 1, \ldots, T + n. \qquad (A1)$$

Under M_1, for large T, fixed z_{ij}'s, and normal ν_{1j}, the dependent variable in (A1) *is* ν_{1j} and γ is zero, so the standard F-statistic testing $\gamma = 0$ is [492] distributed as $F(k_2, n - k_2)$. For stochastic (weakly exogenous) z_{ij}'s, it is distributed as $F(k_2, n - k_2)$ for large n. See Hendry (1979) and Kiviet (1986).

The distribution of the modified forecast-model encompassing test statistic from the auxiliary regression in (21) follows directly from, e.g., Johnston (1963, Chapter 4).

Bibliography

(References marked with an asterisk * are included in this volume.)

Box, G. E. P., and D. A. Pierce (1970) "Distribution of Residual Autocorrelations in Autoregressive-integrated Moving Average Time Series Models", *Journal of the American Statistical Association*, 65, 332, 1509–1526.

Brown, R. L., J. Durbin, and J. M. Evans (1975) "Techniques for Testing the Constancy of Regression Relationships over Time", *Journal of the Royal Statistical Society, Series B*, 37, 2, 149–192 (with discussion).

Campos, J., and N. R. Ericsson (1988) "Econometric Modeling of Consumers' Expenditure in Venezuela", International Finance Discussion Paper No. 325, Board of Governors of the Federal Reserve System, Washington, D.C.

Chong, Y. Y., and D. F. Hendry (1986) "Econometric Evaluation of Linear Macro-economic Models", *Review of Economic Studies*, 53, 4, 671–690.

Chow, G. C. (1960) "Tests of Equality Between Sets of Coefficients in Two [493] Linear Regressions", *Econometrica*, 28, 3, 591–605.

Chow, G. C. (1984) "Random and Changing Coefficient Models", Chapter 21 in Z. Griliches and M. D. Intriligator (eds.) *Handbook of Econometrics*, Amsterdam, North-Holland, Volume 2, 1213–1245.

Clemen, R. T. (1989) "Combining Forecasts: A Review and Annotated Bibliography", *International Journal of Forecasting*, 5, 4, 559–583.

Cox, D. R. (1961) "Tests of Separate Families of Hypotheses" in J. Neyman (ed.) *Proceedings of the Fourth Berkeley Symposium on Mathematical Statistics and Probability*, Berkeley, University of California Press, Volume 1, 105–123.

Cox, D. R. (1962) "Further Results on Tests of Separate Families of Hypotheses", *Journal of the Royal Statistical Society, Series B*, 24, 2, 406–424.

Davidson, R., and J. G. MacKinnon (1981) "Several Tests for Model Specification in the Presence of Alternative Hypotheses", *Econometrica*, 49, 3, 781–793.

Diebold, F. X. (1989) "Forecast Combination and Encompassing: Reconciling Two Divergent Literatures", *International Journal of Forecasting*, 5, 4, 589–592.

Dufour, J.-M. (1980) "Dummy Variables and Predictive Tests for Structural Change", *Economics Letters*, 6, 3, 241–247.

Dufour, J.-M. (1982) "Recursive Stability Analysis of Linear Regression Relationships: An Exploratory Methodology", *Journal of Econometrics*, 19, 1, 31–76.

Durbin, J., and G. S. Watson (1950) "Testing for Serial Correlation in Least Squares Regression. I", *Biometrika*, 37, 3 and 4, 409–428.

Durbin, J., and G. S. Watson (1951) "Testing for Serial Correlation in Least Squares Regression. II", *Biometrika*, 38, 1 and 2, 159–178.

Edison, H. J. (1985) "The Rise and Fall of Sterling: Testing Alternative Models of Exchange Rate Determination", *Applied Economics*, 17, 1003–1021.

Edison, H. J. (1991) "Forecast Performance of Exchange Rate Models Revisited", *Applied Economics*, 23, 187–196.

Edison, H. J., and J. T. Klovland (1987) "A Quantitative Reassessment of the Purchasing Power Parity Hypothesis: Evidence from Norway and the United Kingdom", *Journal of Applied Econometrics*, 2, 309–333.

Engle, R. F. (1982) "Autoregressive Conditional Heteroscedasticity with Estimates of the Variance of United Kingdom Inflation", *Econometrica*, 50, 4, 987–1007.

Engle, R. F., and C. W. J. Granger (1987) "Co-integration and Error Correction: Representation, Estimation, and Testing", *Econometrica*, 55, 2, 251–276.

*Engle, R. F., D. F. Hendry, and J.-F. Richard (1983) "Exogeneity", *Econometrica*, 51, 2, 277–304.

Ericsson, N. R., J. Campos, and H.-A. Tran (1990) "PC-GIVE and David Hendry's Econometric Methodology", *Revista de Econometria*, 10, 1, 7–117; originally cited as (1991), International Finance Discussion Paper No. 406, Board of Governors of the Federal Reserve System, Washington, D.C., forthcoming in *Revista de Econometria*.

Ericsson, N. R., and D. F. Hendry (1985) "Conditional Econometric Modeling: An Application to New House Prices in the United Kingdom", Chapter 11 in A. C. Atkinson and S. E. Fienberg (eds.) *A Celebration of Statistics: The ISI Centenary Volume*, New York, Springer-Verlag, 251–285.

Fair, R. C. (1986) "Evaluating the Predictive Accuracy of Models", Chapter 33 in Z. Griliches and M. D. Intriligator (eds.) *Handbook of Econometrics*, Amsterdam, North-Holland, Volume 3, 1979–1995.

Fisher, F. M. (1970) "Tests of Equality Between Sets of Coefficients in Two Linear Regressions: An Expository Note", *Econometrica*, 38, 2, 361–366.

Fisher, R. A. (1922) "The Goodness of Fit of Regression Formulae, and the [494] Distribution of Regression Coefficients", *Journal of the Royal Statistical Society*, 85, 4, 597–612.

Goldfeld, S. M. (1973) "The Demand for Money Revisited", *Brookings Papers on Economic Activity*, 1973, 3, 577–646 (with discussion).

Goldfeld, S. M., and D. E. Sichel (1990) "The Demand for Money", Chapter 8 in B. M. Friedman and F. H. Hahn (eds.) *Handbook of Monetary Economics*, Amsterdam, North-Holland, Volume 1, 299–356.

Godfrey, L. G. (1978) "Testing Against General Autoregressive and Moving Average Error Models When the Regressors Include Lagged Dependent Variables", *Econometrica*, 46, 6, 1293–1301.

Granger, C. W. J. (1986) "Developments in the Study of Cointegrated Economic Variables", *Oxford Bulletin of Economics and Statistics*, 48, 3, 213–228.

Granger, C. W. J. (1989) *Forecasting in Business and Economics*, Boston, Academic Press, Second Edition.

*Granger, C. W. J., and M. Deutsch (1992) "Comments on the Evaluation of Policy Models", *Journal of Policy Modeling*, 14, 4, 497–516.

Harvey, A. C. (1981) *The Econometric Analysis of Time Series*, Oxford, Philip Allan.

Hendry, D. F. (1979) "Predictive Failure and Econometric Modelling in Macroeconomics: The Transactions Demand for Money", Chapter 9 in P. Ormerod (ed.) *Economic Modelling*, London, Heinemann Education Books, 217–242.

Hendry, D. F. (1983) "Comment", *Econometric Reviews*, 2, 1, 111–114.

Hendry, D. F. (1986) "The Role of Prediction in Evaluating Econometric Models", *Proceedings of the Royal Society of London, Series A*, 407, 25–34 (with discussion).

Hendry, D. F. (1987) "Econometric Methodology: A Personal Perspective", Chapter 10 in T. F. Bewley (ed.) *Advances in Econometrics*, Cambridge, Cambridge University Press, Volume 2, 29–48.

*Hendry, D. F. (1988) "The Encompassing Implications of Feedback versus Feedforward Mechanisms in Econometrics", *Oxford Economic Papers*, 40, 1, 132–149.

Hendry, D. F. (1989) *PC-GIVE: An Interactive Econometric Modelling System*, Version 6.0/6.01, Oxford, University of Oxford, Institute of Economics and Statistics and Nuffield College.

Hendry, D. F., and N. R. Ericsson (1991) "Modeling the Demand for Narrow Money in the United Kingdom and the United States", *European Economic Review*, 35, 4, 833–881.

Hendry, D. F., and A. J. Neale (1991) "A Monte Carlo Study of the Effects of Structural Breaks on Tests for Unit Roots", Chapter 8 in P. Hackl and A. H. Westlund (eds.) *Economic Structural Change: Analysis and Forecasting*, Berlin, Springer-Verlag, 95–119.

Hendry, D. F., and J.-F. Richard (1982) "On the Formulation of Empirical Models in Dynamic Econometrics", *Journal of Econometrics*, 20, 1, 3–33.

Jarque, C. M., and A. K. Bera (1980) "Efficient Tests for Normality, Homoscedasticity, and Serial Independence of Regression Residuals", *Economics Letters*, 6, 3, 255–259.

Johnston, J. (1963) *Econometric Methods*, New York, McGraw-Hill.

Kiviet, J. F. (1986) "On the Rigour of Some Misspecification Tests for Modelling Dynamic Relationships", *Review of Economic Studies*, 53, 2, 241–261.

Lu, M., and G. E. Mizon (1991) "Forecast Encompassing and Model Evaluation", Chapter 9 in P. Hackl and A. H. Westlund (eds.) *Economic Structural Change: Analysis and Forecasting*, Berlin, Springer-Verlag, 123–138.

Marquez, J., and N. R. Ericsson (1993) "Evaluating Forecasts of the U.S. Trade Balance", Chapter 14 in R. C. Bryant, P. Hooper, and C. L. Mann (eds.) *Evaluating Policy Regimes: New Research in Empirical Macroeconomics*, Washington, D.C., Brookings Institution, 671–732; originally cited as (1992), in R. C. Bryant, P. Hooper, C. L. Mann, and R. W. Tryon (eds.) *Empirical Evaluation of Alternative Policy Regimes*, Washington, D.C., Brookings Institution, in press.

[495] Meese, R. A., and K. Rogoff (1983) "Empirical Exchange Rate Models of the Seventies: Do They Fit Out of Sample?", *Journal of International Economics*, 14, 1/2, 3–24.

Mizon, G. E., and J.-F. Richard (1986) "The Encompassing Principle and Its Application to Testing Non-nested Hypotheses", *Econometrica*, 54, 3, 657–678.

Nicholls, D. F., and A. R. Pagan (1983) "Heteroscedasticity in Models with Lagged Dependent Variables", *Econometrica*, 51, 4, 1233–1242.

Pagan, A. (1989) "On the Role of Simulation in the Statistical Evaluation of Econometric Models", *Journal of Econometrics*, 40, 1, 125–139.

Pesaran, M. H. (1974) "On the General Problem of Model Selection", *Review of Economic Studies*, 41, 2, 153–171.

Ramsey, J. B. (1969) "Tests for Specification Errors in Classical Linear Least-squares Regression Analysis", *Journal of the Royal Statistical Society, Series B*, 31, 2, 350–371.

Sargan, J. D. (1958) "The Estimation of Economic Relationships Using Instrumental Variables", *Econometrica*, 26, 3, 393–415.

Sargan, J. D. (1980) "Some Approximations to the Distribution of Econometric Criteria Which Are Asymptotically Distributed as Chi-squared", *Econometrica*, 48, 5, 1107–1138.

Schinasi, G. J., and P. A. V. B. Swamy (1989) "The Out-of-Sample Forecasting Performance of Exchange Rate Models When Coefficients Are Allowed to Change", *Journal of International Money and Finance*, 8, 3, 375–390.

Spanos, A. (1986) *Statistical Foundations of Econometric Modelling*, Cambridge, Cambridge University Press.

Swamy, P. A. V. B., and G. J. Schinasi (1989) "Should Fixed Coefficients Be Re-estimated Every Period for Extrapolation?", *Journal of Forecasting*, 8, 1–17.

Swamy, P. A. V. B., and P. A. Tinsley (1980) "Linear Prediction and Estimation Methods for Regression Models with Stationary Stochastic Coefficients", *Journal of Econometrics*, 12, 2, 103–142.

White, H. (1980) "A Heteroskedasticity-consistent Covariance Matrix Estimator and a Direct Test for Heteroskedasticity", *Econometrica*, 48, 4, 817–838.

White, H. (1989) *Specification Analysis in Econometrics*, Cambridge, Cambridge University Press, forthcoming.

Wilson, A. L. (1978) "When Is the Chow Test UMP?", *American Statistician*, 32, 2, 66–68.

13

Comments on the Evaluation of Policy Models

CLIVE W. J. GRANGER and MELINDA DEUTSCH*

Abstract

This paper examines the evaluation of models claimed to be relevant for policy making purposes. A number of tests are proposed to determine the usefulness of such models in the policy making process. These tests are applied to three empirical examples.

1 Introduction

Applied economic research produces many empirical models of various parts of the economy. The models are evaluated in a variety of ways: some will report the specification search used to reach the final model; some will employ a battery of specification tests looking at missing variables, parameter consistency or heterogeneity; some will use cross-validation or post-sample evaluation techniques; and so forth. Discussion of these procedures and some difficulties that arise can be found in the book of readings, Granger (1990). Many applied papers, as well as some theoretical ones, will end with a section on the "policy implications" of the model. These sections rarely emphasize

* The first author is a Professor of Economics at the University of California, San Diego, and the second author is a graduate student at the same institution. This paper was revised while the first author was a Visiting Scholar at the Federal Reserve Board. This paper represents the views of the authors and should not be interpreted as reflecting the views of the Board of Governors of the Federal Reserve System or members of its staff. Partially supported by NSF grant SES 89-02950.

Reprinted with permission from the *Journal of Policy Modeling* (August 1992), 14, 4, 497–516.

that strictly the policy implications only follow if the model is correct and is the actual data generating mechanism, which is an unreasonably strong assumption. It is also an assumption that cannot be true if one has two competing policy models. Of course models are built for a variety of purposes, and some are fairly easy to evaluate or to compare. For example, if two models are built to provide forecasts, they can be run in real time, after the date [498] of the construction, and the forecasts compared using some pre-agreed cost function or criterion. This approach is less easy to apply to a policy model. A complete evaluation would require some organization, such as the Federal Reserve, to use the model to decide on policy and then to see how well the policy thus achieved actually performs. It is unlikely that most models can be evaluated in such a manner, and so less ambitious methods are required.

In this paper we start with a given model that is claimed to have been built for policy purposes. We consider what the implications are of this model being used by a policy maker to try to keep a single variable of interest near to a series of target values. To do this, a policy variable has its value chosen by use of the model. As background variables change and as targets alter, so the policy variable will take a series of values. It can be argued that each different policy value represents a new "policy regime", but we would prefer to keep this phrase to indicate more momentous, less frequent events such as a change in the variable of interest (from unemployment to inflation) or of the policy variable (from interest rates to money supply) or of the policy model being utilized. In these cases the Lucas critique becomes relevant and tests of super exogeneity can be employed, as in Engle and Hendry (1993). This is an important aspect of policy model evaluation which we will not consider here, but see Hoover and Sheffrin (1992). We will not consider also the argument from the rational expectations literature that policy cannot be successful, although that argument could be used to give an interpretation to some of our results.

It has been suggested that modern policy makers do not consider specific targets and so the type of control mechanism considered here is unrealistic. As a counter-example, it may be noted that the finance ministers of the G–7 countries meet twice a year to give targets for 10 or so indicators of their economies, for use in international policy coordination, as discussed by Frankel (1990). Other examples are also available. It should be noted that the G–7 targets are not made public and so cannot be used by most economists in evaluation exercises.

In what follows we will assume that targets exist but are not known. It is also assumed that policy makers are optimizing rather than satisficing. A good discussion of alternative approaches to policy is given by van Velthoven (1990).

2   The Control Mechanism

Suppose that the proposed policy model takes the form

$$Y_t = a + bC_t + kX_t + e_t, \tag{1}$$

where Y_t is the variable that the decision maker is trying to influence, called   [499]
the variable of interest, such as unemployment; C_t is the variable that the
decision maker has available as a policy variable, such as money supply; X_t is
a vector of other variables that influence Y_t; and e_t is the residual, taken to be
zero-mean white noise. Equation (1) is often called the *plant equation* in the
control literature. For the moment it will be assumed that the coefficients
a, b, k are constant, and in particular do not change as C_t changes. Let T_t
denote a *target series*, which is the desired values of Y_t. Denote $ce_t = Y_t - T_t$,
the control error; and let $S(ce)$ be the cost function of the decision maker,
representing the cost of an error ce.

The objective of the policy maker will be taken to be to manipulate C_{t+1}
so that Y_{t+1} is as close as possible to T_{t+1} when using a one-step horizon.
More precisely the policy maker will chose C_{t+1} to minimize $E_t[S(ce_{t+1})]$.
It should be noted that it is generally not possible to equate Y_{t+1} with T_{t+1}
because X_t and e_t are random variables that are not perfectly forecastable or
controllable. The timing is also important as C_{t+1} and T_{t+1} are *determined*
at time t but in a sense do not become operative until time $t+1$. Replacing
t by $t+1$ in (1) and using a least-squares cost function suggests that the
forecast of Y_{t+1} made at time t is

$$f_{t,1}^Y = a + bC_{t+1} + kf_{t,1}^X, \tag{2}$$

if C_{t+1} is known, as it is potentially for the decision maker. Here $f_{t,1}^X$ is the
optimum one-step forecast of X_t using information available as time t *plus*
C_{t+1}. Requiring this forecast to be equal to the target, gives

$$C_{t+1} = b^{-1}[T_{t+1} - a - kf_{t,1}^X], \tag{3}$$

and then the forecast error will be

$$ec_{t+1} = e_{t+1} + k(X_{t+1} - f_{t,1}^X).$$

Thus *if* the decision maker were using (1) to determine the policy, the values
for the policy variable would be given by (3). Given a satisfactory method
of forecasting X_{t+1}, everything else in (3) can be taken as known.

To an outsider things are rather different as C_{t+1} will not be known at
time t and neither will be T_{t+1}. The first can be forecast but there is often
little direct information about targets.

To an outsider, the best forecast of Y_{t+1} will be

$$g_{t,1}^Y = a + bg_{t,1}^C + kg_{t,1}^X,$$

[500]   according to the model (1), which is being investigated, where $g_{t,1}^X$ is the optimum one-step forecast of X_{t+1} using just information available at time t, not including C_{t+1}. The forecast error will now be

$$
\begin{aligned}
\varepsilon_{t+1} &= Y_{t+1} - g_{t,1}^Y \\
&= ec_{t+1} + b(C_{t+1} - g_{t,1}^C) + k(f_{t,1}^X - g_{t,1}^X).
\end{aligned}
$$

As these two components will be uncorrelated if (1) is correct (as otherwise the size of ec_{t+1} could be reduced), one gets

$$E[\varepsilon_{t+1}^2] \geq E[ec_{t+1}^2] \tag{4}$$

in general. This suggests the following test for evaluating a policy model. The conditional forecast, using information in C_{t+1}, of Y_{t+1} should on average be superior to the unconditional forecast, using just information available at time t to an outsider. Note that both forecasts are constructed directly from the model that is being evaluated. Of course without this constraint, the conditional forecast should always be better than the unconditional forecast, on average, as it is based on more information. It should be noted that equality holds in (4) only if $C_{t+1} = g_{t,1}^C$, that is, the control variable C is perfectly forecastable from the information set I_t. In this case the decision maker cannot influence C and so this variable is irrelevant as a control. If the model in (1) is correct it follows from (3) that if C is perfectly forecastable, so will be the target series, T_t, and also there is no instantaneous causation from C_t to X_t. In these circumstances, the model in (1) or any other model would not be relevant for control purposes. Thus non-rejection of the null hypothesis of equality in (4) is equivalent to rejection of (1) as a control model. As this hypothesis can be rejected in many ways, it does not follow that (1) *is* useful for policy if the hypothesis is rejected. This evaluation technique is clearly relevant for a model that claims to be a policy model and is illustrated in the next section. It is also briefly discussed in Chong and Hendry (1986), reprinted as Chapter 17 of Granger (1990).

Nevertheless, (3) can be used to estimate the target series as

$$\hat{T}_{t+1} = bC_{t+1} + a + kf_{t,1}^X, \tag{5}$$

using the observed value of C_{t+1} and the forecast of X_{t+1}. If some of the estimated target values are unrealistic, such as negative unemployment or very high inflation rates, this would clearly imply that the model is inadequate. A more technical test can be used when Y_t is I(1), so that the change series ΔY_t is stationary, say. It was pointed out in Granger (1988) that if a policy
[501]   control is somewhat successful, then at the very least Y_t and T_t must be cointegrated. It follows that Y_t and $\hat{T}_t$ will be cointegrated, which implies that $Y_t - bC_t - kX_t - a$ is I(0) or stationary, which can be tested using standard unit root tests. This evaluation technique is discussed in Section 4.

To summarize this discussion, there are several evaluation tests that can be applied to a model that is claimed to be relevant for policy selection, assumed to be of the form in (1).

2.1   Test 1

From the model, two (sets of) forecasts can be constructed. The "unconditional" one-step forecast of Y_{t+1} made at time t is

$$g_{t,1}^Y = a + b g_{t,1}^C + k g_{t,1}^X, \tag{6}$$

where $g_{t,1}^C$ is the optimal one-step forecast of C_{t+1} made at time t using the information set $I_t : \{X_{t-j}, C_{t-j}, j \geq 1\}$; and similarly for X. "Conditional" one-step forecasts are now made of the form

$$f_{t,1}^Y = a + b C_{t+1} + k f_{t,1}^X, \tag{7}$$

where now f^Y and f^X are the optimal one-step forecasts based on the large information set $J_t : \{I_t, C_{t+1}\}$, acting as though C_{t+1} is known at time t, which is correct for the decision made in this framework. Forecast errors will result from the two forecasts:

$$\varepsilon_{t+1} = Y_{t+1} - g_{t,1}^Y \tag{8}$$

and

$$ec_{t+1} = Y_{t+1} - f_{t,1}^Y, \tag{9}$$

and the null hypothesis tested is equality of the mean squared errors of ε and ec. Assuming that these errors have zero means, the null hypothesis is easily tested using the procedure discussed in Chapter 9 of Granger and Newbold (1987). Define

$$D_t = \varepsilon_t - ec_t, \tag{10}$$

$$S_t = \varepsilon_t + ec_t, \tag{11}$$

and the null hypothesis is then equivalent to testing $correlation(D_t, S_t) = 0$, which follows by noting that $cov(D_t, S_t) = E[\varepsilon_t^2 - ec_t^2]$. The test employed in the next section is to regress S on a constant and D. If the coefficient of D is significantly different from zero, conclude that SSE of the conditional forecasts is significantly different from the SSE of the unconditional forecasts; otherwise conclude they are not. This is the test that is emphasized in the following section. Non-rejection of the null hypothesis is equivalent to a rejection of the usefulness of the model in (1) for policy purposes. As the forecast horizon used by the policy maker is unknown, the test was repeated [502] for horizons, 1, 2, 3, and 4 of the observational time unit.

2.2   Test 2

If the model in (1) is correctly specified for the control variable, the conditional forecast should forecast-encompass the unconditional forecast, as discussed in Chong and Hendry (1986). This means that the poorer unconditional forecast contains no information that is helpful in improving the quality of the conditional forecast. This has to be true in theory if the forecasts are not being constructed from a given model. The test uses post-sample data to form the regression

$$Y_{t+1} = a_1 + a_2 f_{t,1}^Y + a_3 g_{t,1}^Y + residual, \tag{12}$$

and forecast encompassing occurs if $a_2 = 1$, $a_1 = a_3 = 0$, and the residual is white noise. Similar regressions can be formed for different horizon forecasts but are not reported below.

2.3   Test 3

From (5), under the assumption that the model in (1) is correctly specified, the underlying target series can be estimated. The reasonableness of these estimates can be judged by the evaluator. Clearly, this is not a formal test.

2.4   Test 4

If the target series is $I(1)$, then Y_t will be $I(1)$, and this can be tested by standard techniques such as augmented Dickey-Fuller tests. It will then follow that $z_t = Y_t - bC_t - kX_t - a$ is $I(0)$, or stationary, with zero mean. Again z_t can be tested for the null of $I(1)$ and, if this null is rejected and z_t has declining autocorrelations, one may accept its stationarity. Note that this is equivalent to testing for cointegration between Y_t, C_t, and X_t but with given coefficients, as determined by the model. If these coefficients were unconstrained and X_t included lagged Y_t, the test would be of little interest as z_t should then always be $I(0)$.

2.5   Test 5

In the above test, it is assumed that the target series T_t is unobserved, which is usually the case. If the targets are available, C_{t+1} could be estimated from (3), giving $\hat{C}_{t+1}$, and then a regression run of the form

$$C_{t+1} = \alpha + \beta \hat{C}_{t+1} + error, \tag{13}$$

and the null hypothesis that the model is correct is tested for the joint requirements that $\alpha = 0$, $\beta = 1$, $error = $ white noise. This test is not considered in the following section.

2.6   Test 6

[503]   A further test that can be performed, but which is also not considered in the empirical sections, is to ask if some other policy variable (or its unanticipated component) is missing from the model. Thus, for example, in a model relating money supply to unemployment, unanticipated government expenditure can be considered as a possible missing variable using a Lagrange Multiplier test. If such a potential control variable is missing, the original model cannot be used as a successful policy model.

2.7   Discussion

It should be noted that these tests are not necessarily strong ones and represent only necessary conditions that a policy model should possess. The tests are for a single model and may not be helpful in comparing models. It is also assumed that C_t, or a component of it, is a potentially controllable variable. The tests are not interrelated in a simple way as they concentrate on different types of possible mis-specification of (1).

To perform Tests 1 and 2 it is necessary to form unconditional forecasts of the control variable C_t. This will usually come from a reduced form regression of C_t on various explanatory variables, including lagged C_t. This regression can be thought of as an approximation to a reaction function for C_t. Clearly, if this equation is badly specified then this could be a reason why the null hypothesis considered in the two tests are rejected. In the empirical model considered in the next section, the control variable is taken to be the unanticipated change in money (denoted DMR), and thus its unconditional forecast will just be zero for all horizons.

There is relatively little discussion in econometrics about how to evaluate a policy model as compared to models designed for forecasting or hypothesis testing. In other disciplines there is consideration given to policy evaluation, but it is usually nontechnical, see for example Nagel (1990).

3   An Application to a Model of the Unemployment Rate

The first empirical example examines a model of the unemployment rate proposed by Barro and Rush (1980) which is based on the Natural Rate/Rational Expectations hypothesis. Although this model was not formulated for policy making purposes, it will be used to illustrate some of the concepts presented in this paper. The model of the unemployment rate consists of two equations: the money growth equation and the unemployment rate equation. The [504] money growth equation is given by

$$DM_t = a_0 + \sum_{j=1}^{6} a_{1j}DM_{t-j} + a_2 FEDV_t + \sum_{j=1}^{3} a_{3j} UN_{t-j} + DMR_t, \qquad (14)$$

348

Clive W. J. Granger and Melinda Deutsch

where M is a quarterly average of M1, $DM_t = \log M_t - \log M_{t-1}$, $FEDV_t$ is an estimate of the deviation from the normal value of the real expenditure of the federal government, U is the quarterly average unemployment rate, and $UN_t = \log[U_t/(1 - U_t)]$. The residual, DMR_t, is the unanticipated change in the money supply, and is taken to be the control variable. Thus, for this example, the above equation is used only to estimate the control variable since it is unknown to the investigator.

The equation explaining movements in the unemployment rate is given by

$$UN_t = b_0 + \sum_{j=1}^{10} b_{1j} DMR_{t-j} + b_2 MIL_t$$

$$+ b_3 UN_{t-1} + b_4 UN_{t-2} + residual, \quad (15)$$

where MIL = military personnel/male population aged 15–44 years. This equation is the plant equation. Note that the future values of MIL_t are taken as known when forming the conditional and unconditional forecasts.

In addition, the following univariate model of the unemployment rate was used as a benchmark for comparison.

$$UN_t = a_0 + a_1 UN_{t-1} + a_2 UN_{t-2} + a_3 UN_{t-3} + residual. \quad (16)$$

The above equations were estimated using quarterly data. The estimated money growth equation was

$$DM_t = \underset{(3.05)}{0.02} + \underset{(4.94)}{0.42\ DM_{t-1}} + \underset{(0.55)}{0.05\ DM_{t-2}} + \underset{(1.36)}{0.12\ DM_{t-3}}$$
$$- \underset{(1.71)}{0.15\ DM_{t-4}} + \underset{(3.21)}{0.28\ DM_{t-5}} - \underset{(0.31)}{0.03\ DM_{t-6}}$$
$$+ \underset{(1.45)}{0.01\ FEDV_t} + \underset{(1.15)}{0.01\ UN_{t-1}} + \underset{(0.21)}{0.004\ UN_{t-2}}$$
$$- \underset{(0.87)}{0.009\ UN_{t-3}} + residual, \quad (17)$$

$$T = 148\ [1952(1){-}1988(4)] \quad R^2 = 0.51 \quad dw = 2.00 \quad \hat{\sigma} = 0.00710.$$

[505] (The moduli of t values are shown in parentheses.) The estimate of Barro's unemployment equation was

TABLE 1. Test 1 for Barro's Model
and Root Mean Sum of Squared Forecast Errors

Steps ahead	D		Barro		Univariate
	Coeff.	$|t|$	Cond.	Uncond.	
One	−0.94	0.80	0.08	0.08	0.02
Two	0.08	0.09	0.17	0.16	0.04
Three	0.59	0.80	0.23	0.22	0.05
Four	0.26	0.44	0.27	0.22	0.07

$$
\begin{aligned}
UN_t = &- \underset{(6.03)}{0.50} - \underset{(2.87)}{2.02}\ DMR_t - \underset{(1.64)}{1.19}\ DMR_{t-1} \\
&- \underset{(3.42)}{2.46}\ DMR_{t-2} - \underset{(3.27)}{2.51}\ DMR_{t-3} - \underset{(2.06)}{1.67}\ DMR_{t-4} \\
&- \underset{(2.03)}{1.71}\ DMR_{t-5} - \underset{(2.53)}{2.14}\ DMR_{t-6} - \underset{(1.40)}{1.16}\ DMR_{t-7} \\
&- \underset{(1.24)}{1.00}\ DMR_{t-8} - \underset{(0.01)}{0.08}\ DMR_{t-9} + \underset{(0.05)}{0.04}\ DMR_{t-10} \\
&- \underset{(5.52)}{0.76}\ MIL_t + \underset{(19.64)}{1.40}\ UN_{t-1} - \underset{(9.10)}{0.64}\ UN_{t-2} + residual, \quad (18)
\end{aligned}
$$

$T = 123\ [1954(3)–1985(1)] \quad R^2 = 0.98 \quad dw = 2.06 \quad \hat{\sigma} = 0.04869.$

The univariate model was estimated to be

$$
\begin{aligned}
UN_t = &- \underset{(2.45)}{0.12} + \underset{(19.59)}{1.66}\ UN_{t-1} - \underset{(5.67)}{0.85}\ UN_{t-2} \\
&+ \underset{(1.65)}{0.14}\ UN_{t-3} + residual, \quad\quad\quad\quad\quad (19)
\end{aligned}
$$

$T = 138\ [1950(4)–1985(1)] \quad R^2 = 0.96 \quad dw = 2.01 \quad \hat{\sigma} = 0.06545.$

In order to test the usefulness of this model for policy making purposes the following analysis was performed. First, the conditional and unconditional forecasts were computed for the model using data from 1985(1) to 1988(4). Recall that if the model is useful for policy purposes, then the conditional forecasts should outperform the unconditional forecasts. In order to determine whether this is the case, these forecasts were compared in a number of ways. First, for Test 1, the root mean sum of squared forecast errors (RMSFE) was computed and is displayed in Table 1. Note that for all forecast horizons, the RMSFEs of the unconditional forecasts were smaller than the conditional forecasts.

While this suggests that the conditional forecasts do not outperform the unconditional forecasts, it is desirable to test whether the SSE are significantly different from each other.

[506]   Unfortunately, some of the assumptions necessary for the validity of this test appear to be violated in this example. In particular, the one-step ahead forecast errors appear to be autocorrelated and this serial correlation is not completely corrected for by assuming that the residuals from the relevant regression are AR(1). A similar problem seems to hold for the two-, three-, and four-step ahead forecast errors. In some of the cases, the regression results also indicate that the forecast errors are biased. If, for illustrative purposes, the apparent violation of these two key assumptions is ignored, the conclusion drawn from the test results for all forecast horizons is that the SSE of the conditional and unconditional forecasts are not significantly different.

For Test 2, the one-step regression was completely unsatisfactory, with $f_{t,1}$ having a negative coefficient (of -1.12) and the residuals containing strong serial correlation, with a Durbin-Watson statistic of 0.35. The results clearly indicate that conditions required from Test 2 for the model to be satisfactory for policy purposes are not found.

Test 4 suggests that an additional test of model adequacy should be employed if the variable that the decision maker is trying to influence, Y_t, is I(1): namely, the estimated target from the model under consideration should be cointegrated with Y_t.[1] As a first step in implementing this test, the augmented Dickey-Fuller (ADF) test with two lags and a constant term [see Granger and Newbold (1989) for a discussion of this test] was used to test for stationarity of the unemployment series. The test statistic was 2.95, thus the results are inconclusive as to whether the unemployment series is I(0) or I(1).

[507]   It shall be assumed, however, for illustrative purposes, that U is I(1) so that the test for cointegration can be performed.[2] The cointegrating regression of unemployment on the estimated target from Barro's model and a constant was run, and the ADF test with two lags was used on the residuals from this regression to determine if they were I(0). The t statistic from the Dickey-Fuller test with a constant term is 19.80, indicating that unemployment and the estimated target from Barro's model are cointegrated. Thus, the

---

[1] For this example, it should be noted that the estimated target was approximated by the in-sample fitted values from the unemployment model because the number of out-of-sample values was too small to perform the unit root test. In addition, UN and its associated target were transformed to levels because the unemployment models considered in this section estimate the I(0) variable, $UN_t = \log[U_t/(1-U_t)]$ where U_t is the quarterly average unemployment rate.

[2] It should also be noted that the coefficients of the lagged terms in the univariate model for UN add almost to one $(1.66 - 0.85 + 0.14 = 0.95)$.

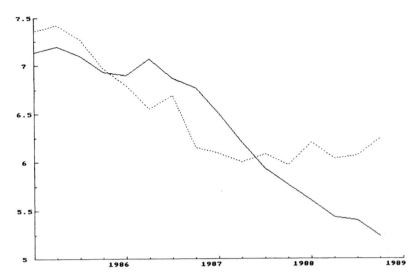

FIGURE 1. The unemployment rate (—) and the estimated target from Barro's model (· · ·).

unemployment model does not fail this simple test.

For Test 3, as a final test of the usefulness of the model for policy purposes, the estimated target series for the model was computed. It does not appear from Figure 1 that these values are unrealistic, so the model does not fail this simple test.

The above results, taken together, strongly suggest that the conditional forecasts are not superior to the unconditional forecasts and, thus, on this basis we conclude that the model is not useful for policy purposes. The error autocorrelation inter alia points to model mis-specification, and the latter may be why the forecast tests are what they are.

4   An Application to Two Models of the Demand for Borrowed Reserves

[508]

The second example examines two models of the demand for borrowed reserves. These models are relevant to policy since the Federal Reserve targets intermediate reserves, and borrowing from the Discount Window has an obvious impact on the reserves. In addition, studies by Keir (1981) and others suggest that the Federal Reserve uses a version of these models. The first model was proposed by Goldfeld and Kane (1966). Briefly, a bank is assumed to have an exogenous reserve need. It can either borrow from the Federal

Reserve or from an alternative source. The bank minimizes its total cost of borrowing by choosing the optimal amount of borrowing from each source. The model proposed by Goldfeld and Kane is

$$R_t^B = a_0 + a_1 K_t + a_2 R_{t-1}^B + a_3 \Delta R_t^{UB} + \varepsilon_t, \qquad (20)$$

where R^B is the level of borrowing from the Discount Window, ΔR^{UB} is the change in unborrowed reserves, $K = i_D - i_S$, and i_D is the discount rate, and i_S is the interest rate of the alternative source.

Dutkowsky (1984) extended Goldfeld and Kane's model by arguing that a switching regression model gave a more accurate representation of the behavior of unborrowed reserves. The switching regression model proposed by Dutkowsky is

$$R_t^B = \begin{cases} a_0^L + a_1^L K_t + a_2^L R_{t-1}^B + a_3^L \Delta R_t^{UB} + \varepsilon_t^L & \text{if } K \leq K^* \\ a_0^U + a_1^U \log K_t + a_2^U R_{t-1}^B + a_3^U \Delta R_t^{UB} + \varepsilon_t^U & \text{if } K > K^*, \end{cases} \qquad (21)$$

where K^* is an unobservable switching point that needs to be estimated. The discount rate i_D is the control variable throughout this section.

The above models were estimated using seasonally adjusted monthly data. Because of the difference in the sample period and the seasonal adjustment of the data, an additional lag of R^B was found to be significant and was included in the regression results. Goldfeld and Kane's model was estimated to be

$$R_t^B = \underset{(6.02)}{97.18} + \underset{(6.19)}{91.06} K_t + \underset{(22.93)}{1.03} R_{t-1}^B$$
$$- \underset{(6.71)}{0.24} R_{t-3}^B - \underset{(4.11)}{0.12} \Delta R_t^{UB} + residual \qquad (22)$$

$$T = 198 \, [1959(7)-1975(12)] \quad R^2 = 0.95 \quad dw = 1.89 \quad \hat{\sigma} = 129.03.$$

For the Dutkowsky model, the unobservable switchpoint, K^*, which max-
[509] imized a likelihood function, was found using a grid search and was estimated to be 0.15. Dutkowsky's estimated model was, for $K_t > 0.15$,

$$R_t^B = \underset{(5.78)}{225.93} + \underset{(4.86)}{107.35} \log(K_t) + \underset{(21.70)}{1.06} R_{t-1}^B$$
$$- \underset{(6.66)}{0.27} R_{t-3}^B - \underset{(4.16)}{0.15} \Delta R_t^{UB} + residual \qquad (23)$$

and, for $K_t \leq 0.15$,

$$R_t^B = \underset{(2.87)}{77.45} + \underset{(1.92)}{64.76} K_t + \underset{(6.74)}{0.81} R_{t-1}^B$$
$$- \underset{(0.83)}{0.07} R_{t-3}^B - \underset{(0.09)}{0.005} \Delta R_t^{UB} + residual \qquad (24)$$

$$T = 192 \, [1960(1)-1975(12)] \quad R^2 = 0.95 \quad dw = 1.91 \quad \hat{\sigma} = 130.06.$$

TABLE 2. Root Mean Sum of Squared Forecast Errors
for Two Models of Borrowed Reserves

	Goldfeld/Kane		Dutkowsky		
Steps ahead	Cond.	Uncond.	Cond.	Uncond.	Univariate
One	0.23	0.23	0.24	0.24	0.29
Two	0.25	0.25	0.27	0.27	0.30
Three	0.27	0.28	0.29	0.32	0.37
Four	0.31	0.32	0.35	0.34	0.45

Note: Values shown are divided by 1,000.

The univariate model was

$$R_t^B = \underset{(2.86)}{48.44} + \underset{(18.32)}{1.28}\ R_{t-1}^B - \underset{(1.36)}{0.16}\ R_{t-2}^B$$
$$- \underset{(2.95)}{0.21}\ R_{t-3}^B + residual \tag{25}$$

$T = 200\ [1959(5)-1975(12)]\quad R^2 = 0.93\quad dw = 2.01\quad \hat{\sigma} = 164.97.$

For Test 1 unconditional forecasts of i_D are required. As i_D is I(1), an AR(3) model for Δi_D was estimated as

$$\Delta i_{D,t} = 0.54\Delta i_{D,t-1} + 0.10\Delta i_{D,t-3} + white\ noise. \tag{26}$$

Thus the unconditional forecast of $i_{D,t+1}$ is the unconditional forecast of $\Delta i_{D,t+1}$ plus $i_{D,t}$. Multiple-step forecasts are easily formed.

The interpretation of the results for this example proved to be less straightforward than for the first example and seemed to depend in part on the forecast horizon considered. Following the analysis above, the RMSFEs of the conditional and unconditional forecasts were computed for both models for 1976(1)–1978(12) and are displayed in Table 2. It can be seen that the conditional RMSFE was less than the unconditional RMSFE for some forecast horizons.

Further investigation was needed to determine whether these differences were statistically significant. In particular, the test involving the sum and [510] differences of the forecast errors was employed and the results are displayed in Table 3.

The conclusion of Test 1 obtained for the Goldfeld and Kane model is that the conditional and unconditional forecasts are not significantly different for any of the forecast horizons. For the Dutkowsky model, the forecast errors

TABLE 3. Test 1 for Two Models of Borrowed Reserves

Steps ahead	D (Dutkowsky)		D (Goldfeld/Kane)	
	Coeff.	$|t|$	Coeff.	$|t|$
One	5.98	2.19	−3.35	0.28
Two	−0.71	0.65	−1.57	0.53
Three	−0.47	0.67	−0.04	0.02
Four	−1.21	2.76	−1.41	1.05

for steps one and four were found to be significantly different, suggesting, surprisingly, that the unconditional forecasts were superior to the conditional forecasts for those forecast horizons. The significantly smaller unconditional RMSFE is prima facie evidence of model mis-specification, and the latter may be why the forecast tests are what they are.

For Test 2, as a further test of the superiority of the conditional forecasts, the conditional and unconditional forecasts were combined using the regression in (12). For a one-step horizon, the estimated parameters were as follows. The regression for Goldfeld and Kane's model is:

$$R_{t+1}^B = \underset{(0.78)}{46.34} - \underset{(1.50)}{9.41}\, f_{t,1} + \underset{(1.64)}{10.36}\, g_{t,1} + residual, \qquad (27)$$

$$T = 36\ [1976(1)\text{--}1978(12)] \quad R^2 = 0.70 \quad dw = 2.47 \quad \hat{\sigma} = 228.39,$$

which is hardly interpretable; and the regression for Dutkowsky's model is:

$$R_{t+1}^B = \underset{(1.37)}{84.00} + \underset{(0.06)}{0.12}\, f_{t,1} + \underset{(0.09)}{0.73}\, g_{t,1} + residual, \qquad (28)$$

$$T = 36\ [1976(1)\text{--}1978(12)] \quad R^2 = 0.66 \quad dw = 2.54 \quad \hat{\sigma} = 244.31.$$

[511] Both of these applications of Test 2 do not support the usefulness of the models for policy purposes.

Lastly, for Test 3, the estimated target series for each model was computed. It does not appear from Figures 2 and 3 that these values are unrealistic.

Taken together, the above results indicate that neither model is useful for policy purposes as the above analysis suggests that the conditional forecasts do not appear to be superior to the unconditional forecasts.

As a final observation it is interesting to note that most of the tests described above can be used to examine the performance of a model during

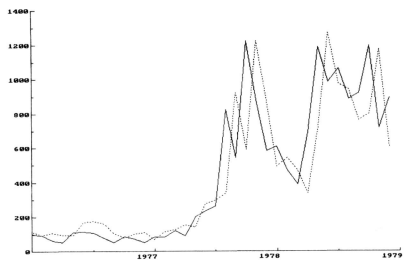

FIGURE 2. Borrowed reserves (—) and the estimated target from the Goldfeld/Kane model (···).

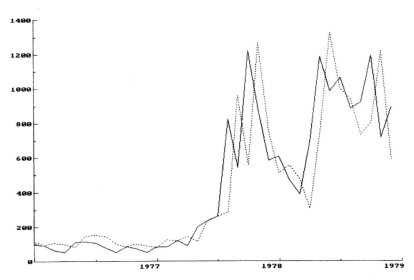

FIGURE 3. Borrowed reserves (—) and the estimated target from the Dutkowsky model (···).

TABLE 4. Sum of Squared Errors
for Each Regime in Dutkowsky's Model

	SSE for $K_t \leq 0.15$		SSE for $K_t > 0.15$	
Steps ahead	Cond.	Uncond.	Cond.	Uncond.
One	0.28	0.24	1.84	1.86
Two	0.07	0.07	2.55	2.62
Three	0.13	0.19	2.95	3.44
Four	0.18	0.24	4.12	4.03

different regimes. ·For example, an investigator may believe that Dutkowsky's
[512] model is only useful for policy making purposes when $K > K^*$. Thus, the
SSE of the conditional and unconditional forecasts for the two regimes may
be calculated. The results are displayed in Table 4. Again, there is not
clear-cut superiority of the conditional forecasts over the unconditional ones.

5   An Application to a Model for the Demand for Narrow Money in the United Kingdom

The final example examines a model of the demand for narrow money in the
[513] United Kingdom. The model proposed by Hendry and Ericsson (1991) is

$$\Delta(m - p)_t = a_0 + a_1 \Delta p_t + a_2 \Delta(m - p - y)_{t-1}$$

$$+ a_3 R_t^* + a_4 (m - p - y)_{t-1} + \varepsilon_t, \qquad (29)$$

where $\Delta(m - p)_t$ is the growth rate of real money, Δp_t is the inflation rate,
$(m - p - y)_t$ is the inverse of velocity, and R_t^* is the learning-adjusted net
interest rate [see Hendry and Ericsson (1991) for a detailed description of
the variables]. For the sample period 1964(1)–1985(2), the above model was
estimated to be

$$\Delta(m - p)_t = \underset{(4.64)}{0.02} - \underset{(5.27)}{0.70} \Delta p_t - \underset{(2.98)}{0.19} \Delta(m - p - y)_{t-1}$$

$$- \underset{(8.24)}{0.62} R_t^* - \underset{(9.94)}{0.09} (m - p - y)_{t-1} + residual \qquad (30)$$

$$T = 86 \; [1964(1)–1985(2)] \quad R^2 = 0.69 \quad dw = 2.15 \quad \hat{\sigma} = 0.01344.$$

TABLE 5. Test 1 and RMSFE for Hendry and Ericsson's Model

Steps ahead	D		Hendry/Ericsson		
	Coeff.	$|t|$	Cond.	Uncond.	Univariate
One	1.34	1.58	1.22	1.52	2.47
Two	0.96	1.48	1.66	1.99	2.82
Three	0.49	1.09	1.77	2.33	3.21
Four	0.83	2.36	1.98	3.20	3.43

The estimated univariate model was

$$\Delta(m-p)_t = \underset{(2.45)}{0.26\ \Delta(m-p)_{t-1}} + \underset{(2.29)}{0.25\ \Delta(m-p)_{t-2}}$$
$$+\ residual, \tag{31}$$

$T = 86\ [1964(1)\text{--}1985(2)]\quad R^2 = 0.16\quad dw = 1.96\quad \hat{\sigma} = 0.02170.$

For Test 1, unconditional forecasts of R_t^* are required. A model for ΔR_t^* was estimated as

$$\Delta R_t^* = 0.01 - 0.13 R_{t-2}^* + white\ noise. \tag{32}$$

The unconditional forecast of R_{t+1}^* is the unconditional forecast of ΔR_{t+1}^*, plus R_t^*. Multiple-step forecasts are easily formed.

Following the analysis in the first example, the RMSFEs of the conditional and unconditional forecasts were computed for both models for 1985(3)–1989(2) and are displayed in Table 5. It can be seen that the conditional RMSFE was less than the unconditional RMSFE for all forecast horizons.

Further investigation was needed to determine whether these differences were statistically significant. In particular, the test involving the sum and differences of the forecast errors was employed and the results are displayed in Table 5. The conclusion of Test 1 obtained for the Hendry and Ericsson [514] model is that the conditional and unconditional forecasts are not significantly different one, two, and three steps ahead but are significantly different for four steps ahead.

For Test 2, as a further test of the superiority of the conditional forecasts, the conditional and unconditional forecasts were combined using regression (12). For a one-step horizon, the estimated parameters were as follows:

$$\Delta(m-p)_{t+1} \;=\; \underset{(0.26)}{0.002} \;+\; \underset{(2.65)}{1.15}\, f_{t,1} \;-\; \underset{(0.62)}{0.31}\, g_{t,1}$$

$$+\; residual, \tag{33}$$

$$T = 16\ [1985(3)-1989(2)] \quad R^2 = 0.56 \quad dw = 2.32 \quad \hat{\sigma} = 0.01316.$$

Lastly, for Test 3, the estimated target series for each model was computed. The estimated target series and the observed $\Delta(m-p)$ are within one to three percentage points of each other, which is not unrealistic.

Taken together, the above results indicate that the usefulness of the above model for policy purposes may depend on the forecast horizon used by the policy maker since the above analysis suggests that the conditional forecasts do not appear to be superior to the unconditional forecasts at one, two, and three steps ahead but are superior for four steps ahead. It should be noted, however, that one interpretation of the failure of the forecast tests to reject is that they lack power because of the small sample size of the forecasts.

6   Conclusion

Despite the importance of reliable models used in the policy making process, there has been little consideration given to the evaluation of policy models in the econometric literature. This paper discussed a number of tests that could be used for such a purpose. While these tests provide only necessary [515] properties that a policy model should possess, they do aid the decision maker by excluding some inadequate models.

Appendix. Description of the Data

	Data for Example 1
M	M1 [1950(1)–1958(12)] (Banking and Monetary Statistics: Board of Governors of the Federal Reserve System, 1976)
M	M1 [1959(1)–1988(12)] (Citibase Series FM1)
U	Unemployment rate, all workers, including resident armed forces (Citibase Series LHURR)
F	Total Federal government expenditures (Citibase Series GGFEX)
$DEFLAT$	Implicit price deflator: Federal government (Citibase Series GDGGF)

Data for Example 1 (con't)

MALE	Male population aged 15–44 years (Sum of Citibase Series PANM4, PANM5, PANM6, PANM7, PANM8, and PANM9)
CIV	Civilian population (Citibase Series POPCIV)
POP	Total population including armed forces overseas (Citibase Series POP)

Variables for Example 1

DM_t	$\log M_t - \log M_{t-1}$
UN_t	$\log[0.01U_t/(1 - 0.01U_t)]$
FED_t	$F_t/DEFLAT_t$
$FEDV_t$	$\log FED_t - [\log FED]_t^*$
$[\log FED]_t^*$	$0.05[\log FED]_t + 0.95[\log FED]_{t-1}^*$
MIL_t	$(POP_t - CIV_t)/MALE_t$

[516]

Data for Example 2

R^B	Total borrowings at reserve banks (Citibase Series F6CMB)
i_D	Discount rate, Federal Reserve Bank of New York (Citibase Series FYGD)
i_S	Federal funds rate (Citibase Series FYFF)
R^{TOT}	Total reserves (Citibase Series FZCMRR)

Variables for Example 2

K	$i_D - i_S$
R_t^{UB}	$R_t^{TOT} - R_t^B$
ΔR_t^{UB}	$R_t^{UB} - R_{t-1}^{UB}$

Notes: For Example 1, the series listed as "data" were converted into quarterly values when appropriate and the "variables" were formed. For Example 2, the series listed as "data" were seasonally adjusted and from them the "variables" were formed.

Bibliography

(References marked with an asterisk * are included in this volume.)

Barro, R. J., and M. Rush (1980) "Unanticipated Money and Economic Activity", in S. Fischer (ed.) *Rational Expectations and Economic Policy*, Chicago, University of Chicago Press (for the NBER).

Chong, Y. Y., and D. F. Hendry (1986) "Econometric Evaluation of Linear Macro-economic Models", *Review of Economic Studies*, 53, 671–690. [Also, Chapter 17 of Granger (1990).]

Dutkowsky, D. (1984) "The Demand for Borrowed Reserves: A Switching Regression Model", *Journal of Finance*, 69, 2, 407–424.

*Engle, R. F., and D. F. Hendry (1993) "Testing Super Exogeneity and Invariance in Regression Models", *Journal of Econometrics*, 56, 1/2, 119–139; originally cited as (1989) "Testing Super Exogeneity and Invariance", Discussion Paper No. 89–51, Economics Department, University of California at San Diego, La Jolla, California, forthcoming in *Journal of Econometrics*.

Frankel, J. A. (1990) "International Nominal Targeting: A Proposal for Overcoming Obstacles to Policy Coordination", Working Paper, Economics Department, University of California, Berkeley.

Goldfeld, S. M., and E. J. Kane (1966) "The Determinants of Member Bank Borrowing: An Econometric Study", *Journal of Finance*, 21, 499–514.

Granger, C. W. J. (1988) "Causality, Cointegration, and Control", *Journal of Economic Dynamics and Control*, 12, 551–559.

Granger, C. W. J. (ed.) (1990) *Modelling Economic Time Series: Readings in Econometric Methodology*, Oxford, Oxford University Press.

Granger, C. W. J., and P. Newbold (1987) *Forecasting Economic Time Series*, New York, Academic Press.

Hendry, D. F., and N. R. Ericsson (1991) "Modeling the Demand for Narrow Money in the United Kingdom and the United States", *European Economic Review*, 35, 4, 833–881.

Hoover, K. D., and S. M. Sheffrin (1992) "Causation, Spending, and Taxes: Sand in the Sandbox or Tax Collector for the Welfare State?", *American Economic Review*, 82, 225–248.

Keir, P. (1981) "Impact of Discount Policy Procedures on the Effectiveness of Reserve Targeting", in *New Monetary Control Procedures*, Volume 1, Federal Reserve Staff Study, Board of Governors of the Federal Reserve System, Washington, D.C.

Nagel, S. S. (1990) *Policy Theory and Policy Evaluation*, New York, Greenwood Press.

van Velthoven, B. C. J. (1990) "The Applicability of the Traditional Theory of Economic Policy", *Journal of Economic Surveys*, 4, 59–88.

14

Confidence Intervals for Linear Combinations of Forecasts from Dynamic Econometric Models

JULIA CAMPOS*

Abstract

This paper derives the approximate distribution of a vector of forecast errors from a dynamic simultaneous equations econometric model. The system may include exogenous variables with known and/or unknown future values. For the latter set of exogenous variables, a stationary and invertible ARMAX process is assumed. Confidence regions are derived for vectors of linear combinations of forecasts. These confidence regions are particularly useful for designing tests of super exogeneity via tests of predictive failure. To illustrate the use of confidence intervals, forecasts are generated for an oil price and for a Venezuelan consumer price index.

1 Introduction

Knowing the potential future evolution of economic variables allows policy makers to anticipate undesirable economic situations and thereby to implement policies that would change the path of economic variables. However, knowledge in economics is not exact, so policies must be based on variables'

---

* The views in this paper do not necessarily coincide with those of the Banco Central de Venezuela. I am grateful to R. Campos, N. R. Ericsson, M. Nerlove, and an anonymous referee for valuable comments, and to L. Barrow and R. Zerpa for help in preparing the graphs. However, I am solely responsible for any errors.

Reprinted with permission from the *Journal of Policy Modeling* (August 1992), 14, 4, 535–560.

forecasts, which are subject to uncertainty. Forecasts are not exact, and all we know is that a particular future observation ought to lie between two values with some probability. Those two values, together with that associated probability, define a confidence interval, which can be derived using statistical techniques.

Forecast confidence intervals themselves, as well as the ex ante forecasts, may be informative to policy makers. To illustrate, consider a country like Venezuela, which earns its international reserves almost entirely from exports of oil. Suppose that the country requires \$10,000 million to pay for imports, [536] that a crude oil price of \$30 a barrel provides \$12,000 million, and that the short-run price elasticity of oil is low. Forecasting that oil prices will be \$29–\$34 a barrel with a 95-percent probability in the near future will very likely lead decision makers to keep related policies unchanged. On the other hand, policy makers may be inclined to implement policies to cover excess imports if oil prices were forecast to lie between \$15 and \$20 a barrel with a 95-percent probability. Finally, a 95-percent confidence interval of \$10–\$60 a barrel would indicate great uncertainty, and could induce yet different policies, depending upon the policy-makers' attitude towards risk.

Lucas (1976) questions the use of econometric models for policy analysis when the processes of the forcing variables change. However, we do not know for sure whether those processes have actually changed and, even if they have, whether those changes have affected the parameters of our econometric model. Forecasts provide us with indirect information on whether the Lucas critique applies by allowing us to test for parameter constancy [see Hendry (1988)]. The distribution of forecasts can be used to define suitable statistics for testing parameter constancy. These statistics can be applied to both the estimated process of the forcing (or control) variables and to the econometric model, in which the latter has the forcing variables as determinants. If the forcing-variable process appears empirically nonconstant but the econometric model is constant, then this is evidence that the econometric model can be used validly for policy simulation, i.e., that the forcing variables are "super exogenous" for the interventions that occurred in sample [Engle, Hendry, and Richard (1983) and Hendry (1988)].

Even for a linear model, derivation of the forecast-based test statistics requires assumptions on the distribution of the model's innovations. Further, obtaining exact results is not straightforward, so authors have resorted to using large sample theory, even though the latter renders only approximate results [usually to $o_p(T^{-1/2})$]. Schmidt (1974) finds the asymptotic distribution of a vector of forecast errors for a system of dynamic equations with exogenous variables [see also Chong and Hendry (1986)]. Yamamoto (1976) finds the asymptotic mean square error of the h-step ahead predictor of a variable from a pure autoregressive (AR) model. Baillie (1979a) derives it for variables from models with AR disturbances and fixed, stochastic, or both kinds of regressors. That leads to an autoregressive distributed lag (AD) model, generalizing Yamamoto's results. Baillie (1979b) extends the former derivation to a multivariate AR process [see also Reinsel (1980)]. Ya-mamoto (1980) obtains the asymptotic distribution of the multi-step ahead prediction error for a simultaneous dynamic model with either AR or moving average (MA) disturbances, assuming known future values of the exogenous variables. Yamamoto (1981) derives the asymptotic mean square error of the h-step forecast for a multivariate autoregressive moving average of order (p, q) [(ARMA(p, q)] model.

    This paper extends Yamamoto's (1980, 1981) results in three complemen-tary ways. First, we extend Yamamoto (1981) by including variables with known future values, thereby allowing for constants and seasonals, which are common in econometric models. Second, we extend Yamamoto (1980) by allowing for exogenous variables with unknown future values. Under the as-sumptions made, that leads to a multivariate ARMA process with exogenous variables (ARMAX) of the kind addressed by Yamamoto (1981). However, the matrices involved in this ARMAX process are special. They contain a number of zeros, and their other elements are implicit functions of the model's reduced form parameters. Hence, we can find simple expressions for those matrices, writing them as linear functions of those parameters. By doing this, we can obtain their covariance matrix directly by estimat-ing separately the two original systems of equations: that of the variables of interest and that of the strongly exogenous variables with unknown fu-ture values. Joint estimation would require a large number of observations, which generally is not available. Third, available econometric models may yield forecasts at a periodicity or in a functional form different from that of interest to policy makers. Thus, the asymptotic distribution of linear com-binations of forecasts is derived, from which we can obtain corresponding confidence intervals.

    Section 2 describes the model, and presents three lemmas and a the-orem on the properties of that model's forecasts. Section 3 illustrates the resulting formulas with models of an oil price and a Venezuelan CPI. Appen-dices A–E prove the lemmas and theorem, Appendix F describes the data, and Appendix G summarizes the notation in Section 2 and the appendices. Sections 2 and 3 are reasonably modular, so a reader primarily interested in applying the results can skip directly to Section 3, referring to Section 2 as necessary.

2 The Model, the Predictor, and the Predictor's Distribution

We wish to consider forecasting future values of endogenous variables from an ARMAX model. Each strongly exogenous variable in that model may have either known or unknown future values. We assume that the strongly exogenous variables with unknown future values are generated by a separate ARMAX process. Because forecasts are computed from reduced form equations, we express the system as a moving average with exogenous variables (MAX), and specify the optimal linear predictor in terms of observed data. Thus, the forecast error is written in terms of observed variables, and estimators whose asymptotic distributions are known. From these results, we can straightforwardly derive the asymptotic distribution of a linear combination of a vector of forecast errors and its corresponding confidence intervals. This section describes the model, the predictor, and the predictor's distribution, relegating proofs to appendices.

[538]

Let us assume that the econometric model in its structural form is ARMAX:

$$B_0 z_t = \sum_{i=1}^{p_1} B_i z_{t-i} + \sum_{i=0}^{p_2} C_i^{+} x_{t-i}^{+} + C_0 x_{1t} + \varphi_t, \tag{1}$$

where z_t, x_t^{+}, and x_{1t} are respectively n_1 endogenous variables, n_2 strongly exogenous variables whose future values are unknown, and K_1 strongly exogenous variables whose values over the forecast period are known exactly, all at time t. The B_i's, C_i^{+}'s, and C_0 are matrices of parameters of dimensions $n_1 \times n_1$, $n_1 \times n_2$, and $n_1 \times K_1$, respectively. B_0 is nonsingular, and φ_t is an n_1 column vector of disturbances normally and independently distributed with zero mean and variance covariance matrix Σ_φ.

The system generating the exogenous variables x_t^{+} is also assumed to be ARMAX:

$$\sum_{i=0}^{p_3} \Phi_i x_{t-i}^{+} = \Upsilon x_{2t} + \sum_{j=0}^{q} \Theta_j \mu_{t-j}, \tag{2}$$

where x_{2t} is a vector of the tth observation on K_2 strongly exogenous variables with known future values. The Φ_i's and Θ_i's are $n_2 \times n_2$ matrices with $\Phi_0 = \Theta_0 = I_{n_2}$ (without loss of generality), Υ is an $n_2 \times K_2$ matrix, μ_t is an n_2 column-vector of innovations normally and independently distributed with zero mean and variance covariance matrix Σ_μ, and $E(\varphi_t \mu_s') = 0$ for all t, s.

In what follows, (1) and (2) are written as a single system in MAX representation, thereby relating the full set of modeled variables y_t $[= (z_t' : x_t^{+\prime})']$ to the exogenous variables with known future values x_t

$[= (x'_{1t} : x'_{2t})']$ and a disturbance e_t. From that relationship, we derive optimal predictors and their asymptotic distribution, and define confidence intervals. Lemma 1 provides the MAX representation.

Lemma 1 *Assuming stationarity, the systems in (1) and (2) have the following MAX representation:* [539]

$$y_t = \Gamma_1(L)e_t + \Gamma_2(L)x_t, \tag{3}$$

where $\Gamma_1(L)$ and $\Gamma_2(L)$ are matrices of one-sided polynomials in the lag operator L. (See Appendix A.)

The MAX representation in (3) expresses y_t as a function of present and past reduced form shocks (e_{t-k}), and present and past known values of the set of exogenous variables with known future values (x_{t-k}). From (3), we can straightforwardly derive the optimal linear predictor.

Let us assume we wish to forecast observation y_{N+h} ($N \geq T$, $h > 0$), where T is the sample size used for estimating the parameters in (1) and (2), and y_t and x_t are known through time N and $N + h$ respectively. From (3), the $(N + h)$th observation is:

$$y_{N+h} = \Gamma_1(L)e_{N+h} + \Gamma_2(L)x_{N+h}, \tag{4}$$

so we can state the following lemma.

Lemma 2 *Conditional upon past observations and all known values of x, the optimal linear predictor of the $(N + h)$th observation y_{N+h} is:*

$$y_{N,h} = \Gamma_1^{**}(L)e_N + \Gamma_2(L)x_{N+h}, \tag{5}$$

where $\Gamma_1^{**}(L)$ is a matrix of polynomials in L. (See Appendix B.)

The forecasts in (5) depend upon the unobserved disturbances, so it is useful to re-express the latter in terms of observed data. Solving for the disturbances in (3), we obtain:

$$e_t = \Psi_1(L)y_t + \Psi_2(L)x_t, \tag{6}$$

where

$$\Psi_1(L) = I_n + \sum_{k=1}^{\infty} H'F^{k-1}(F - A)HL^k \tag{7}$$

and

$$\Psi_2(L) = -\sum_{k=0}^{\infty} H'F^k HCL^k, \tag{8}$$

for suitable matrices H, F, A, and C, defined in Appendix A.

Thus, from (6), the optimal predictor in (5) can be written as:

$$y_{N,h} = [\Gamma_2(L)x_{N+h} + \Gamma_1^{**}(L)\Psi_2(L)x_N] + \Gamma_1^{**}(L)\Psi_1(L)y_N$$

$$= \delta(L)x_N + \eta(L)y_N, \tag{9}$$

[540] where

$$\delta(L) = \sum_{k=-h}^{-1} H'A^{h+k}HCL^k + \sum_{k=0}^{\infty} H'A^{h-1}F^{k+1}HCL^k \tag{10}$$

(see Appendix C), and similarly,

$$\eta(L) = \sum_{k=0}^{\infty} H'A^{h-1}F^k(A-F)HL^k, \qquad h \geq 1. \tag{11}$$

The optimal predictor in (9) is a function of unknown parameters. Hence, we define the feasible predictor as:

$$\hat{y}_{N,h} = \hat{\delta}(L)x_N + \hat{\eta}(L)y_N. \tag{12}$$

The polynomials $\hat{\delta}(L)$ and $\hat{\eta}(L)$ are $\delta(L)$ and $\eta(L)$ with their unknown parameters replaced by suitable estimates.

Equations (3), (5), and (12) express the unknown future value y_{N+h}, its optimal predictor $y_{N,h}$, and its feasible predictor $\hat{y}_{N,h}$ in terms of observables and disturbances. From these equations, we derive the forecast error in terms of disturbances over the forecast period, observables, and estimates of the model parameters.

Lemma 3 *The error in forecasting observation y_{N+h} is:*

$$y_{N+h} - \hat{y}_{N,h} \cong \varepsilon_{(h)} + W_{(h)}Q_{(h)}SM(\hat{\beta} - \beta), \tag{13}$$

where $\varepsilon_{(h)}$ is a vector of disturbances, $W_{(h)}$ depends on observables, $Q_{(h)}$ and M are functions of estimated parameters, S is a selection matrix, and β is the vector of reduced form parameters. (See Appendix D.)

Using Lemma 3, the vector of m prediction errors is:

$$y - \hat{y} \cong \varepsilon + P(\hat{\beta} - \beta), \tag{14}$$

where

$$(y - \hat{y})' = [(y_{N+1} - \hat{y}_{N,1})' \cdots (y_{N+m} - \hat{y}_{N,m})'],$$

$$\varepsilon' = \left[\varepsilon'_{(1)} \cdots \varepsilon'_{(m)}\right], \text{ and}$$

$$P' = M'S' \left[Q'_{(1)}W'_{(1)} \cdots Q'_{(m)}W'_{(m)}\right].$$

Lemma 3 leads to the following theorem, which describes the distribution of the forecast errors and the confidence region for linear combinations of future observations.

Theorem *Let us assume we wish to forecast m observations,*   [541]

$$(y_{N+1} \cdots y_{N+m})'.$$

(i) The vector of forecast errors is approximately normally distributed:

$$(y - \hat{y}) \underset{app}{\sim} \mathsf{N}\left(0, \left[\Lambda + \frac{\mathrm{plim}P\Omega P'}{T}\right]\right), \qquad (15)$$

where $\Lambda = \mathcal{E}(\varepsilon\varepsilon')$ is the variance covariance matrix of ε, and Ω is the asymptotic covariance matrix of $\hat{\beta}$.

(ii) A confidence region for the vector of linear combinations of future observations is given by:

$$\mathrm{Prob}\left[(y - \hat{y})'D'\Sigma_f^{-1}D(y - \hat{y}) \leq \chi_\alpha^2\right] \cong 1 - \alpha, \qquad (16)$$

where D is an $r \times nm$ matrix of fixed elements, χ_α^2 is the critical point in the χ_r^2 distribution corresponding to the significance level α, and

$$\Sigma_f = D(\Lambda + T^{-1}\mathrm{plim}P\Omega P')D'.$$

(iii) In particular, the confidence interval for a linear combination of future observations $d_i'y$ is given by:

$$\mathrm{Prob}\left[d_i'\hat{y} - Z_{\alpha/2}\nu^{1/2} \leq d_i'y \leq d_i'\hat{y} + Z_{\alpha/2}\nu^{1/2}\right] \cong 1 - \alpha, \qquad (17)$$

where d_i' is the i-th row of D, α is the confidence level, $Z_{\alpha/2}$ is the $\alpha/2$ quantile of the normal distribution, and ν is the (i,i)th element in Σ_f.

Part (ii) of the theorem *inter alia* implies that the mean square forecast error (MSFE) is not invariant to linear transformations of the variables being forecast, noting that the diagonal elements of Σ_f in general depend on D. Further, the ranking of empirical MSFEs across models is not invariant to the choice of transformation. For instance, one model may have the smallest MSFE for the changes of a given variable, when compared against several other models. Yet, that same model could have the largest MSFE for the levels of the same variable, even over the same sample period, against the same models, and based on the same underlying forecasts. The reason is that the MSFE ignores the off-diagonal elements of the empirical equivalent to Σ_f. The solution is to look at Σ_f in its entirety, rather than certain pieces of it. See Hendry (1994) for further details.

3 Two Simple Examples

In the following examples, we entertain AR(1) models for the price of Texas Intermediate crude oil and Venezuelan inflation. Both models are mis-specified, thereby allowing us to illustrate the value of constructing fore- [542] cast confidence intervals (a) in testing against specification errors and (b) in evaluating the usefulness of such a model for policy. In Section 3.1, we forecast changes in the logarithm of monthly oil prices, quarterly averages of those changes, the logarithm, and the price itself. Section 3.2 computes monthly and quarterly forecasts for Venezuelan inflation and for the underlying monthly CPI. (See Appendix F for data description.) Both models are AR(1) in the change in the logarithm of the relevant price, so we begin by specifying that model, giving the expressions for the forecasts and for all matrices relevant to computing the covariance matrix of forecast errors.

Denoting monthly changes in logarithms of prices by y_t, the AR(1) model with drift is:

$$(1 - \alpha_1 L)y_t = \alpha_0 + e_t \qquad e_t \sim \mathsf{IN}(0, \sigma_e^2), \tag{18}$$

which is (3) [and also (1)] with $A = \alpha_1$, $F = 0$, $C = \alpha_0$, $H = 1$, $y_t = z_t$, $x_t = x_{1t} = 1 \ (\forall t)$, and $\Sigma_e = \sigma_e^2$. Because $F = 0$, $\delta(L) = \alpha_0 \sum_{k=-h}^{-1} \alpha_1^{k+h} L^k$, and $\eta(L) = \alpha_1^h$, it follows that the h-step forecast is:

$$\hat{y}_{N,h} = \hat{\alpha}_0 \sum_{i=0}^{h-1} \hat{\alpha}_1^i + \hat{\alpha}_1^h y_N, \tag{19}$$

which tends to the estimated unconditional mean $\hat{\alpha}_0/(1 - \hat{\alpha}_1)$ as the forecast horizon $h \to \infty$.

Defining $\hat{\beta} - \beta = (\hat{\alpha}_1 - \alpha_1 : \hat{\alpha}_0 - \alpha_0)'$ and taking $J = 1$, the $(h + 4)$ row vector $W_{(h)}$ is $(1\ 1 \ldots 1\ y_N\ y_{N-1})$ and the $(h + 4) \times 3$ matrix $Q_{(h)}$ is:

$$Q_{(h)} = \begin{bmatrix} 0 & 0 & 1 \\ \hat{\alpha}_0 \sum_{i=0}^0 \alpha_1^{0-i}\hat{\alpha}_1^i & 0 & \alpha_1 \\ \vdots & \vdots & \vdots \\ \hat{\alpha}_0 \sum_{i=0}^{h-2} \alpha_1^{h-2-i}\hat{\alpha}_1^i & 0 & \alpha_1^{h-1} \\ 0 & \hat{\alpha}_0\alpha_1^{h-1} & 0 \\ 0 & 0 & 0 \\ \sum_{i=0}^{h-1} \alpha_1^{h-1-i}\hat{\alpha}_1^i & -\alpha_1^{h-1} & 0 \\ 0 & \hat{\alpha}_1\alpha_1^{h-1} & 0 \end{bmatrix} \qquad h = 2, 3, \ldots, m. \tag{20}$$

[543]   The matrix $Q_{(1)}$ is $Q_{(h)}$ but missing rows 2 through h. In addition, Λ is a symmetric matrix with elements $\Lambda_{ij} = \sigma_e^2 \left(\alpha_1^{j-i} \sum_{\ell=1}^i \alpha_1^{2(\ell-1)} \right)$ for $j \geq i$. The matrix $S \cdot M$ is a 3×2 matrix of zeros except for its elements $(1,1)$ and $(3,2)$, which are unity.

From the estimates of $(\alpha_0 : \alpha_1)'$, their covariance matrix Ω, the starting value y_N, and the expressions for $Q_{(h)}$, $W_{(h)}$, S, M, and Λ, we can compute forecasts of monthly changes in log prices and the covariance matrix of the forecast errors. As $h \to \infty$, the contribution of parameter uncertainty to the variance of the hth forecast error tends to:

$$\frac{\left[\dfrac{\hat{\alpha}_0}{(1-\hat{\alpha}_1)^2}\right]^2 V(\hat{\alpha}_1) + 2\left[\dfrac{\hat{\alpha}_0}{(1-\hat{\alpha}_1)^3}\right] Cov(\hat{\alpha}_0, \hat{\alpha}_1) + \left[\dfrac{1}{1-\hat{\alpha}_1}\right]^2 V(\hat{\alpha}_0)}{T}.$$

3.1 Confidence Intervals for the Price of Texas Intermediate Crude Oil

Let us denote changes in the logarithms of the oil price by Δop. Its h-step ahead forecast is (19), with y replaced by Δop. The covariance matrix of the m corresponding forecast errors can be computed from Λ, $W_{(h)}$, $Q_{(h)}$, S, and M, defined above.

The model in (18) is estimated by OLS from 1984(4) through 1989(12), yielding:

$$\widehat{\Delta op}_t = \underset{(0.21)}{0.26} \Delta op_{t-1} - \underset{(0.010)}{0.004}$$

$T = 1984(4)\text{--}1989(12) \quad R^2 = 0.07 \quad \hat{\sigma} = 8.69\% \quad Cov(\hat{\alpha}_0, \hat{\alpha}_1) = 0.000085$

$\eta_1(5, 62) = 0.58 \quad \eta_2(2, 64) = 3.75 \quad \xi_1(2) = 55.32 \quad \eta_3(15, 67) = 2.08$

$\xi_2(15)/15 = 2.18$.

The numbers below the equation's coefficients are White's standard errors, and $Cov(\hat{\alpha}_0, \hat{\alpha}_1)$ is the covariance between $\hat{\alpha}_0$ and $\hat{\alpha}_1$. $\hat{\sigma}$ is the standard error of the regression. The η and ξ statistics are distributed as F and χ^2 distributions under the null hypothesis of correct specification, with the degrees of freedom indicated in parentheses. Except for residual correlation (η_1), the model fails to satisfy all the test criteria, which are against: heteroscedasticity (η_2); non-normality (ξ_1); and parameter nonconstancy (the Chow statistic η_3 and the χ^2 forecast statistic ξ_2). This is despite a very small R^2.

From the change in oil prices for 1988(12), and the estimates of α_0, α_1, and their covariance matrix Ω, we compute h-step ahead forecasts of changes in the logarithms of oil prices and the covariance matrix of the corresponding forecast errors, for January 1990 through March 1991. Figure 1 plots actual and h-step ahead forecasts, and the confidence bands for actual monthly [544] changes in oil prices, scaled by 100 to obtain percentages. Forecasts and their standard errors reach their limit values rapidly due to the small value of $\hat{\alpha}_1$.

The confidence bands show that the AR(1) model substantially underpredicts August 1990 and, to a lesser extent, September 1990. This is not surprising because there is nothing in the model to pick up the effect of the Gulf War, which started in August 1990. The model also over-predicts February 1991. Both episodes suggest mis-specification. However, h-step ahead forecast errors must be interpreted with care because they are not

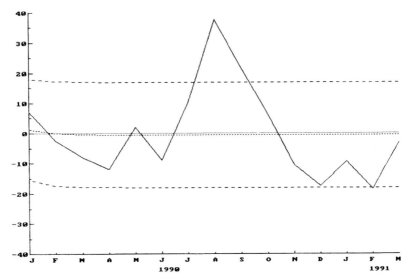

FIGURE 1. Monthly changes in the logarithm of oil prices (×100):
actual values (—), forecasts (···), and confidence bands (– – –).

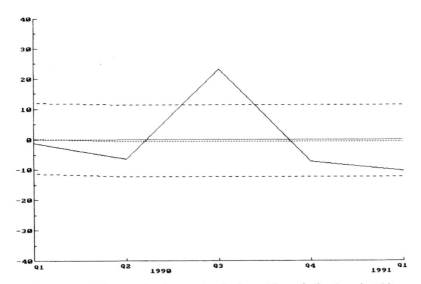

FIGURE 2. Quarterly changes in the logarithm of oil prices (×100,
at monthly rates): actual values (—), forecasts (···), and confidence bands (– – –).

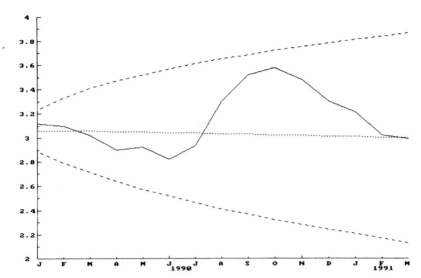

FIGURE 3. The logarithm of oil prices: actual values (—), fore-casts (···), and confidence bands (– – –).

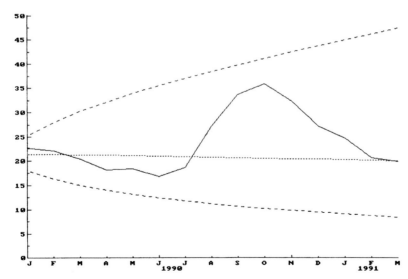

FIGURE 4. Oil prices (US$/barrel): actual values (—), fore-casts (···), and confidence bands (– – –).

independent, as they are linear combinations of 1-step ahead forecast errors. Chong and Hendry (1986) derive the joint test statistic for h-step ahead forecasts, which is:

$$\xi_4(nm) \;=\; (y - \hat{y})' \left(\Lambda + \frac{\operatorname{plim} P\Omega P'}{T} \right)^{-1} (y - \hat{y}).$$

If the parameters were constant, ξ_4 would be approximately distributed as a χ^2 with nm degrees of freedom. Here, $\xi_4(15) = 33.68$, suggesting that the parameters are nonconstant.

In policy making, future observations are unknown, in which case confidence intervals provide an ex ante measure of the forecasts' uncertainty. The results in Figure 1 show that, with a probability of 0.95, actual monthly changes in oil prices from January 1990 to March 1991 could lie between -18.0 and $+18.0$ percent. This confidence interval is large, partly because of mis-specification. However, even correctly specified models may render wide confidence intervals for future observations.

We may also be interested in forecasts of the *average* change in the oil
[545] price over the quarter. To calculate those forecasts and their confidence intervals, D is defined as a 5×15 selection matrix of zeros and $\frac{1}{3}$'s, where the latter elements average the required elements of the vector of monthly forecasts. The results are plotted in Figure 2. With 95-percent probability, quarterly oil price inflation should lie between -12.0 and $+12.0$ percent (at monthly rates). Again, the model under-predicts in the third quarter of 1990.

Instead of changes in logarithms of oil prices, let us now consider computing paths for the *logarithms* of monthly prices. The linear combination is defined by a lower triangular D matrix with all its nonzero elements being unity. Thus, the vector of price forecasts is:

$$(\widehat{op}_{N,1} \ldots \widehat{op}_{N,15})' \;=\; D \cdot (\widehat{\Delta op}_{N,1} \ldots \widehat{\Delta op}_{N,15})' + op_N \cdot \iota,$$

where N is 1989(12) and $\iota' = (1 \ldots 1)$. The confidence interval for h periods ahead is:

$$\left(op_N + \sum_{i=1}^{h} \widehat{\Delta op}_{N,i} \right) \pm 1.96 \nu_h^{1/2},$$

where ν_h is the variance of the h-step ahead forecast error of the logarithms of oil prices, which is the sum of variances and covariances of forecast errors of changes in log oil prices up to time $N + h$, inclusive. Hence, ν_h increases with h unless negative covariances offset the values of the newly added variances. So, confidence intervals for prices are likely to become wider as the forecast horizon increases. Figure 3 shows that they do for this example.

Confidence intervals for monthly prices themselves can be computed from forecasts of their logarithms, although price forecasts so obtained may be biased. Those intervals are: [546]

$$\left[\exp \left\{ op_N + \sum_{i=1}^{h} \widehat{\Delta op}_{N,i} + \nu_h^{1/2} g_1 \right\} ; \ \exp \left\{ op_N + \sum_{i=1}^{h} \widehat{\Delta op}_{N,i} + \nu_h^{1/2} g_2 \right\} \right],$$

where g_1 and g_2 are two values such that:

$$\nu_h^{1/2} + \frac{g_2 + g_1}{2} = 0,$$

and

$$\int_{g_1}^{g_2} (2\pi)^{-1/2} e^{-v^2/2} dv = \gamma,$$

and where γ is the probability associated to the interval, e.g., $\gamma = 0.95$. For these confidence intervals to be optimal, g_1 must be different from g_2 in absolute value. Nonetheless, for this example, we chose $g_2 = -g_1 = 1.96$ for computational ease. Figure 4 plots actual and h-step ahead forecasts of oil prices with these confidence intervals.

3.2 Confidence Intervals for Venezuelan Inflation
[547]

Let us denote Venezuelan inflation by Δp, defined as the change in the logarithm of the monthly consumer price index for Caracas. We construct forecasts and confidence intervals for monthly and quarterly inflation, for the logarithms of prices, and for prices.

Estimating (18) by OLS, we obtain:

$$\widehat{\Delta p_t} = \begin{array}{cc} 0.40 \ \Delta p_{t-1} + & 0.004 \\ (0.09) & (0.001) \end{array}$$

$T = 1968(4)\text{--}1983(12) \quad R^2 = 0.16 \quad \hat{\sigma} = 0.6\% \quad Cov(\hat{\alpha}_0, \hat{\alpha}_1) = -0.00003$
$\eta_1(7, 180) = 2.66 \quad \eta_2(2, 184) = 6.02 \quad \xi_1(2) = 223.21 \quad \eta_3(24, 187) = 2.16$
$\xi_2(24)/24 = 2.17.$

These results suggest that there is residual correlation, heteroscedasticity, non-normality, and parameter nonconstancy.

Figure 5 shows actual and h-step ahead inflation forecasts and the confidence bands for actual inflation from January 1984 to December 1985, scaled by 100 to obtain percentages. The model substantially under-predicts inflation for April and September 1984. Large price increases occurred in the second half of 1984 due to exchange rate changes and the removal of subsidies on some goods. Our simple AR(1) model does not pick up those effects. Chong and Hendry's (1986) statistic $\xi_4(24)$ is 52.5. From Figure 5, actual monthly inflation should lie between a small negative value and 2 percent per month, with 95-percent probability. Hence, assuming our model were correctly specified and the decision maker were risk-averse, he might decide to implement policies to control inflation. Figure 6 shows that the model

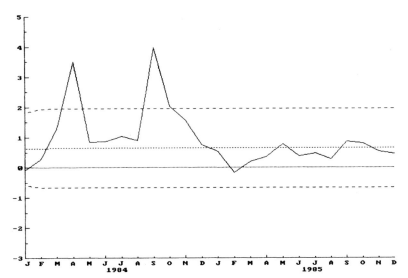

FIGURE 5. Monthly inflation (percent): actual values (—), forecasts (···), and confidence bands (- - -).

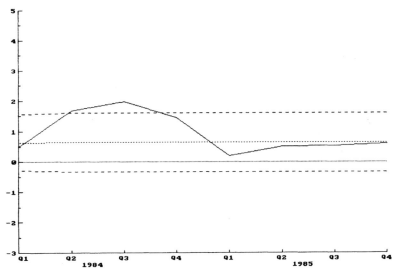

FIGURE 6. Quarterly inflation (percent, at monthly rates): actual values (—), forecasts (···), and confidence bands (- - -).

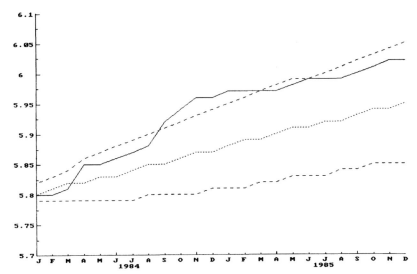

FIGURE 7. The logarithm of the consumer price index: actual values (—), forecasts (···), and confidence bands (– – –).

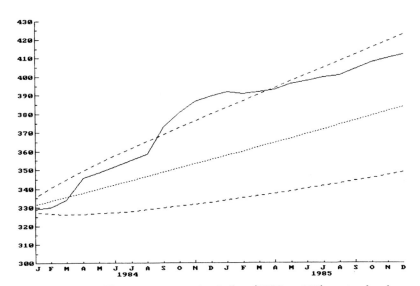

FIGURE 8. The consumer price index (1968 = 100): actual values (—), forecasts (···), and confidence bands (– – –).

under-predicts average quarterly inflation for the second and third quarters
[548] of 1984. With 95-percent probability, quarterly inflation at monthly rates
should lie between -0.3 and $+1.6$ percent. Figure 7 plots the results for the
logarithms of the consumer price index: confidence intervals increase with
the forecast horizon. Figure 8 shows comparable results for the consumer
price index itself.

4   Conclusion

Confidence intervals for future observations of economic variables are defined, based on their forecasts and the distribution of forecast errors. Those
forecasts are obtained from a dynamic simultaneous equations econometric
model (potentially) including two sets of exogenous variables: those with
known future values and those whose forecasts must be computed. A stationary and invertible ARMAX process is assumed to generate the latter set
of variables.

[549]   Confidence intervals show decision makers the most likely future paths of
economic variables, thereby helping them implement policies suitable for at-
taining economic goals. However, the closeness of the *calculated* confidence
intervals to the *unknown* exact confidence intervals will depend upon the
model, the sample size, the estimator employed, and the region of the parameter space. Furthermore, the independence and normality of the disturbances, the consistency and asymptotic normality of the estimators, together
with the exogeneity of x_t^+ all underpin the validity of the confidence intervals
for sample sizes available in econometric studies of time series. Conversely,
confidence intervals themselves may provide us with evidence on whether or
not those assumptions are satisfied.

Appendix A.   Proof of Lemma 1

Ex ante forecasts and their standard errors are based upon the reduced
form of (1) and (2), which we write in a compact form as the multivariate
ARMAX(p, q) process:

$$
\begin{cases}
A_0^* y_t = A_1^* y_{t-1} + \cdots + A_p^* y_{t-p} + C_0^* x_t + \omega_t \\
\\
\omega_t = \psi_t + F_1^* \psi_{t-1} + \cdots + F_q^* \psi_{t-q},
\end{cases}
\tag{A1}
$$

where $p = \max(p_1, p_2, p_3)$, $B_i = 0$ if $i > p_1$, $C_i^+ = 0$ if $i > p_2$, and $\Phi_i = 0$ if
[550] $i > p_3$; and $y_t = (z_t' \, x_t^{+\prime})'$, $x_t = (x_{1t}' \, x_{2t}')'$, and $\psi_t = (\varphi_t' \, \mu_t')'$. For $n \equiv n_1 + n_2$
and $K \equiv K_1 + K_2$, then A_i^*, C_0^*, and F_i^* are $n \times n$, $n \times K$, and $n \times n$ matrices
as follows:

$$A_0^* = \begin{bmatrix} B_0 & -C_0^+ \\ 0 & I_{n_2} \end{bmatrix},$$

$$A_i^* = \begin{bmatrix} B_i & C_i^+ \\ 0 & -\Phi_i \end{bmatrix} \qquad i = 1, \ldots, p,$$

$$C_0^* = \text{diag}(C_0 \, \Upsilon) \qquad n_2 \geq 1, \text{ and}$$

$$F_i^* = \text{diag}(0, \Theta_i) \qquad i = 1, \ldots, q.$$

$A_i^* = B_i$ and $C_0^* = C_0$ for $n_2 = 0$.

Hence, the reduced form of (A1) is the ARMAX(p, q) process:

$$\begin{cases} y_t = A_1 y_{t-1} + \cdots + A_p y_{t-p} + C x_t + u_t \\ \\ u_t = e_t + F_1 e_{t-1} + \cdots + F_q e_{t-q}, \end{cases} \qquad (A2)$$

where $A_i = (A_0^*)^{-1} A_i^*$ $(i = 1, \ldots, p)$, $C = (A_0^*)^{-1} C_0^*$, $u_t = A_0^{*-1} \omega_t$, $F_i = (A_0^*)^{-1} F_i^* A_0^*$ $(i = 1, \ldots, q)$, and $e_t = (A_0^*)^{-1} \psi_t$.

Defining $A(L) = \sum_{j=0}^{p} A_j L^j$ and $F(L) = \sum_{j=0}^{q} F_j L^j$ with $A_0 = F_0 = I_n$, then the model in (A2) can be written as follows:

$$A(L) y_t = F(L) e_t + C x_t. \qquad (A3)$$

Assuming that all roots of $A(L)$ lie outside the unit circle, the MAX representation of (A3) is:

$$y_t = \Gamma_1(L) e_t + \Gamma_2(L) x_t, \qquad (A4)$$

where

$$\Gamma_1(L) = I_n + \sum_{k=1}^{\infty} H' A^{k-1} (A - F) H L^k \qquad (A5)$$

[see Yamamoto (1981)]. The polynomial $\Gamma_2(L)$ can be derived by following the same lines of the proof for $\Gamma_1(L)$, yielding:

$$\Gamma_2(L) = \sum_{k=0}^{\infty} H' A^k H C L^k. \qquad (A6)$$

Also, $H' = (I_n \; 0)$ is an $n \times ns$ matrix; and: [551]

$$A = \begin{bmatrix} A_1 & I_n & 0 & \cdots & 0 \\ A_2 & 0 & I_n & \cdots & 0 \\ \vdots & \vdots & \vdots & \ddots & \vdots \\ A_{s-1} & 0 & 0 & \cdots & I_n \\ A_s & 0 & 0 & \cdots & 0 \end{bmatrix}$$

and

$$
F = \begin{bmatrix}
-F_1 & I_n & 0 & \cdots & 0 \\
-F_2 & 0 & I_n & \cdots & 0 \\
\vdots & \vdots & \vdots & \ddots & \vdots \\
-F_{s-1} & 0 & 0 & \cdots & I_n \\
-F_s & 0 & 0 & \cdots & 0
\end{bmatrix}
$$

are $ns \times ns$ matrices with $s = \max(p,q)$.

Appendix B. The Optimal Predictor

The predictor that minimizes a positive definite quadratic form in the forecast error is shown to be the conditional expectation of the random variable we wish to forecast, given past information. Thus,

$$
y_{N,h} = \mathcal{E}(y_{N+h}|x_{N+h}, x_{N+h-1}, \ldots; e_N, e_{N-1}, \ldots). \tag{B1}
$$

Noting that:

$$
\Gamma_1(L) = \sum_{k=0}^{h-1} \Gamma_{1k}L^k + \sum_{k=0}^{\infty} \Gamma_{1,k+h}L^{k+h},
$$

we can write the $(N+h)$th observation in (4) as follows:

$$
y_{N+h} = \Gamma_1^*(L)e_{N+h} + \Gamma_1^{**}(L)e_N + \Gamma_2(L)x_{N+h}, \tag{B2}
$$

where

$$
\Gamma_1^*(L) = \sum_{k=0}^{h-1} \Gamma_{1k}L^k
$$

and

$$
\Gamma_1^{**}(L) = \sum_{k=0}^{\infty} \Gamma_{1,k+h}L^k. \tag{B3}
$$

Hence (B1) and (B2) imply that the optimal linear predictor of y_{N+h} is:

$$
\begin{aligned}
y_{N,h} &= \mathcal{E}(y_{N+h}|x_{N+h}, x_{N+h-1}, \ldots; e_N, e_{N-1}, \ldots) \\
&= \Gamma_2(L)x_{N+h} + \mathcal{E}(\Gamma_1^*(L)e_{N+h}|x_{N+h}, \ldots; e_N, e_{N-1}, \ldots) \\
&\quad + \mathcal{E}(\Gamma_1^{**}(L)e_N|x_{N+h}, x_{N+h-1}, \ldots; e_N, e_{N-1}, \ldots). \tag{B4}
\end{aligned}
$$

[552]   Because of the assumptions made on the systems in (1) and (2), the e's are serially independent and are independent of the x's, so that:

$$
\mathcal{E}(\Gamma_1^*(L)e_{N+h}|x_{N+h}, \ldots; e_N, e_{N-1}, \ldots) = \mathcal{E}(\Gamma_1^*(L)e_{N+h}) = 0
$$

and

$$\mathcal{E}(\Gamma_1^{**}(L)e_N|x_{N+h}, x_{N+h-1}, \ldots; e_N, e_{N-1}, \ldots) = \Gamma_1^{**}(L)e_N.$$

Thus, the optimal linear predictor in (B4) is:

$$y_{N,h} = \Gamma_1^{**}(L)e_N + \Gamma_2(L)x_{N+h}.$$

See Harvey (1981, pp. 159–160), who finds the optimal predictor for a pure ARMA model.

Appendix C. Derivation of the Lag Polynomial of x_N

Let us first find an expression for $\delta_2(L) = \Gamma_1^{**}(L)\Psi_2(L)$. From (8) and (B3),

$$\delta_2(L) = \Gamma_1^{**}(L)\Psi_2(L)$$

$$= \left(\sum_{k=0}^{\infty} \Gamma_{1,k+h} L^k\right)\left(\sum_{k=0}^{\infty} \Psi_{2k} L^k\right)$$

$$= \sum_{k=0}^{\infty} \delta_{2k} L^k,$$

where

$$\delta_{2k} = \sum_{j=0}^{h} \Gamma_{1,h+j}\Psi_{2,k-j}$$

$$= -H'A^{h-1}(A^{k+1} - F^{k+1})HC, \qquad (C1)$$

using the expressions of the Γ_1's and Ψ_2's in (A5) and (8) and noting that $(A - F)HH' = (A - F)$.

Finally, the whole polynomial of x_N in (9) can be written as follows:

$$\delta(L) = \sum_{k=0}^{h-1} \Gamma_{2k} L^{k-h} + \sum_{k=0}^{\infty}(\Gamma_{2,h+k} + \delta_{2k}) L^k.$$

From the definition of the Γ_{2k}'s and δ_{2k}'s in (A6) and (C1), we have:

$$\Gamma_{2,h+k} + \delta_{2k} = H'A^{h-1}F^{k+1}HC, \qquad (C2)$$

so that (A6) and (C2) yield: [553]

$$\delta(L) = \sum_{k=-h}^{-1} H'A^{h+k}HCL^k + \sum_{k=0}^{\infty} H'A^{h-1}F^{k+1}HCL^k.$$

Appendix D.   Proof of Lemma 3

From (4), (5), (9), and (12), the forecast error is:

$$
\begin{aligned}
y_{N+h} - \hat{y}_{N,h} &= (y_{N+h} - y_{N,h}) + (y_{N,h} - \hat{y}_{N,h}) \\
&= \left[\Gamma_1(L)L^{-h} - \Gamma_1^{**}(L)\right] e_N \\
&\quad - \left[\hat{\delta}(L) - \delta(L)\right] x_N - \left[\hat{\eta}(L) - \eta(L)\right] y_N. \quad (D1)
\end{aligned}
$$

We take the polynomials in the lag operator L in (D1) one by one. First, from (B3),

$$
\Gamma_1(L)L^{-h} - \Gamma_1^{**}(L) = \sum_{k=0}^{h-1} \Gamma_{1k} L^{k-h}. \quad (D2)
$$

Second, from (10),

$$
\mathrm{vec}[\hat{\delta}(L) - \delta(L)]x_N
$$

$$
\begin{aligned}
&\cong \mathrm{vec}\left[\sum_{k=-h}^{-1} (H'\hat{A}^{h+k}H\hat{C} - H'A^{h+k}HC)x_{N-k} \right. \\
&\qquad\quad \left. + \sum_{k=0}^{J}(H'\hat{A}^{h-1}\hat{F}^{k+1}H\hat{C} - H'A^{h-1}F^{k+1}HC)x_{N-k} \right] \\
&= \sum_{k=-h}^{-1} (x'_{N-k} \otimes I_n)\mathrm{vec}\left(H'\hat{A}^{h+k}H\hat{C} - H'A^{h+k}HC\right) \\
&\qquad\quad + \sum_{k=0}^{J}(x'_{N-k} \otimes I_n)\mathrm{vec}\left(H'\hat{A}^{h-1}\hat{F}^{k+1}H\hat{C} - H'A^{h-1}F^{k+1}HC\right), \quad (D3)
\end{aligned}
$$

where vec stands for a column vectoring operation and J is the maximal lag in this representation of $\delta(L)$. Third, and similarly, from (11),

$$
\mathrm{vec}[\hat{\eta}(L) - \eta(L)]y_N \cong
$$

$$
\sum_{k=0}^{J}(y'_{N-k} \otimes I_n)\mathrm{vec}\left[H'\hat{A}^{h-1}\hat{F}^{k}(\hat{A} - \hat{F})H - H'A^{h-1}F^{k}(A - F)H\right]. \quad (D4)
$$

Hence, from (D2), (D3), and (D4), the prediction error in (D1) is:

$$
y_{N+h} - \hat{y}_{N,h} \cong \varepsilon_{(h)} + W_{(h)}(\hat{a}_{(h)} - a_{(h)}), \quad (D5)
$$

where:

$$\varepsilon_{(h)} = \sum_{k=0}^{h-1} \Gamma_{1k} e_{N+h-k}, \tag{D6}$$

[554]

$$W_{(h)} = -\left[(x'_{N+h} \otimes I_n) \dots (x'_{N-J} \otimes I_n) \ (y'_N \otimes I_n) \dots (y'_{N-J} \otimes I_n) \right], \tag{D7}$$

and $(\hat{a}_{(h)} - a_{(h)})$ is a $(h + 2(J+1))$ column vector with

$$\mathrm{vec}(H'\hat{A}^i H\hat{C} - H'A^i HC) \qquad i = 0, \dots, h-1,$$

being its first h elements,

$$\mathrm{vec}(H'\hat{A}^{h-1}\hat{F}^i H\hat{C} - H'A^{h-1}F^i HC) \qquad i = 1, \dots, J+1,$$

being the next $(J+1)$ elements, and

$$\mathrm{vec}[H'\hat{A}^{h-1}\hat{F}^i(\hat{A} - \hat{F})H - H'A^{h-1}F^i(A - F)H] \qquad i = 0, \dots, J,$$

being the last $(J+1)$ elements.

For the first h rows of vecs in $(\hat{a}_{(h)} - a_{(h)})$, we have:

$$H'\hat{A}^\ell H\hat{C} - H'A^\ell HC$$

$$= H'(\hat{A}^\ell - A^\ell)H\hat{C} + H'A^\ell H(\hat{C} - C)$$

$$= H'A^\ell H(\hat{C} - C)$$

$$+ H'\sum_{j=0}^{\ell-1} \hat{A}^j(\hat{A} - A)A^{\ell-1-j}H\hat{C} \qquad \ell = 0, \dots, h-1, \tag{D8}$$

because

$$(\hat{A}^\ell - A^\ell) = \sum_{j=0}^{\ell-1} \hat{A}^j(\hat{A} - A)A^{\ell-1-j} \qquad \ell \geq 1, \tag{D9}$$

where only the first term in (D8) should appear for $\ell = 0$. For the following $(J+1)$ rows of vecs in $(\hat{a}_{(h)} - a_{(h)})$, we have:

$$H'\hat{A}^{h-1}\hat{F}^\ell H\hat{C} - H'A^{h-1}F^\ell HC$$

$$= H'(\hat{A}^{h-1} - A^{h-1})\hat{F}^\ell H\hat{C} + H'A^{h-1}(\hat{F}^\ell - F^\ell)H\hat{C}$$

$$+ H'A^{h-1}F^\ell H(\hat{C} - C)$$

$$= H'A^{h-1}F^\ell H(\hat{C} - C) + H'\sum_{j=0}^{h-2} \hat{A}^j(\hat{A} - A)A^{h-2-j}\hat{F}^\ell H\hat{C}$$

$$+ H'A^{h-1}\sum_{j=0}^{\ell-1} \hat{F}^j(\hat{F} - F)F^{\ell-1-j}H\hat{C} \qquad \ell = 1, \dots, J+1, \tag{D10}$$

where the first summation does not appear for $h = 1$. Finally, for the last $(J+1)$ rows:

$$H'\hat{A}^{h-1}\hat{F}^\ell(\hat{A} - \hat{F})H - H'A^{h-1}F^\ell(A - F)H$$

$$= H'(\hat{A}^{h-1} - A^{h-1})\hat{F}^\ell(\hat{A} - \hat{F})H$$

$$+ H'A^{h-1}(\hat{F}^\ell - F^\ell)(\hat{A} - \hat{F})H$$

$$+ H'A^{h-1}F^\ell[(\hat{A} - \hat{F}) - (A - F)]H$$

$$= H'A^{h-1}F^\ell[(\hat{A} - \hat{F}) - (A - F)]H$$

$$+ H'\sum_{j=0}^{h-2} \hat{A}^j(\hat{A} - A)A^{h-2-j}\hat{F}^\ell(\hat{A} - \hat{F})H$$

$$+ H'A^{h-1}\sum_{j=0}^{\ell-1} \hat{F}^j(\hat{F} - F)F^{\ell-1-j}(\hat{A} - \hat{F})H, \qquad \text{(D11)}$$

where the second term should not appear for $h = 1$ and the third term should
be deleted for $\ell = 0$. Using (D8), (D10), and (D11), $(\hat{a}_{(h)} - a_{(h)})$ is given by:

$$(\hat{a}_{(h)} - a_{(h)}) = Q_{(h)} \begin{bmatrix} \text{vec}(\hat{A} - A) \\ \text{vec}(\hat{F} - F) \\ \text{vec}(\hat{C} - C) \end{bmatrix}. \qquad \text{(D12)}$$

The matrix $Q_{(h)}$ is a 3-column partitioned matrix of size

$$[(J + h + 1)Kn + (J+1)n^2] \times (2n^2s^2 + Kn)$$

with its submatrices defined as:

$$Q_{(h)}(1,1) = 0, \qquad \text{(i)}$$

$$Q_{(h)}(\ell + 2, 1) = \sum_{j=0}^{\ell} [(A^{\ell-j}H\hat{C})' \otimes H'\hat{A}^j] \quad (\ell = 0, \ldots, h-2; h > 1), \qquad \text{(ii)}$$

$$Q_{(h)}(h + \ell, 1) = \sum_{j=0}^{h-2} [(A^{h-j-2}\hat{F}^\ell H\hat{C})' \otimes H'\hat{A}^j] \quad (\ell = 1, \ldots, J+1; h > 1), \text{(iii)}$$

$$Q_{(h)}(h + J + \ell + 1, 1) = (H' \otimes H'A^{h-1}F^{\ell-1})$$

$$+ \sum_{j=0}^{h-2} [(A^{h-j-2}\hat{F}^{\ell-1}(\hat{A} - \hat{F})H)' \otimes H'\hat{A}^j] \quad (\ell = 1, \ldots, J+1), \qquad \text{(iv)}$$

$$Q_{(h)}(i, 2) = 0 \quad (i = 1, \ldots, h), \qquad \text{(v)}$$

$$Q_{(h)}(h+\ell,2) = \sum_{j=0}^{\ell-1}[(F^{\ell-j-1}H\hat{C})' \otimes H'A^{h-1}\hat{F}^j] \quad (\ell=1,\ldots,J+1), \qquad \text{(vi)}$$

$$Q_{(h)}(h+J+2,2) = -(H' \otimes H'A^{h-1}), \qquad \text{(vii)}$$

$$Q_{(h)}(h+J+\ell+2,2) = -(H' \otimes H'A^{h-1}F^\ell)$$
$$+ \sum_{j=0}^{\ell-1}[(F^{\ell-j-1}(\hat{A}-\hat{F})H)' \otimes H'A^{h-1}F^j] \quad (\ell=1,\ldots,J), \qquad \text{(viii)}$$

$$Q_{(h)}(\ell+1,3) = (I_K \otimes H'A^\ell H) \quad (\ell=0,\ldots,h-1), \qquad \text{(ix)}$$

$$Q_{(h)}(h+\ell,3) = (I_K \otimes H'A^{h-1}F^\ell H) \quad (\ell=1,\ldots,J+1), \qquad \text{(x)}$$

$$Q_{(h)}(i+h+J+1,3) = 0 \quad (i=1,\ldots,J+1). \qquad \text{(xi)}$$

Expressions (i), (ii), (iii), (v), and (vi) are $(Kn \times n^2s^2)$ matrices; (iv), (vii), and (viii) are $(n^2 \times n^2s^2)$ matrices; (ix) and (x) are $(Kn \times Kn)$; and (xi) is an $(n^2 \times Kn)$ matrix. In addition, for $h=1$, (iii) is a matrix of zeros, and (ii) and the summation in (iv) do not appear.

The matrices A, F, and C contain a good number of zeros, and their other elements are nonlinear functions of the reduced form parameters of systems (1) and (2). We wish to write those functions explicitly in terms of those parameters so we can derive the variance covariance matrix. In doing so, we write: [556]

$$\hat{a}_{(h)} - a_{(h)} = Q_{(h)}SM(\hat{\beta} - \beta), \qquad \text{(D13)}$$

where β is the vector of parameters of the reduced form of system (1) and those of system (2). That is,

$$\beta = \left[(\text{vec}(B_0^{-1}B_1))' \ldots (\text{vec}(B_0^{-1}B_s))' \right.$$

$$(\text{vec}(B_0^{-1}C_0^+))' \ldots (\text{vec}(B_0^{-1}C_s^+))' \, (\text{vec}(B_0^{-1}C_0))'$$

$$\left. (\text{vec}\Phi_1)' \ldots (\text{vec } \Phi_s)' \, (\text{vec } \Theta_1)' \ldots (\text{vec } \Theta_s)' \, (\text{vec } \Upsilon)' \right]'.$$

The matrix S is $\text{diag}(S_A \ S_F \ S_C)$, which is of dimension:

$$[2n^2s^2 + nK] \times [s(n_1^2 + nn_2) + sn_2n + n_1K_1 + nK_2].$$

S_A, S_F, and S_C are selection matrices of zeros and ones picking up the nonzero elements in A, F, and C. Those matrices and the matrix M are defined as follows.

S_A is a 3×2 partitioned matrix of size $n^2s^2 \times s(n_1^2 + n_2n)$. Submatrices (1,2), (2,1), (3,1), and (3,2) are zero. Its (1,1)st submatrix consists of n_1s

submatrices of n_1^2 columns each. The (i,j)th of those submatrices is defined as the Kronecker product of an $s \times n_1$ matrix of zeros with a one in its (j,i)th position, and the $n \times n_1$ matrix $(I_{n_1}\ 0)'$. Its $(2,2)$nd submatrix is an $nn_2s \times nn_2s$ partitioned matrix of $2sn_2$ submatrices, defined as follows. The $(i,(2j+1))$th $(i = 1,\ldots,n_2;\ j = 0,\ldots,(s-1))$ submatrix is the Kronecker product of an $s \times n_2$ matrix of zeros with a one in its $(j+1,i)$th position, and the $n \times n_1$ matrix $(I_{n_1}\ 0)'$. The $(i,2j)$th $(i = 1,\ldots,n_2;\ j = 1,\ldots,s)$ submatrix is the Kronecker product of an $s \times n_2$ matrix of zeros with a one in its (j,i)th position, and the $n \times n_2$ matrix $(0\ I_{n_2})'$.

S_F is a 3×1 partitioned matrix of size $n^2s^2 \times sn_2n$ with all its submatrices being zero except for the $(3,2)$th one, which is of size $nn_2s \times nn_2s$ and consists of $2sn_2$ submatrices defined in the same way as the $(2,2)$nd element of S_A. S_F is not in S if $n_2 = 0$.

S_C is a 2×3 partitioned matrix of size $nK \times (n_1K_1 + nK_2)$ with its $(1,1)$st element being an $nK_1 \times n_1K_1$ matrix defined as $I_{K_1} \otimes (I_{n_1}\ 0)'$. Its $(2,2)$nd element is an $nK_2 \times n_1K_2$ matrix defined as $I_{K_2} \otimes (I_{n_1}\ 0)'$, and the $(2,3)$th is of size $nK_2 \times n_2K_2$ and defined as $I_{K_2} \otimes (0\ I_{n_2})'$.

M is a matrix of dimension:

$$(n_1^2s + 2nn_2s + n_1K_1 + nK_2) \times$$
$$[n_1^2s + n_1n_2(s+1) + n_1K_1 + 2n_2^2s + n_2K_2],$$

consisting of 24 submatrices, all of which are zero except for the following. The $(1,1)$st submatrix is of size $n_1^2s \times n_1^2s$ defined by $I_s \otimes I_{n_1^2}$. The $(2,2)$nd submatrix is of size $nn_2s \times n_1n_2(s+1)$, defined by two further submatrices: the $(1,1)$st is of size $nn_2s \times n_1n_2$ having all elements equal to zero except the $((2i+1),1)$ $(i = 0,1,\ldots,s-1)$, which are defined by $-(\hat{\Phi}'_{i+1} \otimes I_{n_1})$; and the $(1,2)$th submatrix is of size $nn_2s \times n_1n_2s$ defined as $I_s \otimes (I_{n_1n_2}\ 0)'$.

[557]   The $(2,4)$th and $(3,5)$th $(nn_2s \times n_2^2s)$ submatrices of M are defined as $I_s \otimes [-(I_{n_2} \otimes (B_0^{-1}C_0^+))\ -I_{n_2^2}]'$. The $(3,2)$th $nn_2s \times n_1n_2(s+1)$ submatrix is zero everywhere except at positions $(2i+1,1)$ $(i = 0,\ldots,s-1)$, which are $-(\hat{\Theta}'_{i+1} \otimes I_{n_1})$. The $(4,2)$th $(n_1K_1 + nK_2) \times (s+1)n_1n_2$ submatrix has zeros everywhere except the $(2,1)$st element, which is $(\Upsilon' \otimes I_{n_1})$. The $(4,3)$th $(n_1K_1 + nK_2) \times n_1K_1$ submatrix of M is zero except for its $(1,1)$st element, which is $I_{n_1K_1}$. Finally, the $(4,6)$th $(n_1K_1 + nK_2) \times n_2K_2$ submatrix has its $(1,1)$st element equal to zero, and the $(2,1)$ and $(3,1)$ elements equal to $(I_{K_2} \otimes (B_0^{-1}C_0^+))$ and $I_{n_2K_2}$, respectively.

Having defined all the matrices in (D13), we can write the prediction error in (D5) as:

$$y_{N+h} - \hat{y}_{N,h} \cong \varepsilon_{(h)} + W_{(h)}Q_{(h)}SM(\hat{\beta} - \beta). \tag{D14}$$

Appendix E.   Proof of the Theorem

The vector $\hat{\beta}$ is the vector of the estimates of the parameters of the reduced form model and of those of the process for the exogenous variables x_t^+. We assume $\hat{\beta}$ is asymptotically normal, i.e.,

$$\sqrt{T}(\hat{\beta} - \beta) \underset{a}{\sim} \mathsf{N}(0, \Omega). \tag{E1}$$

The matrix P has dimension $nm \times [n_1^2 s + n_1 n_2 (s+1) + n_1 K_1 + 2n_2^2 s + n_2 K_2]$, which does not change with the sample size T. Thus, we can apply Cramér's (1946, p. 254) linear transformation theorem to obtain:

$$P\sqrt{T}(\hat{\beta} - \beta) \underset{a}{\sim} \mathsf{N}(0, \ \mathrm{plim} P\Omega P'). \tag{E2}$$

Because forecasts are made outside the estimation period, ε and $P(\hat{\beta} - \beta)$ in (14) are mutually uncorrelated. Thus, (14) and (E2) lead to:

$$(y - \hat{y}) \underset{app}{\sim} \mathsf{N}(0, \ \Lambda + T^{-1} \mathrm{plim} P\Omega P'), \tag{E3}$$

where $\Lambda = \mathcal{E}(\varepsilon\varepsilon')$ is the variance covariance matrix of ε with its elements given by:

$$\mathcal{E}(\varepsilon_{(i)}\varepsilon'_{(i)}) = \sum_{k=0}^{i-1} \Gamma_{1k} \Sigma_e \Gamma'_{1k},$$

$$\mathcal{E}(\varepsilon_{(i)}\varepsilon'_{(j)}) = \sum_{k=0}^{i-1} \Gamma_{1k} \Sigma_e \Gamma'_{1,j-i+k} \qquad i < j. \tag{E4}$$

This follows because $e_t \sim \mathsf{IN}(0, \Sigma_e)$ where $\Sigma_e = (A_0^\star)^{-1} \Sigma_\psi (A_0^{\star\prime})^{-1}$ and Σ_ψ is [558] the variance covariance matrix of ψ. The elements below the diagonal (i.e., $i > j$) can be obtained by symmetry.

Let us now assume that D is an $r \times nm$ matrix of fixed elements. Then,

$$D(y - \hat{y}) \underset{app}{\sim} \mathsf{N}(0, \Sigma_f), \tag{E5}$$

where

$$\Sigma_f = D\big(\Lambda + T^{-1} \mathrm{plim} P\Omega P'\big) D'.$$

Furthermore, because Σ_f^{-1} is positive definite, it can be decomposed as $\Sigma_f^{-1} = R'R$ where R is an $r \times r$ nonsingular matrix. Hence,

$$RD(y - \hat{y}) \underset{app}{\sim} \mathsf{N}(0, I_r)$$

so that:

$$(y - \hat{y})' D' \Sigma_f^{-1} D(y - \hat{y}) \underset{app}{\sim} \chi_r^2. \tag{E6}$$

From (E5) and (E6) we can write down confidence intervals and confidence regions for $d_i'y$ and Dy, respectively, where d_i' is the ith row of D.

Appendix F.   Data Description

OP West Texas Intermediate crude oil price, US\$/barrel. Monthly figures from January 1984 to April 1991. Source: International Financial Statistics, IMF, M111M1776AAZ.

P Consumer price index for Caracas, 1968 = 100. Monthly figures from January 1968 to December 1985. Source: Boletín Mensual, Banco Central de Venezuela, several issues. Prices on consumers goods have been subject to governmental regulation for most of the sample period, with the share of regulated goods in total expenditure varying over time. The share was 39.2% in 1981, and decreased over the next two years. Then, the prices of all goods and services, excluding beverages, non-monetary gold, and goods imported through Margarita Island, were put under governmental regulation.

Lower-case letters (op and p) mean logarithms of capitals.

Appendix G.   Notation

[559]

A subscript t denotes "in time period t". "Exogenous" means "strongly exogenous".

A matrix of functions of the reduced form parameters for the y's

B_i $n_1 \times n_1$ matrix of coefficients of z_{t-i}

C matrix of the functions of the reduced form parameters for the x's

C_0 $n_1 \times K_1$ matrix of coefficients of x_{1t}

C_i^+ $n_1 \times n_2$ matrix of coefficients of x_{t-i}^+ in the econometric model

D matrix of constants. D applied to (e.g.) the vector of forecasts gives us its linear combinations.

e_t reduced form innovation in the whole system

F matrix of functions of the reduced form coefficients of the e's

H selection matrix of zeros and ones

J maximal lag in the finite-lag representations associated with $\delta(L)$ and $\eta(L)$

M matrix of functions of parameters in the whole system

p_1 number of lags in the endogenous variables z, in the econometric model

p_2 number of lags in the exogenous variables x^+, in the econometric model

p_3 number of lags in x^+, in the exogenous variables' process

q order of the MA process of the disturbances in the exogenous variables' process

$Q_{(h)}$ matrix of functions of parameters in the whole system

S	selection matrix of zeros and ones
$W_{(h)}$	matrix of observations on all variables
x_t	$(x'_{1t} : x'_{2t})'$, the vector of variables whose future values are known
x_t^+	n_2 stochastic exogenous variables
x_{1t}	K_1 exogenous variables with known future values (in the econometric model)
x_{2t}	K_2 exogenous variables with known future values (in the exogenous variables' process)
y_t	$(z'_t : x_t^{+\prime})'$, the vector of variables whose future values are not known in advance
y_{N+h}	the actual value of y in period $N + h$
$y_{N,h}$	optimal prediction of the $(N + h)$th observation on y
$\hat{y}_{N,h}$	feasible forecast of the $(N + h)$th observation on y
y	vector of all observations on y in the forecast period
$\hat{y}$	vector of feasible forecasts on y
z_t	n_1 endogenous variables in the econometric model
β	vector of the reduced form of parameters
ε	vector of $\varepsilon_{(h)}$'s
$\varepsilon_{(h)}$	vector of linear combinations of h future reduced form innovations (e) [560]
Θ_i	$n_2 \times n_2$ matrix of coefficients of the MA disturbances in the exogenous variables' process
Λ	covariance matrix of ε
μ_t	n_2 vector of disturbances in the exogenous variables' process
ν	(i, i)th element in Σ_f
Σ_f	variance matrix of the linear combinations of the forecast errors
Υ	$n_2 \times K_2$ matrix of coefficients of x_{2t}
φ_t	n_1 vector of disturbances in the econometric model
Φ_i	$n_2 \times n_2$ matrix of coefficients of x_t^+ in the exogenous variables' process
Ω	asymptotic covariance matrix of $\hat{\beta}$, the estimate of β

Bibliography

(References marked with an asterisk * are included in this volume.)

Baillie, R. T. (1979a) "The Asymptotic Mean Squared Error of Multistep Prediction from the Regression Model with Autoregressive Errors", *Journal of the American Statistical Association*, 74, 365, 175–184.

Baillie, R. T. (1979b) "Asymptotic Prediction Mean Squared Error for Vector Autoregressive Models", *Biometrika*, 66, 3, 675–678.

Chong, Y. Y., and D. F. Hendry (1986) "Econometric Evaluation of Linear Macro-economic Models", *Review of Economic Studies*, 53, 671–690.

Cramér, H. (1946) *Mathematical Methods of Statistics*, Princeton, Princeton University Press.

*Engle, R. F., D. F. Hendry, and J.-F. Richard (1983) "Exogeneity", *Econometrica*, 51, 2, 277–304.

Harvey, A. C. (1981) *Time Series Models*, Oxford, Philip Allan.

*Hendry, D. F. (1988) "The Encompassing Implications of Feedback versus Feedforward Mechanisms in Econometrics", *Oxford Economic Papers*, 40, 132–149.

Hendry, D. F. (1994) *Dynamic Econometrics*, Oxford, Oxford University Press, in press; originally cited as (1991) *Lectures on Econometric Methodology*, Oxford, Oxford University Press, forthcoming.

Lucas, R. E., Jr. (1976) "Econometric Policy Evaluation: A Critique", in K. Brunner and A. H. Meltzer (eds.) *The Phillips Curve and Labor Markets, Carnegie-Rochester Conference on Public Policy*, 1, 19–42.

Phillips, P. C. B., and M. R. Wickens (1978) *Exercises in Econometrics*, Volume 2, Oxford, Philip Allan.

Reinsel, G. (1980) "Asymptotic Properties of Prediction Errors for the Multivariate Autoregressive Model Using Estimated Parameters", *Journal of the Royal Statistical Society, Series B*, 42, 3, 328–333.

Schmidt, P. (1974) "The Asymptotic Distribution of Forecasts in the Dynamic Simulation of an Econometric Model", *Econometrica*, 42, 2, 303–309.

Yamamoto, T. (1976) "Asymptotic Mean Square Prediction Error for an Autoregressive Model with Estimated Coefficients", *Journal of the Royal Statistical Society, Series C*, 25, 2, 123–127.

Yamamoto, T. (1980) "On the Treatment of Autocorrelated Errors in the Multiperiod Prediction of Dynamic Simultaneous Equation Models", *International Economic Review*, 21, 3, 735–748.

Yamamoto, T. (1981) "Predictions of Multivariate Autoregressive Moving Average Models", *Biometrika*, 68, 2, 485–492.

15

Testing for Parameter Instability in Linear Models

BRUCE E. HANSEN*

Abstract

Simple tests for parameter instability are presented and discussed. These tests have locally optimal power and do not require *a priori* knowledge of "the breakpoint". Two empirical examples are presented to illustrate the use of the tests. The first examines whether an AR(1) model for annual U.S. output growth rates has remained stable over 1889–1987. The second examines the stability of an error correction model for an aggregate life cycle model of consumption.

1   Introduction

Model stability is necessary for prediction and econometric inference. Because a parametric econometric model is completely described by its parameters, model stability is equivalent to parameter stability. Model instability may be caused simply by the omission of an important variable, or be due to some kind of "regime shift". While model instability generically makes it difficult to interpret regression results, it is of particular importance in policy analysis to know if econometric models are invariant to possible policy interventions. Engle, Hendry, and Richard (1983) incorporated parameter invariance to interventions in their definition of super exogeneity, a condition they argued was a necessary precondition for predictive policy experiments.

* I would like to thank Neil Ericsson and a referee for helpful comments on an earlier draft which improved the exposition and analysis. Research support was provided by NSF Grant No. SES 9022176.

Reprinted with permission from the *Journal of Policy Modeling* (August 1992), 14, 4, 517–533.

A necessary condition for super exogeneity is within sample parameter constancy.

Because of the well-recognized need for stable models, a large literature has emerged developing tests of model stability. The number and variety of testing procedures is quite surprising. Unfortunately, not all tests are equal, and many, developed from ad hoc criteria, are quite poor. Ideally, [518] a test should have known size and possess the maximal power against the alternative of interest for all tests of the same size. In practice, ideal tests rarely exist. Asymptotic theory may be necessary to approximate the null distribution, and direct power comparisons may be impossible. A useful criterion is *local power*, that is, the slope of the power function at the null hypothesis (in the direction of interest). Tests that have maximal local power can be derived [see Cox and Hinkley (1974)], and the local power function can be approximated via the asymptotic local power function.

One of the most common tests in applied econometrics is Chow's (1960, pp. 595–599) simple split-sample test.[1] This test is designed to test the null hypothesis of constant parameters against an alternative of a one-time shift in the parameters at some *known* time. There are several simple ways to calculate this test statistic, each of which involves splitting the sample at the hypothesized time of structural change. One method is to compare (using the appropriate covariance matrix) the estimates obtained from each subsample. A second method is to calculate the estimates using just the data from one subsample, and compare this with the estimates using the full sample. A third method uses dummy variables (intercept and slope) for one subsample, and then tests the significance of the dummy variables. These methods are essentially equivalent and easy to use in practice.

A severe problem arises with this Chow test, however, in the need to select the timing of the structural change that occurs under the alternative hypothesis. The problem is that the date of structural change is not defined (has no meaning) under the null hypothesis, and standard testing theory is not applicable; see Davies (1977, 1987) on this point. A researcher has several options open. First, the timing can be selected in an arbitrary way, such as at the sample midpoint. This solution effectively eliminates the dating question, but is ad hoc and would not be expected to have particularly good power against many alternatives of interest. Second, the data and/or regression residuals can be plotted for indications of structural change. If this is done, the timing is selected conditional on the data and the conventional χ^2 approximation for the distribution of the resulting test statistic is invalid.

---

[1] Chow's test is a straightforward application of the analysis of covariance, a standard statistical method dating back to Fisher (1922). Chow (1960) appears to have been the first, however, to apply the principle to testing stability in a time series context.

What may in effect be done is to select a candidate breakpoint that suggests a structural change, when in fact none may have occurred. Third, the date of structural change may be selected by appeal to events known a priori. If this approach is adopted, it is essential that the researcher can argue that [519] the events are selected exogenously. For example, the oil shock of 1974 is "known" to be associated with a slowdown in aggregate output in many countries. This is known simply because a slowdown did occur after the oil shock. Thus it is impossible to test (using conventional theory) whether the oil shock had an effect upon the GNP process, because the selection of 1974 has been made *after* the data have been informally examined. Fourth, tests for structural change for every breakpoint could be calculated, and the largest test statistic examined. This is the test proposed originally by Quandt (1960), but not used much because of the lack of a distributional theory. This theory has been given recently in Andrews (1993), Chu and White (1992), and Hansen (1990). This procedure is theoretically sound, but may be a computational burden in some cases.

Another commonly applied stability test is the "predictive-failure" test derived by Chow (1960, pp. 594–595)[2] and routinely used by Hendry and his coauthors.[3] This test also requires an a priori selection of a breakpoint, and therefore suffers the same problem as the Chow test.

Recognizing the need for tests that reveal model instability of general form, Brown, Durbin, and Evans (1975) proposed the CUSUM test, which was fairly widely programmed and used in the late 1970s and early 1980s. Theoretical investigations eventually revealed that the CUSUM test is essentially a test to detect instability in the intercept alone [see, for example, Krämer, Ploberger, and Alt (1988)]. Another test proposed from a similar motivation is the CUSUM of squares test. This test, however, has poor asymptotic power against instability in the regression coefficients [Ploberger and Krämer (1990)]. Instead, the CUSUM of squares test can be viewed as a test for detecting instability in the variance of the regression error. For an analysis of the power of these and other tests, see Hansen (1991).

Below we describe a simple yet powerful test for parameter instability. The statistic has a long history in theoretical statistics and econometrics. The test was independently proposed for the Gaussian linear model by Gardner (1969), Pagan and Tanaka (1981), Nyblom and Makelainen (1983), and King (1987). The extensions to nonlinear maximum likelihood and general econometric problems were made by Nyblom (1989) and Hansen (1990), [520]

---

[2] Although Chow developed the predictive failure test, he argued (1960, p. 598) that it would not be as powerful as the analysis-of-covariance test when the number of observations in the prediction interval exceeds the number of coefficients.

[3] See, for example, Hendry and Richard (1982), Engle and Hendry (1993), Hendry (1989), and Hendry and Ericsson (1991).

respectively. The test is approximately the Lagrange multiplier test (or locally most powerful test) of the null of constant parameters against the alternative that the parameters follow a martingale. This alternative incorporates simple structural breaks of unknown timing as well as random walk parameters. These tests can be developed for any econometric model, although this paper concentrates on least squares regression. The analysis includes both static and dynamic regression, for no special treatment of lagged dependent variables is required. It is necessary to exclude, however, nonstationary regressors. That is, we exclude unit root processes and deterministic trends; otherwise, a different distributional theory applies [Hansen (1992)]. One caveat should be noted. The tests discussed here simply test the null of constancy. They are not designed for determining the timing of a "structural break" if one has occurred. Other methods should be used for this purpose, and will not be discussed in this paper.

Section 2 describes the test statistics and discusses their interpretation. Section 3 uses these tests to study U.S. GNP. Section 4 examines error correction models and a simple aggregate consumption equation. Section 5 concludes.

2   Instability Tests

We will examine the standard linear regression model

$$y_t = \beta_1 x_{1t} + \beta_2 x_{2t} + \cdots + \beta_m x_{mt} + e_t$$

$$= \beta' x_t + e_t$$

$$E(e_t \mid x_t) = 0$$

$$E(e_t^2) = \sigma_t^2$$

$$\lim_{n \to \infty} \frac{1}{n} \sum_{t=1}^{n} \sigma_t^2 = \sigma^2. \tag{1}$$

Throughout this paper, we will maintain the assumption that the variables $\{x_t, e_t\}$ are weakly dependent processes. That is, the variables do not contain deterministic or stochastic trends (such as unit roots). See Andrews (1993) or Hansen (1990) for the technical details, and Hansen (1992) for an analysis in the presence of trends in the regressors. We are interested in testing the assumed constancy of the model parameters (β, σ^2). Nyblom (1989) has shown how to derive the locally most powerful test of the hypothesis of constancy against the alternative that the parameters follow a martingale process. We follow this approach here.

[521]   Equation (1) is estimated by least squares, yielding the parameter esti-

mates $(\hat{\beta}, \hat{\sigma}^2)$ and the first-order conditions

$$0 = \sum_{t=1}^{n} x_{it}\hat{e}_t \qquad i = 1, \ldots, m$$

$$0 = \sum_{t=1}^{n} (\hat{e}_t^2 - \hat{\sigma}^2), \qquad (2)$$

where $\hat{e}_t = y_t - x_t'\hat{\beta}$. We can rewrite this by defining

$$f_{it} = \begin{cases} x_{it}\hat{e}_t & i = 1, \ldots, m \\ \\ \hat{e}_t^2 - \hat{\sigma}^2 & i = m+1, \end{cases} \qquad (3)$$

so (2) is equivalent to

$$0 = \sum_{t=1}^{n} f_{it}, \qquad i = 1, \ldots, m+1. \qquad (4)$$

The variables $\{f_{it}\}$ are the first-order conditions (*scores* in a maximum likelihood context). Our test statistics are based upon the cumulative first-order conditions, given by

$$S_{it} = \sum_{j=1}^{t} f_{ij}. \qquad (5)$$

Note that $S_{in} = 0$ by the first-order condition (4). Also note that the sums S_{it} are functions of the full sample estimates, unlike the classic CUSUM of Brown, Durbin, and Evans (1975) (BDE).

We are interested in testing the stability of each parameter individually and the stability of all the parameters jointly. First, the individual stability test statistics[4] are given by

$$L_i = \frac{1}{nV_i} \sum_{t=1}^{n} S_{it}^2, \qquad (6)$$

where

$$V_i = \sum_{t=1}^{n} f_{it}^2. \qquad (7)$$

To obtain the statistic for the joint stability test, it will be most convenient to use matrix notation. Define the vectors

$$f_t = (f_{1t}, \ldots, f_{m+1t})' \qquad [522]$$

$$S_t = (S_{1t}, \ldots, S_{m+1t})'. \qquad (8)$$

The joint stability test statistic is

---

[4] See Nyblom (1989) or Hansen (1990) for the derivations of the test statistic.

$$L_C = \frac{1}{n} \sum_{t=1}^{n} S_t' V^{-1} S_t, \tag{9}$$

where

$$V = \sum_{t=1}^{n} f_t f_t'. \tag{10}$$

Note that the V_i in (7) are the diagonal elements of V in (10).

Expression (9) shows that the test statistic is essentially an average of the squared cumulative sums of first-order conditions. Under the null hypothesis, the first-order conditions are mean zero, and their cumulative sums will tend to wander around zero (in the manner of a tied-down random walk). Under the alternative hypothesis of parameter instability, however, the cumulative sums will develop a nonzero mean in parts of the sample, so S_n will not behave like a random walk, and the test statistic will tend to be large. Thus, the test is to reject the null hypothesis of stability for large values of L_C. The test can be shown to have asymptotic local power against any non-stationary (long-run) movements in β and/or σ^2. This is unlike the CUSUM test, which has asymptotic local power only against movements in $\beta' E(x)$, or the CUSUM of squares test, which has asymptotic local power only against movements in σ^2.[5] In fact, if one regressor is a constant (say x_{1t}), then its associated test statistic (L_1) is an analog of the BDE CUSUM test. Similarly, the test for the stability of the error variance (L_{m+1}) is an analog of the BDE CUSUM of squares test. We can therefore think of the L_i family of tests as expanding, rather than replacing, the CUSUM family of tests.

The following facts about the above construction should be kept in mind. The L_C test statistic given in (9) and (10) is asymptotically robust to heteroscedasticity because the matrix V is exactly the central component in the heteroscedasticity-robust covariance matrix estimator of White (1980). Similarly, the test statistic could be made robust to residual serial correlation as in White and Domowitz (1984). We are explicitly discussing testing via ordinary least squares (OLS) estimation, while in applications generalized least squares (GLS) methods (either for heteroscedasticity or serial correlation) are routinely used. If (1) represents the *transformed* model (after a Cochrane-Orcutt correction or weighting has been made) then all the above analysis is still valid, if the tests are applied to the transformed data. Similarly, in an application involving two-stage least squares (2SLS) estimation, (1) could represent the *transformed* model (after the endogenous regressors have been replaced by their predicted values). The only caution in this case is that the covariance matrix estimate V needs to be calculated differently.

[523]

---

[5] See Krämer, Ploberger, and Alt (1988), Ploberger and Krämer (1990), and Hansen (1991) for analytic studies of the power of these tests.

TABLE 1. Asymptotic Critical Values for L_C

Degrees of Freedom	Significance level					
$(m+1)$	1%	2.5%	5%	7.5%	10%	20%
1	0.748	0.593	0.470	0.398	0.353	0.243
2	1.07	0.898	0.749	0.670	0.610	0.469
3	1.35	1.16	1.01	0.913	0.846	0.679
4	1.60	1.39	1.24	1.14	1.07	0.883
5	1.88	1.63	1.47	1.36	1.28	1.08
6	2.12	1.89	1.68	1.58	1.49	1.28
7	2.35	2.10	1.90	1.78	1.69	1.46
8	2.59	2.33	2.11	1.99	1.89	1.66
9	2.82	2.55	2.32	2.19	2.10	1.85
10	3.05	2.76	2.54	2.40	2.29	2.03
11	3.27	2.99	2.75	2.60	2.49	2.22
12	3.51	3.18	2.96	2.81	2.69	2.41
13	3.69	3.39	3.15	3.00	2.89	2.59
14	3.90	3.60	3.34	3.19	3.08	2.77
15	4.07	3.81	3.54	3.38	3.26	2.95
16	4.30	4.01	3.75	3.58	3.46	3.14
17	4.51	4.21	3.95	3.77	3.64	3.32
18	4.73	4.40	4.14	3.96	3.83	3.50
19	4.92	4.60	4.33	4.16	4.03	3.69
20	5.13	4.79	4.52	4.36	4.22	3.86

Source: Hansen (1990, Table 1).

The asymptotic distribution theory for the stability tests has been given by Nyblom (1989) and Hansen (1990). The distributional theory is non-standard, but depends only upon the number of parameters tested for stability. In the joint tests there are $m+1$ parameters: m regression parameters (which include the intercept if one of the regressors is a constant) and the error variance. Asymptotic critical values are presented in Table 1. The first line of Table 1 gives the relevant critical values for the individual stability tests: since for these tests there is only one "degree of freedom". Note that the 5% significance level for the individual stability test is 0.470. This suggests the informal rule of finding an individual stability test "significant" if the test statistic exceeds one-half, much as we commonly find a t statistic "significant" if its value exceeds 2.0.

One may interpret the individual and joint statistics quite similarly to the interplay between individual and joint tests of significance of regression coefficients. In the latter case, t statistics for each regression coefficient give information regarding the significance of each individual variable, while the F statistic gives the joint significance of all the variables. The difference in the present context is that a significant statistic is bad news, indicating possible instability. It is important as well not to abuse such information. If a large number of parameters are estimated, it should not be surprising to find a small number of "significant" test statistics for individual instability. The joint significance test is a more reliable guide in this context.

One important question that most analysts ask is: If we reject stability, what then? It is important to emphasize that there can be no universal answer, or solution, to the problem of unstable coefficients. Frequently, a significant instability test indicates some form of model mis-specification. For example, omitted variables can induce parameter variation. If an alternative specification appears free of this problem, then it seems reasonable to adopt [524]   the alternative specification. In practice, researchers always estimate a variety of specifications in an attempt to "fit" the data. Instability test statistics can be added to the standard bag of tricks to determine the worth of a particular specification, if used cautiously. Of course, if one *searches* over a variety of specifications to find one whose stability test statistic is "insignificant", a form of data mining has been performed, and the credibility of the resulting regression is suspect.

A more troubling alternative is to explicitly allow the parameters to change over the course of the sample. The most common method is to use intercept and slope dummies to capture "regime shifts". By including dummies, the analyst is admitting that the estimated relationship is not constant, but is attempting to go ahead with the analysis. The immediate questions are the following: Of what use are these regression results? Do they have *any* predictive content? If events can arise which shift the regression slopes in an arbitrary way, how can we exclude such events from arising in the future?

[525]   If it is believed that the regression coefficients are shifting because of economic events, then it is (at least in principle) possible to explicitly model these events. Perhaps simply allowing for interaction among regressors (which can be thought of as allowing the regression coefficients to depend linearly upon other regressors) will adequately capture the "parameter shifts", but more complicated interactions may be required in particular applications.

A final alternative is to use a so-called random coefficient model such as that of Cooley and Prescott (1976). Cooley and Prescott model the regression coefficients as random walks that are independent of the regression error. Such models are highly nonlinear and can be estimated by maximum likelihood. A fundamental feature of this approach is that the coefficient variation is not modeled explicitly. Indeed, the specification is quite non-parametric in spirit. This allows for a large degree of flexibility, but with a reduction of precision vis-à-vis more structural approaches. If the alternative is to include slope dummies for the points of "structural change", then the Cooley-Prescott approach has a natural advantage as it incorporates uncertainty over future values of the parameters into estimated prediction intervals, while inclusion of slope dummies does not. Incidentally, it should be noted that the "meta-parameters" in random coefficient models are of course assumed constant, and the methods described in Nyblom (1989) could be used to design powerful tests of this hypothesis, if desired.

3   Has the Nature of Output Fluctuations Changed?

A major debate in macro-economics concerns the stability of the process describing aggregate output. A common argument by Keynesians is that institutional changes have decreased output fluctuations in the postwar period [see, for example, Tobin (1980, p. 47)]. This view has been challenged recently by Romer (1986a, 1986b, 1989), who argues that the perceived decrease in output fluctuations may be a figment of poorly measured prewar data. It is also commonly asserted that the behavior of output during the great depression is fundamentally different than in neighboring years. De-Long and Summers (1988), for example, argue that shocks to GNP were more persistent during the depression than in the pre-depression and post-World War II years. All of these debates concern whether or not the distribution of the output process has changed. We follow DeLong and Summers in using the corrected GNP data provided by Romer (1989) and excluding the pre-1888 data as unreliable.

An AR(1) model seems a reasonable univariate description for growth [526] rates of U.S. output:

$$\Delta y_t \; = \; \alpha_0 + \alpha_1 \Delta y_{t-1} + e_t \qquad E(e_t^2) = \sigma^2,$$

where Δy_t denotes the first difference of the log of annual per capita real GNP.

DeLong and Summers (1988) argue that the parameter describing persistence, α_1, has changed over time (most importantly, was substantially higher during the Depression and World War II). Table 2 reports model estimates for the periods 1889–1987, 1889–1929, 1930–1947, and 1948–1987 as recommended by DeLong and Summers. The standard errors are calculated using White's heteroscedasticity-robust covariance matrix estimator. The L stability tests are calculated on the full sample.

Bruce E. Hansen

TABLE 2. GNP Equation

	α_0	α_1	σ^2
Sample period			
1889–1987	0.012	0.36	0.0022
	(0.005)	(0.11)	(0.0004)
1889–1929	0.021	−0.12	0.0013
	(0.006)	(0.13)	(0.0003)
1930–1947	0.011	0.60	0.0054
	(0.018)	(0.14)	(0.0015)
1948–1987	0.019	0.05	0.0006
	(0.005)	(0.15)	(0.0001)
Individual L_1	0.03	0.19	0.45*
Joint $L_C = 0.72$			
$R^2 = 0.13$			

* Rejects stability at asymptotic 10% level.

At first sight, the point estimates from the sample subperiods and the L statistics appear to be partially in conflict. The estimates and L statistic agree that σ^2 is not constant, but the estimates of the autoregressive parameter indicate a substantial shift over the periods, while the L_1 statistic fails to reject the null that α_1 is constant. How should we interpret this information?

We first need to think about the finite sample properties of the test statistics. Since the distributional theory presented in the previous section is based upon asymptotic approximations, we should be careful to check if the approximation is useful in the present context. I generated 2,000 sam[527] ples from the full sample model reported in the first line of Table 2 (under the assumption of independently and identically distributed normal errors), and applied the individual stability tests for the autoregressive coefficient and error variance, as well as the joint stability test, using the asymptotic 10 percent critical values. Table 3 presents some simulation results. The first line reports a measure of finite sample size distortion. The table reports rejection frequencies. The tests rejected the null hypothesis at rates close to the nominal values, indicating quite mild size distortion. The second and third lines of Table 3 report the power of the test against particular alter-

TABLE 3.

Finite Sample Rejection Frequencies of Asymptotic 10% Tests

	L_1	$L_2(\sigma^2)$	Joint L_C
Null	0.11	0.08	0.09
α_1 and σ^2 varying	0.11	0.61	0.25
α_1 varying	0.30	0.10	0.17

natives. The numbers reported are rejection frequencies of the test statistics using 1000 samples and the asymptotic 10 percent critical values. The second line used data generated from the same model as used under the null, except that the autoregressive parameter and error variance shift according to the parameter estimates reported in Table 2. The third line of Table 3 has only the autoregressive parameter shifting.

These experiments are designed to answer the question: If the data is generated as suggested by the split-sample estimates, what is the probability that the test statistics will reject the null hypothesis? The answer is quite startling. If both the autoregressive *and* the error variance shift over time, the test will only be able to detect the shift in the error variance. The reason apparently is that the shifting error variance induces too much noise into the series for the test to be able to distinguish parameter variation from sampling variation. But the test is able to reject the constant variance hypothesis 61 percent of the time. When the error variance is held fixed, then the test on the autoregressive coefficient displays some ability to reject the null hypothesis, rejecting 30 percent of the time.

The last simulations suggest that it is difficult to test the stability of one set of parameters, if we allow another subset to be shifting over time (the null hypothesis for all of the tests is that *all* of the parameters are stable, and this is important in the derivation of the distributional theory). Although the results so far seem to suggest strongly that the error variance has changed, we just do not know if the autoregressive parameter was stable or not. We [528] can partially circumvent this problem by using generalized least squares to eliminate the shifts in the error variance. Under the assumption that the error variance shifted twice, in 1930 and 1948, we can use the estimates from Table 2 to re-estimate the equation. This regression is not reported here, but the main results do not change (the L statistic for the AR parameter is 0.18). We conclude that the data are not sufficiently informative to determine whether or not the autoregressive parameter is stable, *given* that the error variance is unstable.

This exercise illustrates the limitations of econometric techniques and the potential dangers of "ocular" or "eyeball" econometrics. The natural impulse to split the sample at some known important date, as done by DeLong and Summers, must be resisted. If conventional critical values are used (which ignore the fact that the sample split point was *selected*), then the tests will be biased towards *spurious rejection* of the stability hypothesis. Similarly, visual displays of recursive estimates or split-sample estimates such as those in Table 2 must be tempered with a large dose of caution. What appears as a significant difference may not in fact be significant once the selection of the sample split is taken into account. The tests advocated in this paper are immune to such criticism since they do not require the selection of a breakpoint. On the other hand, these general tests may have relatively low power against particular alternatives. As a result, we may be unable to extract definitive conclusions from time-series data.

4   Testing Stability in Error Correction Models

Many applied time-series regressions take the form of error correction models (ECMs). We can use the L test statistics to assess the stability of ECMs. ECMs can generally be written in the form

$$\Delta y_{1t} = \mu + \gamma(y_{1t-1} - \alpha' y_{2t-1}) + \beta' x_t + e_t, \qquad (11)$$

where y_{1t} and y_{2t} are individually $\mathsf{I}(1)$ yet jointly cointegrated. The x_t variables should be $\mathsf{I}(0)$, such as lagged values of Δy_{1t} and Δy_{2t}.

The difficulty in applying stability tests in the context of ECMs is that the levels data y_{1t} and y_{2t} contain stochastic or deterministic trends, thus invalidating the distributional theory used to justify the critical values reported in Table 1. Therefore, testing the stability of the cointegrating parameter α requires a different theory, which is given in Hansen (1992). If we are interested in the *dynamics* of an ECM, however, we can use our stability tests [529] to test the stability of the coefficients on $\mathsf{I}(0)$ variables. In (11), if α were known, then the remaining parameters are all coefficients of $\mathsf{I}(0)$ variables. If α is not known but is consistently estimated at a rate faster than the square root of sample size, then the stability test applied to the remaining coefficients can proceed as before.

The easiest way to conduct this test is by using a two-step estimator in the spirit of Engle and Granger (1987). First estimate the cointegrating vector α using either OLS or an asymptotically efficient estimator such as the fully modified (FM) estimator of Phillips and Hansen (1990). Then take the residuals from this first-stage regression and use them in the ECM (11). Because all the variables in this second stage are $\mathsf{I}(0)$, we can apply the testing procedures of Section 2.

This process is illustrated by the following aggregate consumption model using quarterly U.S. data:

$$\Delta c_t = \beta_1 u_{t-1} + \beta_2 \Delta i_t + \beta_3 \Delta \pi_t + \beta_4 + e_t, \tag{12}$$

$$u_t = c_t - \alpha_1 i_t - \alpha_2 \pi_t - \alpha_3. \tag{13}$$

Here, c_t is aggregate consumption expenditure, i_t is aggregate total disposable income, and π_t is the inflation rate. In relation to equation (11), y_{1t} is c_t, y_{2t} is $(i_t, \pi_t)'$, and x_t is $(\Delta i_t, \Delta \pi_t)'$. The sample is 1953:2–1984:4. The consumption and income data are taken from Blinder and Deaton (1985), and the inflation rate is calculated from the implicit GNP deflator in the Citibase data base. We will consider (12) and (13) in both levels and logarithmic specifications for the consumption and income series.

The cointegrating regression (13) in levels without the inflation rate was proposed and analyzed in Campbell (1987) because the model presented in his paper implied that this should be a cointegrating relationship. Deaton (1977) argued that the inflation rate should enter into an aggregate consumption function. He pointed out that a rate of inflation higher than expected is likely to reduce consumption expenditure. This is a disequilibrium (or short-run) mechanism, and suggests that inflation should enter in the dynamic relationship (12), but not in the long-run relationship (13). Deaton's empirical results, however, suggest that inflation is significant in a regression similar to (13). This empirical finding was confirmed by the more extensive study of Davidson, Hendry, Srba, and Yeo (1978). Although there does not appear to be a good theory to explain the presence of inflation in the cointegrating relationship, it seems reasonable to test its presence empirically.

We will estimate and evaluate four competing specifications for the cointegrating relationship.   [530]

Model A: consumption and income in levels; inflation rate excluded.

Model B: consumption and income in levels; inflation rate included.

Model C: consumption and income in logs; inflation rate excluded.

Model D: consumption and income in logs; inflation rate included.

We now explore these alternative specifications using the tests for cointegration and instability. The parameters of (13) were estimated using the fully modified estimator of Phillips and Hansen (1990).[6] Phillips' $Z(t)$ test of the null of no cointegration was applied to the cointegrating residuals $\hat{u}_t$. These same cointegrating residuals were used in the second step estimation

---

[6] To calculate the long-run covariance parameters, the residuals were first pre-whitened as suggested by Andrews and Monahan (1992), and then a quadratic kernel applied using the plug-in bandwidth suggested by Andrews (1991).

Bruce E. Hansen

TABLE 4.
Aggregate Consumption Functions: Estimates and Tests

Parameter	Model A	Model B	Model C	Model D
Equation (13)				
α_1	0.93 (0.01)	0.96 (0.01)	1.00 (0.01)	1.02 (0.01)
α_2		−8.8 (3.6)		−0.002 (0.001)
α_3	−6.9 (43.8)	−54.6 (41.1)	−0.09 (0.10)	−0.23 (0.12)
$Z(t)$	−3.51**	−4.91***	−3.68**	−4.68***
Equation (12)				
β_1	−0.09 (0.05)	−0.14 (0.05)	−0.11 (0.05)	−0.13 (0.05)
L_1	0.06	0.07	0.09	0.09
β_2	0.65 (0.08)	0.65 (0.07)	0.68 (0.08)	0.67 (0.07)
L_2	0.28	0.29	0.15	0.15
β_3		−0.63 (0.69)		−0.00015 (0.00021)
L_3		0.04		0.04
β_4	5.70 (2.52)	5.78 (2.43)	0.0019 (0.0007)	0.0019 (0.0007)
L_4	0.18	0.19	0.07	0.07
σ^2	393 (63)	382 (59)	0.000033 (0.000004)	0.000032 (0.000004)
L_5	1.14***	1.09***	0.21	0.16
R^2	0.47	0.48	0.46	0.47
Joint L_C	1.41**	1.42*	0.44	0.45

*   Rejects at the asymptotic 10% level.
**   Rejects at the asymptotic 5% level.
***Rejects at the asymptotic 1% level.

of (12) by OLS. These results are reported in Table 4. For each parameter in equation (12), the estimate, standard error, and instability statistic are reported.

We first examine the long-run relationship (13). All four specifications yield reasonable parameter estimates. Particularly interesting are the near-unity values for the income elasticities when the model is estimated in logs. The inflation rate coefficient is negative and significant in both specifications. All four specifications reject the null of no cointegration at the 5 percent level, but the specifications with the inflation rate included reject no cointegration at the 1 percent level.

We now turn to the estimates of the dynamic equation, (12). In all specifications, the error correction term is negative and significant, as expected. As predicted by Deaton's theory, when the inflation rate is included, its coefficient has a negative sign, but it is not significantly different from zero. In all four equations, none of the regression coefficients display any evidence of instability. The error variance, however, is apparently unstable in the levels equations (rejecting stability at the 1 percent level), but not in the logarithmic equations.

In summary, the empirical evidence appears to favor the logarithmic specification with the inflation rate included. This model strongly rejects no cointegration, has estimated parameters of the proper sign and magnitude, and passes the stability tests applied to the dynamic equation. It is puzzling, however, that the inflation rate appears significantly in the long-run relationship, but not in the short-run relationship. An explanation of this phenomenon would be a useful enterprise for future research.

5 Conclusion   [531]

This paper has presented a simple yet powerful test for parameter instability. No sample split-points or forecast intervals need to be chosen. The test only requires that the model be estimated once over the full sample. The [532] asymptotic distribution is nonstandard, depending only upon the number of coefficients tested for stability.

If the test statistics are insignificant, then the investigator can be reasonably confident that either the model has been constant over that sample or the data is not sufficiently informative to reject this hypothesis. On the other hand, a significant test statistic suggests the presence of model misspecification. It appears that this test statistic can provide useful information in practice.

Bibliography

(References marked with an asterisk * are included in this volume.)

Andrews, D. W. K. (1991) "Heteroskedasticity and Autocorrelation Consistent Covariance Matrix Estimation", *Econometrica*, 59, 817–858.

Andrews, D. W. K. (1993) "Tests for Parameter Instability and Structural Change with Unknown Change Point", *Econometrica*, 61, 4, 821–856; originally cited as (1990), Cowles Discussion Paper No. 943, Yale University.

Andrews, D. W. K., and J. C. Monahan (1992) "An Improved Heteroskedasticity and Autocorrelation Consistent Covariance Matrix Estimator", *Econometrica*, 60, 4, 953–966; originally cited as (1990), forthcoming in *Econometrica*.

Blinder, A. S., and A. S. Deaton (1985) "The Time Series Consumption Function Revisited", *Brookings Papers on Economic Activity*, 1985, 465–511.

Brown, R. L., J. Durbin, and J. M. Evans (1975) "Techniques for Testing the Constancy of Regression Relationships Over Time", *Journal of the Royal Statistical Society, Series B*, 37, 149–163.

Campbell, J. Y. (1987) "Does Saving Anticipate Declining Labor Income? An Alternative Test of the Permanent Income Hypothesis", *Econometrica*, 55, 1249–1273.

Chow, G. C. (1960) "Tests of Equality Between Sets of Coefficients in Two Linear Regressions", *Econometrica*, 28, 591–605.

Chu, C.-S. J., and H. White (1992) "A Direct Test for Changing Trend", *Journal of Business and Economic Statistics*, 10, 289–299; originally cited as C.-S. J. Chu (1989) "New Tests for Parameter Constancy in Stationary and Nonstationary Regression Models", University of California at San Diego.

Cooley, T. F., and E. C. Prescott (1976) "Estimation in the Presence of Stochastic Parameter Variation", *Econometrica*, 44, 167–184.

Cox, D. R., and D. V. Hinkley (1974) *Theoretical Statistics*, London, Chapman and Hall.

Davidson, J. E. H., D. F. Hendry, F. Srba, and S. Yeo (1978) Econometric Modelling of the Aggregate Time-series Relationship Between Consumers' Expenditure and Income in the United Kingdom", *Economic Journal*, 88, 661–692.

Davies, R. B. (1977) "Hypothesis Testing When a Nuisance Parameter Is Present Only Under the Alternative", *Biometrika*, 64, 247–254.

Davies, R. B. (1987) "Hypothesis Testing When a Nuisance Parameter Is Present Only Under the Alternative", *Biometrika*, 74, 33–43.

Deaton, A. (1977) "Involuntary Saving Through Unanticipated Inflation", *American Economic Review*, 67, 899–910.

DeLong, J. B., and L. H. Summers (1988) "On the Existence and Interpretation of a 'Unit Root' in U.S. GNP", NBER Working Paper No. 2716.

Engle, R. F., and C. W. J. Granger (1987) "Co-integration and Error Correction: Representation, Estimation, and Testing", *Econometrica*, 55, 251–276.

*Engle, R. F., and D. F. Hendry (1993) "Testing Super Exogeneity and Invariance in Regression Models", *Journal of Econometrics*, 56, 1/2, 119–139; originally cited as (1990), forthcoming in *Journal of Econometrics*.

*Engle, R. F., D. F. Hendry, and J.-F. Richard (1983) "Exogeneity", *Econometrica*, 51, 277–304.

Fisher, R. A. (1922) "The Goodness of Fit of Regression Formula, and the [533] Distribution of Regression Coefficients", *Journal of the Royal Statistical Society*, 85, 597–612.

Gardner, L. A., Jr. (1969) "On Detecting Changes in the Mean of Normal Variates", *Annals of Mathematical Statistics*, 40, 116–126.

Hansen, B. E. (1990) "Lagrange Multiplier Tests for Parameter Instability in Non-linear Models", University of Rochester.

Hansen, B. E. (1991) "A Comparison of Tests for Parameter Instability: An Examination of Asymptotic Local Power", University of Rochester; originally cited as (1991a).

Hansen, B. E. (1992) "Tests for Parameter Instability in Regressions with I(1) Processes", *Journal of Business and Economic Statistics*, 10, 3, 321–335; originally cited as (1991b), forthcoming in *Journal of Business and Economic Statistics*.

Hendry, D. F. (1989) *PC-GIVE: An Interactive Econometric Modeling System*, Oxford, University of Oxford, Institute of Economics and Statistics and Nuffield College.

Hendry, D. F., and N. R. Ericsson (1991) "An Econometric Analysis of U.K. Money Demand in *Monetary Trends in the United States and the United Kingdom* by Milton Friedman and Anna J. Schwartz", *American Economic Review*, 81, 8–38.

Hendry, D. F., and J.-F. Richard (1982) "On the Formulation of Empirical Models in Dynamic Econometrics", *Journal of Econometrics*, 20, 3–33.

King, M. L. (1987) "An Alternative Test for Regression Coefficient Stability", *Review of Economics and Statistics*, 69, 379–381.

Krämer, W., W. Ploberger, and R. Alt (1988) "Testing for Structural Change in Dynamic Models", *Econometrica*, 56, 1355–1369.

Nyblom, J. (1989) "Testing for the Constancy of Parameters over Time", *Journal of the American Statistical Association*, 84, 223–230.

Nyblom, J., and T. Makelainen (1983) "Comparisons of Tests for the Presence of Random Walk Coefficients in a Simple Linear Model", *Journal of the American Statistical Association*, 78, 856–864.

Pagan, A. R., and K. Tanaka (1981) "A Further Test for Assessing the Stability of Regression Coefficients", Australian National University.

Phillips, P. C. B., and B. E. Hansen (1990) "Statistical Inference in Instrumental Variables Regression with I(1) Processes", *Review of Economic Studies*, 57, 99–125.

Phillips, P. C. B., and S. Ouliaris (1990) "Asymptotic Properties of Residual-based Tests for Cointegration", *Econometrica*, 58, 165–193.

Ploberger, W. and W. Krämer (1990) "The Local Power of the CUSUM and CUSUM of Squares Tests", *Econometric Theory*, 6, 335–347.

Quandt, R. (1960) "Tests of the Hypothesis That a Linear Regression System Obeys Two Separate Regimes", *Journal of the American Statistical Association*, 55, 324–330.

Romer, C. D. (1986a) "Spurious Volatility in Historical Unemployment Data", *Journal of Political Economy*, 94, 1–37.

Romer, C. D. (1986b) "Is the Stabilization of the Postwar Economy a Figment of the Data", *American Economic Review*, 76, 314–334.

Romer, C. D. (1989) "The Prewar Business Cycle Reconsidered: New Estimates of Gross National Product, 1869–1908", *Journal of Political Economy*, 97, 1–37.

Tobin, J. (1980) *Asset Accumulation and Economic Activity*, Chicago, Basil Blackwell.

White, H. (1980) "A Heteroskedastic-consistent Covariance Matrix Estimator and a Direct Test for Heteroskedasticity", *Econometrica*, 48, 817–838.

White, H., and I. Domowitz (1984) "Nonlinear Regression with Dependent Observations", *Econometrica*, 52, 143–162.

Index

AD, *see* Autoregressive distributed lag

ADF, *see* Augmented Dickey-Fuller

ADL, *see* Autoregressive distributed lag

Adjustment, *see* Partial adjustment, Feedback coefficient

Aggregation, 302, 303

Ahn, S. K., 122, 125

Ahumada, H., 5, 29, 191, 199, 214

Akerlof, G. A., 88

Aldrich, J., 95

Alogoskoufis, G. S., 257, 258, 268

Alt, R., 391, 394

Analysis of covariance test, 314, 390

Andersen, T. M., 168

Anderson, T. W., 125

Andrews, D. W. K., 391, 392, 401

ARCH, 106–9, 112, 170, 177, 201, 202, 211, 213, 229, 260, 321
— test, 108, 170, 230, 260

Argentina, 5, 29, 191–3, 198, 199, 213

ARMA, *see* Autoregressive moving average

ARMAX, *see* Autoregressive moving average

Asymptotic theory, 390

Augmented Dickey-Fuller, 196–9, 346, 350

Aukrust, O., 188

Autonomy, 6, 17, 51, 59, 95, 262, 271, 282

Autoregression, 19, 20, 26; *see also* Vector autoregression

Autoregressive
— conditional heteroscedasticity, *see* ARCH
— distributed lag (ADL), 13, 15, 199–201, 256, 283, 363, 379
— errors, *see* Serial correlation, Residual autocorrelation
— least squares, 56, 57
— process, *see* Vector autoregression
— moving average, 361, 363, 364, 376, 377, 379

Auxiliary regression, 329, 332, 335

Bårdsen, G., 5, 29, 219–21, 227, 228

Baba, Y., 106

Baillie, R. T., 146, 362

Balance, 22, 328

Banerjee, A., 20, 26, 196

Barndorff-Nielsen, O., 5, 40, 44, 48

Barro, R. J., 31, 347–50

Bayesian, 50, 59

BBC (British Broadcasting Corporation), 276–9, 297, 304

Bean, C. R., 257, 258, 268

Behavioural relationship, 64, 97

Bentzel, R., 63

Bera, A. K., 202, 260, 292, 321

Bhargava, A., 26, 196, 197, 260

Bias, 30, 199, 236, 298, 304, 323;

see also Simultaneous equa-
    tions bias
Blanchard, O. J., 253, 254
Blinder, A. S., 401
Block recursiveness, 57, 60, 64
Boswijk, H. P., 25, 130
Bowman, G. W., 278
Box, G. E. P., 321
Brown, R. L., 79, 321, 391, 393
Bruno, M., 254
Budd, A., 275, 288, 298, 299

Cagan, P., 192, 199
Calmfors, L., 254, 261, 270, 271
Calzolari, G., 88
Campbell, J. Y., 20, 401
Campos, J., 5, 7, 20, 27, 31, 125,
    126, 132, 202, 318, 322, 361
Carruth, A. A., 259
CATS, 167
Causality, 39, 40, 47; see also Exo-
    geneity, Granger causality
Cave, M., 275, 278, 299
Chamberlain, G., 43
Charemza, W., 105
Chong, Y. Y., 314, 321, 325, 326,
    328, 344, 346, 362, 372, 373
Chow test, 80, 86, 107, 263, 331,
    390, 391; see also Chow, G. C.
Chow, G. C., 17, 31, 80, 94, 107,
    109, 112, 203, 204, 208, 211,
    213, 230, 263, 266, 312–6, 320–
    2, 329–33, 369, 390, 391
Christ, C. F., 43
Chu, C.-S. J., 391
Clemen, R. T., 326
Cobweb model, 7, 10–12, 16
Coefficient standard errors, 403

Cointegrating
  — exogeneity, 4, 6, 28, 145–9,
    152, 153; see also Exogeneity,
    Granger causality
  — rank, 123, 126, 127
  — relation, 22, 23, 122, 128, 131,
    139, 256
  — vector, 22, 23, 25, 26, 28, 29,
    122, 130, 148, 149, 166, 199,
    204, 227, 230, 234, 256, 292,
    400
Cointegration, 3–6, 15, 17, 19–23,
    25, 26, 28–30, 110, 121–4, 126,
    129, 132, 133, 139, 145–7, 149,
    151, 153, 161–4, 166, 167, 169,
    170, 172, 175, 177, 185, 186,
    191, 192, 194, 196–9, 213, 219,
    220, 223, 225, 228, 229, 251–6,
    269, 284, 285, 290, 292, 298,
    312, 321, 328, 346, 401, 403;
    see also Error correction, Non-
    stationarity, Stationarity, Unit
    root
  — test, 4, 145, 256, 350, 401
Commercial home minutes, 275,
    276, 278, 279, 281, 287, 294,
    297, 298, 300, 304
Common factor, 56, 60, 83
Common trend, 135
Concentrated likelihood, 286
Conditional
  — density, see Conditional model
  — forecasting, 4, 13
  — inference, 46, 47
  — model, 7–11, 14–19, 25–7, 29–
    31, 41, 45–7, 51, 52, 56, 63–6,
    71, 73, 75, 76, 79, 89, 93–5, 97,
    98, 100–2, 111, 129–31, 141,

148, 149, 200, 204, 208, 213, 220, 226, 230, 238, 239, 243, 262, 263, 266, 285

Confidence interval, 31, 115, 298, 361, 363-7, 369, 372, 373, 376, 385

Congruency, 5, 73, 75, 225, 230, 284, 286, 287, 292, 301, 318

Consistency, 16, 26, 48, 53, 56, 57, 64, 74, 79, 80, 101, 107, 132, 170, 287, 341, 376

Constant term, 13, 136, 169, 185, 204, 255, 288, 329, 332, 333, 350

Consumption, 97, 101, 253, 389, 392, 401, 402

Cooley, T. F., 19, 106, 236, 396

Correlation, 59, 194, 294, 299, 300, 302, 304, 345, 369
— coefficient, 106, 260, 294
Squared multiple —, 106, 260

Covariance matrix, see Variance matrix

Cox, D. R., 104, 321, 324, 390

CPI, see Price

Cramér, H., 385

Currency, 29, 191-3, 199, 200, 202, 203, 213, 214, 246

CUSUM, 391, 393, 394

Cuthbertson, K., 27, 73, 79, 80, 82, 83, 86, 89

Data
— admissible, 74
— density, 41-5, 65, 283
— generation process (DGP), 72-4, 76, 77, 97, 170, 227, 282, 284, 298, 301, 313, 314, 316,

318, 319, 322, 323, 327
— mining, 396

Davidson, J. E. H., 20, 72, 194, 268, 401

Davidson, R., 324, 328

Davies, R. B., 390

Deaton, A. S., 401, 403

DeLong, J. B., 397, 400

Denmark, 29, 161-3, 168, 174, 175, 182, 184-8

Deutsch, M., 5, 31, 321, 341

DGP, see Data generation process

Diagnostic test, 29, 103, 107, 108, 182, 202, 229, 261, 294, 299; see also Test

Dickey, D. A., 24, 196, 197, 284

Dickey-Fuller, 25, 26, 165, 166, 197, 260

Diebold, F. X., 326

Difference, 80, 106, 121, 122, 397

Differencing, 20, 164, 253, 284

Discount window, 351, 352

Disequilibrium, 23, 26, 130, 134, 137, 138, 162, 163, 182, 186, 194, 196, 202, 257, 297, 401; see also Equilibrium

Distributed lag, see Autoregressive distributed lag

Dolado, J. J., 20, 26, 165, 196

Domowitz, I., 394

Doornik, J. A., 7, 24

Drèze, J. H., 51, 59

Driffill, J., 254

Dufour, J.-M., 315, 322

Dummy variable, 83, 94, 104, 107, 169, 184, 200, 281, 283, 288, 297, 390; see also Seasonals

Durbin, J., 79, 321, 391, 393

Durbin-Watson (dw), 26, 106, 196, 197, 260, 350
Durlauf, S. N., 26
Dutkowsky, D., 31, 352–4, 356
Dynamic
— models, 44
— modelling, 198
— simulation, 314
— simultaneous equations model (DSEM), 16, 57, 60, 61, 63, 64
— specification, 79, 194, 196, 226, 292
— systems, 48, 49

EC, see Error correction
ECM, see Error correction mechanism
Econometric models, 59, 93, 95, 99, 278, 362, 363, 389
credibility, 66, 301, 327, 396
Lucas critique, 18, 27, 47, 52, 55, 65, 72, 73, 76, 78, 93–5, 99, 100, 161, 178, 204, 252, 268, 285, 342, 362
Economic
— interpretation, 141, 184, 192, 194, 202, 234, 320
— theory, 6, 13, 17, 71, 74, 146, 166, 196, 234, 256, 321, 322
Edison, H. J., 311
Efficiency, 7, 10, 16, 24, 40, 42, 48, 53, 55–7, 63, 64, 105, 129, 131, 132, 141, 162, 165, 166, 169, 204, 227, 319, 400
Ehrenberg, A. S. C., 305
Eigenvalue, 25, 127, 135, 197, 199, 256
Eigenvector, 138, 228

Eitrheim, Ø., 256
EMS, see European Monetary System
Encompassing, 30, 50, 66, 71–7, 104, 110, 167, 194, 251, 252, 258, 268, 269, 286, 287, 312, 320, 321, 323–8, 330–5; see also Restrictions
— test, 331, 333, 335
Forecast —, 312, 313, 321, 324–8, 332, 334, 346
Forecast-model —, 312, 320, 321, 323–6, 332, 334, 335
MSFE —, 325
Parameter —, 104, 312, 321–5
Parsimonious —, 268, 294
Variance —, 78, 104, 167, 312, 321–4, 326
Endogenous variable, 40, 47, 49, 57, 122, 146, 261, 283, 285, 300, 364, 386, 387
Engle, R. F., 4, 6, 10, 14–18, 20, 22, 26–8, 30, 39, 41, 45, 66, 72, 93, 95, 96, 103, 105, 108, 110, 122, 124, 130, 147, 167, 191, 196, 199, 202, 204, 208, 213, 225, 226, 230, 238, 239, 243, 253, 260, 262, 263, 266, 283–5, 321, 342, 362, 389, 391, 400
Equation standard error, 80, 115, 182, 200, 236, 260, 263, 299, 369
Equilibrium, 194, 226, 227, 303; see also Disequilibrium
Ericsson, N. R., 3, 5, 7, 18–20, 26, 27, 30, 31, 104, 106, 121, 125, 126, 132, 165, 202, 211, 223,

238, 243, 282, 311, 318, 322, 330, 333, 356, 357, 391

Eriksson, T., 257–9, 266, 268

Error correction, 6, 15, 20, 22, 23, 28–31, 115, 123, 134, 146, 147, 165, 192, 194, 196, 202, 219, 223, 225–7, 234, 243, 251, 254, 256, 257, 262, 284, 285, 328, 330, 332, 389, 392, 400, 403; see also Cointegration, Non-stationarity, Stationarity, Unit root

— form, 147, 165

— mechanism, 6, 15, 22, 23, 25, 29, 187, 188, 234, 285, 400

European Monetary System (EMS), 175, 182

Evaluation of models, 341; see also Diagnostic test, Test

Model evaluation, 30, 312, 334, 342

Evans, J. M., 79, 321, 391, 393

Excess kurtosis, see Kurtosis

Exchange rate, 24, 28, 107, 145, 146, 149, 164, 175–7, 186, 188, 193, 202, 220, 238, 247, 312, 373

Exogeneity, 3, 4, 6, 7, 10, 11, 13–20, 25, 27–9, 31, 39, 40, 46–52, 55, 57, 61, 63–6, 93, 94, 97–9, 101–3, 106, 110, 122, 129–31, 141, 145–9, 152–4, 192, 204, 211, 213, 219, 225, 236, 239, 252, 285, 299, 320, 321, 376, 390; see also Cointegrating exogeneity, Predetermined-ness, Strict exogeneity, Strong exogeneity, Super exogeneity,

Test, Weak exogeneity

Expectations, 8, 26, 27, 40, 54–8, 60, 71–9, 82, 83, 88, 89, 94, 96, 97, 99–104, 110, 161, 174, 176, 178, 186, 268, 279, 314, 316, 378

Expenditure, 5, 8, 28–31, 79, 214, 219, 222, 223, 230, 236, 238, 239, 242, 243, 246, 278, 287, 297, 299, 303, 347, 348, 386, 401

F-test, 104, 107–9, 131, 182, 184, 234

Factorization, 42, 45, 46, 48, 49, 51, 52

Fair, R. C., 222, 312

Favero, C., 18, 100, 104, 110, 178

Feedback

— coefficient, 127–30, 137–9, 174, 228, 229; see also Cointegration

— model, 178, 182; see also Conditional model

Feedforward, 27, 71–3, 89, 182; see also Expectations

FIML, 64, 99, 258, 286, 293, 300, 302; see also Maximum likelihood

— estimation, 64, 300

Finland, 29, 251, 252, 254, 257, 269–71

Fisher, F. M., 57, 60, 315

Fisher, G., 80

Fisher, P. G., 28, 145, 152

Fisher, R. A., 31, 314, 321, 390

Florens, J.-P., 5, 40, 43, 44, 50, 147

Forecast
  — error, 312, 316, 319, 343, 344,
    364, 366, 369, 372, 378, 380
  — error variance, 316
  — test, 86, 239, 294
  Conditional —, 344, 346
  h-step —, 363, 368
  Unconditional —, 344, 346, 347,
    353, 357
Formulation
  General model, 167, 230, 233
  System —, 283
Forward-looking, *see* Expectations,
    Feedforward
Frankel, J. A., 342
Frequency, 276, 301
Friedman, M., 192
Frisch, R., 41, 95
Fuller, W. A., 24, 130, 196, 197,
    260, 284
Functional form, 42, 223, 236, 292,
    363

Galbraith, J. W., 20
Gardner, L. A., Jr., 391
GDP, 192, 214
General-to-specific, 78, 191, 192,
    194, 196, 234
Germany, 29, 175, 177, 182, 185,
    186, 188
Geweke, J., 39, 43, 66
Giannini, C., 148, 152
GNP, 31, 80, 283, 299, 391, 392,
    397, 401
Godfrey, L. G., 230, 321
Goldfeld, S. M., 31, 220, 221, 322,
    330, 331, 351–4
Goodness-of-fit, 320

Gourieroux, C., 50
Granger
  — causality, 13, 14, 17, 19, 25,
    40–3, 45, 46, 49, 53–5, 60, 62,
    65, 95, 147, 148; *see also*
    Granger, C. W. J.
  — representation theorem, 225,
    284; *see also* Granger, C. W. J.
Granger, C. W. J., 5, 6, 20, 22, 26,
    31, 40, 66, 108, 122, 124, 130,
    134, 147, 191, 194, 196, 225,
    253, 284, 321, 326, 327, 341,
    344, 345, 350, 400
Gregory, A. W., 238
Growth rate, 23, 27, 107, 115, 356
Grubb, D., 254, 257, 258, 268

Haavelmo distribution, 283
Haavelmo, T., 95, 166, 283
Hall, S. G., 328
Hamburger, M. J., 223
Hansen, B., 63
Hansen, B. E., 5, 31, 112, 389, 391–
    5, 400, 401
Harvey, A. C., 79, 200, 227, 260,
    321, 379
Hausman, J., 75, 103
Henderson, J. M., 10
Hendry, D. F., 4, 5, 7, 10, 14–20,
    24–31, 39, 41, 47, 48, 55, 65,
    71–5, 78–80, 88, 93, 95, 96,
    100, 104, 106, 110, 112, 121,
    122, 125, 130, 132, 147, 151,
    167, 176–8, 191, 192, 194, 196,
    198, 202, 204, 208, 211, 213,
    223, 225, 226, 230, 234, 238,
    239, 243, 251, 262, 263, 266,
    268, 275, 276, 280, 282–6, 311–

5, 318, 319, 321–6, 328, 330, 335, 342, 344, 346, 356, 357, 362, 367, 372, 373, 389, 391, 401

Heteroscedasticity, 105, 107, 108, 177, 202, 320, 321, 369, 373, 394; *see also* ARCH

— test, 236

Heteroscedasticity-consistent standard errors, 80, 107

Hinkley, D. V., 390

H. M. Treasury, 106, 155

Holden, S., 274

Hood, W. C., 43

Hoover, K. D., 342

Hunter, J., 4, 6, 28, 145–7

Hurwicz, L., 41, 95

Hylleberg, S., 20, 225, 226, 255

Hyperinflation, 192, 193

Hypothesis

   Alternative —, 186, 197, 321, 390, 394

   Maintained —, 100, 105, 293

   Null —, 25, 93, 96, 100, 102, 103, 111, 166, 184, 197, 203, 227, 266, 314, 315, 321, 327, 332, 344–7, 369, 390, 394, 398, 399

Hysteresis, 29, 199, 251–4, 257, 259, 269, 270

IBA (Independent Broadcasting Authority), 277, 304

Identification, 287, 302

Identities, 59, 62, 286, 292, 293

Incomplete information, 77, 82

Inference, 3–7, 9, 10, 13, 16, 17, 24–6, 39, 40, 46–9, 59, 63–5, 83, 88, 122, 129, 132, 134, 135, 147, 149, 165, 169, 228, 304, 320, 322, 389

Inflation, 24, 28, 29, 88, 93, 108–10, 122, 138, 161–4, 167, 173–7, 182, 184–6, 191–3, 198, 199, 202, 204, 208, 211, 213, 214, 220, 236, 239, 243, 279, 297, 303, 342, 344, 356, 367, 372, 373, 401, 403

Information

   — matrix, 49

   — set, 54, 73, 78, 88, 96, 97, 100, 174, 175, 184, 191, 200, 242, 266, 312, 319, 321, 344, 345

   — taxonomy

   Relative future, 321, 322

   Relative past, 321, 322

   Relative present, 321

   Rival models, 268

   Past —, 74, 106, 378

Initial values, 125

Innovation, 74, 98, 202, 230, 284, 285, 299, 319, 321, 386

Instrument, 75, 79, 82, 99, 101, 103, 104, 242, 261, 298

Instrumental variables, 55, 75, 79, 101, 102, 258, 261, 269, 298, 326

   — estimation, 55, 75, 298; *see also* Recursive estimation

Integrated of order r: $I(r)$, 108, 121, 122, 125, 197, 198, 225, 282, 284, 290, 292, 327

   Integrated, 6, 19, 20, 21, 24, 28, 30, 108, 121, 225, 284, 312, 327, 328

Intercept, *see* Constant term

Interdependence, 275, 276

Interest rate, 8, 16, 19, 24, 28, 29,
79, 80, 88, 93, 97, 106, 108–10,
125, 126, 138, 145, 146, 151,
155, 175, 177, 182, 184, 186,
187, 191–3, 202–4, 208, 211,
213, 214, 219, 220, 222, 223,
230, 238, 243, 246, 247, 330,
342, 352, 356
Intervention, 15, 16, 46, 47, 51, 54,
65, 96, 98, 99, 169, 177, 184,
204, 238, 239, 243, 262, 266,
362, 389; *see also* Invariance,
Super exogeneity
Invariance, 4, 5, 15–18, 27, 30, 39,
41, 44, 46, 47, 51, 52, 54, 55,
57, 59, 65, 72, 93–106, 108,
110, 111, 147, 149, 184, 211,
213, 222, 226, 236, 238, 239,
243, 258, 262, 263, 266, 285,
327, 328, 367, 389
Inversion, 18, 28, 110, 192, 211
ITA (Independent Television Authority), 277
ITV, 277–9, 281, 282, 287, 304

Jackman, R., 253, 254
Jacobian, 48
Jarque, C. M., 202, 260, 292, 321
Jenkinson, T. J., 20
Johansen, S., 4, 6, 17, 20, 21, 24–
6, 28, 121, 122, 126, 128, 130,
131, 133–5, 145–52, 154, 155,
162, 164–7, 191, 197–9, 204,
225–9, 243, 254, 256, 285, 290
Johnston, J., 202, 321, 335
Joint density, 7, 13, 18, 21, 40, 50,
51, 61, 64, 66, 74, 76, 94, 147,
284, 290, 292

Judd, J., 95, 106
Jureen, L., 63
Juselius, K., 4, 20, 24, 25, 28, 29,
122, 125, 126, 128, 130, 131,
135, 145–7, 149–52, 154, 161,
162, 164–7, 173, 175, 182, 184,
186, 197–9, 225, 227, 228, 254,
256

Kane, E. J., 31, 351–4
Keir, P., 351
Kendall, M., 8
King, M. L., 391
Kiraly, J., 105
Kiviet, J. F., 230, 335
Klovland, J. T., 220–2, 238, 311
Koopmans, T. C., 5, 39, 40, 43, 48,
51, 64
Krämer, W., 391, 394
Kremers, J. J. M., 26, 165
Kurtosis, 260, 321

Labour market, 29, 161, 164, 168,
169, 173, 185, 251–3, 259, 261–
3, 266, 270
Laffont, J.-J., 50
Lag polynomial, 256, 283, 379; *see
also* Autoregressive distributed
lag
Lagged
— dependent variable, 297, 327
— residuals, 230
Lagrange multiplier test, *see* LM
test
Laidler, D. E. W., 223, 236
Layard, P. R. G., 253, 254, 257,
258, 268
Lee, L. F., 50, 57

LeRoy, S. F., 19, 106, 236

Likelihood, *see* Maximum likelihood

Lippens, R. E., 146

LM test, 80, 103, 107, 347, 392; *see also* Test

Logit, 50

Long run, 6, 15, 19, 22, 28–30, 88, 108, 109, 122, 123, 128, 129, 131, 133, 141, 146–9, 155, 163–8, 172, 173, 175, 176, 182, 185, 191, 192, 194, 196, 198–200, 202, 213, 219, 222, 223, 225, 227, 228, 233–6, 246, 253, 254, 257–9, 261, 262, 275, 276, 280, 281, 287, 288, 290, 297, 298, 300, 302, 394, 401, 403

Long-run solution, 233

Loretan, M., 20, 228

LR test, 25, 86, 125, 152, 165, 170, 286, 300; *see also* Test

Lu, M., 327

Lucas critique, 6, 17, 18, 27, 72, 73, 76, 78, 93, 94, 99, 100, 161, 178, 204, 252, 268, 342, 362

Lucas, Jr., R. E., 47, 52, 55, 65, 72, 73, 76, 78, 93–5, 99, 100, 161, 178, 204, 252, 268, 285, 342, 362

M1, 27, 71, 79, 80, 88, 89, 95, 106, 108, 112, 125, 214, 219, 261, 270, 348, 358; *see also* Narrow money

MA, *see* Moving average

MacKinnon, J. G., 324, 328

MacMahon, P. C., 146

Maddala, G. S., 50, 57

Makelainen, T., 391

Manning, A., 257, 258, 268

Marginal

— density, *see* Marginal distribution, Marginal model, Marginal process

— distribution, 8, 23, 54, 65, 225, 226

— model, 7, 9, 11, 13, 14, 17, 25, 46, 51, 56, 57, 64, 66, 78, 95, 129–31, 148, 178, 204, 238, 239

— process, 10, 12, 15–18, 45, 52, 101, 149, 208

Marquez, J., 333

Marschak, J., 39, 41, 95

MAX, *see* Moving average

Maximum likelihood, 56, 131, 163, 258, 285, 286, 391, 393, 397

Max statistic, *see* Cointegration

McAleer, M., 80, 238

McCallum, B. T., 101

McFadden, D., 50

Mean square forecast error, 30, 31, 311, 312, 314–6, 318–20, 334, 345, 349, 353, 357, 362, 363, 367; *see also* Forecast error variance

— dominance, 312, 321, 322, 324–6, 334

Meese, R. A., 312

Melnick, R., 199

Milbourne, R., 88

Miller, M. H., 88

Mis-specification, 110, 111, 149, 202, 211, 213, 222, 230, 261, 285, 298, 327, 347, 351, 354, 369, 372, 396, 403; *see also*

Diagnostic test, Test

Mizon, G. E., 20, 24, 72, 75, 104, 125, 130, 132, 167, 194, 225, 226, 255, 268, 282, 286, 321, 323, 324, 327

Model
— design, 202, 322
— evaluation, 30, 312, 334, 342
— specification, 26, 165, 170

Modelling strategy, 5, 7, 71

Monahan, J. C., 401

Monetarism, 161–3, 172, 184, 185

Money demand, 4, 5, 16, 18, 19, 24, 28–31, 79, 82, 88, 89, 93, 97, 106, 108, 110, 112, 123, 125, 129, 133, 136, 139–41, 174, 191, 192, 199, 204, 211, 213, 221–3, 228, 230, 243, 312, 322, 330, 331, 334

Monte Carlo, 25

Montfort, A., 50

Mosconi, R., 148, 152

Mouchart, M., 5, 40, 43, 44, 50, 147

Moving average, 22, 108, 202, 363–5, 377, 386, 387

MSFE, see Mean square forecast error

Muth, J. F., 55, 72

Nagel, S. S., 347

Narrow money, 29, 73, 219–23, 228, 243, 270, 312, 330, 356; see also M1

National Economic Research Associates (NERA), 275, 278, 287, 299

Neale, A. J., 72, 75, 78, 79, 282,

286, 312

Nelson, C. R., 20

NERA, see National Economic Research Associates

Newbold, P., 194, 345, 350

Newell, A., 257, 258, 268

Nicholls, D. F., 202, 321

Nickell, S. J., 74, 185, 253, 257–9, 268

Nonconstancy, see Parameter constancy

Nonstationarity, 122, 126, 162, 164, 166, 284; see also Cointegration, Error correction, Stationarity, Unit root

Normal distribution, 7, 18, 41, 97, 228, 283, 284, 367

Normality, 57, 83, 107, 108, 182, 211, 229, 230, 233, 235, 236, 238, 239, 242, 243, 260, 284, 292, 321, 323, 376
— test, 170, 177, 230

Normalization, 26, 148, 166, 257

Norway, 5, 29, 219, 220, 222, 228, 242, 243, 254, 261

Notes and coin, see Currency

Nuisance parameter, 26

Numerical accuracy, 315

Nyblom, J., 391–3, 395, 397

Nymoen, R., 5, 29, 30, 251, 254, 261, 268, 269, 271

OLS, 16, 49, 53, 56, 57, 64, 83, 196, 202, 233, 258, 260, 294, 313, 316, 369, 373, 394, 400, 403

Omitted variables, 177, 202, 293, 304, 396

Orcutt, G. H., 39

Ordinary least squares, *see* OLS
Orr, D., 88
Orthogonal, 139
Orthogonality, 40, 50
Osterwald-Lenum, M., 229
Oswald, A. J., 259
Ouliaris, S., 406
Output growth, 389

Pagan, A. R., 15, 20, 196, 202, 284,
    314, 321, 391
Pantula, S. G., 126
Parameter
— constancy, 4–6, 15, 17–19, 26,
    27, 30, 31, 46, 66, 71, 73, 75–7,
    79, 80, 82, 83, 88, 89, 93–100,
    103–6, 108–12, 116, 141, 163,
    178, 182, 192, 198, 203, 204,
    208, 211, 213, 219, 223, 230,
    238, 239, 243, 262, 263, 284,
    292, 311–4, 316–20, 322, 326,
    327, 333, 334, 362, 372, 389–
    400, 403
— constancy test, 5, 6, 17, 30,
    31, 94, 103, 314, 320
— instability, 202, 389, 391, 394,
    403
— invariance, 251, 252, 262, 389
— of interest, 5, 7, 10, 11, 13,
    16, 17, 43–5, 47–55, 58, 59, 61,
    63, 64, 72, 74, 95, 97, 98, 130,
    147, 219, 226, 283, 284, 286,
    287, 304
Constant —, 51, 65, 94, 98, 266,
    275, 276, 285, 299
Nuisance —, 40, 44, 47, 56, 63
Variation-free —, 7, 9–13, 44, 46,
    48, 51, 54, 56, 61, 62, 64, 65,

    95, 130, 226, 283
Park, J. Y., 228
Partial adjustment, 330, 332
PcFiml, 88, 151, 230
PcGive, 79, 82, 106, 176, 178, 198,
    228, 251, 275, 311
PDV, *see* Present discounted value
    model
Peacock, A., 276–8, 288, 298, 305
Perron, P., 20
Pesaran, M. H., 104, 321, 324
Phillips curve, 163, 172
Phillips, A. W., 20, 39, 49, 194
Phillips, G. D. A., 79
Phillips, P. C. B., 20, 26, 132, 228,
    400, 401
Pierce, D. A., 321
Piterman, S., 199
Ploberger, W., 391, 394
Plosser, C. I., 20
Policy, 3–7, 15–17, 19, 20, 27, 29–
    31, 46, 47, 53, 64, 65, 72, 88,
    93, 96, 103, 106, 107, 149, 162,
    164, 173, 184, 185, 191, 192,
    213, 219, 220, 230, 238, 246,
    252, 262, 263, 266, 270, 271,
    278, 285, 298, 312, 320, 341–5,
    347, 349–51, 354, 358, 361–3,
    367, 372, 389
Poloz, S. S., 238
Population, 314–6, 327
Power, 26, 31, 66, 78, 89, 94, 96,
    100, 101, 103, 105, 109, 110,
    243, 263, 299, 324, 328, 329,
    358, 389–91, 394, 398, 400
PPP, *see* Purchasing power parity
Predeterminedness, 16, 39, 41, 43,
    48, 50, 51, 53–57, 60, 62–6,

287; *see also* Exogeneity, Strict exogeneity

Predictive failure, 65, 78, 95, 285, 312, 315, 321, 361, 391; *see also* Parameter constancy

Prescott, E. C., 396

Present discounted value model, 102

Press, S. J., 61

Price, 4, 5, 8, 10, 11, 18, 19, 24, 28–30, 79, 93, 101, 102, 106, 108, 109, 112, 122, 125, 128, 138, 145, 146, 149, 161–4, 167–70, 172–5, 177, 182, 184–8, 191–3, 200, 203, 211, 214, 219, 222, 223, 228, 236, 238, 239, 242, 243, 246, 247, 252–4, 257, 259–61, 268–71, 275–82, 287, 288, 290, 294, 297–300, 303, 304, 330, 358, 361, 362, 367, 368, 372, 373, 376, 386
— elasticity, 11, 30, 275–8, 290, 298, 300, 303, 304, 362
Oil —, 146, 149, 150, 152, 155, 162, 185, 361–3, 367–9, 372, 373, 386

Probability, 42, 75, 332, 362, 372, 373, 399

Productivity, 29, 168, 170, 172, 184, 186, 187, 251–4, 257, 259, 261, 268, 269

Progress, 285; *see also* Reduction

Purchasing power parity, 24, 29, 145, 146, 175, 182, 186

Quandt, R. E., 10, 391

Ramsey, J. B., 107, 177, 202, 234, 321

Random coefficient model, 396

Random walk, 20, 392, 394
with drift, 368

Rank conditions, 124, 133, 134

Rational expectation, 31, 47, 55, 72, 93, 96, 100, 101, 146, 342, 347

Recursive
— estimation, 6, 17, 27, 71, 83, 89, 178, 204, 213, 230, 322; *see also* Instrumental variables, OLS, Test
— instrumental variables, 79, 80, 82; *see also* Instrumental variables, Test
— least squares, 79, 80, 82, 88; *see also* OLS, Recursive estimation, Test

Reduced
— form model, 385
— rank, 124, 125, 128, 131–5, 137, 165, 285
Restricted — form, 99, 104

Reduction, 139, 141, 257; *see also* Progress

Regime shifts, 103, 107, 222, 262, 284, 285, 396

Regression
— coefficients, 56, 98, 178, 315, 391, 396, 397, 403
— equation, 96, 97, 112
— estimates, 299
— standard error, 80, 115, 182, 200, 236, 260, 263, 299, 369
Static —, 26, 196, 199

Reinsel, G. C., 122, 125, 363

Reserves
Borrowed —, 31, 351, 353, 354

RESET, 106–9, 112, 177, 201, 211, 213, 321; *see also* Test, Diagnostic test

Residual autocorrelation, 80, 107, 108, 169, 182, 210, 284, 320, 321; *see also* Serial correlation

Restricted reduced form, 99, 104

Restrictions
  Over-identifying —, 49, 52, 59–61, 63, 64, 286, 287, 294, 300, 304

Reverse regression, *see* Inversion

Richard, J.-F., 4, 5, 7, 10, 14–16, 27, 30, 39–41, 45, 51, 55, 57, 59, 62, 66, 72, 75, 95, 96, 104, 110, 122, 130, 147, 167, 202, 204, 226, 234, 238, 262, 268, 282–4, 286, 313, 314, 321–4, 362, 389, 391

Risager, O., 168

Rival models, 268

RMSFE, *see* Mean square forecast error

Rødseth, A., 274

Rogoff, K., 312

Rolin, J.-M., 40, 44, 50, 147

Romer, C. D., 397

Rothenberg, T. J., 69

Rowlatt, P. A., 261

Rush, M., 31, 347

Sachs, J. D., 254

Saikkonen, P., 257, 258, 268

Salmon, M., 20, 47, 96

Sample
  — period, 44, 82, 107, 109, 110, 162, 169, 172, 175, 177, 193, 198, 222, 223, 238, 239, 255, 269, 282, 324, 352, 356, 367, 386, 398
  — size, 80, 198, 210, 230, 290, 299, 300, 358, 365, 376, 385, 400

Sargan, J. D., 15, 20, 26, 60, 82, 104, 194, 196, 197, 260, 261, 284, 321

Sargent, T. J., 47

Scadding, J., 95, 106

Schinasi, G. J., 311

Schmidt, P., 362

Schwartz, A. J., 117

Seasonals, 89, 165, 169, 194, 199, 200, 204, 211, 213, 229, 234, 279, 292, 294, 297, 352

Sequential
  — cut, 9, 10, 44, 45, 49, 50, 63, 147, 148
  — reduction, 200; *see also* Reduction, Progress

Serial correlation, 41, 55, 59, 373, 394

Sheffrin, S. M., 342

Sichel, D. E., 220, 221, 322, 331

Sims, C. A., 39, 41, 43, 66, 228, 286

Simultaneous equations, 41, 43, 48, 52, 64, 66, 103, 361, 376
  — bias, 103

Single equation, 6, 30, 49, 131, 132, 141, 204, 270, 292, 293

Skewness, 260, 321

Smith, G. W., 26, 196

Sosvilla-Rivero, S., 20

Spanos, A., 7, 230, 282, 322

Specification
— test, 28, 75, 93, 94, 155, 341
Model —, 26, 165, 170
Srba, F., 20, 72, 88, 194, 268, 282,
    286, 401
Standard deviation, 106, 169, 200,
    297
Standard error
Coefficient —, 297, 298
Equation —, 80, 112
Starr, R. M., 106
Static regression, 26, 196, 199
Stationarity, 20, 139, 152, 162, 166,
    172, 186, 194, 254, 284, 346,
    350, 365; see also Cointegra-
    tion, Error correction, Nonsta-
    tionarity, Unit root
Statistical
— accuracy, 315
— system, 225, 282, 286
Stochastic variable, 252, 292
Stock, J. H., 26, 101, 106, 196, 227,
    228
Strategy, see Modelling strategy
Strict exogeneity, 4, 16, 27, 39, 41,
    43, 48–51, 53, 54, 57, 60, 62,
    65, 66, 74; see also Exogen-
    eity, Granger causality
Strong exogeneity, 4, 13, 14, 17, 19,
    25, 28, 39, 40, 45, 48–50, 53,
    54, 57, 65, 88, 95, 130, 147,
    148, 226, 302, 363, 364, 386;
    see also Exogeneity, Granger
    causality, Weak exogeneity
Strotz, R. H., 40, 57, 62
Structural
— break, 94, 108, 110, 333, 392
— change, 236, 322, 390, 391,

397
— coefficients, 58, 61
— invariance, see Invariance
— model, 122, 163, 185, 294, 297
Stuart, A., 8
Suits, D. B., 10
Summers, L. H., 253, 254, 397, 400
Super exogeneity, 4, 7, 13, 15–19,
    28–31, 39, 41, 46, 47, 51, 52,
    54, 55, 57, 64, 65, 71–3, 77, 78,
    88, 89, 93, 94, 96, 98–106, 108,
    110, 111, 147, 191, 204, 208,
    210, 211, 213, 220, 222, 226,
    238, 239, 243, 266, 285, 312,
    342, 361, 362, 389; see also
    Exogeneity, Invariance, Weak
    exogeneity
Surrey, M. J. C., 163, 164, 186
Suvanto, A., 257–9, 266, 268
Swamy, P. A. V. B., 311, 329
Swann, P., 275, 278, 299
Symons, J., 257, 258, 268
System
— formulation, 283
— modelling, 29, 302

Tanaka, K., 391
Tanna, S. K., 28, 145, 152
Target, 185, 220, 342–4, 346, 350,
    351, 354, 358
Taxonomy, 30, 31, 312, 319, 334
Teräsvirta, T., 257, 258, 268
Test; see also Diagnostic test
— for autocorrelated squared
    residuals (ARCH), 108, 170,
    230, 260
— for heteroscedasticity, 236
— for normality, 170, 177, 230

— for strong exogeneity, 17
— for super exogeneity, 27, 54, 99, 101, 104
— for weak exogeneity, 24, 25, 28, 103, 122, 131, 141, 154, 226, 243
Chow —, 80, 86, 107, 263, 331, 390, 391
Cointegration —, 256
Constancy —, 104
Durbin-Watson —, 26, 106, 196, 197, 260, 350
Encompassing —, 331, 333, 335
Forecast —, 86, 239, 294
Linear restriction —, 131
Omitted variables —, 177, 202, 293, 304
Parameter constancy —, 5, 17, 18, 30, 31, 46, 66, 80, 88, 93, 94, 103, 106, 110, 203, 204, 311, 313, 314, 316–20, 322, 326, 334, 362, 390
Parameter instability —, 202, 389, 391, 394, 403
RESET —, 106–9, 112, 177, 201, 211, 213, 321
Significance —, 105, 127, 184, 230, 236, 239, 243, 367, 390
Specification —, 28, 75, 93, 94, 155, 341
Unit root —, 350
TFE, see Total final expenditure
Three-stage least squares (3SLS), 258
Time-series properties, 228
Time-varying coefficient model, 329
Tinbergen, J., 10
Tinsley, P. A., 329

Tobin, J., 397
Total final expenditure (TFE), 79, 80, 106, 125, 192, 330
Trace statistic, 25, 125, 256
Tran, H.-A., 7, 20, 125, 126, 132, 322
Transformations, 62, 63, 282, 327, 328, 367
Linear —, 324, 326, 385
Treasury, see H. M. Treasury
Trend, 24, 124–7, 135, 137, 138, 170, 186, 198, 223, 228, 268, 288, 290, 292, 294
Trundle, J. M., 79, 223
Turner, D. S., 28, 145, 152
TV advertising
— expenditure, 30, 288
— time, 275, 276, 278, 287, 288, 294, 297
TVC, see Time-varying coefficient model
Two-stage least squares (2SLS), 99, 394
Typology
Error correction mechanism, 29, 234
Partial adjustment, 330, 332
Static regression, 26, 196, 199

UIP, see Uncovered interest rate parity
Uncovered interest rate parity, 24, 29, 145, 146, 177, 186
Unemployment, 5, 30, 31, 163, 164, 167, 168, 170, 172, 186, 187, 251–4, 257, 259, 261–3, 266, 269–71, 342–4, 347, 348, 350, 358

Unit root, 6, 20, 25, 26, 83, 199, 344, 350, 392; *see also* Cointegration, Error correction, Non-stationarity, Stationarity
— test, 350
United Kingdom, 24, 28, 30, 80, 106, 123, 202, 275–7, 282, 304, 312, 330, 331, 334, 356
United States, 188, 331
Unrestricted reduced form, 62, 104
Urbain, J.-P., 25

VAR, *see* Vector autoregression
Variable
Endogenous —, 40, 47, 49, 57, 122, 146, 261, 283, 285, 300, 364, 386, 387
Instrumental —, 55, 75, 79, 101, 102, 258, 269, 298, 326
Variance
— dominance, 312, 321–4
— matrix, 8, 41, 44, 58, 75, 86, 97, 123, 129, 166, 283, 302, 313, 327, 363, 364, 367, 368, 383, 385, 387, 390, 394, 397
Variation free, 7, 9–13, 44, 46, 48, 51, 54, 56, 61, 62, 64, 65, 95, 130, 226, 283
Vartia, P., 257–9, 266, 268
Vector autoregression (VAR), 7, 13, 19, 22, 24, 79, 86, 88, 89, 123, 129, 132, 134, 141, 146, 147, 149–52, 155, 166, 169, 174, 225, 228–30, 254–6, 290
van Velthoven, B. C. J., 342
Venezuela, 31, 361–3, 367, 373, 386

Wages, 5, 8, 28–30, 161–4, 167, 168,

170, 172, 173, 184–7, 194, 239, 251–4, 256–62, 266, 268–71
Wald test, *see* Test
Wallis, K. F., 28, 47, 55, 72, 96, 145, 152
Watson, G. S., 321
Watson, M. W., 228
Weak exogeneity, 4–7, 9–17, 20, 23, 25, 26, 28, 40, 45, 47–51, 53, 54, 56, 57, 61–6, 72, 88, 95, 96, 98–103, 105, 106, 109, 110, 121, 122, 125, 129–32, 135, 139, 141, 145–9, 152–5, 167, 198, 199, 204, 226, 230, 236, 238, 281, 283–5, 287, 290, 292, 293, 302, 304, 321, 325, 326, 335; *see also* Exogeneity, Strong exogeneity, Super exogeneity
Weiss, A. A., 20, 284
West, K. D., 228
White noise, 202, 255, 329, 343, 346
White, H., 80, 106, 107, 202, 236, 284, 318, 321, 369, 391, 394, 397
Whitley, J. D., 28, 145, 152
Wickens, M. R., 388
Wiener, N., 40
Wilson, A. L., 315
Wold, H. O. A., 40, 57, 62, 63
Wu, D. M., 57, 63, 66, 103

Yamamoto, T., 362, 363, 377
Yeo, S., 20, 72, 194, 268, 401
Yoo, B. S., 20, 199

Zellner, A., 40, 47